W9-BYK-985

A Chanticleer Press Edition

WESTERN FORESTS

By Stephen Whitney

Birds
Miklos D. F. Udvardy, Professor of Biological Sciences, California State University, Sacramento

Butterflies
Robert Michael Pyle, Consulting Lepidopterist, International Union for Conservation of Nature and Natural Resources

Insects and Spiders
Lorus Milne and Margery Milne, Lecturers, University of New Hampshire

Mammals
John O. Whitaker, Jr., Professor of Life Sciences, Indiana State University

Mushrooms
Peter Katsaros, Mycologist

Reptiles and Amphibians
John L. Behler, Curator of Herpetology, New York Zoological Society; and F. Wayne King, Director, Florida State Museum

Trees
Elbert L. Little, Jr., former Chief Dendrologist, U.S. Forest Service

Wildflowers
Richard Spellenberg, Professor of Biology, New Mexico State University

Alfred A. Knopf, New York

This is a Borzoi Book.
Published by Alfred A. Knopf, Inc.

All rights reserved.
Copyright Chanticleer Press, Inc. 1985.
Published in the United States by Alfred A. Knopf, Inc.,
New York, and simultaneously in Canada by Random House of
Canada Limited, Toronto. Distributed by Random House, Inc.,
New York.

Prepared and produced by Chanticleer Press, Inc., New York.

Printed and bound by Dai Nippon, Tokyo, Japan.
Typeset in Garamond by Dix Type Inc., Syracuse, New York.

Published March 1985
Eighth Printing, April 1994

Library of Congress Cataloging in Publication Data
Whitney, Stephen, 1942–
The Audubon Society nature guides. Western forests.
Includes index.
1. Natural history—West (U.S.)—Handbooks, manuals, etc.
2. Forest ecology—West (U.S.)—Handbooks, manuals, etc.
3. Zoology—West (U.S.)—Handbooks, manuals, etc.
4. Botany—West (U.S.)—Handbooks, manuals, etc.   5. Forest
fauna—West (U.S.)—Identification.   6. Forest flora—West
(U.S.)—Identification.
I. National Audubon Society. II. Title. III. Title: Western
forests.
QH104.5.W4W48   1985   574.5'2642'0978   84-48670
ISBN 0-394-73127-1 (pbk.)

National Audubon Society ® is a registered trademark
of National Audubon Society, Inc., all rights reserved.

Cover photograph: A Western Trillium, surrounded by ferns,
grows at the base of a Western Redcedar in Washington's
Olympic National Park.

CONTENTS

ACKNOWLEDGMENTS

This book represents hundreds of hours of labor by a small army of people. I am particularly indebted to Jerry Franklin of the U.S. Forest Service in Corvallis, Oregon, for his meticulous review of the manuscript and excellent suggestions. I would also like to thank the staff at Chanticleer Press, especially Susan Costello, Mary Beth Brewer, Ann Whitman, Marian Appellof, Constance Mersel, David Allen, and Jane Opper. They helped me throughout the project, and worked long after I was done to bring this book to completion.
Stephen Whitney

THE AUTHOR

Stephen Whitney
Author of several field guides, Stephen Whitney holds a
master's degree from the University of California, Santa
Barbara. He has written *A Field Guide to the Cascades and
Olympics, A Field Guide to the Grand Canyon,* and *The Sierra
Nevada, A Sierra Club Naturalist's Guide,* and is the coauthor of
*To Walk with a Quiet Mind: Hikes in the Woodlands, Parks, and
Beaches of the San Francisco Bay Area.* Mr. Whitney is also the
author of many magazine articles, some of which have
appeared in *Backpacker* magazine and *The Mother Earth News.*
Currently he is editorial manager of Mountaineers Books.

HOW TO USE THIS GUIDE

This guide is designed for use both at home and in the field. Its clear arrangement in four parts—habitat essays, color plates, species descriptions, and appendices—puts information at your fingertips that would otherwise only be accessible through a small library of field guides.

The habitat essays enable you to discover the many kinds of forest habitats, the relationships among the plants and animals there, and highlights not to be missed. The color plates feature woodland and forest scenes and over 600 photographs of different plant and animal species. The species descriptions cover the most important information about a plant or animal, including a description, the range, specific habitat, and comments. Finally, the appendices include a bibliography, a glossary, and a comprehensive index.

Using This Guide at Home

Before planning an outing, you will want to know what you can expect to see in a western forest.

1. Begin by leafing through the color plates for a preview of western forests.

2. Read the habitat section. For quick reference, at the end of each chapter you will find a list of some of the most common plants and animals found in that habitat.

3. Look at the color plates of some of the animals and plants so that you will be able to recognize them later in the field. The table called How to Use the Color Plates provides a visual table of contents to the color section, explains the arrangement of the plates, and tells the caption information provided. The habitats where you are likely to encounter the species are listed in blue type so that you can easily refer to the correct habitat chapter. The page number for the full species description is also included in the caption.

4. Turn to the species descriptions to learn more about the plants and animals that interest you. A range map or drawing appears in the margin for birds, mammals, reptiles, and amphibians, and for many of the trees, shrubs, and wildflowers. Poisonous mushrooms and reptiles are indicated by the danger symbol ⊗ next to the species name.

5. Consult the appendices for definitions of technical terms and suggestions for further reading.

Using This Guide in the Field

When you are out in the field, you will want to find information quickly and easily.

1. Turn to the color plates to locate the plant or animal you have seen. At a glance the captions will help you narrow down the possibilities. First, verify the habitat by checking the blue type information to the left of the color plate. Next, look for important field marks, which are also indicated in blue type—for example, when tree flowers bloom or when fruit matures; how a mushroom grows; or an insect's food. To find out whether a bird, mammal, reptile, or amphibian is in your area, check the range map next to the color plate.

2. Now turn to the species description to confirm your identification and to learn more about the species.

First frontispiece. Aspens and Lodgepole Pines in autumn, Jasper National Park, Alberta.

Second frontispiece. Great Gray Owl perched in a dense coniferous forest, Yellowstone National Park, Wyoming.

Third frontispiece. Elk bull feeding in Jasper National Park, Alberta.

Fourth frontispiece. Moose bull browsing at forest's edge, Yellowstone National Park, Wyoming.

Fifth frontispiece. Snow-covered spruce and Lodgepole Pine forest, Grand Teton National Park, Wyoming.

PREFACE

The forests of western North America are among the most magnificent and varied in the world. They include the lush, moss-draped rainforests of the Pacific Northwest as well as dry, sunny stands of Ponderosa Pine in the Rockies; dwarf woodlands of pinyon and juniper in the Southwest, as well as groves of Giant Sequoia in the Sierra Nevada. Dominated by conifers, the Western forests boast the largest, tallest, and oldest trees in the world and surpass all other conifer forests in number of species and the variety of combinations in which they occur. Along the mild, humid coast of the Pacific Northwest, where conifers achieve their planetary climax, old-growth forests exceed even tropical rainforests in their total, exuberant production of living material. Enhancing the beauty of the western forests and woodlands are their spectacular settings—the crags and gorges of the mountains, the canyons and mesas of the Southwest, the cliffs and headlands of the Pacific Coast.

The geographic area covered by this book extends from the Rocky Mountains to the Pacific Ocean and from northern Mexico to an imaginary line running from coastal Alaska southeastward across central British Columbia to near Jasper National Park in Alberta. North and east of that line lies the North American boreal forest, which has affinities with both the western conifer forest and eastern hardwood forest. Because it lies outside our range, the boreal forest is discussed here only briefly. Nevertheless, most of the general principles of conifer forest ecology presented in this book also apply to the boreal forest. Moreover, many of the plants and animals found in the western forests are either present in the boreal forest or have close relatives there.

The western forests offer abundant opportunities—in settings of unsurpassed natural beauty—for hiking, climbing, skiing, camping, fishing, hunting, canoeing, photography, birding, botanizing, and various other activities. In addition, the forests offer quiet, a chance for solitude, perhaps even a bit of adventure. It is therefore little wonder that these forests host millions of visitors each year. Whatever the initial attraction, many people soon find themselves wanting to know more about the forest for its own sake. They want to identify the little yellow flowers growing around camp or the blue, crested bird that swoops down to steal scraps from the table. They may go on to wonder why forest grows in one place and meadows in another or why some forests are dense while others are open and parklike. The purpose of this guidebook is to answer such questions and perhaps to suggest others as well.

Getting Started
The amateur naturalist requires little in the way of special equipment—a notebook and pen or pencil, a pair of binoculars, perhaps a hand lens. Special equipment for collecting specimens is not necessary. Even many butterflies can be identified without recourse to capturing them—much less mounting them. Similarly, it is generally unnecessary to uproot or otherwise damage plants in order to learn their

names. Where such extreme measures are required, they are best left to biologists with legitimate research needs. For the rest of us to damage or even kill a plant or animal merely to learn its name would be to lose sight of what is truly important in our relationship to the natural world. Better to let a butterfly ride the winds unnamed.

A notebook is the single most important piece of equipment a naturalist takes in the field. It is useful for recording daily observations, sketching plants and animals for later reference, taking notes on behavior and habitat, and assisting in identification by recording field marks that otherwise might be forgotten. The naturalist's notebook only increases in value as time goes by and observations accumulate. Soon, patterns begin to emerge from what initially may have been chance encounters with various plants or animals. A well-kept notebook that preserves a record of their activities at a particular place over an extended period of time can contribute information valuable to our understanding of nature.

The notebook you choose should be large enough for sketches and copious notes but small enough to be carried comfortably into the field. When either taking notes or sketching, one should take care to include the date, time of day, location, and weather. The notes themselves, of course, should be as accurate and precise as possible. Notes that are carelessly taken or poorly identified as to time, place, and conditions are likely to be of limited value for later reference.

Binoculars are essential for serious birding and are fast replacing the traditional net for many students of butterflies. Though not necessary for observing mammals, binoculars still greatly enhance that activity as well. Binoculars come in all sizes and shapes, but not all are suitable for observing wildlife. Most birders prefer lightweight models with wide fields of vision. Lightweight binoculars can be moved rapidly to track the flight of birds and can easily be held steady to ensure a clear image. A wide field of vision makes it easier, for example, to locate a bird in a tangle of foliage. Most birders prefer binoculars of $7 \times$, $8 \times$, or $10 \times$ power because those with higher magnification tend to be difficult to hold steady and generally have very narrow fields of vision. Optical quality —clearness and brightness of image, degree of distortion— varies greatly with price. Serviceable binoculars are available for under $100, but the finer models cost $250 and up.

A hand lens is a small magnifying glass, usually of $5 \times$ or $10 \times$ power, that may be used to examine closely the minute organs of plants or invertebrates. Like the macro lens on a camera, a hand lens opens up a fascinating miniature world. It may also be essential for identifying certain species distinguishable solely on the basis of features that are difficult or impossible to observe with the unaided eye. Inexpensive hand lenses are available for as little as a couple of dollars, but professional-quality lenses may cost up to $25 or more.

Nature photography has become tremendously popular over the past two decades. Modern lightweight 35mm single-lens reflex cameras are both easy to carry and capable of a full range of professional results. The wide selection of lenses available for these cameras makes them especially valuable for recording the beauty and variety of nature. Telephoto lenses enable one to record wildlife behavior while remaining far enough away not to disrupt it. Wide-angle lenses allow one to take striking panoramic photos of entire habitats. Macro lenses are ideal for magnified close-ups of natural textures or plant and animal parts too small to be appreciated by the naked eye. Macro zoom lenses, which permit the photographer to switch rapidly from the macro to the telephoto mode, have become very popular with naturalist photographers.

Tips on Observing Wildlife

The ability of animals to move about makes observing them a chancy prospect at best. One may have to look hard to find a particular species of plant, even within its preferred habitat, but once discovered, at least the plant stays in one place for detailed observation. Animals, however, may not only thwart discovery by keeping out of sight but, once observed, may also frustrate prolonged study or enjoyment by moving away at a critical moment. As a result, observing animals is in part a game of wits. One must outsmart the prey; one must think like a predator! The following tips are offered to help beginners increase their chances:

1. The best times for viewing birds and mammals are near dawn and dusk, when both nocturnal and diurnal species may be abroad. The worst time is mid-afternoon, when many creatures rest between bouts of activity.
2. The best places to see birds and mammals are more or less open areas where two or more habitats meet. Open terrain makes observation easier, and the mix of habitats increases the number of species that can be expected to frequent the area.
3. One is likely to see more animals by sitting quietly in one place for a time and then moving on to another station than by continually walking. Mammals in particular are quick to take cover as humans approach. Birds too may fly to higher or less visible perches. Animals soon become accustomed to a person sitting quietly, however, and after a time may go about their business as if no one were present.
4. Birds have excellent color vision, which is why veteran birders always wear drab clothing. Mammals are generally color-blind, but are extremely sensitive to smell. It is best to approach them from downwind.

A Few Precautions

There is less to fear in the Western forests than on the highways traveled to get there. Common sense and simple prudence are enough to ensure a safe, enjoyable visit under ordinary circumstances. The following precautions, however, are good to keep in mind:

1. Do not feed, tease, or otherwise handle or molest wild animals. Bears have been known to bite the hand that feeds them and deer to kick overeager human admirers. Even chipmunks and squirrels may bite, and in some parts of the West—the northern Sierra Nevada, for example—they have

been found to be infested with fleas that carry plague. Nonpoisonous snakes and lizards may inflict painful bites when handled. Under no circumstances approach baby animals. Mother bears, for example, defend their young vigorously and are almost certain to charge anyone who comes too close. Even songbirds may attack someone approaching their nest. At the very least, the young may be harmed or in some cases abandoned as a result of human interference. Do not assume that a young animal by itself has been abandoned. Very likely the mother is nearby, waiting for you to leave. If in doubt, get in touch with a ranger, but do not move or otherwise disturb the animal.

2. In the western national parks, Black Bears have become accustomed to humans and often raid campgrounds for food. These bears are more dangerous than their wilder cousins precisely because they have lost their fear. Discourage bears from visiting your camp by cleaning up thoroughly after dinner, disposing of garbage in appropriate receptacles, and storing food out of reach—either in the back of your car, or if you are backpacking, suspended from a line strung between two trees. Never take food into the tent.

3. The Western Rattlesnake is the only poisonous reptile in most of the forested regions of the West. When in rattlesnake country, watch where you place your hands and feet. Remember, however, that most rattlesnakes are retiring by nature and will flee a human rather than risk confrontation. Moreover, the great majority of rattlesnake bites are not fatal to healthy adults. They are, however, potentially serious and should receive immediate medical attention. Current opinion is sharply divided on the utility of snakebite kits. Before deciding for yourself, you may want to consult your physician. Finally, remember that rattlesnakes are one of nature's ways of keeping the world from being overrun by rodents. The rattlesnake's venom is intended to disable its prey and discourage its enemies, which include hawks, owls, and most large mammalian predators, in addition to humans. Rattlesnakes should not be molested, and there is no need to regard their presence in the world as an affront. They too have their place in the grand scheme of things.

4. Insects are likely to be the most troublesome animal pests encountered in the Western forests. Mosquitoes in particular can be a curse, especially within a few weeks after snow melt. Other insect pests include Black Flies, Deer Flies, Yellowjackets, and biting gnats ("No-see-ems"). The best defense (barring a net suit) is liberal application of repellent containing 100 percent DEET (diethyl toluamide).

5. Learn to recognize such potentially unpleasant plants as Stinging Nettle, Poison Oak, and Poison Ivy; then avoid them. If you inadvertently come into contact with Poison Oak or Poison Ivy, wash the affected area thoroughly with a strong soap—and keep your fingers crossed.

6. Do not attempt to eat wild plants, especially mushrooms, unless you are *absolutely* certain of their edibility. The best way to learn which plants are edible is from someone who already

knows them. Beginners should never rely on their own judgment in this regard.

7. At higher elevations in the mountains, be prepared for sudden changes in weather. Summer thundershowers accompanied by lightning, hail or rain, and plummeting temperatures are common in many parts of the mountainous West. Freezes and snows are possible at any time of year near or above timberline, particularly in the northern Rockies and North Cascades. Always carry appropriate clothing even for short jaunts. Hypothermia is a stealthy killer that can strike even when temperatures are well above freezing. Learn its symptoms and treatment.

8. Do not assume that clear lakes and streams are safe to drink from. Human carelessness has polluted even many back-country waters. Boiling water for at least five minutes removes harmful microorganisms. The new generation of microporous water filters, which also screen out the protozoan *Giardia lamblia,* are portable, easy to use, preserve the excellent flavor of the water, and are now available at reasonable prices.

9. When traveling in winter, avoid areas subject to avalanches. Before traveling in the back country, find out about local avalanche conditions from forest or park rangers or by calling one of the many avalanche information numbers now established for the winter recreation areas in the West.

10. Always carry a map and compass and know how to use them. This is particularly important if you plan any off-trail travel. It is entirely possible to become lost even in a heavily used area only a few dozen yards off the trail.

Listing problems in this way makes them seem more numerous and serious than they really are. Most of those you are likely to encounter in the western forests are merely nuisances, and the rest are generally easy to avoid. Common sense and prudence are the keys to a safe, enjoyable visit.

A Final Note

All forest visitors should take care to leave the woods as little disturbed by their visit as possible. That means camping only in established sites, dousing all fires, disposing of litter properly, and avoiding contamination of lakes and streams by human waste or chemicals, such as soaps and detergents. Visitors should also avoid cutting or defacing living trees and picturesque snags, picking wildflowers, or uprooting plants. It is also important to avoid trampling certain delicate habitats, such as damp meadows, that may take years to recover.

Finally, leave the city and its noises behind you. Savor the quiet, the dappled light, the heady fragrances of the wild forest. Walk the trails and observe firsthand the many plants and animals that give each forest, each patch of woods, its distinctive character. There—near a clear woodland pool, just beyond the first bend in the trail—you may discover, with John Muir, that "Life seems neither long nor short, and we take no more heed to save time or make haste than do the trees and stars. This is true freedom, a good practical sort of immortality."

INTRODUCTION

Across western North America, from the Rocky Mountains to the Pacific Ocean, successive mountain ranges and intervening lowlands form a deeply corrugated landscape characterized by extremes of elevation, climate, and vegetation. Trending north and south, the mountains intercept moist air masses as they move eastward from the Pacific Ocean. This not only increases the moisture on the slopes, but also reduces the precipitation that hits the lowlands and other ranges located downwind. As a result, the cool, moist mountainous areas of western North America stand as climatic islands in a region that is generally characterized by drought. The Rocky Mountains, the Sierra Nevada, the Cascade Range, and most other high ranges in the region bear conifer forests on their flanks, while most of the valleys and basins that lie between them are largely covered by grasslands or desert scrub.

The transition between the moisture-dependent conifer forests upslope and the drought-adapted vegetation below occurs on the lower mountain slopes, where woodlands and brush are commonly found. A woodland differs from a forest in that it consists of smaller, more widely separated trees: Oaks are characteristic of woodlands along the Pacific Coast and in southern Arizona; pinyon pines and junipers are dominant in the woodlands of the Great Basin and southern Rockies. Associated brush formations are commonly lumped together under the term chaparral, but actually include several distinct types, each with its own characteristic shrub species. Only along the humid Northwest Coast and in the northern Rockies and coastal ranges do conifers venture out of the mountains onto the adjacent valleys and plains.

Forest History

About fifty million years ago, early in what geologists call the Tertiary Period, North America had a far warmer, more humid climate than it does today. Mixed temperate forests, rich in both conifers and broadleaf deciduous trees, covered most of the continent from the Arctic Ocean to what is now the northern United States. Most of the genera now occurring both in the eastern deciduous forests and the western conifer forests were well represented in this ancient forest, along with other trees, such as the Ginkgo, that no longer occur naturally in North America. Still other species that were common in this forest, such as the Coast Redwood, are now closely restricted to certain comparatively small geographic areas. Most of the region farther south was covered by a mixed subtropical forest of species with both northern and southern affinities. In the West, semiarid conditions favored woodland, savanna, scrub, and grassland. The common plants consisted mainly of drought-tolerant ancestors of the broadleaf and coniferous evergreens that dominate the region today.

As the Tertiary Period rolled on over the next forty-five million years or so, two major natural events profoundly, though gradually, transformed the vegetation of North America. The first of these events was the slow uplift of the Rocky Mountains and, later, of the Cascade Range and the

Sierra Nevada along the Pacific Coast. The rise of these ranges created increasing aridity to the east and pushed the grasslands into the center of the continent, thereby severing the eastern and western branches of the forest. Desert vegetation spread throughout the Southwest and the Great Basin region. The second major event was a gradual climatic cooling, which caused forests to shift southward along migrational avenues provided by the newly uplifted mountains. By the beginning of the Ice Age—about three million years ago—vegetation had retreated about as far south as it is today, and large areas north of the forest were given over to tundra.

The separation of the eastern and western forests by the grasslands resulted in the differentiated evolution of species with common ancestors. Many dropped out of one forest or the other because of increasingly severe climatic oscillations. In the West, conifers thrived, while most deciduous hardwoods could not survive either the aridity at lower elevations or the cool, brief growing season in the higher mountains.

The continental ice advanced southward at least four times during the Ice Age and formed alpine glaciers in the higher western mountains. Tundra plants from the Arctic persisted on high peaks that protruded above the ice, and grew along the southern margins of the continental ice and the lower margins of the alpine glaciers. These hardy herbs were joined by subalpine conifers such as Whitebark Pine, Mountain Hemlock, Engelmann Spruce, and Subalpine Fir.

The final glacial advance climaxed about 17,000 years ago and was followed by a slow, intermittent retreat. The climate began to warm rapidly about 10,000 years ago and reached a maximum temperature about 7000 years ago. The present distribution of vegetation in North America represents a gradual adjustment to the generally cooler, moister conditions that have prevailed since that time.

Forest Geography
Today, conifers form a forest belt about 500 miles wide, separating the arctic tundra to the north from temperate steppe, scrub, and mixed or broadleaf woodlands and forests to the south. This subarctic, or boreal, conifer forest extends across northern Europe and Siberia and occurs in North America from interior Alaska across northern Canada to the Great Lakes, the Maritime Provinces, and New England. The conifer forests of western North America—the focus of this volume—are essentially southern extensions of the boreal forest, enriched by the addition of numerous species of Mexican origin. This intermingling was made possible by the north–south alignment of the North American mountain ranges, which served as avenues of migration. The resulting conifer forests are unequalled in richness and variety.

Northern, or boreal, conifers—spruces, firs, larches, hemlocks—dominate the western subalpine forests, which are so named because they occur at the edge of or just below the treeless alpine zone. The upper limit of the subalpine forest, which is known as the upper timberline, varies in altitude according to the effect of certain geographic factors, notably latitude and continentality, on local climates. As a general rule, subalpine forests occur at high elevations in zones of cool, brief summers and deep, late-lying snows.

Southern or Mexican species—oaks, pinyons, junipers, and many others—are most conspicuous in the woodlands and chaparral of California, the Great Basin, and the Southwest. Oak or pinyon-juniper woodlands commonly mark the lower timberline, where trees give way to steppe or scrub vegetation. The richest conifer forests occur at middle elevations, where boreal and Mexican species intermingle in varying degrees.

It is convenient to divide these forests into three major geographical divisions: the Northwest coastal forest, the Sierran montane forest, and the Rocky Mountain montane forest. Each group is distinguished by a distinctive mixture of conifers. There is a good deal of overlapping, however, with several species—notably Douglas-fir and Lodgepole Pine— occurring commonly in two, or even all three, divisions.

The Northwest coastal forest occupies the cool, humid lowlands and mountains of the Pacific Northwest from Alaska to central California and from the Pacific shore to the crests of the Coast Mountains of British Columbia and the Cascade Range. The dominant trees are moisture-loving species such as Sitka Spruce, Western Hemlock, Coastal Douglas-fir, and Coast Redwood. Mexican species play a relatively minor role in this forest, but are increasingly important southward through Oregon and northern California.

The Sierran forest replaces the Northwest coastal forest in the interior mountains of southwestern Oregon and northwestern California; it also occurs throughout the Sierra Nevada and the mountains of southern California and northern Baja. Mixed stands containing Ponderosa Pine, Sugar Pine, Incense-cedar, White Fir, and Douglas-fir are characteristic of this forest.

The Rocky Mountain forest occurs throughout the Rocky Mountain region, in the Southwest, and along the eastern side of the Coast Mountains in British Columbia and the Cascade Range. Characteristic trees include Ponderosa Pine, interior Douglas-fir, Lodgepole Pine, and Quaking Aspen.

Climate and Conifers

The oldest conifer fossils date back some 350 million years, to long before the advent of flowering plants, and a time when plants were first colonizing dry land. Instead of flowers, conifers bear small, fleshy, male cones, which provide pollen, and large, woody, female cones, which bear seeds. Pollination is carried out not by insects or birds but by the wind, which broadcasts the fertile dust far and wide. As a group, conifers are prolific seeders, producing large crops every few years, but germination is often difficult in a mature forest.

Conifers dominate the western forests because they are superbly adapted to withstand extremes of cold, heat, and drought. Although deciduous hardwoods, like conifers, are adapted to long, cold winters, they require warm, humid summers in return. In western North America, areas that are moist because of altitude or latitude also tend to be cool, while areas that are warm are invariably also dry. As a result, broadleaf trees in the West either tend to be evergreens (like live oaks and madrones) or, if deciduous, grow mostly in environments where conifers are temporarily precluded. The ability to overcome a brief growing season is essential to the success of trees in cold climates. The evergreen habit of most conifers allows them to lengthen their growing seasons by starting photosynthesis as soon in spring as air temperatures permit; the trees don't have to grow a whole new set of leaves first. Conifers along the Pacific Coast and in the Southwest even have the opportunity to carry on photosynthesis during mild spells in midwinter. On dry sites, almost seventy percent of the year's photosynthesis may occur outside the growing season. This is critical, considering that summer drought is characteristic of even the more humid sections of the region. Both deciduous and evergreen trees shut down for a time in response to moisture stress, resulting from summer drought. But deciduous trees are at a decided disadvantage in this climate, because, unlike evergreens, they cannot carry on additional photosynthesis in the mild winters. Thus deciduous hardwoods in this region grow mainly on sites that are reliably moist in summer.

Because evergreen leaves are exposed continuously, regardless of the weather, they have developed certain features to prevent freezing and moisture loss. The tough, thick, waxy coating on conifer needles provides excellent insulation from cold and heat alike. Resin in the needles acts as antifreeze, and in summer, the waxy coating retards moisture loss by keeping internal temperatures down and reducing surface evaporation. The size and shape of conifer needles also make them ideal in difficult climates. Because the needles are slender and have only a single vein, the flow of water within is concentrated, moisture loss is reduced. The countless slender needles of a conifer expose maximum leaf surface to the sun; but far less damage is done by the loss of any single leaf.

Conifers growing in zones where there is heavy snowfall characteristically have slender, spirelike crowns and flexible branches, both of which enable them to bear heavy snow loads without being damaged. The common and scientific names of the Limber Pine (*Pinus flexilis*) commemorate this trait, which subalpine trees such as Whitebark Pine and Mountain Hemlock also share. Most subalpine conifers can tolerate being pressed flat by heavy snows during the seedling stage; when released, they simply bend upward and continue growing. On steep slopes, snow creep also lays seedlings and saplings low; subalpine conifers may develop "pistol butt" trunks, which extend horizontally for a foot or two, then turn upward.

Regional Climate

The climate of western North America varies greatly with latitude, distance from the Pacific Ocean, and the position of mountain ranges with respect to prevailing westerly winds. Latitude bears directly on both air temperature and the amount and seasonal distribution of precipitation. As a general rule, air temperature in the Northern Hemisphere declines steadily, from south to north. Along this temperature gradient, the evaporation rate gradually decreases, killing frosts increase in frequency and severity, the growing season becomes shorter, and more precipitation falls as snow. In response, conifers increase in numbers relative to broadleaf trees, and the upper and lower elevation limits of the forest are both lowered. Drought-tolerant southern conifers are gradually replaced by cold-resistant northern species.

In summer, a huge subtropical high-pressure (i.e. clear-weather) system sits about half-way between Hawaii and the west coast of North America. Warm, dry air circulates clockwise around its center, bringing fair weather to most of the West. In the winter the high-pressure system shifts southward, and the storms instead move across the western United States. These frontal systems bring heavy rains to coastal lowlands, particularly in the Northwest, and heavy snows to higher elevations in the Cascade Range and the Sierra Nevada. As a result of these seasonal shifts in the storm track, precipitation in western North America tends to decrease from north to south in the region and to be more strictly confined to the winter months. This means that most of the West receives the least precipitation when temperatures—and therefore evaporation rates—are highest.

When moist air is forced to rise over a mountain range, it is cooled in its ascent. Since air's ability to hold water vapor declines with air temperature, rising air masses are able to hold less and less moisture. Excess moisture condenses to form clouds, and with sufficient moisture and cooling, precipitation results. As air passes over the mountain range and descends the leeward slope, it grows warmer and is able to hold increasing amounts of water vapor. Precipitation thus decreases and eventually stops; clouds break up, disappear, or drift in ragged snatches downwind. Desert vegetation gradually replaces forest, with woodland or chaparral marking the transition. Dry regions downwind from high mountain ranges are said to lie in the rain shadow of the peaks; the Great Basin and much of the Southwest lie in the rain shadow of the Sierra. The Cascades have a comparable but less profound effect in eastern Oregon and Washington.

Barrier ranges such as the Cascades and Sierra not only reduce precipitation in regions downwind, but also prevent the passage of marine air into the interior of the continent. Since the temperature of water changes less readily than that of land, the ocean moderates seasonal climatic extremes; thus, regions east of the Cascade–Sierra divide experience greater daily and seasonal shifts in temperature than do coastal areas to the west, where a distinctly maritime climate prevails. West of these mountains, summers are generally cooler, and winters warmer than at comparable latitudes to the east. At the same time, these ranges protect coastal areas from incursions of frigid polar air during the winter.

The most magnificent conifer forests in the world occur in the mountains and humid lowlands of the Pacific Coast region, where mild winters, warm summers, and adequate moisture from late-lying snow or fog combine to create nearly ideal conditions for growing conifers. Most conifer species occurring in the western forests reach their greatest size and longevity in the Pacific states. The Northwestern and Sierran forests also have no equals among conifer forests for numbers of species. In the Rocky Mountain region, where drought and cold create more severe conditions, the forests contain fewer species and generally smaller trees, and occur at higher elevations than forests in California and the Pacific Northwest.

Forest Limits
Facing west from near Denver, Colorado, it is possible to make out the broad band of conifer forest that stripes the eastern wall of the Front Range. The lower limit of the forest occurs in the foothills, where Ponderosa Pines give way to Rocky Mountain chaparral and arid grassland. At the upper limit, Engelmann Spruce and Subalpine Fir are replaced by treeless alpine tundra, which extends to the highest peaks. The upper timberline on mountains and the northern timberline in the Arctic represent the surrender of trees in the face of increasing cold. Beyond either of these timberlines, temperatures are too low to sustain plant activity at a rate essential for growth in such a brief growing season. Summer temperatures are critical, because they govern plant metabolism and growth. Both timberlines coincide roughly with the 50° F isotherm, an invisible boundary beyond which the average daytime temperature in July is below 50° F. The general reason why trees will not grow beyond the timberline is known, but the exact cause or causes remain elusive. One reasonable suggestion is that timberline represents the place where available energy is adequate to maintain basic metabolic processes, but is not sufficient to prompt the addition of new woody tissue. A more recent hypothesis suggests that, although new tissue can be added, the growing season is too short to allow it to completely ripen. This failure of new shoots to ripen is critical; ripening is the process whereby succulent shoots become woody, a necessary transformation for winter survival since woody stems are less vulnerable to freezing and to abrasion by wind-blown snow and ice.
Timberline varies locally in response to topography, snow, wind, and other factors. Trees generally range higher on south-facing slopes, where they also tend to be more stunted and deformed because of greater exposure to wind. In western North America, the prevailing southwesterly storm winds tend to transfer snow from south-facing slopes to northern exposures, where it forms deep drifts. The accumulated snow may linger on north-facing slopes so long that the growing season becomes too brief for tree growth, thereby resulting in a local lowering of timberline. Something similar occurs on the seaward slopes of maritime ranges such as the North Cascades, where deep snows and cloudiness that persists well

into the summer retard melting of the snowpack. As a result,
timberline on the west side of the range is fully 1000 feet
lower than on the sunnier, less snowy eastern flank. At the
same time, too little snow will leave young trees exposed to
winter blasts, which may affect timberline in some areas.
Air temperature declines gradually toward the north,
producing a corresponding lowering of timberline, although
the correlation is not constant. Along the Pacific Coast,
timberline drops from about 11,000 feet in southern
California to 10,000 feet in the northern Sierra Nevada, 7500
feet in the central Oregon Cascades, 5500 feet in the North
Cascades of Washington, 3000 feet in the Alaska Panhandle,
and 1500 feet in south-central Alaska.
The lower limit of the conifer forest on mountainsides is a
moisture frontier, below which precipitation is insufficient to
support forest conifers. As a rule, forests in western North
America occur only where the rainfall averages at least fifteen
inches a year; this figure may be higher or lower, however, as a
result of local conditions. Throughout much of the West,
woodlands and chaparral occupy the foothill zone below the
forest. Where rainfall averages below ten inches a year,
woodlands give way to grasslands or desert vegetation.
From central California northward along the coast to Alaska,
forests extend to sea level. Farther inland, Ponderosa Pines,
the lowest-ranging forest conifers, first appear among foothill
oaks and chaparral at about 3000 feet above sea level on the
western slope of the Sierra Nevada. In the mountains of
southern California, forest pines generally occur only above
4500 feet. On the east side of the Sierra, a conifer forest
extends below 7000 feet only along streams. Farther east,
along the eastern border of California, a sparse Limber Pine-
Bristlecone Pine woodland occurs only above 9000 feet. In the
Colorado Rockies, the lower limit of the Ponderosa Pine forest
is 6000 feet. This forest type extends down to 1200 feet in the
Canadian Rockies, but no lower than 7000 feet in Arizona.

Forest Soil

Forming at the interface of rock and sky, soil is the medium
through which plants absorb moisture from the atmosphere
and nourishment from the earth. Soil begins to form when
water and ice weather bedrock, creating sand grains and
microscopic particles of clay. Coarse sands pack together
loosely, leaving spaces for oxygen. Fine silts and clays improve
moisture retention. The "rich, well-drained loams" of garden
books contain particles in a range of sizes, with just the right
balance of these ingredients to ensure both ample moisture
and good aeration. In addition to their mineral components,
soils also have an organic component, the rich, dark, fragrant
material called humus. Soil fungi and bacteria, with the aid of
numerous invertebrate animals, produce humus by breaking
down the remains of plants and animals. Humus improves the
moisture-holding capacity of sandy soils and the drainage
characteristics of fine-grained soils.
Deeper forest soils are more often deposited than formed in

place, as was long assumed to be the cause. Glaciers, wind, water, and gravity (rockfalls, landslides) all move large quantities of rock debris from one place to another. The resulting aggregations are typically loose, friable, and therefore especially vulnerable to weathering. Volcanic eruptions and the subsequent airborne deposition of ash have also played an important role in soil formation. The Cascade Range would be much rockier and less forested were it not for the volcanic ash generated by volcanoes along its crest.

As a rule, the soils in conifer forest are moderately to highly acidic and deficient in essential nutrients. Needles, with their tough, waxy coats, decompose slowly. This process is further retarded by low temperatures or inadequate moisture, two common conditions in the western conifer forests. As a result, many forests have thick mats of compacted litter, which represents as much as a decade of leaf fall. In other words, potential nutrients are on top of the soil rather than in it. Water that percolates down through the needle mat creates humic acid, which leaches minerals from the uppermost soil horizon, depositing them in the next layer down, out of the reach of most plants. The result is a gray, acidic, nutrient-poor upper horizon, inhospitable for many understory plants. Soils of this type, called podzols, are characteristic of cool, humid climates.

Soil Fungi

Fungi are more important than bacteria in decomposing forest litter because they tolerate soil acidity better. Mushrooms, which are abundant in conifer forests, are merely the exposed fruiting bodies of vast underground networks (mycelia) of probing, branching, hairlike filaments (hyphae). Probing for organic materials in the soil, the hyphae release enzymes that reduce the detritus to a kind of nutrient-rich broth, which fungi can absorb. In the process, the soil is enriched.

In deficient conifer soils, fungi increase their nutrient intake by parasitizing the roots of conifers. In the process, they also enable the trees to extend the range of their root systems and to absorb water and nutrients more efficiently. This union of roots and fungi, known as mycorrhiza, is a classic example of symbiosis, which is an intimate, mutually beneficial relationship between distinct organisms. Some species of fungus form mycorrhiza only with certain host trees; other fungi are less finicky. Although the symbiotic relationship between conifers and fungi has long been recognized, botanists have only recently begun to suspect that mycorrhizae are also widespread among hardwoods as well.

Although soil bacteria are less active in acidic soils, they still play an important role in improving soil fertility. Bacteria such as *Rhizobium* and *Actinomyces* form nodules on the roots of certain host plants, which include legumes, ceanothus, alder, waxmyrtle, buffaloberry, and Antelope Brush. Within these nodules, and only there, the bacteria fix, or bind, atmospheric nitrogen into amino acids, organic compounds useful both to them and their host plants.

Fires and Vegetation

Throughout much of the West, fires have played a critical role in the evolution of forest, woodland, and chaparral vegetation. Each summer, hundreds or thousands of wildfires break out. Most are caused by human carelessness, but a significant number originate with lightning strikes.

Before white settlement of the region, Indians periodically set ground fires to clear out the underbrush and improve the forage conditions for big game. Small, cool ground fires regularly raced through the forests of the Rocky Mountains and the Sierra, removing underbrush but leaving mature trees largely intact. Bigger fires also occurred from time to time, but over the millennia, the forests adjusted to the occasional crown fires that burned entire stands of trees to the ground. In the late nineteenth century, the carelessness of settlers resulted in numerous conflagrations that destroyed thousands of acres of forest. In response, the newly created US Forest Service instituted a strict policy of fire suppression.

As a result of this policy, ground fires were largely eliminated, allowing dangerous build-ups of understory litter in most western forests. By the 1970s, the fuel accumulation had become so alarming that the Forest Service and other resource agencies began to modify their fire-suppression policies. Today they carry out carefully controlled burns on selected sites as a way of reducing fuel accumulation that could lead to far more destructive fires. Research has made it clear that periodic burning confers a number of benefits on forest communities.

The historical role of fire in the coastal, montane, and subalpine forests of the Pacific Northwest is significantly different from that in the Rocky Mountain and Sierran regions. In the Northwest, where cool, humid summers inhibit fires but encourage an enormous accumulation of fuel, fires are infrequent but, when they do occur, are often catastrophic. Such fires tend to happen during intermittent episodes of prolonged drought, when temperatures are high, humidity is low, and wind conditions are ideal for the rapid spread of flames. The interval between these conflagrations averages 300 to 400 years, but may be more than 1000 years; the areas burned may exceed 100,000 or even 200,000 acres. Fire suppression in this century is unlikely to alter this regime over the long run.

Fires promote forest diversity. Periodic fires of varying intensity produce a patchwork of vegetation, ranging from recently burned areas that have been colonized by post-fire herb communities to long-unburned areas that are covered by old-growth forest. This diversity of vegetation and habitats encourages a correspondingly diverse assortment of wildlife. Slow-moving ground fires also improve the soil by transforming needle litter, which is slow to decompose, into a mineral ash that increases soil fertility. Fires also expose areas of mineral soil, which many trees require for successful seed germination. And by removing dead and diseased trees, periodic fires may also hold parasites and insect pests such as Dwarf Mistletoe, Spruce Budworm, and bark beetles in check.

Forest Pests

Insects, fungi, and mistletoe are the principal parasites living on forest conifers. Insects of various kinds feed on all parts of a tree; fungi cause root and heartwood rots; mistletoe deforms trees and saps their vigor, making them more vulnerable to attack by insects and fungi. Even-aged stands of mainly a single species are most vulnerable to epidemic devastation; mixed stands with trees of all ages are least vulnerable.

Under normal conditions, native predators combine with the natural resistance of host trees to keep destructive insects and parasitic fungi in check. Moreover, these so-called pests serve the important and—in human terms—beneficial functions of opening up the forest to new generations of younger trees and creating habitat mosaics that encourage ecological diversity. As a result, forests become more complex, and, because devastating outbreaks of insects or disease are less likely, the forests become more stable as well. Whether destructive insects and fungi are "good" or "bad" therefore depends on one's point of view. If maximizing lumber production in the short term is the sole criterion, then these parasites are evils to be eradicated (which is impossible). When ecological, wildlife, recreational, and aesthetic values are also considered, it becomes apparent that these so-called evils are essential elements in vital forest communities.

The Forest Community

A conifer forest, like all ecological communities, is the collective result of individual plants responding to a shared environment. Each plant in the forest, from tiny mosses to giant conifers, functions according to its particular requirements and capabilities. But since resources are never sufficient to permit the unrestrained development of all resident plants, competition among species is vigorous. A conifer forest, then, manifests the countless accommodations competing plants have made, both to one another and to their physical habitat.

As vegetation evolves on a particular patch of ground, it becomes apparent that there are certain plant species that are naturally better suited to this habitat than to others—and which proliferate faster or grow larger as a result. Such plants, known as dominant species, determine the appearance of vegetation and even alter habitats to reduce competition and perpetuate their own occupation of a site. In the forests of western North America, various conifer species are the dominant plants. By reducing sunlight, monopolizing soil moisture and nutrients, and affecting the habitat in other ways, dominant conifers largely determine which other plants can or cannot grow alongside them. Of course, various plant species long ago evolved forms specially adapted to the habitats created by trees. Some of these associates are so closely adapted to life in the forest that they never occur outside it. Communities include animals as well as plants, although animals are less conspicuous. Nevertheless, they are so important to vegetation that, in their absence, many communities would be significantly different. Most flowering plants depend on insects or birds for pollination, while seeds hitch rides—on the coats or in the stomachs of various birds and mammals—to new seedbeds away from the competition of parent plants. Large grazing or browsing animals can change the appearance and composition of vegetation by cropping certain species and ignoring others; forest insects can completely defoliate a stand of conifers; birds can keep populations of insect pests in check; earthworms aerate the soil. The relationship between plants and animals is so intimate and of such long standing that the evolution of one has proceeded hand in hand with that of the other.

The biotic community and its physical environment constitute an ecosystem, the function of which is to produce and distribute energy. All life depends ultimately on the ability of green plants to carry out photosynthesis, the process in which sunlight is used to synthesize simple sugar from carbon dioxide and water. By incorporating the products of photosynthesis into their tissues, plants make the energy that is bound up in sunlight available to animals. Herbivores obtain their share of the sun by eating plants. Carnivores eat either the herbivores or one another. Among the most successful animals are those that, like crows, skunks, bears, and humans, will eat almost anything. Soil organisms decompose the forest's organic residues, the remains of plant and animal, predator and prey.

Forest Succession

When vegetation colonizes bare ground, such as a rock outcrop or the damp soils at the edge of a pond, a series of plant communities occupies the site in succession, each one altering it somewhat for those that follow. Each stage of vegetation in the process is known as a sere (coined from *series*), and the plants that dominate these seres are called seral species. Eventually, the site is occupied by a community that is so perfectly suited to the habitat that it will persist indefinitely in the absence of further disturbance. Such a community is known as a climax. In a forest, the dominant climax species is the one that is able to reproduce in the shade of its neighbors—the one represented by seedlings and saplings in the understory. Species that are unable to do this are eventually shaded out by those that can, and therefore are not around to be part of the climax forest. A species that is climax in one habitat generally also occurs as a seral species in other habitats, where it may even be dominant for a time.

The climax, however, often represents the potential of vegetation rather than its actual expression in a particular habitat. Disturbances such as fire, logging, or windthrow frequently interrupt the course of plant succession, allowing nonclimax species to maintain themselves on a site. If a nonclimax species lives long enough, repeated disruptions over the course of centuries virtually guarantee its indefinite presence on a site because the climax vegetation is never undisturbed long enough to replace it. This explains the

persistence of Douglas-fir on sites in the Pacific Northwest
where Western Hemlock is the climax tree.
Following fire or logging, opportunistic herbs such as
Fireweed are often the first plants to invade a site and establish
dominance. Arriving as wind-blown seeds from nearby areas,
these fire pioneers form a wild-flower community, which often
persists for several years before being supplanted by shrubs.
Dense brush fields are typical of areas that have been burned
relatively recently, and generally consist of both species that
were present in the former forest and others whose seeds blew
in from outside. Eventually, shrubs are shaded out by rapidly
growing deciduous trees, such as Red Alder or aspen, or
sometimes even by conifers, notably Lodgepole Pine or
Douglas-fir. These trees will shelter the seedlings of the
climax species, which may have to wait a few centuries before
reclaiming the site, or which may never do so. However,
climax species often appear early on in the course of succession
and may even be among the first invaders of a disturbed site.

Ecotones

The boundary between two plant communities forms a
transitional zone, where elements from each community
intermingle to some degree. Such a zone is called an ecotone.
Abrupt ecotones commonly express equally abrupt changes in
environment. For example, throughout the Great Basin,
pinyon woodlands growing on the thin, rocky, well-drained
soils of the lower foothills give way suddenly to sagebrush
steppes on finer, less rapidly draining soils of adjacent flats.
The boundaries between forest and meadow can either be
gradual or rather abrupt. Where trees on well-drained slopes
give way suddenly to meadow or to marsh in poorly drained
basins, abrupt forest-meadow ecotones may occur. During this
century, Subalpine Fir and Mountain Hemlock have invaded
meadows in the Cascades, the Olympics, and the Coast
Mountains of British Columbia, and Lodgepole Pine has done
the same in the Sierra Nevada. Where this invasion has
occurred, a broad ecotone of increasingly tall and more closely
spaced trees leads from meadow to forest. Timberline is
another gradual ecotone.
Even where ecotones are abrupt, the adjacent communities
usually have at least some species in common. The dominant
species in one community often assumes a secondary role in
the neighboring community. In fact, except where unusual
environmental boundaries exist, as in the Klamath Mountains,
one forest community merges gradually into the next. Along
an ecotone, the forest is not only richer in species but virtually
impossible to assign to one type or another.
An ecotone may or may not be stable. The gradual
encroachment of vegetation on a rock outcrop is obviously
unstable, because the boundary will continue to shift as the
vegetation increasingly covers the rock surface. The ecotone
between climax forests, however, represents a long-term
dynamic balance between two communities. But changes in
climate can turn a more or less stable ecotone into an unstable

one; this has happened in the Cascades and the Sierra, where conifers have invaded large areas of meadows.

Forest edges are particularly good places for observing wildlife, because the mixture of vegetation creates a hybrid environment that is appealing to animals from both communities. The variety of vegetation is likely to attract numerous herbivores, which will in turn bring carnivores to the area. Big game animals such as deer and Elk, which commonly move back and forth between forest and meadow, are particularly attracted to forest edges, where resting areas, browse, and succulent herbaceous vegetation are all likely to occur in a restricted area. Birds also increase in both variety and numbers in response to the greater diversity of habitats. This increase in wildlife along ecotones is called the edge effect. Although widely recognized, animal ecologists point out that the increase is more illusory than real: Animals are easier to see and therefore to census at the relatively open forest edge, and invertebrate animals are rarely taken into account. Authorities do not dispute the claim that birds and large game animals are more numerous, but the overall number of creatures, counting invertebrates, is probably not much greater in ecotones than in the middle of a plant formation.

Vegetation Zones

Climatic gradients in mountain ranges occur mainly in response to changes in elevation, and shifts in vegetation correspond to these changes. In ascending a mountain, then, one encounters a sequence of more or less distinct, climatically controlled belts or zones, each of which is defined by a particular type of climax vegetation.

Within a single zone there are typically, in addition to the climax type, numerous communities occupying a variety of habitats. Examples include the following: deciduous woods along streams; aspen groves on especially wet or dry sites; shrubs on rocky, thin soils; and meadows in moist, poorly drained basins. A healthy, well-developed forest complex will include a mosaic of vegetation types and communities.

Zone boundaries seldom follow neat elevational contours, although, for purposes of discussion, it is customary to assign general upper and lower limits to each zone. Actually, zones tend to intermingle along their shared frontier in response to local climates, which result from topography. As a rule, zones in the Northern Hemisphere extend to higher elevations on south-facing slopes and to lower elevations on north-facing slopes, since southern exposures receive more hours and a higher intensity of solar radiation than northern exposures. Consequently, south-facing slopes are warmer, free of snow earlier, and therefore experience longer growing seasons. Zones also tend to extend higher on ridges and lower in adjacent valleys. The ridges are generally sunnier and free of snow earlier, while the valleys are cooler (because of cold air drainage) and tend to keep snow longer. Exceptions to this pattern occur on ridges that are swept free of snow by winds,

where organisms are exposed to severe winter drought and
wind abrasion, which can cause tissue damage.
Zone boundaries tend to be blurred, as one climax community
often merges with its neighbor upslope or down. The plants
that are characteristic of one zone usually occur in cooler,
moister places in the zone below and in warmer, drier ones in
the zone above. As the elevation increases or decreases, certain
plants become less common and may finally disappear from the
mix, while others increase in numbers. Many other understory
plants occur in two or more zones, because the presence of a
forest canopy usually has a greater impact on the distribution
of these plants than do the kinds of trees forming the canopy.

Canopy and Understory

Forests are distinguished from other types of terrestrial
vegetation by their great height—a distinction that is not at
all trivial, however obvious it may seem. They contain vertical
space for the elaboration of vegetation layers other than the
dominant trees. The superimposition of vegetation permits a
maximum number of plants to grow, creating a richness not
present in areas where only shorter types of vegetation can
grow. A well-developed western conifer forest includes several
principal layers: the canopy or overstory layer, which consists
of the dominant conifers; a secondary or understory tree layer,
which usually consists of shade-tolerant hardwoods; a shrub
layer; and an herbaceous layer, which may include grasses,
sedges, and ferns in addition to broadleaf herbs. The lowest
layer, which is best represented in the coastal forests of the
Northwest, consists of low-growing lichens, mosses, and other
cryptogams. One or more layers may be missing or poorly
developed, particularly in forests occupying marginal sites.
In large measure, the density and extent of the canopy
determine the nature of the understory. Dominant forest
conifers modify the climate for plants and animals living
beneath them. Air temperatures within the forest are usually
more moderate than in adjacent open areas. During the day, of
course, the canopy blocks the sunlight and thereby lowers the
temperature on the forest floor. At night, however, the forest
remains warmer than open areas, since the trees prevent the
loss of long-wave radiation to the atmosphere (the common
cause of plummeting nighttime temperatures at high
elevations). Plants within the forest are therefore less subject
to frost damage than those growing in the open. By lowering
temperatures, the canopy also reduces moisture evaporation
from soil and plant surfaces. It also transpires enormous
amounts of water, thereby increasing humidity in the
understory and further lowering the transpiration rates of the
shrubs and herbs on the forest floor. The foliage even traps
moisture from fog, which condenses on needles and then drips
to the ground; fog drip is an important source of supplemental
moisture for coastal forests during summer drought.
Moreover, wind velocity in the forest is usually twenty to sixty
percent less than in the open, the percentage actually
increasing with the speed of the wind. Within a closed forest,

winds rarely exceed one or two miles per hour. The plants within the forest thus enjoy more protection from the chilling, drying, and breaking power of the wind than do those outside. Occasional winds in excess of fifty miles per hour visit every forest at one time or another. Such winds rip through the forest, felling numerous trees, but mainly those that are diseased, weakened, shallow-rooted, or growing on unstable ground. By thus opening up the canopy, winds—like fire, insects, and disease—create opportunities for pioneer plants, thus contributing to renewal and diversity in the forest.

The canopy not only influences the forest understory but is itself a complex ecosystem supporting numerous organisms. In the Pacific Northwest, for example, old-growth Douglas-firs may have sixty-six million needles, with a total surface area of 4000 square meters. These large trees have flat, spraylike branches that are covered with layers of organic "soil" up to several centimeters thick. Several different types of epiphytic plants—mainly mosses and leafy lichens—root in this medium. These lichens are able to fix nitrogen from the atmosphere, and upon their decomposition this essential nutrient becomes available to the forest community.

Adaptations to Shade
Forest conifers receive plenty of light simply by reaching above lesser plants. The pronounced tapering of the crowns of firs, hemlocks, spruces, and other trees not only aids in the shedding of snow but also permits light to penetrate to the lower branches, where flattened sprays are arranged in overlapping whorls around the central trunk. This arrangement is particularly well expressed in understory seedlings and saplings, which need more than their elders to expose maximum leaf surface to the sky. Among conifers growing in open situations, those found in areas of little snow rarely show the classic Christmas-tree shape. For example, the Digger Pine of California's oak woodland has an open, rounded crown not unlike that of a deciduous hardwood. The same is true of pinyons, junipers, and various pines and cypresses occurring in open, droughty woodlands.

Mature forest conifers often shed their lower limbs, which receive minimal light and which would probably use up more water and nutrients than they are worth. Trees such as Douglas-fir, Sitka Spruce, and White Fir may be free of limbs for dozens of feet above the ground. The lowest limb of the General Sherman tree, a giant sequoia in Sequoia National Park in the southern Sierra Nevada, is 130 feet from the ground, measures some fifteen feet at the trunk, and is more than 120 feet long! Self-pruning is another adaptation to understory shade that is rarely seen in the open.

Understory vegetation is usually richest in both quantity and variety in areas where shade and sunlight are mixed to some degree. The amount of light under most forest canopies is sufficient for understory plants to grow and reproduce. The overriding characteristic of plants that have adapted to shade is their ability to carry on photosynthesis at light levels below those tolerable to most plants. The leaves of shade-resistant plants are usually a rich, deep green, partly because they are crammed with chloroplasts, which are the cell structures that manufacture the chlorophyll essential to photosynthesis, and partly because shade leaves have no surface hairs to interfere with the absorption of sunlight. Shade plants also tend to have large, thin leaves so that they can expose maximum surface to the sky. The thinness, of course, is essential if the plant is to develop large leaves without adding weight, which is desirable because too much weight would cause them to droop at angles that are unsuited to the maximum reception of sunlight.

Some plants are able to live in the deepest shade because they have given up the practice of photosynthesis altogether. Plants such as Coralroot, Pinedrops, and Snow Plant contain no chlorophyll, and may be a variety of colors other than green. They also have tiny, nonfunctional, scalelike leaves. As they are unable to manufacture carbohydrates from inorganic materials, these and similar plants instead draw their nutrients from forest humus or, in some cases, the roots of other plants. To do so, they form intimate associations with certain soil fungi, which act as extensions of their root systems.

Tolerance

Some tree species are able when young to grow, often at greatly reduced rates, in the shade of the forest canopy; these trees are said by foresters to be tolerant. Tolerant species such as Western Hemlock, White Fir, and Engelmann Spruce are able to survive in deep shade for decades. Once the canopy is opened by fire, logging, disease, or windthrow, they are able to grow rapidly in response to their new environment. Tolerant trees usually dominate climax forests because intolerant species are gradually eliminated through the inability of their seedlings or saplings to survive in the understory. Intolerant trees are able to reproduce only when natural or human disturbance opens the forest, or on marginal sites, such as arid soils, serpentine, or flooded areas. In such places, the climax dominants often cannot survive, or the vegetation is too sparse to form a more or less closed canopy. The American conifer that is most successful in exploiting such areas is Lodgepole Pine, which is highly intolerant of shade. Ponderosa Pine, another intolerant species, has been able to maintain dominance on some sites only through the agency of periodic fires, which eliminate the seedlings of more tolerant competitors.

Although tolerance traditionally refers to a tree's ability to withstand prolonged shading, low illumination is rarely the only factor operating to inhibit the growth of understory plants. Insufficient soil moisture is often even more critical. Forest trees withdraw enormous amounts of moisture from the soil, producing more or less droughty conditions for understory vegetation. Experiments have been performed in which deep trenches were cut around certain forest plots in order to keep out invasive tree roots; these experiments have consistently shown improved growth of the plants in the protected plots. In many cases, the increase in growth that followed the trenching was even greater than that achieved by tying the canopy back to admit more light. In the open Ponderosa Pine woods of the Rockies, moisture is the chief restricting factor. In the moist forests of the Pacific Northwest, however, low light is apt to be more of a limitation.

Old-growth Forests

Forests that have developed over long periods without catastrophic disturbance of either natural or human origin are known as old-growth forests. They are what most people mean by the phrase "virgin forest," a term that reflects these forests' untouched, primeval quality. Old-growth forests differ from young ones in species composition and structure, as well as in the cycling of energy, nutrients, and water. These differences result mainly from the presence in old-growth forests of large live trees, large snags (standing dead trees), and large downed logs. Old-growth forests are as productive, more complex, and more beautiful than many young forests.

Most current research on the nature of old-growth forests has been carried out in the Pacific Northwest. In this area, these forests, because of their great commercial value, have nearly been eliminated outside of national parks and national wilderness areas. The following description of old-growth forests summarizes the findings of that research. Although old-growth forests in other regions differ from those of the Northwest in various ways, the presence and ecological importance of large living trees, snags, and downed logs are shared characteristics.

Old-growth forests in the Pacific Northwest, where conditions for conifer growth are ideal, require at least 175 years to develop, and most are from 350 to 750 years of age. Stands that are more than 1000 years old are generally restricted to moist pockets—cool river canyons, for example—that are safe from most fires. In other regions, old-growth forests may take longer to develop fully and may not achieve such longevity, but they serve many of the same ecological functions.

Old-growth forests are composed of trees that vary in size and species; the dominant trees are truly impressive. Their multilayered canopies produce heavily filtered light. As a result, the understory layers of shrubs, herbs, and tree seedlings are moderate in density and patchy in distribution, tending to be best developed where terrain or disturbance has created openings. Snags and rotted stubs are common, and numerous large logs in various stages of decay lie strewn over the forest floor and across streams. Small streams may be choked by organic debris; medium-sized ones, however, generally have clear water flowing over gravel beds and plunging over log dams into catch pools below. These stream features—as much as the nature of the understory—are direct results of the structure and composition of old-growth forests. The role of standing trees and of the forest canopy in general has been discussed in preceding sections. But dominant trees continue to influence the forest even after death, first as standing snags and later as downed logs. Snags are most important as a wildlife habitat, serving as nesting sites, food sources, and stages for acting out courtship rituals. Large logs in the Northwest coastal forest take as long as 500 years to decay, depending upon the species. During this period, logs serve a number of important ecological functions that provide a way in which to distinguish old-growth forests. Logs are valuable for wildlife and serve as germination sites for conifers, shrubs, ferns, mosses, lichens, fungi, and other spore-bearing plants. In the humid Northwest forests, lush gardens commonly develop atop these "nurse logs." In addition, logs influence the sociology of the forest by channeling traffic—serving as pathways for some kinds of wildlife and blockades for others.

Fallen logs are also important in the cycling of energy, nutrients, and water through the forest system. They absorb large amounts of moisture, contain carbon, and tend to accumulate nutrients. For example, bacteria that are active in woody debris fix significant amounts of nitrogen. Logs act as storage sites for these various resources, releasing them slowly to the system, but also—more importantly—saving them for times of major disturbance, when other sources may be destroyed. When there is a fire, the nitrogen that is bound up in leaves and branches is vaporized and is thereby lost to the system. However, the nitrogen in logs will remain on the site, where it can be utilized by subsequent vegetation. Eventually, whether burned or consumed through decomposition, logs yield up their stored materials to the forest ecosystem.

They also help the system conserve nutrients that would otherwise be carried away by streams. Logs that fall across small or medium-sized streams create pools with backwaters where organic debris is deposited. Trees thus form the basis of the food chain in small forest streams, as they support the microorganisms that in turn support fish and other vertebrates. Log dams also create habitat diversity and thus increase the number of both aquatic and terrestrial animals able to exist along stream corridors.

Old-growth forests are important as wildlife habitats, recreation areas, and sources of both commercial timber and valuable nutrients and organisms. Even in areas where timber harvesting is the chief activity, it may be advisable to leave some old-growth stands intact so that they can serve as reservoirs for future forests. It may also be advisable to modify cutting techniques in such areas, in order to preserve valuable snags and downed logs.

Wildlife Habitats

Rooted in one place, plants must adjust to the climatic and soil conditions that accompany a particular patch of ground. Animals, however, are able to move through the environment, seeking shelter as needed and searching for food wherever it may be available. Even the most restricted animals are significantly freer than plants to manipulate their environments in ways that enhance their chances of survival. Mobility invests animals with some measure of independence from the elements. As a result, animal habitats depend more upon the types of food and shelter supplied by various kinds of vegetation than they do on climate, soil, or topography.

Some animals are rarely found outside certain habitats. For example, the Dipper, or Water Ouzel, lives almost exclusively along fast-moving streams, where it both feeds and nests. At the other extreme are animals, such as large herbivores and many predators, that commonly wander in and out of various habitats.

Some animals require rather different habitats in close proximity. Beavers, for example, require both ponds to live in and deciduous trees for building dams and lodges, as well as for food. Salamanders mate in pools, but spend most of the year in moist nooks and crannies on dry land. Mountain Bluebirds nest in small trees, which they use as lookouts for spotting insects in adjacent meadows.

The particular way in which an animal uses its habitat—its way of making a living—is called its niche. Forests, because of their layered structure and variety of plant forms, generally offer more kinds of niches than other types of terrestrial vegetation. By occupying different niches, potential competitors can exist side by side. Hawks and owls, for example, both feed on rodents, but hawks hunt during the day, while most owls forage at night. Swainson's Thrush and the Hermit Thrush are closely related insect-eating birds that hunt their prey mainly on the ground. The two may coexist in places, but Swainson's generally prefers lowlands while the Hermit Thrush frequents upper montane and subalpine forests. This separation of potential competitors is called ecological segregation. It permits the maximum utilization of a habitat through the superimposition of several layers of organisms. Ecological segregation has allowed certain groups of animals— notably chipmunks, flycatchers, woodpeckers, warblers, and mice—to fill the western forests with numerous representatives, each occupying a slightly different niche.

Like the vegetation, wildlife habitats in the forest tend to be stratified, with more or less distinctive societies of organisms inhabiting each of the layers. There is, of course, a good deal of movement back and forth between the layers, but most species concentrate their activities in one or two layers.

The ground society consists of animals living on or just beneath the forest floor. It includes the following organisms: wood-processing insects, such as carpenter ants, termites, and certain bugs and beetles; humus digesters, such as pillbugs, sowbugs, and millipedes; and scavengers, such as springtails and Silverfish. Earthworms, of course, are important soil processors. This host of invertebrates is avidly exploited by numerous small predators—including the voracious shrews, Deer Mice, chipmunks—and a variety of birds, among them Robins, thrushes, flickers, and sparrows. These animals are all important in keeping insect populations in check. Burrowing or tunneling animals such as chipmunks, ground squirrels, reptiles, pocket gophers, and moles aerate the soil and carry the remains of plants and prey to lower levels. All of these small birds and mammals in turn support a host of larger predators, such as snakes, Coyotes, foxes, weasels, and owls. Understory shrubs are the principal food of deer and provide winter forage for Elk, while the berries supplied by shrubs are an important food source for numerous birds, rodents, deer, and bears. Shrubbery also provides nesting sites for a variety of birds and serves as cover for small mammals such as hares and chipmunks. Rodents may climb into shrubs in search of food, and woodrats sometimes build their elaborate stick nests in low bushes. Despite all this, no mammals are unique to the shrub layer in western conifer forests.

The most conspicuous mammals living in the forest canopy are the various tree squirrels, which seem forever busy cutting down cones, burying seeds, chasing one another—through the branches, down the trunks, and over the ground—and scolding anyone in the neighborhood. Squirrels nest in tree cavities, which they line with mosses, leaves, and other soft materials. The most important predator of squirrels is the Pine Marten, which resembles an oversized weasel and is able to run down even the fastest squirrel in a treetop chase. Raccoons also nest in tree cavities, but spend most of their time foraging on the ground. Although Porcupines feed in the trees, they most often nest in rock slides—a reverse commute.

Of course, dozens of bird species nest high in the conifers. Each has evolved its own distinctive type of nest and preferred nesting site within the trees; the resulting variety is impressive and represents another form of ecological segregation. Hawks and ravens build large stick platforms, abandoning them after a single season; thereafter, large forest owls use the platforms. Warblers and kinglets hide their soft cuplike nests amid dense foliage high in the trees. Vireos suspend their woven basket nests from the crotches of twigs at various levels. The Evening Grosbeak builds a flimsy nest high in the conifers, but the Pine Grosbeak prefers to use lower branches, understory trees, and shrubs. Jays, tanagers, finches, and Robins all build their nests on horizontal branches far up in the overstory. Woodpeckers are the most ecologically important nest-builders in the forest, as they provide not only homes for themselves, but also hand-me-down nest sites for numerous other creatures. Woodpeckers use their chisel-like beaks to excavate nesting cavities in both living and dead trees, especially the latter, where soft, punky wood makes for easier work. Each year woodpeckers hollow out new nests, abandoning their old ones to countless other birds—including chickadees, House Wrens, owls, and Mountain Bluebirds. Even some mammals, such as squirrels and Raccoons, make use of abandoned woodpecker nests.

Conifers themselves are the most important food plants in the forest. Squirrels, mice, woodrats, chipmunks, and a variety of birds all feed on the nutritious, generally abundant seeds. Pine seeds are particularly prized for their large size and high nutritional value, but the seeds of all conifers are eaten.

Squirrels, by virtue of their size, are able to manipulate entire cones and therefore rarely gather individual conifer seeds, a task that would give less return for comparable energy expenditure. Mice, however, gather individual seeds because they are unable to easily handle cones or to compete effectively with the larger squirrels.

In addition to seeds, the bark and needles of conifers are also important foods. During the winter, Porcupines subsist primarily on bark and may girdle and destroy trees. But in a healthy forest, this pruning may simply serve to open the canopy to younger, more vigorous trees. Several other small mammals, as well as deer, also depend on bark in varying degree. Although conifer needles are favored by fewer animals, they are just about the only food eaten by wintering grouse.

Adaptations to Forest Life

Animal adaptations to life in the forest have generally focused on low light conditions or ways to make a living in the trees. Adaptations to reduced visibility in the forest include dark pigmentation, bold patterning, and an emphasis on voice and hearing for both communication and survival.

Mammals of the forest tend to be darkly pigmented and therefore difficult to detect. The two western red squirrels are both dark, as are the Pine Martens and Fishers that prey upon them. The small rodents of the forest floor are noticeably darker then their counterparts in more open habitats.

Bold color patterns are typical of other kinds of forest animals. The survival value of such coloration seems to be that it breaks up the outline of the animal, making it more difficult to see against the variegated, intricate patterns of light and shadow that are created by limbs and foliage. Forest chipmunks have bolder stripes than those of the open country, and the Golden-mantled Ground Squirrel—the only ground squirrel to specialize in forest living—looks like a giant chipmunk. Woodpeckers and warblers are also rendered in bold patterns.

A number of forest species have also developed excellent hearing and voices to aid communication, since sight alone is not always useful. The large ears of the deer are particularly notable, and are fascinating in the way they constantly shift to pick up every potentially dangerous sound. Squirrels have loud, well-developed voices and spend much of their time scolding either one another or intruders. Male birds sing to mark their territories, attract mates, and warn off rivals; without distinctive, well-developed voices, such activities would be difficult to carry out in the closed forest.

Forest animals also show a number of specific adaptations to arboreal life. Among the most obvious are wings, which may have evolved as special appendages for making use of arboreal habitats. Forest hawks, such as the Goshawk, prey almost entirely on smaller birds; they typically have short wings and long tails for rapid flight and quick maneuvers in the dense forest canopy. Woodpeckers have two toes facing forward and two back, an adaptation that makes possible their method of feeding. The locking mechanism in the feet of perching birds, the sharp claws of certain animals, the large counterbalancing tail of tree squirrels, the gliding cape of flying squirrels, and the prehensile tail of Deer Mice are all good examples of adaptations to arboreal life.

Winter Activities

The chief problem facing animals during the winter is a shortage of food. Many species of birds simply avoid the problem by migrating to warmer climes or, more simply still, to lower elevations. Deer, Elk, and mountain sheep often do likewise, migrating downslope in the fall to their winter grounds and upslope in the spring—attended, of course, by large carnivores such as the Mountain Lion and the Coyote. Most other animals occupy the same ground in winter as in summer, actively hunting or foraging, relying on food caches laid down during the summer, or hibernating.

Animals are only rarely troubled by winter cold, because fur and feathers provide excellent insulation, and cover is readily available. Small animals lose heat faster than do large ones, and they commonly escape cold and carnivores alike by spending most of their time burrowing through the snowpack. They experience the most difficulty when extreme cold combines with a lack of snow cover; this set of conditions either prevents foraging or makes it possible only at the expense of enormous amounts of energy.

Some animals feed heavily in late summer in order to acquire a layer of fat that will sustain them through the winter months. However, this built-in larder is sufficient only if the animal remains inactive, expending a minimum of calories. Therefore, animals that cope with the winter food shortage in this way generally hibernate, spending the season in a state of deep torpor in which the body's metabolism—heartbeat, pulse, respiration rate, and the like—drop to levels far below those normal for the waking state. Marmots are perhaps the champion hibernators of the western forests, remaining in this state of "suspended animation" for as long as seven months. Ground squirrels also hibernate, but waken every couple of weeks to move about and urinate. Surprisingly enough, bears are not true hibernators. They sleep for long periods, but do not enter a torpid state and may venture abroad on warmer days. The Snowshoe Hare, which neither burrows nor hibernates, remains atop the snowpack throughout the winter, where it is almost continuously exposed to both cold and predators. The hare, however, is superbly adapted to this environment. In the fall, its coat changes from brown to white and increases in density. At the same time, a thick pad of hairs grows on the bottom of each hind foot, forming the snowshoes for which the animal is named. The hare relies on its white color for protection and on its broad, padded hind feet for speed and agility in the snow. Its chief predator, the Lynx, has broad, hairy padded feet of its own, and another foe, the weasel, also turns white for the winter. In this manner, predator and prey coevolve to assure their mutual survival.

THE NORTHWEST COASTAL FOREST

Western Hemlock
Tsuga heterophylla
140

Western Redcedar
Thuja plicata
59, 142

Sitka Spruce
Picea sitchensis
116

Douglas-fir
Pseudotsuga menziesii
134

Coast Redwood
Sequoia sempervirens
53, 141

Noble Fir
Abies procera
133

Pacific Silver Fir
Abies amabilis
47

Vine Maple
Acer circinatum
98

Pacific Rhododendron
Rhododendron macrophyllum
209

Blackberry
Rubus ursinus

Salmonberry
Rubus spectabilis
151, 212

Thimbleberry
Rubus parviflorus
152, 181

Twinflower
Linnaea borealis
484

Bigleaf Maple
Acer macrophyllum
102

Sword Fern
Polystichum munitum

The famed redwood groves of northern California and rain forests of western Washington are the finest expressions of a magnificent coastal forest complex that extends northward to southern Alaska. The several conifers presiding over these forests—Western Hemlock, Western Redcedar, Sitka Spruce, Douglas-fir, Coast Redwood, Noble Fir, and Pacific Silver Fir—are among the largest and longest-lived of their kinds, often exceeding 200 feet or more in height, 10 to 15 feet in diameter, and 500 years in age. The forests are spawned by the damp breath of the sea and thrive in a climate of abundant rain, frequent fog, overcast skies, and moderate temperatures year-round. Accordingly, the forests are usually shady and damp, and contain lush understories of shrubs, wildflowers, ferns, and mosses. Dry, open forests and gloomy woods that are too dark for understory plants do exist in the region, but they are not typical. The classic forests of the Pacific Northwest are complex, multistoried formations, ruled by giants.

The finest old-growth stands are often surprisingly spacious. The great trees are seldom crowded, and their columnar trunks may rise dozens of feet skyward before the first branches appear. Even when the canopy is nearly continuous, as it often is, the space beneath may be open enough that light filtered through the upper branches is diffused to create a softly luminous glow throughout. The effect is not one of gloom, but of solemnity.

Among the taller shrubs, the airy Vine Maples seem pruned for placement in a Zen garden, their slender limbs delicately contorted as if for the purpose of holding each spray of leaves at precise right angles to the incidence of light from above. In drier places, large Pacific Rhododendrons sport showy clusters of tubular, pink flowers and whorls of glossy-green, leathery leaves. Huckleberries are numerous, along with Blackberries, Salmonberries, and Thimbleberries. The tiniest shrub is probably Twinflower, which holds its pair of nodding pink blossoms only a few inches above the forest floor.

Giant Bigleaf Maples grow along streams with alders and cottonwoods. Wherever hardwoods are able to take advantage of openings in the canopy, they abandon their broad, rounded crowns to shoot upward like conifers, growing long, straight trunks that culminate in treetop clumps of foliage. In no other conifer forest are hardwoods so few in number or so dearly charged for living space.

Fallen logs lie scattered over the forest floor, no sooner brought low by wind or disease than they are overwhelmed by mosses, ferns, and even young conifers, which find hospitable seed beds elevated above the tangle below. Lichens drape the branches of giant maples. Mosses are everywhere in the damper forests, forming plush carpets, padding boulders the size of houses, clinging to damp cliff faces, and even mantling the trunks and branches of trees. Lush fern gardens, where great clumps of Sword Fern reach nearly to shoulder height, grow on damp, shaded flats and gentle slopes. Other ferns can either attach themselves to tree trunks, rocks, fallen logs—

anywhere a bit of dampness and humus may coexist—or grow
in a more conventional fashion on the ground.

Mushrooms are abundant in the fall, poking their caps above
the moss, growing on wood both living and dead, the great
family of rots and molds and slimes, table delicacies,
toadstools, and mycorrhiza proliferating in these forests
beyond all reckoning.

Among temperate-zone forests, those of the Pacific Northwest
Coast are unique on several counts. First, most other forests in
the middle latitudes are dominated either by deciduous
hardwoods (as in the East) or by a mix of hardwoods and
conifers. In the Northwest coastal forest, hardwoods are a
distinctly minor element and are largely restricted to special,
often temporary habitats that conifers are unable to exploit.
A second unique quality of the Northwest coastal forest is the
size and longevity of its conifers, which, as a group, exceed
the trees of any other type of forest. Among the eleven most
important conifer species that are characteristic of the forest,
six normally live beyond 500 years, and three, beyond 1000
years. The shortest-lived has a life span in excess of 300 years.
Finally, the Northwest coastal forest is the lushest conifer
formation in the world. That, too, is a gift of the rain.

Geographic Distribution

The Northwest coastal forest extends from near Anchorage,
Alaska, south to central California. It occurs along the
immediate coast, but also extends inland to occupy the humid
seaward slopes of adjacent mountain ranges, including the
coastal ranges of Alaska, the Coast Mountains of British
Columbia, the Cascade Range from southern Canada to
southern Oregon, the Klamath Mountains of southwestern
Oregon and northwestern California, and the northern Coast
Ranges of northern and central California. The forest occurs on
both slopes of the Vancouver Island range, the Olympic
Mountains, and the Coast Range in Oregon. Along the U.S.–
Canada border, where maritime conditions extend as far inland
as the Continental Divide, analogous forests occur on the
western slopes of the northern Rockies—in southeastern
British Columbia, northeastern Washington, northern Idaho,
and northwestern Montana. Although essentially similar to
their coastal analogues, these Rocky Mountain forests are, for
reasons of geography, discussed in a separate chapter.

In southern Oregon, the Northwest coastal forest merges
gradually with the Sierran montane forest along the western
slope of the Cascade Range and the eastern slope of the
Siskiyou Mountains. Patches of coastal forest also occur on
suitably humid sites along the eastern slope of the Cascade
Range from southern Canada to northern Oregon, often
forming a belt above montane fir forests similar to those found
in the Rocky Mountains. West of the Cascades, the Northwest
coastal forest covers nearly the entire lowland region of western
Washington and northwestern Oregon. It is absent, however,
from the floor of the Willamette Valley and from anomalously
dry areas in western Washington.

**Alaskan Section of the
Northwest Coastal Forest**

**The Northwest Coastal
Forest**

Climate

Although the climate of the Northwest coastal forest region varies appreciably over its more than 2000-mile span from Alaska to California, the presence of Western Hemlock and Sitka Spruce throughout most of this range suggests an essential climatic unity. Despite differences resulting from latitude and other geographic factors (e.g. topography, cloud cover), the entire region experiences mild, wet winters and cool, often foggy or cloudy summers. Mild winters make possible the year-round growth of conifers; cool summers reduce the effects of drought during that season.

Summer drought is negligible in Canada and southeastern Alaska, where precipitation is distributed more or less evenly throughout the year. Southward along the Pacific Coast, however, it becomes an increasingly critical factor. In western Washington, for example, only six to nine percent of the year's total precipitation falls between June 1 and September 1.

In southern Oregon and northern California, long, relatively warm summers (for the Northwest Coast) permit maximum tree growth where moisture is available. However, the severity of summer drought in that area confines the forest to slopes and valleys that are open to the inland flow of marine air. Coastal fog, which is characteristic of the summer months, is a valuable source of supplemental moisture, as it supplies several inches precisely when it is needed most.

The forest achieves its maximum expression in the coastal lowlands and adjacent foothills of southwestern British Columbia, western Washington, and northwestern Oregon, where neither cold nor drought is a serious limiting factor.

Forest Types

The Northwest coastal forest consists of several forest types, each of which is defined by one or more distinctive dominant trees. Sometimes the dominant trees are also the climax species, as is the case in Sitka Spruce–Western Hemlock forests. In other situations, the dominant species is not climax but is maintained indefinitely on a site by means of recurring disturbances, notably fire and logging. This explains the persistence of Douglas-fir on sites where Western Hemlock is the climax tree. At the same time, Douglas-fir is itself a climax tree on certain other sites. In both instances, the resulting forest is called a Douglas-fir forest.

Sitka Spruce–Western Hemlock forest

The dominant trees in the coastal forest stretching from southern Alaska to northernmost California are Sitka Spruce and Western Hemlock. The spruce-hemlock forest is confined mainly to a relatively narrow strip along the immediate coast, but may extend inland for several miles along major rivers. In California, however, Sitka Spruce grows only along streams near the ocean.

Western Hemlock is the climax species and the only conifer that is commonly represented by seedlings and saplings as well as mature trees. Sitka Spruce, a long-lived associate, is able to maintain its presence through the agency of natural disturbances, which are virtually inevitable over its more than 1000-year lifespan.

For example, high winds often topple shallow-rooted hemlocks and spruces. Although both trees invade the resulting openings, the spruce grows rapidly enough to prevent its being overtopped by the smaller Western Hemlock. Western Redcedar and Douglas-fir are also common associates in the spruce-hemlock forest, except in Alaska. Redcedar is often dominant on boggy ground, and Douglas-fir on burned or unusually dry sites within the forest.

Spruce-hemlock forests support the lushest understory vegetation of any coniferous forest type in North America. Light levels within the forest are generally too low to permit understory trees, but there are abundant shrubs, ferns, wild flowers, mosses, lichens, and liverworts. Common shrubs include Red Huckleberry and Fool's Huckleberry on normal sites, Devil's-club and coastal Red Elderberry in moister habitats, and Salal, Pacific Rhododendron and Evergreen Huckleberry in drier places.

Within the spruce-hemlock forest, conifer reproduction occurs almost entirely on "nurse logs," where seeds happen to fall. These old fallen trees and stumps provide damp, organic nurseries, which are elevated above the dense moss mats and stifling understory herbs and shrubs. Douglas-fir, which requires mineral soil for germination, must wait for fire or some other disturbance to create a suitable seedbed.

Fallen logs commonly persist 300 years or more, providing a long-term source of nutrients and therefore serving to stabilize the forest community. Because of their importance to conifer reproduction, nurse logs also tend to determine the spatial structure of the forest. Vanished nurse logs often betray their former presence in colonnades—straight lines of trees, often with odd, stiltlike roots at their bases.

Western Hemlock is easily bruised and highly susceptible to fungal diseases, which enter through the wounds. Among the various root and butt rots to which it is subject, the most damaging may be the Conifer-base Polypore, which can spread to adjacent trees by way of their root systems. Black-headed Budworm and Hemlock Looper are the only serious insect pests. Dwarf Mistletoe commonly produces clumps of witch's brooms in hemlock crowns. Sitka Spruce, on the other hand, is fairly resistant to fungal disease, and mature trees are little bothered by insect infestations. However, Sitka Spruce Weevil and Spruce Aphid may deform or kill young trees. Western Redcedar also has few insect enemies, but mature trees are subject to yellow ring rots. On the whole, insect pests are a minor element in the Northwest coastal forest. The absence of serious defoliators, such as those that have ravaged the forests of the northern Rockies, is a subject of spirited debate among local foresters and ecologists.

The composition of the Sitka Spruce–Western Hemlock forest varies by region. In southeastern Alaska, Western Hemlock is the dominant tree in most stands, though varying amounts of

Red Huckleberry
Vaccinium parvifolium
150

Fool's Huckleberry
Menziesia ferruginea

Devil's-club
Oplopanax horridum
160

Coast Red Elderberry
Sambucus callicarpa
157, 191

Salal
Gaultheria shallon
214

Evergreen Huckleberry
Vaccinium ovatum

Hemlock Looper
Lambdina fiscellaria

Dwarf Mistletoe
Arceuthobium spp.

Sitka Spruce Weevil
Pissodes strobi

Spruce Aphid
Adelges piceae

Mountain Hemlock
Tsuga mertensiana
49, 139

Alaska Yellow-cedar
Chamaecyparis nootkatensis
56

Red Alder
Alnus rubra
89

Black Cottonwood
Populus trichocarpa
94

Shore Pine
Pinus contorta var. *contorta*

Lodgepole Pine
Pinus contorta
40

Crowberry
Empetrum nigrum

Alpine Laurel
Kalmia microphylla
213

Wild Cranberry
Vaccinium oxycoccos

Grand Fir
Abies grandis
48

Western White Pine
Pinus monticola
121

Port-Orford-cedar
Chamaecyparis lawsoniana
58

Elk
Cervus elaphus
376

Sitka Spruce are present. Douglas-fir is absent and Western Redcedar is a minor element northward only as far as Sitka. Mountain Hemlock and Alaska-cedar are confined in the southern panhandle of Alaska largely to higher forests, but northward gradually extend downslope to the saltwater shores, where they mix with Western Hemlock and Sitka Spruce. A variety of trees occur in marginal sites in southeastern Alaska. Red Alder and Black Cottonwood are pioneers on floodplains and young glacial moraines, where they eventually give way to conifers. Shore Pine, a short, coastal variety of Lodgepole Pine, occurs on rocky shores and, in the company of hemlock or Alaska Yellow-cedar, on sphagnum bogs, where low shrubs such as Crowberry, Alpine Laurel, and wild cranberry also grow.

In western Washington and Oregon, Douglas-fir, Grand Fir, and Pacific Silver Fir occur sparingly in the spruce-hemlock forest. Red Alder grows abundantly on burned areas within the forest and occurs along streams, with Black Cottonwood and willows. Western White Pine, Shore Pine, and Red Alder commonly line coastal sloughs and marshes. Bigleaf Maple is the only hardwood tree to occur regularly in the understory of the spruce-hemlock forest. Along the Oregon coast, Sitka Spruce, Shore Pine, and Douglas-fir form a sparse forest with an understory dominated by heath shrubs such as Pacific Rhododendron, Salal, and Evergreen Huckleberry. Port-Orford-cedar is important in southwestern Oregon and northwestern California.

The famous Olympic rain forest occurs along the Quinault, Queets, Hoh, and Bogachiel river valleys on the western side of the Olympic Peninsula. The special spruce-hemlock forests in this area are characterized by massive, long-lived trees, luxuriant undergrowth, abundant mosses and ferns growing on the trees. The spruce and hemlock form a relatively open canopy, and groves of giant, moss-draped Bigleaf Maples grow on shallow, rocky soils. The spruce in particular are enormous, exceeding 200 feet in height and more than 8 feet in diameter above their flaring bases. These large trees, which are 400 to 700 years old, increase their diameter by as much as two or three feet per century. Browsing by Elk has created an unusually open forest with a more or less open shrub layer. The shrubs in mature spruce-hemlock forests quickly invade recently logged or burned areas, where they form dense brush communities. Red Alder also grows rapidly in these open areas, and soon invades and overtops the shrubs, most of which remain as understory plants in the alder stands. Spruce, hemlock, and Douglas-fir eventually shade out the alders, though the process is often delayed for decades by the inhibiting effect of dense underbrush on the establishment of seedlings. Alternatively, if seed sources are nearby, conifers may establish themselves at once, along with the shrubs.

Coastal Douglas-fir forest
Forests dominated by coastal Douglas-fir, with varying amounts of Western Hemlock, Western Redcedar, Grand Fir,

Sugar Pine
Pinus lambertiana
120

Incense-cedar
Libocedrus decurrens
57

Pacific Yew
Taxus brevifolia

Pacific Madrone
Arbutus menziesii
76, 158

and other conifers, constitute the classic forests of the Pacific Northwest. Although Douglas-fir quickly invades burned and logged areas and even dominates large tracts of old-growth forest (including stands up to 600 years old), Western Hemlock is the climax tree in all but the driest habitats. Douglas-fir seedlings and saplings are seldom in evidence in old-growth forests.

Various other conifer species occur as distinctly minor elements in specific types of habitats. For example, poor, gravelly soils or bogs in the Puget Sound region often support Western White Pine, because in such places the species is able to escape competition from Douglas-fir and other coastal forest conifers. Shore Pine holds its own on rocky headlands, along the borders of lowland sloughs and marshes, and on gravel. Pacific Silver Fir occurs in cold pockets, most often at higher elevations in the forest, while Grand Fir often grows in mixed old-growth stands and in warm lowland valleys. Typically Sierran species such as Sugar Pine and Incense-cedar occur with Douglas-fir in the Oregon Cascades. A common understory tree or tall shrub in most Douglas-fir stands is the Pacific Yew, which apparently thrives in shade.

Bigleaf Maple is common on both moist and dry sites, occupying damp terraces at one extreme and dry talus and scree at the other. Pacific Madrone, a broadleaf evergreen, occurs as an understory tree in drier areas, where it is safe from invasive Western Hemlock and Western Redcedar. Other hardwoods are restricted to special habitats. The most important, Red Alder, is an excellent pioneer species because it is able to fix nitrogen. It commonly grows on soggy bottoms within the forest until it is overtopped by Western Redcedar or Western Hemlock. It also invades areas disturbed by fire or logging and may dominate such sites for decades before being replaced by conifers. In addition, Red Alder grows along streams, often in the company of Black Cottonwood. Other hardwoods that occur with some regularity are Bigleaf Maple and Pacific Madrone.

On the hottest, driest sites—steep, south-facing slopes in the Oregon Cascades—Douglas-fir is the predominant tree in an open forest that may include Sugar Pine, Incense-cedar, Bigleaf Maple, and Pacific Madrone. As habitats become increasingly moist, the percentage of Western Hemlock increases until, on mesic (moderately moist) sites, it is virtually coequal with Douglas-fir. Western Redcedar also becomes increasingly frequent on moister soils, but is typically much less common than either Western Hemlock or Douglas-fir. On sites that are very moist or actually wet, however—such as river terraces in the eastern Olympics and the North Cascades—Western Redcedar may be dominant or may share that role with Western Hemlock. At the same time, Western Redcedar's ability to grow in saturated soils and to take up and transpire large amounts of water also makes it able to withstand drier climates than Western Hemlock. For example, Redcedar ranges farther south than the hemlock both along the coast of California and in the mountains of Idaho. In

Creambush
Holodiscus discolor
192

Beargrass
Xerophyllum tenax
418

White-flowered Hawkweed
Hieracium albiflorum

Western Fescue
Festuca occidentalis

Yerba de Selva
Whipplea modesta
425

Snow Queen
Synthyris reniformis
537

Oregon-grape
Berberis nervosa

Evergreen Violet
Viola sempervirens
449

Oregon Goldthread
Coptis laciniata

Rattlesnake Orchid
Goodyera oblongifolia

Skunk Cabbage
Lysichitum americanum

Canyon Live Oak
Quercus chrysolepis
173

California-laurel
Umbellularia californica
77

Giant Chinkapin
Castanopsis chrysophylla
78, 178

Coast Live Oak
Quercus agrifolia
84

Fireweed
Epilobium angustifolium
493

Pearly Everlasting
Anaphalis margaritacea
422

Oregon's Willamette Valley, it occupies sites well beyond the range of Western Hemlock. The most impressive remaining redcedar stands—in numbers if not tree size—are on the coastal plains of the western Olympic Peninsula.

The characteristic shrubs on dry sites are Salal and Creambush, while Twinflower, Beargrass, White-flowered Hawkweed, Western Fescue, Yerba de Selva, and Snow Queen are among the more common herbs. On mesic sites, Pacific Rhododendron and Oregon-grape are the dominant shrubs. Moist herb gardens commonly feature Twinflower, Evergreen Violet, Oregon Goldthread, Rattlesnake Orchid, and Sword Fern. The shrub layer is sparse in moist habitats, but Sword Fern or Oregon Oxalis—along with a large variety of other species—form a lush herb layer. On the wettest sites, Devil's-club and Skunk Cabbage are typical.

In southwestern Oregon and northwestern California, primarily in the Klamath Mountains and the northern Coast Range, Douglas-fir dominates a mixed evergreen forest that also includes other conifers and a number of broadleaf trees. Tanoak is the most common associate of Douglas-fir in this forest, commonly dominating an understory tree layer that also includes Pacific Madrone and Canyon Live Oak. Moist ravine habitats also support Bigleaf Maple, California-laurel, and Port-Orford-cedar. Giant Chinkapin and Coast Live Oak are locally common. The shrub layer is normally well developed and contains species common to oak woodlands and chaparral, as well as the Northwest coastal forest.

The mixed evergreen forest is one of the most extensive vegetation types within its range. It forms a complicated mosaic along with redwood forest, Sierran montane forest, oak woodlands, chaparral, and grassland balds. It shares species with all of these communities and, along common boundaries, is difficult or impossible to distinguish from adjacent forests or woodlands. The presence of Douglas-fir distinguishes this type of forest from the mixed hardwood forest of central and southern California. In the San Francisco Bay area, where all three types occur in addition to several other types of vegetation, the resulting mosaics are enormously complex. The combination of ample winter rain and pronounced summer drought, changes in slope aspect, steepness, and soil characteristics produces dramatic changes in vegetation over short distances.

Severe insect damage is not a problem in coastal Douglas-fir—hemlock forests, although Douglas-fir Beetle, the Western Budworm, and the Douglas-fir Tussock Moth are present. Nonetheless, Dwarf-mistletoe forms witch's brooms on Douglas-fir, and various shelf and bracket fungi live on mature trees, signaling rot. Fire, which is more common here than in the cooler, more humid coastal spruce-hemlock forests, is the chief source of damage.

After fires or logging, conditions are ripe for the proliferation of opportunistic herbs such as Fireweed, Bracken Fern, Bull Thistle, and Pearly Everlasting. These herbs form weedy communities that persist for a few years until overtopped by

Pacific Blackberry
Rubus ursinus

Snow Bush
Ceanothus velutinus

Subalpine Fir
Abies lasiocarpa
46

Engelmann Spruce
Picea engelmannii
117

Western Larch
Larix occidentalis
51, 131

Thinleaf Huckleberry
Vaccinium membranaceum
163

Foamflower
Tiarella trifoliata

Queen's Cup Beadlily
Clintonia uniflora

Rosy Twisted-stalk
Streptopus roseus
459

Vanilla Leaf
Achlys triphylla
419

Oak Fern
Gymnocarpium dryopteris

Northern Inside-out Flower
Vancouveria hexandra
400

Starry Solomon's Plume
Smilacina stellata

Alaska Huckleberry
Vaccinium alaskense

Oval-leaved Huckleberry
Vaccinium ovalifolium

shrubs. Vine Maple, Pacific Blackberry, Oregon-grape, Salal, Snow Bush, and Pacific Rhododendron, all of which may have been present in the original forest, are among the more common shrubs on logged sites. Within a few years, Red Alder or Douglas-fir overtops the shrubs, and dense stands of second-growth Douglas-fir pole timber are common. As a result, such stands generally lack undergrowth for 50 to 150 years, when natural mortality creates openings in the forest.

True fir forests
The forests that fit this category are essentially cold, snowy versions of the lower forests. Both forms have numerous trees and understory plants in common. The main difference is that Pacific Silver Fir and Noble Fir dominate the true fir forests, while Douglas-fir and hemlock are less common. From southwestern British Columbia to southern Oregon, true fir forests occur just above Douglas-fir and hemlock forests, at elevations of between 2000 and 5000 feet.

Pacific Silver Fir, the climax species, dominates the forest in northwestern Washington and southwestern British Columbia, where Noble Fir is absent. In the Cascades of southern Washington, either fir may predominate, while in northern Oregon, Noble Fir is usually more important. True fir forests occur only on scattered high summits in the Coast Range, and are replaced in the Cascades of southern Oregon by Sierran fir forests.

True fir forests are usually mixed conifer types that include Western Hemlock, Western Redcedar, Douglas-fir, and Western White Pine as important associates. South of Mt. Adams in southern Washington, Grand Fir, Subalpine Fir, Engelmann Spruce, Lodgepole Pine, and Western Larch are also present. Mountain Hemlock and Alaska-cedar, both subalpine trees, commonly occur along the upper margins of the forest. Perhaps the most characteristic understory shrub on favorable sites is Thinleaf Huckleberry, a species noted for its choice fruit. Salal and Oregon-grape are typical of the plants found in the sparse understories on drier slopes or rocky soils. Most stands, however, feature rich herb layers, in which Foam Flower, Queen's Cup Beadlily, Rosy Twisted-stalk, Vanilla Leaf, Oak Fern, Inside-out Flower, and Starry Solomon's Plume are prominent. Wet areas support Devil's-club, Vine Maple, Alaska and Oval-leaved huckleberries, and Skunk Cabbage. Pacific Rhododendron often dominates the understories in Oregon's Western Cascades.

Silver fir replaces Western Hemlock as the climax tree in upper montane forests because hemlock seedlings are damaged by deep snows and litter accumulations. Downslope, however, silver fir is limited by competition from Western Hemlock, which is more tolerant of both shade and drought. At higher elevations, silver fir seedlings cannot withstand the summer frosts common to the subalpine zone.

Noble Fir, the largest and one of the longest-lived of the true firs, is highly intolerant of shade and only regenerates following forest disturbance. However, since it lives longer and is more resistant to insects and diseases than its associates are, it is frequently able simply to outlast them.

Following fires or other disturbances, the reestablishment of the true fir forest commonly occurs in the following way. First, understory shrubs and opportunistic herbaceous plants such as bracken fern and Beargrass form rank brush communities. Gradually, these are overtopped by conifers; Noble Fir and Douglas-fir, either separately or together, are generally the first invaders. Western Hemlock may join them either at the beginning or later on. Pacific Silver Fir, which requires some shade for its seedlings to thrive, is usually the last to invade the site.

Huckleberries are the wild counterparts of the cultivated blueberry. A dozen species of blueberrylike huckleberries grow wild in Washington and Oregon, covering some 100,000 acres. Several species, such as Thinleaf Huckleberry and Delicious Huckleberry, have fruit that rivals or surpasses in quality that of commercial varieties.

Delicious Huckleberry
Vaccinium deliciosum

Most of the blights, rots, and insects that plague trees at lower elevations have dutifully followed them upslope into the true fir forests. In addition, the Balsam Woolly Aphid, a relatively recent European import, has caused severe damage to Silver and Subalpine firs in Washington state. White-pine Blister Rust also inflicts many Western White Pines in this forest.

Balsam Woolly Aphid
Adelges piceae

Coast Redwood forest

The redwood forest is essentially a southern extension of the coastal forests of Oregon and Washington. Throughout the redwood belt, which is about 450 miles long and between 5 and 35 miles wide, Coast Redwood is both the dominant and the climax tree where it occurs. Redwoods grow from sea level to about 3000 feet elevation, but they are most common between 100 and 2500 feet. The finest groves are found on alluvial flats and benches along major streams. Well-developed stands also grow on moist coastal plains, river deltas, moderate seaward slopes, and valleys opening to the ocean.

The two northernmost groves occur along the Chetko River in extreme southwestern Oregon. The majority of redwoods, however, grow in California; they form a more or less continuous belt from the Oregon line to Sonoma County and occur in isolated groves from there southward to Salmon Creek Canyon in the Santa Lucia Mountains of Monterey County. Because redwoods lack root hairs, which extend the moisture-absorbing ability of many trees, they require abundant soil moisture and high humidity throughout the year. Winter precipitation in northern California is ample, but summer drought is extreme. Therefore, redwoods are restricted to areas near the coast, where summer fog supplies seven to twelve inches of moisture during the rainless months. In central California, redwoods require not only summer fog but also moisture from other sources. The Big Sur groves, for example, are confined to stream canyons.

Redwoods, the tallest trees in the world, commonly exceed 250 or even 300 feet in height and characteristically have trunks of ten to fifteen feet in diameter. Redwoods may live 1200 years or more, which gives them a distinct advantage over all of their associates. Moreover, they are extremely tolerant of shade: Small trees can endure more than 400 years of repression beneath a closed canopy without losing their ability to grow rapidly once the canopy is opened.

Redwoods reproduce readily by sprouting new growth from trunks, stumps, or roots. If lightning, wind, or fire destroys the crown of a redwood, the tree sprouts a new one, thereby rapidly closing the canopy and preventing competition from trees, such as Douglas-fir, that require openings to reproduce. Redwoods also can rapidly reassert their dominance on disturbed sites by sprouting roots within two or three weeks following the removal or destruction of trees by logging or fire. Furthermore, new sprouts may grow as much as seven feet in the first year, much faster than any potential competitor grows, and even faster than redwood seedlings. Sprouting is so successful that redwoods seem to be evolving toward the abandonment of seeds as a method of reproduction.

Seed production varies greatly among redwoods. Less than ten percent of the species' seeds are viable, and those that do germinate require bare mineral soil for success. Seedlings tolerate shade and organic soils, but in forest duff, they almost always succumb to root rots and damping-off fungi.

Mature redwoods are highly resistant to fire because their thick, nonresinous bark and moist wood are slow to burn. Many forest veterans show large fire scars from burns that disfigured but did not kill them. Redwood is also highly resistant to insects and fungal diseases. Of the latter, heart rots apparently enter through fire scars, but rarely do enough damage to kill mature trees. Redwood bark beetles also attack weakened or scarred trees but, again, present little real danger. Humans, who highly value redwood lumber for building houses and other outdoor uses, are the chief agents of early demise for this otherwise long-lived conifer.

Pure redwood stands grow on moist streamside flats and terraces that are subject to periodic flooding and deposition of mud, or siltation. Each time a new layer of sediment is deposited, redwoods sprout lateral surface roots from newly buried sections of trunk, giving the trees multilayered root systems. Periodic siltation also destroys understory vegetation and thereby helps to maintain the purity of the stands. The sediments may supply nutrients that contribute to the enormous size of the redwoods growing on alluvial flats. In any case, the tallest trees and the most impressive groves— such as those along the Avenue of the Giants and in Redwood National Park—occur precisely on sites of this kind.

The redwood groves on these streamside flats may be the most famous and impressive, but they are not typical. Most redwoods grow on gentle to moderate slopes, where they dominate mixed forests containing both conifers and hardwoods. Douglas-fir, Coast Redwood's most frequent associate, occurs in nearly every stand. Grand Fir, Western Hemlock, and Sitka Spruce are fairly common north of

Redwood Bark Beetle
Phloeosinus sequoiae

California Torreya
Torreya californica
145

Tanoak
Lithocarpus densiflorus
170

White Alder
Alnus rhombifolia
87

California Hazelnut
Corylus cornuta californica
168

Western Trillium
Trillium ovatum
387

Red Clintonia
Clintonia andrewsiana
473

Bishop Pine
Pinus muricata
128

Eureka, California, but occur more sparingly southward. Pacific Yew, Western Redcedar, California Torreya, and Port-Orford-cedar are occasionally present in the redwood forest. The most important hardwood trees are Tanoak and Pacific Madrone, which grow in the more open, drier forests. White Alder, Bigleaf Maple, and willows are common along streams. Red Alder occurs near the coast.

The understory in mature redwood forests is often rather sparse, consisting of little more than scattered, spindly shrubs, vainly reaching upward for light, and shade-tolerant ground cover plants such as Oregon Oxalis. Where the toppling of redwoods has opened up the forest, understory trees such as Tanoak, madrone, alder, and Bigleaf Maple may develop long, slender, nearly branchless trunks, which culminate perhaps fifty or eighty feet above the ground in a narrow crown of leafy branches. By mimicking the slender growth form of the redwood, these lesser trees strive to obtain their share of available light in the brief span allotted to them. Where groves are more open and moisture is in reasonable supply, a variety of shrubs, ferns, and wild flowers may form two or three distinct layers. Members of the heather family dominate the shrub layer, along with Vine Maple and California Hazelnut. A number of ferns are present, including the nearly ubiquitous Sword Fern. Wild flowers are inconspicuous, although a thorough search may turn up such beauties as Trillium, Red Clintonia, and Evergreen Violet.

California coastal pine forests
Despite their fondness for cool marine air, redwoods rarely grow right along the coast. They are highly intolerant of desiccating winds and salt spray, and therefore leave exposed bluffs and headlands to other types of vegetation. North of Humboldt Bay, a forest of Sitka Spruce, Grand Fir, and Western Hemlock forms a buffer between the redwoods and the sea. Father south, this function is most often performed by open, discontinuous, nearly pure pine forests.

The most common and widespread of these pines is Bishop Pine, which occurs in scattered stands southward along the coast to Santa Barbara County, far beyond the southern limit of redwoods. Often picturesquely twisted and gnarled by wind and salt spray, this pine also forms open forests on the islands off southern and Baja California. In the redwood belt, these forests occur principally on exposed headlands and in shallow, acidic, poorly drained soils from sea level to an elevation of about 1300 feet. Pacific Madrone is a common hardwood companion on these sites, but Redwoods are rarely present. The shrub layer includes numerous acid-tolerant members of the heather family, which may form dense thickets on moist sites. Open floors of grass are also typical.

Periodic fires are essential to the maintenance of Bishop Pine forests. Fires remove all the old trees and prepare the soil for the growth of young, vigorous stands. Bishop Pines are built to burn. Their cones, tightly sealed with resin, generally remain unopened on the branches until fire melts their seals.

Monterey Pine
Pinus radiata

Poison-oak
Toxicodendron diversiloba
114

Creeping Snowberry
Symphoricarpos mollis

Bedstraw
Galium boreale
416

Yerba Buena
Satureja douglasii
421

Great Hedge Nettle
Stachys cooleyae
490

Bolander Pine
Pinus contorta

Mendocino Cypress
Cupressus pygmaea

Raccoon
Procyon lotor
353

Bobcat
Felis rufus
362

Douglas' Squirrel
Tamiasciurus douglasii
340

Winter Wren
Troglodytes troglodytes
270

Varied Thrush
Ixoreus naevius
280

Black Bear
Ursus americanus
359

Fire also prepares the seedbed by exposing bare, mineral soil and enriching it with ash derived from the parent trees and understory shrubs. In the wake of a fire, Bishop Pine seeds germinate readily, and the rapidly growing trees quickly form a new stand on the same ground that was occupied by their parents. Without fire, a stand can be eliminated for good by a combination of fungal disease, squirrel predation, and general debilitation due to old age.

Monterey Pine grows in three small areas along the central California coast, of which the best known is the Monterey Peninsula. Like Bishop Pine, Monterey Pines also bear closed cones and depend on fire for stand rejuvenation. Although Monterey Pines occupy only about 2200 acres within their natural range, they are the most widely planted lumber trees in the world. In California the species is restricted to the fog belt, but appears able to tolerate a variety of habitats. Common understory shrubs include Poison-oak, Creeping Snowberry, and Pacific Blackberry. Bedstraw, Yerba Buena, and Hedge Nettle are among the more common wild flowers.

Shore Pines in northern California are largely restricted to exposed sea bluffs. They are able to withstand a wide range of adverse conditions, but are often stunted or deformed by high winds, salt spray, or hostile soils. Extreme dwarfing occurs in Bolander Pine, a variety of Shore Pine that is endemic to uplifted marine terraces along the Mendocino coast. Flooded in winter and bone-dry in summer, the terraces support a unique pygmy forest dominated by Bolander Pines and Mendocino Cypresses only about two to five feet tall. Adjacent, well-drained slopes, however, support normal redwood forest, where Mendocino Cypresses can grow to be 150 feet tall. Most of the understory shrubs in the pygmy forest are acid-tolerant heath species.

Wildlife

Walking through the Northwest coastal forest, one may be struck by the almost palpable stillness. Other than the occasional bird calls, the infrequent tapping of woodpeckers, or the scolding of a squirrel, there is mostly silence. Nor is wildlife much in evidence. One occasionally spots physical signs, such as the scat of Elk or deer, perhaps the prints of Raccoons or Bobcats, or the dismantled cones left behind by the Douglas' Squirrel. But the animals themselves tend to be aloof. Most birds live in the overstory trees. The few that spend most of their time near the ground, like the Winter Wren and the Varied Thrush, tend to be furtive, well hidden, or both. Small, ground-dwelling mammals such as shrews, mice, and chipmunks are easily missed as they move about. Even really big animals such as Elk, deer, and Black Bear are incredibly adept at keeping out of sight.

Sources of food

Fewer kinds of animals live in the coastal forest than in most other western conifer formations because the habitat offers less diversity of vegetation and fewer types of food. The overwhelming dominance of conifers means that animals

Deer Mouse
Peromyscus maniculatus
329

Pine Siskin
Carduelis pinus
312

Red Crossbill
Loxia curvirostra
310

Blue Grouse
Dendragapus obscurus
224

Red Tree Vole
Phenacomys longicaudus
327

Dusky Tree Vole
Phenacomys silvicola

Porcupine
Erethizon dorsatum
355

Mountain-beaver
Aplodontia rufa
346

Snowshoe Hare
Lepus americanus
350

preferring or requiring deciduous trees are restricted almost entirely to special habitats. There are just fewer niches for wildlife in coastal forests than in more open or mixed forests. Another factor limiting the kinds of wildlife in coastal forests is the scarcity or absence of pine nuts, acorns, and grass seeds, which are among the most important plant foods found in the western forests. Pines and oaks occur only occasionally in coastal forests, and grasses are exceedingly scarce except in forest openings. Highly intolerant of shade, grasses are commonly replaced as ground cover by mosses, which are more beautiful than nutritious.

Nearly all parts of conifers—seeds, bark, twigs, buds, needles, even the cones themselves—are utilized by various birds and mammals for food. Seeds, of course, are the most important. The seeds of Douglas-fir, hemlock, spruce, and fir are far smaller than pine nuts but no less nutritious, containing both proteins and essential fats. During the fall, when cones ripen, the Douglas' Squirrel snips cones at such a furious rate that they seem to rain on the ground below. Chipmunks, Deer Mice, and birds may abscond with part of a squirrel's harvest, but the number of seeds cached so far exceeds the amount required that pilfering is not a serious problem. The populations of Deer Mice and Douglas' Squirrels fluctuate according to the size of the cone crop.

The Pine Siskin, a brown-streaked goldfinch that has adapted to conifers, moves in flocks through the overstory, feeding on buds, young leaves, seeds, and insects. Flocks of Red Crossbills, whose scissorlike beaks are perfect for prying seeds from cones, forage in a similar way. Both species roam widely and tend to time their breeding to coincide with cone crops.

A number of animals feed on conifer needles, especially when the leaves are young and tender. Elk and deer include them in their spring diets. Blue Grouse rely on them throughout the winter. The Red Tree Vole and the closely related Dusky Tree Vole of northwestern Oregon feed almost exclusively on conifer needles, especially those of Douglas-fir. Rarely do these small rodents come down out of the trees.

Conifer bark provides a source of food, particularly in winter, for Porcupines, Mountain-beaver, Snowshoe Hares, and, if other foods are unavailable, squirrels and deer. The Mountain-beaver, which is not a true beaver, resembles a large vole or meadow mouse. During the winter, it relies heavily on the bark of small conifers and alders, which it may girdle and kill. Confined to the coastal forest and the damper forests in the Sierra Nevada, the Mountain-beaver has benefited from the increase in shrubbery that has resulted from logging.

Rodents consume enormous quantities of seeds and inflict damage on young seedlings and saplings. Thus, following fire or logging, they can seriously inhibit the reestablishment of conifers. This is mainly a problem on commercial tree farms, where a reliance on the planting of a single tree species increases the trees' vulnerability to pests.

A second important food source in the coastal forest consists of various types of berries, which are commonly abundant in season. In both forest and openings, berry bushes of one kind or another are often among the more common shrubs. There are huckleberries, blueberries, blackberries, raspberries, currants, and gooseberries, along with a host of other kinds that are relished by animals if not by humans. Ripening in the fall, berries provide a nutritious, fattening food to help animals head into winter. Black Bears, in particular, are noted for gorging on blueberries and huckleberries.

Mushrooms, which are also plentiful in both kinds and numbers, reach their peak after the first rains of autumn. They are probably more important in the diets of many forest mammals than conifer seeds. Chipmunks, hares, mice, and deer make mushrooms an important part of their diets and seem unaffected by the types toxic to humans. Douglas' Squirrel commonly places mushrooms in the crook of a branch or wedges them beneath loose bark to dry out, whereupon it caches them, along with seeds, for future use.

Deer Mice are the most abundant mammals in the forest, spending most of their time foraging on the forest floor, but climbing into shrubbery as the occasion requires. They feed not only on a variety of plant foods, but also eat prodigious amounts of insects, insect larvae, and eggs. The Southern Red-backed Vole, which is abroad both day and night, frequents mossy areas and decaying litter, and feeds mainly on fungi with buried fruiting bodies. This retiring mouse also eats various forest herbs, and stores tubers, bulbs, and seeds for later use. It is found throughout the western conifer forests, but is perhaps most numerous in the coastal forest.

Southern Red-backed Vole
Clethrionomys gapperi

Townsend's Chipmunk is the principal member of its tribe in the Northwest coastal forest. It is larger and darker than other western chipmunks and bears indistinct back stripes. It is thought that the stripes along the backs of chipmunks are a form of camouflage that will confuse predators when the chipmunk is in flight. In the nearly uniform shade of the coastal forest, however, the strongly contrasting white and black stripes characteristic of most other chipmunks might prove to be a disadvantage to Townsend's. The Sonoma Chipmunk, which frequents the shady redwood forests, also has indistinct back stripes.

Townsend's Chipmunk
Eutamias townsendii
332

Sonoma Chipmunk
Eutamias sonomae

Several types of shrews also occur in coastal forests, where they scurry about through the undergrowth in a frenzied search for insects and other invertebrates, or perhaps even a fat mouse. The mild winters favor shrews, whose size requires that they eat more than their weight each day to maintain body heat.

The coastal forest offers damp refuge to creatures such as slugs, snails, and salamanders, which have journeyed only halfway from water to land. Among the more striking slugs is the olive-yellow or green Banana Slug, which can grow as long as six inches. Another giant of its type is the Pacific Giant Salamander, which reaches nearly a foot in length and has been known to feed even on mice and garter snakes. More than a dozen species of salamanders occur in the coastal forest, including several local, rare, or endangered types.

Banana Slug
Ariolimax columbianus

Pacific Giant Salamander
Dicamptodon ensatus
608

Lush understory vegetation is the haunt of the Winter Wren,

American Robin
Turdus migratorius
279

Swainson's Thrush
Catharus ustulatus

Western Tanager
Piranga ludoviciana
294

Evening Grosbeak
Coccothraustes vespertinus
311

Steller's Jay
Cyanocitta stelleri
256

Gray Jay
Perisoreus canadensis
255

Bald Eagle
Haliaeetus leucocephalus

Harlequin Duck
Histrionicus histrionicus

Wood Duck
Aix sponsa

Roosevelt Elk
Cervis elaphus roosevelti

Mountain Lion
Felis concolor
363

Coyote
Canis latrans
370, 371

Columbian Black-tailed
Deer
Odocoileus hemionus columbianus

Mule Deer
Odocoileus hemionus
373

a tiny mite of a bird but an accomplished singer with a loud voice. Another characteristic understory bird is the Varied Thrush, which closely resembles the American Robin but has a black necklace and rust-red bars on the wings. Its song, a sequence of three or four clear, sustained notes in a minor key, is one of the most haunting and memorable sounds of the Northwest coastal forest. Other common understory birds include Swainson's Thrush—another fine singer—and the Blue Grouse. The springtime drumming of the male grouse, by which it marks its territory and announces its amorous intentions, is a cheerful harbinger of an end to winter.

It is often difficult to spot birds in the low light and dense foliage of the Northwest coastal forest. This is particularly true of treetop birds, which may spend the better part of their time dozens of feet above an observer's head. Their calls are often too faint to assist in their discovery; they are absorbed by the smothering foliage and damp air. The Western Tanager is perhaps the showiest treetop species, but the Evening Grosbeak provides close competition. Steller's Jay, with its jaunty blue crest, is the characteristic member of its tribe in the lowland coastal forests. It is replaced at somewhat higher elevations by the Gray Jay, a quieter but far bolder cousin. Other common birds in the canopy include chickadees, kinglets, a variety of warblers, and several species of flycatcher. Numerous streams and rivers support a variety of distinctive birds. The most impressive is the Bald Eagle, which is more common in this region than anywhere else on the continent. The Harlequin Duck, with its striking blue, rust, white, and black pattern, nests along mountain streams and is often seen rafting on the rapids or resting in the intervening pools. The even more striking Wood Duck frequents slower streams and ponds in the wooded lowlands of the Pacific Northwest.

The largest forest herbivores—though not always the most conspicuous—are deer and Elk, which feed chiefly on forest underbrush and young conifers. Roosevelt Elk once roamed widely in the coastal forest region but is now restricted mainly to areas in northwestern California and southwestern Oregon, western Washington—in both the Cascades and the Olympic Mountains—and Vancouver Island. In the Olympic Mountains and the Washington Cascades, some Elk herds summer in the high subalpine parklands, where their diet consists almost entirely of grasses and broadleaf herbs; they move downslope in the fall and spend the winter in densely forested river valleys. Extensive browsing by Elk in the Olympic rain forests is thought to be largely responsible for the unusual thinness of understory vegetation there. In the United States, the Mountain Lion is the chief predator of Roosevelt Elk, but wolves take some Elk on Vancouver Island, and Coyotes occasionally prey upon Elk calves.

The Columbian Black-tailed Deer is a race of western Mule Deer that is restricted to the coastal forest. Like its interior counterpart, the Black-tailed Deer is mainly a browser, or shrub feeder. Its diet differs from that of the Mule Deer, however, in that it includes a higher proportion of conifer

Lynx
Felis lynx
361

Sitka Deer
Odocoileus hemionus

Marten
Martes americana
343

Mink
Mustela vison
345

Spotted Owl
Strix occidentalis

Northern Goshawk
Accipiter gentilis
223

Great Horned Owl
Bubo virginianus
230

Grizzly Bear
Ursus arctos
360

Alaskan Brown Bear
Ursus arctos middendorffi

leaves, principally those of Western Hemlock and Douglas-fir. Black-tails are chiefly preyed upon by Mountain Lions, but Coyotes may take young or sick deer, and wolves prey upon deer in southwestern British Columbia. From Washington northward, Lynx also take an occasional deer.

The Sitka Deer, which closely resembles the Black-tailed Deer, replaces the latter species along the coast and on the offshore islands to the north of Vancouver Island and in southeastern Alaska. During the summer, the Sitka Deer moves upslope to timberline, which is at only about 1500 to 2500 feet in this region. In winter, however, many of these deer migrate to nearby islands. If deep snows in the islands' interiors force the deer to concentrate along the beaches, they provide easy pickings for wolves, Coyotes, and Lynx.

Other important predators in the Northwest coastal forest include weasels, the Marten, Mink, Spotted Owl, Northern Goshawk, and Bald Eagle. The Spotted Owl inhabits dense, unbroken forest, where it feeds on flying squirrels and various other rodents—and virtually anything else it can catch. Never common, this owl quickly retreats before the advance of civilization, often to be replaced by the larger, more adaptable Great Horned Owl.

The Black Bear and the Grizzly Bear prey upon animals, but also enjoy a wide variety of plant foods. Black Bears, which are fairly common in the forest, feed on roots and bulbs, tear apart rotten logs to get at ants and grubs, dig out rodents, and gorge on berries when they are in season. Grizzly Bears occur in sizable populations along nearly every fjord and inlet in British Columbia and southeastern Alaska. The famed Alaskan Brown Bear, a race of the Grizzly, lives on both the mainland and offshore islands, congregating along streams in large numbers during the salmon's spawning season.

THE NORTHWEST COASTAL FOREST: PLANTS AND ANIMALS

SIERRAN MONTANE FORESTS

The most diverse conifer forests in the world adorn the middle-elevation slopes of the Sierra Nevada and other California ranges, and the Siskiyou Mountains and Cascade Range in southern Oregon. Although summer drought is characteristic of the region, long, warm growing seasons and relatively mild winters combine to create a particularly congenial environment for conifers. On sites where the soil is moist and well-drained, these trees regularly attain large, even record, sizes, and form impressive forests. Typical stands in the central Sierra contain five different kinds of conifers, while in parts of the Klamath Mountains, as many as ten species may occur together. Overall, from southern Oregon to Baja California, the Sierran montane forest contains more than two dozen types of conifers and nearly that many species of hardwoods. The latter, though numerous in kind, are comparatively few in number and constitute a distinctly minor element in the forest.

Ponderosa Pine
Pinus ponderosa
38

Black Oak
Quercus kelloggii

Douglas-fir
Pseudotsuga menziesii
134

Just above the oak woodlands and chaparral of the foothills, Ponderosa Pines form open, parklike forests with grassy floors and scattered shrubs. Black Oaks and Douglas-firs may or may not be present, along with various trees that are more commonly found at lower elevations. Water is obviously a problem here. In spring the grasses are green and tough yellow daisies are conspicuous among the annuals sprinkled among the pines. By midsummer the grasses are straw and the flowers have gone to seed. On cool mornings, the forests are lively with the sounds of birds, the scurry of chipmunks and lizards, and the hum and flutter of insects. But as afternoon approaches, life retreats to shady corners and burrows. The air is pungent with the resinous fragrance of pine needles, which quaver ever so slightly in the ruffled afternoon air.

White Fir
Abies concolor
45

Sugar Pine
Pinus lambertiana
120

Incense-cedar
Libocedrus decurrens
57

As elevation increases, the heel of drought lifts, and forests gradually become denser, richer in species, and more complex. White Fir and Douglas-fir are common, along with Sugar Pine and Incense-cedar. Venerable Black Oaks grow large in sunny openings and on rock outcrops. Streamsides are lined with cottonwoods, alders, and willows. There is a variety of shading and texture, of shifting patterns of light and shadow, rock and soil, and bark and foliage, that is reminiscent of certain eastern hardwood forests. Sunny openings—rock outcrops, meadows, stream banks, and brush fields—are more numerous here than in moister forests, and even close stands are rarely so dense that they elicit claustrophobia. The conifers often seem spaced just close enough to provide relief from the nearly constant summer sun, but far enough apart to allow motes and streaks of light to dapple the forest floor. These bright, variegated forests are appropriate in John Muir's "Range of Light."

Higher yet on the mountainsides are somber snow forests in which giant firs are often the only kinds of trees. The huge, columnar trunks of these trees support dense needle canopies that prevent nearly all light from reaching the understory. The forest floor is piled up with fallen logs, old debris, and needle litter, the residues of winter. Routed by deep snow, deep

Quaking Aspen
Populus tremuloides
95

shade, and deep litter, most shrubs and wild flowers huddle in
the relatively few, scattered islands of sunshine. Few plants or
animals can make a living in these somber woods, where the
cold grip of winter restrains the exuberance of summer.

As if in compensation for such austerity, verdant meadows are
more common here than downslope. Watered by snows and
overrun by wild flowers, these fine lawns seem to mock the
surrounding woods with their gaiety. The white trunks and
pale, shimmering leaves of Quaking Aspen, which commonly
grows along meadow fringes, also provide welcome relief from
the darker mood of the forest. On thin, rocky soils, scattered
pines form open woods among rock slabs and boulders; while
some of the showiest wild flowers in the mountains flourish in
moist cranny gardens. Above lies the high country, where the
forest gradually and finally succumbs to the cold.

Geographic Distribution
The Sierran montane forest occurs on all of the higher
mountain ranges of the Pacific Coast region, from southern
Oregon to northern Baja California. In the Oregon Cascades,
the forest forms a distinct belt that ranges from about 2400 to
about 4600 feet from the Crater Lake region south.
Northward, the forest gradually merges with the Northwest
coastal forest. At lower elevations, the forest commonly
borders mixed evergreen forest, oak woodland, or chaparral.
In northern California, the Sierran montane forest splits into
an eastern branch in the Cascades and the Sierra Nevada, and a
western branch in the Klamath Mountains and the Coast
Range. In the California Cascades the forest ranges between
1300 and 6500 feet. It is bounded above by subalpine forest
and below by foothill woodlands on the west and juniper
woodlands or sagebrush on the east.
In the Sierra Nevada, the forest forms a broad belt on the
western slopes at elevations of between 2000 and 6000 feet in
the north, and 5000 and 9000 feet in the south. On the
eastern side of the range, it occurs southward more or less
continuously to Sonora Pass, beyond which it is increasingly
confined to isolated stands in cool, moist canyons at high
elevations. The forest is bordered above by open, mixed,
subalpine forest and below by foothill woodlands on the west
side of the Sierra and pinyon woodland and sagebrush on the
east. Forests enriched by the addition of a few northwestern
species occur in the Klamath Mountains between 2400 and
6500 feet. Below are evergreen forests and oak woodlands;
above, a subalpine forest very much like the one in the Sierra,
but with several additional conifers in attendance. Simpler
forests—more like those in the Sierra—extend southward in
the Coast Range to Napa County, just north of San Francisco.
Scattered stands of Ponderosa Pine also grow in the Coast
Range south of San Francisco, but here they occur without
that species' characteristic Sierran companions.
The Sierran montane forest also occurs in the Tehachapi
Mountains and in the Transverse and Peninsular ranges of
southern California. The forests are bordered below by

Sierran Montane Forests

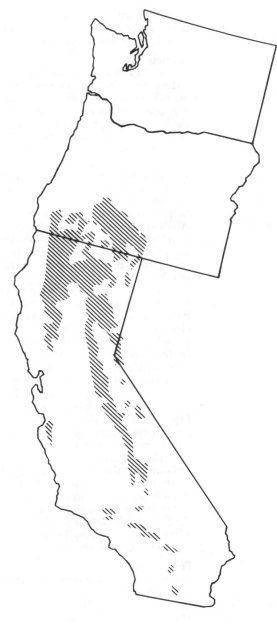

Joshua Tree
Yucca brevifolia

chaparral, coastal sage scrub, or oak woodland on the seaward flanks of the mountains, and by Joshua Tree woodland, pinyon woodland, or desert scrub on the inland sides.

Climate

The Sierran montane forest is a coniferous response to California's mild, wet winters and warm, dry summers. Trees are subject to little cold stress in winter—when the average nighttime lows range from only the mid-teens to the low thirties—and enjoy growing seasons up to seven months long. In return, however, they must withstand prolonged drought in the summer, when daytime temperatures can hit the low nineties.

Precipitation averages between twenty-five inches at the lower forest boundary to as much as eighty inches in the upper montane forest. Less than five percent of those totals, however, falls between June 1 and September 30.

Above 6500 feet, nearly all precipitation takes the form of snow; in favorable locations, the average snowfall exceeds 400 inches a year. The snowpack reaches its maximum depth in mid-March. Below 2000 feet, virtually all precipitation falls as rain.

Summer thunder showers occur on perhaps four or five days a month in the upper montane forest—where many trees bear lightning damage—but such storms are uncommon at lower elevations and in southern California. Overcast days are exceedingly rare in the summer in all areas of the forest except in the western Klamath Mountains, where influxes of marine air make cloud cover more frequent.

The lower limit of the Sierran montane forest generally occurs where mean annual precipitation falls below twenty-five inches. Drought-tolerant montane trees such as Ponderosa Pine, Black Oak, and Incense-cedar can withstand less precipitation, but apparently not when summers are as hot and rainless as they are in California's interior foothills.

At higher elevations, summer drought is somewhat alleviated by occasional thunderstorms, but of far greater importance to conifers is the role played by snow. At elevations of more than about 6500 feet, snowpack depths in excess of one hundred inches are common, and the snow often lingers in the shade of the forest until early July. Gradual melting allows runoff water to penetrate deep forest soils, and trees subsist on this supply throughout the nearly rainless summer.

Forest Types

The Sierran montane forest consists of several forest types, each of which is defined by one or more distinctive dominant trees. In most instances, the dominant trees are also climax species. However, Ponderosa Pine or Lodgepole Pine types may dominate disturbed sites where firs or a mixture of conifers make up the climax forest.

Lodgepole Pine
Pinus contorta
40

Mixed-Conifer forest

This type occurs from southern Oregon to southern California. Stands are dominated by Ponderosa Pine, White Fir, or

Giant Sequoia
Sequoiadendron giganteum
54

Jeffrey Pine
Pinus jeffreyi
37, 126

Shasta Red Fir
Abies magnifica var.
shastensis

Bigcone Douglas-fir
Pseudotsuga macrocarpa
132

Coulter Pine
Pinus coulteri
127

Coast Redwood
Sequoia sempervirens
53, 141

Douglas-fir, but also commonly include Black Oak, Incense-cedar, or Sugar Pine in varying combinations and proportions. The stands are moderately open to fairly dense, with understory layers of trees, shrubs, and herbs. Mountain chaparral is characteristic of burned areas or steep, hot, south-facing slopes. Grasslands occur on seasonally moist flats and basins within the forest.

The composition of a stand depends largely on local moisture levels, which vary sharply with changes in topography. As a general rule, Ponderosa Pine dominates lower, hotter, drier forest sites, extending upslope on dry ridges and hot, south-facing slopes. Either White Fir or Douglas-fir prevails on higher, cooler, moister ground. White Fir reaches a lower limit on cool, moist, northern aspects. Of the species also commonly found in mixed conifer forests, Black Oak tolerates the hottest, driest, rockiest places. Like White Fir, Sugar Pine and Giant Sequoia require cool sites where soil moisture is adequate throughout the summer. Incense-cedar and Douglas-fir have the broadest ranges of tolerance for both moisture and shade and therefore do reasonably well in a variety of habitats. Douglas-fir commonly replaces White Fir as the dominant tree in the mid-slope forests of the northern Sierra and the southern Cascades. However, it is absent south of the Yosemite region. At higher elevations and on serpentine, Jeffrey Pine commonly replaces Ponderosa Pine. Jeffrey Pine also prevails on the eastern side of the Sierra Nevada, where aridity and cold winters combine to discourage Ponderosas. In the Klamath Mountains, Shasta Red Fir and White Fir often occur together in mixed forests, along with Douglas-fir, Sugar Pine, Incense-cedar, Black Oak, and other trees. In the forests of southern California, Douglas-fir is replaced by Bigcone Douglas-fir, and Coulter Pine is added to the mix.

The Giant Sequoia, a distant cousin of the Coast Redwood, grows only in seventy-five groves scattered throughout the central and southern Sierra Nevada. Located on unglaciated ridges at elevations of between 4500 and 8400 feet, the groves occur on deep soils that remain moist throughout the summer. They resemble mixed conifer stands in all respects save the most dramatic: They are dominated by Giant Sequoias, the largest trees in the world and among the oldest as well. Mature Sequoias are typically more than 1500 years old and over 200 feet tall, and they have trunks that are more than 15 feet thick. Exceptional trees are much larger. The General Sherman tree, for example, is 272.2 feet tall and 36.5 feet in diameter at its base. Its age is estimated at 2500 years. Resistance to fire, insects, and disease is no doubt responsible for the Sequoia's longevity. Tannin in the bark makes it unpalatable to insects and fungi. Its thickness and its lack of flammable resins make it resistant to fire and protect the heartwood within. Even so, many old Sequoias have large fire scars. They are able to continue growing even when their trunks have been nearly hollowed out. Sequoias remain vital—even in advanced old age—and seem capable of living much longer than the oldest recorded specimens. Fire damage,

Pacific Dogwood
Cornus nuttallii
69

Giant Chinkapin
Castanopsis chrysophylla
78, 178

Tanoak
Lithocarpus densiflorus
170

California-laurel
Umbellularia californica
77

White Alder
Alnus rhombifolia
87

Bigleaf Maple
Acer macrophyllum
102

California Hazelnut
Corylus cornuta californica
168

Red Huckleberry
Vaccinium parvifolium
150

Greenleaf Manzanita
Arctostaphylos patula
161

Western Peony
Paeonia brownii
466

Sulphur Flower
Eriogonum umbellatum
436

Hooker's Evening Primrose
Oenothera hookeri
448

Pussy Paws
Calyptridium umbellatum
512

Skyrocket
Ipomopsis aggregata
477

Western White Pine
Pinus monticola
121

windthrow, and undermining by erosion seem to be the only significant causes of mortality.

In well-developed mixed conifer stands on deep, moist forest loams, several layers of vegetation may be present. Beneath a moderate canopy of White Fir, Sugar Pine, Douglas-fir, and Incense-cedar, an understory tree layer may, depending on the region, consist of some combination of Pacific Dogwood, Giant Chinkapin, Tanoak, California-laurel, White Alder, Pacific Madrone, or Bigleaf Maple. The shrub layer in such forests commonly includes typical coastal-forest species such as California Hazelnut, Red Huckleberry, and Thimbleberry, along with various gooseberries, currants, and other more typically Sierran plants. Depending on available moisture and sunlight, the herb layer may be either sparse or rather lush. Where moisture is limited, the most common shrubs are drought-hardy species of manzanita and ceanothus. Greenleaf Manzanita is probably the most characteristic shrub of the montane forest.

Shrubs growing in the lower Sierran montane forest commonly show pronounced adaptations to both drought and fire. Most develop deep taproots and sprout from buried root crowns after a fire. Their leaves tend to be rather small, thick, and pale, and are coated with fine hairs, waxy bloom, or shiny varnishlike cutin. All of these features are designed to reduce heating of the leaf surface—and to therefore also minimize moisture loss. Greenleaf Manzanita holds its leaves upright so that incoming sunlight strikes them at their edges at midday. Most species drop some of their leaves and branches during times of drought, thus reducing the amount of tissue that must be supplied with water.

Thin, stony soils and scree slopes within the forest commonly host extensive carpets of Pinemat Manzanita or Squaw Carpet, a species of ceanothus. Pinemat Manzanita, which ranges northward into Washington, is the ecological equivalent of Kinnikinnick, or Bearberry, which occupies similar sites in the Rocky Mountains and the Cascade Range.

The more common wild flowers on dry, open ground include larkspurs, Western Peony, Sulphur Flower, penstemons, Hooker's Evening Primrose, Pussypaws, and Skyrocket. Most herbaceous species in the lower forests are annuals, which bloom and set seed in late spring or early summer, then die. In effect, annuals endure the rainless months in the form of seeds. Their ability to persist for months or years in this way is perhaps the ultimate adaptation to drought.

Owing to the diversity of species in the Sierran montane forest, numerous insect pests and parasitic fungi occur there as well. At the same time, mixed stands tend to discourage serious outbreaks of insects or disease, which often sweep unchecked through a forest consisting mainly or almost entirely of a single tree species. Various root, ring, and trunk rots affect pines and firs alike. Dwarf Mistletoe is a serious pest on firs, Douglas-fir, and Incense-cedar. White Pine Blister Rust has damaged both Sugar Pines and Western White Pines, though losses have not been as extensive as in

Fir Engraver Beetle
Scolytus ventralis

Fir Borer
Melanophila drummondi

Spruce Budworm
Choristoneura fumiferana

Douglas-fir Tussock Moth
Orgyia pseudotsuga

Needleminer
Evagora milleri

Western Pine Beetle
Dendroctonus brevicomis

Mountain Pine Beetle
Dendroctonus ponderosae

Red Fir
Abies magnifica
43

Western Juniper
Juniperus occidentalis
63

Singleleaf Pinyon
Pinus monophylla
137

California Black Oak
Quercus kelloggii
103

Limber Pine
Pinus flexilis
122

Birchleaf Mountain-
mahogany
Cercocarpus betuloides
92, 179

Scrub Oak
Quercus dumosa

the northern Rockies. Firs weakened by fungi or mistletoe are more subject to attack by various insect pests, which include Fir Engraver Beetles, Fir Borers, and defoliators such as Spruce Budworm, Douglas-fir Tussock Moth, and Needleminers. Western Pine Beetle, Mountain Pine Beetle, and bark beetles infest all pine species occurring in the forest.

Jeffrey Pine forest
Ponderosa Pine is restricted in its upslope range by a variety of interlocking factors. First, it requires warm summer weather for best growth. Above about 6500 feet in the central Sierra, air temperatures fall below the minimum necessary for sufficient growth to maintain Ponderosa Pine in the increasingly shaded forest stands. Where shade exceeds fifty percent, Ponderosa seedlings are too spindly to keep from bending under the weight of the snow. In addition, prolonged imprisonment in the snow pack shortens the growing season and exposes seedlings to destructive fungi that live in the snow. Jeffrey Pine, which tolerates all of the above conditions better than the closely related Ponderosa Pine, replaces it in stands at high elevations.

Forests dominated by Jeffrey Pine occur on the eastern side of the southern Cascades, on the Modoc Plateau in extreme northeastern California, on both sides of the Sierra Nevada, in the Klamath Mountains, North Coast Ranges, and in the Transverse and Peninsular ranges of southern California. Stands may be moderately open or dense and often contain scattered or clumped shrubs and an herb layer dominated by grasses. Jeffrey Pine may either form nearly pure stands or constitute the majority of trees in mixed stands.

Because Jeffrey Pine occurs over such a wide range of territory and environments, mixing with most other forest communities throughout California, the species' associates are numerous and vary greatly from place to place. They include Red Fir, Lodgepole Pine, and Western White Pine on the western slopes of the Sierra; while Western Juniper, Ponderosa Pine, and White Fir occur with it on the eastern side of the Cascades and the Sierra. In the mountains of southern California, Jeffrey Pine grows with White Fir, Incense-cedar, Western Juniper, Sugar Pine, Singleleaf Pinyon, California Black Oak, and Limber Pine. Jeffrey Pine also dominates extremely open, woodlandlike stands on serpentine and peridotite barrens in the Klamath Mountains, the Coast Ranges, and the Sierra Nevada. In Oregon, Jeffrey Pine occurs only on serpentine. The understory shrubs in this type of forest also vary greatly by region. East of the Cascades and the Sierra, Great Basin species such as Mountain-mahogany and sagebrush mix with typical western-slope shrubs such as Greenleaf Manzanita. West of the Cascade-Sierra divide, understory thickets commonly include various species of Scrub Oak, manzanita, and ceanothus. In the mountains of southern California, a similar dichotomy in shrub species distinguishes the seaward slopes from the desert slopes. Most of the shrubs are species that also associate with Jeffrey Pine in the Sierra.

California Red Fir
Abies magnifica

Sticky Currant
Ribes viscosissimum

Twinberry
Lonicera involucrata
164

Huckleberry Oak
Quercus vaccinifolia

Mountain Snowberry
Symphoricarpos oreophilus
165

Brewer's Golden-aster
Chrysopsis breweri

White-flowered Hawkweed
Hieracium albiflorum

Mountain Pennyroyal
Monardella odoratissima

Snow Plant
Sarcodes sanguinea
480

Coralroot
Corallorhiza spp.

Indian Pipe
Monotropa uniflora
428

Sugar Stick
Allotropa virgata

Pinesap
Monotropa hypopitys

Bush Chinkapin
Castanopsis sempervirens
169

Rabbitbrush
Chrysothamnus nauseosus

Red-flowering Currant
Ribes sanguineum

Mountain Hemlock
Tsuga mertensiana
49, 139

Noble Fir
Abies procera
133

Red Fir forest

Forests dominated by Red Fir occur above mixed-conifer forests in the southern Cascades, the Klamath Mountains, the North Coast Ranges, and the Sierra Nevada. Two varieties of Red Fir may be present: California Red Fir, which has inconspicuous cone scale bracts, is the more common variety in the Sierra Nevada; Shasta Red Fir, with bracts that extend beyond the scales, is the typical form elsewhere. Stands in the Sierra and the Cascades are often pure, or nearly so, firs forming a closed canopy beneath which shade is nearly complete. The forest floor is typically covered with thick mats of needles, which take a long time to decompose in the short, cool summers of the upper montane zone.

Shade and dense litter act together to severely limit the growth of understory plants. Shrubs are few and largely confined to sunny patches within the forest. The most common species are Sticky Currant, Twinberry, Huckleberry Oak, and Mountain Snowberry. Herbs are somewhat more common, though usually restricted to moister sites such as those along streams or in damp swales. Brewer's Golden-aster, White-flowered Hawkweed, and Mountain Pennyroyal often occur on such sites. Several saprophytic herbs, which do not require any sunlight whatsoever, may occur anywhere in the forest; these include Snow Plant, Coralroot, Indian Pipe, Sugar Stick, and Pinesap.

Steep, hot slopes with dry, rocky soils commonly support dense stands of brush rather than forest. The more common species include Bush Chinkapin, Huckleberry Oak, Mountain Snowberry, Greenleaf Manzanita, Rabbitbrush, Sticky Currant, and Red-flowering Currant. Following a fire, these shrubs replace pioneer herbs until they are in turn shaded out by rapidly growing Lodgepole Pines. Red Fir seedlings, which initially prefer shade, grow beneath the shrubs and eventually overtop the pines. Lightning-caused fires are fairly common in the Red Fir forest and seem to be the most important instigators of secondary succession.

Along the lower margin of the forest, Red and White firs commonly occur together. At higher elevations—particularly from Yosemite northward—Red Fir often grows with Mountain Hemlock. Lodgepole Pine, also a frequent associate, forms thickets on burned ground, generally occupying sites that are either too wet or too dry for Red Firs. Jeffrey Pine often forms moderately dense stands on south-facing slopes with good soil, and occurs with Western White Pine, Lodgepole Pine, and Western Juniper on rocky outcrops and thin, gravelly screes. Aspens occur with Lodgepole Pines on damp flats near meadows or lakes.

In the Klamath Mountains and North Coast Ranges, mixed stands are typical; here Douglas-fir, White Fir, and Mountain Hemlock are important associates. In the western Siskiyou Mountains and in the Cascades north of Crater Lake, the closely related Noble Fir replaces Shasta Red Fir.

The Red Fir forests of the Klamath Mountains are the most diverse conifer forests in the world, containing trees

Brewer Spruce
Picea brewerana
44

Western Yew
Taxus brevifolia
52, 146

Engelmann Spruce
Picea engelmannii
117

Subalpine Fir
Abies lasiocarpa
46

Raccoon
Procyon lotor
353

Western Grey Squirrel
Sciurus griseus
339

Northern Pacific
Rattlesnake
Crotalus viridis oreganus
597

Bushy-tailed Woodrat
Neotoma cinerea
337

Pine Grosbeak
Pinicola enucleator
308

Mountain Yellow-legged
Frog
Rana muscosa
610

Acorn Woodpecker
Melanerpes fornicivorus
241

Band-tailed Pigeon
Columba fasciata
228

Black Bear
Ursus americanus
359

Porcupine
Erethizon dorsatum
355

Snowshoe Hare
Lepus americanus
350

representative of both Sierra and Northwest forests. Aside from the species mentioned above, the Klamath Red Fir forests also include the following conifers: Western White Pine, Brewer Spruce Sugar Pine, Ponderosa Pine, Western Yew, Incense-cedar, Engelmann Spruce, Lodgepole Pine, Subalpine Fir, Pacific Silver Fir, Alaska-cedar, and Port-Orford-cedar. Understory shrubs in the eastern Klamath Mountains are largely Sierran species, while those in the western Klamaths are mostly Northwest forest types.

Wildlife

The Sierran montane forest provides numerous habitats for wildlife. Several factors contribute to this diversity: the large variety of trees, including numerous hardwoods; the moderately open character of most stands, which permits the elaboration of understory vegetation; and the abundance of forest openings in the form of dry grasslands, damp meadows, brush, rock outcrops, cliffs, and stream banks. As a result, the variety of wildlife is impressive. Animals that are more or less confined to conifer forests mingle here with species that are typical of woodlands, brush, meadows, rocky areas, and even deserts. Northern animals mix with southern types. Acorn fanciers rub shoulders with pine-nut connoisseurs and even fir-seed specialists.

Lowland animals such as Raccoon, Western Gray Squirrel, Swainson's Thrush, and Pacific Rattlesnake are most often found in the foothills and valleys of California and southern Oregon, but are also adapted to conditions in the lower montane pine and mixed-conifer forests. In the mountains of California, montane animals such as Douglas' Squirrel, Bushy-tailed Wood Rat, Pine Grosbeak, and Mountain Yellow-legged Frog are confined entirely to middle or upper elevations, but they may occur in lowland forests in the Pacific Northwest and Canada. Changes in latitude are also accompanied by corresponding shifts in the kinds of animals present.

Pine nuts are an abundant source of proteins and fats for numerous animals of the Sierran montane forest, including Gray Squirrel, Douglas' Squirrel, ground squirrels, and other rodents as well as a variety of birds. Since several pine species are present, a poor cone year for one may be offset by a good year for another. Acorns are also plentiful, whether from Black Oak and Canyon Live Oak at lower elevations or from various shrubby oaks in the montane brush of the upper forest. The fauna of the lower montane forest includes a number of acorn specialists, such as Acorn Woodpecker, Band-tailed Pigeon, Gray Squirrel, and Lewis' Woodpecker, all of which are more characteristic of California's oak woodlands. In addition, most birds and mammals that feed on pine nuts also relish acorns, and vice versa. Even such omnivores as Raccoon, skunk, and Black Bear fancy these nuts from time to time, as do Coyotes. When snows are deep and food is scarce, the bark of conifers provides an emergency food for numerous rodents. Porcupines and Snowshoe Hares feed mainly on bark during the winter.

Mountain-beaver
Aplodontia rufa
346

Deer Mouse
Peromyscus maniculatus
329

Bitter Cherry
Prunus emarginata
186

Western Serviceberry
Amelanchier alnifolia
91, 184

Pacific Waxmyrtle
Myrica californica
81

Blue Elderberry
Sambucus cerulea
162

MacGillivray's Warbler
Oporornis tolmiei
292

Wilson's Warbler
Wilsonia pusilla
293

Brown Creeper
Certhia americana
268

Hermit Warbler
Dendroica occidentalis
291

Clark's Nutcracker
Nucifraga columbiana
259

Whitebark Pine
Pinus albicaulis
123

Pika
Ochotona princeps
330

Long-eared Owl
Asio otus
231

Great Gray Owl
Strix nebulosa
233

The hare, along with voles and the Mountain-beaver, favors the thinner, more succulent bark of aspens, cottonwoods, alders, and willows.

Both the seeds of grasses—which are abundant in the Sierran montane forest—and those of the numerous broadleaf herbs that grow on the forest floor are extremely important food sources for Deer Mice, chipmunks, and other small rodents. The abundance of these plants also attracts numerous types of seed-eating birds, which spend most of their time foraging on the forest floor. These include the Dark-eyed Junco, several sparrows, grosbeaks, and the Green-tailed Towhee. The fact that each species has its own particular feeding niche reduces the competition between them. For example, Fox Sparrows feed beneath or near dense stands of mountain brush, Chipping Sparrows prefer grassy openings with small trees nearby, Lincoln's Sparrows forage in damp thickets, and Pine Grosbeaks prefer upper montane forests and meadows.

Rodents, Raccoons, skunks, and bears, along with a host of birds, feast on the abundant berry crops produced in the Sierran montane forest. Bittercherry, Sierra Juniper, Serviceberry, Waxmyrtle, blackberry, and Blue Elderberry are some of the other important berry-producing plants. Juniper berries, which are actually fleshy cones, are particularly important as a winter food source.

Like the seed-eaters, insectivorous birds have also distributed themselves in various suitable niches according to their feeding needs. Ground feeders include Swainson's Thrush, Robins, and various sparrows; other birds, such as Winter Wren, MacGillivray's Warbler, and Wilson's Warbler, are shrub-layer feeders. Nuthatches, woodpeckers, and the Brown Creeper find their quarry in tree bark, while Audubon's Warblers, Hermit Warblers, and Western Tanagers seek food in the foliage.

Steller's Jays seem to be nearly everywhere in the forest, feeding on seeds, nuts, berries, insects, and even the eggs and young of other birds. At the upper levels of the forest, the species is replaced by its relative, Clark's Nutcracker, which also eats a variety of foods, but depends mainly on the nuts of Whitebark Pine, a common subalpine species.

Cooper's and Sharp-shinned hawks prey upon forest birds, mainly at low to middle elevations. They are replaced in the upper montane forests by the Northern Goshawk, a close relative. Red-tailed Hawks nest in tall conifers, but commonly fly upslope during the day to soar over open subalpine meadows in search of ground squirrels, voles, marmots, and Pikas. Among the larger owls present in the forest are the Spotted, Great Horned, Long-eared, and Great Gray, which control the mice and vole populations. Deep woods near large meadows are these birds' especially favored haunts.

Shrubs form the chief staple in the diet of Mule Deer (which here includes the Columbia Black-tailed Deer). These animals prefer Rabbit Brush and various ceanothuses but also feed extensively on Western Serviceberry, wild rose, and most other shrubs. Deer populations in the Sierran montane forest

Mountain Lion
Felis concolor
363

Bobcat
Felis rufus
362

Gray Fox
Urocyon cinereoargenteus
366

Weasel
Mustela spp.

Marten
Martes americana
343

Fisher
Martes pennanti

Yellow-bellied Marmot
Marmota flaviventris
351

Gopher Snake
Pituophis melanoleucus
596

California Mountain
Kingsnake
Lampropeltis zonata
591

Rubber Boa
Charina bottae
599

migrate downslope to the foothills each fall; in spring they follow the receding snow line upslope. Following the Mule Deer in its migrations is its arch predator, the Mountain Lion. To detect the cat's presence, evolution has equipped the Mule Deer with large ears, a sensitive wet nose, and the habit of continually stopping, head erect, to sniff the wind and listen for the crackle of forest litter.

Mule Deer and Mountain Lions have evolved together over the millennia. Left to themselves, the populations achieve a balance, which allows for the number of deer a lion must eat and the number of lions the deer can tolerate. In the first half of this century, thousands of Mountain Lions were killed in the Sierra Nevada; as a result, the Mule Deer population expanded beyond the carrying capacity of its range. By 1940 this range was seriously overbrowsed, and deer were beginning to die in large numbers from starvation and disease. Normally, Mule Deer eat on the run, as it were, nibbling here and there but never pausing too long at one bush. This behavior not only helps them evade predators, but also preserves their food source by spreading the damage of feeding over all of the plants within their range. However, when food is scarce, deer congregate where browse is most plentiful and sometimes eat these plants down to the ground, which further exacerbates the problem. When this happens, increasing numbers of deer die of starvation and disease. Predators such as the Coyote—or even the Black Bear—kill many of the weaker animals.

In addition to the Mountain Lion, important predators in the Sierran montane forest include Bobcat, Coyote, Gray Fox, Weasels, Marten, Fisher, and various reptiles, hawks, and owls. Weasels are the scourge of chipmunks, ground squirrels, and other rodents. Weasels often move into an area and stay until they have rather systematically eliminated the local rodent population. When there are few rodents left, too much energy is needed to catch them, so the weasels move on. In summer, Martens prowl about talus slopes where they hunt down Bushy-tailed Wood Rats, Pikas, and even Yellow-bellied Marmots. In winter they descend into the fir forest, where they run down Douglas' Squirrels in frantic treetop chases. The Fisher, a larger version of the Marten, is the chief predator of Porcupines, which can do significant damage to trees. Fishers also prey upon most other small or medium-sized mammals, including the Marten.

Reptiles are fairly common at lower elevations in the Sierran montane forest, where summers are warm and winters are fairly mild and mercifully brief, with little or no snow. The Pacific Rattlesnake feeds mainly on ground squirrels and chipmunks, but also kills rabbits, birds, and lizards. The Gopher Snake is known to take numerous birds, often climbing into shrubbery to raid nests. The California Mountain Kingsnake preys on a variety of small animals, including most other snakes. The Rubber Boa specializes in nocturnal rodents, while garter snakes frequent damp places, where voles and amphibians are common.

The only conspicuous animals on bare outcrops of rock are

Western Fence Lizard
Sceloporus occidentalis
584

Sagebrush Lizard
Sceloporus graciosus

Northern Alligator Lizard
Gerrhonotus coeruleus
585

Spotted Sandpiper
Actitis macularia

American Dipper
Cinclus mexicanus
271

Belted Kingfisher
Ceryle alcyon

likely to be Western Fence Lizards, which scurry about in a rapid, rather aggressive way. The males frantically perform a series of movements that look like pushups as a way of attracting females or scaring off other males. The smaller but similar Sagebrush Lizard also frequents rock outcrops and nearby brush, where it may be counted among the prey of Alligator Lizards.

Moist, grassy areas within the forest usually support large vole populations, along with the garter snakes that prey upon them. Shrews also frequent such areas in search of insects and other invertebrates, but they occasionally take voles or other small rodents or are taken by garter snakes. The Mountain-beaver also occurs in moist thickets near streams—a habitat that is also preferred by Lincoln's Sparrow. These animals can also be found on the banks of streams, along with the Spotted Sandpiper, American Dipper, and Belted Kingfisher.

SIERRAN MONTANE FORESTS: PLANTS AND ANIMALS

Trees and Shrubs
Bigcone Douglas-fir 132
Bigleaf Maple 102
Birchleaf Mountain-
mahogany 92, 179
Black Cottonwood 94
Blue Elderberry 162
Brewer Spruce 44
California Black Oak 103
California Fremontia 202
California Torreya 145
Canyon Live Oak 173
Cascara Buckthorn 93
Common Chokeberry 156
Common Manzanita 74
Coulter Pine 127
Deer Brush 198, 221
Douglas-fir 134
Giant Chinkapin 78, 178
Giant Sequoia 54
Incense-cedar 57
Jeffrey Pine 37, 126
Knobcone Pine 129
Labrador Tea 185
Lewis' Syringa 188
Lodgepole Pine 40
Mountain Alder 88, 144
Pacific Dogwood 69
Pacific Madrone 76, 158
Pacific Willow 79
Ponderosa Pine 38
Quaking Aspen 95
Red-osier Dogwood 70
Red Shrubby
Penstemon 207
Rocky Mountain Maple 100
Scouler Willow 75
Sugar Pine 120
Tanoak 170
Twinberry 164
Water Birch 90
Wavyleaf Silktassel 71
Western Azalea 208
Western Juniper 63
Western Mountain-ash 108
Western Serviceberry 91
Western White Pine 121
Western Yew 52, 146
White Fir 45

Birds
Acorn Woodpecker 241
American Dipper 271
American Robin 279
Band-tailed Pigeon 228
Bewick's Wren 269
Black-chinned
Hummingbird 235
Black-headed Grosbeak 295
Black-throated Gray
Warbler 289
Blue Grouse 224
Brown Creeper 268
Bushtit 264
Calliope Hummingbird 237
Cassin's Finch 309
Chipping Sparrow 300
Common Raven 260
Dark-eyed Junco 305, 306
Evening Grosbeak 311
Fox Sparrow 301
Golden-crowned
Kinglet 272
Great Gray Owl 233
Great Horned Owl 230
Green-tailed Towhee 297
Hairy Woodpecker 245
Hermit Thrush 278
Lincoln's Sparrow 303
Long-eared Owl 231
MacGillivray's Warbler 292
Mountain Bluebird 276
Mountain Chickadee 261
Mountain Quail 227
Northern Flicker 248
Northern Goshawk 223
Olive-sided Flycatcher 250
Orange-crowned
Warbler 285
Pileated Woodpecker 249
Pine Grosbeak 308
Pine Siskin 312
Pygmy Nuthatch 267
Pygmy Owl 232
Red-breasted Nuthatch 265
Red Crossbill 310
Ruby-crowned Kinglet 273
Rufous-sided Towhee 298
Saw-whet Owl 234
Solitary Vireo 283
Song Sparrow 302
Steller's Jay 256
Townsend's Solitaire 277
Violet-green Swallow 254
Warbling Vireo 284
Western Bluebird 275
Western Flycatcher 252
Western Tanager 294

Long-tailed Wild
Ginger 463
Meadow Goldenrod 433
Merten's Saxifrage 406
Miner's Lettuce 396
Mission Bells 467
Monument Plant 411
Mountain Bluebell 534
Mountain Jewel Flower 462
Nuttall's Larkspur 526
One-sided Wintergreen 407
Orange Agoseris 456
Pearly Everlasting 422
Phantom Orchid 429
Pinedrops 461
Pussy Paws 512
Queen's Cup 393
Red Columbine 483
Richardson's Geranium 386
Rydberg's Penstemon 536
Showy Thistle 479
Sierra Sedum 437
Skyrocket 477
Snow Plant 480
Spotted Coral Root 465
Spreading Dogbane 509
Spring Beauty 392
Stream Violet 450
Sulphur Flower 436
Tough-leaved Iris 528
Twinflower 484
Umbrella Plant 504
Western Blue Flax 520
Western Monkshood 530
Western Pasque Flower 382
Western Peony 466
Western Polemonium 522
Western Starflower 495
Western Wallflower 455
Yarrow 423
Yerba Buena 421

Butterflies
Anicia Checkerspot 553
California Sister 555
California Tortoiseshell 560
Faunus Anglewing 559
Great Spangled
Fritillary 562
Large Wood Nymph 550
Lorquin's Admiral 554
Milbert's Tortoiseshell 561
Nelson's Hairstreak 544
Phoebus Parnassian 541

Pine White 557
Ruddy Copper 543
Western Tiger
Swallowtail 556

Insects and Spiders
Bark Beetles 567
Black Flies 575
Common Water Strider 568
Deer Flies 576
Golden Buprestid 565
Golden Huntsman
Spider 582
Golden Northern Bumble
Bee 578
Orb Weavers 581
Pine and Spruce Engraver
Beetles 566
Short-tailed
Ichneumons 571
Snow Mosquito 574
Violet Tail 569
Western Flying Adder 570
Wood Ticks 579
Yellow Jackets 577

Reptiles and Amphibians
Arboreal Salamander 603
California Mountain
Kingsnake 591
California Newt 602
Common California
Kingsnake 593
Foothill Yellow-legged
Frog 614
Gopher Snake 596
Mountain Yellow-legged
Frog 610
Northern Pacific
Rattlesnake 597
Oregon Ensatina 604
Pacific Treefrog 618
Red-legged Frog 611
Ringneck Snake 590
Rubber Boa 599
Sharptail Snake 598
Striped Racer 589
Wandering Garter
Snake 595
Western Skink 587
Western Toad 617
Western Yellowbelly
Racer 600

Ponderosa Pine
Pinus ponderosa
38

Douglas-fir
Pseudotsuga menziesii
134

Lodgepole Pine
Pinus contorta
40

Quaking Aspen
Populus tremuloides
95

White Fir
Abies concolor
45

Blue Spruce
Picea pungens
118

Western Larch
Larix occidentalis
51, 131

Grand Fir
Abies grandis
48

Western White Pine
Pinus monticola
121

Western Hemlock
Tsuga heterophylla
140

Western Redcedar
Thuja plicata
59, 142

The Rocky Mountain montane forests include several types that occupy the middle elevations between sagebrush steppes or grasslands below and the subalpine forest above. Ponderosa Pine, Douglas-fir, Lodgepole Pine, and Quaking Aspen are the most characteristic and widespread trees, though none of them ranges the entire length of the Rockies. Nonetheless, at least one of the four is likely to be found in every forest stand below the subalpine zone, and together they occur in various combinations and proportions according to an environmental recipe of staggering complexity. The forests are further enriched by the addition of White Fir and Blue Spruce in the southern Rockies, and of Western Larch, Grand Fir, Western White Pine, Western Hemlock, and Western Redcedar in the northern Rockies.

At lower elevations, open forests of Ponderosa Pine reach down to desert and grassland. Few other forest conifers can match the Ponderosa's ability to thrive in these very hot and dry environments. The pines stand aloof even from one another, the intervals separating them determined by competing root systems. Sometimes the transition from grassland to forest is abrupt, with pines forming a shore on gravelly slopes and sandy promontories while sagebrush or grass penetrates the woods in bays and coves of finer alluvium. More often, the shift is gradual. In many areas, mountain brush or pinyon-juniper woodlands form buffer zones between forest and steppe. In others, the forest itself may become gradually attenuated as it marches downslope to drought, the trees spaced ever more widely apart until, finally, they are gone.

Douglas-fir forms thick, shady forests at middle elevations, occupying the choicest sites for conifers in the Rockies. Since most other kinds of trees thrive on the same sites, which have ample moisture and are neither too warm nor too cool, Douglas-fir seldom grows without associate conifers. Indeed, at one place or another it probably grows with virtually every other kind of tree native to the Rockies. Douglas-fir can also rough it, growing in a wider variety of habitats than all but one or two of its companions. In addition, it tolerates shade better than its downslope companions and withstands drought better than its upslope associates.

In the middle and northern Rockies, however, large areas where one would expect to find Douglas-fir are covered instead with Lodgepole Pine. This slim opportunist owes its considerable success in the region to the abundance of sites that have been disturbed by fire or that are somehow unsuitable for potential competitors. In the subalpine forest, Lodgepole Pine often grows on sites that are both too cold and too wet for other conifers; in the montane forest, it may dominate slopes that are too sterile and dry.

Among the glories of the Rocky Mountains—particularly in the south—are the groves of Quaking Aspen, which are more extensive here than anywhere else in the West. Aspens grow in moist, sunny glades, where grasses reach high and wildflowers abound. They are also scar-healers, as they quickly cover burns, logged slopes, and bare talus—places where conifers

have failed. Aspens provide the beauty of contrast. Their
trunks are smooth and white; their crowns, open and rounded;
their leaves, thin, infused with light and wind, pale green in
summer, and gold in fall. Forming pure groves that often
cover entire basins or hillsides, aspens seem to bring the
caprice of youth to the somber rectitude of the conifer forests.
Rocky Mountain forests occupy relatively narrow bands of
moderate climate, squeezed between the extremes of cold
above and drought below. Drought and cold also sandwich the
forests of California, but the two conditions are separated by
thousands of feet of elevation, so trees must contend with
extremes of one or the other, but not of both. In the Rockies,
however, drought often pushes upslope to timberline, while
cold—in the winter at least—descends to the desert floor.
Unfavorable combinations of moisture and temperature are
common in the Rockies, where fully three quarters of the sites
supporting forests provide only the barest minimum of
resources for that purpose.
Throughout most of the Rocky Mountains, drought is never
far away. The desert looms like a terrible possibility just
beyond the last trees. Congregations of grass and sagebrush
surround the mountains, sprawl over valleys and basins, and
advance upslope, even into the forests. The grip of conifers
often seems tenuous in the Rockies; it is as if the merest shift
in climate could initiate an irreversible descent into
desolation. The forest never seems greener, cooler or more
refreshing than here at the desert's edge, and the pines and firs
never appear more magnificent than in the company of
sagebrush.

Geographic Distribution
The Rocky Mountain montane forest forms the lowest forest
belt on all of the principal ranges of the chain from southern
Canada to southern New Mexico. It also occurs on the eastern
side of the Cascade Range, on the higher interior ranges
between the Cascade-Sierra axis and the western front of the
Rockies, and on the high plateaus and mountains in the
Southwest. The forest gradually merges on its northern edge
with the boreal forest.
The elevations at which the upper and lower margins of the
forest occur vary considerably both from region to region and
from range to range. In general, however, the forest occurs at
elevations of 1200 to 6000 feet near the Canadian border,
6000 to 9000 feet in Colorado, and 6500 to 9500 feet in the
Southwest.
The largest expanse of Rocky Mountain montane forest occurs
in the northern Rockies. From Canada the forest extends south
to the Snake River plain in southern Idaho and an isthmus of
High Plains grassland in southwestern Montana, covering the
entire mountain district from the Lewis Range and the Big
Belt Mountains on the east to Washington's Okanogan Valley,
south to northeastern California on the west. Farther south,
scattered islands of forest occur on high, isolated mountain
ranges in southern Oregon and the Great Basin. Islands of

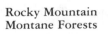

**Rocky Mountain
Montane Forests**

forest are surrounded by grassland in eastern Montana, northeastern Wyoming, and western South Dakota. The Black Hills is the easternmost limit of Ponderosa Pine. There is also a large area of this forest in northwestern Wyoming and adjacent states. Centered around Yellowstone National Park, the forest extends southward through the Teton and Wyoming ranges on the west and the Wind River Range on the east. A large outlier occurs in the Big Horn Mountains of north-central Wyoming. The sagebrush plains of the Wyoming basin constitute the largest forest gap along the Continental Divide, and separate the northern forests from those in the Colorado Rockies.

The Rocky Mountain montane forest is found on all the mountain ranges in Colorado, extending to northern New Mexico. Southern outliers are found on Sierra Blanca Peak, near Alamogordo, New Mexico, and on the Guadalupe Mountains of southern New Mexico and trans-Pecos Texas. From the northern Wasatch Range and Uinta Mountains in Utah, the forest occurs southward intermittently to the high plateaus of southern Utah and northern Arizona, including both rims of the Grand Canyon. It also extends along the Mogollon Rim from central Arizona southeastward through the White Mountains into New Mexico.

Climate

The Rocky Mountain forest region lies in the rain shadow of the Sierra Nevada and the Cascade Range, which together form a lofty barrier across the path of prevailing westerly winds. One effect of the rain shadow is that mountain ranges downwind from the Sierra-Cascade divide receive less precipitation at a given elevation than do slopes west of the divide. This elevates the lower forest limit and narrows the forest belt by squeezing it against the comparatively stable, temperature-controlled upper timberline. The entire forest is pushed upward into colder climatic zones. On some ranges, one or more of the lower forest zones may be missing, because the altitudes at which the precipitation is sufficient to sustain certain conifers are too cold for them. This is why Ponderosa Pine is missing from colder districts in the region. On some desert ranges, only the subalpine zone receives enough precipitation to support forest, so the lower timberline is formed by Bristlecone Pine or Limber Pine at elevations near 10,000 feet.

Numerous individual mountain ranges complicate the general pattern by casting their own rain shadows. Local relief also affects precipitation. Because precipitation around mountains depends largely on the forced uplift and cooling of approaching air masses, a mountain range that rises, say, 10,000 feet above its base will receive more precipitation than one of equal height that rises only 5000 feet above its base. Precipitation along the lower forest boundary ranges from ten to twenty-five inches, though many areas receiving this much do not support conifer forest. The minimum amount of precipitation necessary to support forest conifers depends on

Bristlecone Pine
Pinus aristata
42, 130

Limber Pine
Pinus flexilis
122

several factors, including seasonal distribution of precipitation, evaporation rates, and the kinds of conifers forming the lower timberline. Areas that receive at least some rain during the summer are likely to require less precipitation for the year as a whole. In areas where evaporation rates are reduced, the effectiveness of the precipitation that does fall is increased; in these areas, lower amounts of precipitation are necessary. Evaporation rates tend to decline with increased latitude and elevation, and so will the precipitation requirements for forest growth. Northern exposures also tend to require smaller amounts of precipitation than south-facing slopes. Winds blowing across hot deserts greatly increase the evaporation rates on adjacent mountain slopes, and the degree to which a site is exposed to or sheltered from these winds may well determine whether it supports pinyon-juniper woodlands or Ponderosa Pine forest.

The northern Rockies experience cold, snowy winters and cool, dry summers. Precipitation ranges from as little as fifteen inches at lower elevations to more than sixty inches near timberline on ranges west of the Continental Divide. Nearly all of this precipitation falls as winter snow. Rainfall is scant during the summer, but deep snows and cool temperatures prevent moisture stress at middle and upper elevations. East of the Continental Divide, it is dry and cold in winter. Throughout the region, deep intrusions of continental polar air can cause temperatures to drop well below zero during the winter. West of the Continental Divide, winter cloudiness helps to moderate temperatures, but along the eastern mountain front, where many nights are clear, minimum temperatures of − 40° F occur every winter. Chinook winds also dramatically warm the eastern slopes in winter and early spring. Originating as cool, moist Pacific air, these winds are warmed and dried in their passage over successive mountain ranges. They can raise air temperatures along the eastern base of the northern Rockies by as much as 60° F in an hour, and can melt a foot of snow in a few hours. As a result, trees are subject to desiccation by wind at a time when frozen soils make it impossible for them to replace lost moisture.

In this harsh climate, Ponderosa Pine is absent. On warmer sites at lower elevations, Douglas-fir and Limber Pine occur in scattered, open stands of dwarfed trees. Lodgepole Pine, Quaking Aspen, and White Spruce, a species from the boreal forest, seem to fare best here.

White Spruce
Picea glauca
119

Summers are generally mild and dry in the northern Rockies, but frosts occur at night throughout the summer months. Low relative humidity creates a severe fire hazard in the region, which has been subject to numerous conflagrations in the past. In the northern Rockies, forests are commonly dominated by fire pioneers such as Lodgepole Pine, Western Larch, and Western White Pine. Thunderstorms, which occur with some regularity during the summer, account for most of the fires. Overall, the southern Rocky Mountains are warmer and drier than the northern ranges, with less total precipitation but more varied patterns of seasonal distribution. In the winter, snow is delivered by Pacific storms that enter the region mainly from the northwest. Summer precipitation, which nearly equals the winter amounts in some locations, results from thunderstorms produced both by local convection and by the regular northward incursion of moist tropical air from the gulfs of Mexico and California.

The richest, best-developed montane forests in the region occur in the San Juan Mountains of southwestern Colorado, which are far enough west to intercept a fair share of the moisture delivered by winter storms off the Pacific Ocean, and far enough south to receive ample summer precipitation from tropical air masses moving northward from the Gulf of California.

Summers are warm in the southern Rockies. Most of the days from June through September are clear or partly cloudy along the Front Range and the Sangre de Cristo Mountains, and relative humidities are low throughout the region. The winters are cold, with average January temperatures for Colorado ranging from 10° F near timberline to about 20° F in the valley. In New Mexico and northern Arizona, however, average temperatures in this season rise to about 30° F. Subzero temperatures are common throughout the region, but it rarely gets as bitterly cold as it does in the northern Rockies.

Fire

Wildfires have played an enormous role in shaping the forests of the Rocky Mountains, where the combination of frequent summer thunderstorms and low humidity creates a severe fire hazard. Over large areas, recurrent and sometimes catastrophic fires have favored opportunistic seral species—such as Lodgepole Pine—over climax conifers such as Douglas-fir. In many stands, climax species, if present at all, are represented mainly by understory seedlings and saplings, while climax forests, here more than elsewhere in the West, are often more evident in theory than on the ground. Lodgepole Pine has replaced Douglas-fir on millions of burned acres in the northern and middle Rockies. Quaking Aspen has played a similar role in the southern Rockies, where Lodgepole Pine is absent. Western Larch and Western White Pine are important fire pioneers in the northern ranges west of the Continental Divide. Ponderosa Pine has supplanted Douglas-fir on burns at lower elevations throughout the Rockies.

Before the coming of white settlers, fires were started either by aboriginal residents or lightning and often burned unchecked over millions of acres. Following the fires, opportunistic fire pioneers such as Lodgepole Pine invaded the devastated areas, typically forming pure, even-aged stands that stretched over vast areas. The persistence of Lodgepole Pine forests in the Rockies, in seeming defiance of the normal course of succession to Douglas-fir, remains a subject of some debate. According to the most widely held view, the burned areas were so extensive that reinvasion by climax conifers has been slowed by the remoteness of mature trees to serve as seed sources. Many observers, however, believe that Lodgepole Pine is a climax species on certain types of soils in the Rocky Mountains. The perpetuation of at least some of the extensive stands of Quaking Aspen in the southern Rockies may have a similar explanation. In the northern Rockies, however, the persistence of stands of Western Larch and Western White Pine—also fire pioneers—seems to have a different explanation. Unlike Lodgepole Pine, both of these conifers normally live more than 500 years. During this time, any number of fires or other disturbances are bound to occur. Thus the continued presence of Western Larch and Western White Pine in the forests of the region is guaranteed.

Recurrent fires have also been instrumental in maintaining open, parklike stands of Ponderosa Pines along the lower forest margin. At higher elevations, fires began and perpetuated the dominance of Ponderosa Pine in stands where Douglas-fir is the climax tree. With the suppression of fires in this century, young Douglas-firs now dominate the understories in many of these stands and will eventually succeed the mature pines in the overstories. Selective logging of Ponderosa Pine has furthered this trend.

In the past, fires may also have acted as a natural control of insect pests and parasites, checking the rapid spread of both mistletoe and parasitic fungi and dampening epidemic buildups of insect populations. On the other hand, bark beetles and other insects are often attracted to trees that have been weakened or killed by fire; serious outbreaks of beetles have followed destructive fires in the Rocky Mountain region.

Forest Types

The Rocky Mountain montane forest consists of several forest types, each of which is defined by one or more distinctive dominant trees. Sometimes the dominant tree is also the climax species, as in the case of the Douglas-fir forest. In other situations, the dominant species is not the area's climax tree, but is maintained indefinitely on a site by means of recurring disturbances, notably fire and logging. This explains the persistence of Lodgepole Pine and Quaking Aspen, among other species, on sites where Douglas-fir, Ponderosa Pine, or other montane conifers are climax. At the same time, Quaking Aspen and Lodgepole Pine may themselves be climax species in other, more suitable habitats.

Ponderosa Pine forest

Throughout much of the Rockies, pure stands of Ponderosa Pine form the lower forest boundary, adjoining either grassland, sagebrush, pinyon-juniper woodland, or chaparral. At higher elevations, Ponderosa Pine forest merges with Douglas-fir forest—in which the pine is a common associate— and even dominates burned areas and hot, dry southern exposures. Although Ponderosa Pine is the climax tree at lower elevations, it forms its finest, most productive stands in the zone where Douglas-fir is the climax species.

Ponderosa Pines occupy the warmest, driest forest sites in the Rockies. Stands tend to be open, with the trees widely spaced

Birchleaf Spiraea
Spiraea betulifolia
190

Pacific Ninebark
Physocarpus capitatus

Creambush
Holodiscus discolor
192

Black Hawthorn
Crataegus douglasii
97

Western Serviceberry
Amelanchier alnifolia
91, 184

Western Chokecherry
Prunus virginiana

Antelope Brush
Purshia tridentata
112, 200

Common Juniper
Juniperus communis

Kinnikinnick
Arctostaphylos uva-ursi
149, 215

to minimize competition for water and nutrients. On the most arid sites, the pines may even form a savanna of sorts, in which trees are scattered over an understory of grass or sagebrush. The understories in Ponderosa Pine stands are often sparse because the trees so completely monopolize soil resources. In fact, there may be few or no plants within a thirty- or forty-foot radius around a mature tree.

Ponderosa Pine reproduction in the Rocky Mountain region seems to be infrequent and episodic. Research near the lower timberline in Arizona has shown that good seed crops and favorable conditions must coincide over a period of several years in order to assure germination and seedling establishment. The required conjunction of events apparently occurs only every twenty or more years.

No understory plants are unique to the Ponderosa Pine forest. Instead, understories contain species that are shared with neighboring communities. Moist sites at higher elevations may have well-developed herb and shrub layers featuring species that are also common in forests upslope. On drier sites, the understory plants range from grasses and scattered wildflowers on thin, droughty soils to shrub-grass mixes in stands where some moisture lingers at deeper levels. In the northern Rockies, the more widespread shrubs include Common Snowberry, wild roses, Birchleaf Spiraea, Pacific Ninebark, Creambush, Black Hawthorn, Western Serviceberry, Western Chokecherry, and, on drier sites, Antelope Brush. In the southern Rockies, the understory shrubs include widespread species such as Western Serviceberry, Common Juniper, Mountain Snowberry, and Kinnikinnick. Other species, drawn mainly from the mountain brush communities, intermingle along the lower forest margins. In the Southwest, pinyons and junipers may form an understory tree layer, along with shrubs consisting mainly of woodland and desert species.

Ponderosa Pine tolerates a broader range of environmental conditions than do most of its conifer associates, which consequently are numerous. Although most of these associates join the pine in mixed stands at higher elevations, relatively few occur in the lower Ponderosa Pine forests. Limber Pine occurs on dry, rocky sites in colder locales, where Ponderosa Pine becomes a marginal species. Blue Spruce commonly occurs along streams in the Ponderosa Pine zone, usually in the company of Quaking Aspen and various willows. Along the eastern side of the Cascade Range in southern Oregon, Lodgepole Pine forms extensive forests on poorly drained pumice flats and in frost pockets in the Ponderosa Pine zone, while Ponderosa is restricted to higher, warmer, better-drained sites.

Ponderosa Pine is essentially missing from the middle Rocky Mountains, though stands do occur in the Uinta Mountains of northern Utah and in the Big Horn Mountains of northeastern Wyoming. Throughout most of this region, plateau elevations are above 6000 feet, and conditions at the lower timberline, which occurs at about 7000 feet, are too cold for Ponderosa

Pine. In its place, various combinations of Lodgepole Pine,
Quaking Aspen, and Limber Pine form a lower timberline that
is bordered by sagebrush-grassland. Cold conditions at the
lower timberline have also virtually eliminated Ponderosa Pine
from the mountains of northwestern Colorado and the eastern
front of the northern Rockies in Montana and Alberta.
However, the absence of Ponderosa Pine from the western
slopes of Utah's Wasatch Range seems to have a different
explanation. There, the pine was eliminated from the range
during the Ice Age, when a cooler climate prevailed, and
during the 10,000 years since it has been blocked from
reinvading the area by vast desert basins on the west and the
high crests of the Wasatch Range itself on the east.

Douglas-fir forest
Throughout much of the Rocky Mountain region, Douglas-fir
is the climax conifer in midslope forests above the Ponderosa
Pine zone and below the spruce-fir zone. Douglas-fir forest,
the most widespread type in the northern Rockies, covers
about nine million acres. Southward, its distribution is
spottier. Douglas-fir is usually present in mixed stands, but
other conifers often dominate. Extensive wildfires have allowed
Ponderosa Pine, Lodgepole Pine, Western Larch, and Quaking
Aspen to supplant Douglas-fir in many stands. Unfavorable
temperature and moisture regimes southward also tend to
restrict its distribution and numbers.

In the interior of British Columbia, Douglas-fir extends to the
northern edge of the Fraser Plateau and dominates both closed
forests and open parklands. Prominent associates include
White Spruce and Black Spruce in the north, Ponderosa Pine
and Western White Pine in the south, and Lodgepole Pine
and Quaking Aspen throughout. Understory plants are largely
typical of the Northwest coastal forest.

Black Spruce
Picea mariana
115

Douglas-fir forests in the northern Rockies are confined largely
to ranges west of the Continental Divide. East of the Divide in
Montana and Alberta, it is too cold for the optimum
development of Douglas-fir, which occurs as a regular but
essentially minor element in forests dominated by Lodgepole
Pine. The most extensive Douglas-fir stands occur in central
Idaho. Douglas-fir also forms a distinct belt northward into
British Columbia and westward along the Canadian border to
the eastern slopes of the Cascade Range. The forest is usually
bounded below by Ponderosa Pine forest and above by Grand
Fir or Lodgepole Pine forests, depending on locale. Ponderosa
Pine, Western Larch, and Grand Fir are characteristic
associates in these forests. Ponderosa Pine occurs on warmer
sites; Grand Fir, in moister habitats. Western Larch, an
aggressive fire pioneer, rapidly invades and dominates burned
areas by growing faster than the competition.

Forest understory vegetation ranges from grass on the driest
sites to rather lush associations of shrubs and herbs in moister
habitats. Snowberry, wild roses, and Birchleaf Spiraea are
conspicuous understory shrubs. Wild flowers are abundant and
various in the frequently open stands. Fires have tended to

Engelmann Spruce
Picea engelmannii
117

Subalpine Fir
Abies lasiocarpa
46

Narrowleaf Cottonwood
Populus angustifolia
80

Water Birch
Betula occidentalis
90

Mountain Alder
Alnus tenuifolia
88, 144

Rocky Mountain Juniper
Juniperus scopulorum
64

Corkbark Fir
Abies lasiocarpa var.
arizonica

Southwestern White Pine
Pinus strobiformis
39

Arizona Pine
Pinus ponderosa var.
arizonica

Chihuahua Pine
Pinus leiophylla
124

Creeping Barberry
Berberis repens

produce two-layered stands, in which young Douglas-fir trees grow beneath mature Ponderosa Pines at lower elevations, and beneath Western Larch on higher slopes.

Where climate, soil conditions, or a combination of these factors preclude the presence of Ponderosa Pine, Douglas-fir commonly forms a lower timberline adjacent to sagebrush or grassland. In recent decades, Douglas-fir has aggressively invaded these lower communities, apparently as a result of grazing and strict fire suppression.

Midslope forests in Colorado's Front Range feature mixed stands. Ponderosa Pine dominates the warm, relatively dry, south-facing slopes, while Douglas-fir prevails on the cool, moist, northern exposures and in sheltered mountain valleys. The contrast between the open, yellow-green pine forest and the dense, blue-green Douglas-fir forest is striking, as the margin between them can be rather abrupt. Engelmann Spruce and Subalpine Fir, which dominate subalpine forests, commonly range downslope to mingle with Douglas-fir in its cooler, moister haunts. Lodgepole Pine and Quaking Aspen grow on disturbed sites or in damp but marginal habitats. Blue Spruce grows along streams with Narrowleaf Cottonwood, Quaking Aspen, Water Birch, Mountain Alder, and other hardwoods, but it also joins the forest on cool, north-facing slopes and damp flats. Rocky Mountain Juniper often grows just upslope from Blue Spruce along streams, but may also join Limber Pine on warm, arid, south-facing cliffs.

Forests in the southern Rockies and the Southwest are essentially similar except that Corkbark Fir, a variety of Subalpine Fir, joins Engelmann Spruce and Blue Spruce on cool, damp sites at higher elevations, and White Fir is at least as important as Douglas-fir in many stands. White Fir is most abundant on cool, north-facing slopes at middle elevations, where it may supplant Douglas-fir as the dominant tree, but it also occurs more sparingly with Ponderosa Pine on warmer, drier sites within the forest. Aspen and Blue Spruce ring damp meadows and also border streams. In addition, extensive aspen forests often replace Douglas-firs on the high plateaus of southern Utah. In southern Arizona eastward to the Guadalupe Mountains of western Texas, Southwestern White Pine occurs sparingly on rocky, north-facing slopes. Arizona Pine (a variety of Ponderosa that has five needles per bundle, rather than three) dominates south-facing slopes in the same region, often with Chihuahua Pine, a Mexican species.

Forests on northern slopes may be so dense that needle litter is the principal ground cover. Sunnier aspects, however, commonly feature more open stands with well-developed shrub and herb layers. Kinnikinnick, a prostrate (trailing) species of manzanita, is a common ground cover on thin, rocky soils in sunny openings throughout the Rocky Mountain region. Another common dwarf shrub is Creeping Barberry, which has hollylike leaves, yellow flowers, and sour, purple, grapelike berries. Taller shrubs include numerous species from adjacent stands of mountain brush. Western Serviceberry occupies a variety of sites, from open, windswept ridges to

Gambel Oak
Quercus gambelii
174

New Mexican Locust
Robinia neomexicana
219

moister, shadier spots within the forest. Gambel Oak and New Mexico Locust are common in the southern Rockies and other parts of the Southwest, particularly in the Grand Canyon region.

Lodgepole Pine forest
The most widely ranging North American conifer, Lodgepole Pine, occurs from Alaska and the Yukon to Baja California and central Colorado. In the middle and northern Rockies, it is the most common forest conifer and forms pure stands over vast acreages. It occurs mainly as a pioneer tree on burned ground, but also forms climax stands on certain types of sites. Lodgepole Pine is highly intolerant of shade and depends largely on wildfires to create the openings necessary for its regeneration. Therefore, unlike some other conifers, which are more fire-resistant, Lodgepole Pine has thin, resinous, highly flammable bark. Most of its cones remain on their limbs, tightly sealed with resin, until fire melts the seal and releases the seeds. In this way, a large crop of seeds is broadcast over a newly exposed mineral seedbed that is enriched with ash and largely free of competing vegetation. The resulting stands are generally even-aged—that is, all of the trees are members of a single generation. Although serotinous (late-opening) cones, as they are known, are the rule among Rocky Mountain Lodgepoles, trees producing open cones are not uncommon, occurring in at least small numbers in most stands and even dominating some. By producing both types of cones, Lodgepole Pine is prepared not only for fires, but also for other chance openings of the forest canopy.

In the middle and northern Rockies, extensive stands of Lodgepole Pine show few signs of giving way to climax conifers such as Douglas-fir, Engelmann Spruce, or Subalpine Fir. Lodgepole Pines of all ages are represented in the stands, while the seedlings of climax species are either missing or are sprinkled about with young Lodgepoles along the stand margins. Most of these stands probably originated in the wake of fires that devastated vast areas, in which subsequent reinvasion by climax trees was retarded by the remoteness of seed sources. The prolonged absence of climax conifers produced the uneven-aged structure in Lodgepole stands that is normally associated only with climax stands.

Studies in several areas in the Rockies, however, suggest that Lodgepole Pines may also form climax forests on sandy-gravelly soils that are derived from granitic or other coarse-grained rocks. Around Crested Butte, Colorado, near the southern limit of Lodgepole Pine in the Rockies, the tree is confined largely to north-facing slopes that are underlain by granite or coarse sediments. In the Big Horn Mountains, Lodgepole Pine is the overwhelmingly dominant tree on soils that are underlain by granite, while Douglas-fir is restricted to limestone and other fine-grained sedimentary rocks. Therefore remote seed sources clearly do not explain the absence of Douglas-fir from Lodgepole Pine stands in the Big Horns. Lodgepole Pine also usually dominates marginal habitats—

places that are too cold, too hot, too dry, or too wet for other conifers. In such locales, it is commonly the climax tree; this is the case in subalpine basins that are subject to moisture fluctuations and frequent summer frosts. Engelmann Spruce and Subalpine Fir may be common on adjacent slopes, yet absent from frost-pocket stands dominated by Lodgepole Pine. Along the eastern side of the Oregon Cascades, Lodgepole Pine occurs in pure stands on pumice soils that are either poorly or excessively drained.

Lodgepole Pine commonly forms pure stands, but it also occurs with a wide variety of other conifers in mixed stands representing different stages in forest succession. Douglas-fir, Engelmann Spruce, and Subalpine Fir are its most widespread associates in the Rockies. White Spruce is a frequent companion from the Alberta Rockies south to Montana. West of the Continental Divide, Lodgepole Pine has stiff competition on burned sites from Western Larch and Western White Pine, which occur with it in some stands but replace it in others. Quaking Aspen may also occur with Lodgepole Pine on moist or disturbed ground in the middle Rockies.

Young lodgepole stands are typically dense and monotonous, with little understory vegetation. Older stands are more open and may have sparse to moderate herb and shrub layers consisting largely of species that are also common to adjoining montane or subalpine communities. Since Lodgepole Pine occupies a vast geographic area and a wide range of habitats, its understory associates are accordingly numerous.

Aspen woods

Quaking Aspen occurs widely in forests of western North America, but is nowhere more common than in the Rocky Mountains. It is most widespread in the southern Rockies, where it forms extensive, often pure stands at elevations of between 6500 and 10,000 feet. Even-aged aspen stands are often the first type of woods to develop on recently burned sites. Eventually conifers invade these stands and overtop the aspens, which are highly intolerant of shade. Around the peripheries of meadows, aspens often form narrow fringes, which are gradually invaded by forest conifers bringing up the rear. Aspens are also among the first trees to colonize talus slopes. As a rule, aspens indicate the presence of moisture a few feet below the surface.

In the West, Quaking Aspen stands develop almost exclusively through root suckering, a process that involves the sprouting of new shoots along the length of extensive surface roots. At first these shoots, or suckers, draw water and nourishment from the parent root system, but they eventually develop their own roots and become independent. Aspens also produce seeds, but these rarely survive spring or summer drought. The present distribution of the species in the West probably dates back roughly 10,000 years, to a time when the climate was more congenial to seed and seedling survival.

A typical aspen stand consists of one or more clones, each of which is made up of a parent tree and all of its sucker offspring. Because sexual reproduction is not involved, all of the trees are genetically identical. Nonetheless, each clone, or family group, is genetically distinct from its neighbors, which accounts for differences among them such as the time of budding or leaf drop, which are apparent in most large aspen stands. By regenerating through cloning, aspens can quickly dominate disturbed areas, for suckers grow rapidly, reaching ten feet in height in only six to eight years. Nourished by parent trees, suckers are also insulated from the environmental stresses to which seedlings are routinely subjected. Cloning is a disadvantage, however, when disease strikes, since a disease to which a clone's resistance is low can quickly wipe out an entire stand.

Although Quaking Aspen is widespread in western forests, it is more prominent than conifers only in Utah, western Colorado, and the Great Basin. In many Nevada mountain ranges, which rise like islands from the desert sea, aspens form pure forests in the absence of montane conifers. In western Colorado and Utah, they occur in extensive, pure stands that to all appearances would seem to be climax formations. Trees of all ages are present, and conifers seem to be making little or no headway in invading most stands. Perhaps these stands are true climaxes, and conifers are unable to invade them. Or perhaps the stands originated in the wake of catastrophic fires, and conifer invasion was greatly retarded by aridity, a lack of adequate seed sources, or other factors.

Aspens are excellent pioneer species, contributing abundant leaf litter each year and thereby building up deep, rich soils for invading conifers. The open deciduous canopy allows understory vegetation to flourish. All stands have luxuriant herbaceous layers, which are often dominated by grasses but also contain an enormous variety of wild flowers. Many stands also have well-developed shrub layers. In the northern Rockies, willows, alders, and Kinnikinnick are common in aspen groves. Snowberries, Western Chokecherry, and Western Serviceberry are the more common shrubs in the southern Rockies. Sagebrush may be present in stands along the dry desert margin.

Big Sagebrush
Artemisia tridentata
110

Aspens are subject to a variety of insects and diseases, with clones differing in their resistance to various pathogens. The chief causes of death among aspens are trunk cankers, which are associated with wounds. Butt and trunk rots are also common. Defoliation by Western Tent Caterpillars can kill entire clones. Although aspens normally do not live much beyond a century, stands up to 200 years old are not uncommon in the Rocky Mountains.

Western Tent Caterpillar
Malacosoma californicum

Northwestern humid conifer forests
Forests remarkably like those found on the western slopes of the Washington Cascades are found in the Rockies. These forests occupy humid, midslope habitats on the seaward flanks of mountain ranges in southeastern British Columbia, northeastern Washington, northern Idaho, and Montana west of the Continental Divide.

In these forests, Grand Fir, Western Redcedar, and Western Hemlock, which are all typically coastal conifers, dominate climax stands on progressively moister sites between the Douglas-fir zone below and the subalpine zone above. Western White Pine and Western Larch, which are both splendid timber trees, dominate extensive seral stands that originated from frequent catastrophic wildfires. Douglas-fir is largely a seral species and occurs most commonly with Grand Fir on lower, relatively drier sites.

Throughout most of the Rockies, climates that are sufficiently cool and moist to ward off summer drought occur only in the subalpine zone, where cool, brief growing seasons become a limiting factor. Only in the Northwest, thanks to the eastward penetration of marine air from the Pacific Ocean, are midslope climates simultaneously humid and mild. The Northwestern humid conifer forests experience neither the summer soil drought of the Douglas-fir zone nor the cool weather of the subalpine zone. As a result, they are the richest and most productive forests in the Rockies. Numerous plants found here occur in no other part of the Rockies.

Ponderosa Pine, Douglas-fir, Lodgepole Pine, and Western Larch each dominate seral stands in which Grand Fir is the climax tree. In moister habitats, all of the above species except Ponderosa Pine may still be present, usually along with Grand Fir, although the latter is sometimes replaced by Western Hemlock or Western Redcedar. However, Western White Pine is the principal seral tree on such sites, and it forms extensive forests, particularly in northern Idaho. This species' initial growth exceeds that of all competitors but Lodgepole Pine and Western Larch. Within fifty years, Western White Pine surpasses Lodgepole Pine in height, and at maturity it is as tall as Western Larch. With so many seral conifers present, most stands are mixed.

Relatively dry Grand Fir forests in eastern Oregon and Washington generally feature a rich herbaceous layer that is dominated by grass and sedge but includes herbs such as Heartleaf Arnica, White-flowered Hawkweed, and lupines. The shrub cover, which is generally thin, includes Birchleaf Spiraea, Common Snowberry, wild roses, and willows. Moister forests contain a rich variety of shrubs and herbs, most of which are characteristic of Northwest coastal forests. Dense forests with little sunlight commonly have sparse herb covers that are made up mainly of saprophytes (plants that grow on decayed matter) and partial saprophytes.

Since 1927, when the European fungus White-pine Blister Rust was first detected in northern Idaho, it has infested thousands of acres of Western White Pine, killing millions of trees and turning over many sites to Grand Fir and other conifers. Serious insect pests in these forests include many of the same ones found in Ponderosa Pine–Douglas-fir forests.

Heartleaf Arnica
Arnica cordifolia
443

White-flowered Hawkweed
Hieracium albiflorum

Wildlife
Rocky Mountain montane forests provide an assortment of wildlife habitats, including areas of brush, rock, and meadow;

Mule Deer
Odocoileus hemionus
373

White-tailed Deer
Odocoileus virginianus
374

Elk
Cervus elaphus
376

Caribou
Rangifer tarandus
377

Moose
Alces alces
378

Gray Wolf
Canis lupus
368, 369, 372

Mountain Lion
Felis concolor
363

Coyote
Canis latrans
370, 371

Lynx
Felis lynx
361

Bobcat
Felis rufus
362

Wolverine
Gulo gulo
358

Grizzly Bear
Ursus arctos
360

Golden-mantled Ground
Squirrel
Spermophilus lateralis
335

Marmot
Marmota spp.
351, 352

Black Bear
Ursus americanus
359

flowery aspen groves and streamside woodlands; and a spectrum of forest types, which are scattered from central Canada to the Southwest. The impressive variety of animals in the region results directly from its geographic extent and ecological diversity. Most of the animal species occurring in Rocky Mountain montane forests are generally found throughout the conifer forests of the West. These include virtually all of the major predators, most of the forest birds, all but one of the hoofed mammals, and the majority of reptiles. There is somewhat more regional variation among small mammals and amphibians in the Rockies. Moreover, even among the more generally distributed animals, a good number occur only in the north or the south, with the Wyoming Basin and Green River canyon forming an informal boundary.

The Mule Deer ranges throughout the forest, preferring rough terrain for cover and shrubbery for food. As it flees predators or curious humans, its bounding gait is ideal for negotiating precisely this kind of habitat. The White-tailed Deer, which prefers open woods and brush on gentler terrain, is a graceful runner rather than a leaper. The Elk occurs rather widely in the Rockies, where it grazes in high meadows and parklands during the summer and lower parks and shrublands during the winter. Mountain Caribou are found mostly in the Canadian Rockies, but range southward into northern Washington, Idaho, and Montana. They feed on a variety of plant foods in the summer, but rely mostly on lichen during the winter. The largest American member of the deer family, the Moose, is rather common in the northern Rockies, where it is most often seen along lakes and streams or browsing on twigs in dense willow thickets.

The Gray Wolf and the Mountain Lion are the chief natural predators of the deer family. The Mountain Lion, which hunts alone, largely sticks to Mule Deer and White-tailed Deer. The wolf, which hunts in packs, specializes in the larger Elk and Moose. Smaller predators, namely the Coyote, the Lynx, the Bobcat, and the Wolverine, take fawns whenever they can. The Grizzly Bear generally restricts its hunting to Ground Squirrels and Marmots. The Grizzly is more omnivore than predator, however, roots and berries forming a substantial portion of its diet.

The Grizzly Bear mainly frequents open country such as high subalpine parklands and woodlands. In the forest, it is replaced by its smaller cousin, the Black Bear, an agile climber that readily takes to trees in times of danger and rarely ventures from the safety of the forest. Black Bears give Grizzlies a wide berth, and the climbing ability of the former —particularly of cubs—may largely be an evolutionary response to the greater power and aggressiveness of the latter. Ranging throughout the Rockies, the Black Bear feeds mainly on grasses, roots, bulbs, berries, and other vegetation. It also raids hives for honey and bees, and overturns logs for insects. Three tree squirrels inhabit the Rocky Mountain montane forest. The Northern Flying Squirrel ranges southward largely

Northern Flying Squirrel
Glaucomys sabrinus
336

Abert's Squirrel
Sciurus aberti
342

Red Squirrel
Tamiasciurus hudsonicus
341

Golden-mantled Ground
Squirrel
Spermophilus lateralis
335

Snowshoe Hare
Lepus americanus
350

Vagrant Shrew
Sorex vagrans
325

Deer Mouse
Peromyscus maniculatus
329

Bushy-tailed Woodrat
Neotoma cinerea
337

Western Jumping Mouse
Zapus princeps
328

Red-backed Vole
Clethrionomys gapperi

Heather Vole
Phenacomys intermedius

Marten
Martes americana
343

to Utah's Wasatch Range, but is missing from the southern Rockies. Abert's Squirrel is common in the southern Rockies and the Southwest, but is missing north of Colorado. The Red Squirrel occurs the length of the Rockies.

Where the Red Squirrel and Abert's Squirrel occur in the same range, there is little competition because the two species are segregated by habitat. Abert's is closely confined to Ponderosa Pine forests, where it feeds mainly on pine seeds. The Red Squirrel prefers forests of spruce and fir, where it feeds mainly on the green cones and seeds of those conifers. Where Abert's Squirrel is absent, however, as in the northern Rockies, the Red Squirrel readily moves downslope into the Ponderosa Pine forest. The Northern Flying Squirrel is a common but rarely seen nocturnal mammal. It feeds on a variety of foods, including insects and—when it can get it—even fresh meat. Aside from the tree squirrels, the most conspicuous small mammals on the forest floor are chipmunks, which scurry about in search of seeds, insects, berries, and other edibles, part of which they store for winter use. There are several species of chipmunks in the Rockies, but rarely more than two in any given area. The Golden-mantled Ground Squirrel, which resembles the chipmunks but is larger and lacks facial stripes, is also abroad during the day. It prefers semiopen forests at higher elevations. Often forgotten, its caches of pine seeds can result in clumps of Ponderosa seedlings.

Rarely seen is the Snowshoe Hare, which is nevertheless rather common. It nests in scrapes or depressions under shrubbery and feeds on greenery and berries in summer and on bark and buds in winter. Shrews, the smallest animals, are also common but seldom seen. Feeding day and night in brief shifts that are separated by periods of rest, these tiny, voracious animals are easily missed in the litter and undergrowth.

The Deer Mouse, which is largely nocturnal, is the most abundant animal in the forest. At lower elevations in certain areas, it may be joined by other white-footed mice that frequent adjacent woodlands and brush. The Bushy-tailed Woodrat also forages at night, generally staying near its rock-pile home, where it builds its large stick nest. Several other woodrats occur in the lower forests in the southern Rockies, but only the Bushy-tailed has the distinctive squirrel-like tail.

Damp, grassy areas near lakes and streams, within aspen groves, or in meadows are the haunts of the Western Jumping Mouse, which lives in underground burrows and forages on seeds, fungi, and a variety of other vegetable matter. Several species of voles live in such habitats as well. The remarkable reproductive capacity of these small, blunt-nosed mice can lead to dramatic population explosions that are, in turn, followed by periods of collapse, during which few or no voles are present. As a group, voles are most common in grassy areas, where their presence is betrayed by little runways leading from burrow openings to feeding areas. However, the Red-backed Vole and the Heather Vole are mainly forest animals. Voles and other small mammals are the principal prey of Coyotes, foxes, Bobcats, weasels, Martens, hawks, and owls.

Porcupine
Erethizon dorsatum
355

Beaver
Castor canadensis
347

Dark-eyed Junco
Junco hyemalis
305, 306

Hermit Thrush
Catharus guttatus
278

Blue Grouse
Dendragapus obscurus
224

Ruffed Grouse
Bonasa umbellus
225

Chipping Sparrow
Spizella passerina
300

"Red-shafted" Northern
Flicker
Colaptes auratus
248

Yellow-rumped Warbler
Dendroica coronata
288

Orange-crowned Warbler
Vermivora celata
285

Song Sparrow
Melospiza melodia
302

Fox Sparrow
Passerella iliaca
301

Townsend's Solitaire
Myadestes townsendi
277

Western Wood-Pewee
Contopus sordidulus
251

Olive-sided Flycatcher
Contopus borealis
250

The two largest forest rodents are the Porcupine and the Beaver, both of which feed extensively on the bark of trees. The Porcupine eats a variety of vegetable matter during the summer, but retires to the tops of conifers during the winter, where it subsists entirely on the inner bark, often girdling trees to get it. The Beaver prefers the bark of aspens, cottonwoods, or alders, which it cuts down in order to obtain both food and construction materials for dams and lodges. Some characteristic birds of the forest floor are the Dark-eyed Junco (including both the "Oregon" and "Gray-headed" juncos), the Hermit Thrush, and the Blue, Ruffed, and Spruce grouse, all of which nest and feed on the ground. The Blue Grouse prefers lower, more open forests; the Spruce Grouse, higher, damper forests; and the Ruffed Grouse, deciduous woods and thickets. The Blue and Spruce grouse winter high in spruces or firs, subsisting entirely on needles during that season. The Ruffed Grouse prefers aspens and cottonwoods, where it dines on buds, twigs, and catkins.

Several birds commute to the forest floor from their homes in nearby shrubs and trees. The Chipping Sparrow nests in shrubs or low trees near grassy openings, where it searches for insects, mainly soft caterpillars. The "Red-shafted" Flicker, a western form of the Northern Flicker, nests in tree cavities, but spends much of its time prowling about the forest floor in search of ants, its chief food. Robins nest in shrubs or trees, or occasionally on the ground, while Swainson's Thrush prefers to feed either in shrubbery or on the forest floor near deciduous thickets. Jays, grosbeaks, and the Yellow-rumped Warbler forage at all levels of the forest, frequently descending to the ground for insects or other food.

Some birds have reverse commutes: they nest on the ground but feed in higher vegetation. The Orange-crowned Warbler places its nest on the ground, usually in damp thickets, but forages at moderate heights in aspens, cottonwoods, and other broadleaf trees. The Song Sparrow forages in shrubbery, rarely straying far from damp undergrowth. The Fox Sparrow, similar but larger, prefers drier mountain brush.

Myriads of flying insects constitute a nearly endless food supply for flycatchers and other birds, such as Townsend's Solitaire, that are able to take such prey on the wing. Flycatchers sally forth from lookouts, or special perches, in search of insects, returning to the same spot repeatedly. Each of the several species of flycatchers occurring in the Rocky Mountain forests has its own particular place of operation. For example, the Western Flycatcher chooses shady openings beneath the trees, while the Western Wood-Pewee opts for sunnier perches at middle levels in both coniferous and deciduous woods, and the Olive-sided Flycatcher works from the highest treetops.

The warblers also glean insects from foliage and branches. MacGillivray's works among low, damp shrubbery. The Yellow Warbler is largely restricted to lower, streamside woods. Grace's Warbler, both a gleaner and a fly catcher, frequents the upper branches of pines in the southern Rockies.

Brown Creeper
Certhia americana
268

Red-breasted Nuthatch
Sitta canadensis
265

Pygmy Nuthatch
Sitta pygmaea
267

Red-tailed Hawk
Buteo jamaicensis

Northern Goshawk
Accipiter gentilis
223

Flammulated Owl
Otus flammeolus
229

Great Horned Owl
Bubo virginianus
230

Long-eared Owl
Asio otus
231

Sharp-shinned Hawk
Accipiter striatus

Cooper's Hawk
Accipiter cooperii

Other gleaners include chickadees, wrens, kinglets, and vireos. Chickadees forage at all levels of the forest, from treetops to the ground and from trunks to the outer tips of branches—which are perhaps their specialty. Woodpeckers, with the possible exception of the Northern ("Red-shafted") Flicker, mostly frequent tree trunks, but also feed on the branches. They perform two invaluable services to the forest community: They control bark beetles and other destructive bark insects, and drill or enlarge tree cavities for nests, which are subsequently used by numerous other birds and a few mammals too. The Brown Creeper and the Red-breasted and Pygmy nuthatches also seek bark insects, but—unlike the woodpeckers—go after their prey on the surface. The principal raptors of the Rocky Mountain montane forest include Red-tailed Hawk, Northern Goshawk, Flammulated Owl, Great Horned Owl, and Long-eared Owl. The Goshawk and its close kin, the Sharp-shinned Hawk and Cooper's Hawk, are forest and woodland birds whose chief prey are songbirds. All three have short, broad wings, which are ideal for rapid, agile flight between and around the trees. The Red-tailed Hawk nests high in conifers but ranges upslope to soar over the open parklands and woodlands near timberline, where it feasts on ground squirrels and other rodents. The owls take enormous quantities of rodents and a smaller number of birds, reptiles, and amphibians. The Pygmy Owl is abroad during the day; it feeds largely on insects and lizards and is often mobbed by small forest birds.

ROCKY MOUNTAIN MONTANE FORESTS: PLANTS AND ANIMALS

SUBALPINE FORESTS

Mountain Hemlock
Tsuga mertensiana
49, 139

Subalpine Fir
Abies lasiocarpa
46

Whitebark Pine
Pinus albicaulis
123

Lodgepole Pine
Pinus contorta
40

Foxtail Pine
Pinus balfouriana
41

Engelmann Spruce
Picea engelmannii
117

Bristlecone Pine
Pinus aristata
42, 130

Limber Pine
Pinus flexilis
122

The highest reach of trees into the realm of cold is represented by subalpine forests. Downslope lie mid-elevation montane forests; upslope, the treeless alpine zone. Timberline—the upper limit of trees—is not an abrupt boundary, however, but a more or less broad zone of transition, in which conifers gradually decrease in size and number in the face of an increasingly hostile climate.

Subalpine forests occur on most of the loftier mountain ranges in western North America. Mountain Hemlock and Subalpine Fir are the most important subalpine conifers in the Pacific Northwest. Beyond this region, the pair splits up: Mountain Hemlock joins Whitebark Pine, Lodgepole Pine, and Foxtail Pine in the Sierra Nevada and the Klamath Mountains; Subalpine Fir and Engelmann Spruce dominate Rocky Mountain subalpine forests. Bristlecone and Limber Pine form open timberline woodlands on the high Great Basin ranges. Despite readily apparent regional differences, the subalpine forests of western North America have numerous species in common and represent similar responses to comparable environments. They are essentially southern extensions of the boreal forest. In the steadily cooling climate that culminated in the Ice Age, boreal conifers slowly retreated southward along the Cordillera. Then, as alpine glaciers mantled the higher mountains of the West, these conifers were also forced downslope, where a cooler climate than today's allowed them to spread across intermontane valleys and basins. At the close of the Ice Age, climatic warming caused a general retreat northward and upslope. As grassland and sagebrush invaded the lowlands, many local subalpine forests became more or less isolated on their separate mountain ranges. Gradually the forests were segregated along the lines that exist today.

The subalpine zone generally consists of a lower, closed-forest belt and an upper, parkland or woodland belt. The closed forests are usually similar to adjacent montane forests, except that midslope conifers are gradually replaced by distinctively subalpine species, which are better adapted to deep, long-lasting snowpacks and cool, brief growing seasons. The upper limit of the continuous forest—known as the forest line—occurs where increasingly hostile climate and topography conspire to limit the size of stands and to drastically curtail the number of trees that are able to make a living in any given area. The parkland or woodland portion of the subalpine zone therefore consists of small groves, even smaller tree "islands," or individual conifers widely scattered over great stretches of meadow and rock. Open woodlands are typical of steeper, drier slopes; parklands of gentler, moister terrain. As elevation increases, conifers gradually diminish from tall, erect trees in the closed forest to stunted, but still upright trees in the parkland-woodland belt, and, finally, to sprawling shrubs at timberline. Above timberline, the growing season is too cool and brief to support even shrubby trees, so low herbs and genetically dwarfed shrublets form a tundra similar to that found at sea level in the Arctic.

Where the forest relinquishes its grip, the landscape changes dramatically. Shade yields to sunlight. Panoramic views open up to distant ridges and nearby peaks, and great sweeps of sky and earth. Lingering snowbanks spawn the rivers of the West, fill ice-gouged lake basins, and water some of the most spectacular wildflower gardens on earth. Bonsai trees scattered over exposed bedrock resemble the plantings in a Zen garden or the sculpted woodlands of a Chinese screen painting.

Geographic Distribution

Subalpine forests dominated by Mountain Hemlock occur along Cook Inlet near Anchorage, Alaska, and extend southward on the seaward flanks of the coastal mountain ranges of Alaska and British Columbia to Washington. The forest also occurs at higher elevations on the Queen Charlotte Islands and Vancouver Island. In the conterminous United States, the forest continues southward, mainly on the western side of the Cascade Range, to northern California. There, in the southernmost Cascades and the Klamath Mountains, the Mountain Hemlock forest merges imperceptibly with the Sierran mixed subalpine forest. Mountain Hemlock also dominates subalpine forests in the Olympic Mountains. The species is locally common on the seaward flanks of the northern Rocky Mountain ranges lying west of the continental divide in eastern Washington, northern Idaho, western Montana, and southeastern British Columbia. Forming a timberline at its upper limit, the forest occurs at elevations of sea level to about 1500 feet in south-central Alaska, 2900 to 4900 feet in southern British Columbia, 4300 to 5300 feet in Washington, 5800 to 7800 feet in southern Oregon, and 7500 to 9500 feet in northern California.

Mountain Hemlock, Lodgepole Pine, Whitebark Pine, and Foxtail Pine are the dominant conifers in the Sierran mixed subalpine forest, which extends from Mount Shasta in the California Cascades to the southern end of the Sierra Nevada. The forest occurs on both sides of the Sierra at elevations of approximately 7500 to 9500 feet in the north and 9500 to 12,000 feet in the south. It also occurs on warmer, drier exposures in the Klamath Mountains and Great Basin ranges close to the Sierra.

Engelmann Spruce and Subalpine Fir dominate the Rocky Mountain subalpine forest, which extends through the Rockies on both sides of the Continental Divide from northwestern Alberta and adjacent British Columbia southward to central New Mexico. The higher ranges and plateaus of the Colorado Plateau region also support this type of forest. Impoverished stands occur on mountain ranges in the northeastern Great Basin. The lower and upper limits of the forest are approximately 4500 to 7500 feet in the Canadian Rockies and 9500 to as high as 12,500 feet in the southern Rockies. Similar forests occur on the eastern side of the Coast Mountains in British Columbia and southward along the eastern flanks of the Olympic Mountains and the Cascade Range. The forest is essentially absent from California, where Engelmann Spruce and Subalpine Fir occur only as local,

Subalpine Forests

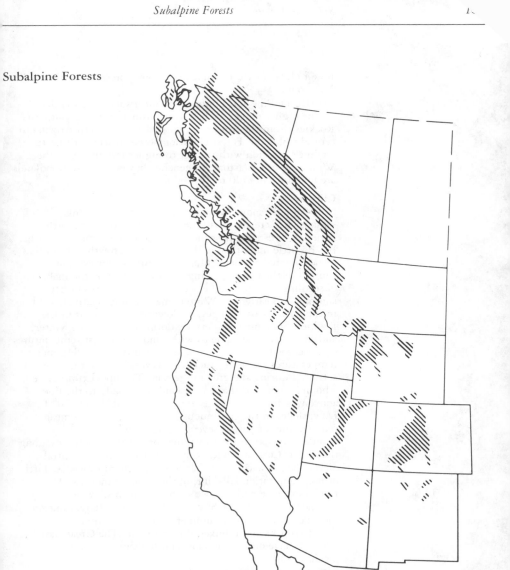

minor elements in the mixed subalpine forest of the Klamath Mountains.

Bristlecone Pine and Limber Pine form subalpine woodlands on the higher ranges of the Great Basin and in the southern Rockies, from the San Francisco Peaks of northern Arizona to central Colorado. Forest elevations vary greatly with latitude, a range's position with respect to higher mountains to the West, and other factors. In general, however, these woodlands are found from 9500 to 11,000 feet.

Climate

Cold, usually snowy winters and cool, brief growing seasons characterize subalpine climates in western North America. Frosts are possible throughout the summer months, but do little more than perhaps slow the growth of trees that are acclimated to them. Montane conifers, however, are limited in their upslope range at least partly by the inability of seedlings to survive the occasional hard frosts of early summer and early fall. Winters may be only relatively cold, as in the Pacific Coast ranges, or downright bitter, as in the Rockies. Subalpine conifers are dormant during the winter, and in this state are able to withstand the coldest temperatures ever recorded in either Siberia or North America. Summer temperatures are more crucial, however, because they govern activities during the growing season. The upper timberline is a boundary of cold that corresponds regionally to the line above which the mean July temperature falls below 50° F. Downslope, in the continuous subalpine forest, the mean temperature for July is several degrees higher.

Annual snowfall in the subalpine zone of the mountains along the Pacific Coast averages about 350 inches in the central Sierra Nevada and 550 inches in the northern Cascades. Little or no precipitation falls during the summer months. The Rockies receive perhaps two thirds as much snow as comparable sites in the Sierra or the Cascade Range, but on the whole receive more summer rainfall from local thunderstorms and influxes of tropical air. The Great Basin ranges receive only scant snow and little or no summer precipitation.

Although air temperature is the most important factor governing the location of timberline, the interplay of wind, topography, and snow is more important in determining the local distribution and growth habits of timberline trees. Timberline areas are subject to frequent gale-force winds during the winter. These generally remove snow from southern slopes and exposed ridgetops and deposit it on northern slopes and in sheltered basins. Snow-free areas offer no protection in winter from wind, cold, and desiccation, and also tend to be droughty for lack of snowmelt. Where conditions are extreme, snow-free slopes and ridges may have no trees whatsoever, while adjacent sheltered areas support thick forest. Sheltered basins that are covered by deep snowdrifts also lack trees because they are not free of snow until midsummer and therefore have growing seasons too brief to establish conifer seedlings. Even where the snow melts earlier, poor drainage in basins produces cold, wet soils better suited for meadow plants than conifers.

Winds damage trees by breaking limbs or, in winter, by blasting them with flying ice pellets and snow crystals. Abrasion is so intense that the windward sides of timberline trees commonly show bare, polished wood, as the bark has been stripped away. High winds are also responsible for the common asymmetric growth form known as flagging, in which foliage and branches, confined to the protected side of a tree, extend straight out in a downwind direction like banners in a full gale. Wind pruning also seems to be chiefly responsible for the shrubby growth habits of most timberline conifers. Known as krummholz (German for "crooked wood") or elfinwood, these tree-shrubs range in height from less than eighteen inches to forty-eight inches or more. However tall they grow, their maximum height generally corresponds to the depth of the local snowpack.

Krummholz trees generally grow in a downwind direction and expand through layering, the rooting of limbs at points where they happen to touch moist ground. Eventually, the older growth—which is upwind from the sprout—dies, but the plant persists in the form of the new, asexual generation. Layering is a common propagation strategy of subalpine trees near the timberline, where short growing seasons and competition from other plants make seeds unreliable.

Timberline trees that are exposed to the elements are also subject to winter desiccation. Both sun and winds can heat up exposed needles and thus cause stomates (tiny, porelike openings on the leaves) to open and moisture to escape through evaporation. In winter, when frozen roots and lower branches are unable to replace lost moisture, young tips may die back. This may account in part for the stunting of erect trees above the forest line. Large trees are more capable of withstanding this pressure because they often have sufficient moisture stored in their trunks and branches to resupply the depleted extremities. They are also better equipped to deal with any foliage losses that might occur. Winter desiccation is one of the main reasons that snow-free areas at timberline generally lack krummholz. Any trees present are usually large, erect, weather-beaten specimens of such drought-hardy types as Foxtail Pine, Bristlecone Pine, or Alpine Larch.

Alpine Larch
Larix lyallii
50

Between the forest line and the upper timberline lies a belt in which trees are stunted in response to wind damage and winter desiccation. These trees are smaller but still erect. They tend to grow in clumps, which provide mutual support and shelter for young trees, as well as a warmer, more humid microclimate than exists in the open.

A single Whitebark Pine can produce a clump all on its own by growing multiple trunks; such clumps often form open woodlands on drier, sheltered sites below timberline. In subalpine parklands, various conifers together form compact clumps, or tree islands. These begin when a conifer manages to establish itself on a favorable site within the meadow—

often a knoll or other rise—where the snow melts earlier and drainage is faster. Other trees are then able to establish themselves more easily because of the shelter provided by the pioneer tree. At the same time, the tree island gradually expands through layering, which is responsible for the skirt of young trees around the periphery. Eventually the pioneer tree, being the eldest, dies, creating a timber atoll—a ring of trees around a vacant center.

Another distinctive form of the tree island is the so-called ribbon forest, a long, narrow strip of trees that grows at a right angle to the wind. Usually several strips run parallel to one another, divided by much wider swaths of meadow. The strips act as wind breaks and allow snow to drift deeply in their lee. The drifts, which persist well into the summer, prevent tree establishment, which accounts for the intervening swaths of meadow. The next ribbon forest occurs far enough downwind from its neighbor that snow is no longer deep enough to inhibit conifer seedlings.

Forest Types

The subalpine forest consists of several forest types, each of which is defined by one or more distinctive dominant trees. Usually the dominant trees are also the climax species, because the disturbances that are necessary to perpetuate the dominance of seral conifers are relatively uncommon in subalpine forests. Nevertheless, fire pioneers such as Lodgepole Pine and Western White Pine dominate certain sites where fire or some other disturbance has eliminated the climax species for a time.

Western White Pine
Pinus monticola
121

Mountain Hemlock forest
The Mountain Hemlock forest consists of a lower, closed forest and an upper, subalpine parkland in which tree islands are scattered over extensive meadows. Individual Mountain Hemlocks also colonize rock outcrops along soil-filled crevices and form krummholz at the upper timberline. Mountain Hemlock ranges downslope into upper montane fir forests, but is limited there by the presence of conifers with greater tolerance for shade.

Mountain Hemlock forms timberlines at elevations ranging from 1000 feet in Alaska to 4500 feet in southern British Columbia, and above 8000 feet in California. This tree remains erect except on the highest, most exposed sites, where it may form huge, sprawling shrubs. Subalpine Fir is a common timberline companion south to the northern California border, and Whitebark Pine, though not always present, is a fairly consistent timberline associate.

Western Hemlock
Tsuga heterophylla
140

Sitka Spruce
Picea sitchensis
116

In southern Alaska, Mountain Hemlock, Western Hemlock, and Sitka Spruce form lush forests that extend from tidewater to 1000 or 1500 feet above sea level. The forests occur in a narrow, often interrupted coastal belt, which ranges eastward from Cook Inlet, then southward along the Alaska Panhandle, where the upper forest limit rises gradually to 3500 feet. In this region, Western Hemlock dominates the lower forest; Mountain Hemlock, the upper. Sitka Spruce ranges

Sitka Alder
Alnus sinuata
85

Alaska Yellow-cedar
Chamaecyparis nootkatensis
56

Pacific Silver Fir
Abies amabilis
47

Copper Bush
Cladothamnus pyroliflorus

Mountain-ash
Sorbus spp.
108

Fool's Huckleberry
Menziesia ferruginea
449

White Mountain Avens
Dryas octopetala

Cascade Azalea
Rhododendron albiflorum
187

Western Mountain-ash
Sorbus scopulina
108

Pacific Rhododendron
Rhododendron macrophyllum
209

Devil's Club
Oplopanax horridum
160

Skunk Cabbage
Lysichitum americanum

Marsh Marigold
Caltha leptosepala
381

Thinleaf Huckleberry
Vaccinium membranaceum
163

Beargrass
Xerophyllum tenax
418

throughout the area, dominating marginal habitats along the shore and the upper timberline, where it forms a krummholz belt above the Mountain Hemlock forest. Southward, Sitka Spruce is confined almost entirely to coastal areas. Shrubby Sitka Alder grows higher yet, while Mountain Hemlock extends downslope along cold-air ravines.

Alaska Yellow-cedar is a minor component of the Mountain Hemlock forest in southeastern Alaska, and Pacific Silver Fir and Subalpine Fir show up in small numbers at the southern end of the panhandle. Conspicuous understory shrubs include Copper Bush, Sitka Mountain-ash, Fool's Huckleberry, and various wild blueberries. Sitka Alder and White Mountain Avens, a lovely mat-forming shrublet, are among the first plants to invade raw glacial moraines.

From southern Alaska to southern Oregon, Pacific Silver Fir, Alaska Yellowcedar, and Subalpine Fir are important associates in the Mountain Hemlock forest. Subalpine Fir is common only in the parkland belt and on the adjacent forest fringe, although it also forms pioneer stands on burned areas in the Oregon Cascades. Pacific Silver Fir, Alaska Yellow-cedar, and Mountain Hemlock together form luxuriant mixed stands below the parkland belt and tree groups within it. Pacific Silver Fir is the climax species in lower, closed-forest stands, but at higher elevations it is less common than Mountain Hemlock. Although its seeds may germinate on snow and survive thereafter, Silver Fir seedlings must occupy a relatively warm microclimate or risk succumbing to frequent summer frosts. Therefore the fir occurs almost exclusively as a latecomer in tree groups, where it enjoys the protection of hardier conifers.

Mixed forests on cool, moist slopes often feature undergrowth that is so dense that cross-country travel is virtually impossible. The most common shrubs forming these tangles are several species of wild blueberry, Cascade Azalea, Fool's Huckleberry, and Mountain-ash. Pacific Rhododendron is conspicuous in the Olympics and in the Cascades of southern Washington and Oregon; Copper Bush, in British Columbia and Washington's North Cascades. Understory wild flowers are numerous in both kind and number. On steep slopes with abundant seepage and a modicum of sunlight, lush herb communities are typical and—in addition to the above species —commonly include many more from adjacent meadow communities. Shady, wet flats typically support Alaska Yellow-cedar, with understories of Devil's Club, Skunk Cabbage, or Marsh Marigold.

Typical stands on drier sites consist almost entirely of Mountain Hemlock and Pacific Silver Fir, with understories of Thinleaf Huckleberry or Beargrass, both of which are among the first to colonize disturbed areas.

The most extensive Mountain Hemlock forests occur on the broad, relatively gentle upland of the central and southern Oregon Cascades. These forests have been little studied but are known to contain fewer species than those described above. Subalpine Fir is a common associate and may succeed

Shasta Red Fir
Abies magnifica var.
shastensis

Grouse Whortleberry
Vaccinium scoparium
450

Pinemat Manzanita
Arctostaphylos nevadensis

California Red Fir
Abies magnifica var.
magnifica

Brewer Spruce
Picea breweriana
44

Port-Orford-cedar
Chamaecyparis lawsoniana
58

Mountain Hemlock on burned sites. Another seral species, Lodgepole Pine, occurs throughout the forest, often forming extensive, nearly pure stands. Along the forest's lower margin, Shasta Red Fir largely replaces Pacific Silver Fir. Alaska Yellowcedar is absent from the region. Drier conditions than in northern Oregon and Washington yield sparser understories, in which Thinleaf Huckleberry and two mat-forming shrubs, Grouse Whortleberry and Pinemat Manzanita, are conspicuous. The region is characterized by extensive pumice barrens—the result of geologically recent eruptions—that support only scant vegetation.

In the California Cascades and northern Sierra Nevada, Mountain Hemlock and Shasta or California Red Fir commonly form mixed forests, with the firs dominating lower stands and the hemlock dominating the higher ones. Lodgepole Pine is a frequent member of these forests, and Whitebark Pine joins the mix at timberline.

The richest conifer forests in the world are found in the Klamath Mountains. Here, Mountain Hemlock occurs in a mixed subalpine forest consisting of a dozen different conifers, a mix of Sierran and Northwestern species, plus the endemic Brewer Spruce. Mountain Hemlock dominates the cooler, moister sites—often on north-facing slopes—and extends upslope to timberline, along with Whitebark Pine and Foxtail Pine. These forests include relict stands of Subalpine Fir, Pacific Silver Fir, Noble Fir, Alaska Yellowcedar, and Engelmann Spruce, which do not occur anywhere else in California. Shasta Red Fir and Lodgepole Pine are important associates in these forests, and Western White Pine and Port Orford-cedar are locally important.

Subalpine parklands represent a broad ecotone in which the forest gradually gives way to alpine tundra. They are best developed in an area extending from southern British Columbia to northern Oregon, and perhaps reach a climax on the slopes of Mt. Rainier. In this region, deep, late-lying snow, which inhibits tree growth, is apparently responsible for the extensiveness of the parklands, which commonly span 1000 to 1300 feet of altitude. The parkland meadows vary greatly in composition, ranging from dwarf heather formations to lush stands of tall herbs, or turfs formed by various sedges and grasses. The wildflower displays in these meadows are among the most spectacular on the continent, with numerous species blooming in succession from late June to early September.

Trees are confined to scattered groups, generally on higher ground where the snow melts earlier and drainage is better. Mountain Hemlock initiates tree groups on moister sites; Whitebark Pine or Subalpine Fir are pioneers on drier sites. Alaska Yellowcedar occurs in many groups, and Pacific Silver Fir invades mature formations.

Sierran Mixed subalpine forest
South of Mt. Shasta in California, the Mountain Hemlock forest gradually merges with the Sierran mixed subalpine

forest. Mountain Hemlock remains prominent, but the forest mix is different. Subalpine Fir, Pacific Silver Fir, and Alaska Yellowcedar are gone. Shasta Red Fir is replaced by California Red Fir, and the Cascade–Rocky Mountain form of Lodgepole Pine is replaced by the rather different Sierran variety. Western White Pine remains in the forest, however, and Whitebark Pine becomes increasingly important southward as the mountains increase in height and ruggedness.

Four different conifer species prevail in different localities of this forest, occurring in various combinations and proportions. Mountain Hemlock and Lodgepole Pine dominate closed forests in the lower subalpine zone and extend upslope to timberline on suitable sites. Whitebark Pine and Foxtail Pine dominate subalpine woodlands that range upslope from the upper forest limit to timberline. Western White Pine and Limber Pine are both locally important associates. Western Juniper, Red Fir, and—very occasionally—White Fir or Jeffrey Pine are minor components.

Western Juniper
Juniperus occidentalis
63

Red Fir
Abies magnifica
43

White Fir
Abies concolor
45

Jeffrey Pine
Pinus jeffreyi
37, 126

The open woodland phase of the forest is poorly represented north of Lake Tahoe, where the uppermost elevations reach timberline only on a few of the highest peaks. The central and southern Sierra Nevada, however, feature vast expanses of bare or sparsely vegetated granite, scoured clean by glaciers and still under attack by invading conifers. The high, rocky timberline zone, with its extraordinary number of glacial lakes and pocket meadows, all overtopped by craggy peaks, is the very essence of the High Sierra.

Parklands such as those in the Cascades are unknown in the Sierra, where summer drought and inadequate soil prevent their formation. However, meadows ranging in size from a few acres to several square miles are abundant in glacial basins and valley floors throughout the subalpine zone. Dominated mainly by sedges and grasses, the meadows range from lush subalpine marshes to sparse sedge and sagebrush communities that experience extreme soil drought in late summer. All meadows, however, are subject to high water tables early in the season, a condition that, in large part, inhibits tree growth and accounts for the meadows' existence. Conifers are mostly confined to the drier margins, where seedlings enjoy longer growing seasons and increased soil oxygen. However, fires seem to be essential to the maintenance of at least the drier meadows. Under the policy of fire control that has prevailed during this century, Lodgepole Pines have been able to invade the margins of meadows throughout the Sierras. The widespread wish to maintain meadows as a scenic element in the High Sierra has led to changes in fire-suppression policies for the future.

Mountain Hemlock is the most important subalpine conifer in the northern Sierra, forming dense, pure stands just above the upper montane Red Fir forest. It occurs less frequently in more open, mixed stands with Red Fir, Lodgepole Pine, and Western White Pine. Well-developed Mountain Hemlock forests occur south to the Yosemite region, but beyond there, this conifer is increasingly restricted to cool sites where

Sierra Lodgepole Pine
Pinus contorta

moisture is available throughout the summer. On damp slopes, Mountain Hemlock commonly ranges to timberline, where it forms huge, sprawling krummholz shrubs. Lodgepole Pine forms closed forests throughout the lower subalpine zone and ranges upslope to timberline on a variety of sites. The Sierra Lodgepole Pine is larger and lives longer than its Rocky Mountain counterpart, attaining heights of 100 feet on favorable sites. It appears to be a climax species in the moist glacial basins of the central and southern Sierra, where stands contain trees ranging in age from very young seedlings to more than 400 years. The success of the Sierra Lodgepole Pine is due in no small part to its ability to adjust its rates of moisture uptake and transpiration to match soil conditions. The pine is especially successful along the margins of lakes and meadows, where damp soils discourage potential competitors. Sierra Lodgepole Pine also occurs as a seral tree in stands where the more shade-tolerant Red Fir or Mountain Hemlock are climax species. The pine is often the first conifer to invade burned sites, but it does not depend on fires for reproduction. Its cones are not serotinous but instead open at maturity and shed seeds over a two-year period. Sierra Lodgepole Pine is an abundant seeder, and usually at least a few trees survive a fire to start a new stand. The species is also an important pioneer on bare granite outcrops, where it colonizes the moist, soil-filled crevices that form along structural joints. The pine's roots probe deeply into the rock and help widen the crevices, thereby hastening the weathering process and, by extension, the ultimate transition from bare rock to forest. At timberline, Lodgepole Pine associates with Whitebark Pine, Limber Pine, Mountain Hemlock, or Foxtail Pine, forming prostrate mats on the windiest sites. Wind-flagged specimens are also common here. Below the timberline zone, Lodgepole Pine is the most abundant tree in the Sierran subalpine forest. Whitebark Pine is the characteristic timberline tree of the northern and central Sierra, as it occurs on sites that are too high and exposed for other conifers. However, the species is overshadowed in the southern Sierra by the more common and imposing Foxtail Pine. On the eastern slopes south of Yosemite, the more drought-tolerant Limber Pine replaces Whitebark at the timberline in some locations. Nevertheless, where the three pines occur together, Whitebark Pine normally attains the highest elevations, forming cushion krummholz at elevations up to 12,000 feet. Common timberline associates from Yosemite northward are Lodgepole Pine and Mountain Hemlock, neither of which ranges as high.

At lower elevations, out of the wind, Whitebark Pine commonly forms erect trees, which reach heights of forty feet or more on deep, well-developed soils. However, it is highly intolerant of shade and rarely grows with other conifers in closed stands. It also seems to fare better in areas where the snow cover is moderate; this probably accounts for its poorer showing on the western flank of the Sierra. Foxtail Pine has an odd, disjunct range: It occurs in the southern Sierra and on the highest peaks in the Klamath Mountains (some 300 miles to the northwest), but nowhere in between. These separate populations may represent survivors from a time when the pine was part of a richer, more widespread subalpine forest. Gnarled, wind-blasted, yet still erect Foxtail Pines form open stands at timberline on exposed slopes and high ridges. Where wind and cold have reduced other conifers to sprawling mats, Foxtail Pine remains upright, often sustained by the merest strip of bark running up the sheltered side of the tree. Mature specimens may be sixty feet tall, more than five feet in diameter, and as much as 2000 years old. They commonly have two or more piggyback trunks, which are formed by branches that, upon the death of successive main trunks, grow upward to take their places. Downslope, in more sheltered locations, Foxtail Pines normally have a full complement of bark and foliage, and young trees are symmetrical and densely needled. Stands may be pure or mixed, but trees are commonly some sixty feet apart. Whitebark, Lodgepole, and Limber pines are the most frequent associates here.

Limber Pine, a common and characteristic timberline tree in the Rocky Mountains and the Great Basin, ranges along the eastern slope of the Sierra from Yosemite southward, forming open timberline stands in the absence of Whitebark Pine. It often occurs on sterile, rocky outcrops, where the competition from other conifers is slight. However, its distribution is uneven: The tree is abundant in some locales, but absent from other, seemingly comparable, sites.

Western White Pine is a common associate of Lodgepole Pine, Mountain Hemlock, and Red Fir in the closed forests of the lower subalpine zone.

Rocky Mountain subalpine forest
Several conifers occur in the subalpine forests of the Rockies. Engelmann Spruce and Subalpine Fir are the climax species and, together or separately, dominate most stands. They form closed forests on suitable sites in the lower subalpine zone, and, above the forest limit, occur in scattered patches, islands, and ribbon forests. They also range upward to timberline, where wind-flagged specimens and cushion krummholz occur. Other conifers commonly dominate disturbed or marginal habitats, especially near timberline. Several species also occur as associates in closed-forest stands dominated by spruce or fir. Understories may contain more young firs than spruces; but these trees are true codominant climax species, each using a different strategy to maintain its competitive edge. Young firs are products of layering. When the parent tree dies, offspring will compete vigorously with one another for resources, and many—perhaps most—will not survive. All young Engelmann Spruces, on the other hand, are seedlings. Fewer of them occur in the understory and they are scattered, so do not compete with one another. Therefore, the percentage of young spruces that survive to become part of the overstory is higher than that of firs. Moreover, since Engelmann Spruce lives 300

to 350 years and Subalpine Fir lives only 150 to 200 years, the latter must produce about twice as many successful offspring to maintain its numbers in the forest.

In the moist maritime climate of the northern Rockies and eastern Cascades, Subalpine Fir may or may not replace Engelmann Spruce in most climax stands. Moreover, Mountain Hemlock, which ranges eastward to the Rockies only in this region, is a successful competitor locally and may also be a climax species in certain areas. Engelmann Spruce commonly occurs without Subalpine Fir in lower-lying, frost-pocket basins and along damp stream bottoms. Subalpine Fir, however, ranges to higher elevations in this region than Engelmann Spruce, consorting at timberline with Alpine Larch, Whitebark Pine, and Mountain Hemlock.

In the southern Rockies, the situation is somewhat reversed: Engelmann Spruce is clearly the dominant tree, and often the only one of the pair existing at timberline. Limber Pine and

Rocky Mountain Bristlecone Pine
Pinus aristata

Corkbark Fir
Abies lasiocarpa var. *arizonica*

Douglas-fir
Pseudotsuga menziesii
134

Rocky Mountain Bristlecone Pine are often present, though generally restricted to particularly hostile sites. In New Mexico and Arizona, Corkbark Fir, a variety of Subalpine Fir, is far more common and widespread than the latter, while Engelmann Spruce forms a shrubby timberline well above both of them. The most important associate trees are Lodgepole Pine and Douglas-fir in the lower, continuous forest; in the parkland-timberline belt, the principal associates are Whitebark Pine, Alpine Larch, Limber Pine, and Rocky Mountain Bristlecone Pine.

The spruce-fir forest and the boreal forest have numerous understory plants in common, and their most important conifers, while not of the same species, are closely related. For example, along the broad transitional zone stretching southeastward across British Columbia and Alberta, Rocky Mountain species commonly hybridize with their boreal

White Spruce
Picea glauca
119

Balsam Fir
Abies balsamea

Jack Pine
Pinus banksiana

Black Spruce
Picea mariana
115

counterparts—Engelmann Spruce with White Spruce, Subalpine Fir with Balsam Fir, and Lodgepole Pine with Jack Pine—to produce trees with intermediate characteristics. White Spruce, an important species in the boreal forest, is a fairly common associate. Black Spruce, another boreal species, commonly occupies boggy sites within the spruce-fir forest of the Canadian Rockies and eastern Coast Mountains, but does not range into the United States.

The undergrowth in dense spruce-fir stands is sparse. Throughout most of the Rockies, the most common understory shrub is Grouse Whortleberry, a mat-forming relative of blueberries and huckleberries that carpets forest floors from New Mexico to Canada. Stands in the southern Rockies characteristically have sparse understories, which contain scattered shrubs and relatively few herbaceous plants. In the northern Rockies and Cascades, however, lush, more varied understories develop; these may consist of three distinct layers, herb, low shrub, and tall shrub, each of which is impressive. Huckleberries and showy flowering shrubs are typical, and the rich herb layer includes species from both the lower forest and adjacent meadows.

Throughout the Rockies, where gentle terrain and sufficient moisture permit, extensive parklands occur above the continuous forest. These are particularly well developed in the northern Rockies: on the Beartooth Plateau in southern Montana, and in the Front Range and the San Juan Mountains of Colorado. Tree islands consisting of Subalpine Fir, Engelmann Spruce, and various other species, depending on locale, are scattered through these parklands, and ribbon forests occur where winds are high. ˙

Throughout the eastern Cascades and in the Rockies south to Wyoming, Whitebark Pine forms sprawling krummholz on the coldest, driest, windiest sites, but also ranges downslope to the upper margins of the spruce-fir forest. On sheltered sites with deeper soils, Whitebark Pine forms small groves of erect trees that reach heights of up to eighty feet.

Alpine Larch grows only in the northern Rockies and North Cascades. It forms open woodlands of stout, erect trees on sites where Whitebark Pine is reduced to krummholz. In more sheltered basins and on cool, snowy northern exposures, Alpine Larch, a deciduous conifer, often covers large areas. In the fall, its gold, lacy foliage provides a spectacular show.

In the southern Rockies, where Whitebark Pine and Alpine Larch are absent, Limber Pine and Rocky Mountain Bristlecone Pine fill comparable ecological niches. Limber Pine forms krummholz on dry, rocky, sterile, generally unsuitable sites. It also ranges well downslope on hot, south-facing cliffs and outcrops, and even forms lower timberlines in the cold, arid foothills along the eastern side of the middle and northern Rockies. The Rocky Mountain Bristlecone Pine grows on the driest, windiest timberline sites from Colorado southward. Like the Alpine Larch in the north, Bristlecone Pine forms open woodlands of upright trees on sites where all other conifers exist as sprawling shrubs. Twisted, wind-blasted trees up to 2000 years old are often sustained merely by narrow strips of bark on their sheltered sides. Rocky Mountain Bristlecone shows a preference for limestone and achieves its highest elevations on that rock.

Great Basin subalpine woodlands

Between the Sierra Nevada and the Wasatch Range lies the Great Basin. It extends from Oregon's Blue Mountains to the Colorado River plateaus and the Mojave Desert. Scattered across the basin are some 200 isolated mountain ranges, which generally run from north to south; many of these exceed 11,000 feet elevation, and one—the White Mountains of eastern California—rises above 14,000 feet. Separating the mountains are desert basins that lie 4000 to 6000 feet above sea level. The region is extremely arid; precipitation sufficient to support forest conifers generally occurs only at subalpine elevations. As a result, montane conifers are missing from many ranges, and pinyon-juniper woodlands extend upslope almost as far as the lower limit of the subalpine woodlands. Some ranges have a so-called double timberline, consisting of a lower, pinyon-juniper band and a higher, subalpine-

woodland band, separated by sagebrush. Drought prevents
subalpine conifers from ranging lower, and cold keeps the
pinyons and junipers from reaching higher.
Limber Pine and Bristlecone Pine are the characteristic
timberline trees of the Great Basin. They form open
woodlands alone, together, or with other conifers. Limber
Pine is invariably shrubby at timberline. Bristlecone Pine may
either form krummholz or grow upright, depending on local
conditions and perhaps other factors. Limber Pine occurs with
Whitebark Pine, Subalpine Fir, and Engelmann Spruce in the
higher northeastern ranges. Whitebark Pine and Sierra
Lodgepole Pine occur on some of the western ranges. White
Fir, the most widespread montane conifer, ranges as far south
as Charleston Peak near Las Vegas and the higher mountains
of the Mojave Desert. Quaking Aspen occurs throughout the
region on appropriately damp sites.

Quaking Aspen
Populus tremuloides
95

**Great Basin Bristlecone
Pine**
Pinus aristata

**Curlleaf Mountain-
mahogany**
Cercocarpus ledifolius
72, 180

Fernbush
Chamaebatiaria millefolium

Rubber Rabbitbrush
Chrysothamnus nauseosus
206

Squaw Currant
Ribes cereum

Great Basin Bristlecone Pine grows in mixed stands with
Limber Pine on a variety of soils. The stands commonly occur
on steep, rocky, south-facing slopes, where thin soils, intense
sunlight, and rapid runoff give the pines a competitive edge
over other conifers. These extremely open woodlands have a
sparse shrub layer, which is usually dominated by sagebrush.
Depending on the locale, other shrubs may include Curlleaf
Mountain-mahogany, Fern Bush, Rubber Rabbitbrush, and
Squaw Currant. Bristlecone Pine often forms pure stands on
limestone or dolomite, which produce sterile soils that are
hostile to most other conifers in these high, dry environments.
Great Basin Bristlecone Pine lives longer than any other tree
in the world. One specimen on Wheeler Peak in eastern
Nevada had more than 4900 annual rings when it was felled.
In the Ancient Bristlecone Pine Forest in the White
Mountains of eastern California, many trees are more than
4000 years old; one of them—the Methuselah Tree—is more
than 4600 years old. Mature trees are often erect but badly
twisted by wind and deformed by cold. On drier sites, they
may consist mostly of dead wood, sustaining small swatches of
foliage by means of a single, narrow strip of bark. They also
commonly form piggyback trunks, in the same way that the
Foxtail Pines in the Sierran mixed subalpine forest do. The
reduction in living tissue may not be an adaptation to high
winds as much as it is an adjustment to extreme drought.

Wildlife
Because animals are less sensitive than plants to the gradual
environmental changes affecting forest composition, the
animals frequenting the lower, closed portions of the
subalpine forests are essentially the same species that are found
in the upper montane forests. The continuity of forest cover is
of far greater consequence to animal habitats than any change
in the dominant conifer species. Where the forest cover ends,
however, at the upper forest limit, the environment changes
drastically, and new kinds of animals, adapted to life in the
open, assume dominance. The following discussion largely
focuses on these animals.

Coyote
Canis latrans
370, 371

White-tailed Ptarmigan
Lagopus leucurus

Clark's Nutcracker
Nucifraga columbiana
259

Gray Jay
Perisoreus canadensis
255

Hermit Thrush
Catharus guttatus
278

Hammond's Flycatcher
Empidonax hammondii

Pine Grosbeak
Pinicola enucleator
308

Evening Grosbeak
Coccothraustes vespertinus
311

Mountain Bluebird
Sialia currucoides
276

American Robin
Turdus migratorius
279

Rufous Hummingbird
Selasphorous rufus
239

Calliope Hummingbird
Stellula calliope
237

Broad-tailed
Hummingbird
Selasphorus platycercus
238

Bumble Bee
Bombus spp.
578

Pika
Ochotona princeps
330

Bobcat
Felis rufus
362

Without continuous forest cover, the animals in the parkland-woodland belt are more exposed to both predators and the elements. Tree islands and woodlands provide essential cover for timberline wildlife. Mule Deer, Elk, Bighorn Sheep, and Mountain Goats may all seek shelter among the trees during storms. Various predators, including Coyotes, foxes, and hawks, also use the trees for cover. The White-tailed Ptarmigan, an alpine grouse, spends the entire winter near timberline, roosting in the highest krummholz at night and during spells of bad weather.

Clark's Nutcracker, a cousin of the jays, is often the most conspicuous timberline bird in areas where Whitebark, Limber, and Foxtail pines are present. The seeds of these pines are the Nutcracker's chief food, while it in turn is the principal agent for seed dissemination. It buries its cargo about one inch below the ground, usually on warm, south-facing slopes or in other areas that will be snow-free early in the year. Some caches are forgotten, and—under the right conditions—one or more of the buried seeds may germinate. Following a bad seed year, Nutcrackers often wander great distances in search of alternate foods.

The Gray Jay is more of a scavenger than Clark's Nutcracker. Roaming throughout the upper montane and subalpine forests in loose bands of a few birds, the Gray Jay eats most anything —seeds, nuts, insects, birds' eggs, nestlings, and handouts. Other common subalpine songbirds include the Hermit Thrush, Hammond's Flycatcher, and Pine and Evening grosbeaks.

The usual pattern among subalpine birds is to nest among the trees and feed in adjoining meadows. The Mountain Bluebird uses small trees at the edges of a meadow as lookouts, and sallies forth after flying insects. It also hovers above the meadow in search of ground insects. Robins and Brewer's Blackbirds also venture into meadows to feed. The Rufous, Calliope, and Broad-tailed hummingbirds nest in low trees and shrubs near meadows and other openings where wild flowers are abundant. The tubular shape of many subalpine flowers is an adaptation that accommodates pollination by hummingbirds or bumble bees.

Subalpine meadows and parklands offer abundant herbaceous vegetation, which attracts voles, lemmings, and their kin, pocket gophers, ground squirrels, Pikas, and marmots. These in turn attract predators such as Badgers, Martens, Coyotes, foxes, Bobcats, weasels, hawks, owls, and eagles. The numerous insects that feed upon meadow herbs supplement the diets of small mammals and draw a host of insectivorous birds. Most small mammals living within the meadows nest in underground tunnels or burrows, which afford a measure of protection from predators.

Talus slopes and boulder fields, which are abundant in the upper subalpine zone, provide excellent cover and nesting sites for Pikas, marmots, and Bushy-tailed Woodrats. All three den in the rocks but require nearby meadows for foraging. Both Pikas and marmots are abroad during the day and are often

Bushy-tailed Woodrat
Neotoma cinerea
337

Weasel
Mustela spp.

Marten
Martes americana
343

Wolverine
Gulo gulo
358

American Elk
Cervus elaphus
376

Mule Deer
Odocoileus hemionus
373

Bighorn Sheep
Ovis canadensis
375

Mountain Goat
Oreamnos americanus

Grizzly Bear
Ursus arctos
360

Black Bear
Ursus americanus
359

Snowshoe Hare
Lepus americanus
350

Ermine
Mustela erminea
344

Long-tailed Weasel
Mustela frenata

heard uttering shrill whistles of alarm. Bushy-tailed Woodrats, on the other hand, forage mostly at night, when they may pilfer utensils or other objects from campsites, often leaving a rock or other item in return.
Because of their long, slim bodies and small size, Weasels are especially adept at running down prey among the rocks. The Marten, a larger edition of the weasel, commonly hangs about rockslides during the summer, preying upon small mammals unwary enough to show themselves to this efficient predator. The notorious Wolverine is a rare timberline resident; it ranges over hundreds of square miles in search of prey.
The American Elk, or Wapiti, is the principal large grazing animal of the subalpine parklands in the Rocky Mountains, the Cascade Range, and the Olympic Mountains, where it feeds on meadow vegetation throughout the summer. During the fall, Elk move downslope to lowland ranges, where they depend mainly on evergreen shrubs. Mule Deer, which prefer shrubs to herbs, also graze the high meadows, but less frequently than Elk. Moreover, the deer rarely venture very far beyond the cover of the forest. The other hoofed animals of the high country—Bighorn Sheep and Mountain Goats—live mainly on rocky, inaccessible slopes, where they feed on crevice vegetation.
The Grizzly Bear, now extirpated from most of its former range in the conterminous United States, ranges widely but generally prefers parklands over forests. Grizzlies feed on a variety of plant and animal foods, including roots, bulbs, herbage, mushrooms, berries, rodents, fish, deer, and Elk. During the fall, Grizzly and Black bears both feed heavily on huckleberries and other fruits to put on fat for the winter.
Subalpine animals have various strategies for coping with winter. Most of the birds are migratory, though some do little more than fly downslope into the closed forest, where food and shelter are more abundant. Deer, Elk, and Bighorn Sheep also move downslope in winter. Most other mammals, however, remain in the high country. Marmots and ground squirrels truly hibernate, living off the fat they accumulated during the late summer and fall. Bears also live off their fat during the winter, but do not enter the torpor of true hibernation; they may awaken, or even venture abroad, from time to time. Chipmunks also retire to winter dens, but, like the bears, are light sleepers, rousing now and again to feed on stored foodstuffs. The Pika winters within snow-covered talus slopes, where it is protected from the wind and cold. It subsists on hay, which it makes from herbs that were gathered and cured during the summer months, but it also feeds on lichen.
The Snowshoe Hare feeds mainly on bark and buds during the winter. Its coat thickens and changes color from brownish-gray to white, thus affording excellent protective coloration for life on the snow. Its large, furred feet ("snowshoes") allow easy movement over the snowpack. The Ermine and Long-tailed Weasel also turn white in winter, with the exception of the tips of their tails, which remain black. These predators too are difficult to spot on the snow—until it is too late.

SUBALPINE FORESTS: PLANTS AND ANIMALS

Trees and Shrubs

Alpine Larch 50
Alpine Laurel 213
Black Spruce 115
Bog Birch 113
Brewer Spruce 44
Bristlecone Pine 42, 130
Cascade Azalea 187
Engelmann Spruce 117
Foxtail Pine 41
Kinnikinnick 149, 215
Labrador Tea 185
Lewis' Syringa 188
Limber Pine 122
Lodgepole Pine 40
Lowbush Penstemon 218
Mountain Hemlock 49, 139
Pacific Willow 79
Quaking Aspen 95
Red Mountain-heather 216
Red-osier Dogwood 70
Rocky Mountain Maple 100
Scouler Willow 75
Shrubby Cinquefoil 203
Sitka Alder 85
Subalpine Fir 46
Twinberry 164
Western Juniper 63
Western Mountain-ash 108
Western White Pine 121
Western Serviceberry 91
White Alder 87
White Mountain-
heather 193
White Spruce 119
Whitebark Pine 123

Birds

American Dipper 271
Black-chinned
Hummingbird 235
Blue Grouse 224
Brown Creeper 268
Calliope Hummingbird 237
Cassin's Finch 309
Cedar Waxwing 282
Chipping Sparrow 300
Clark's Nutcracker 259
Common Raven 260
Dark-eyed Junco 305, 306
Evening Grosbeak 311
Fox Sparrow 301
Golden-crowned
Kinglet 272

Gray Jay 255
Great Gray Owl 233
Great Horned Owl 230
Hairy Woodpecker 245
Hermit Thrush 270
Lincoln's Sparrow 303
Long-eared Owl 231
Mountain Bluebird 276
Mountain Chickadee 261
Northern Flicker 248
Northern Goshawk 223
Olive-sided Flycatcher 250
Pileated Woodpecker 249
Pine Siskin 312
Pygmy Owl 232
Red-breasted Nuthatch 265
Red Crossbill 310
Ruby-crowned Kinglet 273
Rufous Hummingbird 239
Saw-whet Owl 234
Steller's Jay 256
Three-toed
Woodpecker 247
Townsend's Solitaire 277
Townsend's Warbler 290
Violet-green Swallow 254
Warbling Vireo 284
Western Flycatcher 252
Western Tanager 294
Western Wood Pewee 251
White-crowned
Sparrow 304
White-headed
Woodpecker 246
Williamson's Sapsucker 243
Wilson's Warbler 293
Yellow-rumped
Warbler 288

Mushrooms

Black Morel 320
Chanterelle 316
Chicken Mushroom 323
Emetic Russula 315
Fluted White Helvella 319
Fly Agaric 314
King Bolete 318
Red-belted Polybore 324
Sculptured Puffball 321
Tomentose Suillus 317

Mammals

Beaver 347
Black Bear 359

Bobcat 362
Bushy-tailed Woodrat 337
Caribou 377
Coyote 370
Deer Mouse 329
Douglas' Squirrel 340
Elk 376
Ermine 344
Gray Wolf 368
Grizzly Bear 360
Hoary Bat 338
Hoary Marmot 352
Long-tailed Vole 326
Lynx 361
Marten 343
Mink 345
Mountain Lion 363
Mule Deer 373
Northern Flying
Squirrel 336
Pika 330
Porcupine 355
Red Fox 364
Red Squirrel 341
Western Jumping
Mouse 328
Wolverine 358
Yellow-bellied Marmot 351

Wildflowers
Arrowhead Groundsel 444
Avalanche Lily 390
Beargrass 418
Beautiful Sandwort 395
Bedstraw 416
Bluebell 532
California Corn Lily 413
Cliff Penstemon 510
Common Monkeyflower 439
Coyote Mint 535
Cusick's Speedwell 521
Elegant Death-camas 399
Elephant Head 492
Explorer's Gentian 533
Felwort 525
Fendler's Waterleaf 426
Few-flowered Shooting
Star 485
Fireweed 499
Freckled Milkvetch 471
Fringed Grass of
Parnassus 391
Giant Red Paintbrush 472
Glacier Lily 446

Heartleaf Arnica 443
Hooker's Onion 507
Leafy Aster 506
Lewis' Monkeyflower 503
Lousewort 431
Maiden Blue-eyed Mary 531
Marsh Marigold 381
Meadow Goldenrod 433
Meadow Rue 460
Monument Plant 411
Mountain Bluebell 534
Northern Fairy
Candelabra 394
Orange Agoseris 456
Pearly Everlasting 422
Pussy Paws 512
Red Columbine 483
Rocky Mountain Lily 481
Roseroot 469
Rosy Twisted Stalk 459
Round-leaved Rein
Orchid 405
Rydberg's Penstemon 536
Sierra Sedum 437
Silky Phacelia 540
Silvery Luina 435
Skyrocket 477
Spotted Coral Root 465
Spring Beauty 392
Subalpine Buttercup 451
Sulfur Paintbrush 434
Sulphur Flower 436
Tiger Lily 458
Western Monkshood 530
Western Pasque Flower 382
Yarrow 423
Yellow Bell 447

Butterflies
Anicia Checkerspot 553
California Tortoiseshell 560
Chryxus Arctic 552
Common Alpine 548
Faunus Anglewing 559
Great Spangled
Fritillary 562
Lorquin's Admiral 554
Milbert's Tortoiseshell 561
Northern Blue 542
Northwest Ringlet 547
Phoebus Parnassian 541
Pine White 557
Queen Alexandra's
Sulphur 546

Ruddy Copper 543
Western Tiger
Swallowtail 556

Insects and Spiders
Bark Beetles 567
Black Flies 575
Common Water Strider 568
Deer Flies 576
Golden Buprestid 565
Golden Northern Bumble
Bee 578
Orb Weavers 581
Pine and Spruce Engraver
Beetles 566
Short-tailed
Ichneumons 571
Snow Mosquito 574
Violet Tail 569
Yellow Jackets 577

Reptiles and Amphibians
Cascades Frog 613
Long-toed Salamander 606
Mountain Yellow-legged
Frog 610
Northern Leopard Frog 616
Rubber Boa 599
Spotted Frog 612
Wandering Garter
Snake 595
Western Toad 617

WOODLANDS

Throughout southwestern North America, as in all other semiarid regions of the world, woodlands form a transition between moister conifer forests and drier grasslands or deserts. Woodlands are generally more open than forests and feature smaller trees, though many stands defy such easy categorization. North American woodlands are further distinguished because they have trees different from those found in the forests. There is some overlapping, to be sure, but the dominant woodland trees are chiefly drought-tolerant oaks, pines, and junipers derived from Mexican sources, while forest conifers are mainly cold-tolerant firs, spruces, and hemlocks of boreal origin. Forest pines are different species from the pine species found in the woodlands, but as a group, the pines form a clear link between the two ecological communities, as they are the most drought-hardy of the forest conifers and the most cold-resistant of the woodland trees. Where woodland and forest meet, interesting mixed stands are the rule.

Oak woodlands cover the foothills and lower mountain slopes in areas such as California, southern Arizona, and New Mexico, where winters are usually mild. In areas where the winters are cold, such as the Great Basin and the Colorado Plateau, woodlands are dominated by pinyons or junipers rather than oaks. Transitional areas, where oaks grow together with pinyons and junipers, occur in southern Arizona, southern California, and northeastern California. Various brush communities, most notably chaparral, coexist with all of these woodlands throughout much of their range, often replacing them on dry, rocky slopes, but also occurring in other situations as well. Differences in soil and local climate generally account for the segregation of woodland and chaparral, but the specific causes in particular locales are not always readily apparent.

Woodlands are favored places of both people and animals alike, offering the shelter of trees and the vistas and sunlight of open places. The human race apparently evolved in the woodlands of East Africa, and in villages and neighborhoods around the world, people attempt to recreate the woodland environment either by clearing sections of the forest or by planting trees and shrubs in open areas. The goal is always a mixture of trees and openings, shade and sun, shelter and spaciousness. It isn't surprising, then, that the woodlands of western North America have borne the brunt of settlement in the region. Large areas of oak woodland in California have been lost to suburban housing, as foothills near urban areas are subdivided into "lots with a view." As the Southwest and the Great Basin continue to attract new settlement, their pinyon-juniper and oak woodlands will almost certainly suffer a similar fate.

Geographic Distribution

Throughout California, from the outer Coast Ranges near the ocean to the western slopes of the Sierra Nevada, woodlands that are dominated by deciduous or evergreen oaks or by

Oregon White Oak
Quercus garryana
176

Limber Pine
Pinus flexilis
122

Rocky Mountain Juniper
Juniperus scopulorum
64

associated hardwoods occur on foothill slopes and valley floors. These woodlands range southward into northern Baja California and northward into the interior foothills and valleys of western Oregon. Small stands of Oregon White Oak occur northward sporadically through the Puget Sound region to the southern tip of Vancouver Island.

Woodlands dominated by pinyons or junipers occur throughout the Great Basin, Colorado Plateau, and Rocky Mountain regions, from eastern Oregon, southern Idaho, and southwestern Wyoming southward into Mexico, and from the eastern slopes of the Sierra Nevada to the eastern slopes of Colorado's Front Range. Pinyon-juniper woodlands also occur on the desert slopes of mountain ranges in southern California and northern Baja California. From Arizona the woodlands extend eastward to the Big Bend and Edwards Plateau regions of Texas.

Chaparral and related brush communities occur along the Pacific Coast from southwestern Oregon to northern Baja California, and from the ocean to the foothills of both the Sierra and the Peninsular Ranges of southern California. Chaparral ranges eastward in the higher mountains and plateaus of central and southern Arizona and New Mexico to trans-Pecos Texas, and southward into northern Mexico.

Rocky Mountain brush extends from northern Arizona and New Mexico to southeastern Washington, southern Idaho, and southern Montana. It occurs on the eastern side of Colorado's Front Range, ranging northward to the vicinity of Denver.

Climate

Areas that are warm enough to support woodlands generally occur at elevations that are so low that drought becomes a problem. Conversely, areas moist enough for woodlands are too cold. As a result, forest usually merges directly with grassland or sagebrush steppe, without an intervening woodland belt. Patches of woodland in northwestern Oregon, the Puget Sound region, and southeastern Washington owe their existence to exceptional circumstances. Along the eastern front of the Rockies north of the Denver area, Limber Pine and Rocky Mountain Juniper form a woodland of sorts along the lower forest margin in some locales. These formations are cold-climate analogues of pinyon-juniper woodlands to the south. The fabled California climate features hot, dry summers and mild, moist winters. Summer daytime highs in the foothills and valleys west of the Sierra Nevada usually exceed 80° F, and top 90° or even 100° on at least a few days each summer month; winter lows generally range in the thirties or low forties. Most woodland sites receive fifteen to twenty-five inches of rain a year, more than seventy percent falling between December and March, and the remainder in the spring and fall. There is no rainfall in the summer, and snow is virtually unknown in this region. Such conditions not only create severe moisture stress, but also result in frequent, often highly destructive fires.

California's climate is like that of the Mediterranean region,

Woodlands and
Chaparral

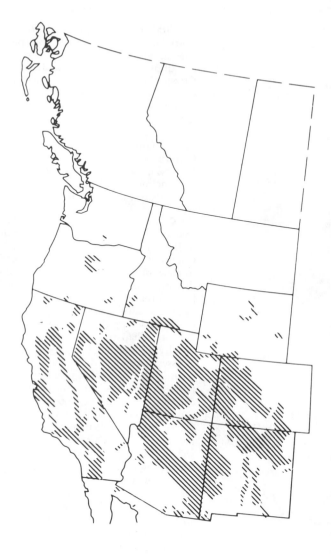

and similar climates prevail on the western coasts of all the continents poleward of the subtropical arid belts. The vegetation in these regions is also similar, consisting of broadleaf woodland, grassland, and brush.

Classic chaparral, such as that in California, consists mostly of evergreen shrubs with small, thick, leathery leaves; such plants are known as broadleaf sclerophyll (Greek for "hard leaf") shrubs. The so-called Rocky Mountain chaparral, while containing some evergreen sclerophylls, is actually a deciduous brush community adapted to cold winters.

California's woodlands enjoy neither winter snow nor summer fog and grow in a region where hot, dry weather produces extreme moisture stress. The various ways in which vegetation responds to this harsh climate largely account for the patchwork of woodland, chaparral, and grassland that covers the California foothills. Topography, slope aspect, and soil characteristics are chiefly important insofar as they ameliorate or intensify summer drought.

Oaks and other woodland trees generally rely on long taproots to reach deep moisture reservoirs and therefore prefer well-drained soils that allow water to pass quickly downward beyond the reach of evaporation.

Chaparral shrubs also develop long taproots, but can survive on less moisture than trees because they have less bulk to support. Chaparral therefore commonly occurs on sites that are too dry for woodland and too rocky for grassland.

Grasses commonly dominate woodland understories, but also form treeless stands on sites where the rainfall or the water table—or both—is insufficient to support woodland or chaparral. Within the woodland belt, such conditions commonly occur on flats, depressions, and gentle slopes, where fine-grained, poorly drained soils largely keep moisture near the surface. During the rainy season, these soils are often wet, but with hot weather, they quickly dry out.

The oak woodlands of southern Arizona and New Mexico receive less precipitation overall (about twelve to eighteen inches a year), but the greater part of it falls during the summer months. In the winter, Pacific storms deliver smaller amounts of rainfall. Spring and fall are accompanied by pronounced periods of drought. Because moisture is generally available during the growing season, these woodlands tend to be more productive and richer in species than those in California.

Pinyon-juniper woodlands develop in a very different climate than that which fosters California's oak woodlands. Summers in the Great Basin and Colorado Plateau areas are comparably warm to those in the Golden State, but winters are much colder. Rainfall ranges from as little as eight inches in the most ideal habitats to as much as twenty-five inches on sites where hot, dry desert winds suck up moisture from plants and soil alike. The minimum necessary precipitation increases southward and eastward from the Great Basin. Most stands, however, receive ten to twenty inches of precipitation a year, with the greater part falling as winter snow.

In the Great Basin—and probably elsewhere as well—pinyon-juniper woodlands occupy thermal belts, where conditions are warmer than at either higher or lower elevations. The colder climate upslope is largely a function of elevation; downslope, it results from the nighttime drainage and accumulation of cold air from the heights.

Fire

The role of fire in the California oak woodlands has not received much study and is generally poorly understood. The current openness of the woodlands, however, may be a result —at least in part—of the periodic fires that were deliberately set by Indians prior to white settlement. This idea is largely conjecture; the fact that there are few eyewitness accounts makes it difficult to assess the frequency and extent of this early burning. The picture is complicated by the fact that the early miners and ranchers started numerous fires, some of which burned for weeks. The California woodlands are still recovering from these extensive burns.

Fires caused by lightning occur only rarely in the California foothills and result almost entirely from tropical storms pushing northward from Mexico. Although these storms invade California every few years, a given woodland stand might grow for several decades between lightning strikes. Even when lightning does hit, the open nature of most woodland stands and the scarceness of understory shrubs and litter tend to inhibit the spread of fire, keeping it from burning out of control.

Fire is a major factor in the development and maintenance of California chaparral and other brush formations. Chaparral shrubs are specifically adapted to fire, and the vegetation as a whole depends on periodic fires for its renewal and continued presence in a given area.

A chaparral stand can be expected to burn every ten to forty years. Many of the shrubs actually contain volatile resins that burn like gasoline. They also commonly carry numerous dead branches and strips of sloughed bark, both of which burn readily. Moreover, litter is normally thick in mature stands. As a result, chaparral ignites easily, and fires can be extremely hot, reaching temperatures as high as 1200° F.

In overmature chaparral stands, litter is more abundant than living tissue, and when shrubs die off, toxins released into the soil over the years by parent plants inhibit the establishment of replacement vegetation. These aged chaparral stands need fire to remove old growth, to stimulate sprouting and seed germination, to vaporize soil toxins, to return nutrients that are bound up in plant materials to the soil, and to prepare a mineral seedbed for the next generation.

About half of the chaparral shrub species reproduce following fires by sprouting new shoots from living root crowns, which are located just below the soil surface. Supported by the extensive root systems that are already in place, these new shoots avoid the hazards that seedlings must face. As a result, individual climax chaparral shrubs succeed themselves, since

Big Sagebrush
Artemisia tridentata
110

Antelope Brush
Purshia tridentata
112, 200

Western Chokecherry
Prunus virginiana var.
demissa

the climax species is present in the first post-fire season.
Most chaparral shrubs, including the sprouters, also produce
abundant seed crops at early ages in order to ensure
reproduction in the event of fire. In most cases, the seeds lie
dormant for years, as they require fire—or some combination
of conditions that is created by fire—in order to germinate.
The large number of seeds guarantees that numerous seedlings
will appear in the first season after a burn.

Although chaparral shrubs reassert their dominance within five
years of a fire, rich herbaceous communities develop on
chaparral sites in the early post-fire seasons. Dominated by
drought-evasive annuals, these communities include a number
of fire endemics—plant species that rarely or never occur
outside of burned areas. The seeds produced by one of these
plants in the first post-fire season may lie dormant in the
ground for decades—until fire once again removes the
dominant shrubs and stimulates germination.

In pinyon-juniper woodlands, fire has been historically
infrequent—but never more so than in this century of strict
fire control. All-consuming fires lead to the temporary
replacement of pinyons and junipers by shrubs; these include
prolific seeders—such as Big Sagebrush—and crown
sprouters, such as Antelope Brush, rabbit brush, and Western
Chokecherry. Birds and animals initiate the reestablishment of
woodland by transporting pinyon and juniper seeds from
nearby groves to burned areas. Repeated fires, however, can
lead to semipermanent shrub communities. Fire suppression,
on the other hand, favors trees, and may have contributed to
the recent spread of junipers into adjoining shrub steppes and
grasslands.

Woodland Types

Western woodlands encompass several distinct types, each of
which is defined by one or more dominant trees. These trees
are also generally the climax species. For convenient discussion
in the limited space available, the large number of woodland
types found in western North America are grouped together
into two extremely general types: broadleaf woodlands and
pinyon-juniper woodlands. The several types within each
group are close enough in structure and ecology to merit being
discussed together. For similar reasons, the several brush
communities occurring in conjunction with western woodlands
are discussed together under the general heading of chaparral.

Broadleaf woodlands

Woodlands dominated by oaks or other hardwoods occupy an
intermediate position between cool, moist conifer forests and
warm, dry grasslands or scrub. Stands vary in structure and
composition largely according to the availability of moisture,
ranging from widely scattered oaks on the driest woodland
sites to rich mixed hardwood forests at the moister end of the
spectrum.

Four species of deciduous oaks and four of evergreen, or live,
oaks occur in the foothill woodlands of California, forming
pure stands or growing together in various mixtures with one

another and other hardwoods and conifers. (Two additional species—one deciduous and one evergreen—occur on the Channel Islands off southern California.) The deciduous oaks tend to be more common in the foothills and valleys of the interior, where the climate is marked by winter frosts and summer heat and drought. In contrast, the evergreen oaks are more often found in moist, frost-free areas—such as the coastal hills from San Francisco southward into southern California—where adequate moisture and mild temperatures allow them to carry out photosynthesis through the winter. However, these distributions are merely rules of thumb: Deciduous oaks also occur on the cooler, drier sites in the Coast Ranges, and live oaks and other evergreen hardwoods grow on the moister interior sites.

The deciduous oaks include Oregon White Oak, Blue Oak, California Black Oak, and Valley Oak. Oregon White Oak forms woodlands and savannas in the North Coast Ranges, the Klamath Mountains, and the interior valleys of western Oregon. It ranges northward in sporadic groves to the southern tip of Vancouver Island and eastward through the Columbia River gorge to form a woodland in a small area on the eastern side of the Cascade Range. Blue Oak is the principal woodland species in the foothills surrounding California's Central Valley, where its frequent companions are the open, rangy Digger Pine and the evergreen Interior Live Oak, which is confined largely to moister sites. California Black Oak is common in the Sierra mixed-conifer forest and also dominates woodlands in Oregon's interior valleys and southward through the Klamath Mountains and the Coast Ranges. Valley Oak, the largest, most stately California oak, forms open savannas in relatively deep, moist soils, both in interior valleys and on adjacent foothill slopes. It also dominates the sinuous forest corridors lining the major Sierran rivers that course across California's Central Valley.

The evergreen oaks include Canyon Live Oak, Interior Live Oak, Coast Live Oak, and Engelmann Oak. The first of these is abundant on rocky canyon sides in the Klamath Mountains, the northern Coast Ranges, and the northern Sierra Nevada, where it occurs with a variety of woodland and montane-forest trees. Interior Live Oak, which is the most drought-resistant of the evergreen hardwoods in California, forms nearly pure stands on the drier woodland sites in the outer Coast Ranges and on the moister ones in the interior Coast Ranges and the Sierra foothills. Although Coast Live Oak is the least tolerant of heat and drought, it is still able to endure extremes of both. The species is largely confined to coastal hills from the San Francisco Bay area southward. Engelmann Oak forms extensive woodlands in southern California, often in the company of Coast Live Oak or California Walnut.

On cooler, moister sites in the Coast Ranges, oak woodlands merge imperceptibly with mixed hardwood forests in which Tanoak, California-laurel, and Pacific Madrone are the common, locally dominant trees. California-laurel often grows in pure, extremely dense stands on moist northern slopes or in

Blue Oak
Quercus douglasii
177

California Black Oak
Quercus kelloggii
103

Valley Oak
Quercus lobata

Digger Pine
Pinus sabiniana
125

Interior Live Oak
Quercus wislizeni
82

California Black Oak
Quercus kelloggii
103

Canyon Live Oak
Quercus chrysolepis
173

Coast Live Oak
Quercus agrifolia
84

Engelmann Oak
Quercus engelmannii

California Walnut
Juglans californica

Tanoak
Lithocarpus densiflorus
170

California-laurel
Umbellularia californica
77

Pacific Madrone
Arbutus menziesii
76, 158

Douglas-fir
Pseudotsuga menziesii
134

California Buckeye
Aesculus californica
105

Emory Oak
Quercus emoryi
83, 171

Arizona White Oak
Quercus arizonica
175

Mexican Blue Oak
Quercus oblongifolia

Silverleaf Oak
Quercus hypoleucoides

Gray Oak
Quercus grisea

Gambel Oak
Quercus gambelii
174

Apache Pine
Pinus engelmannii

Chihuahua Pine
Pinus leiophylla
124

canyon bottoms. Pacific Madrone tolerates drier sites and is especially well-suited to rocky areas. Tanoak has the greatest range of tolerance, dominating many stands and growing as the principal understory tree in mixed evergreen forests dominated by Douglas-fir. Mixed hardwood forests are part of a complex coastal mosaic that includes coastal brush, grassland balds, oak woodlands, and redwood forests.

Dominant woodland trees show several adaptations to summer drought. Most develop long taproots to reach deep pockets of moisture. They prefer soils that are coarse enough to permit rapid drainage and root growth. Thick, leathery leaves retard moisture loss by insulating inner tissues and thereby preventing them from overheating. The leaves also tend to have fewer and recessed stomates, which are the microscopic openings through which moisture and gases are exchanged. Some trees, like Blue Oak, may drop a few leaves at midsummer to reduce the bulk of tissue requiring water. The common California Buckeye, which can occur either as a small deciduous tree or as a large shrub, does not resist drought, but rather avoids it. Its practice of setting its leaves in February and dropping them in August allows the Buckeye to take advantage of ample moisture and warm temperatures in spring while avoiding the hot weather and drought of late summer and early fall.

Four evergreen oaks—Emory, Arizona White, Mexican Blue, and Silverleaf—dominate the open oak-pine woodlands in the foothills and mountains of southern Arizona and New Mexico. The deciduous Gray and Gambel oaks, which are more widespread, may also be present here, along with Apache and Chihuahua pines. The oak-pine woodlands merge with montane forests higher up and with pinyon-juniper northward.

Drier woodland margins from Oregon to New Mexico generally feature extremely open, parklike stands in which individual oaks or small oak clumps are widely scattered over a grassland understory. Known as savanna, such stands represent a broad ecological boundary between woodland and grassland. In this transitional zone, the trees decrease in number and are more widely spaced as moisture levels steadily decline. All of the tree-forming oak species along the Pacific Coast and in the Southwest form savannas on appropriate sites. Understory grasses rely on surface moisture, which in California is plentiful during the winter and spring, but nonexistent in summer. Oaks rely on deeper sources, which are subject to less fluctuation. Shrubs are generally absent, because they cannot compete with trees on these drier sites.

In late winter and spring, the California foothills are emerald green from newly sprouted grasses. By early summer, the hills have turned golden as the grasses die, leaving behind only their seeds to endure the season of drought. The native perennial grasses that once occupied these areas could not compete with introduced, aggressive European grasses. In southern Arizona and New Mexico, however, where most precipitation comes in the summer, perennial bunchgrasses persist in both savanna and woodland.

Poison-oak
Toxicodendron diversiloba
114

Oregon Ash
Fraxinus latifolia
106

Red Alder
Alnus rubra
89

White Alder
Alnus rhombifolia
87

Bigleaf Maple
Acer macrophyllum
102

Fremont Cottonwood
Populus fremontii
96, 167

Boxelder
Acer negundo

California Sycamore
Platanus racemosa
101

Western Redbud
Cercis occidentalis
67, 166, 217

Arizona Cypress
Cupressus arizonica
60, 143

Arizona Sycamore
Platanus wrightii

Arizona Walnut
Juglans major

Arizona Madrone
Arbutus arizonica

Netleaf Hackberry
Celtis reticulata

Texas Mulberry
Morus microphylla

Understory shrubs are largely confined to moister sites on steeper, rockier terrain, where they are better able to coexist with woodland trees. On sites between those favored by woodland and those where brush occurs, trees may form savannas with understories of shrubs rather than grasses. Most woodland shrubs are derived from adjacent brush communities. Poison-oak, however, is a notorious exception. Occurring either as a shrub or a climbing vine, Poison-oak is nearly ubiquitous and nowhere more abundant or characteristic than in broadleaf woodlands. The moister mixed hardwood stands in the Coast Ranges of California may include shrubs that are characteristic of the Northwest coastal forest. Distinctive woodlands form along streams, where moisture stress is not a problem. In northern California and Oregon, these riparian (streamside) woodlands commonly feature Oregon Ash, Red Alder, White Alder, Bigleaf Maple, California-laurel, Oregon White Oak, and various willows. In California's Central Valley, Fremont Cottonwood, Boxelder, and Oregon Ash are present, together with willows. The undergrowth is often a dense tangle, for numerous kinds of shrubs find these perennially moist soils to their liking, including several that are rarely found in adjacent open woodlands. In the southern half of California, California Sycamore is an important riparian tree. There it may be joined by many of the same streamside species found farther north, as well as by Western Redbud. In southeastern Arizona and adjacent New Mexico, Arizona Cypress dominates riparian woodlands that include Arizona Sycamore, Arizona Walnut, Arizona Madrone, Netleaf Hackberry, and Texas Mulberry.

Pinyon-juniper woodlands
Four species of pinyons and seven species of junipers, alone or in various mixtures, form savannalike woodlands with grasses and scattered shrubs. In typical stands, the trees are less than thirty feet tall, and their crowns do not touch. The woodlands occur on lower mountain slopes and plateaus throughout the Great Basin and Colorado Plateau regions.
At their lower limits, they give way to grasslands or shrub-steppes. At higher elevations, they generally merge with lower montane forests. On certain mountain ranges in the Great Basin, however, a band of sagebrush lies between the woodlands and the higher forests. This double timberline occurs because the intervening midslope sagebrush belt is too dry for montane conifers and too cold for pinyons or junipers. The composition and density of pinyon-juniper woodland stands vary greatly. Pinyons, or nut pines, generally favor higher elevations, and junipers, lower ones. As a result, stands often consist of a lower fringe of pure juniper, an upper fringe of pure pinyon, and a middle belt in which both types of trees occur. Pinyons and junipers both grow best on the fringes, where they don't have to compete with one another.
Understory composition also changes with the overstory: Big Sagebrush prevails in the middle belt; lower sagebrushes, in the woodland margins. The herb cover is also highest in the

Singleleaf Pinyon
Pinus monophylla
137

Utah Juniper
Juniperus osteosperma
65

California Juniper
Juniperus californica
61

Colorado Pinyon
Pinus edulis
136

Oneseed Juniper
(Redberry Juniper)
Juniperus monosperma
66

Rocky Mountain Juniper
Juniperus scopulorum
64

Alligator Juniper
Juniperus deppeana
62

Mexican Pinyon
Pinus cembroides

Parry Pinyon
Pinus quadrifolia
138

Western Juniper
Juniperus occidentalis
63

more open fringe areas, but is very sparse in any case, often accounting for less than one percent of the total plant cover. Singleleaf Pinyon is the only representative of its tribe in the Great Basin, where it commonly occurs with Utah Juniper. On the eastern side of the Sierra Nevada, it forms pure stands; it grows with either California Juniper or, less often, Utah Juniper, in southern California. Colorado Pinyon is confined to the Colorado Plateau and the southern Rocky Mountain region, where it occurs with Oneseed Juniper, Utah Juniper, Rocky Mountain Juniper, Redberry Juniper, and Alligator Juniper. Mexican Pinyon and Parry Pinyon are more limited in their distribution in the United States. Mexican Pinyon is found from southern Arizona and New Mexico south into the Sierras of central Mexico. Parry Pinyon is associated with chaparral in the Peninsular ranges of California and Baja.

When subjected to drought, junipers tolerate a much broader range of habitats than pinyons, and they apparently act as pioneers on many sites. Junipers seed and grow under the protective cover of shrubs; pinyons, in the shelter of junipers. Many sites that now host junipers alone will some day, in the absence of disturbance, probably support pinyons as well.

In the northern Rockies and the Pacific Northwest, Rocky Mountain Juniper and Western Juniper grow beyond the limit of pinyons. Both occur on open, rocky slopes, ranging upslope almost as far as timberline, but they also form woodlands along the lower forest margin. Rocky Mountain Juniper is less drought-tolerant than its cousins, but can withstand colder temperatures than most of them. As a result, it ranges northward into British Columbia and Alberta. Western Juniper occurs in open woodlands on the high lava plateaus of eastern Oregon and northeastern California, where its understories are composed of grasses and shrubs much like those of the mixed pinyon-juniper stands farther south. Near Mt. Shasta, it even forms a savanna with Oregon White Oak. California Juniper occurs with Singleleaf Pinyon in southern California, but ranges by itself northward through the Coast Ranges and Sierra Nevada foothills, growing in isolated groves along the lower woodland margin or on rock outcrops.

Pinyons and junipers alike are able to weather both severe winters and pronounced summer drought. Their compact form exposes a minimum of plant surface to the elements. Their slow growth is an adaptation to drought—an alternative to not growing at all. Pinyons are perhaps the slowest-growing pines. In thin, dry soils, an eighty- to one-hundred-year-old tree may have a trunk diameter of only four to six inches. Their growth is more rapid in deeper soils, but still only produces ten- to twelve-inch trunks at a comparable age. Mexican Pinyon, the most drought-resistant of American species, may reach a diameter of only seven to ten inches in 125 to 185 years. Root growth, on the other hand, is rapid for both pinyons and junipers. In deep soils, they send down taproots to moister, lower levels. In shallow soils, they elaborate the lateral surface roots and compete vigorously with grasses for ephemeral moisture.

Mountain-mahogany
Cercocarpus spp.
72, 92, 179, 180

Cliffrose
Cowania mexicana
201

Rubber Rabbitbrush
Chrysothamnus nauseosus
206

Mormon tea
Ephedra spp.

Chamise
Adenostoma fasciculatum
109

Scrub Oak
Quercus ilicifolia

Toyon
Heteromeles arbutifolia
159

Flannel Bush
Fremontia californica

Bush Buckwheat
Eriogonum fasciculatum

Bitter Cherry
Prunus emarginata
186

Silktassel
Garrya spp.
71

Buckthorn
Rhamnus spp.
93, 148

Sumac
Rhus spp.
220

Birchleaf Mountain-
mahogany
Cercocarpus betuloides
92, 179

Other than the dominant trees, no plants are endemic to the pinyon-juniper woodlands. All of the relatively few species of herbs and shrubs are derived from adjacent forest, grassland, or shrub-steppe formations. The more common and widespread shrub associates include ceanothus, mountain mahogany, Antelope Brush, Cliffrose, Big Sagebrush, Rubber Rabbitbrush, and Mormon tea.

Brush formations
Tracts of continuous brush are intimately associated with woodlands and forests throughout western North America, where they occupy sites that for reasons of disturbance or drought are unsuitable for trees. Mountain brush communities are briefly described in connection with the forest types with which they occur. Climax brush formations, however, do occur along the drier forest-woodland margins of the West, and they are described here.

True chaparral consists mainly of evergreen broadleaf sclerophyll shrubs adapted to fire and drought. Chaparral is most widespread in and characteristic of the foothills of California, but ranges northward into Oregon, southward into Baja California, and eastward through central and southern Arizona and New Mexico. Throughout this range, it forms complex vegetation mosaics with various woodland and grassland types.

Chamise, Scrub Oak, and several species of manzanita and ceanothus are the most important chaparral shrubs. Chamise dominates most climax stands in southern California, typically forming nearly pure and usually impenetrable stands. Ceanothus chaparral is the principal type in northern California and southwestern Oregon; any one of several species of ceanothus may be dominant. Manzanita chaparral generally grows at higher elevations on sites that are intermediate in characteristics between those preferred by Chamise chaparral and locales favored by montane forest. Various kinds of manzanitas may dominate nearly pure stands. Scrub Oak chaparral is a rich, mixed-shrub type that prefers moister sites, where it may merge with oak woodland. It occurs throughout California and ranges eastward into Arizona and New Mexico. Dozens of different kinds of shrubs occur in chaparral, a large number of which may be at least locally prominent. Among the more important shrubs are Toyon, Flannel Bush, Bush Buckwheat, Poison-oak, Bittercherry, Western Chokecherry, and various species of sage (not sagebrush), yucca, silktassel, buckthorn, sumac, and Birchleaf Mountain-mahogany. Chaparral shrubs are highly tolerant of drought, having evolved a variety of mechanisms for coping with it. Chief among these is the evergreen habit, which allows the shrubs to carry out photosynthesis during the wet winter season and whenever moisture conditions are favorable. Chaparral shrubs become semidormant in the summer, stopping growth and reducing photosynthesis to maintenance levels. The ability of chaparral shrubs to withstand severe seasonal drought also depends largely on their dual root systems, which consist of long taproots for reaching deep sources of moisture, and extensive lateral root systems for absorbing ephemeral moisture near the soil surface. Root growth among seedlings is extremely rapid: A three-month-old ceanothus seedling may have a forty-inch-long taproot and lateral roots that are about twenty-four inches long.

Coastal sage scrub, a low-shrub formation, is restricted to the coastal hills of California from San Francisco southward into Baja California. It often occurs adjacent to chaparral on lower or otherwise drier sites and can be distinguished from its neighbor by its lower stature and more open stands. In contrast to chaparral shrubs, most plants of the coastal sage scrub are semiwoody, less than three feet tall, and summer-deciduous. They cope with drought by avoiding it, confining growth to the wet season and shedding leaves by early summer. As further insurance, the leaves of most of these shrubs are covered with pale, downy hairs, which give the formation a gray-green appearance. These hairs reflect heat and insulate the leaves, thereby reducing moisture loss. California Sagebrush, several species of wild sage, Bush Buckwheat, and a number of other shrubs are characteristic of coastal sage scrub. Cacti and other succulents are prominent in Baja California.

California Sagebrush
Artemisia californica

North coastal scrub occurs on coastal hills and terraces from Monterey County northward to southern Oregon. Stands of this type vary greatly in composition and structure, ranging from shrub savannas with an understory of coastal grasses to dense, multilayered thickets containing tall, medium, and low shrubs, along with a variety of ferns and wild flowers. North coastal scrub is but one element in a complex mosaic of coastal vegetation. It is likely that north coastal scrub is climax on some sites but seral on others. Fire can maintain it indefinitely.

North coastal scrub is restricted to the fog belt, where cool summers, fog drip, and ample winter rain all combine to ameliorate seasonal drought. Coyote Brush, Orange Bush Monkeyflower, and several woody lupines are particularly characteristic of the formation, but several other shrubs—including a number from adjacent woodlands and forest—are also common. Southern stands also contain shrubs that are common to coastal sage scrub, which displaces this formation southward. Among the more common ferns and wild flowers are Cow Parsnip, paintbrush, iris, and Bracken.

Coyote Brush
Baccharis pilularis consanguinea
111

Orange Bush Monkeyflower
Mimulus aurantiacus
204

Cow Parsnip
Heracleum lanatum

Bracken
Pteridium aquilinum

Ponderosa Pine
Pinus ponderosa
38

Rocky Mountain brush forms interrupted thickets between Ponderosa Pine forest above and desert scrub or grassland below. This formation is found from northern Arizona and New Mexico northward through the southern and middle Rockies to Idaho and Montana. It is essentially a cold-winter variant of true chaparral, with which it shares many important species and genera. Gambel Oak, which is characteristic of Rocky Mountain brush from Arizona and New Mexico northward to central Colorado and northern Utah, often forms dense clonal stands on gentler slopes, while it occurs in mixed stands on higher, steeper slopes. A variety of other shrubs are

Apache Plume
Fallugia paradoxa
183

California Ground Squirrel
Spermophilus beecheyi

Western Spadefoot Toad
Scaphiopus hammondi

Western Gray Squirrel
Sciurus griseus
339

Acorn Woodpecker
Melanerpes fornicivorus
241

Scrub Jay
Aphelocoma coerulescens
257

Dusky-footed Wood Rat
Neotoma fuscipes

Plain Titmouse
Parus inornatus
263

Orange-crowned Warbler
Vermivora celata
285

Black-headed Grosbeak
Pheucticus melanocephalus
295

Western Pocket Gopher
Thomomys mazama

also locally important. The showy Apache Plume and Cliffrose, to mention just two, are common in this community in the Grand Canyon. For reasons that are not entirely clear, Rocky Mountain brush and pinyon-juniper woodlands are mutually exclusive: Where one occurs the other is absent. Like the woodlands, Rocky Mountain brush thrives in thermal belts where temperatures are higher than those found either above or below. These sites are also free of snow most of the winter, which means that the growing season can commence earlier in the spring. Like true chaparral, Rocky Mountain brush occupies dry, rocky slopes that are unsuitable for grassland, sagebrush, or forest. Where coarse soils on slopes give way to fine soils in basins or valleys, the boundary between brush and grassland is often abrupt. Rocky Mountain brush also contains numerous sprouting species, although fire is less common in this formation than in true chaparral.

Wildlife

The mosaic of woodland, grassland, and chaparral or other brush provides excellent food and cover for a large variety of wildlife. Moreover, mild winters, lack of snow cover, and the onset of plant growth as early as November make the woodland areas of California hospitable all year. Along with a number of full-time residents, the woodlands host both winter and summer visitors, mostly migrating birds.

Summer is the season of stress, when drought causes a marked decline in both plant and insect activity and, as a result, in animal populations as well. Nesting birds generally take advantage of abundant food and moisture in the spring, and finish rearing their young by late in the season. A few animals, such as the California Ground Squirrel, Western Spadefoot Toad, and a number of invertebrates, retire to burrows and become dormant during all or part of the dry season, emerging only when rains sufficiently dampen the soil. Most foothill mammals, however, escape summer heat by being active at night. Small rodents obtain sufficient moisture from their food, which they may supplement with drafts of dew. Larger mammals tend to congregate near the relatively few perennial streams and springs in the region.

Woodland oaks are important sources of both food and cover. Acorns are diet staples for several animals, including the Gray Squirrel, Acorn Woodpecker, Scrub Jay, Dusky-footed Wood Rat, and chipmunks. Abundant insects attract numerous kinds of birds. Those that forage in the leaves include the Plain Titmouse, Orange-crowned Warbler, and Black-headed Grosbeak.

The open, grass-covered woodland floor offers little cover for animals, but provides green herbage in winter and spring, abundant grass seeds in summer, and mushrooms and fallen acorns in the fall. Burrowing animals such as the California Ground Squirrel, pocket gophers, and the Western Spadefoot Toad are the only permanent residents, but numerous other species venture into the area from their home bases in nearby

Coyote
Canis latrans
370, 371

Bobcat
Felis rufus
362

White-footed Mouse
Peromyscus spp.

Merriam's Chipmunk
Eutamias merriami

California Pocket Mouse
Perognathus californicus

Wrentit
Chamaea fasciata
281

Rufous-sided Towhee
Pipilo erythrophthalmus
298

California Quail
Callipepla californica
226

Ash-throated Flycatcher
Myiarchus cinerascens
253

Ringtail
Bassariscus astutus
354

Raccoon
Procyon lotor
353

Gray Fox
Urocyon cinereoargenteus
366

Mountain Lion
Felis concolor
363

Mule Deer
Odocoileus hemionus
373

Grizzly Bear
Ursus arctos
360

shrubs or the trees overhead. Throughout their ranges, woodlands and chaparral are so intimately intertwined that the latter is essentially the shrub layer of the woodland transplanted to a neighboring plot. Although each formation has its characteristic animals, most species move back and forth freely between trees and shrubs.

The Western Gray Squirrel is a conspicuous woodland resident. Remaining active throughout the winter, it relies to a great degree on stored acorns during that season. It also pilfers acorns from the Acorn Woodpecker, which stashes them in specially drilled holes in dead trees, utility poles, fence posts, and the sides of old buildings. The Gray Squirrel is relatively safe from predators when in the trees, but on the ground it is vulnerable to hawks, owls, foxes, Coyotes, and Bobcats.

The small mammals that frequent woodlands live largely in chaparral or other shrubbery, from which they venture abroad. Small rodents such as the White-footed Mouse, Merriam's Chipmunk, and the California Pocket Mouse feed upon fresh greenery, berries, and seeds as the year progresses. The Dusky-footed Woodrat builds an elaborate, multichambered stick nest in which it lives and stores food. A number of other creatures, including mice, quail, snakes, and spiders, may share this spacious abode.

Among the many kinds of birds that make use of chaparral, the most distinctive is undoubtedly the Wrentit, which rarely ventures more than a few feet from the cover of shrubs. The Wrentit feeds mostly on insects during spring and summer, and depends heavily on berries during fall and winter.

Another year-round resident, the Rufous-sided Towhee, forages for seeds and insects on the ground beneath the shrubs, where it scratches amongst the litter like a chicken. The California Quail commonly feeds in grassy areas beneath the oaks, but retreats to the chaparral at the first sign of danger. Summer visitors to the chaparral include the Ash-throated Flycatcher and the Orange-crowned Warbler, both insect eaters; several species of hummingbirds, which come for the flowers; and a number of different sparrows, which feed on insects and seeds alike. Abundant winter berry crops attract numerous birds from northern and mountain areas.

Chaparral provides excellent cover from predators, particularly hawks and owls overhead. However, weasels and snakes are slim and well-suited to negotiating dense tangles of brush. The Ringtail, a slender, agile relative of the Raccoon, is also adept in this environment. The Coyote, the Gray Fox, and the Bobcat fare better in more open situations. The Mountain Lion, though its populations are greatly reduced, still ranges through the broken foothill country, seeking Mule Deer among the woodlands and chaparral. The Grizzly Bear, which was once abundant in this habitat, was hunted to extinction here and has not been seen since the 1920s.

The oak-pine woodlands of southeastern Arizona and southwestern New Mexico are the northernmost extensions of a woodland type that is widespread in the foothills of northern and central Mexico. Although these woodlands provide ecological niches that are comparable to those in the woodlands of California, the species within them are largely different, as they are primarily Mexican. This exotic fauna—which includes a number of species that are not found anywhere else north of Mexico—has made these woodlands renowned among naturalists.

Rugged topography creates diverse habitats in the pinyon-juniper woodland. Steep cliffs often feature solitary, stunted trees, while better sites may support dense stands. The shrub cover between and beneath the trees also varies greatly. Numerous kinds of animals use these woodlands for breeding or wintering, but only the Pinyon Jay, Plain Titmouse, and Bushtit are restricted to these habitats within the Great Basin and the southern Rocky Mountain regions. All other animals are just as common, or more so, in adjacent forest or desert communities. Among the mammals, the Desert Woodrat and the Pinyon Mouse are the most characteristic. Various lizards and snakes range into the community from the desert downslope, but none are particularly typical of the woodland.

Pinyon Jay
Gymnorhinus cyanocephalus
258

Bushtit
Psaltriparus minimus
264

Desert Woodrat
Neotoma lepida

Pinyon Mouse
Peromyscus truei

Pinyon nuts and juniper berries are abundant, nutritious, and easily obtained foods, so they attract numerous birds and mammals. Pinyon cones ripen in the fall of every other year; in a good seed year, all of the pinyons over a large area produce seeds simultaneously, oversupplying the animals that feed upon them and thereby increasing chances of germination. Juniper berries, on the other hand, ripen only in either their first or second year, depending on the species. Since juniper berries remain on the trees throughout the winter, they are one of the most important foods during that season.

Large and wingless, pinyon seeds drop to the ground beneath the parent trees, where the competition for resources makes seedling survival unlikely. The Pinyon Jay, whose geographic range coincides with that of pinyon woodlands, performs the necessary service of disseminating seeds to new areas. In turn, it helps to assure the continued regeneration and spread of pinyons—and therefore of its principal food source. The jay's behavior is so closely attuned to the seeding cycles of pinyons that it would surely perish in their absence. Rabbits, chipmunks, mice, Robins, and waxwings also help to disperse pinyon seeds.

American Robin
Turdus migratorius
279

Juniper seeds germinate readily only when their fleshy covers have been removed in the course of passing through the digestive tract of a bird or other animal. The seed is deposited, unharmed, along with the feces—a kind of ready-made fertilizer—usually at a place that is well away from parent trees. Robins and waxwings are voracious consumers of juniper berries, but most other woodland birds also eat them. The foliage of pinyons and junipers is also a source of food for various animals, albeit to a much lesser degree than the seeds. Mule Deer highline some juniper trees—that is, they consume all of the foliage as far up as they can reach—yet steadfastly ignore neighboring trees. The reasons for this preference are unclear, but they are undoubtedly chemically based.

Porcupine
Erethizon dorsatum
355

Elk
Cervus elaphus
376

Bighorn Sheep
Ovis canadensis
375

Long-tailed Weasel
Mustela frenata

Badger
Taxidea taxus

Red-tailed Hawk
Buteo jamaicensis

Great Horned Owl
Bubo virginianus
230

Mountain Bluebird
Sialia currucoides
276

Black-throated Gray
Warbler
Dendroica nigrescens
289

Broad-tailed
Hummingbird
Selasphorus platycercus
238

Blue-gray Gnatcatcher
Polioptila caerulea
274

Steller's Jay
Cyanocitta stelleri
256

Clark's Nutcracker
Nucifraga columbiana
259

Rosy Finch
Leucosticte arctoa

Townsend's Solitaire
Myadestes townsendi
277

Cedar Waxwing
Bombycilla cedrorum
282

Porcupines, which are locally common in pinyon-juniper woodlands, feed on the cambium (inner bark) layer of pinyons. A number of birds and mammals also use the shreddy bark of the juniper as nest-building material.

Mule Deer depend on pinyon-juniper woodlands for cover, shelter from the elements, and emergency food during the winter. Elk winter in the woodlands as well, generally preferring areas where Mountain Mahogany is present.

Bighorn Sheep are locally common in the woodlands, because they favor the same rimrock country that is so often utilized by pinyons and junipers. However, Bighorns have no special relationship to the trees, as they feed largely on herbs and shrubs that are widely available.

Major woodland predators include Mountain Lions and Coyotes, which follow the deer downslope during the winter, as well as Bobcats, which prey on birds and smaller mammals. Long-tailed Weasels and Badgers are also present wherever small burrowing mammals provide a sufficient food source.

Pinyons and junipers host several species of hawks, which require the trees for both nesting and lookouts, and the adjacent steppelands for hunting. Permanent raptorial residents include the Red-tailed and Swainson's hawks, the American Kestrel, and the Golden Eagle. Also present are Cooper's Hawk (which preys mainly on adult birds), the Great Horned Owl, and several other birds of prey.

In addition to the Pinyon Jay, summer nesting birds include the Mountain Bluebird, Black-throated Gray Warbler, Broad-tailed Hummingbird, Ash-throated Flycatcher, Blue-gray Gnatcatcher, and various hawks. Winter visitors, which are attracted to the abundant pinyon seeds and juniper berries, include juncos, nuthatches, Steller's Jay, Clark's Nutcracker, and even Rosy Finch. One snake, the swift Striped Racer, is a major predator of both birds' eggs and nestlings; it climbs among the trees and shrubs in search of prey.

Most of the same animals that frequent pinyon-juniper woodlands also occur in Rocky Mountain brush. However, there are no distinctive brush animals. Vertebrate species, at least, are transitory, seasonal, or equally common in adjacent communities. Although Rocky Mountain brush consists mostly of deciduous shrubs, the several evergreen types—ceanothus, mountain mahogany, Antelope Brush, and Cliffrose—provide an important source of winter browse for deer. Stands of brush are also favored wintering grounds for numerous birds, including juncos, jays, Townsend's Solitaire, the Cedar Waxwing, and the American Robin. These and other species live on southern and western slopes, which remain snow-free throughout most of the season. They feed on abundant seeds, winter fruits, dormant buds, and galls containing insect nymphs.

WOODLANDS: PLANTS AND ANIMALS

1 Spruce-hemlock forest Hoh Rain Forest, Olympic National Park, Washington

Northwest Coastal Forest

2 Spruce-hemlock forest Quinault Rain Forest, Olympic National Park, Washington

Northwest Coastal Forest

3 Spruce-hemlock forest Hoh Rain Forest, Olympic National Park, Washington

Northwest Coastal Forest

4 Pacific Rhododendron, Olympic National Forest, Washington
Douglas-firs, hemlocks

Northwest Coastal Forest

5 Redwood grove Redwood National Park, California

Northwest Coastal Forest

6 Bishop Pine forest Point Reyes National Seashore, California

Northwest Coastal Forest

7 Mixed conifer forest   Northern Sierra Nevada, California

Sierran Montane Forest

8 Jeffrey Pine with White Fir   Near Mammoth Lakes region, California

Sierran Montane Forest

9 Red Fir forest   Yuba Pass, Sierra Nevada, California

Sierran Montane Forest

10 Ponderosa Pines   Salmon River region, Idaho

Rocky Mountain
Montane Forest

11 Ponderosa Pines   Salmon River region, Idaho

Rocky Mountain
Montane Forest

**12 Ponderosa Pines and   Northern rim of the Grand Canyon, Arizona
Quaking Aspens**

Rocky Mountain
Montane Forest

13 Western Hemlocks and Redcedars

Kaniksu National Forest, Idaho

Rocky Mountain
Montane Forest

14 Lodgepole Pine forest

Yellowstone National Park, Wyoming

Rocky Mountain
Montane Forest

15 Lodgepole Pine forest

Yellowstone National Park, Wyoming

Rocky Mountain
Montane Forest

16 Aspen stand   Ouray, Colorado

Rocky Mountain
Montane Forest

17 Aspen stand   Medicine Bow National Forest, Wyoming

Rocky Mountain
Montane Forest

18 Aspen stand   Flagstaff, Arizona

Rocky Mountain
Montane Forest

**19 Sierran mixed
subalpine forest**
Bullfrog Lake Basin, Kings Canyon National Park, California

Subalpine Forest

**20 Sierran mixed
subalpine forest**
Near Lee Vining, California

Subalpine Forest

**21 Engelmann Spruce
forest**
Timberline, Snowy Range, Wyoming

Subalpine Forest

22 Engelmann Spruce forest Rocky Mountain National Park, Colorado

Subalpine Forest

23 Englemann Spruce, fir, and aspen Maroon Creek Canyon, White River National Forest, Colorado

Subalpine Forest

24 Engelmann Spruce Snowy Range, Medicine Bow National Forest, Wyoming

Subalpine Forest

25 Bristlecone Pines — Mount Washington, Snake Range, Nevada

Subalpine Forest

26 Bristlecone Pines — Mount Hamilton, Nevada

Subalpine Forest

27 Bristlecone Pines — Mount Evans, Arapaho National Forest, Colorado

Subalpine Forest

28 Oak woodlands   Santa Ynez Valley, California

Woodlands

29 Oak woodlands   Figueroa Mountains, California

Woodlands

30 Live oak woodlands   Del Rey Oaks, California

Woodlands

31 Pinyon-juniper woodlands   Silver City, New Mexico

Woodlands

32 Pinyon-juniper woodlands   Scipio, Utah

Woodlands

33 Pinyon-juniper woodlands   Providence Mountains, California

Woodlands

34 Alligator Junipers   Coronado National Forest, Arizona

Woodlands

35 Oak woodlands and chaparral boundary   Napa County, California

Woodlands

36 Chaparral   Santa Ynez Mountains, California

Woodlands

HOW TO USE THE COLOR PLATES

The color plates on the following pages include eight major groups of plants and animals: trees and shrubs, birds, mushrooms, mammals, wildflowers, butterflies, insects and spiders, and reptiles and amphibians.

Table of Contents
For easy reference, a table of contents precedes the color plates. The table is divided into two sections. On the left, we list each major group of plants or animals. On the right, the major groups are usually subdivided into smaller groups, and each small group is illustrated by a symbol. For example, the large group of trees and shrubs is divided into small groups based on characteristics such as leaf shape, fruit type, or flower color. Similarly, the large group of reptiles and amphibians is divided into small groups made up of distinctive animals such as lizards or snakes.

Captions for the Color Plates
The black bar above each color plate contains the following information: the plate number, the common and scientific names of the plant or animal, its dimensions, and the page number of the full species description. To the left of each color plate, the habitats where you are likely to encounter the species are always indicated in blue type. Additionally, you will find either a fact helpful in field identification, such as the food that an insect eats (also in blue type), or a range map or drawing.

The chart on the facing page lists the dimensions given and the blue-type information, map, or drawing provided for each major group of plants or animals.

CAPTION INFORMATION

Dimensions	Blue Type/Art
Trees and Shrubs	
Leaf, leaflet, or needle length; fruit length, width, or diameter; flower width or length	Winter tree silhouette or time when fruit matures or flowers bloom
Birds	
Length, usually of adult male, from tip of bill to tail	Range map showing breeding, winter, and/or permanent range
Mushrooms	
Approximate size of mature mushroom: height of stalked mushroom; width of round or unusually shaped mushroom	Specific habitat
Mammals	
Length of adult	Range map
Wildflowers	
Plant height and flower length or width	Drawing of plant or flower
Butterflies	
Wingspan of fully spread adult	Caterpillar's host plants
Insects and Spiders	
Length of adult, excluding antennae and appendages	Major food
Reptiles and Amphibians	
Maximum length of adult	Range map

Trees and Shrubs

Needle-leaf and Scale-leaf Conifers
37–66

Simple Leaves
67–104, 109–113

Compound Leaves
105–108, 114

Cones
115–144

Berrylike Fruit
145–165

Pods and Capsules
166–167

Nuts
168–169, 178

Acorns
170–177

Tufted Fruit
179–180

White or Cream-colored Flowers
181–198

Trees and Shrubs (*continued*)

Yellow or Orange Flowers
199–206

Red or Pink Flowers
207–220

Blue Flowers
221–222

Birds

Hawk
223

Grouse and Quail
224–227

Pigeon
228

Owls
229–234

Hummingbirds
235–239

Trogon
240

Woodpeckers
241–249

Wildflowers (*continued*)	Brownish-purple 459–470	
	Red 471–483	
	Pink 484–514	
	Blue or Purple 515–540	
Butterflies	White-patterned 541–543, 557	
	Blue 542	
	Orange, Yellow, or Green 543–547, 558	
	Eyespot Patterns 548–552	
	Boldly Patterned 553–556, 559–564	
Insects and Spiders	Beetles 565–567	

37 Jeffrey Pine
Pinus jeffreyi
p. 355
Needle length: 5–10″

Sierran Montane Forest

38 Ponderosa Pine
Pinus ponderosa
p. 355
Needle length: 4–8″

Sierran Montane and Rocky Mountain Montane forests

39 Southwestern White Pine
Pinus strobiformis
p. 356
Needle length: 2½–3½″

Rocky Mountain Montane Forest

40 Lodgepole Pine   *Pinus contorta*   Needle length: 1¼–2¾"
p. 356

Sierran Montane, Rocky
Mountain Montane, and
Subalpine forests

41 Foxtail Pine   *Pinus balfouriana*   Needle length: ¾–1½"
p. 357

Subalpine Forest

42 Bristlecone Pine   *Pinus aristata*   Needle length: ¾–1½"
p. 358

Subalpine Forest

43 Red Fir
Abies magnifica
p. 358

Needle length: ¾–1⅜"

Sierran Montane and
Subalpine forests

44 Brewer Spruce
Picea brewerana
p. 359

Needle length: ¾–1"

Northwest Coastal, Sierran
Montane, and Subalpine
forests

45 White Fir
Abies concolor
p. 359

Needle length: 1½–2½"

Sierran Montane and Rocky
Mountain Montane forests

46 Subalpine Fir *Abies lasiocarpa* Needle length: 1–1¾"
p. 360

Subalpine Forest

47 Pacific Silver Fir *Abies amabilis* Needle length: ¾–1½"
p. 361

Northwest Coastal and
Subalpine forests

48 Grand Fir *Abies grandis* Needle length: 1¼–2"
p. 361

Northwest Coastal and
Rocky Mountain Montane
forests

49 Mountain Hemlock   *Tsuga mertensiana*   Needle length: ¼–1"
p. 362

Subalpine Forest

50 Alpine Larch   *Larix lyallii*   Needle length: 1–1¼"
p. 362

Subalpine Forest

51 Western Larch   *Larix occidentalis*   Needle length: 1–1½"
p. 363

Rocky Mountain Montane
Forest

52 Western Yew
Taxus brevifolia
p. 363
Needle length: ½–¾"

Northwest Coastal, Sierran Montane, and Rocky Mountain Montane forests

53 Coast Redwood
Sequoia sempervirens
p. 364
Needle length: ⅜–¾"

Northwest Coastal Forest

54 Giant Sequoia
Sequoiadendron giganteum
p. 365
Leaf length: to ½"; scalelike

Sierran Montane Forest

55 MacNab Cypress
Cupressus macnabiana
p. 366
Leaf length: ¹⁄₁₆"; scalelike

Oak Woodlands and
Chaparral

56 Alaska Yellow-cedar
Chamaecyparis nootkatensis
p. 366
Leaf length: ⅛"; scalelike

56 Alaska Yellow-cedar

57 Incense-cedar
Libocedrus decurrens
p. 367
Leaf length: ⅛–½"; scalelike

Northwest Coastal and
Sierran Montane forests

58 Port-Orford-cedar   *Chamaecyparis lawsoniana*   Leaf length: ¹⁄₁₆″; scalelike
p. 367

Northwest Coastal Forest

59 Western Redcedar   *Thuja plicata*   Leaf length: ¹⁄₁₆–¹⁄₈″; scalelike
p. 368

Northwest Coastal and
Rocky Mountain Montane
forests

60 Arizona Cypress   *Cupressus arizonica*   Leaf length: ¹⁄₁₆″; scalelike
p. 369

Oak and Pinyon-juniper
woodlands

61 California Juniper   *Juniperus californica*   Leaf length: ¹⁄₁₆–¹⁄₈″; scalelike
p. 369

Oak and Pinyon-juniper
woodlands

62 Alligator Juniper   *Juniperus deppeana*   Leaf length: ¹⁄₁₆–¹⁄₈″; scalelike
p. 370

Oak and Pinyon-juniper
woodlands

63 Western Juniper   *Juniperus occidentalis*   Leaf length: ¹⁄₁₆″; scalelike
p. 370

Sierran Montane and
Subalpine forests; Pinyon-
juniper Woodlands

64 Rocky Mountain Juniper
Juniper scopulorum
p. 371
Leaf length: $1/16''$; scalelike

Rocky Mountain Montane and Subalpine forests

65 Utah Juniper
Juniperus osteosperma
p. 371
Leaf length: $1/16''$; scalelike

Pinyon-juniper Woodlands

66 Oneseed Juniper
Juniperus monosperma
p. 372
Leaf length: $1/16''$; scalelike

Pinyon-juniper Woodlands

67 Western Redbud
Cercis occidentalis
p. 372
Leaf length: 1½–3½"

Oak and Pinyon-juniper
woodlands; Chaparral

68 Singeleaf Ash
Fraxinus anomala
p. 373
Leaf length: 1½–2"

Rocky Mountain Montane
Forest and Pinyon-juniper
Woodlands

69 Pacific Dogwood
Cornus nuttallii
p. 373
Leaf length: 2½–4½"

Northwest Coastal and
Sierran Montane forests

70 Red-osier Dogwood *Cornus stolonifera* Leaf length: 1½–3½"
p. 374

Northwest Coastal, Sierran
Montane, Rocky Mountain
Montane, and Subalpine
forests; Woodlands

71 Wavyleaf Silktassel *Garrya elliptica* Leaf length: 2–3¼"
p. 375

Sierran Montane Forest
Oak Woodlands, and
Chaparral

72 Curlleaf Mountain- *Cercocarpus ledifolius* Leaf length: ½–1¼"
mahogany *p. 375*

Rocky Mountain Montane
Forest; Oak and Pinyon-
juniper woodlands; and
Chaparral

73 Bebb Willow · *Salix bebbiana* p. 376 · Leaf length: 1–3½"

Rocky Mountain Montane
Forest

74 Common Manzanita · *Arctostaphylos manzanita* p. 377 · Leaf length: 1–1¾"

Sierran Montane Forest,
Oak Woodlands, and
Chaparral

75 Scouler Willow · *Salix scouleriana* p. 377 · Leaf length: 2–5"

Northwest Coastal, Sierran
Montane, Rocky Mountain
Montane, and Subalpine
forests

76 Pacific Madrone *Arbutus menziesii* Leaf length: 2–4½"
p. 378

Northwest Coastal and
Sierran Montane forests;
Oak Woodlands

77 California-laurel *Umbellularia* Leaf length: 2–5"
californica
p. 379

Northwest Coastal Forest
and Woodlands

78 Giant Chinkapin *Castanopsis* Leaf length: 2–5"
chrysophylla
p. 379

Northwest Coastal and
Sierran Montane forests

79 Pacific Willow   *Salix lasiandra*   Leaf length: 2–5″
p. 380

Northwest Coastal, Sierran
Montane, and Rocky
Mountain Montane forests;
Woodlands

**80 Narrowleaf
Cottonwood**   *Populus angustifolia*   Leaf length: 2–5″
p. 380

Rocky Mountain Montane
Forest

81 Pacific Waxmyrtle   *Myrica californica*   Leaf length: 2–4½″
p. 381

Northwest Coastal Forest

82 Interior Live Oak   *Quercus wislizeni*   Leaf length: 1–2"
p. 382

Oak Woodlands

83 Emory Oak   *Quercus emoryi*   Leaf length: 1–2½"
p. 382

Oak and Pinyon-juniper
woodlands

84 Coast Live Oak   *Quercus agrifolia*   Leaf length: ¾–2½"
p. 383

Oak Woodlands

85 Sitka Alder

Alnus sinuata
p. 383

Leaf length: 2½–5"

Northwest Coastal, Rocky
Mountain Montane, and
Subalpine forests

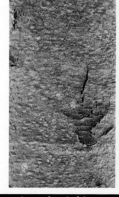

86 Arizona Alder

Alnus oblongifolia
p. 384

Leaf length: 1½–3¼"

Woodlands

87 White Alder

Alnus rhombifolia
p. 385

Leaf length: 2–3½"

Northwest Coastal and
Sierran Montane forests;
Woodlands

88 Mountain Alder
Alnus tenuifolia
p. 385
Leaf length: 1½–4"

Northwest Coastal, Sierran Montane, and Rocky Mountain Montane forests

89 Red Alder
Alnus rubra
p. 386
Leaf length: 3–5"

Northwest Coastal Forest

90 Water Birch
Betula occidentalis
p. 387
Leaf length: 1–2"

Sierran Montane and Rocky Mountain Montane forests; Woodlands

91 Western Serviceberry   *Amelanchier alnifolia*   Leaf length: ³⁄₁–2″
p. 387

All western forests and
woodlands

92 Birchleaf Mountain-mahogany   *Cercocarpus betuloides*   Leaf length: 1–1¼″
p. 388

Sierran Montane Forest,
Oak Woodlands, and
Chaparral

93 Cascara Buckthorn   *Rhamnus purshiana*   Leaf length: 2–6″
p. 388

Northwest Coastal and
Sierran Montane forests

94 Black Cottonwood

Populus trichocarpa
p. 389

Leaf length: 3–6"

Northwest Coastal and
Sierran Montane forests

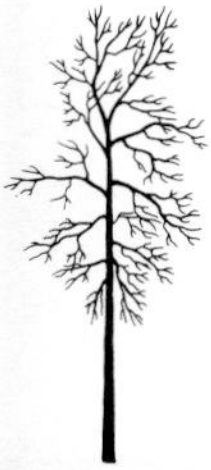

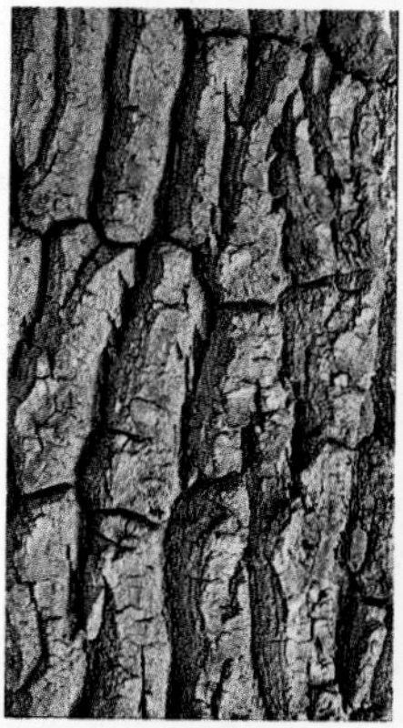

95 Quaking Aspen

Populus tremuloides
p. 390

Leaf length: 1¼–3"

Sierran Montane, Rocky
Mountain Montane, and
Subalpine forests

96 Fremont Cottonwood

Populus fremontii
p. 391

Leaf length: 2–3"

Oak and Pinyon-juniper
woodlands

97 Black Hawthorn   *Crataegus douglasii*   Leaf length: 1–3"
                         p. 391

Northwest Coastal and
Rocky Mountain Montane
forests

98 Vine Maple   *Acer circinatum*   Leaf length: 2½–4½"
                     p. 392

Northwest Coastal Forests

99 Bigtooth Maple   *Acer grandidentatum*   Leaf length: 2–3¼"
                         p. 393

Woodlands

100 Rocky Mountain Maple   *Acer glabrum*   Leaf length: 1½–4½"
p. 393

Northwest Coastal, Sierran Montane, Rocky Mountain Montane, and Subalpine forests

101 California Sycamore   *Platanus racemosa*   Leaf length: 6–9"
p. 394

Woodlands

102 Bigleaf Maple   *Acer macrophyllum*   Leaf length: 6–10"
p. 394

Northwest Coastal and Sierran Montane forests; Woodlands

103 California Black Oak   *Quercus kelloggii*   Leaf length: 3–8″
p. 395

Sierran Montane Forest and Woodlands

104 Cliffrose   *Cowania mexicana*   Leaf length: ¼–⅝″
p. 396

Pinyon-juniper Woodlands

105 California Buckeye   *Aesculus californica*   Leaflet length: 3–6″
p. 396

Oak Woodlands and Chaparral

106 Oregon Ash

Fraxinus latifolia
p. 397

Leaflet length: 2–5"

Northwest Coastal and
Sierran Montane forests

107 Velvet Ash

Fraxinus velutina
p. 398

Leaflet length: 1–3"

Rocky Mountain Montane
Forest and Woodlands

108 Western Mountain-ash

Sorbus scopulina
p. 398

Leaflet length: 1¼–2½"

Sierran Montane, Rocky
Mountain Montane, and
Subalpine forests

109 Chamise

Adenostoma fasciculatum
p. 399

Plant height: 2–12'
Flower length: 1½–4"

Chaparral

Flowers
Bloom May–June

110 Big Sagebrush

Artemisia tridentata
p. 400

Plant height: 1½–15'
Flowers: minute

Sierran Montane, Rocky Mountain Montane, and Subalpine forests; Pinyon-juniper Woodlands

Flowers
Bloom July–November

111 Coyote Brush

Baccharis pilularis consanguinea
p. 400

Plant height: 2–10';
Flower length: ³⁄₁₆"

Chaparral

Flowers
Bloom August–October

112 Antelope Brush

Purshia tridentata
p. 401

Plant height: 3–10'
Leaf length: about ½"

Rocky Mountain Montane
Forest; Pinyon-juniper
Woodlands; and Chaparral

Flowers
Bloom May–July

113 Bog Birch

Betula glandulosa
p. 402

Plant height: 1–6'
Flowers: tiny; in catkins ¾–1"

Northwest Coastal, Rocky
Mountain Montane, and
Subalpine forests

Flowers
Bloom in late spring

114 Poison-oak

*Toxicodendron
diversiloba*
p. 402

Plant height: to 6'
Flowers: minute

Northwest Coastal and
Sierran Montane forests;
Oak Woodlands

Flowers
Bloom April–May

115 Black Spruce — *Picea mariana* p. 403 — Cone length: ⅝–1¼"

Subalpine Forest

116 Sitka Spruce — *Picea sitchensis* p. 404 — Cone length: 2–3½"

Northwest Coastal Forest

117 Engelmann Spruce — *Picea engelmannii* p. 404 — Cone length: 1½–2½"

Rocky Mountain Montane and Subalpine forests

118 Blue Spruce *Picea pungens* Cone length: 2¼–4″
p. 405

Rocky Mountain Montane
Forest

119 White Spruce *Picea glauca* Cone length: 1½–2½″
p. 405

Subalpine Forest

120 Sugar Pine *Pinus lambertiana* Cone length: 11–18″
p. 406

Northwest Coastal and
Sierran Montane forests

121 Western White Pine *Pinus monticola* Cone length: 5–9"
p. 407

Northwest Coastal, Sierran
Montane, Rocky Mountain
Montane, and Subalpine
Forests

122 Limber Pine *Pinus flexilis* Cone length: 3–6"
p. 407

Rocky Mountain Montane
and Subalpine Forests

123 Whitebark Pine *Pinus albicaulis* Cone length: 1½–3¼"
p. 408

Subalpine Forest

124 Chihuahua Pine

Pinus leiophylla
p. 408

Cone length: 1½–2½"

Rocky Mountain Montane
Forest

125 Digger Pine

Pinus sabiniana
p. 409

Cone length: mostly 6–10"

Oak Woodlands

126 Jeffrey Pine

Pinus jeffreyi
p. 355

Cone length: 5–10"

Sierran Montane Forest

127 Coulter Pine
Pinus coulteri
p. 410
Cone length: 8–12"

Sierran Montane Forest and
Oak Woodlands

128 Bishop Pine
Pinus muricata
p. 410
Cone length: 2–3½"

Northwest Coastal Forest

129 Knobcone Pine
Pinus attenuata
p. 411
Cone length: 3¼–6"

Sierran Montane Forest,
Oak Woodlands, and
Chaparral

130 Bristlecone Pine *Pinus aristata* Cone length: 2½–3½"
p. 358

Subalpine Forest

131 Western Larch *Larix occidentalis* Cone length: 1–1½"
p. 363

Rocky Mountain Montane
Forest

132 Bigcone Douglas-fir *Pseudotsuga macrocarpa* Cone length: 4–6"
p. 411

Sierran Montane Forest and
Oak Woodlands

133 Noble Fir
Abies procera
p. 412
Cone length: 4½–7″

Northwest Coastal Forest

134 Douglas-fir
Pseudotsuga menziesii
p. 412
Cone length: 2–3½″

Northwest Coastal, Sierran
Montane, and Rocky
Mountain Montane forests

135 Bristlecone Fir
Abies bracteata
p. 413
Cone length: 2½–4″

Woodlands

136 Colorado Pinyon   *Pinus edulis*   Cone length: 1½–2″
p. 414

Pinyon-juniper Woodlands

137 Singleleaf Pinyon   *Pinus monophylla*   Cone length: 2–3″
p. 414

Pinyon-juniper Woodlands

138 Parry Pinyon   *Pinus quadrifolia*   Cone length: 1½–2½″
p. 415

Oak and Pinyon-juniper
woodlands

139 Mountain Hemlock

Tsuga mertensiana
p. 362

Cone length: 1–3"

Subalpine Forest

140 Western Hemlock

Tsuga heterophylla
p. 415

Cone length: ¾–1"

Northwest Coastal and
Rocky Mountain Montane
forests

141 Coast Redwood

Sequoia sempervirens
p. 364

Cone length: ½–1⅛"

Northwest Coastal Forest

142 Western Redcedar

Thuja plicata
p. 368

Cone length: ½"

Northwest Coastal and
Rocky Mountain Montane
forests

143 Arizona Cypress

Cupressus arizonica
p. 369

Cone length: ¾–1¼"

Oak and Pinyon-juniper
woodlands

144 Mountain Alder

Alnus tenuifolia
p. 385

Cone length: ⅜–⅝"

Northwest Coastal, Sierran
Montane, and Rocky
Mountain Montane forests

| 145 California Torreya | *Torreya californica*
 p. 416 | Male or pollen cone length: ³⁄₈″
 Seed length: 1–1½″ |

Northwest Coastal and
Sierran Montane forests

| 146 Western Yew | *Taxus brevifolia*
 p. 363 | Male or pollen cone diameter: ⅛″
 Seed length: ¼″ |

Northwest Coastal and
Sierran Montane forests

| 147 Hollyleaf Cherry | *Prunus ilicifolia*
 p. 416 | Fruit diameter: ½–⅝″ |

Oak Woodlands and
Chaparral

148 California Buckthorn

Rhamnus californica
p. 417

Fruit length: about ¼″

Sierran Montane Forest, Woodlands, Chaparral

Fruit
Matures in summer

149 Kinnikinnick

Arctostaphylos uva-ursi
p. 418

Fruit width: ⅜″

Northwest Coastal, Rocky Mountain Montane, and Subalpine forests

Fruit
Matures in summer

150 Red Huckleberry

Vaccinium parvifolium
p. 418

Fruit diameter: about ¼″

Northwest Coastal Forest

Fruit
Matures in late summer and fall

151 Salmonberry
Rubus spectabilis
p. 419
Fruit length: ½–1″

Northwest Coastal Forest

Fruit
Matures in summer

152 Thimbleberry
Rubus parviflorus
p. 419
Fruit diameter: ½–¾″

Northwest Coastal and
Rocky Mountain Montane
forests

Fruit
Matures in summer

153 Sierra Gooseberry
Ribes roezlii
p. 420
Fruit diameter: about ½″

Sierran Montane Forest

Fruit
Matures in late summer
and fall

154 Wax Currant

Ribes cereum
p. 421

Fruit diameter: about ½″

Sierran Montane,
Subalpine, and Rocky
Mountain Montane forests

Fruit
Matures in fall

155 Squawbush

Rhus trilobata
p. 422

Fruit diameter: about ¼″

All western forests and
woodlands except
Northwest Coastal Forest

Fruit
Matures in summer

156 Common
Chokecherry

Prunus virginiana
p. 422

Fruit diameter: ¼–⅜″

Northwest Coastal, Sierran
Montane, and Rocky
Mountain Montane forests;
Woodlands

Fruit
Matures in summer

157 Coast Red Elderberry

Sambucus callicarpa
p. 423

Fruit diameter: ⁵⁄₁₆″

Northwest Coastal Forest

Fruit
Matures in summer

158 Pacific Madrone

Arbutus menziesii
p. 378

Fruit diameter: ⅛–½″

Northwest Coastal and
Sierran Montane forests;
Oak Woodlands

Fruit
Matures in autumn

159 Toyon

Heteromeles arbutifolia · Fruit length: ¼–⅜″
p. 424

Oak Woodlands and
Chaparral

Fruit
Matures in autumn,
remaining attached in
winter

160 Devil's Club — *Oplopanax horridum* p. 424 — Fruit diameter: 1/3"

Northwest Coastal and
Rocky Mountain Montane
forests

Fruit
Matures in fall

161 Greenleaf Manzanita — *Arctostaphylos patula* p. 425 — Fruit diameter: 1/4–1/2"

Sierran Montane and Rocky
Mountain Montane forests

Fruit
Matures in summer

162 Blue Elderberry — *Sambucus cerulea* p. 426 — Fruit diameter: nearly 1/4"

All western forests and Oak
Woodlands

Fruit
Matures in summer and
autumn

**163 Thinleaf
Huckleberry**

*Vaccinium
membranaceum*
p. 426

Fruit diameter: ¼" or more

Northwest Coastal, Rocky
Mountain Montane, and
Subalpine forests

Fruit
Matures in summer

164 Twinberry

Lonicera involucrata
p. 427

Fruit diameter: about ⅓"

All western forests and
woodlands

Fruit
Matures in summer

**165 Mountain
Snowberry**

*Symphoricarpos
oreophilus*
p. 427

Fruit length: about ⅜"

Subalpine and Rocky
Mountain Montane forests

Fruit
Matures in fall, remaining
attached in winter

166 Western Redbud   *Cercis occidentalis*   Fruit length: 2–3½"
p. 372

Oak and Pinyon-juniper
woodlands; Chaparral

Fruit
Matures in late summer

**167 Fremont
Cottonwood**   *Populus fremontii*   Fruit length: about ½"
p. 391

Oak and Pinyon-juniper
woodlands

Fruit
Matures in spring

168 California Hazelnut   *Corylus cornuta
californica*
p. 428   Fruit length: ⅜–⅝"

Northwest Coastal Forest

Fruit
Matures in summer

169 Bush Chinkapin

Castanopsis sempervirens
p. 429

Fruit diameter: ¾–1¼″

Northwest Coastal Forest

Fruit
Matures in fall

170 Tanoak

Lithocarpus densiflorus
p. 429

Acorn length: ¾–1¼″

Northwest Coastal and
Sierran Montane forests

Fruit
Matures second year

171 Emory Oak

Quercus emoryi
p. 382

Acorn length: ½–¾″

Oak and Pinyon-juniper
woodlands

Fruit
Matures first year

172 Turbinella Oak
Quercus turbinella
p. 430
Acorn length: ⅝–1″

Oak Woodlands, Pinyon-
juniper Woodlands, and
Chaparral

Fruit
Matures first year

173 Canyon Live Oak
Quercus chrysolepis
p. 430
Acorn length: ¾–2″

Northwest Coastal and
Sierran Montane forests;
Oak Woodlands

Fruit
Matures second year

174 Gambel Oak
Quercus gambelii
p. 431
Acorn length: ½–¾″

Rocky Mountain Montane
Forest, Woodlands, and
Chaparral

Fruit
Matures first year

175 Arizona White Oak

Quercus arizonica
p. 432

Acorn length: ¾–1″

Woodlands

Fruit
Matures first year

176 Oregon White Oak

Quercus garryana
p. 432

Acorn length: 1–1¼″

Northwest Coastal Forest
and Oak Woodlands

Fruit
Matures autumn of first
season

177 Blue Oak

Quercus douglasii
p. 433

Acorn length: ¾–1¼″

Oak Woodlands

Fruit
Matures first season

178 Giant Chinkapin   *Castanopsis*   Fruit diameter: 1–1½"
                           chrysophylla
                           p. 379

Northwest Coastal and
Sierran Montane forests

Fruit
Matures in autumn of
second year

179 Birchleaf Mountain-   *Cercocarpus betuloides*   Fruit length: ⅜"
mahogany   *p. 388*

Sierran Montane Forest,
Oak Woodlands, and
Chaparral

Fruit
Matures in late summer

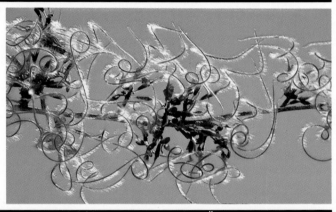

180 Curlleaf Mountain-   *Cercocarpus ledifolius*   Fruit length: ¼"
mahogany   *p. 375*

Rocky Mountain Montane
Forest; Oak and Pinyon-
juniper woodlands; and
Chaparral

Fruit
Matures in summer

181 Thimbleberry — *Rubus parviflorus* — Flower width: 1–2″
p. 419

Northwest Coastal and
Rocky Mountain Montane
forests

Flowers
Bloom April–July

182 Mountain Misery — *Chamaebatia foliosa* — Flower width: about 1″
p. 433

Sierran Montane Forest

Flowers
Bloom May–July

183 Apache Plume — *Fallugia paradoxa* — Flower width: 1–1½″
p. 434

Rocky Mountain Montane
Forest and Pinyon-juniper
Woodlands

Flowers
Bloom May–October

184 Western Serviceberry	*Amelanchier alnifolia* p. 387	Flower width: ¾–1¼"

All western forests and woodlands

Flowers
Bloom in spring

185 Labrador Tea	*Ledum glandulosum* p. 434	Flower width: about ½"

Northwest Coastal, Sierran Montane, Rocky Mountain Montane, and Subalpine forests

Flowers
Bloom June–August

186 Bitter Cherry	*Prunus emarginata* p. 434	Flower width: ½"

All western forests and woodlands except Northwest Coastal Forest

Flowers
Bloom in spring

187 Cascade Azalea

Rhododendron albiflorum
p. 435

Flower width: ⅝–¾"

Subalpine Forest

Flowers
Bloom June–August

188 Lewis' Syringa

Philadelphus lewisii
p. 435

Flower width: ¾–1¼"

Northwest Coastal, Sierran Montane, Rocky Mountain Montane, and Subalpine forests; Oak Woodlands

Flowers
Bloom May–July

189 Moosewood Viburnum

Viburnum edule
p. 436

Flower width: tiny; in an inflorescence to 1¼"

Subalpine and Rocky Mountain Montane forests

Flowers
Bloom in summer

190 Birchleaf Spiraea

Spiraea betulifolia
p. 436

Flower width: about ¼″

Subalpine and Rocky
Mountain Montane forests

Flowers
Bloom July–August

191 Coast Red Elderberry

Sambucus callicarpa
p. 423

Flower width: ¼″

Northwest Coastal Forest

Flowers
Bloom in spring and early
summer

192 Creambush

Holodiscus discolor
p. 437

Flower width: about ⅛″

All western forests and
woodlands except
Chaparral

Flowers
Bloom May–August

193 White Mountain-heather
Cassiope mertensiana
p. 437
Flower length: ¼"

Subalpine Forest

Flowers
Bloom July–August

194 Common Manzanita
Arctostaphylos manzanita
p. 377
Flower length: ⁵⁄₁₆"

Sierran Montane Forest, Oak Woodlands, and Chaparral

Flowers
Bloom in late winter and early spring

195 Greenleaf Manzanita
Arctostaphylos patula
p. 425
Flower length: ¼"

Sierran Montane and Rocky Mountain Montane forests

Flowers
Bloom May–June

196 Blue Yucca

Yucca baccata
p. 438

Flower length: 2–4"

Rocky Mountain Montane
Forest and Pinyon-juniper
Woodlands

Flowers
Bloom April–July

197 Our Lord's Candle

Yucca whipplei
p. 438

Flower length: 1–1½"

Chaparral

Flowers
Bloom April–May

198 Deer Brush

Ceanothus integerrimus
p. 439

Flower cluster length: 3–6"

Sierran Montane and Rocky
Mountain Montane forests;
Chaparral

Flowers
Bloom May–June

199 Creeping Oregon Grape

Berberis repens
p. 439

Flower width: about ½"

Rocky Mountain Montane Forest

Flowers
Bloom March–June

200 Antelope Brush

Purshia tridentata
p. 401

Flower width: about ½"

Rocky Mountain Montane Forest; Pinyon-juniper Woodlands; and Chaparral

Flowers
Bloom May–July

201 Cliffrose

Cowania mexicana
p. 396

Flower width: ¾–1"

Pinyon-juniper Woodlands

Flowers
Bloom in spring and summer

202 California Fremontia

Fremontodendron californicum
p. 440

Flower width: 1¼–2"

Sierran Montane Forest,
Oak Woodlands, and
Chaparral

Flowers
Bloom in spring and early
summer

203 Shrubby Cinquefoil

Potentilla fruticosa
p. 440

Flower width: about 1"

Rocky Mountain Montane
and Subalpine forests

Flowers
Bloom June–August

204 Orange Bush Monkeyflower

Mimulus aurantiacus
p. 441

Flower width: ¾–1"

Chaparral

Flowers
Bloom March–September

205 Twinberry

Lonicera involucrata
p. 427

Flower length: ½"

All western forests and
woodlands

Flowers
Bloom March–July

206 Rubber Rabbitbrush

*Chrysothamnus
nauseosus*
p. 441

Flower length: ⅛"

Pinyon-juniper Woodlands
and Rocky Mountain
Chaparral

Flowers
Bloom July–October

207 Red Shrubby Penstemon

Penstemon corymbosus
p. 442

Flower length: 1–1½"

Northwest Coastal and
Sierran Montane forests;
Oak Woodlands

Flowers
Bloom June–October

208 Western Azalea
Rhododendron occidentale
p. 442
Flower width: 1½–2½"

Northwest Coastal and
Sierran Montane forests

Flowers
Bloom April–August

209 Pacific Rhododendron
Rhododendron macrophyllum
p. 443
Flower length: about 1½"

Northwest Coastal Forest

Flowers
Bloom May–June

210 Chaparral Pea
Pickeringia montana
p. 443
Flower length: about ¾"

Chaparral

Flowers
Bloom May–August

211 Nootka Rose *Rosa nutkana* Flower width: 2–3"
p. 444

Northwest Coastal and
Rocky Mountain Montane
forests

Flowers
Bloom May–July

212 Salmonberry *Rubus spectabilis* Flower width: 1–1½"
p. 419

Northwest Coastal Forest

Flowers
Bloom March–July

213 Alpine Laurel *Kalmia microphylla* Flower width: ½"
p. 444

Subalpine Forest

Flowers
Bloom June–September

214 Salal
Gualtheria shallon
p. 444
Flower length: ⅜"

Northwest Coastal Forest

Flowers
Bloom May–July

215 Kinnikinnick
Arctostaphylos uva-ursi
p. 418
Flower width: ¼"

Northwest Coastal, Rocky
Mountain Montane, and
Subalpine forests

Flowers
Bloom in late spring and
early summer

216 Red Mountain-heather
Phyllodoce
empetriformis
p. 445
Flower length: about ¼"

Subalpine Forest

Flowers
Bloom June–August

217 Western Redbud   *Cercis occidentalis*
p. 372   Flower length: ½"

Oak and Pinyon-juniper
woodlands; Chaparral

Flowers
Bloom in early spring

**218 Lowbush
Penstemon**   *Penstemon fruticosus*   Flower length: 1–2"
p. 445

Northwest Coastal, Rocky
Mountain Montane, and
Subalpine forests

Flowers
Bloom May–August

**219 New Mexican
Locust**   *Robinia neomexicana*   Flower length: ¾"
p. 446

Oak and Pinyon-juniper
woodlands; Chaparral

Flowers
Bloom in late spring and
early summer

220 Sugar Sumac *Rhus ovata* Flower width: ¼″
p. 446

Chaparral

Flowers
Bloom in early spring

221 Deer Brush *Ceanothus integerrimus* Flower cluster length: 3–6″
p. 439

Sierran Montane and Rocky
Mountain Montane forests;
Chaparral

Flowers
Bloom May–June

222 Blueblossom *Ceanothus thyrsiflorus* Flower width: ³⁄₁₆″
p. 447

Northwest Coastal Forest,
Oak Woodlands, and
Chaparral

Flowers
Bloom in spring

223 Northern Goshawk

Accipiter gentilis
p. 452

Length: 20–26″

All western conifer forests

224 Blue Grouse

Dendragapus obscurus
p. 452

Length: 15½–21″

All western conifer forests

225 Ruffed Grouse

Bonasa umbellus
p. 453

Length: 16–19″

Northwest Coastal and
Rocky Mountain Montane
forests

226 California Quail
Callipepla californica
p. 453
Length: 9–11″

Northwest Coastal Forest,
Woodlands, and Chaparral

227 Mountain Quail
Oreortyx pictus
p. 454
Length: 10½–11½″

Northwest Coastal and
Sierran Montane forests

228 Band-tailed Pigeon
Columba fasciata
p. 454
Length: 14–15½″

Northwest Coastal, Sierran
Montane, and Rocky
Mountain Montane forests;
Oak Woodlands

229 Flammulated Owl
Otus flammeolus
p. 454
Length: 6–7"

Rocky Mountain Conifer
Forest

230 Great Horned Owl
Bubo virginianus
p. 455
Length: 18–25"

All western forests and
woodlands

231 Long-eared Owl
Asio otus
p. 455
Length: 13–16"

All western forests and
woodlands

232 Northern Pygmy-Owl   *Glaucidium gnoma*   Length: 7–7½"
p. 456

All western conifer forests;
Oak Woodlands

233 Great Gray Owl   *Strix nebulosa*   Length: 24–33"
p. 456

All western conifer forests

234 Northern Saw-whet Owl   *Aegolius acadicus*   Length: 7–8½"
p. 457

All western conifer forests

235 Black-chinned Hummingbird *Archilochus alexandri* Length: 3¼–3¾"
p. 457

Sierran Montane, Rocky Mountain Montane, and Subalpine forests; Woodlands; and Chaparral

236 Anna's Hummingbird *Calypte anna* Length: 3½–4"
p. 457

Oak Woodlands and Chaparral

237 Calliope Hummingbird *Stellula calliope* Length: 2¾–4"
p. 458

Northwest Coastal, Sierran Montane, Rocky Mountain Montane, and Subalpine forests

238 Broad-tailed Hummingbird

Selasphorus platycercus
p. 459

Length: 4–4½"

Rocky Mountain Montane
and Subalpine forests;
Pinyon-juniper Woodlands

239 Rufous Hummingbird

Selasphorous rufus
p. 459

Length: 3–4"

Northwest Coastal, Rocky
Mountain Montane, and
Subalpine forests

240 Elegant Trogon

Trogon elegans
p. 460

Length: 11–12"

Woodlands

241 Acorn Woodpecker — *Melanerpes formicivorus* — Length: 8–9½"
p. 460

Sierran Montane Forest and
Oak Woodlands

242 Yellow-bellied Sapsucker — *Sphyrapicus varius* — Length: 8–9"
p. 461

Northwest Coastal, Sierran
Montane, and Rocky
Mountain Montane forests;
Woodlands

243 Williamson's Sapsucker — *Sphyrapicus thyroideus* — Length: 9½"
p. 461

Rocky Mountain Montane,
Sierran Montane, and
Subalpine forests

244 Nuttall's Woodpecker
Picoides nuttallii
p. 462
Length: 7–7½"

Oak Woodlands

245 Hairy Woodpecker
Picoides villosus
p. 462
Length: 8½–10½"

All western conifer forests

246 White-headed Woodpecker
Picoides albolarvatus
p. 462
Length: 9"

Sierran Montane, Rocky Mountain Montane, and Subalpine forests

247 Three-toed Woodpecker

Picoides tridactylus
p. 463

Length: 8–9½"

Northwest Coastal, Rocky Mountain Montane, and Subalpine forests

248 Northern Flicker

Colaptes auratus
p. 463

Length: 12½–14"

All western forests and woodlands

249 Pileated Woodpecker

Dryocopus pileatus
p. 464

Length: 16–19½"

Northwest Coastal, Sierran Montane, Rocky Mountain Montane, and Subalpine forests

250 Olive-sided Flycatcher

Contopus borealis
p. 464

Length: 7–8"

All western conifer forests

251 Western Wood-Pewee

Contopus sordidulus
p. 465

Length: 6–6½"

All western conifer forests;
Oak Woodlands

252 Western Flycatcher

Empidonax difficilis
p. 465

Length: 5½–6"

All western conifer forests

253 Ash-throated Flycatcher
Myiarchus cinerascens
p. 465
Length: 7½–8½"

Woodlands and Chaparral

254 Violet-green Swallow
Tachycineta thalassina
p. 466
Length: 5–5½"

All western forests and woodlands except Chaparral

255 Gray Jay
Perisoreus canadensis
p. 466
Length: 10–13"

Northwest Coastal, Rocky Mountain Montane, and Subalpine forests

256 Steller's Jay   *Cyanocitta stelleri*   Length: 12–13½"
                                       p. 467

All western conifer forests

257 Scrub Jay   *Aphelocoma coerulescens*   Length: 11–13"
                                       p. 467

Woodlands and Chaparral

258 Pinyon Jay   *Gymnorhinus*   Length: 9–11¾"
                                       cyanocephalus
                                       p. 468

Pinyon-juniper Woodlands

259 Clark's Nutcracker   *Nucifraga columbiana*   Length. 12–13″
p. 468

Subalpine Forest

260 Common Raven   *Corvus corax*   Length: 21½–27″
p. 469

All western conifer forests;
Woodlands

261 Mountain Chickadee   *Parus gambeli*   Length: 5–5¾″
p. 469

All western conifer forests

262 Chestnut-backed Chickadee
Parus rufescens
p. 469
Length: 4½–5"

Northwest conifer forest

263 Plain Titmouse
Parus inornatus
p. 470
Length: 5–5½"

Oak Woodlands

264 Bushtit
Psaltriparus minimus
p. 470
Length: 3¾–4"

All western forests except Subalpine; Woodlands; and Chaparral

265 Red-breasted Nuthatch
Sitta canadensis
p. 471
Length: 4½–4¾"

All western conifer forests

266 White-breasted Nuthatch
Sitta carolinensis
p. 471
Length: 5–6"

Northwest Coastal and Sierran Montane forests; Woodlands

267 Pygmy Nuthatch
Sitta pygmaea
p. 472
Length: 3¾–4½"

Sierran Montane and Rocky Mountain Montane forests

268 Brown Creeper
Certhia americana
p. 472
Length: 5–5¾"

All western conifer forests

269 Bewick's Wren
Thryomanes bewickii
p. 472
Length: 5–5½"

All western forests except Subalpine; Woodlands; Chaparral

270 Winter Wren
Troglodytes troglodytes
p. 473
Length: 4–4½"

Northwest Coastal and Sierran Montane forests

Northwest Coastal, Sierran
Montane, Rocky Mountain
Montane, and Subalpine
forests

All western conifer forests

All western conifer forests

Woodlands and Chaparral

Northwest Coastal, Sierran
Montane, and Rocky
Mountain Montane forests;
Woodlands

Sierran Montane, Rocky
Mountain Montane, and
Subalpine forests

277 Townsend's Solitaire
Myadestes townsendi
p. 476
Length: 8–9½"

All western conifer forests

278 Hermit Thrush
Catharus guttatus
p. 477
Length: 6½–8"

All western conifer forests

279 American Robin
Turdus migratorius
p. 477
Length: 9–11"

Northwest Coastal, Sierran Montane, and Rocky Mountain Montane forests; Woodlands

280 Varied Thrush

Ixoreus naevius
p. 478

Length: 9–10″

Northwest Coastal and
Rocky Mountain Montane
forests

281 Wrentit

Chamaea fasciata
p. 478

Length: 6–6½″

Northwest Coastal Forest,
Woodlands, and Chaparral

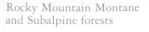

282 Cedar Waxwing

Bombycilla cedrorum
p. 479

Length: 6½–8″

Rocky Mountain Montane
and Subalpine forests

283 Solitary Vireo

Vireo solitarius
p. 479

Length: 5–6"

All western conifer forests
except Subalpine;
Woodlands

284 Warbling Vireo

Vireo gilvus
p. 480

Length: 4½–5½"

Deciduous trees in conifer
forests; Woodlands

285 Orange-crowned Warbler

Vermivora celata
p. 480

Length: 4½–5½"

All forests except
Subalpine; Oak
Woodlands; and Chaparral

286 Nashville Warbler   *Vermivora ruficapilla*   Length: 4–5"
p. 480

Rocky Mountain Montane
Forest

287 Virginia's Warbler   *Vermivora virginiae*   Length: 4–4¼"
p. 481   Adult female

Woodlands and Chaparral

**288 Yellow-rumped
Warbler**   *Dendroica coronata*   Length: 5–6"
p. 481

All western conifer forests

289 Black-throated Gray Warbler   *Dendroica nigrescens*   Length: 4½–5″
p. 482

Northwest Coastal, Sierran Montane, and Rocky Mountain Montane forests

290 Townsend's Warbler   *Dendroica townsendi*   Length: 4¼–5″
p. 482

Rocky Mountain Montane and Subalpine forests

291 Hermit Warbler   *Dendroica occidentalis*   Length: 4½″
p. 483

Northwest Coastal Forest

292 MacGillivray's Warbler

Oporornis tolmiei
p. 483

Length: 4¾–5½"

All western conifer forests
except Subalpine Forests
and Chaparral

293 Wilson's Warbler

Wilsonia pusilla
p. 484

Length: 4½"

All western conifer forests;
Woodlands

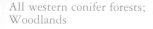

294 Western Tanager

Piranga ludoviciana
p. 484

Length: 6–7½"

All western conifer forests

295 Black-headed Grosbeak

Pheucticus melanocephalus
p. 485

Length: 6½–7¾"

Northwest Coastal, Rocky Mountain Montane, and Sierran Montane forests; Woodlands

296 Lazuli Bunting

Passerina amoena
p. 485

Length: 5–5½"

Woodlands and Chaparral

297 Green-tailed Towhee

Pipilo chlorurus
p. 486

Length: 6¼–7"

Rocky Mountain Montane and Sierran Montane forests; Pinyon-juniper Woodlands; and Chaparral

298 Rufous-sided Towhee

Pipilo erythrophthalmus
p. 486

Length: 7–8½"

Northwest Coastal, Sierran Montane, and Rocky Mountain Montane forests; Woodlands; and Chaparral

299 Brown Towhee

Pipilo fuscus
p. 486

Length: 8–10"

Northwest Coastal Forest, Woodlands, and Chaparral

300 Chipping Sparrow

Spizella passerina
p. 487

Length: 5–5¾"

All western conifer forests; Oak Woodlands

301 Fox Sparrow
Passerella iliaca
p. 487
Length: 6–7¼″

All western conifer forests

302 Song Sparrow
Melospiza melodia
p. 488
Length: 5–7″

Northwest Coastal, Sierran Montane, and Rocky Mountain Montane forests; Woodlands

303 Lincoln's Sparrow
Melospiza lincolnii
p. 488
Length: 5–6″

Northwest Coastal, Sierran Montane, Rocky Mountain Montane, and Subalpine Forests

304 White-crowned Sparrow

Zonotrichia leucophrys
p. 489

Length: 5½–7"

Northwest Coastal, Rocky Mountain Montane, Sierran Montane, and Subalpine forests; Woodlands

305 Dark-eyed Junco

Junco hyemalis
p. 489

Length: 5–6½"
"Oregon" Junco

All western conifer forests

306 Dark-eyed Junco

Junco hyemalis
p. 489

Length: 5½–6"
"Gray-headed" Junco

Rocky Mountain Montane and Subalpine forests

307 Northern Oriole   *Icterus galbula*   Length: 7–8½"
bullockii   "Bullock's" Oriole
p. 490

Oak Woodlands

308 Pine Grosbeak   *Pinicola enucleator*   Length: 8–10"
p. 491

Rocky Mountain Montane
and Sierran Montane forests

309 Cassin's Finch   *Carpodacus cassinii*   Length: 6–6½"
p. 491

Sierran Montane, Rocky
Mountain Montane, and
Subalpine forests

310 Red Crossbill

Loxia curvirostra
p. 492

Length: 5¼–6½"

All western conifer forests

311 Evening Grosbeak

Coccothraustes
vespertinus
p. 493

Length: 7–8½"

All western conifer forests

312 Pine Siskin

Carduelis pinus
p. 493

Length: 4½–5¼"

All western conifer forests

313 Bulbous Cort

Cortinarius glaucopus
p. 495

Height: 2–5"

Northwest Coastal, Sierran
Montane, and Rocky
Mountain Montane forests;
Oak Woodlands

Habitat
Usually under spruce, fir,
or oak

314 Fly Agaric

Amanita muscaria
p. 495

Height: 2–10"

⊗

All western forests and
woodlands

Habitat
Most often under pine,
spruce, or birch

315 Emetic Russula

Russula emetica
p. 495

Height: 1–3"

⊗

All western forests

Habitat
Most frequently in
sphagnum moss but also on
the ground in mixed woods

316 Chanterelle *Cantharellus cibarius* Height: ⅜–6″
p. 496

All western forests and Oak Woodlands

Habitat
Mixed woods, or under conifers or oaks

317 Tomentose Suillus *Suillus tomentosus* Height: 2–4″
p. 496

All western forests

Habitat
Under 2-needle and 3-needle pines

318 King Bolete *Boletus edulis* Height: ¾–10″
p. 497

All western forests

Habitat
Under conifers, and under birch and aspen

**319 Fluted White
Helvella**

Helvella crispa
p. 497

Height: ⅝–5⅛"

All western forests

Habitat
Under conifers or
hardwoods, or in grassy
areas

320 Black Morel

Morchella elata
p. 497

Height: 2¾–6"

All western forests

Habitat
Coniferous woods or under
aspens

321 Sculptured Puffball

Calbovista subsculpta
p. 498

Width: 3¼–6"

All western forests

Habitat
Open woods, along paths,
but not in lowland areas

322 Western Rhizopogon

Rhizopogon occidentalis Width: ⅜–2"
p. 498

Northwest Coastal, Sierran Montane, and Rocky Mountain Montane forests

Habitat
Under conifers, preferring sandy soil

323 Chicken Mushroom

Laetiporus sulphureus Cap width: 2–12"
p. 498

Northwest Coastal, Sierran Montane, and Subalpine forests

Habitat
Logs and stumps of coniferous and deciduous trees; also on living trees

324 Red-belted Polypore

Fomitopsis pinicola Cap width: 2–12"
p. 499

All western forests

Habitat
Dead trees and stumps of conifers and hardwoods; sometimes living trees

325 Vagrant Shrew   *Sorex vagrans*   Length: 3¾–4¾"
                           p. 501

Northwest Coastal, Sierran
Montane, and Rocky
Mountain Montane forests

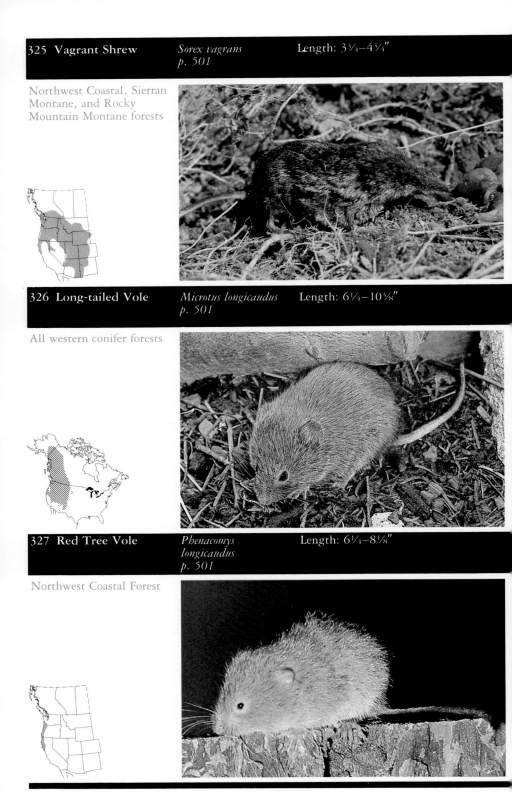

326 Long-tailed Vole   *Microtus longicaudus*   Length: 6¼–10⅜"
                              p. 501

All western conifer forests

327 Red Tree Vole   *Phenacomys*   Length: 6¼–8⅛"
                           longicaudus
                           p. 501

Northwest Coastal Forest

328 Western Jumping Mouse

Zapus princeps
p. 502

Length: 8½–10¼"

All western conifer forests

329 Deer Mouse

Peromyscus maniculatus
p. 502

Length: 4¾–8¾"

All western forests and woodlands

330 Pika

Ochotona princeps
p. 503

Length: 6⅜–8½"

Mostly Subalpine Forest

331 Uinta Chipmunk
Eutamias umbrinus
p. 503
Length: 7¾–9⅝"

Rocky Mountain
Montane Forest

332 Townsend's Chipmunk
Eutamias townsendii
p. 504
Length: 8⅞–12½"

Northwest Coastal Forest

333 Least Chipmunk
Eutamias minimus
p. 504
Length: 6⅝–8⅞"

Rocky Mountain Montane
Forest; Pinyon-juniper and
Great Basin Subalpine
woodlands

**334 Yellow-pine
Chipmunk**

Eutamias amoenus
p. 505

Length: 7⅛–9⅝"

Sierran Montane and Rocky
Mountain Montane forests

**335 Golden-mantled
Ground Squirrel**

Spermophilus lateralis
p. 505

Length: 9⅛–12⅛"

Northwest Coastal and
Sierran Montane forests

**336 Northern Flying
Squirrel**

Glaucomys sabrinus
p. 506

Length: 10⅜–14½"

All western conifer forests

337 Bushy-tailed Woodrat
Neotoma cinerea
p. 506

Length: 11½–18½"

All western conifer forests

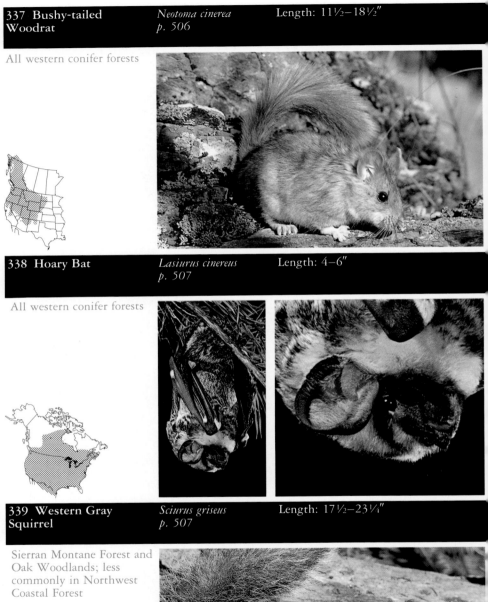

338 Hoary Bat
Lasiurus cinereus
p. 507

Length: 4–6"

All western conifer forests

339 Western Gray Squirrel
Sciurus griseus
p. 507

Length: 17½–23¼"

Sierran Montane Forest and Oak Woodlands; less commonly in Northwest Coastal Forest

340 Douglas' Squirrel   *Tamiasciurus douglasii*   Length: 10⅝–14"
p. 507

Northwest Coastal, Sierran Montane, and Subalpine forests

341 Red Squirrel   *Tamiasciurus hudsonicus*   Length: 10⅝–15¼"
p. 508

Rocky Mountain Montane and Subalpine forests

342 Abert's Squirrel   *Sciurus aberti*   Length: 18¼–23"
p. 509

Rocky Mountain Montane Forest

343 Marten *Martes americana* Length: 19¼–26⅞"
p. 509

All western conifer forests

344 Ermine *Mustela erminea* Length: 7½–13½"
p. 510

All western conifer forests

345 Mink *Mustela vison* Length: 19¼–28¼"
p. 510

All western conifer forests

Northwest Coastal and
Sierran Montane forests

Most western forests and
woodlands

Northwest Coastal, Sierran
Montane, and Rocky
Mountain Montane forests

| 349 Brush Rabbit | *Sylvilagus bachmani*
p. 514 | Length: 11⅛–14¾" |

Northwest Coastal Forest,
Chaparral, and Oak
Woodlands

| 350 Snowshoe Hare | *Lepus americanus*
p. 514 | Length: 15–20½" |

Northwest Coastal, Sierran
Montane, Rocky Mountain
Montane, and Subalpine
forests

| 351 Yellow-bellied
Marmot | *Marmota flaviventris*
p. 515 | Length: 18½–27⅝" |

Sierran Montane, Rocky
Mountain Montane, and
Subalpine forests

352 Hoary Marmot
Marmota caligata
p. 515
Length: 17¾–32¼″

Northwest Coastal, Rocky Mountain Montane, and Subalpine forests

353 Raccoon
Procyon lotor
p. 516
Length: 23¾–37⅜″

All western forests and woodlands except Subalpine

354 Ringtail
Bassariscus astutus
p. 517
Length: 24½–31⅞″

Sierran Montane Forest, Woodlands, and Chaparral

All western conifer forests;
Pinyon-juniper woodlands

All forests and woodlands
except Subalpine

Oak Woodlands

358 Wolverine *Gulo gulo* Length: 31½–44¼"
p. 520

All western conifer forests

359 Black Bear *Ursus americanus* Length: 4½–6¼'
p. 520

All western forests and woodlands

360 Grizzly Bear, *Ursus arctos* Length: 6–7'
including Brown Bears *p. 522*

Northwest Coastal, Rocky Mountain Montane, and Subalpine forests

361 Lynx

Felis lynx
p. 523

Length: 29⅛–41⅞″

Northwest Coastal, Rocky Mountain Montane, and Subalpine forests

362 Bobcat

Felis rufus
p. 524

Length: 28–49⅛″

All western forests and woodlands

363 Mountain Lion

Felis concolor
p. 525

Length: 59⅛–108″

All western forests and woodlands

364 Red Fox   *Vulpes vulpes*   Length: 35⅜–40⅜″
                     p. 526

All western conifer forests

365 Red Fox   *Vulpes vulpes*   Length: 35⅜–40⅜″
                     p. 526

All western conifer forests

366 Gray Fox   *Urocyon*   Length: 31½–44¼″
                     cinereoargenteus
                     p. 527

Northwest Coastal and
Rocky Mountain Montane
forests; all western
woodlands

367 Red Fox *Vulpes vulpes* Length: 35⅜–40⅜″
p. 526

All western conifer forests

368 Gray Wolf *Canis lupus* Length: 39½–80⅝″
p. 528

Northwest Coastal, Rocky
Mountain Montane, and
Subalpine forests

369 Gray Wolf *Canis lupus* Length: 39½–80⅝″
p. 528

Northwest Coastal, Rocky
Mountain Montane, and
Subalpine forests

370 Coyote
Canis latrans
p. 529
Length: 41⅜–52″

All western forests and woodlands

371 Coyote
Canis latrans
p. 529
Length: 41⅜–52″

All western forests and woodlands

372 Gray Wolf
Canis lupus
p. 528
Length: 39½–80⅝″

Northwest Coastal, Rocky Mountain Montane, and Subalpine forests

373 Mule Deer
Odocoileus hemionus
p. 530
Length: 3¾–6½′

All western forests and woodlands

374 White-tailed Deer
Odocoileus virginianus
p. 531
Length: 4½–6¾′

Northwest Coastal and Rocky Mountain Montane forests

375 Bighorn Sheep
Ovis canadensis
p. 532
Length: rams: 5¼–6′; ewes: 4¼–5¼′

Sierran Montane and Rocky Mountain Montane forests; Pinyon-juniper woodlands

376 Elk *Cervus elaphus* Length: 6¾–9¾'
p. 533

Northwest Coastal, Rocky
Mountain Montane, and
Subalpine forests

377 Caribou *Rangifer tarandus* Length: 4½–6¾'
p. 534

Rocky Mountain and
Subalpine forests

378 Moose *Alces alces* Length: 6¾–9'
p. 535

Rocky Mountain Montane
Forest

379 Engelmann Aster   *Aster engelmannii*   Plant height: 1½–5'
p. 538   Flower width: 1½–2½"

Rocky Mountain Montane
Forest

380 Stemless Daisy   *Townsendia exscapa*   Plant height: 1–2"
p. 538   Flower width: 1–2"

Pinyon-juniper Woodlands

381 Marsh Marigold   *Caltha leptosepala*   Plant height: 1–8"
p. 538   Flower width: ½–1½"

Subalpine Forest

| 382 Western Pasque Flower | *Anemone occidentalis* p. 539 | Plant height: 8–24″ Flower width: 1¼–2″ |

Northwest Coastal, Sierran Montane, and Subalpine forests

| 383 Bunchberry | *Cornus canadensis* p. 539 | Plant height: 2–8″ Flower width: to 4″ |

Northwest Coastal and Rocky Mountain Montane forests

| 384 Canada Violet | *Viola canadensis* p. 539 | Plant height: 4–16″ Flower width: nearly 1″ |

Northwest Coastal and Rocky Mountain Montane forests

| 385 Dwarf Bramble | *Rubus lasiococcus*
p. 540 | Creeper
Flower width: about ½" |

Northwest Coastal and
Sierran Montane forests

| 386 Richardson's
Geranium | *Geranium richardsonii*
p. 540 | Plant height: 8–32"
Flower width: about 1" |

Sierran Montane and Rocky
Mountain Montane forests;
Pinyon-juniper Woodlands

| 387 Western Trillium | *Trillium ovatum*
p. 541 | Plant height: 4–16"
Flower width: 1½–3" |

Northwest Coastal Forest

388 Sego Lily *Calochortus nuttallii* Plant height: 6–18"
p. 541 Flower width: 1–2"

Rocky Mountain Montane
Forest and Pinyon-juniper
Woodlands

389 Washington Lily *Lilium* Plant height: 2–7'
washingtonianum Flower width: 3–4"
p. 541

Northwest Coastal Forest

390 Avalanche Lily *Erythronium montanum* Plant height: 6–10"
p. 542 Flower width: about 2½"

Subalpine Forest

391 Fringed Grass of Parnassus   *Parnassia fimbriata*   Plant height: 6–20″
p. 542   Flower width: about 1″

Northwest Coastal, Sierran
Montane, Rocky Mountain
Montane, and Subalpine
forests

392 Spring Beauty   *Claytonia lanceolata*   Plant height: 2–10″
p. 543   Flower width: ¼–¾″

Northwest Coastal, Sierran
Montane, Rocky Mountain
Montane, and Subalpine
forests

393 Queen's Cup   *Clintonia uniflora*   Plant height: 2½–6″
p. 543   Flower width: 1–1½″

Northwest Coastal, Sierran
Montane, and Rocky
Mountain Montane forests

394 Northern Fairy Candelabra

Androsace septentrionalis
p. 543

Plant height: 1–10"
Flower width: ⅛"

Rocky Mountain Montane and Subalpine forests

395 Beautiful Sandwort

Arenaria capillaris
p. 544

Plant height: 2–12"
Flower width: ¼–½"

Northwest Coastal, Rocky Mountain Montane, and Subalpine forests

396 Miner's Lettuce

Montia perfoliata
p. 544

Plant height: 1–14"
Flower width: ⅛–¼"

Northwest Coastal, Sierran Montane, and Rocky Mountain Montane forests; Oak Woodlands

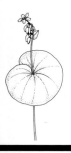

| **397 Broad-leaved Montia** | *Montia cordifolia* p. 544 | Plant height: 4–16" Flower length: about ½" |

Northwest Coastal, Sierran Montane, and Rocky Mountain Montane forests

| **398 Wood Nymph** | *Moneses uniflora* p. 545 | Plant height: 2–6" Flower width: ¾" |

Northwest Coastal and Rocky Mountain Montane forests

| **399 Elegant Death-camas** | *Zigadenus elegans* p. 545 | Plant height: 6–28" Flower width: about ¾" | ⊗ |

Northwest Coastal, Rocky Mountain Montane, and Subalpine forests

400 Northern Inside-out Flower

Vancouveria hexandra
p. 546

Plant height: 6–20"
Flower length: about ½"

Northwest Coastal Forest

401 White Globe Lily

Calochortus albus
p. 546

Plant height: 1–2'
Flower length: about 1"

Oak Woodlands and Chaparral

402 Wartberry Fairybell

Disporum trachycarpum
p. 546

Plant height: 1–2'
Flower length: ⅜–⅝"

Rocky Mountain Montane Forest

403 Broad-leaved Twayblade

Listera convallarioides
p. 547

Plant height: 2–14"
Flower length: ⅜–½"

Northwest Coastal, Sierran Montane, and Rocky Mountain Montane forests

404 Five-point Bishop's Cap

Mitella pentandra
p. 547

Plant height: 4–16"
Flower width: about ¼"

Northwest Coastal, Sierran Montane, and Rocky Mountain Montane forests

405 Round-leaved Rein Orchid

Habenaria orbiculata
p. 548

Plant height: 8–24"
Flower length: ½–¾"

Northwest Coastal, Rocky Mountain Montane, and Subalpine forests

| 406 Merten's Saxifrage | *Saxifraga mertensiana*
 p. 548 | Plant height: 4–16"
 Flower width: nearly ¼" |

Northwest Coastal, Sierran Montane, and Rocky Mountain Montane forests

| 407 One-sided Wintergreen | *Pyrola secunda*
 p. 548 | Plant height: 2–8"
 Flower length: ¼" |

Northwest Coastal, Sierran Montane, and Rocky Mountain Montane forests

| 408 False Lily of the Valley | *Maianthemum dilatatum*
 p. 549 | Plant height: 6–14"
 Flower length: about ⅛" |

Northwest Coastal Forest

409 False Mitrewort

Tiarella unifoliata
p. 549

Plant height: 8–16"
Flower width: about ¼"

Northwest Coastal and
Rocky Mountain Montane
forests

410 Fringe Cups

Tellima grandiflora
p. 550

Plant height: to 32"
Flower width: about ½"

Northwest Coastal, Sierran
Montane, and Rocky
Mountain Montane forests

411 Monument Plant

Frasera speciosa
p. 550

Plant height: 4–7'
Flower width: 1–1½"

Sierran Montane, Rocky
Mountain Montane, and
Subalpine forests; Pinyon-
juniper Woodlands

412 False Solomon's Seal *Smilacina racemosa* Plant height: 1–3'
p. 550 Flower length: about ¹⁄₁₀"

Northwest Coastal, Sierran
Montane, and Rocky
Mountain Montane forests

413 California Corn Lily *Veratrum californicum* Plant height: 4–8'
p. 551 Flower length: ½–¾"

Northwest Coastal, Sierran
Montane, Rocky Mountain
Montane, and Subalpine
forests

414 Goatsbeard *Aruncus sylvester* Plant height: 3–7'
p. 551 Flower width: less than ⅛"

Northwest Coastal and
Sierran Montane forests

| 415 Poker Alumroot | *Heuchera cylindrica*
p. 551 | Plant height: 6–36"
Flower depth: ¼–½" |

Northwest Coastal and
Rocky Mountain Montane
forests

| 416 Bedstraw | *Galium boreale*
p. 552 | Plant height: 8–32"
Flower length: less than ⅛" |

All western forests and
woodlands

| 417 Baneberry | *Actaea rubra*
p. 552 | Plant height: 1–3'
Flower length: ⅛" |

Northwest Coastal, Sierran
Montane, and Rocky
Mountain Montane forests

418 Beargrass   *Xerophyllum tenax*   Plant height: to 5'
p. 553   Flower length: ⅜"

Northwest Coastal, Sierran
Montane, Rocky Mountain
Montane, and Subalpine
forests

419 Vanilla Leaf   *Achlys triphylla*   Plant height: 10–20"
p. 553   Flower length: 1–2"

Northwest Coastal Forest

420 Rattlesnake Plantain   *Goodyera oblongifolia*   Plant height: 12–18"
p. 553   Flower length: ¼"

Northwest Coastal and
Rocky Mountain Montane
forests; Oak Woodlands

421 Yerba Buena

Satureja douglasii
p. 554

Creeper
Flower length: about ¼"

Northwest Coastal and
Sierran Montane forests;
Oak Woodlands

422 Pearly Everlasting

Anaphalis
margaritacea
p. 554

Plant height: 8–36"
Flower length: about ¼"

All western conifer forests
and woodlands

423 Yarrow

Achillea millefolium
p. 555

Plant height: 12–40"
Flower length: ⅛"

Northwest Coastal, Sierran
Montane, Rocky Mountain
Montane, and Subalpine
forests

| **424 Nuttall's Pussytoes** | *Antennaria parvifolia* p. 555 | Plant height: to 6" Flower length: nearly ½" |

Rocky Mountain Montane
Forest and Pinyon-juniper
Woodlands

| **425 Yerba de Selva** | *Whipplea modesta* p. 555 | Creeper Flower length: about ⅛" |

Northwest Coastal Forest

| **426 Fendler's Waterleaf** | *Hydrophyllum fendleri* p. 556 | Plant height: 8–32" Flower width: ¼–⅜" |

Northwest Coastal, Rocky
Mountain Montane, and
Subalpine forests

427 Case's Fitweed   *Corydalis caseana*   Plant height: 2–7'
                            p. 556   Flower length: ¾–1"

Sierran Montane and Rocky
Mountain Montane forests

428 Indian Pipe   *Monotropa uniflora*   Plant height: 2–10"
                            p. 557   Flower length: about ¾"

Northwest Coastal Forest

429 Phantom Orchid   *Eburophyton austinae* Plant height: 9–20"
                            p. 557   Flower length: ½–¾"

Northwest Coastal and
Sierran Montane forests

| 430 Golden Pea | *Thermopsis montana*
p. 557 | Plant height: 2–4'
Flower length: ¾–1" |

Northwest Coastal, Sierran
Montane, and Rocky
Mountain Montane forests;
Pinyon-juniper Woodlands

| 431 Bracted Lousewort | *Pedicularis bracteosa*
p. 558 | Plant height: to 3'
Flower length: ½–¾" |

Northwest Coastal, Rocky
Mountain Montane, and
Subalpine forests

| 432 Yellow Skunk
Cabbage | *Lysichitum americanum*
p. 558 | Plant height: 12–20"
Flower height: to 8" |

Northwest Coastal Forest

433 Meadow Goldenrod *Solidago canadensis* Plant height: 1–5′
  p. 559 Flower length: about ⅛″

All western conifer forests

434 Sulfur Paintbrush *Castilleja sulphurea* Plant height: 6–20″
  p. 559 Flower length: ¾–1¼″

Rocky Mountain Montane
and Subalpine forests

435 Silvery Luina *Luina hypoleuca* Plant height: 6–16″
  p. 559 Flower length: nearly ⅜″

Northwest Coastal and
Subalpine forests

436 Sulphur Flower

Eriogonum umbellatum
p. 560

Plant height: 4–12"
Flower width: 2–4"

Sierran Montane, Rocky
Mountain Montane, and
Subalpine forests; Pinyon-
juniper Woodlands

437 Sierra Sedum

Sedum obtusatum
p. 560

Plant height: 1–7"
Flower length: about ⅜"

Sierran Montane and
Subalpine forests

438 Deer Weed

Lotus scoparius
p. 561

Plant height: 1–3'
Flower length: about ⅜"

Chaparral

439 Common Monkeyflower   *Mimulus guttatus* p. 561   Plant height: to 3' Flower length: ½–1½"

Northwest Coastal, Sierran Montane, Rocky Mountain Montane, and Subalpine forests; Woodlands.

440 Golden Aster   *Chrysopsis villosa* p. 562   Plant height: 8–20" Flower width: about 1"

Rocky Mountain Montane Forest and Pinyon-juniper Woodlands

441 Golden Yarrow   *Eriophyllum lanatum* p. 562   Plant height: 4–24" Flower width: 1½–2"

Northwest Coastal, Sierran Montane, and Rocky Mountain Montane forests; Oak Woodlands; and Chaparral

442 Arrowleaf Balsam Root *Balsamorhiza sagittata*
p. 562
Plant height: 8–32"
Flower width: 4–5"

Sierran Montane and Rocky Mountain Montane forests; Pinyon-juniper Woodlands

443 Heartleaf Arnica *Arnica cordifolia*
p. 563
Plant height: 4–24"
Flower width: 2–3½"

Northwest Coastal, Sierran Montane, Rocky Mountain Montane, and Subalpine forests; Woodlands

444 Arrowhead Groundsel *Senecio triangularis*
p. 563
Plant height: 1–5'
Flower width: 1–1½"

All western conifer forests

445 Golden Columbine

Aquilegia chrysantha
p. 564

Plant height: 1–4'
Flower width: 1½–3"

Rocky Mountain Montane
Forest

446 Glacier Lily

*Erythronium
grandiflorum*
p. 564

Plant height: 6–12"
Flower length: 1–2"

Northwest Coastal, Rocky
Mountain Montane, and
Subalpine forests

447 Yellow Bell

Fritillaria pudica
p. 564

Plant height: 4–12"
Flower length: ½–1"

Rocky Mountain Montane
and Subalpine forests;
Pinyon-juniper Woodlands

| 448 Hooker's Evening Primrose | *Oenothera hookeri* p. 565 | Plant height: 2–3' Flower width: 2–3" |

Northwest Coastal, Sierran Montane, and Rocky Mountain Montane forests; Woodlands and Chaparral

| 449 Evergreen Violet | *Viola sempervirens* p. 565 | Creeper Flower width: about ½" |

Northwest Coastal Forest

| 450 Stream Violet | *Viola glabella* p. 566 | Plant height: 2–12" Flower width: about ½–¾" |

Northwest Coastal, Sierran Montane, and Rocky Mountain Montane forests

451 Subalpine Buttercup

Ranunculus eschscholtzii
p. 566

Plant height: 2–10″
Flower width: ¾–1½″

Subalpine Forest

452 California Poppy

Eschscholtzia californica
p. 566

Plant height: 8–24″
Flower width: 1–2″

Oak Woodlands

453 Fire Poppy

Papaver californicum
p. 567

Plant height: 12–24″
Flower width: about 1″

Oak Woodlands and
Chaparral

454 Scarlet Globemallow *Sphaeralcea coccinea*
p. 567

Plant height: to 20″
Flower width: 1–1¼″

Pinyon-juniper Woodlands

455 Western Wallflower *Erysimum capitatum*
p. 568

Plant height: 6–36″
Flower width: about ¾″

Sierran Montane and Rocky
Mountain Montane forests;
Oak and Pinyon-juniper
woodlands

456 Orange Agoseris *Agoseris aurantiaca*
p. 568

Plant height: 4–24″
Flower width: about 1″

Northwest Coastal, Sierran
Montane, Rocky Mountain
Montane, and Subalpine
forests

| 457 Amber Lily | *Anthericum torreyi*
p. 568 | Plant height: to 3'
Flower width: about 1" |

Rocky Mountain Montane
Forest and Pinyon-juniper
Woodlands

| 458 Tiger Lily | *Lilium columbianum*
p. 569 | Plant height: 2–4'
Flower width: 2–3" |

Northwest Coastal and
Subalpine forests

| 459 Rosy Twisted-stalk | *Streptopus roseus*
p. 569 | Plant height: 6–16"
Flower length: ¼–½" |

Northwest Coastal and
Subalpine forests

460 Western Meadow Rue	*Thalictrum occidentale* p. 570	Plant height: 1–3' Flower width: about ⅜"

Northwest Coastal, Rocky Mountain Montane, and Subalpine forests

461 Pinedrops	*Pterospora andromedea* p. 570	Plant height: 1–3' Flower length: about ¼"

Northwest Coastal, Sierran Montane, and Rocky Mountain Montane forests

462 Mountain Jewel Flower	*Streptanthus tortuosus* p. 570	Plant height: 8–40" Flower length: ½"

Sierran Montane Forest

463 Long-tailed Wild Ginger

Asarum caudatum
p. 571

Creeper
Flower width: 1½–5"

Northwest Coastal, Sierran Montane, and Rocky Mountain Montane forests

464 Vase Flower

Clematis hirsutissima
p. 571

Plant height: 8–24"
Flower length: about 1"

Rocky Mountain Montane Forest and Pinyon-juniper Woodlands

465 Spotted Coral Root

Corallorhiza maculata
p. 572

Plant height: 8–32"
Flower width: about ¾"

Northwest Coastal, Sierran Montane, Rocky Mountain Montane, and Subalpine forests

466 Western Peony

Paeonia brownii
p. 572

Plant height: 8–24"
Flower width: 1–1½"

Sierran Montane and Rocky
Mountain Montane forests;
Pinyon-juniper
Woodlands; and Chaparral

467 Mission Bells

Fritillaria lanceolata
p. 572

Plant height: 1–4'
Flower length: ¾–1½"

Northwest Coastal, Sierran
Montane, and Rocky
Mountain Montane forests;
Oak Woodlands; and
Chaparral

468 Clustered Lady's Slipper

Cypripedium fasciculatum
p. 573

Plant height: 2–8"
Flower width: about 1½"

Northwest Coastal, Sierran
Montane, and Rocky
Mountain Montane forests

469 Roseroot	*Sedum rosea* *p. 573*	Plant height: 1¼–12″ Flower length: about ⅛″

Subalpine Forest

470 California Ground Cone	*Boschniakia strobilacea* *p. 574*	Plant height: 4–10″ Flower length: about ⅝″

Northwest Coastal Forest,
Oak Woodlands, and
Chaparral

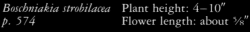

471 Freckled Milkvetch	*Astragalus lentigenosus* *p. 574*	Plant height: 4–16″ Flower length: ⅜–¾″

Sierran Montane, Rocky
Mountain Montane, and
Subalpine forests; Pinyon-
juniper Woodlands

472 Giant Red Paintbrush

Castilleja miniata
p. 574

Plant height: 1–3'
Flower length: ¾–1½"

Northwest Coastal, Sierran
Montane, Rocky Mountain
Montane, and Subalpine
forests

473 Red Clintonia

Clintonia andrewsiana
p. 575

Plant height: 10–20"
Flower length: about ½"

Northwest Coastal Forest

474 Cardinal Flower

Lobelia cardinalis
p. 575

Plant height: 1–3'
Flower length: 1–1½"

Pinyon-juniper Woodlands
and Chaparral

| 475 California Fuchsia | *Zauschneria californica* p. 576 | Plant height: 1–3′ Flower length: 1½–2½″ |

Sierran Montane Forest, Oak Woodlands, and Chaparral

| 476 Scarlet Bugler | *Penstemon centranthifolius* p. 576 | Plant height: 1–4′ Flower length: 1–1¼″ |

Oak Woodlands and Chaparral

| 477 Skyrocket | *Ipomopsis aggregata* p. 577 | Plant height: 6–84″ Flower length: ¾–1¼″ |

Northwest Coastal, Sierran Montane, Rocky Mountain Montane, and Subalpine forests; Pinyon-juniper Woodlands

478 Candystick

Allotropa virgata
p. 577

Plant height: 4–12"
Flower length: about ¼"

Northwest Coastal and
Sierran Montane forests

479 Showy Thistle

Cirsium pastoris
p. 577

Plant height: 2–4'
Flower length: 1½–2½"

Sierran Montane Forest and
Woodlands

480 Snow Plant

Sarcodes sanguinea
p. 578

Plant height: 8–24"
Flower length: ½–¾"

Sierran Montane Forest

481 Rocky Mountain Lily   *Lilium philadelphicum*   Plant height: 12–28″
p. 578   Flower width: 2–2½″

Rocky Mountain Montane and Subalpine forests

482 Scarlet Fritillary   *Fritillaria recurva*   Plant height: 1–3′
p. 578   Flower length: ¾–1¼″

Oak Woodlands

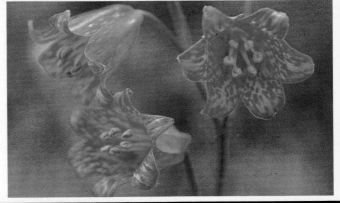

483 Red Columbine   *Aquilegia formosa*   Plant height: 6–36″
p. 579   Flower width: about 2″

Northwest Coastal, Sierran Montane, Rocky Mountain Montane, and Subalpine forests

484 Twinflower *Linnaea borealis* Creeper
p. 579 Flower length: about ½″

Northwest Coastal, Sierran
Montane, and Rocky
Mountain Montane forests

485 Few-flowered *Dodecatheon pulchellum* Plant height: 4–24″
Shooting Star p. 579 Flower length: ¾–1″

Northwest Coastal, Rocky
Mountain Montane, and
Subalpine forests; Pinyon-
juniper Woodlands

486 Western Bleeding *Dicentra formosa* Plant height: 8–18″
Heart p. 580 Flower length: about ¾″

Northwest Coastal Forest

487 Fairy Slipper

Calypso bulbosa
p. 580

Plant height: to 8"
Flower length: about 1¼"

Northwest Coastal and
Rocky Mountain Montane
forests

488 American Vetch

Vicia americana
p. 581

Plant height: 2–4'
Flower length: ½–1¼"

Northwest Coastal, Sierran
Montane, and Rocky
Mountain Montane forests;
Woodlands; and Chaparral

489 Purple Loco

Oxytropis lambertii
p. 581

Plant height: 4–16"
Flower length: ½–1"

Rocky Mountain Montane
Forest and Pinyon-juniper
Woodlands

| 490 Great Hedge Nettle | *Stachys cooleyae* p. 582 | Plant height: 2–5′ Flower length: 5/8–1″ |

Northwest Coastal Forest

| 491 Common Owl's Clover | *Orthocarpus purpuracens* p. 582 | Plant height: 4–16″ Flower length: 1–1 1/4″ |

Woodlands

| 492 Elephant Head | *Pedicularis groenlandica* p. 582 | Plant height: to 28″ Flower length: about 1/2″ |

Subalpine Forest

493 Fireweed

Epilobium angustifolium
p. 583

Plant height: 2–7'·
Flower length: ½–¾"

Northwest Coastal, Sierran
Montane, Rocky Mountain
Montane, and Subalpine
forests

494 Scarlet Gaura

Gaura coccinea
p. 583

Plant height: usually 6–24"
Flower width: about ½"

Pinyon-juniper Woodlands

495 Balloon Flower

Penstemon palmeri
p. 584

Plant height: 2–7'
Flower length: 1–1½"

Rocky Mountain Montane
Forest and Pinyon-juniper
Woodlands

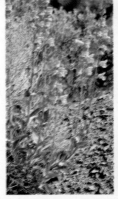

Oak Woodlands

Subalpine Forest

Northwest Coastal and
Sierran Montane forests

499 Mountain Globemallow	*Iliamna rivularis* p. 585	Plant height: 3–7' Flower width: 1–2"

Rocky Mountain Montane Forest

500 Little Pipsissewa	*Chimaphila menziesii* p. 586	Plant height: 2–6" Flower width: about ½"

Northwest Coastal and Sierran Montane forests

501 Western Starflower	*Trientalis latifolia* p. 586	Plant height: 4–10" Flower width: about ½"

Northwest Coastal, Sierran Montane, and Rocky Mountain Montane forests

502 Mustang Clover   *Linanthus montanus*   Plant height: 4–24"
p. 587   Flower width: about ¾"

Oak Woodlands

503 Red Maids   *Calandrinia ciliata*   Plant height: 2–16"
p. 587   Flower width about ½"

Oak Woodlands

504 Indian Pink   *Silene californica*   Plant height: 6–16"
p. 587   Flower width: 1–1½"

Sierran Montane Forest and
Oak Woodlands

505 Showy Daisy — *Erigeron speciosus* — p. 588 — Plant height: 1–3' — Flower width: 1½–2"

Northwest Coastal and Rocky Mountain Montane forests

506 Leafy-bract Aster — *Aster foliaceus* — p. 588 — Plant height: 8–20" — Flower width: 1–2"

Northwest Coastal, Sierran Montane, Rocky Mountain Montane, and Subalpine forests

507 Hooker's Onion — *Allium acuminatum* — p. 589 — Plant height: 4–12" — Flower length: about ½"

Northwest Coastal, Sierran Montane, Rocky Mountain Montane, and Subalpine forests

| 508 Redwood Sorrel | *Oxalis oregana* | Plant height: 2–7″ |
| | *p. 589* | Flower width: ½–¾″ |

Northwest Coastal Forest

509 Spreading Dogbane	*Apocynum*	Plant height: 8–20″
	androsaemifolium	Flower length: ¼–⅜″
	p. 589	

Northwest Coastal, Sierran
Montane, and Rocky
Mountain Montane forests

| 510 Cliff Penstemon | *Penstemon rupicola* | Creeper |
| | *p. 590* | Flower length: 1–1½″ |

Northwest Coastal, Sierran
Montane, and Subalpine
forests

511 Farewell to Spring	*Clarkia amoena* *p. 590*	Plant height: 6–36" Flower width: ¾–1½"

Oak Woodlands

512 Pussy Paws	*Calyptridium* *umbellatum* *p. 591*	Creeper Flower length: to ½"

Sierran Montane, Rocky
Mountain Montane, and
Subalpine forests

513 Bitterroot	*Lewisia rediviva* *p. 591*	Plant height: ½–2" Flower width: 1½–2½"

Rocky Mountain Montane
Forest and Pinyon-juniper
Woodlands

| 514 Colorado Four O'Clock | *Mirabilis multiflora* p. 591 | Plant height: to 18″ Flower width: about 1″ |

Pinyon-juniper Woodlands

| 515 Tufted Phlox | *Phlox caespitosa* p. 592 | Plant height: 2–6″ Flower width: ½–¾″ |

Rocky Mountain Montane Forest and Pinyon-juniper Woodlands

| 516 Baby Blue Eyes | *Nemophila menziesii* p. 592 | Plant height: 4–12″ Flower width: ½–1½″ |

Oak Woodlands and Chaparral

| 517 Hound's Tongue | *Cynoglossum grande* p. 592 | Plant height: 12–32″ Flower width: about ½″ |

Northwest Coastal Forest
and Oak Woodlands

| 518 Blue Violet | *Viola adunca* p. 593 | Plant height: to 4″ Flower width: ½–¾″ |

Northwest Coastal, Sierran
Montane, and Rocky
Mountain Montane forests

| 519 Blue-eyed Grass | *Sisyrinchium angustifolium* p. 593 | Plant height: 4–20″ Flower width: ½–1½″ |

Northwest Coastal, Sierran
Montane, and Rocky
Mountain Montane forests;
Oak Woodlands

| 520 Western Blue Flax | *Linum perenne*
p. 594 | Plant height: 6–32″
Flower width: ¾–1½″ |

Northwest Coastal, Sierran
Montane, and Rocky
Mountain Montane forests;
Woodlands

| 521 Cusick's Speedwell | *Veronica cusickii*
p. 594 | Plant height: 2–8″
Flower width: about ½″ |

Subalpine Forest

| 522 Western
Polemonium | *Polemonium occidentale*
p. 594 | Plant height: 1–3′
Flower width: ½–¾″ |

Northwest Coastal, Sierran
Montane, and Rocky
Mountain Montane forests

| 523 Blue Anemone | *Anemone oregana* p.` 595 | Plant height: 4–12″ Flower width: 1–1½″ |

Northwest Coastal Forest

| 524 Common Camas | *Camassia quamash* p. 595 | Plant height: 12–20″ Flower width: 1½–2½″ |

Northwest Coastal, Sierran Montane, and Rocky Mountain Montane forests

| 525 Felwort | *Swertia perennis* p. 595 | Plant height: 2–20″ Flower width: about ¾″ |

Northwest Coastal, Sierran Montane, Rocky Mountain Montane, and Subalpine forests

526 Nuttall's Larkspur | *Delphinium nuttallianum* p. 596 | Plant height: 4–16" Flower width: about 1"

Sierran Montane and Rocky Mountain Montane forests; Pinyon-juniper Woodlands

527 Douglas' Iris | *Iris douglasiana* p. 596 | Plant height: 6–32" Flower width: 3–4"

Northwest Coastal Forest and Oak Woodlands

528 Tough-leaved Iris | *Iris tenax* p. 597 | Plant height: to 16" Flower width: 3–4"

Northwest Coastal and Sierran Montane forests; Oak Woodlands

| 529 Western Dayflower | *Commelina dianthifolia* p. 597 | Plant height: to 20″ Flower width: about ¾″ |

Rocky Mountain Montane Forest and Pinyon-juniper Woodlands

| 530 Western Monkshood | *Aconitum columbianum* p. 598 | Plant height: 1–7′ Flower length: ⅝–1¼″ |

Northwest Coastal, Sierran Montane, Rocky Mountain Montane, and Subalpine forests

| 531 Maiden Blue-eyed Mary | *Collinsia parviflora* p. 598 | Plant height: 2–16″ Flower width: about ¼″ |

Northwest Coastal, Rocky Mountain Montane, and Subalpine forests; Woodlands

532 Roundleaf Bluebell

Campanula rotundifolia
p. 599

Plant height: 4–40″
Flower length: ½–1″

Northwest Coastal, Rocky Mountain Montane, and Subalpine forests

533 Explorer's Gentian

Gentiana calycosa
p. 599

Plant height: 2–12″
Flower length: 1–1½″

Northwest Coastal, Sierran Montane, Rocky Mountain Montane, and Subalpine forests

534 Mountain Bluebell

Mertensia ciliata
p. 599

Plant height: 6–60″
Flower length: ½–¾″

All western conifer forests

535 Coyote Mint

*Monardella
odoratissima*
p. 600

Plant height: 6–14"
Flower length: ⅜"

Sierran Montane, Rocky
Mountain Montane, and
Subalpine forests; Pinyon-
juniper Woodlands

536 Rydberg's Penstemon

Penstemon rydbergii
p. 600

Plant height: 8–24"
Flower length: ½–¾"

Sierran Montane, Rocky
Mountain Montane, and
Subalpine forests

537 Snow Queen

Synthyris reniformis
p. 601

Plant height: to 6"
Flower length: about ¼"

Northwest Coastal Forest

538 Blue-pod Lupine
Lupinus polyphyllus
p. 601

Plant height: 2–5′
Flower length: about ½″

Northwest Coastal, Sierran
Montane, and Rocky
Mountain Montane forests

539 Cascade Penstemon
Penstemon serrulatus
p. 601

Plant height: 8–28″
Flower length: ¾–1″

Northwest Coastal Forest

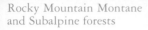

540 Silky Phacelia
Phacelia sericea
p. 602

Plant height: to 16″
Flower length: about ¼″

Rocky Mountain Montane
and Subalpine forests

541 Phoebus Parnassian

Parnassius phoebus
p. 604

Wingspan: 2⅛–3"

All western conifer forests

Host Plants
Stonecrops (*Sedum lanceolatum, S. obtusatum,* and perhaps other species of *Sedum*)

542 Northern Blue

Lycaeides argyrognomon
p. 604

Wingspan: ⅞–1¼"

Subalpine Forest

Host Plants
Lupines (*Lupinus*), crowberry (*Empetrum*), and laurel (*Kalmia*) among others

543 Ruddy Copper

Chalceria rubidus
p. 605

Wingspan: 1⅛–1¼"

All western conifer forests

Host Plants
Wild rhubarb (*Rumex hymenosepnalus*), dock (*R. triangularis*), and others

544 Nelson's Hairstreak

Mitoura nelsoni
p. 605

Wingspan: ⅞–1″

Northwest Coastal, Sierran
Montane, and Rocky
Mountain Montane forests;
Pinyon-juniper Woodlands

Host Plants
Incense cedar (*Libocedrus
decurrens*) and other
members of the cypress
family

545 Northern Blue

Lycaeides argyrognomon
p. 604

Wingspan: ⅞–1¼″

Subalpine Forest

Host Plants
Lupines (*Lupinus*),
crowberry (*Empetrum*), and
laurel (*Kalmia*) among
others

546 Queen Alexandra's Sulphur

Colias alexandra
p. 606

Wingspan: 1½–1⅞″

Rocky Mountain Montane
and Subalpine forests

Host Plants
Golden pea (*Thermopsis*)
and many other legumes

547 Northwest Ringlet   *Coenonympha ampelos*   Wingspan: 1–1⅞"
p. 606

Northwest Coastal, Rocky
Mountain Montane, and
Subalpine forests;
Woodlands

Host Plants
Grasses (Poaceae)

548 Common Alpine   *Erebia epipsodea*   Wingspan: 1¾–2"
p. 607

Rocky Mountain Montane
and Subalpine forests

Host Plants
Grasses (Poaceae)

549 Common Alpine   *Erebia epipsodea*   Wingspan: 1¾–2"
p. 607

Rocky Mountain Montane
and Subalpine forests

Host Plants
Grasses (Poaceae)

550 Large Wood Nymph
Cercyonis pegala
p. 607

Wingspan: 2–2⅞"

Sierran Montane and Rocky
Mountain Montane forests;
Woodlands

Host Plants
Grasses (Poaceae)

551 Large Wood Nymph
Cercyonis pegala
p. 607

Wingspan: 2–2⅞"

Sierran Montane and Rocky
Mountain Montane forests;
Woodlands

Host Plants
Grasses (Poaceae)

552 Chryxus Arctic
Oeneis chryxus
p. 608

Wingspan: 1¾–2"

Northwest Coastal, Sierran
Montane, Rocky Mountain
Montane, and Subalpine
forests; Woodlands

Host Plants
Grasses (Poaceae), possibly
Idaho fescue (*Festuca
idahoensis*) in Washington

553 Anicia Checkerspot
Occidryas anicia
p. 609
Wingspan: 1⅛–1⅞″

Sierran Montane, Rocky Mountain Montane, and Subalpine forests

Host Plants
Indian paintbrush (*Castilleja*), beardtongue (*Penstemon*), other plants in several families: figworts (Scrophulariaceae), plantain (Plantaginaceae), borage (Boraginaceae)

554 Lorquin's Admiral
Basilarchia lorquini
p. 609
Wingspan: 2¼–2¾″

Northwest Coastal, Sierran Montane, Rocky Mountain Montane, and Subalpine forests; Woodlands

Host Plants
Willows (*Salix*), poplars (*Populus*), chokecherry (*Prunus virginiana*), and others

555 California Sister
Adelpha bredowii
p. 610
Wingspan: 2⅞–3⅜″

Northwest Coastal and Sierran Montane forests; Woodlands; Chaparral

Host Plants
Canyon live oak (*Quercus chrysolepis*) and coast live oak (*Q. agrifolia*), perhaps giant chinkapin (*Chrysolepis chrysophylla*)

556 Western Tiger Swallowtail

Pterourus rutulus
p. 611

Wingspan: 2¾–3⅞"

All western forests and woodlands

Host Plants
Willows, poplars, and aspens (Salicaceae), several alders (*Alnus*), sycamores (Platanaceae), and others

557 Pine White

Neophasia menapia
p. 611

Wingspan: 1¾–2"

All western forests; Pinyon-juniper Woodlands

Host Plants
Pines (*Pinus*), true firs (*Abies*), and Douglas-fir (*Pseudotsuga*)

558 Queen Alexandra's Sulphur

Colias alexandra
p. 606

Wingspan: 1½–1⅞"

Rocky Mountain Montane and Subalpine forests

Host Plants
Golden pea (*Thermopsis*) and many other legumes

559 Faunus Anglewing
Polygonia faunus
p. 612
Wingspan: 1⅞–2″

Northwest Coastal, Sierran Montane, Rocky Mountain Montane, and Subalpine forests; Woodlands

Host Plants
Birch (*Betula*), alder (*Alnus*), willow (*Salix*), currant (*Ribes*), perhaps wild rhododendron and azalea (*Rhododendron*) in West

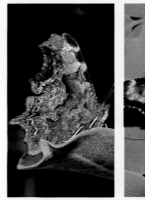

560 California Tortoiseshell
Nymphalis californica
p. 613
Wingspan: 1⅞–2⅜″

Northwest Coastal, Sierran Montane, Rocky Mountain Montane, and Subalpine forests; Woodlands

Host Plants
Buckthorns (*Ceanothus*); probably also other plants

561 Milbert's Tortoiseshell
Aglais milberti
p. 613
Wingspan: 1¾–2″

Northwest Coastal, Sierran Montane, Rocky Mountain Montane, and Subalpine forests; Woodlands

Host Plants
Nettles (*Urtica*)

562 Great Spangled Fritillary

Speyeria cybele
p. 614

Wingspan: 2⅛–3″

Northwest Coastal, Sierran Montane, Rocky Mountain Montane, and Subalpine forests; Woodlands

Host Plants
Violets (*Viola rotundifolia*)

563 Great Spangled Fritillary

Speyeria cybele
p. 614

Wingspan: 2⅛–3″

Northwest Coastal, Sierran Montane, Rocky Mountain Montane, and Subalpine forests; Woodlands

Host Plants
Violets (*Viola rotundifolia*)

564 Anicia Checkerspot

Occidryas anicia
p. 609

Wingspan: 1⅛–1⅞″

Sierran Montane, Rocky Mountain Montane, and Subalpine forests

Host Plants
Indian paintbrush (*Castilleja*), beardtongue (*Penstemon*), other plants in several families: figworts (Scrophulariaceae), plantain (Plantaginaceae), borage (Boraginaceae)

565 Golden Buprestid

Buprestis aurulenta
p. 616

Length: ½–¾"

All western conifer forests

Food
Pollen, nectar, and some foliage; larva feeds on the wood of conifers

566 Pine and Spruce Engraver Beetles

Ips spp.
p. 616

Length: ⅛–¼"

All western conifer forests

Food
Cambium bark and phloem tissues of inner bark

567 Bark Beetles

Scolytus spp.
p. 616

Length: ⅛–¼"

Northwest Coastal, Sierran Montane, Rocky Mountain Montane, and Subalpine forests

Food
Inner bark of various trees

All western forests and
woodlands

Food
Aquatic insects

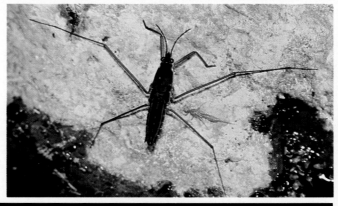

All western forests and
woodlands

Food
Small, soft-bodied insects;
naiad preys on aquatic
insects

Northwest Coastal and
Sierran Montane forests;
Woodlands

Food
Flying insects; naiad eats
small insects, tadpoles,
worms

571 Short-tailed Ichneumons

Ophion spp.
p. 618

Length: ⅜–¾"

All western forests and woodlands

Food
Nectar; larva eats internal tissues of some caterpillars

572 California Oak Gall Wasp

Andricus quercuscalifornicus
p. 618

Length: ⅛–¼"

Oak Woodlands

Food
Adult may not eat; larva feeds on soft tissues inside large galls on oak twigs

573 Giant Carpenter Ant

Camponotus laevigatus
p. 619

Length: ⅝"

All western forests

Food
Other insects, honeydew, fruit juices, grains of sugar, and other sweets

Northwest Coastal, Sierran
Montane, Rocky Mountain
Montane, and Subalpine
forests

Food
Male drinks plant juices;
female takes blood of
mammals and birds

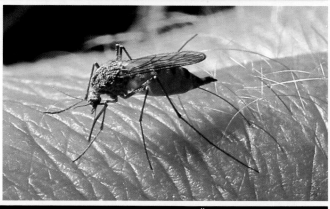

All western conifer forests

Food
Male and female feed on
nectar; female sucks blood
from birds and mammals

All western conifer forests

Food
Male drinks plant juices;
female sucks blood from
mammals

577 Yellow Jackets

Vespula spp.
p. 620

Length: ½–⅝"

All western conifer forests

Food
Nectar; larva feeds on
insects pre-chewed by
adults

578 Golden Northern Bumble Bee

Bombus fervidus
p. 621

Length: ⅜–⅝" (male drones); ½–¾"
(workers); ¾–⅞" (queen)

All western forests and
woodlands

Food
Nectar and honey

579 Wood Ticks

Dermacentor spp.
p. 621

Length: ¼"

Sierran Montane and Rocky
Mountain Montane forests;
Woodlands

Food
Larger animals and blood
of mammals, especially
deer

580 Forest Wolf Spider

Lycosa gulosa
p. 621

Length: ⅜" (males); ⅜–½" (females)

Rocky Mountain Montane
Forest

Food
Small insects

581 Orb Weavers

Araneus spp.
p. 622

Length: ¼" (males); ⅜–¾" (females)

All western forests and
woodlands

Food
Insects

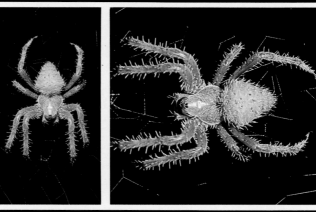

582 Golden Huntsman Spider

Olios fasciculatus
p. 622

Length: ½–⅝" (males); ¾–⅞"
(females)

Sierran Montane and Rocky
Mountain Montane forests;
Woodlands; Chaparral

Food
Insects

Rocky Mountain Montane Forest

Northwest Coastal and Sierran Montane forests; Woodlands

Northwest Coastal and Rocky Mountain Montane forests; Woodlands

586 Plateau Striped Whiptail

Cnemidophorus velox
p. 625

Length: 8–10¾"

Rocky Mountain Montane Forest and Woodlands

587 Western Skink

Eumeces skiltonianus
p. 626

Length: 6½–9⁵⁄₁₆"

Northwest Coastal, Sierran Montane, and Rocky Mountain Montane forests; Woodlands

588 Striped Whipsnake

Masticophis taeniatus
p. 626

Length: 40–72"

Rocky Mountain Montane Forest, Woodlands, and Chaparral

589 Striped Racer   *Masticophis lateralis*   Length: 30–60″
p. 627

Sierran Montane Forest,
Woodlands, and Chaparral

590 Ringneck Snake   *Diadophis punctatus*   Length: 10–30″
p. 627

Northwest Coastal, Sierran
Montane, and Rocky
Mountain Montane forests;
Woodlands

591 California Mountain   *Lampropeltis zonata*   Length: 20–40″
Kingsnake   *p. 628*

Northwest Coastal and
Sierran Montane forests;
Woodlands

592 Sonoran Mountain Kingsnake	*Lampropeltis pyromelana* p. 629	Length: 20–41"

Rocky Mountain Montane Forest, Woodlands, and Chaparral

593 California Kingsnake	*Lampropeltis getulus californiae* p. 630	Length: 36–82"

Sierran Montane Forest, Woodlands, and Chaparral

594 California Red-sided Garter Snake	*Thamnophis sirtalis infernalis* p. 630	Length: 18–51⅝"

Northwest Coastal Forest and Woodlands

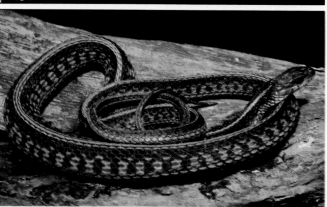

595 Wandering Garter Snake

Thamnophis elegans vagrans
p. 630

Length: 18–42"

Northwest Coastal, Sierran Montane, Rocky Mountain Montane, and Subalpine forests; Woodlands; Chaparral

596 Gopher Snake

Pituophis melanoleucus
p. 631

Length: 48–100"

Rocky Mountain Montane and Sierran Montane forests; Woodlands; Chaparral

597 Northern Pacific Rattlesnake

Crotalus viridis oreganus
p. 632

Length: 16–64"

⊗

Most western forests and woodlands

598 Sharp-tailed Snake	*Contia tenuis*	Length: 10–19″
	p. 632	

Northwest Coastal and
Sierran Montane forests;
Woodlands

599 Rubber Boa	*Charina bottae*	Length: 14–33″
	p. 632	

Northwest Coastal, Sierran
Montane, Rocky Mountain
Montane, and Subalpine
forests

600 Western Yellowbelly Racer	*Coluber constrictor mormon*	Length: 34–77″
	p. 633	

Northwest Coastal, Sierran
Montane, and Rocky
Mountain Montane forests;
Woodlands

601 Roughskin Newt   *Taricha granulosa*   Length: 5–8½"
p. 633

Northwest Coastal Forest

602 California Newt   *Taricha torosa*   Length: 5–7¾"
p. 634

Sierran Montane Forest and
Woodlands

**603 Arboreal
Salamander**   *Aneides lugubris*   Length: 4¼–7¼"
p. 635

Sierran Montane Forest and
Oak Woodlands

604 Oregon Ensatina

Ensatina eschscholtzi oregonensis
p. 635

Length: 3–5⅞"

Northwest Coastal and
Sierran Montane forests;
Woodlands

605 Olympic Salamander

Rhyacotriton olympicus
p. 636

Length: 3–4⅝"

Northwest Coastal Forest

606 Long-toed Salamander

Ambystoma macrodactylum
p. 636

Length: 4–6⅜"

Northwest Coastal, Rocky
Mountain Montane, and
Subalpine forests

Northwest Coastal Forest

Northwest Coastal and
Rocky Mountain Montane
forests

Rocky Mountain Montane
and Subalpine forests;
Pinyon-juniper Woodland

| 610 Mountain Yellow-legged Frog | *Rana muscosa* p. 638 | Length: 2–3¼" |

Sierran Montane and Subalpine forests

| 611 Red-legged Frog | *Rana aurora* p. 639 | Length: 2–5⅜" |

Northwest Coastal and Sierran Montane forests; Woodlands

| 612 Spotted Frog | *Rana pretiosa* p. 639 | Length: 2–4" |

Northwest Coastal, Rocky Mountain Montane, and Subalpine forests

| **613 Cascades Frog** | *Rana cascadae* p. 640 | Length: 1¾–2⁵⁄₁₆″ |

Northwest Coastal and
Subalpine forests

| **614 Foothill Yellow-legged Frog** | *Rana boylei* p. 640 | Length: 1⅝–3″ |

Sierran Montane Forest and
Woodlands

| **615 Tailed Frog** | *Ascaphus truei* p. 641 | Length: 1–2″ |

Northwest Coastal and
Rocky Mountain Montane
forests

616 Northern Leopard Frog
Rana pipiens
p. 641
Length: 2–5″

Rocky Mountain Montane and Subalpine forests

617 Western Toad
Bufo boreas
p. 642
Length: 2½–5″

Northwest Coastal, Sierran Montane, Rocky Mountain Montane, and Subalpine forests; Woodlands

618 Pacific Treefrog
Hyla regilla
p. 642
Length: ¾–2″

Northwest Coastal, Sierran Montane, and Rocky Mountain Montane forests; Woodlands

TREES AND SHRUBS

A walk through any of the forests of the West will reveal a diverse assortment of trees and shrubs. Some—like the majestic Sequoias and Redwoods—are themselves reason enough to visit the forests; others, such as the wide variety of pines that grow in these forests, are less well known but equally fascinating. The descriptions included here are of typical trees and shrubs of the West.

Jeffrey Pine
Pinus jeffreyi
37, 126

Large tree with straight axis and open, conical crown of spreading branches and with large cones. Both bark and twigs give off odor of lemon or vanilla when crushed.
Height: 80–130' (24–39 m). Diameter: 2–4' (0.6–1.2 m), sometimes much larger.
Needles: evergreen; 3 in bundle: 5–10" (13–25 cm) long. Stout, stiff; light gray-green or blue-green, with broad white lines on all surfaces.
Bark: dark reddish brown, thick, furrowed into scaly plates.
Twigs: stout, hairless, gray-green with whitish bloom, smooth.
Cones: 5–10" (13–25 cm) long; conical or egg-shaped, light reddish brown, almost stalkless; opening and shedding at maturity, leaving a few cone-scales on twig; cone-scales numerous, raised, and keeled, ending in long prickle.

Habitat
Dry slopes of mountains, especially on soils derived from lava, serpentine, and granite; best developed on deep, well-drained soils; often forming pure stands and with other conifers.

Range
SW. Oregon south through the Sierra Nevada (especially eastern slopes) to W. Nevada and S. California; also N. Baja California; mostly at 6000–9000' (1829–2743 m); less frequently down to 3500' (1067 m) and up to 10,000' (3048 m).

Comments
This pine can be told from the very similar Ponderosa Pine by its more reddish bark and, mainly, by its much larger, less prickly-feeling cones. The scent of crushed twigs has been likened to the scent of lemons, vanilla, violets, pineapples, and apples.

Ponderosa Pine
Pinus ponderosa
38

Large to very large tree with broad, open, conical crown of spreading branches; 3 distinct geographic varieties.
Height: 60–130' (18–39 m). Diameter: 2½–4' (0.8–1.2 m), sometimes larger.
Needles: evergreen; usually 3 in bundle (2–5 in varieties); generally 4–8" (10–20 cm) long. Stout, stiff, dark green.
Bark: yellowish or reddish brown and irregularly furrowed into large, flat, scaly plates; on young trees, blackish, rough, and furrowed into ridges.
Cones: 2–6" (5–15 cm) long; conical or egg-shaped, almost stalkless, light reddish brown; opening and shedding at maturity, leaving a few cone-scales on twig; cone-scales raised and keeled, end in sharp prickle: small, long-winged seeds.

Habitat
Mostly in mountains in pure stands, forming extensive forests; also in mixed coniferous forests.

Range
Widely distributed; S. British Columbia east to SW. North

Dakota, south to Trans-Pecos Texas, and west to S. California; also northern Mexico; from sea level in north to 9000' (2743 m) in south; the best developed stands at 4000–8000' (1219–2438 m).

Comments
This is the most widely distributed and common pine in North America. Arizona Pine or Arizona Ponderosa Pine (var. *arizonica*), occurring mainly in southeastern Arizona, has 5 slender needles in a bundle. David Douglas, the Scottish botanical explorer, found the Ponderosa Pine in 1826 and named it for its ponderous, or heavy, wood. This valuable timber tree is the most commercially important western pine.

Southwestern White Pine
Pinus strobiformis
39

Tree with straight trunk and narrow, conical crown of horizontal branches.
Height: 50–80' (15–24 m). Diameter: 1½–3' (0.5–0.9 m).
Needles: evergreen; 5 in bundle, sheath shedding first year; 2½–3½" (6–9 cm) long. Slender, finely toothed at least near tip; bright green, with white lines on inner surfaces only.
Bark: gray and smooth; becoming dark gray or brown and deeply furrowed into narrow, irregular ridges.
Cones: 6–9" (15–23 cm) long; cylindrical, yellow-brown, short-stalked; opening at maturity; cone-scales slightly thickened, very long, the thin, narrow tip spreading and curved back; seeds large, edible, very short-winged.

Habitat
Dry, rocky slopes and canyons in high mountains; a minor component of coniferous forests.

Range

Trans-Pecos Texas west to east-central Arizona; also northern Mexico; at 6500–10,000' (1981–3048 m).

Comments
The large seeds are consumed by wildlife and were eaten by Southwestern Indians. This species of the Mexican border region was formerly considered a southern variety of Limber Pine.

Lodgepole Pine
Pinus contorta
40

Widely distributed pine that may grow tall with narrow, dense, conical crown, or remain small with broad, rounded crown; 3 geographic varieties.
Height: 20–80' (6–24 m). Diameter: 1–3' (0.3–0.9 m).
Needles: evergreen; 2 in bundle; 1¼–2¾" (3–7 cm) long. Stout, slightly flattened and often twisted; yellow-green to dark green.
Bark: light brown, thin, and scaly; or in Shore Pine (the coastal variety), dark brown, thick, furrowed into scaly plates.
Cones: ¾–2" (2–5 cm) long; egg-shaped, stalkless, oblique or 1-sided at base, shiny yellow-brown; remaining closed on tree many years (or in varieties opening); cone-scales raised, rounded, keeled, with tiny, slender prickle.

Habitat
High mountains, mostly on marginal or disturbed sites, often in pure stands; Shore Pine on rocky shores and in peat bogs, muskegs, and dry, sandy sites.

Range
SE. Alaska and central Yukon south on Pacific Coast to N. California, south through Sierra Nevada to S. California, and south in Rocky Mountains to S. Colorado; also local in Black Hills of South Dakota and N. Baja California; coastal variety from sea level to 2000′ (610 m); inland varieties at 1500–3000′ (457–914 m) in north and at 7000–11,500′ (2134–3505 m) in south.

Comments
Lodgepole Pine is one of the most widely distributed New World pines and the only conifer native in both Alaska and Mexico. Its name refers to the use by American Indians of the slender trunks as poles for their conical tents or teepees. Shore Pine (var. *contorta*), the Pacific Coast variety, is a small tree with spreading crown, thick, furrowed bark, short leaves, and oblique cones pointing backward, opening at maturity but remaining attached. Also known as Shore Pine.

Foxtail Pine
Pinus balfouriana
41

Pine with very short needles crowded against twigs suggesting a foxtail, and irregular crown of short, spreading branches; a shrub at timberline.
Height: 20–50′ (6–15 m). Diameter: 1–2″ (0.3–0.6 m).
Needles: evergreen; 5 in bundle, with sheath shedding after first year; ¾–1½″ (2–4 cm) long. Crowded in long, dense mass curved against twig; stout, sharp-pointed; dark green, with white lines on inner surfaces; persisting 10–20 years.
Bark: whitish gray and smooth, becoming reddish brown and deeply furrowed into irregular ridges.
Cones: 3½–5″ (9–13 cm) long; cylindrical but tapering, almost stalkless, dark reddish brown; opening at maturity; thick, 4-sided cone-scales, with tiny prickle. Purple, mottled seeds more than ¼″ (6 mm) long; wing about ⅞″ (22 mm), remaining attached.

Habitat
Exposed, dry, rocky slopes and ridges of high mountains in subalpine zone to timberline.

Range
Local in Klamath Mountains of N. California and Sierra Nevada of east-central California; at 6000–11,500′ (1829–3505 m).

Comments
Foxtail Pine is closely related to Bristlecone Pine, which is sometimes also called Foxtail Pine because of the similar foliage. Their ranges, however, do not overlap. Foxtail Pine is the characteristic timberline tree of the southern Sierra Nevada.

Bristlecone Pine
Pinus aristata
42, 130

Tree with very short needles crowded into mass suggesting a foxtail and a broad, irregular crown of spreading branches; a low shrub at timberline.
Height: 20–40' (6–12 m). Diameter: 1–2½' (0.3–0.8 m).
Needles: evergreen; 5 in bundle, with sheath shedding after first year; ¾–1½" (2–4 cm) long. Crowded in long, dense mass curved against twig; stout, stiff, blunt-pointed; persisting 10–20 years. Dark green, with white lines on inner surfaces; needles often marked with whitish resin dots on outer surface.
Bark: whitish gray, smooth; becoming reddish brown and furrowed into irregular, scaly ridges.
Cones: 2½–3½" (6–9 cm) long; cylindrical, dark purplish brown, almost stalkless; opening at maturity; cone-scales 4-sided, with slender, curved bristle: seeds brown mottled with black and with detachable wing.

Habitat
Exposed, dry, rocky slopes and ridges of high mountains in subalpine zone to timberline; often in pure stands.

Range
Colorado and N. New Mexico west to E. California; at 7500–11,500' (2286–3505 m).

Comments
The oldest known dated living trees are Bristlecone Pines more than 4600 years old, protected at Inyo National Forest near Bishop, in eastern California. Other very old Bristlecone Pines are found at Wheeler Peak Scenic Area, in the Humboldt National Forest of eastern Nevada. Although these trees are classed among the oldest known living things, some shrubs and trees that spread in colonies or clumps from the same root system may be older. The age of a tree is dated by counting the annual rings: wood cells formed in the spring are generally large, while those formed in the summer are smaller; the contrast in cell size is visible as a line.

Red Fir
Abies magnifica
43

Large, handsome fir with an open conical crown rounded at tip and short, nearly horizontal branches.
Height: 60–120' (18–37 m). Diameter: 1–4' (0.3–1.2 m).
Needles: evergreen; spreading in 2 rows; crowded and curved upward on upper twigs; ¾–1⅜" (2–3.5 cm) long. 4-sided, blue-green with whitish lines.
Bark: thick, reddish brown, furrowed into narrow ridges.
Twigs: stout, brown, with fine hairs when young.
Cones: 6–8" (15–20 cm) long; cylindrical, purplish brown, upright on topmost twigs; cone-scales with fine hairs, with yellowish bracts either mostly short and hidden (Shasta Red Fir), or long and exposed (California Red Fir), pointed and finely toothed; paired, long-winged seeds.

Habitat
High mountains with dry summers and deep snow in winter; often in pure stands, also in mixed conifer forests.

Range
Cascade Mountains of SW. Oregon south to Coast Ranges of California and through Sierra Nevada to central California and extreme W. Nevada. At 6000–9000' (1829–2743 m) in south, to 4500' (1372 m) in north.

Comments
Named for its characteristic bark, this magnificent conifer forms almost pure forests. Symmetrical, young trees, with whorls of horizontal branches, are the prized "silvertip firs" of the Christmas tree trade.

Brewer Spruce
Picea brewerana
44

Large tree crowned with long, slender, horizontal branches ending in ropelike, drooping branches; trunk enlarged and buttressed at the base and tapering above.
Height: 70–100' (21–30 m). Diameter: 1½–3' (0.5–0.9 m).
Needles: evergreen; spreading on all sides of twig; ¾–1" (2–2.5 cm) long; flattish; blunt-pointed, 4–6 whitish lines above, shiny dark green beneath.
Bark: reddish brown, thin, scaly.
Twigs: reddish brown, long and slender, finely hairy, rough with peglike leaf bases.
Cones: 2½–4" (6–10 cm) long; cylindrical, short-stalked, dull orange-brown; cone-scales thin, rounded, not toothed; paired, brown, long-winged seeds.

Habitat
High mountain ridges near timberline; with Red Fir and other conifers; seldom in pure stands.

Range
Chiefly in Siskiyou Mountains of SW. Oregon and NW. California; at 3300–7500' (1006–2286 m).

Comments
The weeping habit serves to reduce breakage of branches by heavy snowfall. Rare even as a cultivated ornamental, this local species is found in 5 National Forests and a special preserve, the Brewer Spruce Natural Area.

White Fir
Abies concolor
45

Very large fir, widespread in western mountains, with narrow, pointed crown of short, symmetrical, horizontal branches.
Height: 70–160' (21–49 m). Diameter: 1½–4' (0.5–1.2 m).
Needles: evergreen; spreading almost at right angles in 2 rows; curved upward on upper twigs; 1½–2½" (4–6 cm) long. Flat, flexible, almost stalkless; with tip short-pointed, rounded, or notched. Light blue-green with whitish lines on both surfaces.
Bark: light gray, smooth, becoming very thick near base and deeply furrowed into scaly, corky ridges.
Twigs: light brown or gray; stout, hairless.
Cones: 3–5" (7.5–13 cm) long; cylindrical; greenish, purple or yellow; upright on topmost twigs; cone-scales finely hairy, with short, hidden bracts; paired, long-winged seeds.

Habitat
Moist, rocky mountain soils; in pure stands and with other firs.

Range
Extreme SE. Idaho southeast to New Mexico, west to California, and north to SW. Oregon; local in northwestern Mexico. At 5500–11,000′ (1676–3353 m) in south; to 2000′ (610 m) in north.

Comments
Rocky Mountain White Fir (var. *concolor*), of the Rocky Mountain region, grows in the warmest and driest climate of all native firs. California White Fir (var. *lowiana*), the Pacific Coast variety, is grown for ornament, shade, and Christmas trees. The scientific name, meaning "of uniform color," refers to both needle surfaces. The winged seeds of this and other firs are eaten by songbirds and various mammals, especially squirrels and chipmunks. Deer and grouse feed on the foliage; porcupines gnaw the bark.

Subalpine Fir
Abies lasiocarpa
46

The most widespread western true fir, with dense, long-pointed, spirelike crown and rows of horizontal branches reaching nearly to base; shrubby at timberline.
Height: 50–100′ (15–30 m). Diameter: 1–2½′ (0.3–0.8 m).
Needles: evergreen; spreading almost at right angles in 2 rows; crowded and curved upward on upper twigs; 1–1¾″ (2.5–4.5 cm) long. Flat; dark green, with whitish lines on both surfaces.
Bark: gray, smooth, with resin blisters, becoming fissured and scaly.
Twigs: gray, stout, with rust-colored hairs.
Cones: 2¼–4″ (6–10 cm) long; cylindrical, upright on topmost twigs, dark purple; cone-scales finely hairy with short, hidden bracts; paired, long-winged seeds.

Habitat
Subalpine zone of high mountains to timberline; forming spruce-fir forest with Engelmann Spruce, and with other conifers.

Range
Central Yukon and SE. Alaska southeast to S. New Mexico; at 8000–12,000′ (2438–3658 m) in south; to sea level in north.

Comments
The spires of Subalpine Fir add beauty to subalpine parklands. When weighted down to the ground with snow, the lowest branches sometimes take root, forming new shoots. The bark of this and related firs is browsed by deer, elk, bighorn sheep, and moose; the leaves are eaten by grouse, and the seeds are consumed by songbirds and mammals. The scientific name, meaning "hairy-fruited," refers to the cones. Corkbark Fir (var. *arizonica*), a variety found from Arizona to Colorado, has thin, whitish, corky bark. Also known as Alpine Fir.

Pacific Silver Fir
Abies amabilis
47

Large fir with beautiful, spirelike, conical crown of short,
down-curving branches and flat, fernlike foliage.
Height: 80–150' (24–46 m). Diameter: 2–4' (0.6–1.2 m).
Needles: evergreen; crowded and spreading forward in 2 rows;
curved upward on upper twigs; ¾–1½" (2–4 cm) long. Flat,
shiny dark green and grooved above, silvery white beneath.
Bark: light gray, smooth; becoming scaly and reddish gray or
reddish brown.
Cones: 3–6" (7.5–15 cm) long; cylindrical, upright on
topmost twigs, purple; cone-scales with fine hairs, bracts short
and hidden; paired, long-winged seeds.

Habitat
Cool, wet regions, including coastal fog belt and interior
mountain valleys; in coniferous forests.

Range
Pacific Coast from extreme SE. Alaska south to W. Oregon;
local in NW. California; to 1000' (305 m) in north; to 6000'
(1829 m) in south.

Comments
David Douglas (1798–1834), the Scottish botanical explorer
and discoverer of this species, named it *amabilis,* meaning
"lovely."

Grand Fir
Abies grandis
48

One of the tallest true firs, with narrow, pointed crown of
stout, curved, and slightly drooping branches.
Height: 100–200' (30–61 m). Diameter: 1½–3½'
(0.5–1 m).
Needles: evergreen; spreading almost at right angles in 2
rows; crowded and curved upward on upper twigs; 1¼–2"
(3–5 cm) long. Flat, flexible; shiny dark green above, silvery
white beneath.
Bark: brown; smooth, with resin blisters, becoming deeply
furrowed into narrow scaly ridges.
Twigs: brown; slender, with fine hairs when young.
Cones: 2–4" (5–10 cm) long; cylindrical, upright on topmost
twigs, green or brown; cone-scales hairy, bracts short and
hidden. Paired, long-winged seeds.

Habitat
Valleys and mountain slopes in cool, humid climate; in
coniferous forests.

Range
S. British Columbia south along coast to California; also south
in Rocky Mountain region to central Idaho; to 1500' (457 m)
along coast; to 6000' (1829 m) inland.

Comments
This tree's common and scientific names refer to its large size;
the champion in Olympic National Park, Washington, is 231'
(70.4 m) tall with a circumference of 20'8" (6.3 m). As with
related species, small trunks have swellings or blisters; when
pinched, fragrant, transparent resin or balsam squirts out.

Mountain Hemlock
Tsuga mertensiana
49, 139

Tree with tapering trunk, conical crown of slender horizontal or drooping branches, and very slender, curved, drooping leader; a prostrate shrub at timberline.
Height: 30–100' (9–30 m). Diameter: 1–3' (0.3–0.9 m).
Needles: evergreen; usually crowded at ends of short side twigs; spreading on all sides and curved upward; ¼–1" (0.6–2.5 cm) long. Short-stalked, flattened above, and half-round, stout, and blunt; blue-green, with whitish lines.
Bark: gray to dark brown; thick, furrowed into scaly ridges.
Twigs: light reddish brown, mostly short, slender, finely hairy, rough with peglike bases.
Cones: 1–3" (2.5–7.5 cm) long; cylindrical, purplish turning brown, stalkless, hanging down, with many rounded cone-scales; paired, long-winged seeds.

Habitat
Moist, coarse or rocky soils, from sheltered valleys to exposed ridges; with firs and in mixed coniferous forests.

Range
S. Alaska southeast along Pacific Coast to British Columbia and in mountains to central California; also SE. British Columbia south in Rocky Mountains to N. Idaho and NE. Oregon; to 3500' (1067 m) in Alaska and at 5500–11,000' (1676–3353 m) in south.

Comments
Mountain Hemlock is a characteristic species of high mountains, varying greatly in size from a large tree at low altitudes to a dwarf, creeping shrub at timberline. Hemlock groves provide cover, nesting sites, and seeds for birds, as well as foliage for mountain goats and other hoofed browsers.

Alpine Larch
Larix lyallii
50

Deciduous tree with straight trunk, short branches, and irregular, spreading crown.
Height: 30–50' (9–15 m). Diameter: 1–2' (0.3–0.6 m).
Needles: deciduous; 1–1¼" (2.5–3 cm) long, ¹⁄₃₂" (1 mm) wide. Many crowded in cluster on spur twigs; also alternate and scattered on leader twigs; 4-angled, stiff, short-pointed. Pale blue-green, turning yellow in autumn before shedding.
Bark: dark red-brown, thin, becoming fissured into irregular scaly plates.
Twigs: 2 kinds; long leaders densely covered with whitish hairs, and many short spurs.
Cones: 1½–2" (4–5 cm) long; elliptical, upright, nearly stalkless, composed of many densely hairy, dark reddish-purple cone-scales shorter than dark purple, 3-toothed bracts; paired, brown, long-winged seeds.

Habitat
At timberline on rocky soils in Engelmann Spruce-Subalpine Fir forest; locally in pure stands.

Range
SE. British Columbia and SW. Alberta south to W. Montana

and west to NE. Washington; at 4000–8000' (1219–2438 m).

Comments
Subalpine Larch is seldom seen because of its isolated timberline location in high mountains. For most of the year the branches are bare, except for the blackened dead cones.

Western Larch
Larix occidentalis
51, 131

Very large deciduous tree with narrow, conical crown of horizontal branches.
Height: 80–150' (24–46 m). Diameter: 1½–3' (0.5–0.9 m), sometimes larger.
Needles: deciduous; 1–1½" (2.5–4 cm) long, ⅓₂" (1 mm) wide. Crowded in cluster on spur twigs; also alternate and scattered on leader twigs; 3-angled, stiff, sharp-pointed. Light green, turning yellow in autumn before falling.
Bark: reddish brown, scaly, becoming deeply furrowed into flat ridges with many overlapping plates.
Twigs: 2 kinds; long leaders (orange-brown and hairy when young), and many short spurs.
Cones: 1–1½" (2.5–4 cm) long; elliptical, brown, upright on short stalks; many rounded, hairy cone-scales shorter than long-pointed bracts; paired, pale brown, long-winged seeds.

Habitat
Mountain slopes and valleys on porous, gravelly, sandy, and loamy soils; with other conifers.

Range
SE. British Columbia south to NW. Montana and N. Oregon; at 2000–5500' (610–1676 m) in north; to 7000' (2134 m) in south.

Comments
Western Larch often follows or survives fires, later being replaced by other conifers. The natural sugar, or galactan, in the gum and wood resembles a slightly bitter honey and can be made into medicine and baking powder. Grouse eat the buds and leaves.

Western Yew
Taxus brevifolia
52, 146

Poisonous, nonresinous, evergreen tree with angled trunk often twisted or irregular and with broad crown of slender, horizontal branches; sometimes shrubby.
Height: 50' (15 m). Diameter: 2' (0.6 m).
Needles: evergreen; alternate; spreading in 2 rows; ½–¾" (12–19 mm) long. ¹⁄₁₆" (1.5 mm) or more wide. Flattened, short-pointed at both ends, soft and flexible, short-stalked. Deep yellow-green above, light green with 2 broad, whitish bands beneath.
Bark: purplish brown, very thin, smooth, with red-brown papery scales.
Twigs: green, becoming light brown; slender and slightly drooping, with 2 lines below each leaf.
Seeds and Male Cones: on separate trees. Elliptical seeds ¼"

(6 mm) long; stalkless, blunt-pointed, 2- to 4-angled, brown; nearly enclosed by scarlet cup ⅜" (10 mm) in diameter; soft, juicy, and sweet; scattered and single on leafy twigs. Male or pollen cones ⅛" (3 mm) in diameter; pale yellow, short-stalked, single at leaf bases.

Habitat
Moist soils of stream banks and canyons; in understory of coniferous forests.

Range
Extreme SE. Alaska south along coast to central California; also SE. British Columbia south in Rocky Mountains to central Idaho; from sea level in north to 7000' (2134 m) in south.

Comments
The strong wood has been used for archery bows, poles, canoe paddles, and small cabinetwork. Most parts of yew plants, including seeds and foliage, are poisonous and, if eaten, can be fatal. However, the red, juicy cup around the seed is reported to be edible, provided the poisonous seed is not chewed or swallowed. Birds eat these cups and scatter the seeds.

Coast Redwood
Sequoia sempervirens
53, 141

The world's tallest tree, with reddish-brown trunk much enlarged and buttressed at base and often with rounded swellings or burls and slightly tapering; crown short, narrow, irregular and open with horizontal or drooping branches. Height: 200–325' (61–99 m). Diameter: 10–15' (3–4.6 m), sometimes larger.
Leaves: evergreen; of 2 kinds. Mostly needlelike and unequal, ⅜–¾" (10–19 mm) long; flat and slightly curved; stiff and sharp-pointed, extending down twig at base; dark green above, whitish green beneath; spreading in 2 rows. Leaves on leaders scalelike, as short as ¼" (6 mm); keeled, concave, spreading around twig.
Bark: reddish brown, very tough and fibrous, very thick, deeply furrowed into broad, scaly ridges; inner bark cinnamon-brown.
Twigs: slender, dark green, forking in 1 plane, ending in scaly bud.
Cones: ½–1⅛" (1.2–3 cm) long; elliptical, reddish brown, with many flat, short-pointed cone-scales; hanging down at end of leafy twig; maturing in 1 season; 2–5 seeds under cone-scale, light brown, 2-winged.

Habitat
Foggy but sheltered flats and slopes just inland from coast; best stands on alluvial soils of river benches and floodplains, where it forms pure stands of giant trees.

Range
Extreme SW. Oregon south to central California in fog belt, a coastal strip 5–35 miles (8–56 km) wide; from sea level to 3000' (914 m).

Comments

The world's tallest tree is a Coast Redwood, 368' (112 m) high. The age of these trees at maturity is 400–500 years; the maximum age counted in annual rings is 2200. Circles of trees grow from sprouts around stumps and dead trunks. The genus name commemorates the Indian named Sequoyah (also spelled Sequoia) (1770?–1843), the inventor of the Cherokee alphabet. Existing stands of Coast Redwood occupy only a fraction of the large area in California and Oregon where they originally grew before the arrival of European settlers. Virgin forests remain in several state parks, as well as in the Redwoods National Park and along the Redwoods Highway. But there is still some question concerning the status of the species outside of these parks. The Redwood industry maintains that selective logging, leaving seed trees, and planting in tree farms assure the future of this species. Conservationists feel that every effort should be made to maintain this magnificent tree at its present levels.

Giant Sequoia
Sequoiadendron giganteum
54

One of the world's largest trees with fibrous, reddish-brown trunk much enlarged and buttressed at base, fluted into ridges, and conspicuously narrowed or tapered above; narrow, conical crown of short, stout, horizontal branches reaches nearly to base. Giant trees have tall, bare trunk and irregular, open crown.
Height: 150–250' (46–76 m). Diameter: 20' (6 m), sometimes larger.
Leaves: evergreen; crowded and overlapping; ⅛–¼" (3–6 mm) long, to ½" (12 mm) on leaders. Scalelike; ovate or lance-shaped, sharp-pointed; blue-green with 2 whitish lines.
Bark: reddish brown, fibrous, very thick, deeply furrowed into scaly ridges.
Twigs: much-branched, slender, drooping; blue-green turning brown.
Cones: 1¾–2¾" (4.5–7 cm) long; elliptical, reddish brown; many flat, short-pointed cone-scales; maturing in 2 seasons; hanging down at end of leafy twig and remaining attached; 3–9 seeds under cone-scale, light brown, 2-winged, falling gradually.

Habitat
Granitic and other rocky soils in scattered groves in moist mountain sites, usually canyons or slopes; in coniferous forests.

Range
Scattered groves on western slope of Sierra Nevada, central California; at 4500–7500' (1372–2286 m); rarely at 3000–8900' (914–2713 m).

Comments
This rare species ranks among the world's oldest trees; felled trees show annual rings indicating up to 3200 years of age. Almost all Giant Sequoias are protected in Yosemite, Kings Canyon, and Sequoia national parks, in 4 national forests, and

in state parks and forests. It is a popular, large ornamental tree in moist, cool temperate climates along the Pacific Coast and around the world. The lumber is no longer used, although many trees were cut and wasted in the early logging days. Seedlings and saplings are killed by forest fires, but the very thick bark of mature trees offers resistance. Douglas squirrels cut and store quantities of mature cones, and sparrows, finches, and chipmunks destroy many seedlings. Also called Big Tree.

MacNab Cypress
Cupressus macnabiana
55

Small evergreen tree or shrub with stout trunk, several forks, and spreading crown broader than high.
Height: 30′ (9 m). Diameter: 1′ (0.3 m).
Leaves: opposite in 4 rows; ¹⁄₁₆″ (1.5 mm) long. Scalelike; dull gray-green, with gland-dot that exudes whitish resin; very fragrant.
Bark: gray, rough, furrowed, fibrous.
Twigs: slender, spreading in 1 plane in flat sprays.
Cones: ¾–1″ (2–2.5 cm) in diameter; angular, brown or gray, with 6 or 8 irregular scales with prominent raised point; remaining closed and attached; many irregular brown seeds.

Habitat
Dry, rocky soils in foothills and lower mountain zones in chaparral and with Digger Pine.

Range
Mountains of N. California, including Coast Ranges and Sierra Nevada foothills; to 2600′ (792 m).

Comments
MacNab Cypress is perhaps the most widely distributed cypress in California.

Alaska Yellow-cedar
Chamaecyparis nootkatensis
56

Tree with narrow crown and horizontal or drooping branches.
Height: 50–100′ (15–30 cm). Diameter: 1–4′ (0.3–1.2 m).
Leaves: evergreen; opposite in 4 rows; ⅛″ (3 mm) long. Scalelike, pointed and spreading. Bright yellow-green, generally without gland-dot.
Bark: gray-brown, thin, with long narrow fissures, fibrous and shreddy.
Twigs: slightly stout, flattened or 4-angled, regularly branched and spreading horizontally, becoming reddish brown.
Cones: ½″ (12 mm) in diameter; rounded, reddish brown, with 4 or 6 rounded cone-scales ending in long point; maturing in 2 seasons; 2–4 seeds under a cone-scale.

Habitat
Wet mountain soils; mainly in mixed conifer forests, sometimes in pure stands.

Range
Pacific Coast region from S. and SE. Alaska southeast to

mountains of W. Oregon and extreme NW. California; local farther inland; at 2000–7000′ (610–2134 m); to sea level farther north.

Comments
The durable wood has a pleasant, resinous odor; it is used for furniture, interior finish, and boats. Northwest Coast Indians made canoe paddles from the wood and carved ceremonial masks from the trunks.

Incense-cedar
Libocedrus decurrens
57

Large, resinous, aromatic tree with tapering, irregularly angled trunk and narrow, columnar crown, becoming open and irregular.
Height: 60–150′ (18–46 m). Diameter: 3–5′ (0.9–1.5 m).
Leaves: evergreen; opposite in 4 rows; ⅛–½″ (3–12 mm) long. Scalelike; side pair keeled, long-pointed, overlapping next pair, extending down twig; very aromatic when crushed; shiny green.
Bark: light or reddish brown; thick, deeply and irregularly furrowed into shreddy ridges.
Twigs: much-branched and flattish; with wedge-shaped joints longer than broad; composed of scalelike leaves.
Cones: ¾–1″ (2–2.5 cm) long; oblong; hanging down at end of slender, leafy stalk; reddish brown; composed of 6 paired, hard, flattened, pointed cone-scales. Seeds 4 or fewer in cone, paired, with 2 unequal wings.

Habitat
Mountain soils; in mixed coniferous forests, seldom in pure stands.

Range
W. Oregon south to S. California and extreme W. Nevada; also N. Baja California; at 1200–7000′ (366–2134 m).

Comments
An important timber species, Incense-cedar is also the leading wood for the manufacture of pencils, because it is soft but not splintery, and can be sharpened in any direction with ease. Although stands of young trees are killed by fire, the very thick bark protects mature trees.

Port-Orford-cedar
Chamaecyparis lawsoniana
58

Large evergreen tree with enlarged base, narrow, pointed, spirelike crown, and horizontal or drooping branches.
Height: 70–200′ (21–61 m). Diameter: 2½–4′ (0.8–1.2 m).
Leaves: opposite in 4 rows; ¹⁄₁₆″ (1.5 mm) long. Scalelike; dull green above, whitish beneath, with gland-dot.
Bark: reddish brown, very thick, deeply furrowed into long fibrous ridges.
Twigs: very slender, flattened, regularly branched and spreading horizontally in fernlike spray.
Cones: ⅜″ (10 mm) in diameter; many in clusters, reddish brown, often with a bloom; with 8 or 10 blunt cone-scales; maturing in 1 season; 2–4 seeds under a cone-scale.

Habitat
Sandy and clay loams, also rocky ridges; with other conifers, sometimes in pure stands.

Range
SW. Oregon and NW. California in narrow coastal belt and Klamath Mountains; to 5000' (1524 m).

Comments
Port-Orford-cedar is adapted to the humid climate of the Pacific Coast with its wet winters and frequent summer fog. Logs of the aromatic wood are exported to Japan for woodenware and toys and for construction of shrines and temples; a special use is for arrow shafts. The names honor Port Orford, Oregon, located in the center of the range, and Peter Lawson and his sons, Scottish nurserymen who introduced this species into cultivation in 1854.

Western Redcedar
Thuja plicata
59, 142

Large to very large tree with tapering trunk, buttressed at base, and a narrow, conical crown of short, spreading branches drooping at ends: foliage is resinous and aromatic.
Height: 100–175' (30–53 m) or more. Diameter: 2–8' (0.6–2.4 m) or more.
Leaves: evergreen; opposite in 4 rows; 1/16–1/8" (1.5–3 mm) long. Scalelike, short-pointed; side pair keeled, flat pair usually without gland-dot; shiny dark green, usually with whitish marks beneath.
Bark: reddish brown, thin, fibrous, and shreddy.
Twigs: much branched in horizontal plane, slightly flattened in fanlike sprays, jointed.
Cones: 1/2" (12 mm) long; clustered and upright from short, curved stalk; elliptical, brown; with 10–12 paired, thin, leathery, sharp-pointed cone-scales; 6 usually bearing 2–3 seeds with 2 wings.

Habitat
Moist, slightly acid soils; forming widespread forests with Western Hemlock, also with other conifers.

Range
SE. Alaska southeast along coast to NW. California; also SE. British Columbia south in Rocky Mountains to W. Montana; to 3000' (914 m) in north; to 7000' (2134 m) in south.

Comments
Particularly resistant to rot, Western Redcedar is the chief wood for shingles and one of the most important for siding and boatbuilding. Indians of the Northwest Coast carved their famous totem poles and split lumber for their lodges from this durable softwood. Indians also used the wood for boxes, batons, and helmets and the fibrous inner bark for rope, roof thatching, blankets, and cloaks. The largest Western Redcedar measures 21' (6.4 m) in diameter, ranking second only to the Giant Sequoia among native trees; however, this species is not among the tallest.

Arizona Cypress
Cupressus arizonica
60, 143

Evergreen tree with conical crown and stout branches.
Height: 40–70' (12–21 m). Diameter: 1–2' (0.3–0.6 m).
Leaves: opposite in 4 rows; ¹⁄₁₆" (1.5 mm) long. Scalelike,
keeled; dull gray-green, mostly with gland-dot that exudes
whitish resin.
Bark: varying from gray or dark brown, rough, and furrowed,
to reddish brown, smooth, thin, and peeling.
Twigs: 4-angled, slightly stout, branching almost at right
angles.
Cones: ¾–1¼" (2–3 cm) in diameter; dark reddish brown
with a bloom, becoming gray; with 6 or 8 rounded, short-
pointed, hard scales, sometimes slightly warty; usually
remaining closed and attached. Many brown seeds ⅛–³⁄₁₆"
(3–5 mm) long.

Habitat
Coniferous woodlands on coarse, rocky soils; in pure stands or
with pinyons and junipers.

Range
Local and rare from Trans-Pecos Texas west to SW. New
Mexico, Arizona, and S. California; also northern Mexico; at
3000–5000' (914–1524 m).

Comments
Arizona Cypress is often grown for Christmas trees. The
durable wood is used locally for fenceposts. As many as 5
varieties, based on minor differences of foliage and bark, have
been distinguished.

California Juniper
Juniperus californica
61

Evergreen shrub or small tree with broad, irregular crown.
Height: 30' (9.1 m). Diameter: 1–2' (0.3–0.6 m).
Leaves: usually in 3s: ¹⁄₁₆–⅛" (1.5–3 mm) long. Scalelike,
blunt, forming stout, stiff, rounded twigs; yellow-green, with
gland-dot.
Bark: gray, fibrous, furrowed, shreddy.
Cones: ½–¾" (12–19 mm) long; berrylike, longer than
broad, bluish with a bloom, becoming brown, hard, and dry;
mealy and sweetish; 1–2 seeds.

Habitat
Dry slopes and flats of foothills and lower mountain zones;
with pinyons in woodland and with Joshua-trees in semidesert
zone.

Range
Mountains of California, extreme S. Nevada, and W. Arizona;
also N. Baja California; at 1000–5000' (305–1524 m).

Comments
Able to withstand heat and drought, this species extends
farther down into the semidesert zone than other junipers and
is important in erosion control on dry slopes. Indians used to
gather the "berries" to eat fresh and to grind into meal for
baking.

Alligator Juniper
Juniperus deppeana
62

Evergreen tree with short, stout trunk and rounded, spreading crown, becoming irregular and with branches partly dead in vertical strips.
Height: 20–50′ (6–15 m). Diameter: 2–4′ (0.6–1.2 m).
Leaves: opposite; in 4 rows, forming slender, 4-angled twigs; 1/16–1/8″ (1.5–3 mm) long. Scalelike, sharp-pointed; blue-green, with gland-dot and often whitish resin drop.
Bark: blackish or gray; thick and rough, deeply furrowed into checkered plates, suggesting an alligator's back.
Cones: 1/2″ (12 mm) in diameter; berrylike, brownish with whitish bloom, hard and dry, mealy; 3–5 seeds; maturing second year.

Habitat
Rocky hillsides and mountains; with pinyons, other junipers, oaks, and Ponderosa Pine.

Range
Trans-Pecos Texas northwest to N. Arizona; also Mexico; at 4500–8000′ (1372–2438 m).

Comments
Alligator Juniper is easily recognized by its distinctive bark. One of the largest junipers, it is used for fuel and fenceposts. New sprouts often appear at the base of cut stumps. The large "berries" are consumed by birds and mammals. Large trees often have a partially dead crown of grotesque appearance with some branches that die and turn light gray instead of falling; other branches die only in a vertical strip and continue to grow on the other side.

Western Juniper
Juniperus occidentalis
63

Evergreen tree with short trunk and broad crown of stout, spreading branches, becoming ragged and gnarled with age; or a shrub.
Height: 15–30′ (4.6–9 m). Diameter: 1′ (0.3 m), sometimes much larger.
Leaves: mostly in 3s; 1/16″ (1.5 mm) long. Scalelike, forming stout, rounded twigs; gray-green, with gland-dot.
Bark: reddish-brown, furrowed, shreddy.
Cones: 1/4–3/8″ (6–10 mm) in diameter; short, elliptical, berrylike, blue-black with a bloom, soft, juicy, resinous; maturing second year; 2–3 seeds.

Habitat
Mountain slopes and plateaus, mostly on shallow, rocky soils.

Range
Central and SE. Washington south to S. California; to 10,000′ (3048 m).

Comments
Giants reach a trunk diameter of 16′ (5 m) and an estimated age of more than 2000 years. This species may develop thick, long roots that entwine rock outcrops, mimicking the shape of the branches.

Rocky Mountain Juniper
Juniperus scopulorum
64

Evergreen tree with straight trunk, narrow, pointed crown, and slender branches of aromatic, gray-green foliage often drooping at ends.
Height: 20–50' (6–15 m). Diameter: 1½' (0.5 m).
Leaves: opposite in 4 rows, forming slender, 4-angled twigs; ¹⁄₁₆" (1.5 mm) long. Scalelike, pointed, gray-green.
Bark: reddish brown, thin, fibrous, shreddy.
Cones: ¼" (6 mm) in diameter; berrylike, bright blue with whitish coat, soft, juicy, sweetish, resinous; usually 2-seeded; maturing second year. Male or pollen cones on separate trees.

Habitat
Rocky soils, especially on limestone and lava outcrops; in open woodlands at lower border of trees to the north; in foothills with pinyons to the south.

Range
Generally in mountains, from central British Columbia, east to W. North Dakota, and south to Trans-Pecos Texas; also northern Mexico; at 5000–9000' (1524–2743 m); almost to sea level in north.

Comments
A graceful ornamental, often with narrow crown of drooping foliage, several varieties differ in form and in leaf color. The aromatic wood is especially suited for cedar chests and is also used for lumber, fenceposts, and fuel. Wildlife eat the "berries."

Utah Juniper
Juniperus osteosperma
65

Tree with short, upright trunk, low, spreading branches, and rounded or conical, open crown.
Height: 15–40' (4.6–12 m). Diameter: 1–3' (0.3–0.9 m).
Leaves: generally opposite in 4 rows, forming stout, stiff twigs; ¹⁄₁₆" (1.5 mm) long. Scalelike, short-pointed; yellow-green, usually without gland-dot.
Bark: gray, fibrous, furrowed, shreddy.
Cones: ¼–⅝" (6–15 mm) in diameter; berrylike, bluish with a bloom, becoming brown, hard and dry; mealy and sweetish; 1–2 seeds.

Habitat
Dry plains, plateaus, hills, and mountains, mostly on rocky soils; often in pure stands or with pinyons.

Range
Nevada east to Wyoming, south to W. New Mexico, and west to S. California; local in S. Montana; at 3000–8000' (914–2438 m).

Comments
The most common juniper in Arizona, it is conspicuous at the south rim of the Grand Canyon and on higher canyon walls. Utah Juniper grows slowly, becoming craggier and more contorted with age. American Indians used the bark for cordage, sandals, woven bags, thatching, and matting. They also ate the "berries" fresh or in cakes. Birds and small

mammals also consume quantities of juniper "berries."
Junipers are also called cedars, and Cedar Breaks National
Monument and nearby Cedar City in southwestern Utah are
named for this tree.

Oneseed Juniper
Juniperus monosperma
66

Evergreen shrub or small tree with several branches curving up
from ground, sometimes with short trunk, and much-
branched, spreading, and often scraggly crown.
Height: 10–25' (3–7.6 m). Diameter: 1' (0.3 m).
Leaves: opposite; in 4 rows on short, stout, crowded twigs;
1/16" (1.5 mm) long. Scalelike; yellow-green, usually with
gland-dot.
Bark: gray, fibrous, shreddy.
Cones: 1/4" (6 mm) in diameter; berrylike, dark blue with a
bloom, soft, juicy, sweetish and resinous, 1-seeded. Male or
pollen cones on separate trees.

Habitat
Dry plains, plateaus, hills, and mountains, mostly on rocky
soils; often in pure, orchardlike stands.

Range
Central Colorado south to NW. and Trans-Pecos Texas and
west to central Arizona; also northern Mexico; at 3000–7000'
(914–2134 m).

Comments
This abundant juniper is one of the most common small trees
in New Mexico. The wood is important for fenceposts and
fuel, and Indians used to make mats and cloth from the fibrous
bark. Birds and mammals consume the juicy "berries," and
goats browse the foliage.

Western Redbud
Cercis occidentalis
67, 166, 217

Large flowering shrub or small tree with rounded crown of
many spreading branches.
Height: 16' (5 m). Diameter: 4" (10 cm).
Leaves: alternate; 1½–3½" (4–9 cm) long and broad. Nearly
round, long-stalked, with 7–9 veins from notched base,
thickened, mostly hairless. Dark green above, paler beneath.
Bark: gray, smooth, and becoming fissured.
Twigs: reddish brown when young, becoming dark gray;
hairless.
Flowers: ½" (12 mm) long; 1 broad upper petal and 2 lateral
petals nearly enclosing 2 bottom petals that are joined and
shaped like the prow of a boat; petals slightly unequal and
purplish pink, rarely white; 2–5 flowers in clusters on slender
stalks; scattered along twigs; in early spring before leaves.
Fruit: 2–3½" (5–9 cm) long; narrowly oblong, flat, thin
pods; brown or purplish; maturing in late summer and
splitting open on 1 edge; many hanging in clusters along
twigs; several beanlike seeds.

Habitat
Canyons and slopes of foothills and mountains.

Range
N. California east to S. Utah and south to S. Arizona; at 500–
6000' (152–1829 m).

Comments
Western Redbud is a handsome ornamental with showy
flowers that cover the twigs in early spring. Indians used to
make bows from the wood. Deer browse the foliage.

Singleleaf Ash
Fraxinus anomala
68

Shrub or small tree with short trunk and rounded crown of
stout, curved branches.
Height: 25' (7.6 m). Diameter: 6" (15 cm).
Leaves: opposite; simple or occasionally pinnately compound,
with 2–3 leaflets; 1½–2" (4–5 cm) long, 1–2" (2.5–5 cm)
wide (leaflets slightly smaller). Broadly ovate or nearly round,
rounded or short-pointed at tip, blunt or notched at base;
inconspicuously wavy-toothed or without teeth; slightly thick
and leathery; becoming hairless; long-stalked. Dark green
above, paler beneath.
Bark: dark brown, furrowed into narrow ridges.
Twigs: brown, hairless, 4-angled or slightly winged.
Flowers: ⅛" (3 mm) long; greenish, without petals; many
together in small hairy clusters on previous year's twigs back
of leaves in spring; bisexual and female.
Fruit: ¾" (19 mm) long; a flattened key with elliptical,
rounded wing ⅛" (10 mm) wide, extending to base; maturing
in summer.

Habitat
Dry canyons and hillsides including rocky slopes in upper
desert; woodland and Ponderosa Pine forest.

Range
W. Colorado to E. California, Arizona, and extremely NW.
New Mexico; usually at 2000–6500' (610–1981 m); in
California to 11,000' (3353 m).

Comments
Singleleaf Ash is common in Grand Canyon National Park. As
the scientific name suggests, this species is distinct in its
genus, which is characterized by pinnately compound leaves.

Pacific Dogwood
Cornus nuttallii
69

Tree with dense, conical or rounded crown of often horizontal
branches and with beautiful white flower clusters.
Height: 50' (15 m). Diameter: 1' (0.3 m), rarely larger.
Leaves: opposite; 2½–4½" (6–11 cm) long, 1¼–2¾"
(3–7 cm) wide. Elliptical, edges slightly wavy, with 5–6
long, curved veins on each side of midvein. Shiny green and
nearly hairless above, paler with woolly hairs beneath, turning
orange and red in autumn.
Bark: reddish brown, thin, smooth or scaly.
Twigs: slender; light green and hairy when young, becoming
dark red or blackish.
Flowers: ¼" (6 mm) wide; with 4 greenish-yellow petals;

many crowded together in a head 1″ (2.5 cm) wide; bordered by usually 6 (sometimes 4–7) large, elliptical, short-pointed, white (sometimes pinkish), petal-like bracts 1½–2½″ (4–6 cm) long, altogether forming a huge "flower" 4–6″ (10–15 cm) wide; in spring and early summer, often again in late summer or autumn.
Fruit: ½″ (12 mm) long; elliptical, shiny red or orange; thin, mealy, bitter pulp; stone containing 1–2 seeds; many crowded together in head 1½″ (4 cm) across; maturing in autumn.

Habitat
Moist soils in understory of coniferous forests.

Range
SW. British Columbia south to W. Oregon and in mountains to S. California; to 6000′ (1829 m).

Comments
Pacific Dogwood is one of the most handsome native ornamental trees on the Pacific Coast, with very showy flowers and fruit. This tree is also known as Flowering Dogwood and Mountain Dogwood.

Red-osier Dogwood
Cornus stolonifera
70

Large, spreading, thicket-forming shrub with several stems, clusters of small white flowers, and small whitish fruit; rarely a small tree.
Height: commonly 3–10′ (0.9–3 m), rarely to 15′ (4.6 m).
Diameter: 3″ (7.5 cm).
Leaves: opposite; 1½–3½″ (4–9 cm) long, ⅝–2″ (1.5–5 cm) wide. Elliptical or ovate, short- or long-pointed, without teeth; 5–7 long, carved, sunken veins on each side of midvein. Dull green above, whitish green and covered with fine hairs beneath; turning reddish in autumn.
Bark: gray or brown, smooth or slightly furrowed into flat plates.
Twigs: purplish red, slender, hairy when young, with rings at nodes.
Flowers: ¼″ (6 mm) wide; with 4 spreading, white petals; many, crowded in upright, flattish clusters 1¼–2″ (3–5 cm) wide; in late spring and early summer.
Fruit: ¼–⅛″ (6–10 mm) in diameter; whitish, juicy, with 2-seeded stone; maturing in late summer.

Habitat
Moist soils, especially along streams; forming thickets and in understory of forests.

Range
Central Alaska east to Labrador and Newfoundland, south to N. Virginia, and west to California; also northern Mexico; to 5000′ (1524 m); to 9000′ (2743 m) in the Southwest.

Comments
One of the most common and widespread shrubs across Canada and the northern states, it is planted as an ornamental, especially for the showy twigs in winter. Red-osier Dogwood

is useful for erosion control on stream banks. The common name recalls the resemblance of the reddish twigs to those of some willows, called osiers, used in basketry.

Wavyleaf Silktassel
Garrya elliptica
71

Evergreen shrub or small tree with tassel-like clusters of flowers and fruit and paired, leathery, wavy-edged leaves. Foliage and other parts have bitter taste.
Height: 20' (6 m). Diameter: 4" (10 cm).
Leaves: evergreen; opposite; 2–3¼" (5–8 cm) long. Elliptical; thick; shiny green and nearly hairless above, paler with thick coat of woolly hairs beneath.
Bark: gray, smooth, becoming fissured and slightly scaly.
Twigs: 4-angled and densely hairy when young; greenish, becoming brown or blackish; bitter.
Flowers: tiny, scaly, greenish, and without petals; many crowded together in drooping, narrow, catkinlike clusters 2–5" (5–13 cm) long; male and female on separate plants; in late winter and very early spring.
Fruit: ⅜" (10 mm) in diameter; rounded, berrylike, dark purple to black, densely covered with white hairs; becoming dry, with bitter pulp; 1-seeded; maturing in summer and splitting open.

Habitat
Dry slopes and ridges; often in thickets, chaparral, and mixed evergreen forests.

Range
W. Oregon south to S. California and Santa Cruz Island; to 2000' (610 m).

Comments
This is the only native species of *Garrya* reaching tree size. This distinct genus of shrubs and small trees is often placed separately in the Silktassel Family (Garryaceae). Several other species also occur in the western United States.

Curlleaf Mountain-mahogany
Cercocarpus ledifolius
72, 180

Slightly resinous and aromatic evergreen shrub or small tree with compact, rounded crown of widely spreading, curved, and twisted branches and many stiff twigs.
Height: 15–30' (4.6–9 m). Diameter: ½–1½' (0.15–0.5 m).
Leaves: evergreen; alternate; usually clustered; ½–1¼" (1.2–3 cm) long, less than ⅜" (10 mm) wide. Narrowly lance-shaped or elliptical, thick and leathery, with edges rolled under, slightly resinous and aromatic, almost stalkless. Shiny dark green with grooved midvein and obscure side veins above, pale and with fine hairs beneath.
Bark: reddish brown, thick, deeply furrowed into scaly ridges.
Twigs: reddish brown, hairy when young.
Flowers: ⅜" (10 mm) long; funnel-shaped, slightly 5-lobed, yellowish, hairy, without petals, stalkless; 1–3 at leaf bases; in early spring.

Fruit: ¼" (6 mm) long; narrowly cylindrical, hairy, with twisted tail 1½–3" (4–7.5 cm) long, covered with whitish hairs; maturing in summer.

Habitat
Dry, rocky mountain slopes; in grassland, with sagebrush, pinyons, and oaks, and in coniferous forests.

Range
Extreme SE. Washington east to S. Montana, south to N. Arizona, and west to S. California; at 4000–10,500' (1219–3200 m).

Comments
This species is a small tree characteristic of lower mountain slopes throughout the Great Basin. Deer browse the evergreen foliage year-round. The hard, heavy wood is an important source of fuel in local mining operations; it is also used for novelties, as it takes a high polish. The name "Mountain-mahogany" applied to this genus is misleading; these shrubby trees are not related to true mahogany (*Swietenia*), a valuable cabinetwood of tropical America. The dark reddish-brown, mahogany-colored heartwood may have led to this name.

Bebb Willow
Salix bebbiana
73

Much-branched shrub or small tree with broad, rounded crown.
Height: 10–25' (3–7.6 m). Diameter: 6" (15 cm).
Leaves: alternate; 1–3½" (2.5–9 cm) long, ⅜–1" (1–2.5 cm) wide. Elliptical, often broadest beyond middle, short-pointed at ends; slightly saw-toothed or wavy; firm, slightly hairy. Dull green above, gray or whitish and net-veined beneath.
Bark: gray, smooth, becoming rough and furrowed.
Twigs: reddish purple, slender, widely forking; with pressed hairs when young.
Flowers: catkins ¾–1½" (2–4 cm) long; with yellow or brown scales; on short, leafy stalks; before or with leaves.
Fruit: ⅜" (10 mm) long; very slender capsules; hairy, light brown, ending in long point, long-stalked; maturing in early summer.

Habitat
Moist, open uplands and borders of streams, lakes, and swamps.

Range
Central and SW. Alaska south to British Columbia and east to Newfoundland, south to Maryland, west to Iowa, and south in Rocky Mountains to S. New Mexico; to 11,000' (3353 m) southward.

Comments
Bebb Willow is the most important "diamond willow," a term applied to several species that sometimes have diamond-shaped patterns on their trunks. These are caused by fungi, usually in shade or poor sites.

Common Manzanita
Arctostaphylos manzanita
74, 194

Large evergreen shrub, sometimes a small tree commonly branching near base, with stout, crooked, twisted trunks and branches and dense, rounded crown as broad as high.
Height: 20' (6 m) or more. Diameter: 6" (15 cm).
Leaves: evergreen; alternate 1–1¾" (2.5–4.5 cm) long, ¾–1¼" (2–3 cm) wide. Elliptical or nearly round; without teeth; thick; short-stalked; shiny or dull green on both surfaces, sometimes finely hairy.
Bark: dark reddish brown, smooth.
Twigs: crooked, densely covered with gray hairs.
Flowers: ⁵⁄₁₆" (8 mm) long; jug-shaped, white or pale pink corolla ending in 5 tiny lobes; numerous, in many-branched clusters, drooping at end of twig; in late winter and early spring.
Fruit: ⁵⁄₁₆–½" (8–12 mm) in diameter; berrylike, round or slightly flattish, white, turning deep reddish brown; with mealy pulp and several nutlets; maturing in late summer.

Habitat
Dry slopes and in mountain canyons, chaparral, foothill and oak woodlands, and in Ponderosa Pine forest.

Range
N. and central California in northern Coast Ranges and foothills of Sierra Nevada; at 300–4000' (91–1219 m).

Comments
Whether manzanitas should be considered trees is debatable; a few of the approximately 40 native shrubby species mainly in California (including this one) reach tree size. However, they generally branch or fork near the ground, thus lacking the single trunk of a tree. Whiteleaf Manzanita (*Arctostaphylos viscida*), with whitish-green leaves, is the most common chaparral species. *Manzanita* is a Spanish word meaning "little apple." The mealy berries are consumed by wildlife and were eaten by Indians, who also made them into manzanita cider.

Scouler Willow
Salix scouleriana
75

Shrub or small tree with erect trunk and compact, rounded crown; sometimes medium-sized. Freshly stripped bark of twigs usually has skunklike odor.
Height: 15–50' (4.6–15 m). Diameter: 1½' (0.5 m).
Leaves: alternate; spreading, fanlike; 2–5' (5–13 cm) long, ½–1½" (1.2–4 cm) wide. Variable in shape; mostly obovate to elliptical and broadest beyond middle, short-pointed at tip and tapering to base; without teeth to sparsely wavy-toothed. Dark green and nearly hairless above, whitish with gray hairs or with few reddish hairs beneath.
Bark: gray, smooth, thin; becoming dark brown and fissured into broad, flat ridges.
Twigs: yellow to reddish brown, stout; densely hairy when young, with reddish buds.
Flowers: catkins 1–2" (2.5–5 cm) long; stout, stalkless or nearly so, with black, long-haired scales; abundant in early spring before leaves.

Fruit: ⅜" (10 mm) long; narrow, stalkless, light brown capsules, with gray, woolly hairs; maturing in early summer.

Habitat
Upland coniferous forests under larger trees, in cutover areas, and in clearings, including dry sites.

Range
Central Alaska east to Manitoba and southwest to Idaho and California; also in Black Hills of South Dakota and in mountains to S. New Mexico; to 10,000' (3048 m) in mountains.

Comments
The species is sometimes called Fire Willow because it rapidly occupies burned areas, forming blue-green thickets. A pussy willow and one of the earliest flowering species, it is an important browse plant for moose in Alaska and for sheep and cattle elsewhere.

Pacific Madrone
Arbutus menziesii
76, 158

Handsome evergreen tree with tall, reddish brown trunk and open, narrow, rounded or irregular crown of stout, smooth red branches.
Height: 20–80' (6–24 m). Diameter: 2' (0.6 m).
Leaves: evergreen; 2–4½" (5–11 cm) long, 1–3" (2.5–7.5 cm) wide. Elliptical, blunt at tip, not toothed or sometimes saw-toothed; thick and leathery; hairless except when young. Shiny dark green above, paler or whitish beneath; turning red before falling.
Bark: red, smooth, thin, and peeling off in thin, papery scales on branches; dark reddish brown and divided into square plates on trunks.
Twigs: light red or green, turning reddish brown; hairless.
Flowers: ¼" (6 mm) long; jug-shaped or urn-shaped, white or pink-tinged corolla; short-stalked; in branched clusters 2–6" (5–15 cm) long and wide at twig ends; in early spring.
Fruit: ⅜–½" (10–12 mm) in diameter; berrylike, orange-red, finely warty; with mealy pulp, large stone, and many flattened seeds; maturing in autumn.

Habitat
Upland slopes and canyons; in oak and coniferous forests, often in understory.

Range
Pacific Coast from SW. British Columbia south to W. Oregon and in Coast Ranges to S. California; also Sierra Nevada of central California and Santa Cruz Island; to 5000' (1524 m); sometimes to 6000' (1829 m).

Comments
Pacific Madrone is one of the most beautiful broadleaf flowering evergreens, with its glossy foliage, large clusters of small white flowers, orange-red fruits, and very showy, reddish, peeling bark. It is the northernmost New World tree of its family, ranging to Canada.

California-laurel
Umbellularia californica
77

Giant Chinkapin
Castanopsis chrysophylla
78, 178

Evergreen tree with short trunk, usually forked into several large, spreading branches, forming a broad, rounded, dense crown of aromatic, peppery foliage; in exposed situations a low, thicket-forming shrub.
Height: 40–80' (12–24 m). Diameter: 1½–2½' (0.5–0.8 m).
Leaves: evergreen; 2–5" (5–13 cm) long, ½–1½" (1.2–4 cm) wide. Elliptical or lance-shaped, short-pointed or rounded at ends, thick and leathery, with edges slightly turned under. Shiny dark green above, dull and paler beneath with prominent network of veins; turning yellow or orange before shedding gradually after second year.
Bark: dark reddish brown, thin, with flat scales.
Twigs: stout, hairy; yellow-green when young, becoming reddish brown.
Flowers: ¼" (6 mm) long; pale yellow, numerous; clustered on stalk at leaf bases; in late winter or early spring.
Fruit: ¾–1" (2–2.5 cm) long; an elliptical or nearly round berry, greenish to purple, with thin pulp and large brown seed; maturing in late autumn.

Habitat
Moist soils, especially in mountain canyons and valleys; in mixed forests.

Range
SW. Oregon south in Coast Ranges and Sierra Nevada to S. California; to 4000' (1219 m); at southern limit, 2000–6000' (610–1829 m).

Comments
A handsome ornamental and street tree on the West Coast, it is also known as California-bay and Oregon-myrtle. When crushed, the foliage, twigs, and other parts are pungently aromatic.

Evergreen tree with straight trunk, becoming grooved or fluted, and with stout, spreading branches and broad, rounded crown; also a shrub variety (Golden Chinkapin).
Height: 40–80' (12–24 m). Diameter: 1–3' (0.3–0.9 m).
Leaves: evergreen; alternate; 2–5" (5–13 cm) long, ⅝–1½" (1.5–4 cm) wide. Lance-shaped or oblong; thick and leathery; edges slightly turned under, without teeth. Shiny dark green with scattered scales above, covered with tiny golden-yellow scales beneath; turning yellow before falling. Shrub variety has leaves folded upward.
Bark: gray and smooth when young, becoming reddish brown, thick, deeply furrowed into plates; inner bark bright red.
Twigs: stiff, scurfy with tiny, golden-yellow scales when young, turning dark reddish brown.
Flowers: about ⅛" (3 mm) long; whitish, stalkless; many in catkins 2–2½" (5–6 cm) long; upright near ends of twigs; mostly male; few female at base or in separate clusters; mostly in early summer.

Fruit: 1–1½" (2.5–4 cm) in diameter; a nearly stalkless, spiny bur; maturing in autumn of second year, splitting irregularly into 4 parts. 1–2 nuts ⁵⁄₁₆–½" (8–12 mm) long; broadly egg-shaped or rounded, light brown, hard-shelled, edible.

Habitat
Gravelly and rocky soils in mountain slopes and canyons in Redwood and evergreen forests. Shrub variety on dry ridges in chaparral and Knobcone Pine stands.

Range
Pacific Coast region from SW. Washington south to central California; also local in the Sierra Nevada of central California; to 1500' (457 m); Golden Chinkapin to 6000' (1829 m).

Comments
A handsome tree with a massive trunk, this species attains a large size. The showy, whitish blossoms have a strong odor. The edible nuts, like small chestnuts, are borne in small quantities; they are usually consumed by chipmunks and ground squirrels. Also known as Golden Chinkapin.

Pacific Willow
Salix lasiandra
79

Tree with open, irregular crown; sometimes a thicket-forming shrub.
Height: 20–50' (6–15 m). Diameter: 2' (0.6 m).
Leaves: alternate; 2–5" (5–13 cm) long, ½–1" (1.2–2.5 cm) wide. Narrowly lance-shaped, very long-pointed, mostly rounded at base; finely saw-toothed, becoming almost hairless; leafstalks slender, with glands at upper end. Shiny green above, whitish beneath.
Bark: gray or dark brown; becoming rough and deeply furrowed into flat, scaly ridges.
Twigs: shiny reddish to brownish or yellow, hairless.
Flowers: catkins 1½–4" (4–10 cm) long; with hairy, yellow or brown scales; at ends of leafy twigs; with leaves in spring.
Fruit: ¼" (6 mm) long; light reddish brown, hairless capsules; maturing in early summer.

Habitat
Wet soils along streams, lakes, and roadsides; in valleys and on mountains.

Range
Central and SE. Alaska east to Saskatchewan and south mostly in mountains to S. New Mexico and S. California; to 8000' (2438 m).

Comments
As the common name suggests, Pacific Willow is familiar along riverbanks and valleys through the Pacific states.

Narrowleaf Cottonwood
Populus angustifolia
80

Tree with narrow, conical crown of slender, upright branches and with resinous, balsam-scented buds.
Height: 50' (15 m). Diameter: 1½' (0.5 m).

Leaves: alternate; 2–5″ (5–13 cm) long, ½–1″ (1.2–2.5 cm) wide. Lance-shaped, long-pointed at tip, rounded at base; finely saw-toothed, hairless or nearly so, short-stalked. Shiny green above, paler beneath; turning dull yellow in autumn.
Bark: yellow-green, smooth; becoming gray-brown and furrowed into flat ridges at base.
Twigs: yellow-green, slender, hairless.
Flowers: catkins 1½–3″ (4–7.5 cm) long; reddish; male and female on separate trees; in early spring before leaves.
Fruit: about ¼″ (6 mm) long; broadly egg-shaped capsules, light brown, hairless; maturing in spring, splitting into 2 parts; many cottony seeds.

Habitat
Moist soils along streams in mountains; with willows and alders in coniferous forests.

Range
Mountains from S. Alberta and extreme SW. Saskatchewan south to Trans-Pecos Texas and California; also northern Mexico; at 3000–8000′ (914–2438 m).

Comments
Discovered in 1805 by Lewis and Clark on their expedition to the Northwest, this is the common cottonwood of the northern Rocky Mountains. It is easily distinguishable from related species by the narrow, short-stalked, willowlike leaves. Its root system makes it suitable for erosion control.

Pacific Waxmyrtle
Myrica californica
81

Evergreen, much-branched shrub or small tree with a narrow, rounded crown and waxy brownish berries.
Height: 30′ (9 m). Diameter: 1′ (0.3 m).
Leaves: alternate; evergreen; 2–4½″ (5–11 cm) long, ½–¾″ (12–19 mm) wide. Reverse lance-shaped, usually broadest near short-pointed tip; saw-toothed except near long-pointed base, aromatic, slightly thickened, hairless. Shiny dark green above, yellow green with tiny black gland-dots beneath.
Bark: gray or brown, smooth, thin.
Twigs: green or brown, slender, hairy when young.
Flowers: tiny yellowish male flowers in almost stalkless clusters ⅜–¾″ (10–19 mm) long; at base of lower leaves. Tiny reddish-green female flowers in clusters ⁵⁄₁₆–½″ (8–12 mm) long; at base of upper leaves of same plant. Both in early spring.
Fruit: ¼–⁵⁄₁₆″ (6–8 mm) in diameter; brownish purple, warty with whitish wax coat, 1-seeded; several along stalk at leaf base; maturing in early autumn.

Habitat
Moist sand dunes, hillsides, and canyons; forming thickets with coastal scrub, Redwood, and Shore Pine.

Range
SW. Washington south near Pacific Coast to S. California; to 500′ (152 m).

Comments
Pacific Waxmyrtle is sometimes planted as an ornamental
shrub for the showy berries and dense, shiny evergreen foliage.
The fruit is eaten in small quantities by yellow-rumped
warblers and many other birds. The waxy covering of the fruit
apparently is not used; colonists extracted the wax from related
eastern bayberries or waxmyrtles in boiling water and made
fragrant-burning candles. Sierra Waxmyrtle (*Myrica hartwegii*)
occurs only in the Sierra Nevada.

Interior Live Oak
Quercus wislizeni
82

Evergreen tree with short trunk and broad, rounded crown of
stout, spreading branches; sometimes a shrub.
Height: 30–70' (9–21 m). Diameter: 1–3' (0.3–0.9 m).
Leaves: evergreen; alternate; 1–2" (2.5–5 cm) long, ½–1¼"
(1.2–3 cm) wide. Lance-shaped to elliptical, short-pointed at
tip, blunt or rounded at base, often with short, spiny teeth,
thick and leathery, hairless. Shiny dark green above, light
yellow-green with prominent network of veins beneath.
Bark: gray, becoming furrowed into narrow, scaly ridges.
Acorns: ¾–1½" (2–4 cm) long; egg-shaped, long-pointed,
often with long, dark lines, about ½ enclosed by deep, thin,
scaly cup; 1 or 2 on short stalks or stalkless; maturing second
year.

Habitat
Valleys and slopes in foothill woodlands; with other oaks and
Digger Pine.

Range
N. to S. California, mostly in foothills of Sierra Nevada and
inner Coast Ranges, and N. Baja California; at 1000–5000'
(305–1524 m).

Comments
This species is named for its discoverer, Friedrich Adolph
Wislizenus (1810–89), a German-born physician of St. Louis.
Although slow growing, it is planted as an ornamental. Deer
browse the foliage, and the wood is used for fuel.

Emory Oak
Quercus emoryi
83, 171

Medium-sized evergreen tree with straight trunk, rough black
bark, rounded crown, and shiny yellow-green leaves.
Height: 60' (18 m). Diameter: 2½' (0.8 m).
Leaves: evergreen; alternate; 1–2½" (2.5–6 cm) long, ⅜–1"
(1–2.5 cm) wide. Broadly lance-shaped, with short, spiny
point and few short, spiny teeth, rounded or notched at base;
thick, stiff, leathery. Both surfaces shiny yellow-green and
nearly hairless; shedding gradually in spring as new leaves
unfold.
Bark: black, thick, deeply furrowed into scaly plates.
Twigs: slender, stiff, finely hairy.
Acorns: ½–¾" (12–19 mm) long; oblong, ⅓–½ enclosed by
deep, scaly cup; almost stalkless; slightly bitter but edible;
maturing first year.

Habitat
On slopes of foothills and mountains and in canyons; common to abundant in oak woodland with other evergreen oaks.

Range
Trans-Pecos Texas west to central Arizona; also northwestern Mexico; at 4000–7000' (1219–2134 m); rarely to 8000' (2438 m).

Comments
Emory Oak is the most characteristic tree of the oak woodland in mountains along the Mexican border. The acorns are only slightly bitter and are gathered and eaten locally. They are also consumed in quantities by quail, wild turkeys, squirrels, and other wildlife. The foliage is browsed by deer and, to a lesser extent, by livestock.

Coast Live Oak
Quercus agrifolia
84

Evergreen tree with short, stout trunk; many large, crooked, spreading branches; and broad, rounded crown; sometimes shrubby.
Height: 30–80' (9–24 m). Diameter: 1–3' (0.3–0.9 m) or more.
Leaves: evergreen; alternate; ¾–2½" (2–6 cm) long, ½–1½" (1.2–4 cm) wide. Oblong or elliptical, short-pointed or rounded at both ends; with edges turned under and bearing spiny teeth; thick and leathery. Shiny dark green above, yellow-green and often hairy beneath.
Bark: dark brown, thick, deeply furrowed.
Acorns: 1–1½" (2.5–4 cm) long; narrowly egg-shaped, ⅓ enclosed by deep, thin cup with many brownish, finely hairy scales outside and silky hairs inside; 1 or few together; stalkless; maturing first year.

Habitat
In valleys and on slopes, usually in open groves; often with Canyon Live Oak and California Black Oak.

Range
Coast Ranges mostly, central to S. California, including Santa Cruz and Santa Rosa Islands; also N. Baja California; to about 3000' (914 m).

Comments
This is the common oak of the California coastal hills, forming parklike groves that often appear in the scenery of motion pictures made in Hollywood. The acorns were among those preferred by Indians; after removing the shells, they ground the seeds into meal, which was washed to remove the bitter taste, and boiled into mush or baked in ashes as bread.

Sitka Alder
Alnus sinuata
85

Thicket-forming shrub or small tree, often with several trunks, and with shiny yellow-green leaves, gummy when young.
Height: 30' (9 m). Diameter: 8" (20 cm).

Leaves: alternate; 2½–5" (6–13 cm) long, 1½–3" (4–7.5 cm) wide. Ovate, shallowly wavy-lobed and doubly saw-toothed with long-pointed teeth and 6–10 nearly straight parallel veins on each side; gummy or sticky when young. Shiny, speckled yellow-green on both surfaces, paler and often slightly hairy beneath.
Bark: gray to light gray, smooth and thin; inner bark red.
Twigs; gummy, finely hairy, and orange-brown when young; becoming light gray, slender, and slightly zigzag.
Flowers: tiny; in spring with or after leaves. Male flowers yellowish, drooping, narrowly cylindrical; in catkins 3–5" (7.5–13 cm) long, ⅜" (10 mm) wide. Female flowers reddish, in narrow cones ⅜" (10 mm) long.
Cones: ½–¾" (12–19 mm) long; 3–6 clustered on slender, spreading, long stalks; elliptical, with many hard, black scales; remaining attached. Tiny, elliptical, flat nutlets with 2 broad wings; maturing in summer.

Habitat
Along streams and lakes and in valleys; also avalanche tracks, talus, moraines.

Range
SW. and central Alaska and Yukon southeast to NW. California and central Montana; in Alaska to alpine zone above timberline; in NW. California to 7000' (2134 m).

Comments
In Alaska, Sitka Alder is a pioneer in disturbed areas, following landslides, logging, and glacial retreat. Adapted to soils too barren for other trees, this species improves soil conditions by adding organic matter and nitrogen from bacteria in its root nodules. It acts as a nurse tree for Sitka Spruce, later dying when shaded by the larger conifer.

Arizona Alder
Alnus oblongifolia
86

Tall, straight-trunked tree with open, rounded crown.
Height: 80' (24 m). Diameter: 2' (0.6 m).
Leaves: alternate; in 3 rows; 1½–3¼" (4–8 cm) long, 1–1½" (2.5–4 cm) wide. Ovate or elliptical, usually doubly saw-toothed but not lobed, with 7–10 nearly straight parallel veins on each side. Dark green and almost hairless above, paler and often finely hairy with tufts of rust-colored hairs in vein-angles beneath.
Bark: dark gray, smooth, thin, becoming fissured and scaly.
Twigs: slender, brown, finely hairy when young, with 3-angled pith.
Flowers: tiny; in early spring before leaves. Male yellowish, in 3–4 drooping, narrowly cylindrical catkins 2–3" (5–7.5 cm) long. Female reddish, in narrow cones ¼" (6 mm) long.
Cones: ½"–¾" (12–19 mm) long; 3–8 clustered on short stalks, elliptical, with many hard black scales; remaining attached; tiny, elliptical, flat nutlets; maturing in summer.

Habitat
Wet canyon soils in mountains and along streams.

Range
SW. New Mexico and Arizona; local in N. New Mexico; also in northern Mexico; at 4500–7500' (1372–2286 m).

Comments
This is one of the largest native alders and a handsome tree of rocky canyon bottoms.

White Alder
Alnus rhombifolia
87

Medium-sized to large tree with tall, straight trunk and open, rounded crown; showy in winter with long, golden-colored male catkins hanging from slender, leafless twigs.
Height: 70' (21 m). Diameter: 2' (0.6 m).
Leaves: alternate; in 3 rows; 2–3½" (5–9 cm) long, 1½–2" (4–5 cm) wide. Ovate or elliptical, finely saw-toothed but not lobed, slightly thickened, with 9–12 nearly straight, parallel veins on each side. Dull dark green, hairless or nearly so, and often with tiny gland-dots above, light yellow-green and slightly hairy beneath.
Bark: light or dark brown, fissured into flat, scaly ridges.
Twigs: slender, light green, finely hairy when young, with 3-angled pith.
Flowers: tiny; in winter and early spring before leaves. Male yellowish in drooping, narrowly cylindrical catkins 1½–5" (4–13 cm) long. Female reddish in cones ⅜" (10 mm) long.
Cones: ⅜–¾" (10–19 mm) long; 3–7 clustered on short stalks, elliptical, with many hard, black scales; remaining closed until early spring; tiny, elliptical, flat nutlets; maturing in late summer.

Habitat
Streamsides.

Range
W. Idaho and Washington south in mountains to W. Nevada and S. California; at 100–8000' (30–2438 m); generally below 5000' (1524 m).

Comments
White Alder, named for its pale foliage, is the only alder native to southern California. Limited to permanent streams, it is a good indicator of water. It is sometimes planted as an ornamental in wet sites.

Mountain Alder
Alnus tenuifolia
88, 144

Shrub with spreading, slender branches or sometimes a small tree with several trunks and a rounded crown; often forming thickets.
Height: 30' (9 m). Diameter: 6" (15 cm).
Leaves: alternate; in 3 rows; 1½–4" (4–10 cm) long, 1–2½" (2.5–6 cm) wide. Ovate or elliptical, wavy-lobed and doubly saw-toothed, rounded at base, with 6–9 nearly straight parallel veins on each side. Dull dark green above, light yellow-green and sometimes finely hairy beneath.
Bark: gray, thin, smooth, becoming reddish gray and scaly.
Twigs: slender, reddish and hairy when young, becoming

gray, with 3-angled pith.
Flowers: tiny; in early spring before leaves. Male yellowish, in catkins 1–2¾″ (2.5–7 cm) long. Female brownish, in narrow cones ¼″ (6 mm) long.
Cones: ⅜–⅝″ (10–15 mm) long; 3–9 clustered on short stalks; elliptical, with many hard black scales; maturing in late summer and remaining attached. Tiny, elliptical, flat nutlets.

Habitat
Banks of streams, swamps, and mountain canyons in moist soils.

Range
Central Alaska, Yukon, and Mackenzie southeast mostly in mountains to New Mexico and central California; near sea level in north; to 9000′ (2743 m) in south.

Comments
This is the common alder throughout the Rockies. The Navajo Indians made a red dye from the powdered bark. It is also called Thinleaf Alder.

Red Alder
Alnus rubra
89

Graceful tree with straight trunk, pointed or rounded crown, and mottled, light gray to whitish, smooth bark.
Height: 40–100′ (12–30 m). Diameter: 2½′ (0.8 m), sometimes larger.
Leaves: alternate; in 3 rows; 3–5″ (7.5–13 cm) long, 1¾–3″ (4.5–7.5 cm) wide. Ovate to elliptical, short-pointed at both ends, slightly thickened, wavy-lobed and doubly saw-toothed, edges slightly turned under, with 10–15 nearly straight parallel veins on each side. Dark green and usually hairless above, gray-green with rust-colored hairs beneath.
Bark: mottled light gray to whitish, smooth or becoming slightly scaly, thin; inner bark reddish brown.
Twigs: slender, light green, covered with gray hairs when young, with 3-angled pith.
Flowers: tiny; in spring before leaves. Male yellowish, in drooping, narrowly cylindrical catkins 4–6″ (10–15 m) long, ¼″ (6 mm) wide. Female reddish, in narrow cones ⅜–½″ (10–12 mm) long.
Cones: ½–1″ (1.2–2.5 cm) long; 4–8 on short stalks, elliptical, with many hard black scales; remaining attached; tiny, rounded, flat nutlets with 2 narrow wings; maturing in late summer.

Habitat
Moist soils including loam, gravel, sand, and clay, along streams and lower slopes; often in nearly pure stands.

Range
SE. Alaska southeast to central California; also local to N. Idaho; to 2500′ (762 m).

Comments
The leading hardwood in the Pacific Northwest, Red Alder is

used for pulpwood, furniture, cabinetwork, and tool handles.
It is planted as an ornamental in wet soils and is a pioneer on
landslides, roadsides, and moist sites after logging or fire. Red
Alder thickets are short-lived and serve as a cover for seedlings
of the next coniferous forest. Alder roots, like those of
legumes, often have swellings or root nodules containing
nitrogen-fixing bacteria, which enrich the soil by converting
nitrogen from the air into chemicals like fertilizers that the
plants can use.

Water Birch
Betula occidentalis
90

Shrub or small tree with rounded crown of spreading and
drooping branches; usually forming clumps and often in
thickets.
Height: 25' (7.6 m). Diameter: 6–12" (15–30 cm).
Leaves: alternate; 1–2" (2.5–5 cm) long, ¾–1" (2–2.5 cm)
wide. Ovate, sharply and often doubly saw-toothed, usually
with 4–5 veins on each side. Dark green above, pale yellow-
green with tiny gland-dots beneath; turning dull yellow in
autumn.
Bark: shiny, dark reddish brown, smooth, with horizontal
lines, not peeling.
Twigs: greenish, slender, with gland-dots.
Flowers: tiny; in early spring. Male yellowish, with 2 stamens,
many in long, drooping catkins near tip of twigs. Female
greenish in short, upright catkins back of tip of same twig.
Cones: 1–1¼" (2.5–3 cm) long; cylindrical, brownish,
upright or spreading on slender stalk; with many 2-winged
nutlets; maturing in late summer.

Habitat
Moist soils along streams in mountain canyons; usually in
coniferous forests and with cottonwoods and willows.

Range

NE. British Columbia east to S. Manitoba and south to N.
New Mexico and California; at 2000–8000' (610–2438 m).

Comments
This uncommon but widespread species is the only native
birch in the Southwest and the southern Rocky Mountains.
Sheep and goats browse the foliage. It is also called Red Birch
and Black Birch.

Western Serviceberry
Amelanchier alnifolia
91, 184

Shrub or small tree, usually with several trunks, and with star-
shaped, white flowers.
Height: 30' (9 m). Diameter: 8" (20 cm).
Leaves: alternate; ¾–2" (2–5 cm) long and almost as broad.
Broadly elliptical to nearly round, rounded at both ends,
coarsely toothed above middle, usually with 7–9 straight veins
on each side. Dark green and becoming hairless above, paler
and hairy when young beneath.
Bark: gray or brown, thin, smooth or slightly fissured.
Twigs: red-brown, slender, hairless.

Flowers: ¾–1¼" (2–3 cm) wide; with 5 narrow, white petals; in small, terminal clusters; in spring with leaves.
Fruit: ½" (12 mm) in diameter; like a small apple, purple or blackish, edible, juicy and sweet; with several seeds; in early summer.

Habitat
Moist soils in forests and openings.

Range
Central Alaska southeast to Manitoba, W. Minnesota, and Colorado and west to N. California; local east to SE. Quebec; to 6000' (1829 m).

Comments
The fruits of this and related species are eaten fresh, prepared in puddings, pies, and muffins, and dried like raisins and currants. They are also an important food for wildlife from songbirds to squirrels and bears. Deer and livestock browse the foliage.

Birchleaf Mountain-mahogany
Cercocarpus betuloides
92, 179

Large evergreen shrub or small tree with single trunk and spreading crown.
Height: 20' (6 m). Diameter: 6" (15 cm).
Leaves: evergreen; alternate; 1–1¼" (2.5–3 cm) long, ⅜–½" (10–12 mm) wide. Elliptical, rounded at tip, broadest and finely toothed beyond middle, tapering toward short-stalked base, slightly leathery, 5–8 straight sunken veins on each side. Dark green above, pale green or grayish and slightly hairy beneath.
Bark: dark brown, smooth, becoming scaly.
Twigs: reddish brown, hairy when young.
Flowers: ⅜" (10 mm) long; funnel-shaped, slightly 5-lobed, yellowish, hairy, without petals, nearly stalkless; 1–3 at leaf base; in early spring.
Fruit: ⅜" (10 mm) long; narrowly cylindrical, with twisted tail 2–3¼" (5–8 cm) long, covered with whitish hairs, 1-seeded; maturing in late summer.

Habitat
Dry, rocky soils of mountain slopes; in chaparral and oak woodland.

Range
SW. Oregon south to N. Baja California and east to Arizona; at 3500–6500' (1067–1981 m).

Comments
Birchleaf Mountain-mahogany is a common shrub in chaparral vegetation, sprouting after fire. It is also an important browse plant for deer, cattle, and sheep.

Cascara Buckthorn
Rhamnus purshiana
93

Large shrub or small tree with short trunk and crown of many stout, upright branches.
Height: 30' (9 m). Diameter: ½–1' (0.15–0.3 m).

Leaves: usually alternate, sometimes opposite; often clustered near ends of twigs; 2–6′ (5–15 cm) long, 1–2½″ (2.5–6 cm) wide. Broadly elliptical, finely wavy-toothed, with many nearly straight side veins. Dull green and nearly hairless above, paler and slightly hairy beneath, turning pale yellow in late autumn.
Bark: gray or brown, thin, fissured into short, thin scales; inner bark yellow, turning brown upon exposure; very bitter.
Twigs: gray, slender; hairy when young; ending in bud of tiny brown leaves covered with rust-colored hairs.
Flowers: ³⁄₁₆″ (5 mm) wide; bell-shaped, with 5 pointed, greenish-yellow sepals; in clusters at leaf bases; in spring and early summer.
Fruit: ⅜″ (10 mm) in diameter; berrylike; red, turning to purplish black; with thin, juicy, sweetish pulp and 2–3 seeds; maturing in late summer or autumn.

Habitat
Moist soils in open areas, along roadsides, and in understory of coniferous and mixed evergreen forests.

Range

S. British Columbia south to N. California; also Rocky Mountain region south to N. Idaho and W. Montana; to 5000′ (1524 m).

Comments
The bark is the source of the laxative drug, Cascara Sagrada, meaning "sacred bark" in Spanish. It is harvested commercially in Washington and Oregon by stripping bark from wild trees. When a tree is cut down, several sprouts grow from the stump. The berries are consumed by songbirds and bears, raccoons, and other mammals.

Black Cottonwood
Populus trichocarpa
94

The tallest native cottonwood, with open crown of erect branches and sticky, resinous buds with balsam odor.
Height: 60–120′ (18–37 m). Diameter: 1–3′ (0.3–0.9 m), sometimes much larger.
Leaves: alternate; 3–6″ (7.5–15 cm) long, 2–4″ (5–10 cm) wide, larger on young twigs. Broadly ovate; short- or long-pointed at tip, rounded or slightly notched at base; finely wavy-toothed, slightly thickened, hairless or nearly so. Shiny dark green above, whitish and often with rusty veins beneath; turning yellow in autumn. Leafstalks slender, round, hairy.
Bark: gray, smooth, becoming thick and deeply furrowed into flat, scaly ridges.
Twigs: brownish, stout, often hairy when young.
Flowers: catkins 1½–3¼″ (4–8 cm) long; reddish purple; male and female on separate trees; in early spring.
Fruit: ¼″ (6 mm) in diameter; round capsules, light brown, hairy; maturing in spring, splitting into 3 parts; many cottony seeds.

Habitat
Moist to wet soils of valleys, mainly on stream banks and flood

plains, also on upland slopes; often in pure stands and with willows and Red Alder.

Range
S. Alaska south to S. California and east in mountains to extreme SW. Alberta and Montana; also local in SW. North Dakota and N. Baja California; to 2000′ (610 m) in north; to 9000′ (2743 m) in south.

Comments
Black Cottonwood is the tallest native western hardwood. The current champion in Yamhill County, Oregon, measures 147′ (44.8 m) in height, 30.2′ (9.2 m) in trunk circumference, and 97′ (29.6 m) in crown spread.

Quaking Aspen
Populus tremuloides
95

The most widely distributed tree in North America, with a narrow, rounded crown of thin foliage.
Height: 40–70′ (12–21 m). Diameter: 1–1½′ (0.3–0.5 m).
Leaves: alternate; 1¼–3″ (4–7.5 cm) long. Nearly round, abruptly short-pointed, rounded at base; finely saw-toothed, thin. Shiny green above, dull green beneath; turning golden yellow in autumn before shedding. Leafstalks slender, flattened.
Bark: whitish, smooth, thin; on very large trunks becoming dark gray, furrowed, and thick.
Twigs: shiny brown, slender, hairless.
Flowers: catkins 1–2½″ (2.5–6 cm) long; brownish; male and female on separate trees; in spring before leaves.
Fruit: ¼″ (6 mm) long; narrowly conical, light green capsules in drooping catkins to 4″ (10 cm) long; maturing in late spring and splitting in 2 parts. Many tiny, cottony seeds; rarely produced in West, where propagation is by root sprouts.

Habitat
Many soil types, especially sandy and gravelly slopes; often in pure stands and in western mountains in an altitudinal zone below spruce-fir forest.

Range
Across northern North America from Alaska to Newfoundland, south to Virginia, and in Rocky Mountains south to S. Arizona and northern Mexico; from near sea level in north to 6500–10,000′ (1981–3048 m) in south.

Comments
The names refer to the leaves, which tremble in the slightest breeze on their flattened leafstalks. The soft, smooth bark is sometimes marked by bear claws. A pioneer tree after fires and logging and on abandoned fields, it is usually short-lived and replaced by conifers. The twigs and foliage are browsed by deer, elk, and moose, as well as by sheep and goats. Beavers, rabbits, and other mammals eat the bark, foliage, and buds, and grouse and quail feed on the winter buds. It is also known as Trembling Aspen.

Fremont Cottonwood
Populus fremontii
96, 167

Tree with broad, flattened, open crown of large, widely spreading branches.
Height: 40–80' (12–24 m). Diameter: 2–4' (0.6–1.2 m).
Leaves: alternate; 2–3" (5–7.5 cm) long and wide. Broadly triangular, often broader than long, short-pointed, nearly straight at base; with coarse, irregular, curved teeth; thick, hairless; leafstalks long, flattened. Shiny yellow-green; turning bright yellow in autumn.
Bark: gray, thick, rough, deeply furrowed.
Twigs: light green, stout, hairless.
Flowers: catkins 2–3½" (5–9 cm) long; reddish; male and female on separate trees; in early spring.
Fruit: about ½" (12 mm) long; egg-shaped capsules, light brown, hairless; maturing in spring, splitting into 3 parts; many cottony seeds.

Habitat
Wet soils along streams, often with sycamores, willows, and alders; in deserts, grasslands, and woodlands.

Range

S. and W. Colorado west to N. California and southeast to Trans-Pecos Texas; also northern Mexico; to 6500' (1981 m).

Comments
This species, including varieties, is the common cottonwood at low altitudes along the Rio Grande and Colorado River and in the rest of the Southwest, as well as in California. Fremont Cottonwood grows only on wet soil and is an indicator of permanent water and shade. Easily propagated from cuttings, it is extensively planted in its range along irrigation ditches, and although it grows rapidly, it is short-lived. To this day, Hopi Indians of the Southwest carve cottonwood roots into kachina dolls, the representations of supernatural beings, which have become valuable collectors' items. Horses gnaw the sweetish bark of this species; beavers also feed on the bark and build dams with the branches. Greenish clumps of parasitic mistletoes are often scattered on the branches.

Black Hawthorn
Crataegus douglasii
97

Small tree with compact, rounded crown of stout, spreading branches; often a thicket-forming shrub.
Height: 30' (9 m). Diameter: 1' (0.3 m).
Leaves: alternate; 1–3" (2.5–7.5 cm) long, ⅝–2" (1.5–5 cm) wide. Obovate to ovate, broadest toward short-pointed tip, sharply saw-toothed and often slightly lobed. Shiny dark green becoming nearly hairless above, paler beneath.
Bark: gray or brown, smooth or becoming scaly.
Twigs: shiny red, slender, hairless, often with straight or slightly curved spines to 1" (2.5 cm) long.
Flowers: ½" (12 mm) wide; with 5 white petals, 10–20 pink stamens, and 3–5 styles; on long, slender stalks in broad, leafy clusters; in spring.
Fruit: ½" (12 mm) in diameter; turning shiny black, with thick, light yellow pulp and 3–5 nutlets; sweetish and mealy

but somewhat insipid-tasting; several on long stalks in
drooping clusters, maturing in late summer.

Habitat
Moist soils of mountain streams and valleys; with sagebrush
and conifers.

Range
Local in S. Alaska and from British Columbia south to central
California, east to New Mexico, and north to S. Saskatchewan;
also local near Lake Superior; near sea level in north; to 6000'
(1829 m) in south.

Comments
This species is a handsome ornamental with showy white
flowers, glossy foliage, and odd, shiny black fruits. It is
named for its discoverer, David Douglas (1798–1834), the
Scottish botanical explorer. Cattle and sheep browse the
foliage; pheasants, partridges, quail, and other birds consume
the berries.

Vine Maple
Acer circinatum
98

Shrub or small tree with short trunk or several branches
turning and twisting from base, often vinelike and leaning or
sprawling.
Height: 25' (7.6 m). Diameter: 8" (20 cm).
Leaves: opposite; 2½–4½" (6–11 cm) long and wide.
Rounded, with 7–11 long-pointed lobes, sharply doubly
toothed, with 7–11 main veins from notched base; long
leafstalks with enlarged bases joined. Bright green above,
paler with tufts of hairs in vein angles beneath; turning orange
and red in autumn.
Bark: gray or brown; smooth or finely fissured.
Twigs: green to reddish brown, with whitish bloom; slender.
Flowers: ½" (12 mm) wide; spreading purple sepals and
whitish petals; in broad, branched clusters at end of short
twigs; with new leaves in spring; usually male and female on
same plant.
Fruit: 1½" (4 cm) long; paired, long-winged keys spreading
almost horizontally; reddish when young; 1-seeded; maturing
in autumn.

Habitat
Moist soils, especially along shaded stream banks; in
understory of coniferous forests.

Range
Pacific Coast from SW. British Columbia south to N.
California; to 5000' (1524 m).

Comments
This handsome ornamental is dramatically colored in most
seasons with bright green foliage turning orange and red in
autumn, purple and white flowers in spring, and young red
fruit in summer. The seeds of this and other maples are
consumed by songbirds, game birds, and mammals.

Bigtooth Maple
Acer grandidentatum
99

Small to medium-sized tree with short trunk and spreading, rounded, dense crown; often a shrub.
Height: 40' (12 m). Diameter: 8" (20 cm).
Leaves: opposite; 2–3¼" (5–8 cm) long and wide. 3 broad, blunt lobes and 2 small basal lobes; few blunt teeth, 3 or 5 main veins from notched or straight base; slightly thickened; long leafstalks. Shiny dark green above, pale and finely hairy beneath; turning red or yellow in autumn.
Bark: gray or dark brown; thin; smooth or scaly.
Twigs: reddish, slender, hairless.
Flowers: ³⁄₁₆" (5 mm) long; with bell-shaped, 5-lobed, yellow calyx; in drooping clusters on long, slender, hairy stalks; male and female in same or different clusters; with new leaves in early spring.
Fruit: 1–1¼" (2.5–3 cm) long; paired, forking, long-winged keys; reddish or green, mostly hairless, 1-seeded; maturing in autumn.

Habitat
Moist soils of canyons in mountains and plateaus; in woodlands.

Range
SE. Idaho south to Arizona and east to S. New Mexico and Trans-Pecos Texas; local in Edwards Plateau of south-central Texas, SW. Oklahoma, and northern Mexico; at 4000–7000' (1219–2134 m); locally to 1500' (457 m).

Comments
The western relative of Sugar Maple, Bigtooth Maple has sweetish sap used locally to prepare maple sugar. The common and scientific names both refer to the leaves.

Rocky Mountain Maple
Acer glabrum
100

Shrub or small tree with short trunk and slender, upright branches, hairless throughout.
Height: 30' (9 m). Diameter: 1' (0.3 m).
Leaves: opposite; 1½–4½" (4–11 cm) long and wide, sometimes smaller. 3 short-pointed lobes (sometimes 5) or divided into 3 lance-shaped leaflets; doubly saw-toothed, 3 or 5 main veins from base; long, reddish leafstalks. Shiny dark green above, paler or whitish beneath; turning red or yellow in autumn.
Bark: gray or brown; smooth, thin.
Twigs: reddish brown, slender.
Flowers: ¼" (6 mm) wide; greenish yellow; 4 narrow sepals and 4 petals on drooping stalks; in branched clusters; male and female usually on separate plants; with new leaves in spring.
Fruit: ¾–1" (2–2.5 cm) long; paired, forking, long-winged keys; reddish, turning light brown; 1-seeded; maturing in late summer or autumn.

Habitat
Moist soils, especially along canyons and mountain slopes in coniferous forests.

Range
SE. Alaska, British Columbia, and SW. Alberta, south mostly in mountains to S. New Mexico and S. California; to 5000–9000' (1524–2743 m) in south.

Comments
The northernmost maple in the New World, it extends through southeastern Alaska. Deer, elk, cattle, and sheep browse the foliage.

California Sycamore
Platanus racemosa
101

Tree with enlarged base, stout trunk, often branched near base, and broad, irregular, open crown of thick, spreading branches.
Height: 40–80' (12–24 m). Diameter: 2–4' (0.6–1.2 m), sometimes much larger.
Leaves: alternate; 6–9" (15–23 cm) long and wide. Slightly star-shaped; deeply divided about halfway to base into 5 (sometimes 3) narrow, long-pointed lobes, wavy edges with few large teeth, 5 (sometimes 3) main veins from notched or blunt base. Light green above, paler and hairy beneath. Leafstalk long, stout, covering side bud at enlarged base.
Bark: whitish, smooth, thin on branches; peeling in brownish flakes and mottled on trunk, becoming dark gray or brown; rough, thick, deeply furrowed at base.
Twigs: slender, zigzag, light brown, with ring scars at nodes; hairy when young.
Flowers: tiny; male and female in 2–7 separate, ball-like clusters; in spring with leaves.
Fruit: ⅞" (22 m) in diameter; 2–7 balls or heads hanging on long stalk, composed of many narrow nutlets with tuft of hairs at base; maturing in autumn, separating in winter.

Habitat
Wet soils of stream banks in valleys, foothills, and mountains.

Range
N. to S. California and N. Baja California; to 4000' (1219 m).

Comments
Common in the valleys of California, it is also a shade and ornamental tree. Giant trees with massive, barrel-shaped trunks often lean and fork into picturesque shapes. The champion at Santa Barbara, California, when measured in 1945, was 116' (35.4 m) high, 27' (8.2 m) in trunk circumference, and 158' (48.2 m) in crown spread. The mottled bark and coarse, light green foliage are distinctive.

Bigleaf Maple
Acer macrophyllum
102

Small to large tree with broad, rounded crown of spreading or drooping branches and the largest leaves of all maples.
Height: 30–70' (9–21 m). Diameter: 1–2½' (0.3–0.8 m).
Leaves: opposite; 6–10" (15–25 cm) long and wide. Rounded, with 5 deep, long-pointed lobes (sometimes 3); edges with few small, blunt lobes and teeth; 5 main veins; slightly thickened.

Shiny dark green above, paler and hairy beneath; turning orange or yellow in autumn. Leafstalks to 10' (25 cm), stout, with milky sap when broken.
Bark: brown, furrowed into small 4-sided plates.
Twigs: green, stout, hairless.
Flowers: ¼" (6 mm) long; many on slender stalks; yellow; fragrant; male and female together in narrow, drooping clusters to 6" (15 cm) long at end of leafy twig; in spring.
Fruit: 1–1½" (2.5–4 cm) long; paired, long-winged keys; brown, with stiff yellowish hairs; 1-seeded; maturing in autumn.

Habitat
Stream banks and in moist canyon soils sometimes in pure stands.

Range
SW. British Columbia to S. California; to 1000' (305 m) in north; at 3000–5500' (914–1676 m) in south.

Comments
The common and scientific names describe the very large leaves. A handsome shade tree and particularly showy in autumn, Bigleaf Maple is popular on the Pacific Coast. The only western maple with wood of commercial importance, it is used for veneer, furniture, handles, woodenware, and novelties. Indians made canoe paddles from the wood, and maple sugar can be obtained from the sap.

California Black Oak
Quercus kelloggii
103

Tree with large branches and irregular, broad, rounded crown of stout, spreading branches.
Height: 30–80' (9–24 m). Diameter: 1–3' (0.3–0.9 m).
Leaves: alternate; 3–8" (7.5–20 cm) long, 2–5" (5–13 cm) wide. Elliptical, usually 7-lobed about halfway to midvein, each lobe with few bristle-pointed teeth; slightly thick. Shiny dark green above, light yellow-green and often hairy beneath; turning yellow or brown in autumn.
Bark: dark brown, thick, becoming furrowed into irregular plates and ridges; on small trunks, smooth, light brown.
Acorns: 1–1½" (2.5–4 cm) long; elliptical, ⅓–⅔ enclosed by deep, thin, scaly cup; 1 or few on short stalk; maturing second year.

Habitat
Sandy, gravelly, and rocky soils of foothills and mountains; often in nearly pure stands and in mixed coniferous forests.

Range
SW. Oregon south in Coast Ranges and Sierra Nevada to S. California; at 1000–8000' (305–2438 m).

Comments
This is the common oak in valleys of southwestern Oregon and in the Sierra Nevada. The large, deeply lobed leaves with bristle-tipped teeth differ from all other western oaks, but resemble those of Black Oak (*Quercus velutina*) of the eastern

United States. Slow-growing and long-lived, it is a popular
fuelwood and hardy shade tree in dry soils. Deer and livestock
browse the foliage.

Cliffrose
Cowania mexicana
104, 201

Small-leaf, evergreen, resinous, spreading shrub or small tree
with crooked trunk, irregular, open crown of many short,
stiff, erect branches, and showy white flowers.
Height: 20' (6 m). Diameter: 6" (15 cm).
Leaves: evergreen; alternate; crowded; ¼–⅝" (6–15 mm)
long. Wedge-shaped, divided into 3–7 narrow lobes, thick
and leathery, edges rolled under, with white sticky resin-dots;
bitter-tasting. Dark green and often loosely hairy above,
densely covered with white, woolly hairs beneath.
Bark: reddish brown or gray; shreddy, splitting into long,
narrow strips.
Twigs: reddish brown, hairy, gland-dotted.
Flowers: ¾–1" (2–2.5 cm) wide; with 5 broad white or pale
yellow; spreading petals; borne singly at end of side twigs
fragrant; in spring and summer.
Fruit: ¼" (6 mm) long; each with long whitish, feathery tail
to 2" (5 cm) long; 5–10 in cluster, developed from 1 flower;
in autumn.

Habitat
Dry, rocky hills and plateaus, especially limestone; in deserts
and with oaks, pinyons and junipers.

Range
SE. Colorado to N. Utah, E. California, and SW. New
Mexico; also south to central Mexico; at 3500–8000' (1067–
2438 m).

Comments
An attractive ornamental, Cliffrose is also planted for erosion
control. It is an important browse plant for deer, cattle, and
sheep, especially in winter. Indians used to make rope,
sandals, and clothing from the shreddy bark and arrow shafts
from the stems. It is also called Quinine-bush because of the
bitter-tasting foliage. This species is abundant on the south
rim at Grand Canyon National Park, Arizona. Another
alternate name is Stansbury Cliffrose.

California Buckeye
Aesculus californica
105

Thicket-forming shrub or small tree with a short trunk often
enlarged at base, a broad, rounded crown of crooked branches,
and many showy flowers.
Height: 25' (7.6 m). Diameter: 1' (0.3 m).
Leaves: opposite; palmately compound; long-stalked.
Generally 5 leaflets (sometimes 4–7) 3–6" (7.5–15 cm) long,
1–2" (2.5–5 cm) wide; narrowly elliptical, finely saw-toothed,
short-stalked. Dark green above, paler with whitish hairs on
veins beneath; turning dull brown and shedding in late
summer.
Bark: light gray, smooth, thin.

Twigs: reddish brown, stout, ending in resinous bud.
Flowers: 1–1¼" (2.5–3 cm) long; with 4–5 nearly equal,
white or sometimes pale pink petals and 5–7 much longer
stamens; fragrant; in upright, narrow clusters 4–8" (10–20
cm) long; in late spring and early summer.
Fruit: 2–3" (5–7.5 cm) long; pear-shaped capsules, pale
brown, smooth, splitting usually on 3 lines; maturing in late
summer; usually 1 large, rounded, shiny brown, poisonous
seed.

Habitat
Moist soils of canyons and on hillsides in chaparral and oak
woodland.

Range
California in Coast Ranges and Sierra Nevada foothills; to
4000′ (1219 m).

Comments
The only native buckeye in the West, this species is
sometimes grown as an ornamental. California Indians made
flour from the poisonous seeds after leaching out the toxic
element with boiling water. The ground, untreated seeds were
thrown into pools of water to stupefy fish, which then rose to
the surface and were easily caught. Chipmunks and squirrels
consume the seeds, but bees are poisoned by the nectar and
pollen.

Oregon Ash
Fraxinus latifolia
106

Tree with long, straight trunk and narrow, dense crown.
Height: 80′ (24 m). Diameter: 2′ (0.6 m).
Leaves: opposite; pinnately compound; generally 5–12" (13–
30 cm) long; axis usually hairy. Leaflets 5 or 7 (sometimes 9),
paired except at end; 2–5" (5–13 cm) long, 1–1½" (2.5–4
cm) wide; elliptical, short-pointed at ends; without teeth or
slightly saw-toothed; with prominent network of veins;
stalkless or nearly so. Light green above, paler and hairy
beneath; turning yellow or brown in autumn.
Bark: dark gray or brown, thick, furrowed into forking, scaly
ridges.
Twigs: stout, covered with soft hairs.
Flowers: ⅛" (3 mm) long; without corolla; male yellowish and
female greenish on separate trees; many together in small
clusters on twigs; before leaves in early spring.
Fruit: 1¼–2" (3–5 cm) long; a light brown key with broad,
rounded wing extending nearly to base of slightly flattened
body; many hanging in dense clusters; maturing in early
autumn.

Habitat
Wet soils along streams and in canyons; with Red Alder,
Black Cottonwood, willows, and Oregon White Oak.

Range
W. Washington, W. Oregon, and south in Coast Ranges and
Sierra Nevada to central California; to 5500′ (1676 m).

Comments
Oregon Ash is the only ash native to the Northwest and the only western ash with commercially important wood; it is used for furniture, flooring, millwork, paneling, boxes, and fuel. It is also planted as a shade tree along the Pacific Coast.
According to an old superstition in the Northwest, poisonous snakes are unknown where this ash grows.

Velvet Ash
Fraxinus velutina
107

Tree with open, rounded crown of spreading branches and leaflets quite variable in shape and hairiness.
Height: 40' (12 m). Diameter: 1' (0.3 m).
Leaves: opposite; pinnately compound; 3–6" (7.5–15 cm) long. Commonly 5 leaflets (to 9) 1–3" (2.5–7.5 cm) long, ⅜–1¼" (1–3 cm) wide; paired except at end; lance-shaped to elliptical, pointed at ends, slightly wavy-toothed or sometimes without teeth; often slightly thickened and leathery; short-stalked. Shiny green above, paler and densely covered with soft hairs or sometimes hairless beneath; yellow in autumn.
Bark: gray, deeply furrowed into broad, scaly ridges.
Twigs: gray or brown, often hairy when young.
Flowers: ⅛" (3 mm) long; without corolla; male yellowish and female greenish on separate trees; many together in small clusters on twigs; before leaves in early spring.
Fruit: ¾–1¼" (2–3 cm) long; a light brown, narrow key with long wing not extending to base; many hanging in dense clusters; maturing in summer and early autumn.

Habitat
Moist soils of stream banks, washes, and canyons, mainly in mountains, desert, desert grassland; in oak woodland and Ponderosa Pine forest.

Range
Trans-Pecos Texas west to extreme SW. Utah, S. Nevada, and S. California and south to northern Mexico; at 2500–7000' (762–2134 m).

Comments
This variable species is the common ash in the Southwest, where it is planted as a shade and street tree. It is hardy in alkaline soils and fast growing. In the desert, ash trees indicate a permanent underground water supply.

Western Mountain-ash
Sorbus scopulina
108

A shrub forming dense clumps or, rarely, a small tree, with many small white flowers and small, applelike fruit.
Height: 20' (6 m). Diameter: 4" (10 cm).
Leaves: alternate; pinnately compound; 4–9" (10–23 cm) long. 11–15 stalkless leaflets 1¼–2½" (3–6 cm) long; lance-shaped, pointed at tip, sharply saw-toothed almost to unequal, rounded base; becoming hairless. Shiny dark green above, slightly paler beneath.
Bark: gray or reddish, smooth.
Twigs: light brown, slender, with whitish hairs when young.

Flowers: ⅜" (10 mm) wide; with 5 white rounded petals, fragrant; many in upright, rounded clusters 1¼–3" (3–7.5 cm) wide; in early summer.
Fruit: less than ⅜" (10 mm) in diameter; like a tiny apple, shiny red, bitter, with several seeds; fewer than 25 in a cluster; maturing in summer and persisting into winter.

Habitat
Moist soils, in openings and clearings; in coniferous forests.

Range
Alaska east to SW. Mackenzie and south in mountains to central California and S. New Mexico, locally beyond; down to sea level in north; at 4000–9000' (1219–2743 m) in south.

Comments
This shrubby species takes the form of a small tree in southeastern Alaska. Birds and mammals eat the fruit. The similar Sitka Mountain-ash (*Sorbus sitchensis*) of the Northwest Coastal Forest, Subalpine Forest, and Sierran Montane Forest occurs from southeastern Alaska south to northern Idaho and California.

Chamise
Adenostoma fasciculatum
109

An erect evergreen shrub with alternating clusters of tiny needlelike leaves and large basal burl.
Height: 2–12' (0.6–3.6 m).
Leaves: evergreen; in bundles or less often single and alternate; to ⅜" (1 cm) long, pointed, stiff, smooth, numerous.
Bark: reddish, nearly smooth on twigs but becoming shreddy with age.
Flowers: tiny, white or rarely pinkish, in dense panicles 1½–4" (3.8–10 cm) long at ends of branchlets; petals 5, sepals 5, persistent, united at base to form cuplike calyx; stamens 10–15, with clusters of 2–3 alternating with petals; May–June.

Habitat
Dry, rocky slopes and ridges among chaparral.

Range
N. California to Baja California west of the deserts.

Comments
This is the dominant chaparral plant throughout most of California, often forming pure, impenetrable stands. Also known as Greasewood, the shrub contains highly flammable resins, which cause it to burn rapidly when ignited. Following a fire, Chamise sprouts rapidly from its basal burl (root crown) and soon outgrows most competitors. Chamise further reduces competition by releasing toxins into the soil that inhibit or prevent the growth of most other plants. Its principal value to wildlife lies in providing cover, for the tough, resinous foliage is unpalatable. Chamise becomes dormant during the hottest, driest period of summer, and sheds both branches and bark in an effort to reduce the amount of tissue requiring moisture. These sloughed materials then serve as fuel for the next fire.

Big Sagebrush
Artemisia tridentata
110

Much-branched gray-green shrub with pungent sagelike aroma; with short, thick trunk or a few stems rising from base.
Height: 1½–15' (0.5–4.5 m).
Leaves: evergreen; alternate or in bundles. Usually to ¾" (2 cm) long. Upper leaves may be linear or oblanceolate and untoothed. Narrowly wedge-shaped, usually with 3 terminal lobes, covered with fine gray hairs.
Bark: gray, shreddy.
Flowers: heads ovoid, silver-green, numerous; usually 3–6 minute disk flowers (ray flowers absent) in erect, leafy panicles from ends of branchlets; July–November.
Fruit: resinous achenes.

Habitat
Deep, fine soils in arid basins and on mountain slopes to near timberline; often with pinyons and junipers.

Range
British Columbia east to North Dakota, south to S. California, Arizona, and New Mexico.

Comments
Big Sagebrush is the dominant shrub over vast areas of the Great Basin region. Several subspecies have been identified, all more or less similar to the typical form. Before the coming of white settlers to the West, bunchgrasses and sagebrush together formed vast steppes, with the shrubs distinctly subordinate. Overgrazing by sheep and cattle, however, has resulted in the elimination or severe reduction of grasses throughout most of the region, with the result that sagebrush has become the dominant plant cover on these arid steppelands. Sagebrush is a valuable forage plant for wildlife, particularly during the winter. It is browsed by deer, moose, elk, antelope, and bighorn sheep, especially in late winter and spring. Sage grouse also feed heavily on sagebrush, which also provides nesting sites for a variety of songbirds. Even more nutritious than alfalfa, this shrub consists of 16 percent proteins, 15 percent fats, and 47 percent carbohydrates. Humans have used the plant primarily as firewood—the volatile oils responsible for its pungent aroma are so flammable that they can cause even green plants to burn. Sagebrush reproduces entirely from seed and after fire may be replaced for a time by sprouting shrubs.

Coyote Brush
*Baccharis pilularis
consanguinea*
111

Erect, much-branched, evergreen shrub with green, angular branchlets in new growth.
Height: 2–10' (0.6–3 m).
Leaves: alternate, ½–1½" (1.3–4 cm) long. Obovate or oblanceolate, tapering to base. 1- or 3-veined, leathery, coarsely and irregularly toothed or almost untoothed. Dark green and hairless.
Flowers: male and female flower heads on different plants; heads rayless, solitary or often several in leaf axils or at ends of

leafy branchlets; August–October.
Fruit: small, clustered achenes.

Habitat
Low, open hills in grassland, brush, and woodland.

Range
S. Oregon to S. California from coast east to Sierra Nevada.

Comments
Coyote Brush is perhaps the most common and widespread
shrub in coastal brush communities in northern and central
California, becoming gradually less common southward.
Dwarf Baccharis (*B. pilularis*), the variety of this species that
was first discovered and named, is a prostrate dune plant found
only along the coast of central California. Coyote Brush,
though named later, is actually the more common widespread
variety. Except for differences in size and growth pattern, the
forms are similar, and plants with characteristics of both are
common where their ranges overlap. *Baccharis* refers to the
Roman god Bacchus, a god of vegetation and of wine;
pilularis, meaning "pill-shaped," refers to the round, flat
flower heads.

Antelope Brush
Purshia tridentata
112, 200

An erect, much-branched silvery shrub with fragrant yellow
flowers and many small, wedge-shaped 3-lobed leaves.
Height: 3–10' (1–3 m).
Leaves: evergreen or sometimes deciduous; alternate but
crowded and apparently in bundles, about ½" (1.3 cm) long,
with margins turned under slightly; gray-green and downy
above, white and covered with feltlike hairs beneath.
Bark: gray or brown, with young branches more or less sticky
and covered with fine hairs.
Flowers: about ½" (1.3 cm) across, fragrant, creamy yellow,
usually solitary at ends of short branchlets; 5 petals, 5 sepals,
about 25 stamens; May–July.
Fruit: a leathery, hairy, teardrop-shaped achene tapering in a
persistent style.

Habitat
Dry, well-drained slopes, usually with sagebrush but ranging
upslope in pinyon-juniper woodlands and dry, open conifer
forests nearly to timberline.

Range
British Columbia and Montana south to central California and
New Mexico.

Comments
Antelope Brush is one of the West's most important forage
plants for mule deer, elk, moose, bighorn sheep, and
pronghorns (the "antelope" for which it is named), especially
in the winter, when other food may be scarce. Domestic
livestock also favor the plant. On overgrazed lands, Antelope
Brush is usually severely pruned and therefore unavailable to
wildlife. Among the rodents that gather and cache the

teardrop-shaped seeds of this shrub are chipmunks, deer mice, pocket mice, and the golden-mantled ground squirrel. Some Antelope Brush populations are able to sprout after a fire and thereby quickly reinvade a burned area. Other populations do not sprout and may thereby be eliminated from extensive areas following a rangefire. Where this occurs on lands already overgrazed, the resulting damage can be disastrous.

Bog Birch
Betula glandulosa
113

Small, erect, or sometimes prostrate shrub with stiff, rather leathery leaves and finely haired, warty-glandular twigs.
Height: 1–6′ (.3–2 m); occasionally to 9′ (2.7 m).
Leaves: alternate, ½–1½″ (3–4 cm) long, nearly as wide. Broadly ovate or nearly round, wedge-shaped or rounded at base, rounded at tip, with rounded teeth. Dark green and hairless above, paler and glandular beneath; petioles reddish.
Bark: dark brown; smooth.
Flowers: male and female on same plant. Male flowers tiny, numerous in drooping catkins about 1″ (2.5 cm); catkins near end of twigs. Female flowers tiny, numerous in erect catkins about ¾″ (2 cm) long in leaf axils.
Nutlets: ovoid, about ⅛″ (3 mm) long, with narrow wings.

Habitat
Damp places, often forming low thickets in wet meadows and swamps.

Range
Alaska southward to N. California and Colorado, eastward to Newfoundland and New England states; to 7500′ (2250 m) in N. California.

Comments
The leaves are about the size and shape of quarters, and turn a coppery red in autumn.

Poison-oak
Toxicodendron diversiloba
114

An erect or spreading shrub or a climbing vine with 3-parted leaves and brown or whitish berries.
Height: shrub to 6′ (2 m); as a climbing vine may ascend tree trunks to great heights.
Leaves: alternate; compound, 3–6″ (7.5–15 cm) long, shiny dark green above, turning red in fall; leaflets 3, 1–4″ (2.5–10 cm) long, more or less ovate or oblong, the edges variously blunt- or round-toothed or lobed (rarely untoothed); terminal leaflet has distinct petiole.
Bark: grayish.
Flowers: small, usually in panicles that droop from leaf axils; 5 petals, 5 sepals, and 5 stamens; April–May, appearing with the leaves.
Fruit: brown or whitish berry about ¼″ (6 mm) in diameter; falling shortly after ripening.

Habitat
Shady to open woods, streambanks, thickets in damp bottomlands.

Range
Washington to Baja California, east to Arizona.

Comments
Poison-oak is not a true oak, but a close relative of Poison Ivy (*Toxicodendron radicans*). Poison Ivy also has 3-parted compound leaves, but the leaflets are not lobed and have more slender, pointed tips. Poison Ivy replaces Poison-oak east of the Pacific Coast region. Like Poison Ivy, Poison-oak secretes an oily juice to which many people are severely allergic. Merely touching any part of the plant is enough to cause painful dermatitis characterized by a blistery, oozing, extremely itchy rash. Coming into contact with the smoke of burned Poison-oak may cause severe eye and lung irritation. Nonetheless, livestock and deer commonly browse the plant without ill effect. Poison-oak is so widespread and common in California that it almost qualifies as the state shrub. Anyone spending time in the lowlands and foothills of the state should learn to recognize the plant and avoid it at all costs. Some people initially show little response to Poison-oak only to become sensitive later. Washing exposed parts with a strong soap such as Fels Naptha shortly after contact has been known to prevent dermatitis. Over-the-counter cortisone creams provide some relief from itching in mild cases; where dermatitis is more severe, victims may want to see their physician.

Black Spruce
Picea mariana
115

Tree with open, irregular, conical crown of short, horizontal or slightly drooping branches; a prostrate shrub at timberline.
Height: 20–60′ (6–18 m). Diameter: 4–12″ (0.1–0.3 m).
Needles: evergreen; ¼–⅝″ (6–15 mm) long. Spreading on all sides of twig from very short leafstalks; 4-angled, stiff, sharp-pointed. Ashy blue-green with whitish lines.
Bark: gray or blackish, thin, scaly; brown beneath; cut surface of inner bark yellowish.
Twigs: brown, slender, hairy, rough, with peglike bases.
Cones: ⅝–1¼″ (1.5–3 cm) long; egg-shaped or rounded, dull gray; curved downward on short stalk and remaining attached, often clustered near top of crown; cone-scales stiff and brittle, rounded and finely toothed; paired, brown, long-winged seeds.

Habitat
Wet soils and bogs including peats, clays, and loams; in coniferous forests; often in pure stands.

Range
Across northern North America near northern limit of trees from Alaska and British Columbia east to Labrador, south to N. New Jersey, and west to Minnesota; at 2000–5000′ (610–1524 m).

Comments
Black Spruce is one of the most widely distributed conifers in North America. Uses are similar to those of White Spruce;

however, the small size limits lumber production. The lowest branches take root by layering when deep snows bend them to the ground, forming a ring of small trees around a large one.

Sitka Spruce
Picea sitchensis
116

The world's largest spruce, with tall, straight trunk from buttressed base, and broad crown of horizontal branches.
Height: 160' (49 m). Diameter: 3–5' (0.9–1.5 m), sometimes much larger.
Needles: evergreen; spreading on all sides of twig; ⅝–1" (1.5–2.5 cm) long. Flattened and slightly keeled, sharp-pointed; dark green.
Bark: gray, smooth, thin; becoming dark purplish brown with scaly plates.
Twigs: brown, stout, hairless, rough, with peglike bases.
Cones: 2–3½" (5–9 cm) long; cylindrical, short-stalked, light orange-brown; hanging at ends of twigs; opening and falling at maturity; cone-scales long, stiff, thin, rounded, and irregularly toothed. Paired, brown, long-winged seeds.

Habitat
Coastal forests in fog belt, a narrow strip of high rainfall and cool climate; in pure stands and with Western Hemlock.

Range
Pacific Coast from S. Alaska and British Columbia to NW. California; to timberline at 1500' (457 m) in Alaska; below 1200' (366 m) in California.

Comments
The main timber tree in Alaska, Sitka Spruce produces high-grade lumber for many uses and wood pulp for newsprint.

Engelmann Spruce
Picea engelmannii
117

Large tree with dark or blue-green foliage; dense, narrow, conical crown of short branches spreading in close rows.
Height: 80–100' (24–30 m). Diameter: 1½–2½' (0.5–0.8 m).
Needles: evergreen; ⅝–1" (1.5–2.5 cm) long. Spreading on all sides of twig from very short leafstalks; 4-angled, sharp-pointed, slender, flexible; with disagreeable skunklike odor when crushed; dark or blue-green, with whitish lines.
Bark: grayish brown or purplish brown; thin, with loosely attached scales.
Twigs: brown, slender, hairy, rough, with peglike leaf bases.
Cones: 1½–2½" (4–6 cm) long; cylindrical, shiny light brown; hanging at end of leafy twig; cone-scales long, thin, and flexible, narrowed and irregularly toothed; paired, blackish, long-winged seeds.

Habitat
Dominant with Subalpine Fir in subalpine zone up to timberline; also with other conifers.

Range
Central British Columbia and SW. Alberta south to Oregon

and New Mexico; at 8000–12,000′ (2438–3659 m) in south; down to 2000′ (619 m) in north.

Comments
Its resonant qualities make the wood of Engelmann Spruce valuable for piano sounding boards and violins.

Blue Spruce
Picea pungens
118

Large tree with blue-green foliage and a conical crown of stout, horizontal branches in rows.
Height: 70–100′ (21–30 m). Diameter: 1½–3′ (0.5–0.9 m). Needles: evergreen; spreading on all sides of twig from very short leafstalks; ¾–1⅛″ (2–2.8 cm) long. 4-angled, sharp-pointed, stiff; with resinous odor when crushed. Dull blue-green or bluish, with whitish lines.
Bark: gray or brown; furrowed and scaly.
Twigs: yellow-brown, stout, hairless, rough, with peglike leaf bases.
Cones: 2¼–4″ (6–10 cm) long; cylindrical, mostly stalkless, shiny light brown; cone-scales long, thin, and flexible, narrowed and irregularly toothed; paired, long-winged seeds.

Habitat
Narrow bottomlands along mountain streams; also cool, damp north slopes; often in pure stands.

Range
Rocky Mountain region from S. and W. Wyoming and E. Idaho south to N. and E. Arizona and S. New Mexico; at 6000–11,000′ (1829–3353 m).

Comments
Cultivated varieties of Blue Spruce include several with dramatic bluish-white and silvery-white foliage. It is a popular Christmas tree and is also used in shelterbelts.

White Spruce
Picea glauca
119

Tree with rows of horizontal branches forming a conical crown; smaller and shrubby at tree line.
Height: 40–100′ (12–30 m). Diameter: 1–2′ (0.3–0.6 m). Needles: evergreen; ½–¾″ (12–19 mm) long. Spreading mainly on upper side of twig, from very short leafstalks; 4-angled, stiff, sharp-pointed. Blue-green, with whitish lines; exuding skunklike odor when crushed.
Bark: gray or brown, thin, smooth or scaly; cut surface of inner bark whitish.
Twigs: orange-brown, slender, hairless, rough, with peglike bases.
Cones: 1½–2½″ (4–6 cm) long; cylindrical, shiny light brown, hanging at end of twigs, falling at maturity; cone-scales thin and flexible, margins nearly straight and without teeth; paired brown, long-winged seeds.

Habitat
Many soil types in coniferous forests; sometimes in pure stands.

Range
Across northern North America near northern limit of trees from Alaska and British Columbia east to Labrador, south to Maine, and west to Minnesota; local in NW. Montana, South Dakota, and Wyoming; from near sea level to timberline at 2000–5000' (610–1524 m).

Comments
This is the foremost pulpwood and generally the most important commercial tree species of Canada. As well as providing lumber for construction, the wood is valued for piano sounding boards, violins, and other musical instruments. White Spruce and Black Spruce are the most widely distributed conifers in North America after Common Juniper, which rarely reaches tree size. Various kinds of wildlife, including deer, rabbits, and grouse, browse spruce foliage in winter.

Sugar Pine
Pinus lambertiana
120

Large, very tall tree with a straight trunk unbranched for a long span and open, flat-topped crown of long, nearly horizontal branches, bearing giant cones near the ends; becoming flat-topped.
Height: 100–160' (30–49 m). Diameter: 3–6' (0.9–1.8 m), sometimes much larger.
Needles: evergreen; 5 in bundle, with sheath shedding first year; 2¾–4" (7–10 cm) long. Twisted, slender, stiff, sharp-pointed; blue-green, with white lines on all surfaces.
Bark: brown or gray, furrowed into irregular scaly ridges; gray and smooth on branches.
Cones: 11–18" (28–46 cm) long; cylindrical, shiny light brown; hanging down on long stalk near ends of upper branches; cone-scales thick, rounded, ending in blunt point, spreading widely; seeds large, long-winged, edible.

Habitat
Many kinds of mountain soils; not forming pure stands but occurring in mixed coniferous forests.

Range
Cascade Range from N. Oregon south through Sierra Nevada to S. California; at 1100–5400' (335–1646 m) in north, 2000–7800' (610–2377 m) in Sierra Nevada, and 4000–10,500' (1219–3200 m) in south.

Comments
A major lumber species, Sugar Pine is one of the most beautiful and largest pines and has been called the "king of pines." The trunk diameter occasionally reaches 6–8' (1.8–2.4 m); the current champion is 10' (3 m) in diameter, and the tallest tree recorded was 241' (73.5 m) high. No other conifer has such long cones, which reach a maximum of 21" (53 cm). Sugar Pine provided early settlers of California with wood for their houses, especially shingles or shakes, and with fences. Forty-niners made ample use of the wood for flumes, sluice boxes, bridges, and mine timbers. American Indians

gathered and ate the large, sweet seeds. The common name refers to the sweetish resin that exudes from cut or burned heartwood, which was also eaten by Indians.

Western White Pine
Pinus monticola
121

Large to very large tree with straight trunk and narrow, open, conical crown of horizontal branches.
Height: 100' (30 m). Diameter: 3' (0.9 m), sometimes much larger.
Needles: evergreen; 5 in bundle, with sheath shedding first year; 2–4" (5–10 cm) long. Slightly stout; blue-green, with whitish lines on inner surfaces.
Bark: gray and thin, smooth, becoming furrowed into rectangular, scaly plates.
Cones: 5–9" (13–23 cm) long; narrowly cylindrical, yellow-brown, mostly long-stalked; opening and shedding at maturity; cone-scales thin, rounded, ending in small point, spreading widely; long-winged seeds.

Habitat
Moist mountain soils; in mixed forests and occasionally in almost pure stands.

Range
Northern Rocky Mountains from British Columbia southeast to NW. Montana; also along Pacific Coast south through the Sierra Nevada to central California; to 3500' (1067 m) in north; at 6000–9800' (1829–2987 m) in south.

Comments
An important timber tree, Western White Pine is also a leading match wood, because of its uniformly high grade without knots, twisted grain, or discoloration. It is one of the worlds largest pines; the champion near Medford, Oregon, is 239' (72.8 m) tall. White pine blister rust, caused by an introduced fungus (*Cromartium ribicola*), is a serious disease of this and other 5-needle white pines.

Limber Pine
Pinus flexilis
122

Medium-sized tree with short trunk and broad, rounded crown of annual rows of stout branches nearly down to ground; or a windswept, deformed shrub at timberline.
Height: 40–50' (12–15 m). Diameter: 2–3' (0.6–0.9 m).
Needles: evergreen; 5 in bundle, with sheath shedding first year; 2–3½" (5–9 cm) long. Slender, long-pointed, not toothed; light or dark green, with white lines on all surfaces.
Bark: light gray and smooth; becoming dark brown and furrowed into scaly ridges or rectangular plates.
Twigs: slender, very tough and flexible.
Cones: 3–6" (7.5–15 cm) long; egg-shaped, yellow-brown, short-stalked; opening at maturity; cone-scales thick, rounded, ending in blunt point; seeds large and edible, with short wing.

Habitat
Dry, rocky slopes and ridges of high mountains up to timberline; often in pure stands.

Range
Rocky Mountain region chiefly, from SE. British Columbia
and SW. Alberta south to N. New Mexico and west to E. and
S. California; also local in NE. Oregon, SW. North Dakota,
Black Hills of South Dakota, and W. Nebraska; at 5000–
12,000′ (1524–3658 m).

Comments
The names refer to the very tough and flexible twigs, which
can sometimes be twisted into a knot. Plants on exposed
ridges and at timberline are shaped by the wind into stunted
shrubs with crooked or twisted branches that are bent over and
are longer on one side. Birds and mammals, especially
squirrels, consume the large seeds.

Whitebark Pine
Pinus albicaulis
123

Tree with short, twisted or crooked trunk and irregular,
spreading crown; a shrub at timberline; foliage has sweetish
taste and odor.
Height: 20–50′ (6–15 m). Diameter: 1–2′ (0.3–0.6 m).
Needles: evergreen; 5 in bundle, with sheath shedding first
year; crowded at ends of twigs; 1½–2¾″ (4–7 cm) long.
Stout, stiff, short-pointed; dull green, with faint white lines
on all surfaces.
Bark: whitish gray, smooth, thin, becoming scaly.
Twigs: stout, tough and flexible, brown; with fine hairs when
young.
Cones: 1½–3¼″ (4–8 cm) long; egg-shaped or rounded,
almost stalkless, purple to brown; shedding at maturity but
not opening; cone-scales very thick, with sharp edge ending in
raised, stout point. Large, elliptical, dark brown, thick-
walled, wingless, edible seeds.

Habitat
Dry, rocky soils on exposed slopes and ridges in subalpine
zone to timberline; sometimes forms pure stands and thickets.

Range .
Central British Columbia east to SW. Alberta, south to W.
Wyoming and west to central California. At 4500–7000′
(1372–2134 m) in north; at 8000–12,000′ (2438–3658 m)
in south.

Comments
American Indians gathered the cones and ate the seeds of this
species. Whitebark Pine is considered the most primitive
native pine because its cones do not open until they decay.

Chihuahua Pine
Pinus leiophylla
124

Pine with trunk bearing short, leafy twigs, very thick bark,
and thin, open, spreading crown of upturned branches.
Height: 30–80′ (9–24 m). Diameter: 1–2′ (0.3–0.6 m).
Needles: evergreen; 3 in bundle, with sheath shedding first
year; 2½–4″ (6–10 cm) long. Stout, stiff; blue-green, with
white lines on all surfaces.
Bark: dark brown or blackish, as much as 2–3″ (5–7.5 cm)

thick, and deeply furrowed into broad, scaly ridges.
Cones: 1½–2½" (4–6 cm) long; narrowly egg-shaped, shiny
light brown, long-stalked; usually opening but remaining
attached; cone-scales flattened, mostly with tiny prickle.

Habitat
Rocky ridges and slopes of mountains; with Arizona Pine and
Apache Pine.

Range
SW. New Mexico, E. central and SE. Arizona, and Mexico; at
5000–7800' (1524–2377 m).

Comments
Unlike most pines, this species often produces new shoots or
sprouts from cut stumps. The cones mature in 3 growing
seasons, instead of the usual 2; cones in 3 stages of ⌐
development, as well as many old, open cones, are usually
present.

Digger Pine
Pinus sabiniana
125

Tree with crooked, forking trunk and branches; open, very
thin, irregular, broad, or rounded crown; and very large,
heavy cones.
Height: 40–70' (12–21 m), sometimes much larger.
Diameter: 2–4' (0.6–1.2 m).
Needles: evergreen; 3 in bundle; 8–12" (20–30 cm) long.
Slender and drooping; dull gray-green, with many white lines.
Bark: dark gray, thick, deeply and irregularly furrowed into
scaly ridges, becoming slightly shaggy; light gray, smooth on
branches.
Cones: mostly 6–10" (15–25 cm) long; egg-shaped, brown,
bent down on long stalks; opening late and remaining on tree
many years; cone-scales very long, thick, sharply keeled and 4-
sided, narrowed into very large, stout, straight or slightly
curved spine. Very large, elliptical, thick-walled, edible seeds
with detachable wing.

Habitat
Dry slopes and ridges in foothills and low mountains; mainly
with oaks.

Range
N. to S. California through the Coast Ranges and the Sierra
Nevada; mostly at 1000–3000' (305–914 m); rarely down to
100' (30 m) and up to 6000' (1829 m).

Comments
The soft, lightweight wood of this common and widespread
pine is not durable; the crooked, forking trunks also make the
wood impractical to use except as fuel. The common name
refers to the Digger Indians (a pioneer term grouping all
California Indian tribes together), who dug up roots for food
and harvested quantities of the large seeds.

Coulter Pine
Pinus coulteri
127

Straight-trunked tree with rows of nearly horizontal branches formed annually, an open, thin, irregular crown, and very large, heavy cones.
Height: 40–70' (12–21 m). Diameter: 1–2½' (0.3–0.8 m).
Needles: evergreen; 3 in bundle; crowded at ends of stout, brown twigs; 8–12" (20–30 cm) long. Very stout, stiff, sharp-pointed; light gray-green, with many white lines.
Bark: dark gray, thick, deeply furrowed into scaly ridges, becoming slightly shaggy; blackish gray, very rough, divided into rectangular plates on branches.
Cones: 8–12" (20–30 cm) long; egg-shaped, bent down on very stout stalk, very heavy, slightly shiny yellow-brown, resinous; opening gradually and remaining on tree; cone-scales very long, thick, sharply keeled, with very long, stout spine flattened and curved forward. Seeds very large, eliptical, dark brown, thick-walled, edible, with detachable wing.

Habitat
Dry, rocky slopes and ridges in foothill woodlands and lower mountain forests.

Range
Central and S. California; also N. Baja California; at 3000–6000' (914–1829 m); rarely at 1000–7000' (305–2134 m).

Comments
This pine has the heaviest cone of all pines in the world, often weighing 4–5 pounds (1.8–2.3 kilos). Indians once gathered and ate the large seeds; now squirrels and other wildlife consume the annual crop.

Bishop Pine
Pinus muricata
128

Tree with conical, rounded, or irregular crown of stout, spreading branches and with numerous spiny cones remaining closed many years.
Height: 40–80' (12–24 m). Diameter: 2–3' (0.6–0.9 m).
Needles: evergreen; 2 in bundle; 4–6" (10–15 cm) long. Stout, slightly flattened, stiff, blunt-pointed, dull green.
Bark: dark gray, very thick, furrowed into scaly plates; smoothish on branches.
Cones: 2–3½" (5–9 cm) long; conical or egg-shaped, shiny yellow-brown, stalkless; oblique or 1-sided at base; many clustered in rings or whorls; cone-scales raised and keeled, those on outer part much enlarged, ending in stout, flattened, straight or curved spine.

Habitat
Low hills and plains along coast in fog belt; in scattered groves and with other pines.

Range
Coast of central and N. California and Santa Cruz and Santa Rosa islands; also local in Baja California; a variety on Cedros Island, Mexico; near sea level.

Comments
The numerous cones remain closed and may be enclosed by the

bark and wood of the expanding trunk. Fossil cones form the Pleistocene, or glacial, epoch indicate that this pine was associated with extinct vertebrates, including the woolly mammoth.

Knobcone Pine
Pinus attenuata
129

Tree with narrow, pointed crown of slender, nearly horizontal branches turned up at ends, becoming irregular with age, and with abundant cones remaining closed many years.
Height: 30–80' (9–24 m). Diameter: 1–2½' (0.3–0.8 m).
Needles: evergreen; 3 in bundle; 3–7" (7.5–18 cm) long; slender, stiff, yellow-green.
Bark: gray and smooth, becoming dark gray and fissured into large, scaly ridges.
Cones: 3¼–6" (8–15 cm) long; egg-shaped, clustered in many rings or whorls, stalkless and turned back, shiny yellow-brown, cone-scales raised and keeled, ending in short, stout spine. Blackish seeds about ¼" (6 mm) long; narrow wing 1–1¼" (2.5–3 cm) long.

Habitat
Forms almost pure stands on poor, coarse, rocky, mountain soils, including those derived from serpentine.

Range
SW. Oregon south to S. California; local in N. Baja California; at 1000–2000' (305–610 m) in north; 1500–4000' (457–1219 m), sometimes higher, in south.

Comments
The whorls of many knobby, closed cones help identify this species. Since the cones may become imbedded within the wood of the expanding trunk, this species has been called "the tree that swallows its cones." When fires kill the trees, cones as much as 30 years old are opened by the heat and shed their seeds. The abundant seedlings then begin a new stand.

Bigcone Douglas-fir
Pseudotsuga macrocarpa
132

Evergreen tree with open, broad, conical crown of long, spreading branches.
Height: 40–80' (12–24 m). Diameter: 2–3' (0.6–0.9 m).
Needles: evergreen; spreading mostly in 2 rows; ¾–1¼" (2–3 cm) long. Flattened, sharp-pointed, almost stalkless; blue-green or blue-gray.
Bark: dark reddish brown, thick, deeply furrowed into broad, scaly ridges.
Twigs: dark reddish brown, slender, often drooping, slightly hairy when young, ending in dark brown, pointed, scaly, hairless bud.
Cones: 4–6" (10–15 cm) long; narrowly egg-shaped, brown, short-stalked; with many thick, stiff, rounded cone-scales each above a short, 3-pointed bract. Paired, long-winged seeds.

Habitat
Dry slopes and canyons in various soils; with chaparral, Canyon Live Oak, and in mixed coniferous forests.

Range
Mountains of S. California; at 900–8000′ (274–2438 m).

Comments
Bigcone Douglas-fir is native only to the mountains of southern California. This species is distinguishable from Douglas-fir by its much larger cones and by its sharp-pointed, bluish needles. The trees recover from fire damage and injuries by sprouting vigorously from trunks and branches.

Noble Fir
Abies procera
133

The largest native true fir, with conical crown rounded at tip and with short, nearly horizontal branches.
Height: 100–150′ (30–46 m), often much taller. Diameter: 2½–4′ (0.8–1.2 m).
Needles: evergreen; spreading in 2 rows; 1–1⅛″ (2.5–3.5 cm) long. Flat, grooved above, often notched, blue-green with whitish lines; shorter, crowded and curved upward, 4-sided, pointed on upper twigs.
Bark: gray-brown and smooth, becoming brown to red-brown; slightly thickened, and furrowed into irregular, scaly plates.
Twigs: stout, brown, with rust-colored hairs when young.
Cones: 4½–7″ (11–18 cm) long; cylindrical, upright on topmost twigs, green becoming purplish brown: cone-scales with fine hairs and mostly covered by large papery bracts, finely toothed, long-pointed, and bent downward; paired, long-winged seeds.

Habitat
Moist soils in high mountains with short, cool growing season and deep winter snow. With other conifers; not in pure stands.

Range
Cascade Mountains and Coast Ranges from Washington south to NW. Calfornia; at 3000–7000′ (914–2134 m); occasionally at 200–8800′ (61–2682 m).

Comments
A handsome tree with large, showy cones mostly covered by papery bracts, Noble Fir was named by the Scottish botanical explorer David Douglas (1798–1834). It is the tallest true fir; the champion in the Gifford Pinchot National Forest in southwestern Washington has a height of 278′ (85 m), a trunk circumference of 28′ (8.6 m), and a crown spread of 47′ (14 m).

Douglas-fir
Pseudotsuga menziesii
134

Large to very large tree with narrow, pointed crown of slightly drooping branches.
Height: 80–200′ (24–61 m). Diameter: 2–5′ (0.6–1.5 m), sometimes much larger.
Needles: evergreen; spreading mostly in 2 rows; ¾–1¼″ (2–3 cm) long. Flattened, mostly rounded at tip, flexible; dark yellow-green or blue-green; very short, twisted leafstalks.
Bark: reddish brown, very thick, deeply furrowed into broad ridges; often corky.

Twigs: orange, turning brown; slender, hairy, ending in dark red, conical, pointed, scaly, hairless bud.
Cones: 2–3½″ (5–9 cm) long; narrowly egg-shaped, light brown, short-stalked; with many thin, rounded cone-scales each above a long, protruding, 3-pointed bract; paired, long-winged seeds.

Habitat
Coast Douglas-fir forms vast forests on moist, well-drained soils; often in pure stands. Rocky Mountain Douglas-fir is chiefly on rocky soils of mountain slopes; in pure stands and mixed coniferous forests.

Range
Central British Columbia south along Pacific Coast to central California; to 2700′ (823 m) in north and to 6000′ (1829 m) in south; also in Rocky Mountains to SE. Arizona and Trans-Pecos Texas; down to 2000′; (610 m) in north and at 8000–9500′ (2438–2896 m) in south; also local in mountains of northern and central Mexico.

Comments
One of the world's most important timber species, Douglas-fir ranks first in the United States in total volume of timber, in lumber production, and in production of veneer for plywood. It is one of the tallest trees as well and a popular Christmas tree.

Bristlecone Fir
Abies bracteata
135

The rarest of the firs, with narrow, conical, spirelike crown of short, slightly drooping branches.
Height: 40–100′ (12–30 m). Diameter: 1–3′ (0.3–0.9 m).
Needles: evergreen; spreading almost at right angles in 2 rows; 1½–2¼″ (4–6 cm) long, ⅛″ (3 mm) wide. Flat, sharp-pointed, stiff. Shiny dark green above, with 2 broad, whitish bands beneath.
Bark: light reddish brown, smooth, becoming scaly and slightly fissured at base.
Twigs: stout, light reddish brown, hairless.
Cones: 2½–4″ (6–10 cm) long; egg-shaped, purple-brown, upright on topmost twigs; cone-scales thin, rounded, hairless, finely toothed each with bract ending in very long, spreading, yellow-brown bristle; paired, long-winged seeds.

Habitat
Steep, rocky slopes and canyons; in mixed evergreen forests.

Range
Santa Lucia Mountains of S. California; at 2000–5000′ (610–1524 m); locally at 600′ (183 m).

Comments
The entire natural range of this rare species is limited to a coastal strip about 60 miles (97 km) long, within Los Padres National Forest. Aromatic resin from the trunk was used as incense in the early Spanish mission nearby.

Colorado Pinyon
Pinus edulis
136

Small, bushy, resinous tree with short trunk and compact, rounded, spreading crown.
Height: 15–35' (4.6–10.7 m). Diameter: 1–2' (0.3–0.6 m) or more.
Needles: evergreen; 2 in bundle (sometimes 3 or 1); ¾–1½" (2–4 cm) long; stout, light green.
Bark: gray to reddish brown, rough, furrowed into scaly ridges.
Cones: 1½–2" (4–5 cm) long; egg-shaped, yellow-brown, resinous or sticky; opening and shedding; with thick, blunt cone-scales; seeds large, wingless, slightly thick-walled, oily.

Habitat
Open, orchardlike woodlands, alone or with junipers; on dry, rocky foothills, mesas, plateaus, and lower mountain slopes.

Range
Southern Rocky Mountain region from Utah and Colorado south to New Mexico and Arizona; local in SW. Wyoming, extreme NW. Oklahoma, Trans-Pecos Texas, SE. California, and Mexico. Mostly at 5000–7000' (1524–2134 m).

Comments
The edible seeds, known as pinyon nuts, Indian nuts, pine nuts, and *piñones* (Spanish), are a wild, commercial nut crop. Eaten raw, roasted, and in candies, they were once a staple food of southwestern Indians. Every autumn, local residents, especially Navajo Indians and Spanish-Americans, harvest quantities for the local and gourmet markets. However, most of these oily seeds are promptly devoured by Pinyon Jays, Wild Turkeys, woodrats or "pack-rats," bears, deer, and other wildlife. Small Pinyons are popular Christmas trees. This species is the most common tree on the south rim of Grand Canyon National Park.

Singleleaf Pinyon
Pinus monophylla
137

Slow-growing, small pine with spreading, rounded, gray-green crown and low, horizontal branches; often shrubby.
Height: 16–30' (5–9 m). Diameter: 1–1½' (0.3–0.5 m).
Needles: evergreen; 1 in bundle (rarely 2), sheath shedding after first year; 1–2¼" (2.5–6 cm) long. Stout, stiff, sharp-pointed; straight or slightly curved; dull gray-green, with many whitish lines; resinous.
Bark: dark brown or gray, smoothish, becoming furrowed into scaly plates and ridges.
Cones: 2–3' (5–7.5 cm) long; egg-shaped or rounded, dull yellow-brown, almost stalkless, resinous; opening and shedding; with thick, 4-angled cone-scales, often with tiny prickle; seeds large, wingless, thin-walled, mealy, edible.

Habitat
Dry, gravelly slopes of mesas, foothills, and mountains; in open, orchardlike, pure stands and with junipers.

Range
SE. Idaho and N. Utah south to NW. Arizona and west to

S. California; also N. Baja California; at 3500–7000' (1067–2134 m).

Comments
This species is easily recognized by the needles borne singly, instead of in bundles of 2–5, as in other native pines. The large seeds, or pine nuts used to be a staple of Indians in the Great Basin region, many birds and mammals eat the seeds.

Parry Pinyon
Pinus quadrifolia
138

Small resinous tree with spreading, rounded crown and low, horizontal branches; often shrubby.
Height: 16–30' (5–9 m). Diameter: 1–1½' (0.3–0.5 m).
Needles: evergreen; 4 in bundle (sometimes 3 or 5), sheath shedding after first year; 1–2¼" (2.5–6 cm) long. Stout, stiff, sharp-pointed; bright green with whitish inner surfaces.
Bark: light gray and smooth, becoming reddish brown and furrowed into scaly ridges.
Cones: 1½–2½" (4–6 cm) long; egg-shaped or nearly round, almost stalkless, dull yellow-brown, resinous; opening and shedding; cone-scales thick, 4-angled, often with tiny prickle; large, wingless, edible seeds.

Habitat
Dry, gravelly slopes of foothills and mountains; in woodlands or with junipers.

Range
S. California and N. Baja California; at 4000–6000' (1219–1829 m).

Comments
The edible seeds are not gathered commercially because of the tree's limited distribution. Rodents (especially woodrats), other mammals, and birds consume the small annual crop.

Western Hemlock
Tsuga heterophylla
140

The largest hemlock, with long, slender, often fluted trunk; narrow, conical crown of short, slender, horizontal or slightly drooping branches; very slender, curved, drooping leader.
Height: 100–150' (30–46 m). Diameter: 3–4' (0.9–1.2 m).
Needles: evergreen; spreading in 2 rows; ¼–¾" (6–19 mm) long. Flat, flexible, rounded at tip, very short-stalked. Shiny dark green above, with 2 broad, whitish bands and indistinct green edges, often with tiny teeth beneath.
Bark: reddish brown to gray-brown, thick, deeply furrowed into broad, scaly ridges; cut surface of inner bark red.
Twigs: very slender, yellow-brown, finely hairy, rough with peglike bases.
Cones: ¾–1" (2–2.5 cm) long; elliptical, brown, stalkless; with many rounded, elliptical cone-scales; hanging down at ends of twigs; paired, long-winged seeds.

Habitat
Moist, acid soils, especially flats and lower slopes; in dense pure stands and with Sitka Spruce and other conifers.

Range
S. Alaska southeast along Pacific coast to NW. California; also
SE. British Columbia south in Rocky Mountains to N. Idaho
and NW. Montana; to 2000' (610 m) along coast; to 6000'
(1829 m) inland.

Comments
Western Hemlock is one of the most common trees in the
Pacific Northwest. This important timber species is one of the
best pulpwoods and a source of alpha cellulose for making
cellophane, rayon yarns, and plastics. Indians of southeastern
Alaska used to make coarse bread from the inner bark.

California Torreya
Torreya californica
145

Strongly aromatic tree with conical or rounded crown and rows
of slender, spreading branches.
Height: 16–70' (5–21 m). Diameter: 8"–2' (0.2–0.6 m),
sometimes larger.
Needles: evergreen; alternate; spreading in 2 rows; 1–2¾"
(2.5–7 cm) long, less than ⅛" (3 mm) wide. Mostly paired;
flattish and slightly curved; long, sharp point at tip, short-
pointed and almost stalkless at base; stiff. Shiny dark green
above, green with 2 narrow, whitish lines beneath.
Bark: gray-brown, thin, irregularly fissured into narrow scaly
ridges.
Twigs: mostly paired, slender, with 2 lines below base of each
leaf; yellow-green, turning reddish brown.
Seeds and Male Cones: on separate trees. Seeds 1–1½" (2.5–4
cm) long; elliptical; fleshy outer layer green with purplish
markings and shedding; inner layer yellow-brown, thick-
walled, stalkless; scattered and single on leafy twigs; maturing
in 2 seasons. Male or pollen cones ⅜" (10 mm) long;
elliptical, pale yellow, single at leaf bases.

Habitat
Mixed evergreen forests along mountain streams, especially in
shady canyon bottoms; also on exposed slopes.

Range
Mountains of central and N. California including Coast
Ranges and western slope of Sierra Nevada; at 3000–6500'
(914–1981 m), also down almost to sea level near coast.

Comments
This tree is also known as California-nutmeg because of the
resemblance of the aromatic seeds, with a deeply folded seed
coat, to those of the unrelated commercial spice, nutmeg
(*Myristica fragrans*). The crushed foliage and other parts have a
disagreeable resinous odor. Indians used to make bows from
the strong wood.

Hollyleaf Cherry
Prunus ilicifolia
147

Small evergreen tree with short trunk, dense crown of stout,
spreading branches, spiny-toothed leaves, and red cherries;
hairless throughout; often a shrub.
Height: 25' (7.6 m). Diameter: 1' (0.3 m).

Leaves: evergreen; alternate; 1–2″ (2.5–5 cm) long, ¾–1¼″ (2–3 cm) wide. Ovate to rounded, short-pointed or rounded at ends, coarsely spiny-toothed, thick and leathery, crisp, with odor of almond when crushed. Shiny green above, paler beneath.
Bark: dark reddish brown, fissured into small, square plates.
Twigs: gray or reddish brown, slender.
Flowers: ¼″ (6 mm) wide; with 5 rounded white petals; in upright, narrow, unbranched clusters less than 2½″ (6 cm) long at leaf bases; in early spring.
Fruit: ½–⅝″ (12–15 mm) in diameter; a rounded cherry; red, sometimes purple or yellow, with thin, juicy, sweetish pulp and smooth stone marked by branching lines; maturing in late fall.

Habitat
Dry slopes and in moist soils along streams; in chaparral and foothill woodland.

Range

Pacific Coast from central California south to Baja California: to 5000′ (1524 m).

Comments
Hollyleaf Cherry has been planted as an ornamental and a hedge plant from the time of the Spanish settlement in California. Although sweetish and edible, the cherries are mostly stone and are consumed only by wildlife. Indians used to crack the dried fruit and prepare meal from the ground and leached seeds. The common and scientific names both refer to the hollylike leaves, which are used as Christmas decorations.

California Buckthorn
Rhamnus californica
148

Usually a tall shrub with leathery, elliptical leaves and black berries.
Height: Usually 4–6′ (1.2–1.8 m), less often 10–20′ (3–6 m).
Leaves: evergreen; alternate; 1–3″ (2.5–7.5 cm) long. Usually more or less elliptical; margins without teeth or sharply to bluntly toothed. Dark green and hairless above, paler and hairless or sparsely downy beneath. In hot, dry places leaves smaller, thicker, and often hairy on one or both surfaces. In shady places leaves larger, thinner, less leathery, and mostly hairless.
Bark: gray-brown or reddish.
Flowers: inconspicuous, greenish, several in stalked umbels; April–June.
Fruit: about ¼″ (6 mm) long; 2–3-parted berrylike drupe; green, turning red and then black at maturity.

Habitat
Chaparral, woodland, lower montane forest.

Range
S. Oregon to Baja California, east to western slope of the Sierra Nevada and the mountains of the Mohave Desert.

Comments
California Buckthorn is one of the most common shrubs of canyons and hillsides in the California Coast ranges, where it occurs in redwood forest, Douglas-fir forest, coastal pine forest, oak woodland, mixed evergreen woodland, and chaparral. It is one of 5 buckthorns occuring in California. Various birds and mammals relish the fruits and foliage.

Kinnikinnick
Arctostaphylos uva-ursi
149, 215

A low, matted plant with smooth, red-brown, woody trailing stems, leathery, dark green leaves, and small, pink, lantern-shaped flowers in racemes on short branches.
Flowers: corolla ¼" (6 mm) long, with 5 lobes around small opening; March–June.
Leaves: ¼–1¼" (1.3–3.1 cm) long, oblong, widest near blunt tips.
Fruit: bright red berry ⅜" (9 mm) wide.
Height: creeper, the leaves and flower clusters about 6" (15 cm) high, the stems to 10' (3 m) long.

Habitat
Open places near the coast or high in the mountains.

Range
Coastal N. California north to Alaska; east from Oregon and Washington to the Rocky Mountains, south to New Mexico.

Comments
Kinnikinnick, an Indian word for many tobacco substitutes, is most frequently applied to this species, which also had many medicinal uses, including the alleged control of several sexually transmitted diseases.

Red Huckleberry
Vaccinium parvifolium
150

Erect, somewhat sparse shrub with sharply angled green branches and twigs, red berries, and thin leaves.
Height: generally 4–12' (1.2–3.6 m).
Leaves: alternate, ½–1" (1.3–2.5 cm) long. Thin, oval or elliptic; light green above, paler below, entire, nearly without petioles.
Bark: bright green.
Flowers: greenish to whitish, single or in pairs from leaf axils; corolla about ¼" (6 mm) long, globular, 5-lobed, calyx slightly 5-lobed; May–June.
Fruit: bright red, sweet edible berry about ¼" (6 mm) in diameter.

Habitat
Shady, humid forests.

Range
British Columbia south through W. Washington and Oregon to central California, both along the coast and in the Sierra Nevada.

Comments
In early summer Red Huckleberry, with its red berries

seeming like tiny Christmas ornaments on the bright green branches, is unmistakable. The berries are eaten by birds and small mammals, as well as bears. Deer and domestic livestock browse the foliage. This is the only tall red-berried *Vaccinium* in the West. It is especially common in Northwest coastal forests below 1500 feet.

Salmonberry
Rubus spectabilis
151, 212

An erect or sometimes leaning shrub with weakly armed stems, bright pink flowers, and yellow or salmon-red fruits that resemble a cultivated blackberry in all but color.
Height: 3–12' (0.9–3.6 m).
Leaves: alternate; compound with 3 leaflets or simple and incompletely divided in 3; leaflets oblong to ovate, 1–3" (2.5–7.5 cm) long, doubly toothed, pointed at tip, round at base. Green and slightly downy above, covered with dense white, feltlike hairs beneath. Petioles shorter than leaf blade, armed with prickles.
Bark: golden or reddish brown, satiny, peeling in strips.
Flowers: 1–1½" (2.5–4 cm) across, dark pink or red, solitary or 2–3 in open cluster; petals 5, sepals 5, hairy, sharply pointed; March–July.
Fruit: ovoid or globose, ½–1" (1.3–2.5 cm) long, yellow, orange, or salmon-red, consisting of numerous individual small drupelets tightly packed around a central receptacle that comes off with the fruit when picked. Sweet and juicy but insipid.

Habitat
Moist woods, streambanks, sunny slopes well watered by seeps.

Range
Alaska to NW. California, mostly along the coast and in adjacent mountains, but also eastward to N. Idaho and W. Montana.

Comments
On moist, sunny slopes in the Cascades, Salmonberry can form impenetrable thickets. The juicy fruit, which looks like a yellow or orange blackberry, is a welcome trailside snack, though too bland for some tastes. Indians ate not only the berries but also the tender young shoots. Numerous birds and animals also feast on the fruits, which may be abundant in good years. The deep pink flowers are distinctive and may occur along with the fruits.

Thimbleberry
Rubus parviflorus
152, 181

Erect, unarmed shrub with palmately lobed leaves and raspberrylike fruits.
Height: 3–6' (1–3 m).
Leaves: alternate; 2–7" (5–18 cm) long and and wide; 3- or 5-lobed, coarsely toothed; smooth or slightly hairy above, downy below. Petioles usually bristly and more or less glandular.
Bark: gray, eventually peeling in strips.

Flowers: 1–2″ (2.5–5 cm) across, white (rarely pinkish), 4–7 in open, terminal cluster; petals 5, sepals 5 with slender, elongate tips; April–July.
Fruit: resembles a cultivated raspberry, consisting of numerous individual drupelets packed around a central receptacle, from which the fruit detaches when ripe. Edible and sweet, but rather insipid.

Habitat
Moist places, such as streamsides, in more or less open forest or in coastal scrub.

Range
Alaska south to S. California and New Mexico, east to the Great Lakes region.

Comments
The genus *Rubus*, Latin name meaning "bramble," includes cultivated raspberries and blackberries, as well as a host of wild species, including more than a dozen native to western North America. Thimbleberry derives its name from the shape of its fruit. The species name *parviflorus* means "small-flowered," a curious choice for this shrub, whose flowers are among the largest in the genus. The fruits are important seasonal foods for numerous birds and mammals, including bears, and are a welcome, if not inspired, trailside snack. Wild Red Raspberry (*R. idaeus*) has much smaller flowers, prickles on stem, and compound leaves with 3 or 5 leaflets. Black Raspberry (*R. leucodermis*) has recurved thorns, small white flowers whose sepals are longer than the petals, compound leaves, and black fruits.

Sierra Gooseberry
Ribes roezlii
153

Stout shrub with long, spreading branches and 1–3 stiff, straight spines at the stem nodes.
Height: 1–4′ (0.3–1.2 m).
Leaves: alternate; clustered at the ends of short lateral branchlets, ½–1″ (1.3–2.5 cm) across, round in outline but deeply 3–5-lobed, toothed, dark green and minutely haired above, paler and downy beneath.
Bark: light brown.
Flowers: tubular, calyx longer than broad, ovary covered with spines and shorter glandular bristles; sepals purplish; petals whitish; June–July.
Fruit: berry red to purple; covered with nonglandular spines and shorter gland-tipped bristles; unpalatable.

Habitat
Dry, open slopes.

Range
California mountain ranges on both sides of the Central Valley and from the far northern to the far southern ends of the state; at 3500–8500′ (1050–2590 m).

Comments
This is the most common wild gooseberry at middle elevations

on the west slope of the Sierra Nevada, where it occurs with pines and firs. Altogether, 15 species of gooseberries and currants occur in the Sierra and nearly twice that many in all of California. Many species have delicious berries that attract birds, rodents, bears, and humans. A number of others, including Sierra Gooseberry, are edible and acceptable as an emergency food but otherwise unpalatable. Earlier programs to control white pine blister rust by eradicating *Ribes,* a host for the destructive fungus, dramatically affected most species. Attempts to breed resistant strains show great promise.

Wax Currant
Ribes cereum
154

A shrub with intricate, spineless branches, downy twigs, fragrant, glossy green leaves, creamy flowers, and red berries.
Height: 2–8′ (0.6–2.4 m).
Leaves: alternate; ½–1″ (1.3–2.5 cm) long and wide; fragrant, clustered on short lateral branchlets, more or less round and obscurely 3–5-lobed, finely toothed, glossy green and hairless above, finely haired and glandular beneath.
Bark: smooth, hairless, gray or brown.
Flowers: white, creamy, or pinkish, 2–8 in short, drooping racemes; the calyx tube 5-lobed; the stamens attached about three quarters of the way up calyx tube and alternate with the petals; June–July.
Fruit: Bright red berry about ½″ (12 mm) in diameter, slightly sticky-haired, becoming smooth at maturity; edible but acrid.

Habitat
Dry, rocky habitats upslope to near timberline.

Range
British Columbia south to S. California and east to the Rocky Mountains and W. Nebraska.

Comments
About 150 species of gooseberries and currants are found mainly in the northern hemisphere but extend southward into the mountains of South America. The greatest number of species (more than 30) in any one region occur along the Pacific Coast. About 15 species occur in the Sierra Nevada and perhaps 25 throughout the Rockies. Gooseberries and currants, members of the same family, differ mainly in that the former generally have spiny stems while the latter generally do not. Wild currants and gooseberries vary greatly in palatability, ranging from sweet and juicy through bland to terribly bitter. They are an important food source for wildlife, including bears, rodents, and birds. Indians added the berries of palatable species to dried buffalo meat and rendered fat to make pemmican, a nutritious, concentrated food source that was easy to carry and lasted indefinitely. Among the showier species of *Ribes* are the spectacular Red Flowering Currant (*R. sanguineum*) of the Pacific Coast and Golden Currant (*R. aureum*), found mainly in the Rocky Mountains.

Squawbush
Rhus trilobata
155

Erect, bushy, stiffly branched shrub with highly aromatic 3-parted leaves and clusters of red berries.
Height: 3–6′ (0.9–1.8 m).
Leaves: alternate, usually pinnately compound with 3 leaflets or, rarely, simple and 3- or 5-lobed; up to 3″ (7.5 cm) long. Terminal leaflet about 2″ (5 cm) long, broadly wedge-shaped and tapering to junction with the 2 smaller, rounder side leaflets. Teeth/color; finely haired.
Bark: smooth, brown.
Flowers: tiny, pale yellow, clustered in spikes ½–1″ (1.25–2 cm) long; 5 petals, 5 sepals, and 5 stamens; March–June.
Fruit: about ¼″ (6 mm) in diameter; fleshy red berry with sticky secretion and fine hairs, in tight clusters.

Habitat
Open slopes and canyons; often in chaparral.

Range
Alberta south in the Rockies to Mexico, east to Iowa, west to Idaho and SE. Oregon, and from there south through California to Baja California.

Comments
Squawbush is one of the more widespread sumacs in the West. It is most common in the Rockies, where it is a common constituent of mountain brush communities on dry, often rocky slopes in open montane forest. The plant is less common in California, where it mainly occurs in canyons and washes in the foothills. The fruit, which ripens in the fall, is an important source of winter food for many game birds, as well as songbirds and a number of small mammals. In severe winters, game birds have been known to stay close to sumac patches until the berries are exhausted. Indians used the berries of Squawbush and other sumacs to make drinks resembling pink lemonade, hence the name Lemonade Berry that is applied to this and several other members of the genus. The name Squawbush no doubt derives from the fact that Indian women used the flexible stems of this plant to make baskets. A less flattering name, Skunkbush, refers to the unpleasant odor emitted when the plant is crushed.

Common Chokecherry
Prunus virginiana
156

Shrub or small tree, often forming dense thickets, with dark red or blackish chokecherries.
Height: 20′ (6 m). Diameter: 6″ (15 cm).
Leaves: alternate; 1½–3¼″ (4–8 cm) long, ⅝–1½″ (1.5–4 cm) wide. Elliptical, finely and sharply sawtoothed, slightly thickened. Shiny dark green above, light green and sometimes slightly hairy beneath; turning yellow in autumn. Leafstalks slender, usually with 2 gland-dots.
Bark: brown or gray, smooth or becoming scaly.
Twigs: brown, slender, with disagreeable odor and bitter taste.
Flowers: ½″ (12 mm) wide; with 5 rounded white petals; in unbranched clusters to 4″ (10 cm) long; in late spring.

Fruit: ¼–⅜″ (6–10 mm) in diameter; a chokecherry; shiny
dark red or blackish skin; juicy, astringent or bitter pulp;
large stone; maturing in summer.

Habitat
Moist soils, especially along streams in mountains and
clearings and along forest borders and roadsides.

Range

N. British Columbia east to Newfoundland, south to W.
North Carolina, and west to S. California; to 8000′ (2438 m)
in the Southwest.

Comments
As the common name suggests, chokecherries are astringent or
puckery, especially when immature or raw. They can be made
into preserves and jelly; however, the fruit stones are
poisonous.

Coast Red Elderberry
Sambucus callicarpa
157, 191

Clump-forming shrub or sometimes small tree with many
small, white flowers in clusters and bright red berries; flowers
and crushed foliage have unpleasant odor.
Height: 20′ (6 m). Diameter: 6″ (15 cm).
Leaves: opposite; pinnately compound; 5–10″ (13–25 cm)
long; with unpleasant odor; 5 or 7 leaflets 2–5″ (5–13 cm)
long, 1–2″ (2.5–5 cm) wide; paired except at end, lance-
shaped or elliptical, finely and sharply saw-toothed. Green and
nearly hairless above, paler and hairy beneath.
Bark: light to dark gray or brown; smooth, becoming fissured
into small, scaly or shaggy plates.
Twigs: gray, stout, hairy when young; with ringed nodes and
thick, whitish pith becoming yellow-orange or brown.
Flowers: ¼″ (6 mm) wide; with white, 5-lobed corolla; in
upright, many-branched clusters to 4″ (10 cm) long; in spring
and early summer.
Fruit: ⁵⁄₁₆″ (8 mm) in diameter; a round berry, bright red or
sometimes orange, juicy, with 1-seeded, poisonous nutlets;
maturing in summer.

Habitat
Moist soils, especially in open areas such as cutover coniferous
forests.

Range

SW. Alaska southeast along coast to W. central California; to
2000′ (610 m).

Comments
The red fruit, inedible when raw, can be made into wine and
is also eaten by birds and mammals. The seeds are considered
poisonous, causing diarrhea and vomiting. The specific name
means "beautiful fruit." The similar Mountain Red Elderberry
(*Sambucus microbotrys*), a shrub to 6½′ (2 m) tall, occurs in the
Rocky Mountain Montane Forest and in the Sierran Montane
Forest. The Black Elderberry (*Sambucus melanocarpa*), a low
shrub with black or deep purple fruit, is also found in the

Rockies and the Sierra. These shrubs and the Coast Red Elderberry are considered by some authorities to be varieties of the single species *Sambucus racemosa*.

Toyon
Heteromeles arbutifolia
159

One of the most beautiful native shrubs or small trees, evergreen, with short trunk, many branches, and rounded crown.
Height: 30' (9 m). Diameter: 1' (0.3 m).
Leaves: evergreen; alternate; 2–4" (5–10 cm) long, ¼–1½" (2–4 cm) wide. Oblong lance-shaped, sharply saw-toothed, thick, short-stalked. Shiny dark green above, paler beneath.
Bark: light gray, smooth, aromatic.
Twigs: dark red, slender; hairy when young.
Flowers: ¼" (6 mm) wide; with 5 white petals; many in upright clusters 4–6" (10–15 cm) wide; in early summer.
Fruit: ¼–⅜" (6–10 mm) long; like small apples, red (sometimes yellow), mealy and sour, usually 2-seeded; maturing in autumn and remaining attached in winter.

Habitat
Along streams and on dry slopes; in chaparral and woodland zones.

Range
California in Coast Ranges and Sierra Nevada foothills and Channel Islands; also Baja California; to 4000' (1219 m).

Comments
The only species-in its genus, Toyon is very showy in winter with evergreen leaves and abundant red fruit and is popular for Christmas decorations. A pioneer plant on eroded soil, it sprouts vigorously after fire or cutting. The common name Toyon apparently is of American Indian origin.

Devil's Club
Oplopanax horridum
160

A sparsely branched, somewhat rangy shrub with giant maplelike leaves and crooked, pithy, canelike stems with long, stiff, yellow thorns.
Height: 3–12' (0.9–3.6 m).
Leaves: 4–14" (10–36 cm) wide; palmately 7–9-lobed, toothed; with thorny petioles and veins.
Bark: thin, light brown.
Flowers: tiny, greenish white, in pyramid-shaped cluster at top of main stem; June–August.
Fruit: Bright red berry in terminal clusters.

Habitat
Wet, swampy places in shady forest.

Range
Alaska south in coastal forests to Oregon, east to both slopes of the Cascade Range, Idaho, Montana, Michigan, and Ontario.

Comments
Devil's Club is a conspicuous understory shrub in boggy places

within the Northwest coastal forest, where it makes off-trail travel difficult or impossible. The barbed thorns inflict wounds sufficiently unpleasant as to have given rise to the persistent myth that they are tipped with poison. Nevertheless, the plant is a beautiful, or at least unusual, component of the forest understory. Its giant leaves are adaptations to the dim light of its environment. Indians dried and pulverized the bark for use as a deodorant. Certain tribes made a reddish cosmetic paint by mixing burned stems with grease. Believing that Devil's Club had magical powers, the Northwest Coast Indians made charms from its wood and tied bits of bark onto fish hooks to increase the chances of a large catch.

Greenleaf Manzanita
Arctostaphylos patula
161, 195

A large, erect, spreading, much-branched shrub with smooth, reddish-brown bark and several stout stems growing from a swollen burl (root crown).
Height: 3–8' (0.9–2.4 m).
Leaves: 1–1¾" (2.5–4.5 cm) long, broadly ovate to nearly round. Generally smooth and bright green.
Bark: smooth and reddish brown on older branches; branchlets covered with downy hairs and yellowish-green glands.
Flowers: ¼" (6 mm) long, in branched clusters. Pinkish, urn-shaped; calyx 5-lobed, corolla united nearly to tip, where there are 5 small recurved lobes; May–June.
Fruit: a smooth, dark brown berry.

Habitat
Open conifer forests, especially burned or logged areas.

Range
S. Washington south to central California, east to Colorado and Arizona.

Comments
Greenleaf Manzanita is common in postfire brush communities in the Sierra Nevada, often forming dense thickets with a number of other shrubs that may cover many acres. Following a fire, the shrub is able to regenerate rapidly by sprouting new shoots from its basal burl, or root crown. The genus name *Arctostaphylos* means "bear grape" and refers to the fondness shown by bears for the fruits of these shrubs, many of which are known as Bearberry. The more widespread common name *manzanita* is Spanish for "little apple," again referring to the berries. There are about 50 species of manzanitas, only one of which is circumpolar in distribution. The rest are found from Central America northward, and about 40 of these are native to California, the undisputed center of the genus. They are especially abundant in California chaparral but occur in most other forest and woodland communities as well. Manzanitas provide important browse for deer, and the berries are relished by birds and various small mammals, as well as bears.

Blue Elderberry
Sambucus cerulea
162

Large, many-branched, thicket-forming shrub or small tree often with several trunks with compact, rounded crown, numerous small, whitish flowers in large clusters, and bluish fruit.
Height: 25' (7.6 m). Diameter: 1' (0.3 m).
Leaves: opposite; pinnately compound; 5–7" (13–18 cm) long; sometimes nearly evergreen southward; 5–9 leaflets 1–5" (2.5–13 cm) long, ⅜–1½" (1–4 cm) wide; paired except at end, narrowly ovate or lance-shaped, long-pointed at tip, short-pointed and unequal at base; sharply saw-toothed; short-stalked. Yellow-green above, paler and often hairy beneath.
Bark: gray or brown, furrowed.
Twigs: green, stout, angled, often hairy; with ringed nodes and thick, white pith.
Flowers: nearly ¼" (6 mm) wide; with yellowish-white, 5-lobed corolla; fragrant; in upright, flat-topped, many-branched clusters 4–8" (10–20 cm) wide; in summer.
Fruit: nearly ¼" (6 mm) in diameter; dark blue berry with whitish bloom, thick, juicy, sweet pulp, and 3 1-seeded nutlets; many clusters; maturing in summer and autumn.

Habitat
Moist soils along streams and canyons of mountains, in open areas in coniferous forests; also along roadsides, fencerows, and clearings.

Range
S. British Columbia south along coast to S. California, east in mountains to Trans-Pecos Texas, and north to W. Montana; also in northwestern Mexico; to 10,000' (3048 m).

Comments
The sweetish, edible berries are used in preserves and pies. Lewis and Clark first reported Blue Elderberry as an "alder" with "pale, sky blue" berries. Whistles can be made by removing the pith from cut twigs; California Indians made flutes in a similar fashion. A remedy for fever has been concocted from the bark. Blue Elderberry is planted as an ornamental for the numerous whitish flowers and bluish fruits.

Thinleaf Huckleberry
Vaccinium membranaceum
163

Erect, much-branched shrub with thin, toothed leaves; relatively large, deep purple berries; and branchlets that are slightly angled in cross-section.
Height: 1–5' (0.9–1.5 m).
Leaves: alternate, 1–2⅜" (2.5–6 cm) long. Ovate to obovate, slender-pointed at tip; minutely toothed. Bright green, turning brilliant red in autumn.
Flowers: about ¼" (6 mm) in diameter; yellow/globose, with 5 tiny lobes at tip; calyx entire or with wavy margin; May–July.
Fruit: deep purple to nearly black berry ¼" (6 mm) or more in diameter.

Habitat
Shaded woods and moist places to open, sunny slopes on recent burns.

Range
Alaska south to extreme N. California, east to Idaho, Montana, and Michigan.

Comments
Thinleaf Huckleberry is one of the choicer wild blueberries in the West and fortunately is also one of the most abundant within its range. It is perhaps the most common forest shrub at mid- to high elevations in the Washington Cascades, where the appearance of abundant fruit in August and September proves a great temptation to hikers. Oval-leaved Huckleberry (*V. ovalifolium*), frequently found with the thinleaf variety, has entire rather than toothed leaves. The name *Vaccinium* is Latin for blueberry. More than a dozen species occur in western North America and are perhaps most common in the Pacific Northwest. Huckleberries are extremely important sources of food for forest birds and mammals; the black bear gorges on the fruits each fall in preparation for winter hibernation.

Twinberry
Lonicera involucrata
164, 205

Erect, deciduous shrub with opposite leaves and both flowers and fruits in pairs growing from leaf axils.
Height: 2–10' (0.6–3 m).
Leaves: opposite, 2–5" (5–12.5 cm) long, ovate, tapering at tip. Dark green and hairless above, paler and downy beneath or losing hairs with age; untoothed, often with hairlike fringe.
Bark: light brown, shreddy.
Flowers: about ½" (12 mm) long; yellow, sometimes tinged red, tubular, 5-lobed. In pairs on stalks emerging from leaf axils; bractlets at base of flowers forming saclike cups; March–July.
Fruit: Black, oval or globose berries about ⅜" (9 mm) in diameter.

Habitat
Moist, shady places such as streamsides and canyon bottoms.

Range
Alaska and British Columbia east to Quebec and south to S. California, Arizona, Utah, and Colorado.

Comments
The berries are edible but not particularly tasty. Some birds and bears are known to eat the fruit, but these plants are not common enough to be important to wildlife. Twinberry is widespread, however, and the yellow flowers and paired fruits often attract attention. Several other honeysuckles, both shrubs and woody vines, occur in the West. The common garden honeysuckle (*Lonicera japonica*) is a close relative that sometimes escapes into the wild. The genus, *Lonicera,* is named after a 16th-century German herbalist.

Mountain Snowberry
Symphoricarpos oreophilus
165

Erect, much-branched shrub with white berries, tubular flowers, and hairy young twigs.
Height: 3–5', (1–1.5 m).

Leaves: opposite, ⅜–1¼" (1–3 cm) long; oval, entire or toothed, usually hairless, somewhat paler beneath.
Bark: shreddy grayish or brownish.
Flowers: tubular, rose-colored, about ½" (12 mm) long, with spreading lobes much shorter than the tube; June–July.
Fruit: white berries about ⅜" (1 cm) long.

Habitat
Riverbanks, other moist places.

Range
Colorado and Nevada south to Mexico and Texas.

Comments
One of several species of snowberry found in the West. All are similar in appearance and are most easily distinguished from one another by the shape of the flower. There are also other small differences. The berries ripen in late summer and remain on the plants through the winter, constituting a valuable food source for grouse, pine grosbeaks, and robins. Deer browse the foliage, and rabbits and other small mammals find cover beneath these shrubs.

California Hazelnut
Corylus cornuta californica
168

Open, spreading shrub with numerous ascending stems; thin, downy, double-toothed leaves; and nuts wrapped in an "envelope" of leafy bracts.
Height: 3–20' (.9–6 m).
Leaves: alternate, 1½–3" (4–7.5 cm) long. Rounded to obovate, more or less unequal at base; doubly toothed and sometimes slightly 3-lobed. Glandular-hairy until early summer, becoming hairless or nearly so with age; paler below.
Bark: smooth but with more or less down-covered branchlets.
Flowers: male and female on same plant. Male flowers tiny, numerous, in elongated, drooping, stalkless catkins at ends of previous year's branchlets; appearing in spring before leaves. Female flowers fewer, but borne severally in small, rounded, scaly buds; each flower with 2 protruding red stigmas.
Nut: ovoid to nearly globular, ⅜–⅝" (.6–1.5 cm) long, hard-shelled; enclosed by 2–3 stiff-hairy bracts united to form an "envelope" extending to form a fringed tube longer than the nut.

Habitat
Moist, well-drained sites in woodlands and forests at lower elevations.

Range
British Columbia southward to central California, east to N. Idaho; to 7000' (2100 m) in the south.

Comments
The nuts, very similar to the commercial hazelnut or filbert, are relished by squirrels, which may hang precariously from the slender branches to reach them. Deer and livestock browse the foliage. This large shrub is a common understory species in cool, moist forests of the Pacific states.

Bush Chinkapin
Castanopsis sempervirens
169

Low, spreading, round-topped evergreen shrub with burred fruit and round-tipped evergreen leaves.
Height: 1–8' (0.3–2.4 m).
Leaves: evergreen; alternate; 1–3" (2.5–7.5 cm) long, ½–1" (1.3–12.5 cm) wide, oblong or oblong-lanceolate, rounded at tip, flat, gray-green above, golden or rusty below due to dense, feltlike hairs.
Bark: smooth; brown or gray.
Flowers: male and female on same plant. Male flowers tiny, ill-smelling, in 3's, in the axils of bracts, forming stiff, erect catkins 1–3" (2.5–7.5 cm) long. 1–3 female flowers borne in an involucre (circle of bracts) at the base of the male catkin or in short, separate catkins.
Nut: about ⅜" (1 cm) long, hard-shelled, bitter; 1–3 enclosed by spiny burr ¾–1¼" (2–3 cm) thick.

Habitat
Rocky, sunny mountain slopes and ridges, mostly 2500–11,000' (750–3300 m).

Range
S. Oregon to S. California.

Comments
This tough shrub is one of the dominant members of the montane chaparral community found on dry, rocky sites within the Sierran montane forest. The name *Castanopsis*, meaning "resembling a chestnut" in Greek, refers to the burred fruit of this and other members of the genus. This species is told from the Golden Chinkapin, a shrubby form of the Giant Chinkapin (*C. chrysophylla*), by the Golden's pointed leaves, which are sometimes folded up along the midrib.

Tanoak
Lithocarpus densiflorus
170

Evergreen tree with a great central trunk and crown varying from narrow and conical to broad and rounded; sometimes a shrub.
Height: 50–80' (15–24 m). Diameter: 1–2½' (0.3–0.8 m).
Leaves: evergreen; alternate; 2½–5" (6–13 cm) long, ¾–2¼" (2–6 cm) wide. Oblong, thick and leathery, with many straight, parallel, sunken side veins; with wavy-toothed border sometimes turning under stout, hairy leafstalks. Shiny light green and becoming hairless or nearly so above; with whitish or yellowish hairs, woolly when young, beneath.
Bark: brown, thick, deeply furrowed into ridges and plates.
Twigs: stout, with dull yellow hairs.
Flowers: numerous, tiny, stalkless, whitish flowers in catkins 2–4" (5–10 cm) long; with unpleasant odor; upright from base of leaf; in early spring, sometimes also in autumn; usually all male, sometimes also 1–2 tiny, greenish female flowers at base.
Acorns: ¾–1¼" (2–3 cm) long; egg-shaped; 1–2 on stout, long stalk; yellow-brown, with shallow, saucer-shaped cup covered by long, slender, spreading scales; maturing second year.

Habitat
Moist valleys and mountains slopes; in oak forests and sometimes in nearly pure stands.

Range
Pacific Coast from SW. Oregon south to S. California and in Sierra Nevada to central California; to 5000' (1524 m).

Comments
Tanoak is placed in a separate genus with more than 100 species native to southeast Asia and Indomalaysia. While the acorns somewhat resemble those of true oaks, the flowers are like those of chinkapins and chestnuts. Tanoak bark was once the main commercial western source of tannin. Indians ground flour from the large acorns after removing the shells and washing the seeds in hot water to remove the bitter taste.

Turbinella Oak
Quercus turbinella
172

Evergreen, much-branched, thicket-forming shrub or small tree with a spreading crown.
Height: 5–15' (1.5–4.6 m), sometimes larger. Diameter: 4" (10 cm).
Leaves: evergreen; alternate; small; ⅝–1½" (1.5–4 cm) long, ⅜–¾" (10–19 mm) wide. Elliptical or oblong, short-pointed at tip, rounded or notched at base, spiny-toothed, thick and stiff. Blue-green with whitish bloom and nearly hairless above, yellow-green and with fine hairs beneath.
Bark: gray, fissured and scaly.
Acorns: ⅝–1" (1.5–2.5 cm) long; narrowly oblong, a quarter to a third enclosed by shallow, scaly cup; 1 or few at end of stalk; maturing first year.

Habitat
On mountain slopes, forming thickets; also with other oaks, pinyons, and junipers.

Range
SW. Colorado south S. New Mexico, west to S. California, and south to Baja California; at 4000–8000' (1219–2438 m).

Comments
The name *turbinella,* meaning "like a little top," refers to the acorns. Turbinella Oak is the characteristic shrub in the chaparral vegetation of Arizona mountain slopes. The foliage is browsed by wildlife and occasionally by livestock.

Canyon Live Oak
Quercus chrysolepis
173

Evergreen tree with short trunk, large, spreading, horizontal branches, and broad, rounded crown; sometimes shrubby.
Height: 20–100' (6–30 m). Diameter: 1–3' (0.3–0.9 m) or more.
Leaves: evergreen; alternate; 1–3" (2.5–7.5 cm) long, ½–1½" (1.2–4 cm) wide. Elliptical to oblong; short-pointed at tip, rounded or blunt at base; with edges turned under and often with spiny teeth (especially on young twigs); thick and leathery. Shiny green above; with yellow hairs or becoming

gray and nearly hairless beneath.
Bark: light gray, nearly smooth or scaly.
Acorns: ¾–2″ (2–5 cm) long; variable in size and shape, egg-shaped, turbanlike with shallow, thick cup of scales densely covered with yellowish hairs; stalkless or short-stalked; maturing second year.

Habitat
In canyons and on sandy, gravelly, and rocky slopes; in pure stands and mixed forests.

Range
SW. Oregon south through Coast Ranges and Sierra Nevada to S. California; local in W. Nevada and in W. and central Arizona; at 1000–6500′ (305–1981 m); in Arizona at 5500–7500′ (1676–2286 m).

Comments
Many consider this to be the most beautiful of the California oaks. The species name, meaning "golden-scale," refers to the yellowish acorn cups.

Gambel Oak
Quercus gambelii
174

Tree with rounded crown, often in dense groves; or a thicket-forming shrub.
Height: 20–70′ (6–21 m). Diameter: 1–2½′ (0.3–0.8 m).
Leaves: alternate; 2–6″ (5–15 cm) long, 1¼–3¼″ (3–8 cm) wide. Elliptical or oblong, rounded at tip, short-pointed at base; deeply 7- to 11-lobed halfway or more to middle, edges straight or wavy; varying in size, lobing, and hairiness. Shiny dark green and usually hairless above, paler and with soft hairs below; turning yellow and reddish in autumn.
Bark: gray, rough, thick, deeply furrowed or scaly.
Acorns: ½–¾″ (12–19 mm) long; egg-shaped, about a third enclosed by deep, thick, scaly cup; 1–2 on short stalk or nearly stalkless; maturing first year.

Habitat
Slopes and valleys, in mountains, foothills, plateaus; scattered with Ponderosa Pine.

Range
N. Utah east to extreme S. Wyoming, south to Trans-Pecos Texas, and west to S. Arizona; local in extreme NW. Oklahoma and S. Nevada; also northern Mexico; at 5000–8000′ (1524–2438 m).

Comments
Gambel Oak is the common oak of the Rocky Mountains, abundant in Grand Canyon National Park. It is closely related to White Oak (*Quercus alba*) of the eastern United States. The foliage is browsed by deer and sometimes by livestock. Wild turkeys, squirrels, and other wildlife, as well as hogs and domestic animals eat the sweetish acorns.

Arizona White Oak
Quercus arizonica
175

Medium-sized evergreen tree with irregular, spreading crown of stout branches.
Height: 30–60' (9–18 m). Diameter: 1–2' (0.3–0.6 m).
Leaves: evergreen; 1½–3" (4–7.5 cm) long, ¾–1½" (2–4 cm) wide. Oblong or obovate; slightly wavy-lobed and toothed toward tip, base notched or rounded; thick and stiff. Dull blue-green and nearly hairless with sunken veins above paler and densely hairy with raised veins beneath; shedding gradually in spring as new leaves unfold.
Bark: light gray, furrowed into narrow, scaly plates and ridges.
Acorns: ¾–1" (2–2.5 cm) long; oblong, about a third enclosed by deep cup of finely hairy scales thickened at base; 1–2 on short stalk or stalkless; maturing first year.

Habitat
Mountain slopes and canyons; in oak woodland with other evergreen oaks.

Range
Trans-Pecos Texas west to Arizona; also northern Mexico; at 5000–7500' (1524–2286 m).

Comments
One of the largest southwestern oaks, this handsome tree reaches its greatest size in canyons and other moist sites.

Oregon White Oak
Quercus garryana
176

Tree with dense, rounded, spreading crown of stout branches; sometimes shrubby.
Height: 30–70' (9–21 m). Diameter: 1–2½' (0.3–0.8 m).
Leaves: alternate; 3–6" (7.5–15 cm) long, 2–4" (5–10 cm) wide. Elliptical, blunt or rounded at both ends; deeply lobed halfway or more to midvein, with blunt or slightly toothed lobes; slightly thickened. Shiny dark green above, light green and usually hairy beneath; sometimes reddish in autumn.
Bark: light gray or whitish; thin; scaly or furrowed into broad ridges.
Acorns: 1–1¼" (2.5–3 cm) long; elliptical, a quarter to a third enclosed by shallow, thin, scaly cup; stalkless or short-stalked; sweetish and edible.

Habitat
In valleys and on mountain slopes; often, in pure stands and with other oaks.

Range
SW. British Columbia south to central California in Coast Ranges and Sierra Nevada; to 3000' (914 m) in north and at 1000–5000' (305–1524 m) in south.

Comments
The oak of greatest commercial importance in the West, this species is used for furniture, shipbuilding, construction, cabinetwork, interior finish, and fuel. It is the only native oak in Washington and British Columbia. The sweetish acorns, often common in alternate years, are relished by animals.

Blue Oak
Quercus douglasii
177

Tree with short, leaning trunk; short, stout branches; broad, rounded crown; and brittle, hairy twigs; sometimes shrubby.
Height: 20–60' (6–18 m). Diameter: 1' (0.3 m).
Leaves: alternate; 1¼–4" (3–10 cm) long, ¾–1¾" (2–4.5 cm) wide. Oblong or elliptical, rounded or blunt at both ends; shallowly 4- or 5-lobed, coarsely toothed or without teeth; thin but stiff. Pale blue-green and nearly hairless above, paler and slightly hairy beneath.
Bark: light gray, thin, scaly.
Acorns: ¾–1¼" (2–3 cm) long; elliptical, broad or narrow, with shallow cup of warty scales; stalkless or nearly so, maturing first season.

Habitat
Dry, loamy, gravelly, and rocky slopes, with other oaks and Digger Pine.

Range
N. to S. California mostly in foothills of Coast Ranges and Sierra Nevada; at 300–3500' (91–1067 m).

Comments
Recognized from a distance by the bluish foliage, this handsome California oak was named for its discoverer, David Douglas (1798–1834), the Scottish botanical explorer. It is used principally for fuel. The acorns, often abundant, are eaten by livestock as well as by wildlife. This oak commonly grows in open woodlands with Digger Pine.

Mountain Misery
Chamaebatia foliosa
182

Low, spreading shrub with pungent, sticky, fernlike leaves; often forms dense carpets.
Height: 8–24" (20.3–61 cm).
Leaves: evergreen; alternate; ¾–4" (2–10 cm) long, pinnately divided 3 times, with ultimate segments crowded, elliptical and tipped with stalked gland, making the foliage sticky.
Bark: smooth; bluish to brown.
Flowers: white, about 1" (2.5 cm) across, in loose terminal clusters; petals 5, sepals 5, united at base to form a persistent calyx; May–July.
Fruit: an achene.

Habitat
Dry, open conifer forests.

Range
West slope of Sierra Nevada, California; a related form occurs in extreme S. California and N. Baja California.

Comments
Mountain Misery got its name from what many forest visitors consider to be an unpleasant combination of sticky leaves and a medicinal aroma. The shrub forms dense carpets in ponderosa pine and mixed-conifer stands in the Sierra, often covering extensive areas. Hikers walking through such tracts soon discover that the plant's black gum sticks to boots and clothing. The resin makes Mountain Misery highly flammable,

and it is among the several Sierra shrubs that invade recently
burned areas. California's Miwok Indians, who called the plant
Kit-kit-dizze, drank a tea steeped from the leaves as a cure for a
number of ailments.

Apache Plume
Fallugia paradoxa
183

A shrub with white flowers and silvery puffs of fruit heads
borne at the tips of very dense, intertangled, twiggy, slender
branches.
Flowers: 1–1½" (2.5–3.8 cm) wide; petals 5, round, growing
from rim of a small cup; stamens many; May–October.
Leaves: ½–1" (1.3–2.5 cm) long, thick, divided into 5 or 7
narrow lobes, edges strongly curled downward.
Fruit: styles form a feathery plume ¾–2" (2–5 cm) long,
above a seedlike base; many in a head.
Height: to 7' (2.1 m).

Habitat
Gravelly or rocky slopes and in washes, from deserts to open
pine forests.

Range
SE. California and S. Nevada to S. Colorado, W. Texas, and
northern Mexico.

Comments
These rather thick shrubs appear unkempt, but in full flower
their white petals are attractive against the dark foliage.

Labrador Tea
Ledum glandulosum
185

White flowers bloom in roundish clusters at ends of branches
of this shrub.
Flowers: about ½" (1.3 cm) wide; petals 5, white; stamens 5–
12, the lower part of the stalks hairy; June–August.
Leaves: ½–2½" (1.3–6.3 cm) long, closely placed on stem,
ovate or elliptic, with white, feltlike hairs beneath.
Fruit: roundish, 5-chambered capsule.
Height: 2–7' (60–210 cm).

Habitat
Wet places in the mountains.

Range
British Columbia; south to the Sierra Nevada of California,
NE. Oregon, central Idaho, and NW. Wyoming.

Comments
As with many shrubby species in this family, Labrador Tea is
poisonous.

Bitter Cherry
Prunus emarginata
186

Thicket-forming shrub or small tree with rounded crown,
slender, upright branches, bitter foliage, and small, bitter
cherries.
Height: 20' (6 m). Diameter: 8" (20 cm).
Leaves: alternate; 1–2½" (2.5–6 cm) long, ⅜–1¼" (1–3 cm)
wide. Oblong to elliptical, rounded or blunt at tip, short-

pointed at base, with 1–2 dotlike glands; finely saw-toothed, with blunt, gland-tipped teeth. Dark green above, paler and sometimes hairy beneath.
Bark: dark brown, smooth, very bitter.
Twigs: shiny red, slender, hairy when young.
Flowers: ½" (12 mm) wide; with 5 rounded, notched, white petals; 3–10 on slender stalks; in spring with leaves.
Fruit: ⁵⁄₁₆–³⁄₈" (8–10 mm) in diameter; a round cherry, with thick, red to black skin, thin, juicy, bitter pulp, and pointed stone; maturing in summer.

Habitat
Moist soils of valleys and on mountain slopes; in chaparral and coniferous forests.

Range
British Columbia, Washington, and W. Montana south to S. California and SW. New Mexico; to 9000' (2743 m) in south.

Comments
This is the most common western cherry. The fruit is not edible; like the bark and leaves, it is intensely bitter. However, the fruit is consumed by many songbirds and mammals and the foliage is browsed by deer and livestock.

Cascade Azalea
Rhododendron albiflorum
187

A shrub with 1–4 white, bowl-shaped flowers clustered in leaf axils along the stem.
Flowers: corolla ⁵⁄₈–³⁄₄" (1.5–2 cm) wide, with 5 round lobes; stamens 10, hairy near base; June–August.
Leaves: 1½–4" (3.8–10 cm) long, broadly lanceolate, with short petioles.
Height: 3–7' (90–210 cm).

Habitat
Wet places in the mountains.

Range
British Columbia south to Oregon and east to W. Montana.

Comments
This species does not produce the spectacular brilliant flowers that many of its relatives do, yet its dainty clusters of mildly citrus-scented white flowers and green leaves are delightful.

Lewis' Syringa
Philadelphus lewisii
188

A loosely branched shrub, covered in the spring by many white flowers.
Flowers: ¾–1¼" (2–3.1 cm) wide; in clusters at ends of short branches; petals 4 or 5; stamens many; May–July.
Leaves: 1¼–3" (3.1–7.5 cm) long, opposite, on short stalks, ovate, smooth or minutely toothed on edges.
Fruit: woody capsule.
Height: 4–10' (1.2–3 m).

Habitat
Rocky slopes and banks in open forest and mixed woodland.

Range
British Columbia to central California; east to W. Montana.

Comments
Idaho's state flower; when in full bloom the flowers scent the air with a delightfully sweet fragrance reminiscent of orange blossoms. The genus is named for the Egyptian king Ptolemy Philadelphus, and the species and common names honor the scientist-explorer Meriwether Lewis, who first discovered and collected it during his exploration of the Louisiana Purchase. Indians used this shrub's straight stems in making arrows. Also known as Mockorange.

Moosewood Viburnum
Viburnum edule
189

Straggly shrub with opposite, 3-lobed leaves and sour, edible red berries.
Height: 1½–8′ (0.5–2.4 m).
Leaves: opposite, 2¼–4″ (5.5–10 cm) long, more or less round but 3-lobed, each lobe tapering to a point, edges toothed; turns crimson in fall.
Bark: grayish.
Flowers: white, tiny, 3–30 in inflorescence up to 1¼″ (3 cm) across.
Fruit: Smooth, fragrant, sour, edible red berry.

Habitat
Wooded margins of lakes and streams.

Range
Alaska and the Yukon east to Newfoundland and south to Oregon, Idaho, Colorado, Minnesota, and Pennsylvania.

Comments
Except in fall, when this plant adds a vivid splash of color to northern forests, Moosewood Viburnum is often overlooked, being rather straggly in appearance. There are more than 100 species of viburnum in the world, 15 of which occur in North America, primarily in the northern latitudes. Many birds and mammals eat the tart berries of the viburnums.

Birchleaf Spiraea
Spiraea betulifolia
190

Low, erect shrub with small white flowers in showy, flat-topped clusters.
Height: 8–32″ (20.5–81.5 cm).
Leaves: alternate, ¾–2¼″ (2–5.5 cm) long; oval to obovate, glossy green above, paler beneath, coarsely toothed, especially above the middle; without stipules.
Bark: brown and smooth.
Flowers: white, turning brown, about ¼″ (6 mm) across, with 3 sepals, 5 petals, 5 pistils, and numerous stamens; July–August.
Fruit: Small podlike fruits that open down one side.

Habitat
Moist places in open woods and treeless areas, including moraines and lakeshores.

Range
British Columbia and Alberta south to Oregon, Wyoming, SW. Saskatchewan, and South Dakota.

Comments
Several species of spiraea occur in western conifer forests. The others have inflorescences that are either pyramid-shaped or, if flattened, consist of rose-colored flowers. Spiraeas are also known by the name Meadowsweet, which refers to their fragrant flowers. Those of Birchleaf Spiraea, however, are less fragrant than those of the others. Blue grouse eat the leaves in the spring, and deer browse the shrub in summer. Insects often lay eggs inside the flowers, causing galls to form.

Creambush
Holodiscus discolor
192

A much-branched shrub with shreddy bark and showy pyramidal clusters of small, creamy-white flowers.
Height: 3–20′ (1–6 m).
Leaves: alternate; 1–3″ (2.5–7.5 cm) long; ovate, broadly wedge-shaped at base; coarsely toothed. Green and slightly hairy above, often with impressed veins; more or less white-haired and prominently veined beneath.
Bark: light brown or ashy gray, often shreddy on older shoots.
Flowers: about ⅛″ (3 mm) wide; petals 5, sepals 5, persistent in fruit, stamens 20, from ringlike disk; densely clustered in panicles at the end of branchlets; May–August.
Fruit: 1-seeded, hairy achene less than ⅛″ (3 mm) long.

Habitat
Coastal bluffs to moist woods and streamsides in both conifer and broadleaf forests and in woodlands.

Range
British Columbia to S. California and Montana.

Comments
Also known as Ocean Spray and Mountain Spray, Creambush is exceptionally showy when in flower, with clusters up to a foot long covering the entire plant. Creambush is a common understory plant in the Northwest Coastal Forest, where it indicates sites that elsewhere would be considered moist but are among the drier ones in this humid forest. Indians made arrows from the straight branches and the shrub is now widely planted as an ornamental.

White Mountain-heather
Cassiope mertensiana
193

Flowers like small white bells hang from the tips of slender stalks that grow from the axils near the ends of the branches on this matted plant.
Flowers: corolla ¼″ (6 mm) long, with 5 bluntly pointed lobes; July–August.
Leaves: ⅛–¼″ (3–6 mm) long, very narrow, angled upward, opposite and arranged in 4 rows that hide stem.
Fruit: 4- or 5-chambered capsule that opens along back of each chamber.
Height: 2–12″ (5–30 cm).

Habitat
Open slopes near and above the timberline.

Range
Alaska and Canada south to central California, N. Nevada, and W. Montana.

Comments
The white flowers, somewhat starlike, may have inspired the genus name of this plant, for in Greek mythology Cassiopeia was set among the stars as a constellation.

Blue Yucca
Yucca baccata
196

Rigid, spine-tipped leaves in 1 or several rosettes, and a long cluster of whitish flowers on a stalk about as tall as the leaves.
Flowers: 6 petal-like segments, each 2–4" (5–10 cm) long, white or cream and often also purplish tinged, waxy; April–July.
Leaves: to about 3' (90 cm) long, edges with a few whitish fibers.
Fruit: pod 2½–10" (6.3–25 cm) long, fleshy, cylindrical, round at ends.
Height: to 5' (1.5 m), the trunks up to 20" (50 cm).

Habitat
Rocky soil in deserts, grasslands, and open woods.

Range
SE. California across S. Nevada and Utah to SW. Colorado; south through much of Arizona, all of New Mexico, and W. Texas to northern Mexico.

Comments
The baked fruit of Blue Yucca tastes somewhat like sweet potato. Yucca flowers are still eaten by Mexican Indians to such an extent that some species now rarely show mature pods. Identification of the many Yucca species is often difficult. Those with broad leaves are sometimes called Spanish-daggers, a name generally applied to the treelike species of western Texas.

Our Lord's Candle
Yucca whipplei
197

Long, massive cluster of several thousand white or cream flowers, often tinged with purple, on a stout stalk growing from a dense basal rosette of gray-green, spine-tipped leaves.
Flowers: 6 petal-like segments, each 1–1½" (2.5–3.8 cm) long, form a bell; April–May.
Leaves: 3' (90 cm) long.
Height: 4–11" (1.2–3.3 m).

Habitat
Stony slopes in chaparral.

Range
S. California and N. Baja California.

Comments
Showiest of the yuccas. Hundreds in bloom provide a

spectacular sight on brushy slopes. After flowering, the plants die. All yuccas have a reciprocal relationship with the Yucca Moth. After gathering pollen from a flower and rolling the pollen into a little ball, the moth lays its eggs in the ovary of another flower and then packs the pollen into holes on the stigma, thus both pollinating the flower and ensuring seed-set. The moth's larvae feed on some of the developing seeds, then burrow out of the fruit when mature.

Deer Brush
Ceanothus integerrimus
198, 221

An openly branched shrub with thin leaves, gray bark, and tiny white or pale blue flowers in conical clusters at ends of flexible twigs.

Flowers: cluster 3–6″ (7.5–15 cm) long; sepals 5, petal-like, triangular, curved toward center; petals 5, spoon-shaped; May–June.
Leaves: to 2½″ (6.3 cm) long, elliptic, with 3 main veins.
Fruit: small, 3-lobed capsule.
Height: 3–13′ (90–390 cm).

Habitat
Dry slopes in chaparral and open forests.

Range
E. Washington to SW. Oregon, California and Baja California; east to W. New Mexico.

Comments
In the spring, Deer Brush covers hillsides with a mixture of white and pale blue, and fills the air with its sweet, spicy, honey scent.

Creeping Oregon Grape
Berberis repens
199

A plant with 2 or 3 pinnately compound leaves with leathery, hollylike leaflets on low, short stems ending in dense, branched clusters of small yellow flowers.

Flowers: about ½″ (1.3 cm) wide; sepals 6, in 2 whorls; petals 6, also in 2 whorls, slightly shorter than sepals; 3 small bracts outside sepals; stamens 6, lying against petals and moving toward the single style when touched; March–June.
Leaves: 5–7 (occasionally 3 or 9) ovate, spiny-margined leaflets 1¼–3″ (3.1–7.5 cm) long, shiny on upper side.
Fruit: chalky-blue berry about ¼″ (6 mm) wide.
Height: 4–8″ (10–20 cm).

Habitat
Dry, open pine forests.

Range
Western Canada to NE. California and S. Nevada; east to W. Montana, South Dakota, Colorado, and W. Texas.

Comments
This plant grows from a creeping underground rhizome, its erect stems surfacing here and there in the woods. Another low-growing species, Cascade Oregon Grape (*B. nervosa*), found from southwestern British Columbia to central

California, has 7—21 leaflets. A shrubby species, Tall Oregon
Grape (*B. aquifolium*), is the state flower of Oregon. The sour
berries are eaten by wildlife and make good jelly. Indians
made a yellow dye from the bark and wood of shrubby species.

California Fremontia
Fremontodendron californicum
202

Evergreen, many-branched, thicket-forming shrub or small
tree with short trunk, open crown, and large, showy, bright
yellow flowers.
Height: 20′ (6 m). Diameter: 8″ (20 cm).
Leaves: evergreen; alternate; ½—1½″ (1.2—4 cm) long and
wide. Rounded or broadly ovate, usually with 3 blunt lobes
and 3 main veins; thick; long-stalked; mostly on short side-
twigs. Dull dark green and sparsely hairy above, covered with
rust-colored and scurfy hairs and showing raised veins beneath.
Bark: brownish gray, fissured and scaly; inner bark
mucilaginous.
Twigs: stout, stiff; densely covered with rust-colored hairs
when young; becoming reddish brown.
Flowers: 1¼—2″ (3—5 cm) wide; with 5 broad, bright yellow
calyx lobes and without petals; borne singly on short side-
twigs or opposite leaves; in spring and early summer.
Fruit: 1—1¼″ (2.5—3 cm) long; pointed, densely hairy, egg-
shaped capsule; 4- or 5-celled; ripening in late summer and
splitting open on 4—5 lines; many elliptical, dark reddish-
brown seeds.

Habitat
Dry, rocky mountain slopes and canyons; with chaparral,
pinyons, junipers, and Ponderosa Pine.

Range

California, central Arizona, and N. Baja California; at 3000—
6500′ (914—1981 m).

Comments
The beautiful masses of large yellow flowers and odd, small
leaves covered with scurfy hairs makes this plant an attractive
ornamental. When flowering, the showy plants are
conspicuous from a distance. The alternate common name
Flannelbush refers to the densely hairy foliage. Under a hand
lens, the many-branched hairs on various parts look like stars.

Shrubby Cinquefoil
Potentilla fruticosa
203

A small shrub with reddish-brown, shredding bark on the
young twigs, and yellow flowers, 1 in each upper leaf axil, or
a few in clusters at ends of branches.
Flowers: about 1″ (2.5 cm) wide; petals 5, broad, stamens
25—30; June—August.
Leaves: pinnately divided, generally with 5 crowded leaflets,
each ½—¾″ (1.3—2 cm) long, hairy and grayish, especially on
lower side.
Height: 6—36″ (15—90 cm).

Habitat
Ridges, open forests, and plains from low to high elevations.

Range
Throughout the West.

Comments
This handsome shrub, common in the West, adapts well to cultivation. Among the many horticultural variants are dwarf, low-growing, and unusually large-flowered forms, some with white flowers, others with yellowish-orange ones.

Orange Bush Monkeyflower
Mimulus aurantiacus
204

A plant with woody, branched stems, covered with a sticky, varnishlike secretion and pale to deep orange, bilaterally symmetrical flowers.
Flowers: 1¼–2″ (3.1–5 cm) long; upper lip of corolla has 2 lobes bent upward, lower lip has 3 lobes bent downward; calyx smooth; March–August.
Leaves: to 3″ (7.5 cm) long, lanceolate, dark green on top, pale and sparsely hairy on underside, edges with fine teeth.
Height: 2–4′ (60–120 cm).

Habitat
Slopes and banks in chaparral and open woods.

Range
SW. Oregon to S. California; inland to the base of the Sierra Nevada.

Comments
Its long blooming season makes Orange Bush Monkeyflower a reliable source of nectar for hummingbirds. At the end of the style, two flaps (the stigmas) will slowly but visibly move and close together when touched by a blade of grass, a pollen-laden insect, or a hummingbird, providing a protective chamber for the pollen to begin its growth.

Rubber Rabbitbrush
Chrysothamnus nauseosus
206

Shrub with several stems growing erect from the base and with flexible branchlets covered with grayish or white feltlike hairs.
Height: 1–7′ (0.3–2 m).
Leaves: alternate; ¾–2½″ (2–6.5 cm) long, linear to nearly threadlike. More or less covered with fine, feltlike hairs.
Bark: shreddy.
Flowers: yellow disk flowers in rounded, often compound terminal clusters, usually covering plant in late summer and fall; ray flowers absent; July–October.
Fruit: 5-angled achenes.

Habitat
Dry, open slopes and flats; waste places.

Range
E. British Columbia east to Saskatchewan and south to E. California, Arizona, New Mexico, and Texas.

Comments
In season, flowering Rubber Rabbitbrush may seem to carpet dry slopes and flats with gold, as the shrubs are covered with

blossoms. Rubber Rabbitbrush frequents waste places and roadsides, where soil is poor or eroded. It also occurs with Big Sagebrush and Antelope Brush on better sites, often among pinyons and junipers or along the margins of ponderosa pine forests. The plant provides forage for rabbits, deer, elk, antelope, bighorn sheep, and jackrabbits, but is generally less favored than companion shrubs. The common name refers to the presence of latex in the sap. The genus name means "gold shrub," in reference to the flowers. All 13 species of rabbitbrush are rather similar and occur only in western North America.

Red Shrubby Penstemon
Penstemon corymbosus
207

A low, dark green shrub with bright, brick-red, bilaterally symmetrical flowers in bunches at ends of branches.
Flowers: 1–1½" (2.5–3.8 cm) long, the 2 lobes of upper lip project forward, the 3 lobes of lower lip bend downward; stamens 5, with stalks hairy at base, the fifth stamen lacking an anther but tipped with golden hairs; June–October.
Leaves: ¾–1½" (2–3.8 cm) long, opposite, leathery, ovate, often with small teeth.
Height: 12–20" (30–50 cm).

Habitat
Open rocky slopes and cliffs.

Range
Coast Ranges and Sierra foothills of N. California.

Comments
After the summer heat dries the low mountains, driving most wildflowers to seed and browning the grasses, Red Shrubby Penstemon begins to flower, providing a final source of nectar before the hummingbirds must seek food higher in the cooler mountains or, if late in the season, migrate south.

Western Azalea
Rhododendron occidentale
208

Large white to deep pink, very fragrant flowers bloom in large clusters at ends of stems on this shrub.
Flowers: corolla 1½–2½" (3.8–6.3 cm) wide, with narrow, tubular base and 5 wavy, pointed lobes, the upper lobe with yellow-orange patch; stamens 5, with hairy stalks; April–August.
Leaves: 1¼–3½" (3.1–8.8 cm) long, thin, green, elliptic.
Height: 4–17' (1.2–5.1 m).

Habitat
Moist places; in open areas near the coast, otherwise where partly shaded.

Range
S. California to SW. Oregon.

Comments
Flower variations include mixtures of pale pink, deep pink, and yellow-orange.

Pacific Rhododendron
Rhododendron macrophyllum
209

Evergreen shrub with large, deep green, leathery leaves and rounded clusters of large, pink, tubular flowers.
Height: 4–10′ (1.2–3 m); less commonly to 20′ (6 m) nearly treelike.
Leaves: evergreen; alternate but often so closely spaced as to seem whorled; 2½–8″ (6–20 cm) long; petioles stout. Leathery, thick, not toothed, oblong to elliptical; dark green and hairless above, paler and sometimes rusty beneath.
Flowers: pink to rose-purple, rarely white, about 1½″ (3.8 cm) long, with 5 wavy-margined petals united to form a broadly bell-shaped corolla about 1½″ (3.8 cm) long; in rounded clusters up to 6″ (15 cm) across; May–June.
Fruit: capsule about ¾″ (2 cm) long.

Habitat
Acidic soils in open or shady forest.

Range
SW. British Columbia south along coast and in Cascades to central California.

Comments
This is the showiest flowering shrub in the forests of western North America, with flower clusters that nearly rival in size and number those of its cultivated relatives. Pacific Rhododendron is confined to drier forest environments in western Washington, where it is the state flower. These same environments, however, are among the moister ones occurring in northern California, at the southern limit of this shrub's range. The plant is most abundant in Oregon, where mass displays provide a spectacular show in late spring and early summer.

Chaparral Pea
Pickeringia montana
210

A spiny dark green shrub, often forming impenetrable thickets, with bright reddish-lavender flowers near the ends of branches.
Flowers: about ¾″ (2 cm) long; 1 broad upper petal and 2 lateral petals nearly enclosing 2 bottom petals that are joined like the prow of a boat; May–August.
Leaves: 3 leaflets, less than ½″ (1.3 cm) long, stiff, broadly lanceolate.
Fruit: pod 1¼–2″ (3.1–5 cm) long, flat, straight.
Height: to 7′ (2.1 m).

Habitat
Dry hillsides in chaparral.

Range
Central to S. California.

Comments
Chaparral Pea is the only species in a genus confined to California. It is one of an unusually large number of endemic species that make the state's flora so distinctive. Rarely reproducing from seed, it grows new stems from roots that spread, especially after fires.

Nootka Rose
Rosa nutkana
211

A thorny shrub with pale pink flowers, the largest (often only) thorns in pairs near leafstalks.
Flowers: 2–3" (5–7.5 cm) wide; petals 5, broad; sepals 5, slender, usually tapered from base to narrow middle, then expanded slightly near tip; stamens many; May–July.
Leaves: pinnately compound, with 5–9 ovate leaflets ½–3" (1.3–7.5 cm) long, sharply toothed on edges.
Fruit: berrylike, ½–¾" (1.3–2 cm) long, round, smooth, reddish purple.
Height: 2–13' (60–400 cm).

Habitat
Woods and open places in the mountains.

Range
Alaska to N. California, NE. Oregon, N. Utah, and Colorado.

Comments
The hips, or fruit, of any wild roses may be eaten and are often used to make jams and jellies. Several species of wild rose occur in forests throughout the West. Woods Rose (*R. woodsii*) is the most common Rocky Mountain species.

Alpine Laurel
Kalmia microphylla
213

Several deep pink, bowl-shaped flowers face upward on slender stalks growing near the top of the leafy stems of this low, matted plant.
Flowers: corolla ½" (1.3 cm) wide, with 5 lobes and 10 little pouches that hold the 10 stamens, which spring up suddenly as corolla expands or is bent back; June–September.
Leaves: ½–1½" (1.3–3.8 cm) long, opposite, lanceolate, smooth and dark green on upper side, gray and hairy on lower, edges often curled downward.
Height: 4–20" (10–50 cm).

Habitat
Bogs and wet mountain meadows.

Range
Alaska and Canada; south to S. California and central Colorado.

Comments
Leaves, in spite of the name, are not to be used as a seasoning as they are suspected of being poisonous. The smaller Western Swamp Laurel (*K. occidentalis*), from lowlands of Alaska to Oregon, has flowers ⅝–¾" (1.5–2 cm) wide.

Salal
Gualtheria shallon
214

Shrublike, with spreading or erect hairy stems, often in large, dense patches, the pale pink, urn-shaped flowers hanging along reddish or salmon-colored racemes in upper axils.
Flowers: corolla hairy, ⅜" (9 mm) long, with 5 pointed lobes around opening; May–July.
Leaves: 2–4" (5–10 cm) long, ovate, with many minute teeth on edges.

Fruit: dark purple berry ¼–½" (6–13 mm) in diameter.
Height: 4–48" (10–120 cm).

Habitat
Conifer forest, moist woodland, coastal shrub.

Range
British Columbia to central California; rare and local south to
S. California.

Comments
The berries are a source of food for wildlife and were once
eaten by coastal Indians. The leaves are often used in floral
arrangements.

Red Mountain-heather
Phyllodoce empetriformis
216

A low, matted shrub with short, needlelike leaves and deep
pink, bell-shaped flowers that hang at the ends of slender
stalks in upper leaf axils.
Flowers: corolla about ¼" (6 mm) long, with 5 lobes tightly
curled back; stamens 10, shorter than corolla; June–August.
Leaves: ⅜–⅝" (9–15 mm) long, with groove on lower side.
Fruit: 5-chambered capsule that splits open along the walls
between chambers.
Height: 4–6" (10–40 cm).

Habitat
Open rocky slopes or in forests high in the mountains.

Range
Alaska to N. California, Idaho, and Colorado.

Comments
Brewer Mountain-heather (*P. breweri*), from the California
mountains, has pink flowers and stamens longer than the
corolla. Yellow Mountain-heather (*P. glandulifera*), growing in
the mountains from Oregon and Wyoming northward, has
glandular hairs on a yellowish or greenish-white corolla. Also
known as Pink Mountain Heather.

Lowbush Penstemon
Penstemon fruticosus
218

A bushy plant usually much broader than tall, with large,
showy, pale lavender or pale blue-violet, bilaterally
symmetrical flowers in crowded, narrow clusters at ends of
stems.
Flowers: corolla 1–2" (2.5–5 cm) long, plump, with long
white hairs inside near base of lower lip, the 2 lobes of upper
lip arched forward, the 3 lobes of lower lip bent downward; 4
stamens have hairy pollen sacs, the fifth stamen has a bearded
tip but no pollen sac; May–August.
Leaves: to 2½" (6.3 cm) long, opposite, lanceolate or ovate,
the edges with or without teeth.
Height: 6–16" (15–40 cm).

Habitat
Rocky open or wooded sites from the foothills well into the
mountains.

Range
S. British Columbia to central Oregon; east to W. Montana
and Wyoming.

Comments
In a genus with many beautiful species, this one may be the
most spectacular. Bright green leafy patches cascade down
banks and between rocks, topped with a dense display of
subtly shaded flowers that butterflies find especially attractive.

New Mexican Locust
Robinia neomexicana
219

Spiny shrub or small tree with open crown and showy,
fragrant, purplish-pink flowers; often forming thickets.
Height: 25' (7.6 m). Diameter: 8" (20 cm).
Leaves: alternate; pinnately compound; 4–10" (10–25 cm)
long; 13–21 leaflets, paired except at end, ½–1½" (1.2–4
cm) long, ¼–1" (0.6–2.5 cm) wide; elliptical, rounded at
ends, with tiny bristle tip; not toothed; finely hairy when
young; pale blue-green; nearly stalkless.
Bark: light gray, thick, furrowed into scaly ridges.
Twigs: brown, with rust-colored gland hairs when young;
with stout, brown, paired spines ¼–½" (6–12 mm) long at
nodes.
Flowers: ¼" (19 mm) long; 1 broad upper petal and 2 lateral
petals nearly enclosing 2 bottom petals that are joined and
shaped like the prow of a boat; petals unequal and purplish
pink; on stalks with sticky hairs; many in large, unbranched,
drooping clusters at base of leaves; in late spring and early
summer.
Fruit: 2½–4½" (6–11 cm) long; a narrowly oblong, flat, thin
brown pod with bristly and often glandular hairs; splitting
open, maturing in early autumn; 3–8 beanlike, flattened,
dark brown seeds.

Habitat
Canyons and moist slopes; with Gambel Oak, Ponderosa Pine,
and pinyons.

Range
Mountains from SE. Nevada east to S. and central Colorado,
south and east to Trans-Pecos Texas, and west to SE. Arizona;
also northern Mexico; at 4000–8500' (1219–2591 m).

Comments
Spectacular flower displays of New Mexican Locust can be seen
at the north rim of Grand Canyon National Park in early
summer. It is sometimes planted as an ornamental for the
handsome flowers and is also valuable for erosion control,
sprouting from roots and stumps and rapidly forming thickets.
Livestock and wildlife browse the foliage and cattle relish the
flowers. Indians also ate the pods and flowers.

Sugar Sumac
Rhus ovata
220

Evergreen shrub or small tree with rounded crown.
Height: 15' (4.6 cm). Diameter: 5" (13 cm).
Leaves: evergreen; alternate; 1½–3¼" (4–8 cm) long, 1–2"

(2.5–5 cm) wide. Ovate, short-pointed at tip, rounded at base, without teeth, thick and leathery; curved or folded up at midvein; shiny light green on both surfaces.
Bark: gray-brown, rough, shaggy and very scaly.
Twigs: reddish, stout, hairless.
Flowers: ¼" (6 mm) wide; with 5 rounded, whitish petals, from pink or reddish buds; many crowded in clusters 2" (5 cm) long, at end of twig; in early spring.
Fruit: more than ¼" (6 mm) in diameter; slightly flattened, red, covered with short, sticky, red hairs, 1-seeded; many in clusters; maturing in summer.

Habitat
Dry slopes in chaparral zone.

Range
Mountains of central Arizona and S. California including Santa Cruz and Santa Catalina islands south to N. Baja California; from near sea level to 2500' (762 m); in Arizona to 5000' (1524 m).

Comments
Sometimes planted for erosion control and landscaping in mountainous areas, this common species is also an attractive ornamental. The edible fruit was used as a sweetener by Indians; however, the large seeds are not eaten.

Blueblossom
Ceanothus thyrsiflorus
222

Large evergreen shrub or small tree with short trunk, many spreading branches, and showy blooms resembling lilacs; some plants prostrate.
Height: up to 20' (6 m). Diameter: 8" (20 cm).
Leaves: evergreen; alternate; ¾–2" (2–5 cm) long, ½–¾" (12–19 mm) wide; Oblong or elliptical, rounded to short-pointed at both ends; finely wavy, saw-toothed; 3 main veins; slightly thickened. Shiny green above, paler and slightly hairy on raised veins beneath.
Bark: red-brown, fissured into narrow scales.
Twigs: pale yellow-green, angled; slightly hairy when young.
Flowers: ³⁄₁₆" (5 mm) wide; with 5 light to deep blue petals (rarely almost white); fragrant; crowded on slender stalks in branched clusters 1–3" (2.5–7.5 cm) at base of upper leaves; in spring.
Fruit: ³⁄₁₆" (5 mm) in diameter; smooth, sticky, black capsules slightly 3-lobed, splitting into 3 1-seeded nutlets; maturing in summer.

Habitat
Mountain slopes and in canyons in chaparral, Redwood, and mixed evergreen forests.

Range
SW. Oregon south to S. California in outer Pacific Coast Range; to 2000' (610 m).

Comments
This is the hardiest and largest ceanothus. Each spring the

highways of the West Coast display masses of Blueblossom flowers. Plants can be grown in screens, in hedges, and against walls. Elk and deer browse the foliage. The shrubs form dense thickets after fires and logging.

Birchleaf Buckthorn
Rhamnus betulifolia

Upright shrub with oval green leaves and small stalked clusters of flowers or berries in the leaf axils.
Height: to 8¼' (2.5 m).
Leaves: mostly alternate, 2–6" (5–15 cm) long, usually thin; ovate to obovate or oval; edges untoothed or finely toothed. Green above and below; sparsely to densely haired below but not matted and woolly.
Bark: smooth and grayish.
Flowers: small, greenish, in loose clusters; May–June.
Fruit: black berry.

Habitat
Streamsides.

Range
Utah; possibly SW. Colorado south through Arizona to Mexico.

Comments
This buckthorn is a common streamside shrub in the canyonlands of the Southwest. Deer and bighorn sheep browse the foliage. A variety of songbirds and small mammals feed on the berries, which are edible but scarcely palatable. Of some 60–100 buckthorns in the world, 10–15 occur in North America, most of them in the West.

Evergreen Huckleberry
Vaccinium ovatum

Tall, stout, much-branched shrub with numerous small, dark green, leathery, evergreen leaves and small, black, sweet berries.
Height: 2–8' (0.6–2.4 m).
Leaves: evergreen; alternate; ½–1¼" (1.3–3 cm) long. Ovate, toothed, glossy green, leathery.
Flowers: about ¼" (6 mm) long; pink, bell-shaped, 1–5 in raceme; April–May.
Fruit: about ⅛" (3 mm) long, nearly as wide; black berries without whitish bloom; broadly egg-shaped to nearly round, sweet and edible.

Habitat
Drier portions of the Northwest coastal forest, often in deep shade beneath Coast Redwood or Douglas-fir.

Range
British Columbia south along coast and in adjacent mountains to S. California.

Comments
An important evergreen of the Northwest coastal forest, this lovely shrub is a conspicuous, often dominant plant beneath Douglas-firs and coast redwoods, where its common

associates are Salal, Oregon-grape, and Sword Fern. Preferring relatively dry sites with gravelly soils, Evergreen Huckleberry becomes more common southward to central California, where it is abundant in appropriate habitats. In Washington and British Columbia it is less common and widespread than several other huckleberry species. The berries are of moderate quality when eaten raw but are excellent for jams and pies. The plant produces them in abundance, providing a choice and plentiful food source for a variety of birds and mammals from September through November. The handsome branchlets of this shrub are widely used in floral displays.

Fernbush
Chamaebatiaria millefolium

A stout, densely branched shrub with fragrant, fernlike leaves and sticky branchlets.
Height: 2–6' (0.6–2 m).
Leaves: ¾–2" (2–5 cm) long, pinnately divided into 15–20 pairs of leaflets that are themselves divided into tiny segments, the result being distinctly fernlike; clustered more or less at tips of branchlets, hairless above, with star-shaped hairs beneath; petioles short, stipules present.
Bark: brownish gray.
Flowers: about ½" (12 mm) across, white, with 5 petals and 5 sepals, in panicles 2–4" (5–10 cm) long at ends of branchlets; stamens numerous; June–September.
Fruit: composed of 5 small, smooth, several-seeded pods.

Habitat
Dry, rocky ground in sagebrush scrub, pinyon-juniper woodlands, pine forest, and subalpine woodlands.

Range
S. Idaho and E. Oregon south along east side of Sierra Nevada to SE California, east to Arizona and north to Wyoming.

Comments
Though nowhere common, Fernbush grows conspicuously outside the Visitor Center at the South Rim of the Grand Canyon. It is perhaps most common in pinyon-juniper woodlands and dry pine forests, where it often is a pioneer plant in rock crevices. Fernbush is the only member of its genus and occurs nowhere else in the world.

Fool's Huckleberry
Menziesia ferruginea

Straggling or slender, ascending shrub with rusty-haired leaves and coppery urn-shaped flowers.
Height: 6–15' (1.8–4.5 m).
Leaves: alternate, but closely spaced to form whorl-like clusters at branchlet tips, 1¼–2¾" (3–7 cm) long; thin, elliptic-oblong to obovate, finely toothed. Deep green above, paler beneath, with scattered rusty hairs on both surfaces; petioles with long hairs.
Flowers: Copper-colored or yellowish, appearing with the leaves, borne in terminal clusters, the calyx saucerlike and fringed with fine bristles, the corolla urn-shaped, 4- (rarely 5-)

lobed, about ½" (12 mm) long; June–July.
Fruit: ovoid, woody, 4-celled capsule about ¼" (6 mm) long.

Habitat
Moist slopes to near timberline, often in subalpine tree
clumps.

Range
Alaska south to NW. California, east to Cascades and Rockies
of British Columbia, Idaho, and W. Montana.

Comments
Fool's Huckleberry is one of the more common shrubs at
middle to high elevations in the mountains of the Pacific
Northwest, where it may be confused with huckleberries
(*Vaccinium*) or Cascade Azalea (*Rhododendron albiflorum*). Fool's
Huckleberry, however, does not produce berries and lacks the
distinctive white flower of Cascade Azalea. All these shrubs
commonly occur together either in the understory of upper
montane and subalpine forests of the Pacific Northwest. Fool's
Huckleberry also occurs downslope to sea level, where it
coexists with still other members of the heath family.

Grouse Whortleberry
Vaccinium scoparium

Low, carpet-forming shrublet with green, broomlike twigs
and small, sweet red berries.
Height: 4–12" (10.2–30.5 cm).
Leaves: alternate, about ½" (12 mm) long. Somewhat ovate;
toothed.
Bark: green.
Flowers: about ⅛" (3 mm) long; pink, calyx barely 5-lobed,
corolla nearly round with 5 tiny lobes at tip; June–July.
Fruit: red huckleberries to ¼" (6 mm) in diameter; edible and
very pleasant to the taste.

Habitat
Dry forest floors, especially of Lodgepole Pine, from mid- to
high elevation.

Range
British Columbia south along east side of Cascade Range to
extreme N. California, and south in Rocky Mountains from
Alberta to New Mexico.

Comments
The combination of red berries, green twigs, and mat-forming
habit make Grouse Whortleberry distinctive among the many
species of blueberries and huckleberries found in the western
forests. Grouse Whortleberry is often the only ground cover in
dry, shady conifer stands in the Rockies and is particularly
common beneath Lodgepole Pine. Numerous birds and
mammals, including humans, relish the berries of this and
other members of the genus *Vaccinium,* which also includes
cultivated blueberries and cranberries.

BIRDS

A tremendous number of birds—large and small, silent and noisy—find a congenial home in the forests of the West. The attentive visitor will find that a trip into the forests offers many chances to observe birds: inconspicuous and shy towhees, brilliantly colored hummingbirds, and the imposing, mysterious owls. This section covers many of the most typical birds of the western forests; learning to identify some of these birds of prey, game and ground birds, and songbirds will enrich your forest visits.

Northern Goshawk
Accipiter gentilis
223

20–26" (51–66 cm). Wingspan 42–48" (1–1.2 m).
Uniformly gray above, white with light gray cross-barring
below. Dark gray crown and ear patch separated by white eye-
stripe. Flies with several short, rapid flaps followed by a glide.
As in most birds of prey, female is larger and stronger than
male. Juveniles brown above with brown-streaked creamy
underparts and light eye-stripe.

Voice
A repeated *kek kek kek* and a harsh scream at nest site.

Habitat
Taiga; the northern coniferous forests and western extensions.

Range
Circumpolar. In the West, from Alaska through the Rocky
Mountains to New Mexico; also the mountains and forests of
Washington, Oregon, and interior California. Migrates and
winters in lowlands as far south as northern Mexico.

Comments
The male supplies food while the female incubates and broods.
As the young grow and demand more food, both parents hunt.
Although Northern Goshawks can kill animals as large as
jackrabbits, they feed mainly on grouse and smaller birds.

Blue Grouse
Dendragapus obscurus
224

15½–21" (39–53 cm). Large grouse. Male dusky gray or
bluish gray overall with orange-yellow comb over the eyes,
some mottling on wings. Light gray terminal band on dark
tail may be lacking in birds in the northern Rockies. Females
and immatures mottled brown with dark tail.

Voice
A deep series of hoots: *whoop, whoop, whoop* . . . increasing in
volume and tempo toward the end of the series. Calling birds
are often extremely difficult to find.

Habitat
Burns, edge of brush in coastal rain forest; montane forests,
slashes, and subalpine forest clearings.

Range
Coastal forest area from SE. Alaska to San Francisco Bay; the
Sierra Nevada and Rocky Mountains.

Comments
The spring display of the territorial male is an imposing sight.
Perched on a stump or fallen log, the male produces "booms"
or "hoots" by inflating and deflating the sound-magnifying
pouches on each side of his neck. The yellow or purple
featherless pouch is ringed by the white downy bases of
surrounding feathers. In winter this grouse feeds exclusively
on pine needles; in summer, on insects, seeds, and berries.

Ruffed Grouse
Bonasa umbellus
225

16–19" (41–48 cm). Chicken-sized. Slight crest. Mottled, brownish with buff streaks above, gray-brown cross-barring below. Fan-shaped tail has contrasting cross-barring on gray or red base, and broad black terminal band emphasized by lighter margins. Male has ruff of erectile black feathers on side of neck. Female is plainer, with smaller ruff and tail.

Voice
The drumming of the male is a hollow-toned, low-pitched accelerating series of beats made with the wings. The voice is used only in close communication, as in the soft murmur of a female with chicks, or a series of sharp notes when alarmed.

Habitat
Deciduous woodland; edges within the coniferous forest zone.

Range

From the northern tree limit across North America south to the limit of good coniferous growth: NE. California, N. Utah and Colorado, and from the Great Lakes forest south along the Appalachian chain.

Comments
The male's spring display consists of the "drumming" described above. The female raises the chicks alone. In summer the birds feed on berries and fruits; in winter they take to the treetops and forage on buds, catkins, and twigs, preferring aspen and poplar.

California Quail
Callipepla californica
226

9–11" (23–28 cm). Colorfully and intricately patterned. Small and plump with black forward-curving plume arising from chestnut crown. Creamy forehead and black throat. Crown and throat edged in white. Grayish-blue breast and softly mottled nape; unstreaked brown back and creamy belly scaled with brown markings. Creamy diagonal flank streaking. Female less boldly marked than male.

Voice
A loud, distinctive *ka ka kow,* the second note highest. Sometimes expressed as *chi-ca-go* or *who are you?* Often with 2-noted "warmup" phrases. Calls include loud *pit!* notes.

Habitat
Brush with open areas such as coastal or foothill chaparral and live-oak canyons; also adjacent desert and suburbs.

Range

Originally, both California and Baja California. Introduced to southern Vancouver Island, British Columbia; also found in W. Washington, S. Oregon and N. Nevada.

Comments
Perched on tree or fence post, the male claims his territory by cackling and posturing; the entire family takes to trees for roosting as well as for safety. After the breeding season, these birds become gregarious and gather in large coveys, often visiting city parks, gardens, and yards.

Mountain Quail
Oreortyx pictus
227

10½–11½" (27–29 cm). Largest North American quail. Grayish-blue head, neck, and breast; chestnut throat patch framed by creamy forehead and side streak. Olive-brown back, heavy white diagonal markings on chestnut flanks. Female duller. Both sexes have long, straight, black head plume.

Voice
Its frequent call is a single haunting, low, owl-like, slightly ascending whistled: *woook?* "Conversational" notes include a series of soft whistles.

Habitat
Dry mountains; brushy wooded areas and chaparral.

Range
Washington, Idaho, Oregon, and California. Introduced to southern Vancouver Island, British Columbia.

Comments
This quail migrates on foot from high territory, where it breeds, to protected valleys, where it winters in coveys of 6 to 12 birds. They are usually found in very dense cover.

Band-tailed Pigeon
Columba fasciata
228

14–15½" (36–39 cm). Larger than the Domestic Pigeon. Dark gray above; tail has pale gray terminal band. Head and underparts purplish-plum, whitening toward vent. Adults have narrow white semi-collar at nape. Yellow bill is tipped with black; yellow legs.

Voice
A deep, owl-like *whoo-hoo*.

Habitat
Coniferous forests along the northwestern Pacific Coast, but in the southwestern part of its range it prefers oak woodlands or pine-oak forests where it can feed on acorns.

Range
From S. British Columbia to Baja California in and near coastal forests and hills; in mountain chains extending from Utah and Colorado south through Mexico to South America.

Comments
This shy forest pigeon is adapting to parks and gardens, where it feeds on lawns and ornamental berries, especially holly. Already a city bird in the Northwest, it has spread from natural redwood pockets to suburban conifer plantings in California towns. In fall these birds feast on acorns.

Flammulated Owl
Otus flammeolus
229

6–7" (15–18 cm). Slightly larger than a sparrow. Small, indistinct ear tufts and dark eyes. Grayish above, light below, with white and rust-colored markings. Sexes look similar but female larger than male.

Voice
A monotonous low hoot, single or double, is repeated almost

endlessly, and sounds as mechanical as the time signals of a radio station.

Habitat
Coniferous woodlands and forest edges in the Northwest; dry ponderosa pine woods in the Southwest.

Range
From the interior forest of British Columbia through the Rocky Mountain and Pacific states, east of the Cascade-Sierra divide, south to the mountains of the Mexican Plateau.

Comments
As with other owls, the male Flammulated supplies food and protection, while the female is the chief nest-tender. Mice and similar prey are usually decapitated, the male feeding on the head, the female and young consuming the softer parts of the body.

Great Horned Owl
Bubo virginianus
230

18–25" (46–64 cm). Large owl. Ear tufts set wide apart, yellow eyes. Mottled gray-brown above with fine dark gray horizontal barring below.

Voice
A deeply resonant hooting, *hoo, hoo-hoo-hoo, hoo;* also 3 hoots.

Habitat
In all habitats, including deserts, as long as shelter such as woods or cliffs is close.

Range
Common in North America up to the northern tree limit.

Comments
This owl hunts rabbits, rodents, and birds, including crows, ducks, and other owls. On occasion, it even captures skunks. It is the largest and best known of the common owls. Since owls can see in the dark, they were believed to possess supernatural powers.

Long-eared Owl
Asio otus
231

13–16" (33–41 cm). Similar to but smaller than the Great Horned Owl. It lacks the white throat, has vertical chest markings rather than horizontal, and its long, dark ear tufts, when raised, are much closer together than those on other "eared" owls.

Voice
In spring its hooted *hoooo,* repeated at intervals, and catlike calls reveal its presence in woods.

Habitat
Deciduous and mixed woods, conifer groves, near open country, and even sagebrush desert.

Range
In temperate areas of North America from Canada to Baja California.

Comments
This forest owl is strictly nocturnal; during the day it rests near the trunk of a tree, where its camouflage makes it hard to detect. It is sometimes mobbed by other birds, but seldom attacks them. It feeds mainly on rodents, like other owls locating prey more by hearing than sight.

Northern Pygmy-Owl
Glaucidium gnoma
232

7–7½" (18–19 cm). Sparrow-sized. Small round head and long, finely barred tail, often cocked at an angle. Varying shades of brown with fine buff spotting above; buff with bolder brown streaks below; two white-edged black spots at back of neck suggest "eyes." Undulating flight.

Voice
Most common call is a series of hollow whistles on one pitch. Also a thin rattle around the nest.

Habitat
Open coniferous forests or mixed aspen and oak woods; dense canyon growth.

Range
From SE. Alaska throughout the West, with the eastern limit formed by prairies adjacent to the Rocky Mountain forest; south to the mountains of Mexico and Guatemala.

Comments
This small owl sometimes hunts by day, attacking birds even larger than itself. In spring the male is conspicuous, uttering a staccato whistle every few seconds, while flicking his long tail upward and sideways. In response, the small forest birds scold and mob this tiny owl, just as they would any larger owl.

Great Gray Owl
Strix nebulosa
233

24–33" (61–84 cm). Largest owl in North America. Large rounded head lacks ear tufts; enormous pale facial disk patterned in concentric gray circles with yellow eyes and bill and black chin spot. Mottled gray and brown above, grayish lengthwise streaking below. Relatively long tail.

Voice
Very deep *hooo* note at irregular intervals.

Habitat
Bogs and forests of the taiga; in the southern fringes of its range, montane conifers near openings and alpine meadows.

Range
From Alaska to Ontario, south along mountains east of the coastal ranges from British Columbia to central California (the Sierra Nevada) and from the northern Rockies to Yellowstone. Rare and local; common only in the Far North.

Comments
Like most large owls, it has a remarkably small body within a large mass of feathers that provide excellent insulation in the rugged climate it prefers. It often hunts in the late afternoon.

Northern Saw-whet Owl
Aegolius acadicus
234

7–8½" (18–22 cm). Small owl. Brown above, lightly streaked with white on the forehead and crown; white below with broad reddish-brown streakings. Lacks ear tufts; has yellow eyes, dark bill, and short tail. Immatures are tawny-rust with broad white eyebrows that form a "V."

Voice
A monotonous series of low, whistled notes on one pitch. Also an upslurred whistle.

Habitat
Coniferous or deciduous woodlands, from bogs and moist alder thickets to drier ponderosa pine slopes.

Range
Breeds in SE. Alaska and S. Canada east to the Atlantic Coast; in the West south along wooded mountain ranges to Mexico. Also in winter on forested lowlands across North America.

Comments
A nocturnal hunter of forest rodents and large beetles, it is tame and approachable during the day while resting. Though widespread in Canada and all of the northern and western United States, its distribution is spotty.

Black-chinned Hummingbird
Archilochus alexandri
235

3¼–3¾" (8–10 cm). Small hummingbird. Male green above with black chin, underlined by violet-purple throat band. Female green above with white throat and breast, buff sides, and white-tipped outer tail feathers.

Voice
Calls are a low *tup* and a buzz. Male makes a dry buzz with wings in flight.

Habitat
Mountain and alpine meadows, woodlands, canyons with thickets, chaparral, and orchards.

Range
British Columbia south to Mexico and W. Texas; absent from humid N. Pacific Coast. Winters in Mexico.

Comments
The male Black-chinned, like all hummingbirds, maintains a mating and feeding territory in spring. He courts his female with a dazzling aerial display involving a pendulumlike flight pattern. When mating interest wanes, the male often takes up residence elsewhere, near a good food supply. Later, when the blooming season and insect swarming subside, both male and female move south.

Anna's Hummingbird
Calypte anna
236

3½–4" (9–10 cm). Medium-sized hummingbird. Both sexes metallic green above; male has dark rose-red crown and gorget and grayish chest. Female has spotted throat with central patch of red spots, grayish-white underparts, and white-tipped outer tail feathers. Throat of juveniles frequently unmarked.

Voice
Song of male is a series of coarse squeaking notes continuing in a definite pattern for several seconds; delivered from a perch. Common calls include a sharp *chip* and a rapid *chee-chee-chee-chee-chee*. When displaying, the male climbs high in the air and plummets rapidly earthward, giving an explosive *peeep!* as he levels off just above the ground. This sound issues from the specialized, narrow tail feathers spread out during the descent.

Habitat
Chaparral, coastal scrub, brushy oak woodland, and gardens.

Range
Principally from N. Baja California and coastal foothills up to S. Oregon; summer pioneers reach Vancouver Island, British Columbia. With the planting of eucalyptus trees and increased use of window feeders in California's Central Valley, food is always available and this species now stays year round. Other inland populations are migratory.

Comments
Anna's and other hummingbirds vigorously defend their feeding territories, which, although often as small as a few clumps of fuchsias, provide adequate nectar and small nectar-feeding insects. From July to late fall, however, transient and juvenile birds disregard territorial claims, and competition at feeders increases greatly.

Calliope Hummingbird
Stellula calliope
237

2¾–4″ (7–10 cm). Smallest North American hummer. Male metallic green above, gorget white with purple-violet rays, which can be raised to give a whiskered effect. (All other North American hummers have solid-colored gorgets.) Female green above, white below, with dark streaks on throat, buffy flanks, and white-tipped tail corners.

Voice
A series of light *chip* notes. Displaying male utters a high *see-ree* note as it dives over female.

Habitat
Breeds and feeds in montane and subalpine forest clearings, brushy edges, and alpine meadows.

Range
From interior and southern coastal British Columbia to Baja California in the West, and from Alberta to Wyoming in the Rocky Mountains. Winters in Mexico.

Comments
In mating display or in defending their feeding flowers, male hummers (and occasionally females) put on a striking show, rising out of sight and then swooping down to buzz the female or an opponent. Each species has its own flight pattern.

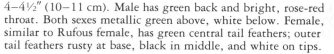

Broad-tailed Hummingbird
Selasphorus platycercus
238

4–4½″ (10–11 cm). Male has green back and bright, rose-red throat. Both sexes metallic green above, white below. Female, similar to Rufous female, has green central tail feathers; outer tail feathers rusty at base, black in middle, and white on tips.

Voice
Call is a sharp *chick*. Adult male makes a *unique loud musical trill with wings* in flight, which distinguishes it.

Habitat
Varies widely from mountain meadows, pinyon-juniper woodland, dry ponderosa pine, to fir or mixed forest and canyon vegetation.

Range
Mountainous areas from E. California to N. Wyoming, the Great Basin, and Rocky Mountain states, south through the Mexican Plateau. Winters in Central America.

Comments
The Broad-tailed is the common hummingbird of the Rocky Mountains. Accounts of this species mention that it nests in the same tree or bush year after year, a phenomenon known as philopatry—faithfulness to the previous home area. It will return to the same branch and even build a new nest atop an old one.

Rufous Hummingbird
Selasphorus rufus
239

3–4″ (8–10 cm). Male's non-iridescent, rufous upperparts and sides contrast with bright orange-red gorget and white breast. Female is green above, with rufous on sides and at base of tail.

Voice
Low chipping and buzzy notes. An excited *zeee-chuppity-chup* is often heard. The wings of adult males may produce a musical buzz in flight.

Habitat
Forest edges, thickets in coniferous or deciduous forests, woodlands, mountain chaparral, and alpine meadows.

Range
The Pacific Northwest, northward through interior valleys and coastal slopes to the Alaskan panhandle.

Comments
This is perhaps the most pugnacious hummingbird north of Mexico. The first bird to discover a source of food defends it. Although satiated, it perches nearby and intercepts an intruder in the air with angry buzzing. If a female is disturbed when feeding, she gives a "no trespassing" signal by fanning and waving her tail. Females, therefore, have developed distinct tail patterns, whereas males, facing the opponent, signal with their brilliant throat patches, called gorgets. The sexes have separate territories; the female visits the male at mating time. In California's redwood forests, this species is replaced by the very similar Allen's Hummingbird, which has a green back.

Elegant Trogon
Trogon elegans
240

11–12" (28–30 cm). Robin-sized. Unmistakable combination of stout, hooked yellow bill, upright posture, and long, square-cut tail. Male glossy, dark emerald-green on upperparts, head, and upper breast; white breast band; crimson belly and undertail coverts. Copper-red tail has black terminal band, but viewed from below it is gray with broad white bars. Female plain brown where male is green, with white patch on cheek; pink where male is crimson, with white and light coffee bands on breast.

Voice
The calls, described as *ko-ah ko-ah ko-ah* and *kum! kum! kum!*, carry quite far but are hard to locate even when the bird sits close by, because it usually stays in the middle level of the forest canopy.

Habitat
Thick deciduous mountain growth; sycamore canyons.

Range
From SE. Arizona to Central America.

Comments
This beautiful trogon is related to the bird of the Maya emperor-gods, the Quetzal. Finding it is a prime objective of birders, since its range barely extends into the United States. Trogons are insectivorous, but also eat small fruits.

Acorn Woodpecker
Melanerpes formicivorus
241

8–9½" (20–24 cm). Smaller than Robin. Male has yellowish-white forecrown; red crown, light eyes, black nape, back, wings, and tail. Black chin, yellowish-white throat and sides of head with heavy dark streaking on breast and flanks; white belly, wing patches, and rump. Female has black forecrown; otherwise identical to male.

Voice
This noisy woodpecker gives a variety of calls, including a distinctive *JA-cob, JA-cob* or *WAKE-up, WAKE-up*. Also a rolling drum with bill against a dead limb.

Habitat
Open oak and pine-oak forests.

Range
S. Oregon through California and Arizona; New Mexico, and W. Texas south to Colombia.

Comments
This well-named woodpecker harvests acorns and, in agricultural or suburban areas, almonds and walnuts as well. In autumn the birds store their crops of nuts tightly in individual holes so that no squirrel can pry them out. The storage trees are usually mature or dead pines, or Douglas-firs with thick, soft bark, but dead oak branches, utility poles, and fence posts are also used. The holes made by a colony are re-used year after year. Acorns seem to be emergency provisions; on mild winter days these birds catch insects.

Yellow-bellied Sapsucker
Sphyrapicus varius
242

8–9″ (20–23 cm). 2 subspecies, sometimes considered different species, are all characterized by a long white wing patch, barred back, and white rump. Rocky Mountain and Great Basin birds ("Red-naped" Sapsucker) have red nape, forehead, and throat (female's throat is only partly red). Both these subspecies have black chest band separating throat from yellow belly. Immatures dusky brown with light spots above, lighter below, with black-and-white checked wings and tail.

Voice
A soft, slurred *whee-ur* or *mew*. The display communication of the spring pair is not a drum but a tap in a broken series: *prrrrrrp, prrp, prp, prp.*

Habitat
Edges of coniferous forest; woodlands, groves of aspen and alder.

Range
In the West, the Rocky Mountain areas harbor the "Red-naped"; the "Yellow-bellied" occurs in cottonwood and aspen groves of the prairie provinces. All forms winter from southern United States to Central America.

Comments
Sapsuckers feed mainly on insects extracted from bark, thus keeping down the number of boring insects that destroy healthy trees. The similar and closely related Red-breasted Sapsucker (*Sphyrapicus ruber*) inhabits the coastal forest from the Alaska panhandle to southern California. It has an all-red hood and white "mustache."

Williamson's Sapsucker
Sphyrapicus thyroideus
243

9½″ (24 cm). Male has black head, breast, and back, white facial stripes, bright red throat, and large white wing and rump patches. Lemon yellow belly is bordered with black-and-white-barred flanks. Sexes very dissimilar: female has brown head, dark brown and white zebra stripes above and on flanks; large dark bib and smaller, less brilliant yellow area on belly.

Voice
A soft nasal *churrr,* descending in pitch. Drum has an intermittent cadence.

Habitat
Ponderosa pine forests and open coniferous forests; subalpine forests of the Southwest.

Range
Throughout the West in drier forests from SE. British Columbia to New Mexico; not found in coastal ranges. Winters in southern Pacific states from Arizona to Mexico.

Comments
The distribution of this woodpecker, like that of many birds, is tied to a certain climatic belt. In southern areas, cool climates occur at high elevations, whereas in northern latitudes such conditions occur closer to sea level.

Nuttall's Woodpecker
Picoides nuttallii
244

7–7½" (18–19 cm). Small "ladder-backed" woodpecker. Black head with white markings; male has red cap on midcrown; light side spotting on unstreaked white underparts.

Voice
Rolling call, *prreep*, often expanded into a long, rolling *prree-prree-prrreeeee*. Drums frequently in spring.

Habitat
Canyon scrub oaks, oak woodlands, and streamside growth.

Range
California, with a slight extension to S. Oregon and Baja California.

Comments
Although some sources indicate that this species is restricted to interior and coastal foothills with extensive stands of oaks, it sometimes also nests in suburban areas and riparian woods.

Hairy Woodpecker
Picoides villosus
245

8½–10½" (22–27 cm). Medium-sized. White head with black crown, eye-mask, and "whiskers." Male has red patch at base of crown; light underparts; white back; black wings with white spots. Tail black with white outer tail feathers. Female similar but lacks red patch.

Voice
A loud, sharp *peek!*

Habitat
Deciduous trees; coniferous stands, especially in montane forests and river groves.

Range
All of wooded North America from the subarctic treeline of Canada to the tropics of Panama, where it is a highland bird.

Comments
Woodpeckers secure their food by hammering holes through bark and then extracting grubs with their extremely long, flexible tongues. They begin their work with a gentle tapping, which helps them detect the exact location of the food. When drumming to proclaim their territory, they select a dry limb and tap rapidly, increasing in loudness, then fading away. The Downy Woodpecker (*Picoides pubescens*) is nearly identical but smaller, with a shorter bill and usually black bars on the white outer tail feathers. It prefers broadleaf trees to conifers.

White-headed Woodpecker
Picoides albolarvatus
246

9" (23 cm). Small woodpecker. Black overall with white head, throat, and wing patch. Male has red patch on nape.

Voice
Calls include a sharp *pee-dink* and a more prolonged *pee-dee-dee-dink*. Drum is a short, even series.

Habitat
Ponderosa pine belt of mountains; also subalpine belt of firs.

Range
Extreme south-central British Columbia, NE. Washington and Idaho, south to S. California and just across the Nevada line, but avoids the Pacific Coast rain forest.

Comments
An inconspicuous bird, hard to find due to its silent habits, it rarely taps or drums, vocalizing only around the nest. It feeds by scaling bark off the tree to reach the insects underneath. Its black-and-white pattern, striking in flight, provides good camouflage when the bird perches in a shady forest.

Three-toed Woodpecker
Picoides tridactylus
247

8–9½″ (20–24 cm). Yellow cap, black head with white facial stripes; black-and-white barred "ladder back"; black wings, rump, and tail; barred flanks and white underparts. Female lacks yellow cap.

Voice
Call is a sharp *pik* or *kik*. Drums like the Black-backed Three-Toed Woodpecker.

Habitat
Coniferous forests; from light woodland muskeg or burns to open pine woods and dense stands.

Range
In the North, from Alaska across the Canadian taiga belt to Newfoundland, south along the western mountains to the Oregon Cascades in the West, and east to Arizona and New Mexico.

Comments
The very similar Black-backed Woodpecker (*Picoides arcticus*), which also has 3 toes, is told by its solid black back and slender eyebrow stripe but is otherwise very similar to the Three-toed Woodpecker.

Northern Flicker
Colaptes auratus
248

12½–14″ (32–36 cm). A large woodpecker. Barred cinnamon-brown back and white rump. Head brown, with gray face and throat, and red mustache (male only); black crescent on breast; underparts white, boldly spotted with black; salmon-pink wing and tail linings are conspicuous in flight.

Voice
A piercing *keee-ar*. Also *flicka-flicka-flicka,* and a loud prolonged series: *wick wick wick wick wick.*

Habitat
Deciduous or mixed woods, semiopen country, edge or replacement growth in northern conifer belt, saguaros and woods along desert washes.

Range
Woodlands from Alaska to Mexico and coast to coast, including deserts of the Southwest.

Comments
The Northern Flicker occurs in 3 color variants, the "Red-shafted" of the West; the "Gilded," living in the desert; and the "Yellow-shafted," found east of the Rocky Mountains. The "Red-shafted" and "Yellow-shafted" hybridize in the Great Plains. Flickers are important in the woodland community, providing nesting cavities for many hole-nesting birds. They feed on ants and other ground insects and, in winter, also on berries.

Pileated Woodpecker
Dryocopus pileatus
249

16–19½" (41–50 cm). Almost crow-sized. Male is predominantly black with red crest and mustache; white face, black eye-mask and long white throat stripe. White flanks and underwing linings flash in flight. Female similar, but red less extensive on crest and absent on mustache.

Voice
A loud *kak kak kak kak*.

Habitat
Mature coniferous and mixed woods, with dead stumps.

Range
Breeds across the continent in the Canadian taiga; coastal forest down to central California, the Sierra Nevada, and the Cascades of Oregon. Rare in the Rocky Mountain states, but widespread in the East.

Comments
With the probable extinction of the Ivory-billed Woodpecker, this is now the largest woodpecker in America. Its staple food consists of carpenter ants living in fallen timber, dead roots, and stumps. The woodpecker excavates thumb-sized rectangular cavities, then uses its enormously long, sticky tongue to reach the ant burrows.

Olive-sided Flycatcher
Contopus borealis
250

7–8" (18–20 cm). Large, stocky, thick-headed flycatcher. Dark brownish-gray above, broad olive-gray flanks that almost meet in center of dusky white chest. White "downy" tufts on lower back frequently visible behind folded wing.

Voice
Song is a clearly whistled *whip-three-beers!*, the middle note highest in pitch. Call is an incessant *pilt, pilt*.

Habitat
Northern coniferous woodlands, burns, and clearings. Also favors eucalyptus (in California), aspens, birches, and maples.

Range
Across the boreal forest from Alaska through Canada, and south through the forested West to Baja California, Nevada, Arizona, and New Mexico. Winters in South America.

Comments
This flycatcher hunts insects from a high branch of a conifer.

Analysis of stomach contents shows that everything it eats is winged; it takes no spiders, caterpillars, or other larvae. It habitually chooses the leader or highest branches of a conifer as its hunting and singing perch and is therefore often unseen.

Western Wood-Pewee
Contopus sordidulus
251

6–6½" (15–17 cm). Dark olive-gray above with slightly lighter breast and sides. Light yellowish chin and belly and 2 whitish wing bars. No eye-ring.

Voice
Once heard, easy to recognize. Mainly in the morning and at twilight, it utters a *pee-wee*.

Habitat
Coniferous, deciduous, or mixed woods near water.

Range
Throughout the West, from S. Alaska through Mexico to Central America. Northern populations migratory.

Comments
This flycatcher is found in a large variety of wooded habitats, so long as there are clear areas for foraging. It is also found in forest edges and perches on branches over roads or streams.

Western Flycatcher
Empidonax difficilis
252

5½–6" (14–15 cm). Olive-brown above, with yellow throat and belly separated by dusky olive breast; white eye-ring and light wing bars. Fall birds may be duller. Bill long and wide, lower mandible bright yellow.

Voice
Quite distinct, rising *pseet, ptsick, seet.* First part alone is often used as a call, or is repeated on a drawn-out, almost sibilant high pitch. Second part is rapid and louder.

Habitat
Moist, shaded coniferous or mixed forests; canyons.

Range
From Alaska to Baja California, and through forests of the western mountains to Montana and New Mexico. Winters in Mexico and Central America.

Comments
The Western Flycatcher makes use of shady airspace between tangled ground cover and the low branches of the towering conifers. It is the most frequently observed *Empidonax* in most of its western range.

Ash-throated Flycatcher
Myiarchus cinerascens
253

7½–8½" (19–22 cm). Slender bill and gray-white throat. Olive-brown above, light yellow underparts, with cinnamon-rust primaries and tail feathers. 2 white wing bars.

Voice
Common call is a rolling *quee-eerr* suggestive of a low-pitched

playground whistle. Also various *pip* or *pwit* notes and various croaking sounds.

Habitat
Open woodland, pinyon-juniper, chaparral, oak canyons, deserts, and riverside groves.

Range
S. Washington and Idaho south into California and Mexico, east to Colorado and Texas. Winters from extreme S. California and Arizona southward.

Comments
These birds launch their pursuit of insects from the dead upper branches of mature trees at the edge of woodlands. Although this flycatcher nests in tree cavities, it still builds a nest and has streaked, camouflaged eggs like its open-nesting ancestors.

Violet-green Swallow
Tachycineta thalassina
254

5–5½" (13–14 cm). Dark metallic bronze-green upperparts, iridescent violet rump and tail, the latter slightly forked; white underparts. White cheek extending above eye and white on the sides above rump.

Voice
A high *dee-chip* given in flight. Also varying *tweet* notes.

Habitat
Forests, wooded foothills, mountains, and suburban areas.

Range
From Alaska east to South Dakota, south to Baja California, Texas, and central Mexico. Winters south to Central America, and irregularly in coastal S. California.

Comments
Like many other swallows, it lives in colonies, basically because of its feeding needs; where one finds food there is usually enough for all, and when feeding communally these birds can more readily defend themselves against hawks.

Gray Jay
Perisoreus canadensis
255

10–13" (25–33 cm). Dark gray above, with narrow, light band across back; light below. Blackish nape contrasts with almost white forehead and face. Juveniles are dark slaty overall, with light whisker.

Voice
A whistled *pwee-ah* note. Also a great variety of other notes, some harsh and grating.

Habitat
Northern coniferous forests.

Range
Taiga from Alaska to the Atlantic Coast, the coastal rain forest to N. California, and the interior and Rocky Mountain ranges to NE. California, Arizona, Colorado, and N. New Mexico.

Comments
Anyone who has camped in the mountains of the northern
forests is familiar with this bird, formerly called Canada Jay
and popularly known as the Whiskey Jack or Camp Robber.
This bird is attracted to campsites, where it appropriates as
much food as possible. It stores scraps of frozen meat, suet, or
hide, gluing them into balls with its saliva and hiding them
among the needles.

Steller's Jay
Cyanocitta stelleri
256

12–13½" (30–34 cm). Only western jay with crest. Front half
of bird sooty black, rear dark bluish-gray, with tight black
cross-barring on secondaries and tail. Lightly streaked
eyebrow, chin, and forehead markings vary considerably.

Voice
A harsh *shack-shack-shack-shack* or *chook-chook-chook* call reveals
its presence. May also mimic the screams of hawks.

Habitat
Coniferous forests: pine and oak woods in the South, small
groves and stands of mixed oak and redwood in northern
California. In the Northwest, a bird of dense coniferous
forests. In fall it moves to oak trees at lower elevations, often
leaving the conifers it prefers at nesting time.

Range
Throughout the West, from coastal Alaska to the prairies and
from the Rockies to S. California and Central America.

Comments
Somewhat reticent, Steller's Jay nevertheless quickly becomes
accustomed to campsites and human providers. It is often seen
sitting quietly on treetops, surveying the surroundings. Near
the nest site, it is silent and shy.

Scrub Jay
Aphelocoma coerulescens
257

11–13" (28–33 cm). Robin-sized, but large, strong bill and
long tail make it appear larger. Head, wings, and tail blue
(conspicuous when it glides after a long, undulating flight);
back dull brown and underparts light gray; white throat offset
by incomplete blue necklace.

Voice
Call is a loud, throaty *jayy?* or *jree?* In flight, a long series of
check check check notes.

Habitat
Woodland and chaparral, but does not breed in low scrub
because it needs watch posts; also inhabits suburban gardens.

Range
SW. Washington east to Wyoming, south to Texas,
California, and Mexico; also in Florida.

Comments
Like all jays, this species may be secretive and silent around its
nest or while perching in a treetop in early morning but is

frequently noisy and conspicuous. Many condemn it as a nest robber, although in summer it is mainly insectivorous. These birds also eat acorns and have been described as "uphill planters," counterbalancing the tendency of acorns to bounce downhill. The jays bury many more acorns than they consume and help regenerate oak forests destroyed by fire or drought.

Pinyon Jay
Gymnorhinus cyanocephalus
258

9–11¾" (23–30 cm). Robin-sized. Long, slender bill. Gray-blue, darkest on head, with white streaking on throat. Rather short tail. Crowlike flight and flocking habits. Yearlings gray.

Voice
A high-pitched *caa*, often quavering at the end to resemble a laughing *haa-a-a-a*.

Habitat
Mainly pinyon-juniper woodlands, ranging into forests of ponderosa pine or mixed pine and oak.

Range
Central Plateau area, extending to Oklahoma, E. California, and N. Baja California.

Comments
Although they sometimes pull up earthworms from lawns in the fashion of Robins, Pinyon Jays feed principally on pine nuts, which they store in fall and consume during winter and spring. Their local abundance varies from year to year with the success of the nut crop. They nest early after a good harvest; in poor years they delay breeding until August.

Clark's Nutcracker
Nucifraga columbiana
259

12–13" (30–33 cm). Almost crow-sized, with flashing black, white, and gray pattern. Light gray with dark eye and long, sharply pointed bill. Black wing with large white wing patch at trailing edge; black tail with white outer tail feathers. Face white from forehead to chin, white belly. Crowlike flight.

Voice
A guttural *kraaaa* . . .

Habitat
Subalpine forests near timberline, especially where whitebark or limber pines are present. Ranges lower in winter.

Range
From the Great Basin area, including S. British Columbia and Alberta, throughout the pine-clad western mountains south to California and to N. Baja California.

Comments
An erratic winter wanderer, this nutcracker's periodic irruption in great numbers, bringing it all the way to the Pacific Coast, is related to failure of the pine seed crop. It can hold several nuts in a special cheek pouch under the tongue in addition to those it holds in the beak.

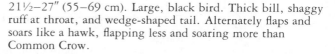

Common Raven
Corvus corax
260

21½–27" (55–69 cm). Large, black bird. Thick bill, shaggy ruff at throat, and wedge-shaped tail. Alternately flaps and soars like a hawk, flapping less and soaring more than Common Crow.

Voice
Utters a hoarse, croaking *kraaak* and a variety of other notes, including a hollow, knocking sound and a melodious *klookluk,* usually in flight.

Habitat
A great variety, including deserts, mountains, canyons, boreal forests, Pacific Coast beaches.

Range
Aleutians and throughout Alaska and Canada to Greenland. South, in the West, to Central America and east to the foothills of the Rockies.

Comments
A very "intelligent" bird, it seems to apply reasoning in situations entirely new to it. Its "insight" behavior at least matches that of a dog. It is a general predator and opportunistic feeder, like other members of its family, and often feeds at garbage dumps.

Mountain Chickadee
Parus gambeli
261

5–5¾" (13–15 cm). Gray above, paler below. White eye-stripe, black cap and bib; pale gray flanks.

Voice
A hoarse *chick-a-zee-zee, zee.* Spring song is a 3-toned *fee-bee-bee,* the *bees* at a lower pitch.

Habitat
High-altitude coniferous forests.

Range
Mountains of interior British Columbia through Rockies and Cascade-Sierra chains to Baja California and W. Texas.

Comments
A fearless, constantly active insect-gleaner of the mountain forest, it frequently descends into the lowlands in winter. In November an occasional flock can be found near sea level in desert oases containing conifers, while other flocks will still be at 8500 feet in the subalpine forest. The similar Black-capped Chickadee (*Parus atricapillus*), found southward in the West to NW. California and N. New Mexico, has no eye stripe.

Chestnut-backed Chickadee
Parus rufescens
262

4½–5" (11–13 cm). Dusky, black-capped and black-bibbed chickadee with chestnut flanks and back.

Voice
Its *chick-a-dee* call is somewhat shriller and the beat faster than in other chickadees. Often simply utters a thin *tsee-deee* and thin lisping notes.

Habitat
The Northwest coastal forest; moist areas containing conifers.

Range
From coastal Alaska south to the redwood pockets of central California; in the western ranges of the Rocky Mountains in S. British Columbia and W. Montana.

Comments
In the coastal forest of the Northwest, where the ranges of the Chestnut-backed and Black-capped chickadees overlap, the former prefers the top half of conifers, while the latter feeds in the lower half of trees, very frequently oaks. Thus they do not compete for space even within the same area.

Plain Titmouse
Parus inornatus
263

5–5½" (13–14 cm). Sparrow-sized. Gray with small crest, usually erect, and lighter underparts.

Voice
A harsh, fussy *see dee dee* or *chica-dee-dee*. A variety of other repeated notes, such as *teed le-doo*.

Habitat
Live oaks and deciduous growth of all kinds; oak woodlands, streamside cottonwoods, forest edges, and oak-juniper woodlands.

Range
From S. Oregon, N. Nevada, Utah, and SW. Wyoming, east to Oklahoma and south to Baja California, Arizona, S. New Mexico, and W. Texas.

Comments
Whereas chickadees gather into winter flocks, the related Plain Titmouse is usually found singly or in pairs. This bird is conspicuous, for it calls often as it feeds among juniper and elderberry bushes or high in the spring growth of freshly sprouted oaks. It also frequents gardens in suburbs of western towns adjacent to its native habitat.

Bushtit
Psaltriparus minimus
264

3¾–4" (10 cm). Gray above with light underparts, small bill, and relatively long tail. Pacific Coast birds have brown crown, pale ear patch; Rocky Mountain birds have gray crown, brown ear patch. Birds in mountains near Mexican border with black ear patch formerly called "Black-eared" Bushtit.

Voice
Contact calls are light *tsip* and *pit* notes, constantly uttered. Alarm call, warning of an approaching predator, is a high trill.

Habitat
Deciduous growth, usually streamside. In the coastal forest, it lives in second-growth alder thickets, or edges of coniferous forest composed of maple, dogwood, and birch; also in oak woodland, chaparral, and juniper brush.

Range
In the West, from extreme SW. British Columbia down the Pacific states to S. Baja California; in the Southwest, from the southern Rockies (south to Sonora) east to Oklahoma.

Comments
Bushtits flock in small bands, flitting nervously through trees and bushes, hanging, prying, picking, and gleaning, and keeping contact through a constant banter of soft chirps. They pervade a small area, then vanish, and reappear a couple of hundred yards away.

Red-breasted Nuthatch
Sitta canadensis
265

4½–4¾" (11–12 cm). Blue-gray above, with black cap bounded by white line above broad black eye-stripe. Rusty breast, belly, and undertail coverts. Female and juveniles have slate-gray cap and are paler below.

Voice
A high, nasal *yank-yank-yank;* its nasal quality recalls the tooting of a tin horn.

Habitat
Coniferous or mixed woods.

Range
Northern coniferous forests from coast to coast, south along the coastal interior and Rocky Mountain chains to California in the West, and to the Appalachians in the East.

Comments
Nuthatches hoard excess food and will transport seed from a tree heavily laden with mature cones to their distant larders. In years of bad harvest, they migrate in large numbers to more southerly forests. They also feed on bark insects, maneuvering with agility around the tips of outer branches or in treetops.

White-breasted Nuthatch
Sitta carolinensis
266

5–6" (13–15 cm). Sparrow-sized. Blue-gray above, white below, crown and nape black; the only nuthatch with a wholly white face.

Voice
A low *yank* or *yair.* Song is a nasal, whistled series on one pitch: *whee, whee, whee, whee . . .*

Habitat
Widespread in various habitats; western birds frequent coniferous forests as well as oak woods and pinyon-juniper woodlands.

Range
S. Canada, coast to coast in the United States and in Mexico. Absent in large areas that lack suitable forested habitat.

Comments
Its habit of creeping headfirst down a tree trunk, then stopping and looking around with head held at a 90° angle,

is characteristic of nuthatches. The White-breasted is an inquisitive, acrobatic bird, pausing occasionally to hang and hammer at a crack. Essentially nonmigratory, it stores food during fall for winter in crevices behind loose tree bark.

Pygmy Nuthatch
Sitta pygmaea
267

3¾–4½" (10–11 cm). Small nuthatch. Bluish-gray above, with gray-brown cap terminated by indistinct black eye-line. Faint white smudge at base of nape. Creamy white below. Usually in flocks.

Voice
A monotonous *peep, peep-peep*.

Habitat
Primarily ponderosa pine forests with undergrowth of bunchgrass. Less common in stands of other pines, Douglas-fir, and western larch.

Range
Widespread from S. British Columbia eastward through the Black Hills, and south to Baja California, mainland Mexico, including the scattered pine-capped desert mountains of the Southwest.

Comments
The Pygmy Nuthatch keeps mostly to pine woodlands. It feeds on bark and twig insects, as well as stored nuts, seeds, eggs, and hibernating larvae in winter.

Brown Creeper
Certhia americana
268

5–5¾" (13–15 cm). Small, slender bird with mottled brown upperparts, a whitish eyebrow, and white underparts. Long downcurved bill; stiff tail braces it like a woodpecker.

Voice
High-pitched song consists of about 6 notes falling and then rising: *see-see-see-whee-see-see*.

Habitat
Mature coniferous or mixed forests.

Range
Mainly in the taiga belt, in North America from Alaska to Newfoundland; has also spread south into the montane conifer groves, as far as Central America.

Comments
As it searches for bark insects the Brown Creeper always moves in an upward direction, circling tree trunks in spirals, then plunging to the base of the next tree.

Bewick's Wren
Thryomanes bewickii
269

5–5½" (13–14 cm). Slightly larger than House Wren. Plain, unpatterned warm brown above, white or grayish white below, with distinct long white eyebrow-stripe. When tail is fanned, white outer tips of tail feathers are conspicuous, as is its unique slow flicking of tail sideways.

Voice
The loud, cheerful song usually begins with a soft buzz, as if the bird is inhaling, followed by a trill and a series of slurred notes. As in many birds, its singing perches are often higher than its foraging areas. Scold notes include a harsh *vit vit vit* and a harsh, drawn-out buzzing note.

Habitat
On or near the ground in a brush-covered, partly open area, including the edge of deciduous forests, coniferous woods with underbrush, chaparral, and pinyon-juniper woodland.

Range
Locally from British Columbia east to the Appalachians and south to S. Mexico.

Comments
Bewick's Wren uses its long, narrow, slightly downcurved bill for scavenging on the ground and picking in crevices for insects and spiders. Searching for food, it may venture into hollow trunks, rock crevices, or barns. The more widespread House Wren (*Troglodytes aedon*), also a brush dweller, has an indistinct eye stripe and no white tail stripes.

Winter Wren
Troglodytes troglodytes
270

4–4½″ (10–11 cm). Tiny, dark, reddish-brown wren. Indistinct light eye-line; barred both above and below, more heavily on belly. Short, often uptilted tail, which it flicks conspicuously.

Voice
A clear, trilling, musical song, high in pitch, lasting for several seconds and repeated often; like a bubbling stream rushing over stones. Call is a double *chimp-chimp.*

Habitat
Shady secluded underbrush in coniferous forests.

Range
All other wrens are found exclusively in the Americas, but this species breeds from the British Isles across N. Asia and from Alaska to the Atlantic Coast. In North America, its range extends south of the boreal forest in the coastal forest and Sierra Nevada forest in California and the Appalachians.

Comments
In the open the male builds a large, elaborate (though unlined), domed structure with a side entrance. This mock or dummy nest is not used for nesting and is thought to be a diversionary tactic against would-be nest robbers.

American Dipper
Cinclus mexicanus
271

7–8½″ (18–22 cm). Uniformly slate gray, chunky bird with stubby tail; feet yellowish.

Voice
Vigorous singers, their loud bubbling song carries over the noise of rapids. Call is a sharp *zeet.*

Habitat
Near clear fast streams with rapids.

Range
From Alaska to mountains of Central America, and from Pacific Coast to eastern slope of the Rockies. It may move to lowlands in winter.

Comments
The Dipper feeds on insect life in streams. Where water is shallow and runs over gravel, it appears to "water-ski" on the surface. At deeper points it dives into the water and runs along the bottom with half-open wings.

Golden-crowned Kinglet
Regulus satrapa
272

3¼–4″ (8–10 cm). One of the smallest North American birds. Olive green above, dirty white below, with small, slender bill, white wing bars, and slightly notched tail. White eyebrow; black-bordered orange-yellow (male) or yellow (female) crown.

Voice
A high-pitched *see-see-see.*

Habitat
Dense, first-growth conifer stands.

Range
Coast to coast across the boreal forest zone from S. Alaska and Canada south, in the East, into the N. Appalachians; in the West, southward through the Douglas-fir and subalpine fir zones of the western mountain chains and the cool, wet coastal rain forest. Winters as far south as Central America.

Comments
Outside the breeding season, these tiny, energetic birds are frequently seen in the company of Ruby-crowned Kinglets, Brown Creepers, nuthatches, and chickadees. These groups move through the trees, searching out insects and larvae.

Ruby-crowned Kinglet
Regulus calendula
273

3¾–4½″ (10–11 cm). Olive-gray above, shaded white below, with white wing bars. Incomplete white eye-ring, and small, scarlet crown patch in male (frequently concealed); crown patch lacking in female. Differentiated from warblers and vireos by its smaller size; short, slightly forked tail; continuous, rapid movements and nervous wing-flicking habit.

Voice
Call is harsh *ji-dit.* Song begins with several high, thin notes followed by loud, whistled phrases.

Habitat
Coniferous forests in summer; mixed coniferous and deciduous thickets in winter.

Range
Coast to coast in the taiga, from Alaska through Canada; along

the Rocky Mountains to Arizona, and along the Pacific coastal mountains to the mountains of S. California. Winters south to Gulf states and Central America.

Comments
Because kinglets weigh little, they are able to feed on the tips of branches of conifers. The Ruby-crowned feeds lower in the canopy than the Golden-crowned and characteristically hovers above a twig looking for caterpillars and other insects.

Blue-gray Gnatcatcher
Polioptila caerulea
274

4–5″ (10–13 cm). Small, slender bird. Bluish-gray above, white below; long black tail with white outer feathers is cocked. Male's crown and forehead bordered with black. Female less bluish and lacks black markings on head. Narrow white eye-ring and white edging of secondary wing feathers conspicuous in both sexes.

Voice
Call is a thin *speeeee*. Song is a jumble of fussing, warbled notes.

Habitat
Deciduous woodland, streamside thickets, live oaks, pinyon-juniper, chaparral.

Range
From N. California east to W. and S. Colorado, S. Ontario, and New York south to Central America. Winters in southern United States and Central America.

Comments
These gnatcatchers are lively birds, constantly flicking their conspicuous long tails upward while gathering insects from the branches of trees or bushes.

Western Bluebird
Sialia mexicana
275

6–7″ (15–18 cm). Long-winged, rather short-tailed. Male has deep blue hood and upperparts; rusty red breast and crescent mark across upper back; white belly. Female sooty gray above, with dull blue wings and tail. Juveniles like female but grayer, with speckled underparts.

Voice
Soft calls sound like *phew* and *chuck*. Song is a short, subdued *cheer, cheer-lee, churr*.

Habitat
Open woodland and pine forest with old trees for nest sites.

Range
From southern half of British Columbia and W. Alberta south to Baja California, central Mexico; west along the Rocky Mountains to W. Texas.

Comments
Females are attracted by the vivid blue of the male and by the availability of nesting holes, which are often in short supply.

Once the male secures a nesting hole he entices the female
with a colorful display that repels rivals. His red breast is a
signal of aggression toward other males.

Mountain Bluebird
Sialia currucoides
276

6½–8" (17–20 cm). Male turquoise blue with lighter blue
breast and white belly. Female gray-brown with trace of blue
on wings, rump, and tail. Juveniles are brown above, lightly
spotted below, with pale blue wash on the wings and tail.

Voice
A quiet warbling dawn song. Calls, which vary with the
species, include a soft *phew, ior,* and *terr.* This bluebird's notes
are harsher and more nasal than those of other species.

Habitat
Open areas where mountain meadows and pastures are
interspersed with loose stands or single coniferous trees. In the
North, nests at low elevations in pine woodlands and wooded
areas; farther south, in subalpine forests among alpine
meadows, aspen groves, and other montane woodlands.

Range

From Alaska, N. British Columbia and Alberta, and central
Manitoba south to the mountains of S. California and to W.
Oklahoma. Winters in southern part of its breeding area at
low elevations and in Mexico.

Comments
These birds hover low over the ground and drop down to catch
insects, or dart out from a branch, flycatcher-fashion, and then
return to another perch.

Townsend's Solitaire
Myadestes townsendi
277

8–9½" (20–24 cm). Overall gray, unstreaked, slightly darker
above, with thin white eye-ring and white outer tail feathers;
pale rusty wing patch. It sits upright, usually high on a
branch. Juveniles are mottled gray and white.

Voice
Usually utters the loud, melodious, fluty rising and falling
phrases of its somewhat thrushlike song from a high perch,
but it may also fly up and sing over the nesting territory. Call
is a bell-like *heep.*

Habitat
Open coniferous forests, edges, or burns with single standing
trees in the mountains.

Range

From the high mountains of the West to the Sierra Madre
ranges of Mexico and the ranges of N. Baja California. In the
North, it reaches Alaska and N. British Columbia. Usually
winters in lowlands.

Comments
This is the northernmost of a number of mountain-forest
thrushes (solitaires) of the New World and the only species

north of Mexico. Like other thrushes, it forages on the ground for berries and insects; in winter, it descends to lower elevations, and may even occur in desert oases.

Hermit Thrush
Catharus guttatus
278

6½–8″ (17–20 cm). Olive-brown above, with rufous tail; whitish below, with streaked throat; blackish-brown spots on breast. Flicks its wings and tail nervously.

Voice
Loud, slow, repetitive phrases spiraling down the scale carry and echo in the still of the evening forest; it also sings at dawn. Many consider this the most beautiful bird song in America. Call note is a soft *chup* or *chup-chup.*

Habitat
Mixed woods or open coniferous forests. In the Northwest, mostly at timberline but nests along ocean shores on the Queen Charlotte Islands.

Range
Breeds from Aleutians west to Unimak Island, Alaska to Newfoundland, south to California in the West, to Maryland in the East. Winters mainly in southern United States and in wooded lowlands of the Pacific Coast from Washington south.

Comments
These thrushes forage on the ground, most of the time under dense cover, hopping around and then watching in an upright position like a Robin.

American Robin
Turdus migratorius
279

9–11″ (23–28 cm). Perhaps the best known of all North American birds. Puffed-out breast is fox-red or orange; dark gray-brown upperparts; throat white, head and tail blackish, paler in the female. Juveniles are brown-spotted below, and lack the characteristic red breast of adults.

Voice
Many regard the rich caroling of the male, uttered from a high perch, as the true herald of spring. It consists of clear rising and falling phrases recalling the words "cheer-up, cheerily," etc. The call note is a vibrant *weep.* It also gives a loud *put-put-put* and, in flight, a lisping *see-lip.*

Habitat
Open woods, forest borders, cut-over areas, meadows. Also lawns and parks in suburbs.

Range
Most of North America between the tundra and the desert. In winter, they leave colder areas and fly to the southern states to harvest winter berries.

Comments
Robins feed on a variety of animal and plant foods. They forage on the ground for earthworms, grubs, and adult insects and also relish berries and other fruits, especially in winter.

Overwintering robins are common in lowland forests and woodlands, west of the Sierra-Cascade divide.

Varied Thrush
Ixoreus naevius
280

9–10" (23–25 cm). Similar to Robin. Upperparts are slate gray; rusty orange throat and breast interrupted by broad slaty or black breast band; off-white belly. Female is similar but paler. Juveniles' breast band incomplete, often with orange and dusky speckles. Flight more undulating than Robin's.

Voice
Song is not melodious, but is nevertheless remarkable. Whistles 2 or 3 buzzy notes, each drawn out until it fades away, followed by a short silence. The thrush sings, concealed high in a tree, its song echoing in the dark of the silent forest. Calls are a low *took* and a soft buzz.

Habitat
Dense coniferous or deciduous forests with abundant water sources.

Range
In the coastal rain forest of the Pacific Northwest from central Alaska south to N. California. Winters in great numbers in the madrona forests of SW. British Columbia and southward.

Comments
This thrush lives on the shaded floor of coniferous forests. Like the American Robin, it feeds on earthworms and insects in open, bare areas. In winter it migrates to lowlands or flies south to California parks, habitats it shares with Robins.

Wrentit
Chamaea fasciata
281

6–6½" (15–17 cm). Uniformly brown with streaked breast, white eyes, and long, slender, rounded, cocked tail.

Voice
An accelerating series of musical notes running together into a trill and dropping slightly in pitch toward the end: *peep peep peep-pee-pee-peepeepepeprrrr*. Call is a prolonged dry "growling" note. Far more often heard than seen.

Habitat
Chaparral, understory shrubs, and brush.

Range
From the Columbia River, on the northern border of Oregon, south along the coastal chaparral into Baja California, and in the foothills of the Central Valley of California.

Comments
The Wrentit spends all its adult life within the territory chosen in its first year. Individuals hesitate to cross open spaces of even 30 to 40 feet, and it is believed that the wide Columbia River effectively stops this bird from entering Washington, even though that side of the river offers suitable habitat. Common but elusive, and seldom seen at close range, the Wrentit even sings from dense brush.

Cedar Waxwing
Bombycilla cedrorum
282

6½–8" (17–20 cm). Trim, crested bird. Grayish-brown, with black mask and chin; yellow belly, white undertail coverts; yellow terminal tail band. Juveniles have indistinct gray-streaked breast.

Voice
A high, sibilant *see-e-e-e*. Voice is often the only means of detecting its presence.

Habitat
Edges of coniferous or mixed forests; orchards or fruiting trees where second-growth stands, such as alders, maples, and dogwoods, follow a watercourse; city parks with berry-bearing trees and shrubs.

Range
Breeds from coast to coast in deciduous or mixed forest and around parks and gardens from SE. Alaska to central California in the West and from Newfoundland to Georgia in the East. Winters in most of its range and southern United States.

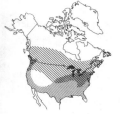

Comments
In summer Cedar Waxwings are rather inconspicuous, but in winter they travel in flocks of 40 or more, incessantly calling, turning, and twisting in flight, and frequently alighting in the same tree. Berries are their main food source in winter, but they revert to flycatching in milder seasons.

Solitary Vireo
Vireo solitarius
283

5–6" (13–15 cm). Gray crown, olive-green back, white throat and underparts. 2 broad white wing bars and large white spectacles. The olive-backed birds of the Pacific states have yellowish flanks; those in the Rocky Mountains are gray-backed with no yellowish tinge below.

Voice
Loud, rich, slurred notes with pauses between notes usually longer than the duration of the notes themselves: *chuwee, cheereo, bzurrp, chuweer.* Scolding call is a harsh *chv chv chv chv.*

Habitat
Deciduous or mixed woodland, second growth or streamside groves in the West; junipers and yellow pine stands in the southern Rockies.

Range
Widespread in wooded areas of the West; also in most parts of the East. Winters in Mexico and Central America, where breeding populations are also found.

Comments
The song of most vireos consists of a variety of staccato notes, the basic theme being *vi-rio, vi-reii, vi-reyo,* with the accent on the second syllable. Those who named the genus in 1807 heard in the song the Latin word *vireo,* meaning "I am green" —as are most species of these foliage-inhabiting birds.

Warbling Vireo
Vireo gilvus
284

4½–5½" (11–14 cm). Small, inconspicuous vireo. Olive-gray above, lighter below; white eye-stripe; no wing bars.

Voice
A long, variable, languid warble. Call note is a soft *vit*.

Habitat
Deciduous and mixed woods, from mature stands to low thickets.

Range
Throughout wooded North America from Canada to Mexico and Central America. Winters in Mexico and Central America.

Comments
This species is confined to broadleaf trees, but occurs in conifer forests where broadleaf trees, such as aspens and alders, are present. Males sing almost nonstop in the nesting season.

Orange-crowned Warbler
Vermivora celata
285

4½–5½" (11–14 cm). Olive green above with orange crown feathers, which usually remain hidden. Olive-yellow underparts with very faint breast streaking. No eye-ring or wing bars.

Voice
Song is a simple trill going up or down the scale toward the end. Call is a sharp *stick*.

Habitat
Forest edges, especially in low deciduous growth, burns, clearings, and thickets. In migration often seen in riverside willows and in scrub-oak chaparral.

Range
Breeds from Alaska east to Labrador and Quebec, and south to Baja California, Arizona, and New Mexico. Winters from the southern United States to Central America.

Comments
The Orange-crowned Warbler is one of the commonest western warblers. Its very lack of conspicuous field marks is an aid to its identification. Like other birds with concealed crown patches, this warbler displays the crown only during courtship or when alarmed.

Nashville Warbler
Vermivora ruficapilla
286

4–5" (10–13 cm). Male has gray head, olive-green upperparts, bright yellow chin, throat, and underparts fading into whitish on belly. Distinctive white eye-ring. Chestnut crown patch sometimes visible. Female, immatures, and fall male somewhat duller olive green above, bright yellow below.

Voice
Song is a rapid series of sweet 2-part notes, followed by a short trill of single notes: *see-pit see-pit see-pit see-pit tititititi*. Call note is a sharp *plink*.

Habitat
Sparse second growth, burns, edges of deciduous woodland, particularly aspens and cottonwoods; also bogs.

Range
S. British Columbia east to W. Montana and south through the Cascades and Sierras to S. California, avoiding coastal forests. In the East from S. Manitoba to Newfoundland and south into the northeastern states. Winters in Mexico.

Comments
This warbler prefers areas in early stages of forest succession, when brush provides cover, and scattered, small trees serve as singing posts.

Virginia's Warbler
Vermivora virginiae
287

4–4¼" (10–11 cm). Male gray above, with yellow breast, rump, and undertail coverts. Throat and belly white. Chestnut crown patch and white eye-ring visible at close range. Female is duller.

Voice
The male delivers a *seedle seedle seedle sweet sweet* from a high perch. Call is a sharp *plink*.

Habitat
Scrub oak and other chaparral, pinyon-juniper brushland, pine and oak.

Range
Southern parts of the Central Plateau and the Rockies, from Nevada to Colorado, and extreme E. California to New Mexico. Winters in Mexico.

Comments
This warbler forages for insects and spiders in scrub oaks near the ground. Though the male occasionally uses a song post such as the top of a juniper, he also sings while feeding in the middle of the chaparral. It closely resembles three other warblers: the Nashville, Lucy's, and the rare Colima.

Yellow-rumped Warbler
Dendroica coronata
288

5–6" (13–15 cm). Bright yellow cap, flanks, and rump. Dark gray above with black streaks, white belly; in spring and summer, males have black breast. Conspicuous white eye-ring and tail spots. The white-throated northern population with 2 white wing bars was formerly known as the "Myrtle Warbler"; the western race, with yellow throat and one broad white wing bar, was called "Audubon's Warbler." The two have been found to interbreed and are now considered one species, the Yellow-rumped Warbler. Females in all plumages, as well as fall and winter males, are brownish beige with 2 light wing bars, faintly streaked underparts, and some yellow on throat, flanks, and rump.

Voice
Song of the male is a loud trilling, rising or falling at the end.

Flocks that winter in desert oases, live-oak canyons, and parks and gardens of the Southwest utter a sharp *chep* or *chip*.

Habitat
Coniferous forests in open areas, even when mixed with such deciduous edge growth as dogwood, maple, and alder; in winter, in any kind of woodland.

Range
The "Myrtle Warbler" lives in the boreal forest across North America; "Audubon's Warbler" ranges from north-central British Columbia and S. Alberta south into Mexico. They winter in the Southwest and in Central America.

Comments
Yellow-rumped Warblers are vivid and conspicuous birds that search for food both high and low in Douglas-firs or pines. They most often sing from the high canopy of trees. During winter they disperse in loose flocks, so two or three birds at most are observed at a time. The birds constantly chirp a "contact call" that keeps the flock together.

Black-throated Gray Warbler
Dendroica nigrescens
289

4½–5″ (11–13 cm). Head striped black and white, black bib on throat, white below with black stripes on sides, blue-gray back with black striping; yellow spot between bill and eyes. 2 white wing bars and white outer tail feathers. Winter male, female, and juveniles lack black bib.

Voice
The song is a series of buzzes, rising in pitch and intensity, then falling: *zee zee zee zee bzz bzz*. Call is a dull *tup*.

Habitat
Shrubby openings in coniferous forest or mixed woods, dry scrub oak, pinyon and juniper, chaparral, and other low brushy areas; also in forests.

Range
S. British Columbia to N. Baja California. Also in Great Basin states. Winters in the Southwest and northern Mexico, but mainly in central Mexico.

Comments
This bird resembles Townsend's Warbler in every respect except that it lacks the green and yellow colors of the latter. The drab appearance of the Black-throated Gray is a good adaptation to the bluish gray-green of western junipers.

Townsend's Warbler
Dendroica townsendi
290

4¼–5″ (11–13 cm). Adult male has black crown and nape, ear patch, throat, and bib. Face and breast bright yellow; sides heavily streaked with black; white belly. Wings and tail dusky with 2 white wing bars and white outer tail feathers. In winter black bib of male, female, and immatures is replaced by dark streaking; black elsewhere becomes dusky olive. Back is green in all plumages.

Voice
A rising series of notes, usually with 2 phrases, the first repeated 3 or 4 times, the second once or twice: *weazy weazy weazy weazy twea or dee dee dee-de de.* Call is a soft *chip.*

Habitat
Coniferous forests; in old stands of Douglas-firs, where it forages in the upper canopy.

Range
Coastal forests of the Pacific Northwest from Alaska and British Columbia to N. Washington; Idaho, Montana, and Wyoming. Winters to Central America.

Comments
In winter, this striking but seldom seen warbler occurs along the coast from Oregon southward into Mexico.

Hermit Warbler
Dendroica occidentalis
291

4½" (11 cm). Yellow head, with black chin and throat, gray back; white underparts with black-streaked flanks. Gray wings and tail with white wing bars and outer tail feathers. Female and immatures have little or no dark throat markings; gray of back extends to top of crown. No other western warbler is as white underneath.

Voice
A series of high notes, somewhat less buzzy than the song of a Townsend's Warbler; recalls a Yellow Warbler in pattern but less emphatic. Call is a soft *chup.*

Habitat
Mature coniferous forests.

Range
Pacific coastal states from Washington to NW. California and the Sierra Nevada. Winters in Mexico and Central America.

Comments
This species lives high in the canopy of the tallest redwoods and Douglas-fir trees and is therefore difficult to observe. It has been occasionally found to hybridize with Townsend's Warbler. The similarity in their songs indicates that the species are close relatives.

MacGillivray's Warbler
Oporornis tolmiei
292

4¾–5½" (12–14 cm). Slate-gray hood extending from mantle to breast, where it darkens to black. Olive-green above, yellow below; female slightly paler. Both sexes have broken white eye-ring. In fall, hood lighter, with little or no eye-ring.

Voice
Song, a chanting *tree tree tree tree sweet sweet!* Call is a loud *tik,* sharper than the calls of most other western warblers.

Habitat
Coniferous forest edges, burns, brushy cuts, or second-growth alder thickets and streamside growth.

Range
From the Pacific coastal forest of SE. Alaska eastward to the Rocky Mountains and the prairies, and south to the desert. Winters in Mexico and South America.

Comments
This bird is common but seldom seen. It spends most of its time foraging in dense, damp thickets or brush.

Wilson's Warbler
Wilsonia pusilla
293

4½" (11 cm). Male is olive-green above with black cap, underparts yellow. Female similar but lacks black cap.

Voice
Song is a rapid series of light *chips,* accelerating in tempo and increasing in intensity: *chip chip chip chip chip chip chip.* Call is a soft *timp.*

Habitat
Deciduous shrubbery or thickets; in the Northwest, windfall openings, cuts and burns growing up in shrubs and second-growth alders, poplars, or other trees at the edge of woods; elsewhere, streamside growth and alpine willow-fir thickets.

Range
From Alaska across Canada to New England in the boreal forest zone; in the West, widespread north of the desert areas. Winters from Mexico to Central America.

Comments
It is easy to observe this common warbler because it has little fear of man and because it searches the outside of leafy branches, often catching flying insects on the wing. Early in summer, the foraging male utters long bursts of vivid song.

Western Tanager
Piranga ludoviciana
294

6–7½" (15–19 cm). Adult male has brilliant red head, bright yellow body, with black back, wings, and tail. 2 wing bars; smaller uppermost bar yellow, lower white. Female is yellow-green above, yellow below; wing bars similar to male's.

Voice
Song is strong and carries far; short fluty stanzas rendered with a pause in between, like song of American Robin. The quality is much hoarser, however. Call is a dry *pit-r-ick.*

Habitat
Open coniferous forests.

Range
Widespread in the West, from Alaskan panhandle and S. Mackenzie south to N. Baja California, skirting the deserts; in the mountains of the Southwest. Winters in Mexico and Central America.

Comments
In late spring and early summer it flycatches for insects; later it feeds on berries and other small fruits.

Black-headed Grosbeak
Pheucticus melanocephalus
295

6½–7¾" (17–20 cm). Plump finch. Male has black head, large pale bill, rusty orange collar, breast, sides, and rump, yellow belly and wing linings. Black-and-white-patterned wing and tail prominent in flight. Female and yearling male are buff with the fine black streaking on crown, back, and undersides. Prominent black-and-white face pattern and sparsely streaked buffy breast distinguish it from other female grosbeaks.

Voice
Song, delivered from a high perch and occasionally in flight, is a rapid, melodious series of rising and falling whistles interspersed with low *whirr* notes. Call is a sharp *eek!* Young birds give a complaining *whee-oh*.

Habitat
Dense woods along rivers, edges of second-growth deciduous woods, stands of tall oaks, mountain forest edges; orchards and gardens.

Range
From S. British Columbia and Saskatchewan south to its wintering grounds in W. Mexico.

Comments
The Black-headed Grosbeak is a rather still and secretive bird throughout the summer. Its song, delivered from high in the trees, is very similar to that of the American Robin.

Lazuli Bunting
Passerina amoena
296

5–5½" (13–14 cm). Male has bright turquoise hood, back, rump; cinnamon breast and sides; white belly. Wings dark with 2 white wing bars. Female is light brown above, unstreaked buffy below with paler throat and belly; blue tinge on primaries, rump, and tail; light wing bars.

Voice
The territorial male sings a typical finch song: a sequence of 10–12 beats, beginning at a high pitch and falling toward the end, with some of the beats repeated, such as *sweet-sweet chew-chew seet chew*. Call is a soft *chip*. In flight, a dry buzz.

Habitat
Deciduous brushland and edges, clearings in woods, chaparral, streamsides.

Range
Southern British Columbia to North Dakota south to Oklahoma and northern Baja California. Winters in extreme southern Arizona and in Mexico.

Comments
A diligent songster, the male patrols the perimeter of his territory, spending much time on his song perches. The brilliant turquoise upperparts distinguish it easily from the somewhat similarly colored Western Bluebird.

Green-tailed Towhee
Pipilo chlorurus
297

6¼–7″ (16–18 cm). Smaller than other towhees. Sexes similar; rufous cap, olive-green above, with white throat and belly, gray breast. White between eye and base of bill, with dark mustache stripe. Yellow wing linings.

Voice
Song loud and lively, consisting of slurred notes and short, buzzy trills, usually delivered from atop a shrub or young conifer. Call is a short, nasal, catlike mew.

Habitat
Sagebrush, mountain chaparral, pinyon-juniper stands, and thickets bordering alpine meadows.

Range
Central Oregon south through mountains to S. California and the Great Basin to SE. New Mexico. Winters at lower elevations and south to S. Arizona, South-central Texas and into Mexico.

Comments
This shy bird hops and scratches for food under low cover, flicking its tail and erecting its rufous cap into a crest. It prefers low scrub and occurs in brushy openings in western mountain forests, as well as in sagebrush habitats.

Rufous-sided Towhee
Pipilo erythrophthalmus
298

7–8½″ (18–22 cm). Smaller than a Robin. Male has black hood, wings, and back with white wing bars and spots. Black tail has white edging on outer feathers. White breast and belly with bright rufous sides. Female has same pattern but is brown where male is black. Both sexes have red eyes.

Voice
The song varies, often with a few introductory notes and usually ending with a long trill, such as *drink-your-teeaaa* or *to-wheeeee*. On the Pacific Coast, the buzzy trill makes up the entire song. Call is an inquisitive *meeu'u'w?*

Habitat
Forest edges, thickets, woodlands, gardens, and park areas.

Range
S. Canada to S. United States and N. Central America. Widely distributed except for the dense forests of the Alaskan and N. British Columbian coasts and treeless prairies. In winter, northwestern and mountain-area towhees migrate to the lowlands of the southwestern states and Mexico.

Comments
Suburban gardens as well as chaparral perfectly suit this towhee, which is not as secretive as other towhees.

Brown Towhee
Pipilo fuscus
299

8–10″ (20–25 cm). Earth brown above with buffy, faintly streaked throat, light brown underparts, and rust-colored undertail coverts. Birds of the Southwest are paler and grayer and have a rufous cap.

Voice
Song is a series of squeaky *chips* on the same pitch, accelerating into a rapid trill. The pattern varies according to the area. The call is a sharp *chink* and thin *tseeee.*

Habitat
Shady underbrush, open woods, pinyon-juniper woodlands, and suburban gardens.

Range
Coastal and foothill chaparral from Oregon to S. Baja California; brush country of the southwestern states of Arizona, Colorado, Oklahoma and Texas to S. Mexico.

Comments
The Brown Towhee often forages quietly among chaparral bushes or garden cover. Although its range in the chaparral overlaps during winter with that of the Rufous-sided Towhee, it lives in low scrub, whereas the Rufous-sided keeps to scrub oaks and other taller "forest edge" areas.

Chipping Sparrow
Spizella passerina
300

5–5¾" (13–15 cm). Rufous cap bordered by white eyebrow-stripe; black eye-line. Cheek, collar, and underparts are unstreaked gray. Mantle brown with dark streaking; 2 white wing bars. Sexes similar. Winter adults have duller rufous cap and eye-stripe with brown-tinged gray areas. Immatures have light median stripe through crown, brownish cap, buffy eye-stripe and underparts.

Voice
An insectlike trill on one pitch. Call is a high, sweet *seep.*

Habitat
Coniferous and deciduous woodland edges; orchards and parks.

Range
Widespread in the boreal forest as well as the eastern deciduous forest, and lowland montane areas of the West, southwest to Mexico and the mountains of Central America.

Comments
This sparrow is inconspicuous even when it feeds in the open, for it moves slowly among the grass or litter. The singing territorial male is also hard to find as he sits inconspicuously among the branches of a conifer.

Fox Sparrow
Passerella iliaca
301

6–7¼" (15–18 cm). A chubby, large sparrow, dusky brown, fox red, or slaty, often so dark that no back pattern can be discerned; heavy streaking of underparts converges at midbreast into a large brown spot. Heavy bill with lighter-colored lower mandible, slightly notched rust-colored tail, and rounded head outline.

Voice
A lively song that opens with one or more clear whistles and follows with several short trills or *churrs.* Call, a sharp *chink.*

Habitat
Mountain brush or thickets; forest undergrowth; chaparral.

Range
Widespread in the Far North from the taiga-tundra transition region of Alaska to Unalaska Island in the Aleutians and the Canadian Northwest Territories east to New England; south to the coast of the Pacific Northwest and to S. California, the central Rockies, and other western mountains at timberline. Winters in lowlands along Pacific Coast and in the Southwest.

Comments
This species spends much time in the shade of shrubs and bushes, scratching in litter for insects and seeds. It sings from a high but not prominent post, and nests near the ground.

Song Sparrow
Melospiza melodia
302

5–7" (13–18 cm). Heavy brown streaking on white underparts with prominent central breast spot (sometimes lacking in juveniles). Variation in size of subspecies is considerable and colors range from pale sandy to deep black-brown. "Pumps" its relatively long, rounded tail in flight.

Voice
Cheerful song often begins with 3 clear piping notes, followed by a lower note and a rapid jumble of notes. Call is *chimp.*

Habitat
Forest edges, clearings, thickets and marshes with open grassy feeding areas, low dense scrub for nesting, and some high vantage points for singing.

Range
The Aleutians east to Newfoundland below the Arctic tree-line scrub and south to Baja California, central Mexico, Nebraska, and North Carolina.

Comments
The Song Sparrow is one of the most widespread, diverse and geographically variable of North American birds. The species ranges from very large, dark-colored, large-billed birds on the rocky beaches of the humid Aleutian Islands to small, sandy, short-billed birds in scrub desert areas on the Lower Colorado River Valley. Song Sparrows prefer moist habitats and in drier parts of the West are confined largely to streamside areas.

Lincoln's Sparrow
Melospiza lincolnii
303

5–6" (13–15 cm). Resembles Song Sparrow, but cheek gray, mustache stripe pale buffy, and buffy breast finely streaked with brown. Central breast spot usually missing.

Voice
Song a low gurgling stanza that ends after some rising phrases. Calls are *tik* and a buzzy *tzeee.*

Habitat
Brush-covered bogs, meadows; also mountain meadows with willow thickets or other dense clumps of vegetation.

Range
Breeds in the boreal forest from coast to coast, and along western mountain chains to S. California and New Mexico. Winters from the southwestern states to Central America.

Comments
When not singing, it is wary and secretive. In winter, a lone Lincoln's Sparrow is often seen among other sparrows wintering on the Pacific Coast and in bushy areas inland.

White-crowned Sparrow
Zonotrichia leucophrys
304

5½–7" (14–18 cm). Crown white, bordered by black stripes. Eyebrow white with narrow black line behind eye. Cheek, neck, and breast are gray; belly whitish. Back streaked gray and brown; white wing bars. First winter birds have brown-and-buff crown pattern. Bill pink or yellowish.

Voice
The song is variable geographically but basically consists of a clear introductory whistle followed by 4–8 whistles or wheezy trills on different pitches. Call note is a metallic *chink* or *pink*.

Habitat
Forest edges and clearings, often found along streams or surrounding bogs; alpine meadows; brushy burns, fields, parks, and suburban gardens. Essential for its breeding habitat are patches of grass and open ground for foraging, with low shrubbery nearby for escape and nesting.

Range
Widespread across Alaska and Canada, south in W. United States, to California and New Mexico. Winters in the Southwest and Mexico, though some coastal breeding populations are not migratory.

Comments
The northern, northwestern, and mountain subspecies have slightly different head patterns and songs. Song dialects vary locally as well.

Dark-eyed Junco
Junco hyemalis
305, 306

5–6½" (13–16.5 cm). This species shows much geographic variation in color. 5 subspecies, formerly considered distinct species, occur in the West. All have pink bills, white outer tail feathers, white bellies, and dark eyes. The male "Oregon" Junco has a black hood, chestnut mantle, and white underparts with buff sides. Females are similar but have grayer hoods. The male "Slate-colored" Junco is dark slate gray on the head, upper breast, flanks, and upperparts. The "White-winged" form is similar to the "Slate-colored" but with 2 white wing bars and extensive white outer tail feathers. Females of these 2 subspecies are similar but duller. The "Gray-headed" Junco has an ash-gray head, neck, sides, rump, and tail, and a rufous back; in this subspecies, the sexes are alike. The "Pink-sided" Junco has broad pink sides, with no distinct contrast between the hood and back. The female is similar to the male.

Voice
Song a loose, rolling trill on one pitch. Members of a flock may spread out widely, keeping contact by constantly giving call notes, a tsick or tchet. Also gives a soft, buzzy trill in flight.

Habitat
Coniferous forest edges and light stands where the ground is mostly open but shaded, with nearby ground cover for shelter; in winter: fields, woodland edges, roadsides, parks, and suburban gardens; pine-oak woodland in the South.

Range
Boreal and mountainous coniferous forest of North America from Alaska to Newfoundland and south across northern United States. In the West, south through coastal rain forest and mountain forests of Northwest through Baja California. "Gray-headed" breeds from NW. Nevada, S. Idaho, and Wyoming south through mountains to SE. California, N. Arizona, S. New Mexico, and W. Texas. Western birds winter mostly in Pacific coastal areas, occasionally wandering to the East Coast. "Gray-headed" winters at lower elevations and south to northern Mexico.

Comments
This lively territorial bird is a ground dweller. It also moves through the lower branches of trees and seeks shelter in tangles of shrubs. The most widespread race of the Dark-eyed Junco is the "Slate-colored"; this bird ranges extensively through the coniferous forests of the Far North, in the East as well as the West, where its song is frequently heard. Where their ranges overlap, the various races of the Dark-eyed Junco interbreed, and thus intermediate forms may be seen in the field. Such intermediates can be puzzling to identify. The "Gray-headed" Junco was formerly considered a separate species, and has only recently been combined with the Dark-eyed. The Yellow-eyed Junco (*Junco phaeonotus*) inhabits the pine-oak woodlands of southern Arizona and New Mexico and ranges south into northern Mexico; it resembles the "Gray-headed" Junco but has a distinctly yellow, rather than a dark, eye.

Northern Oriole
Icterus galbula bullockii
307

7–8½" (18–22 cm). Male is orange-yellow with black crown, nape, and mantle; narrow black eye-stripe and narrow black bib. Wings have broad white patch and white edges on flight feathers. Central tail feathers and tips of outer tail feathers are black. Female unstreaked olive-gray above with yellow throat and chest and white belly.

Voice
A loud series of whistles: *chuk chucky wheew wheew wheew*. Call is a rolling chatter.

Habitat
Woodland and savannas, streamside growth, farms and ranches, oak woods, city parks and suburbs with tall shade trees.

Range
Across wooded areas of S. Canada and the United States south into Mexico. Also Great Plains. Winters in Central America.

Comments
The Northern Oriole is among the brightest of western songbirds. The western subspecies, still called "Bullock's" Oriole by many birders, was once considered to be a separate species from the eastern "Baltimore" Oriole; however, these birds were found to interbreed where their ranges overlap in the Great Plains, and were subsequently combined into one species, the Northern Oriole. The majority of colorful western birds inhabit woodlands or forests, where dense cover and scattered sunlight permits the elaboration of brilliant plumage among the males. In more open environments, drabber colors make for more certain camouflage from would-be predators. The related Scott's Oriole (*Icterus parisorum*) is a lemon-yellow-and-black resident of pinyon-juniper woodlands and open desert. Frequently found in canyons, they give a melodious, clear whistle that often reverberates and can be heard for long distances.

Pine Grosbeak
Pinicola enucleator
308

8–10" (20–25 cm). Large, plump finch. Stubby, strongly curved black bill. Dull rose-red body with dark streaking on back, dark wings with 2 white wing bars; dusky, notched tail. Juvenile male dull pinkish-red on head and rump with gray body. Females similar to first-year males in pattern, with dull mustard head and rump markings.

Voice
Call, a 3-note whistle; song has whistles, trills, and warbles.

Habitat
Coniferous forests.

Range
Breeds across boreal forest; in the West extends south into the pine and fir forests of high mountains from the northern Sierra Nevada and Rockies to New Mexico.

Comments
During snowy winters these grosbeaks can be located in scattered open forests by the feeble calls that keep the flock together. They settle in a tree and feed, snapping off buds or seeking the pits in fruit, until sated or disturbed. When food is scarce, they may descend into woods at sea level.

Cassin's Finch
Carpodacus cassinii
309

6–6½" (15–17 cm). Male's breast coloration paler rose-red; brown-streaked nape and mantle make rosy crown and rump, especially crown, appear more brilliant. Unstreaked flanks and belly pale pink to whitish. Female finely streaked above and below, with indistinct eye-line and jaw stripe.

Voice
Song is a series of fluty, varied warbles. Call note, a high *pwee-de-lip,* is distinctive to this species.

Habitat
Open conifer stands at high elevations.

Range
Interior mountain ranges or valleys of the West, from the southern Canadian Rockies to the mountains of Baja California and to the southern rim of the Central Plateau. Northernmost populations migratory; many winter in Mexico.

Comments
The closely related Cassin's, House, and Purple finches are each found in different altitudes and habitats; thus there is no competition among them. In California the House Finch (*Carpodacus mexicanus*) is common in the arid, hot plains, deserts, and the foothills, nesting widely in chaparral and oak woodland. In the montane forest belt, the Purple Finch (*C. purpureus*) is found at the edges of coniferous stands and the shady oak growth of canyons. Cassin's is found higher up in firs and yellow pines.

Red Crossbill
Loxia curvirostra
310

5¼–6½″ (13–17 cm). Sparrow-sized finch with crossed mandibles. Head and body of male dusky brick-red, wings and tail dark. Female is drab olive-gray with dull yellow on rump and underparts. Immature males have orange tint with dusky streaks on mantle and breast. Plumage of both sexes has overall mottled appearance.

Voice
A repeated *kip-kip* or *jeep-jeep* betrays its presence. Song is a short series of chipping and tinkling notes.

Habitat
Coniferous forests, favoring pines.

Range
Resident throughout the boreal forest from Alaska to Newfoundland; south in coniferous forests to Baja California, Nicaragua, and the southern Appalachians.

Comments
Holding a pine cone with one foot, the bird inserts its specialized bill between the cone and the scales, pries the scales apart by opening its bill, and extracts the seed with its flexible tongue. Dependent on pine seeds, the Red Crossbill is erratic and nomadic. When cone crops fail, these birds gather in flocks and may wander far from their normal haunts. They may breed at any season, so long as the food supply is adequate. The White-winged Crossbill (*Loxia leucoptera*) is rose-red, with 2 white wing bars. It is a boreal forest species that ranges irregularly southward.

Evening Grosbeak
Coccothraustes vespertinus
311

7–8½" (18–22 cm). A plump bird, with heavy conical bill. Wings and tail black, large white wing patch. Body dark yellow, with yellow on forehead and eyebrows; head, neck, and breast dark olive-brown. Bill yellowish-green in breeding birds; ivory in winter. Female and immatures dusky, wings and tail marked with white.

Voice
Calls incessantly to maintain contact within the flock. In flight, *tchew tchew tchew* or a shrill *p-teer*. Also a clear, downslurred *tew*.

Habitat
For breeding, coniferous and mixed forests. In fall, large flocks gather in woods where seeds or fruits are available, remaining into late spring.

Range
In the West, the southern part of the coniferous forest belt in the Canadian provinces; the coastal forest and the mountain chains, through the latter south to Mexico. It spread eastward during the last half century into the Great Lakes region and even farther east.

Comments
Major Delafield, an explorer of the 1820s, was the first to write about this grosbeak. He sighted some of these birds near his tent at twilight, and believed that they hid in dark shade during the day and dispersed at sunset; this led to its subsequent Latin designation by Cooper: *Hesperiphona vespertina*, "Evening Night-singer." Until recently, the misnomer stuck both in Latin and in English.

Pine Siskin
Carduelis pinus
312

4½–5¼" (11–13 cm). Grayish-brown above, buffy below, with dusky streaking overall; yellow on wing and tail. Sharp, slender bill and deeply notched tail. Females have less yellow.

Voice
In flight, a scratchy *shick-shick* and a thin *tseee*. Also a rising, buzzy *schhrreeee*.

Habitat
Coniferous forests; second-growth alders, aspens, and broadleaf trees along the fringes of boreal forests.

Range
From S. Alaska and Canada south through the W. United States and across the Mexican border; north-central and NE. United States. Found irregularly farther south in winter.

Comments
Siskins, redpolls, and goldfinches are a closely related group of seed specialists. All have short, conical beaks, short, slightly forked tails, bright wing markings, and "nervous" behavior. They feed in flocks, which, after breeding, may contain hundreds of birds. They are all acrobats, often hanging upside down, plucking seeds from seed pods and catkins.

MUSHROOMS

The damp, shady forest floor provides exactly the right kind of habitat for many kinds of mushrooms. Some of these grow on the ground, while others spring to life on fallen tree trunks and branches. Some species are quite inconspicuous; others lend a touch of unexpected color—bright reds and oranges—to somber areas. This section provides descriptions of some of the most familiar and conspicuous mushrooms that grow in our western forests.

Bulbous Cort
Cortinarius glaucopus
313

Cap 2–5" (5–12.5 cm) wide; stalk 2–4" (5–10 cm) tall. Cap reddish-brown and streaked, with a wavy margin, and sticky. The crowded gills change from purple to brownish as spores mature. Purplish stalk with a bulbous base; remains of cobwebby veil usually present higher up.

Season
Differs with locale. July to August in Rocky Mountains; September to October in Pacific Northwest; November to March in California.

Habitat
Usually under spruce, fir, or oak.

Range
Widespread throughout the United States.

Comments
Because so many other species closely resemble this one, it is not recommended that the Bulbous Cort be eaten. The best way to become acquainted with safe, edible species is to accompany an experienced mushroom hunter on as many field trips as possible. Learning to distinguish safe species from those that are poisonous or even deadly can take years, and beginners should never eat what they gather.

Fly Agaric ⊗
Amanita muscaria
314

Cap 2–10" (5–25 cm) wide; stalk 2–7" (5–18 cm) tall. Cap bright red to reddish-orange, adorned with white warts or patches, and sticky in humid weather. Gills white, crowded, and not attached to the stalk (or just touching it). Concentric bands of tissue just above bulbous base of stalk, with a white ring higher up.

Season
July to October, and also in winter in California.

Habitat
Most often under pine, spruce, or birch.

Range
Pacific Coast to the Rocky Mountains.

Comments
This species is famous in mushroom lore. An Asiatic form has been used to induce visions, and the species has also been used as a fly poison. Forms that grow in the East have orange or yellow caps. Fly Agarics are poisonous and should be avoided.

Emetic Russula ⊗
Russula emetica
315

Cap 1–3" (2.5–7.5 cm) wide; stalk 2–4" (5–10 cm) tall. Cap bright red varying to deep pink. The cap is sticky with a striate margin. Gills are off-white, close, and attached to the stalk. The white to off-white stalk may widen at the base. There is no ring.

Season
August to September.

Habitat
Most frequently in sphagnum moss but also on the ground in mixed woods.

Range
Widely distributed throughout North America.

Comments
Usually regarded as poisonous, the Emetic Russula is nevertheless eaten by some. The extremely acrid taste will discourage most people. In any event, it cannot be recommended for the table since it closely resembles other species whose toxic properties are unknown.

Chanterelle
Cantharellus cibarius
316

Cap 1–4" (2.5–10 cm) wide; stalk 1–3" (2.5–7.5 cm) tall. Cap is yellow to orange-yellow, and slightly hairy or smooth. Gill-like blunt ridges, with much cross-veining, run down the pale stalk. The entire mushroom is funnel-shaped.

Season
September to February.

Habitat
Mixed woods, or under conifers or oaks.

Range
Northwest U.S. to California (but widely distributed in North America).

Comments
This beautiful mushroom is highly regarded and widely sought as a choice edible. It usually emits an apricot fragrance. *Omphalotus illudens,* a similar and poisonous species, has gills; the gills are not cross-veined.

Tomentose Suillus
Suillus tomentosus
317

Cap 2–4" (5–10 cm) wide; stalk 1–4½" (2.5–11 cm) tall. Cap yellow with yellow to orange-yellow scales, bun-shaped, dry above but sticky beneath scales. Undersurface of cap has pores; changes from cinnamon-color to yellowish with maturity, turning blue when rubbed. Stalk yellowish with brownish dots.

Season
September to October in Pacific Northwest; November to January in California.

Habitat
Under 2-needle and 3-needle pines.

Range
Pacific Northwest, California, Rocky Mountains, and farther east.

Comments
If you cut this mushroom with a knife, its yellow interior will slowly change to greenish-blue.

King Bolete
Boletus edulis
318

Cap 3–10″ (8–25 cm) wide; stalk 4–10″ (10–25 cm) tall. Cap reddish-brown (varying to lighter or darker), bun-shaped; sticky in humid weather. Pore-bearing undersurface is white at first, maturing to greenish-yellow. Stalk stout, usually bulbous, pale, with fine, white network on upper part.

Season
June to October.

Habitat
Under conifers, and under birch and aspen.

Range
Widespread throughout North America.

Comments
A choice edible, the King Bolete has a nutty flavor. It occurs in several variations. One bitter-tasting look-alike species has a pinkish undersurface.

Fluted White Helvella
Helvella crispa
319

Cap ¾–2½″ (2–6 cm) wide; stalk 1–3½″ (2.5–9 cm) tall. Cap cream-colored to buff, wavy and lobed, suggesting a small saddle. Stalk similarly colored, and coarsely ribbed with a few pits.

Season
September to October in the Northwest; December to April in the Southwest.

Habitat
Under conifers or hardwoods, or in grassy areas.

Range
Widely distributed across the United States.

Comments
In the young mushroom, the cap is rolled inward, but with maturity the cap unrolls and flares out. Although this species can be eaten, it is not a popular edible.

Black Morel
Morchella elata
320

Cap ¾–1¾″ (2–4 cm) wide, ½–2″ (1.3–5 cm) tall; stalk 2–4″ (5–10 cm) tall. Cap conical with overall blackish hue, and honeycombed throughout with ridges and pits. Stalk is off-white with a granular coating.

Season
Spring.

Habitat
Coniferous woods or under aspens.

Range
Widely distributed throughout North America.

Comments
The Black Morel is one member of a complex of similar appearing species. They cannot easily be distinguished without microscopic examination. In any event, none should

be eaten since at least one of the species has caused many incidents of gastrointestinal disturbances.

Sculptured Puffball
Calbovista subsculpta
321

Mushroom 3–6″ (7.5–15 cm) wide, 2½–3½″ (6.5–9 cm) high; no stalk. Shaped like a mound of dough, usually broader than tall. White, covered with low warts except at smooth base. Warts have brownish hairs at center. Interior of mushroom firm and white, becoming brown as spores mature.

Season
April to August.

Habitat
Open woods, along paths, but not in lowland areas.

Range
Pacific Coast mountain ranges and Rocky Mountains.

Comments
This is a good edible species when it is young and the interior is white. As the mushroom matures and the interior darkens, however, it loses its flavor.

Western Rhizopogon
Rhizopogon occidentalis
322

Mushroom ⅜–2″ (1–5 cm) wide; no stalk. Shaped like a potato; whitish when young, becoming lemon-yellow, with a network of brown threads. Surface of mushroom stains darker when handled. Internally olive-colored at maturity.

Season
May to September.

Habitat
Under conifers, preferring sandy soil.

Range
Pacific Coast states and Idaho.

Comments
This species is one of a large group of related mushrooms. It is usually difficult to find because it grows deep in needle beds, sometimes so deeply that it is practically subterranean.

Chicken Mushroom
Laetiporus sulphureus
323

Cap 2–12″ (5–30 cm) wide; stalk very small or absent. Cap orange-red to orange-yellow, usually bright orange; smooth; whitish in age. Deep yellow on undersurface, with pores. Fan-shaped, usually growing in clusters.

Season
May to November, but more typically found in autumn.

Habitat
Logs and stumps of coniferous and deciduous trees; also on living trees.

Range
Widespread throughout North America.

Comments
The Chicken Mushroom, so named because its taste resembles that of chicken, has long been considered a choice edible. However, current reports indicate that stomach upsets can result from eating this species; and some people have been known to suffer an allergic reaction. It should particularly never be eaten raw. *L. sulphureus* sometimes grows in large clusters of up to 50 or more. A color variety exists that has a white, rather than yellow, undersurface.

Red-belted Polypore
Fomitopsis pinicola
324

Cap 2–12" (5–30 cm) wide; no stalk. Cap shaped like a hoof or somewhat flatter, reddish brown or brown, covered with resinous crust. Margin rounded and reddish. Pores on white or light yellow undersurface, which turns yellow when rubbed.

Season
All year.

Habitat
Dead trees and stumps of conifers and hardwoods; sometimes living trees.

Range
Throughout North America.

Comments
This widespread species causes decay in a large number of useful trees.

MAMMALS

The forests are teeming with life, yet some of the most interesting animals can be shy and hard to observe. The visitor who learns to wait and watch—quietly, and with patience— will be rewarded by the sight of a Moose, Elk, deer, fox, or other animal that lives in the forests of the West. This section includes descriptions of many typical mammals of the forests, from the tiny shrews and mice of the forest floor to the formidable Grizzly Bear.

Vagrant Shrew
Sorex vagrans
325

3¾–4¾" (9.5–11.9 cm) long. In summer: brownish to grayish above; grayish tinged with brown or red below. In winter: all parts grayish or blackish. Long tail 1 color or grading to lighter below.

Habitat
Mixed forests.

Range
S. British Columbia south to N. California, N. Nevada, Arizona, E. New Mexico.

Comments
This shrew's common and scientific names allude to its extraordinary activity in pursuit of food, rather than its wanderings, which are no greater than those of other shrews. The Vagrant Shrew is one of 12 very similar shrew species found in western North America.

Long-tailed Vole
Microtus longicaudus
326

6¼–10⅜" (15.5–26.5 cm) long. Large. Grayish brown above; light grayish below. Feet dusky white. Long tail bicolored.

Habitat
Dry grassy areas far from water; mountain slopes; alder and willow sedge areas.

Range
SE. Alaska through Yukon and SW. Mackenzie to California, Nevada, NE. Arizona, New Mexico; W. South Dakota.

Comments
In winter these voles spread out across the mountain slopes in search of food; in summer they usually retreat into grassy areas. They feed on roots and bark when green vegetation is scarce.

Red Tree Vole
Phenacomys longicaudus
327

6¼–8⅛" (15.8–20.6 cm) long. Bright reddish above; whitish below. Long tail blackish, well haired.

Sign
Bulky nests in Douglas-fir trees.

Habitat
Primarily Douglas-fir forests; also redwood or Sitka Spruce–Salal areas if ample Douglas-fir not available.

Range
Coastal Oregon and NW. California.

Comments
This highly specialized tree-dweller rarely descends to the ground. Its nests are built 6–150' above ground, usually in Douglas-fir. Nests are composed of twigs from the host tree, though the voles may base them on old nests of squirrels, woodrats, or birds, with the inner nest composed of resin ducts from leaves discarded by the vole when feeding.

Additional twigs and food refuse are used to enlarge the nest continually, with urine and fecal pellets helping to mold it together and secure it to the tree. Generations of voles may use the same nest, and a large nest may have several chambers.

Western Jumping Mouse
Zapus princeps
328

8½–10¼" (21.5–26 cm) long. Yellow sides; dark band down middle of back; belly white, sometimes tinged with yellow. Long tail darker above, whitish below. Enlarged hind feet.

Breeding
Mating occurs soon after emergence from hibernation. Young usually born in June or July, sometimes much later, in a spherical nest of interwoven broad-leaved grasses or, if in a bog, of sphagnum moss.

Habitat
Variable: primarily moist fields, thickets, or woodlands, especially where grasses, sedges, or other green plant cover is dense; grassy edges of streams, ponds, or lakes.

Range
S. Yukon, all of British Columbia, southern half of Alberta and Saskatchewan, extreme SW. Manitoba, south through NE. South Dakota, NE. and W. Montana to central New Mexico and east-central Arizona, Utah, N. Nevada, W. California, W. Oregon.

Comments
Although it often runs on all 4 feet, the Western Jumping Mouse may make a series of jumps 3–5' long when startled from its hiding place, then "disappear" by remaining motionless in a new one. It can also swim and climb.

Deer Mouse
Peromyscus maniculatus
329

4¾–8¾" (11.9–22.2 cm) long. Grayish to reddish brown above; white below; tail distinctly bicolored and short-haired.

Sign
Tracks: In dust, hindprint ⅝" long, with 5 toes printing; foreprint slightly smaller, with 4 toes printing; straddle, 1⅜"; with foreprints behind and between hindprints. In mud, both fore- and hindprints ⁵⁄₁₆" wide, straddle 1½".

Habitat
Forests; woodlands; brush.

Range
Mexico to S. Yukon and Northwest Territories; in the East, Hudson Bay to Pennsylvania, the southern Appalachians, central Arkansas, and central Texas.

Comments
The Deer Mouse is the most common and widespread of more than half a dozen species of white-footed mice native to wooded areas of western North America. These species are difficult or impossible for amateur naturalists to distinguish in the field.

Pika
Ochotona princeps
330

6⅜–8½" (16.2–21.6 cm) long. Brownish. Small rounded ears. No visible tail.

Sign
Tracks: Seldom visible except in patches of snow or mud; complete cluster, showing all 4 feet, no more than 3" wide, less than 4" from hind- to foreprints. Front feet have 5 toes, but often the reduced fifth toe does not print; hind feet, with 4 toes, slightly larger than forefeet but not greatly elongated, so there is no mistaking track for a rabbit's.

Breeding
2–6 young born blind and naked May–June; a second litter may be produced in late summer.

Habitat
Talus slides; rocky banks; steep, boulder-covered hillsides; usually at elevations of 8000–13,500'.

Range
Western North America from central California and N. New Mexico north to middle British Columbia.

Comments
The Pika feeds on many species of green plants, eating some on the spot and carrying cuttings of others to boulders near its home. It spreads them to dry in the sun, curing its "hay" as a farmer does; haystacks are not high but may contain up to a bushel of vegetation, primarily grasses and sedges but including fireweed, dryad, stonecrop, sweetgrass, and thistles. Later, the dried vegetation is stored in the Pika's den.

Uinta Chipmunk
Eutamias umbrinus
331

7¾–9⅝" (196–243 mm) long. Grayish above, including crown, with wide, dark brown side stripes; white below; tawny wash on sides. Tail back-tipped, white-bordered, tawny below. Ears blackish in front, whitish behind.

Breeding
Young born in early summer depending on latitude and elevation.

Habitat
Coniferous forests, mixed woods, open areas; in yellow pines, white pines, junipers, scrub oaks.

Range
Wyoming, Nevada, W. California, Utah, north-central Arizona, north-central Colorado.

Comments
This tree-dwelling species often occurs together with the Golden-mantled Ground Squirrel. It accumulates much fat, which is used in hibernation during the long winters of its range. Nuts, seeds, fruits, and berries are chief foods.

Townsend's Chipmunk
Eutamias townsendii
332

8⅞–12½″ (22.1–31.7 cm) long. Large. Dark brown, often with rather wide, diffuse or indistinct blackish and light stripes on head and continuing down body. Lighter in summer than winter. Backs of ears bicolor: dusky on front half; gray on back half. Tail long and bushy: blackish above with many white-tipped hairs, bright reddish brown below bordered with black and finely edged with white-tipped hairs. Brownish stripe below ears.

Breeding
Mates in spring; 1 litter of 2–6 young born May–June.

Habitat ·
Rank vegetation, usually among dense hardwood or humid coniferous forests.

Range
Extreme S. British Columbia south through most of W. Oregon.

Comments
One of the largest western chipmunks and the darkest in color (as is common among species in moist climates), it has a looser, less sleek coat than the others. It is active all day, like other chipmunks, but rather shy. It lives in a burrow about 2″ across and comparatively short at 5′ in length. A very good climber, it often suns itself in trees and may run up a tree to flee a predator. It forages within a home range of 1½ acres. Three similar, closely related species also inhabit forested areas in NW. California and W. Oregon.

Least Chipmunk
Eutamias minimus
333

6⅝–8⅞″ (16.7–22.5 cm) long. Small. Color varies; in drier regions, muted yellowish gray above with dark tan stripes; in moister areas, brownish gray with black side stripes. Stripes continue to base of tail. Sides orange-brown; belly grayish white. Long tail light brown above, yellowish below, with hairs black-tipped. Ears tawny in front.

Breeding
1 litter of 5–7 young born in May in an underground nest; nest may also be in a tree.

Habitat
Sagebrush deserts; pastures; pine forests; rocky cliffs; often abundant in open coniferous forests.

Range
Most of southern Canada from Ontario to S. Yukon; western United States from W. North Dakota to New Mexico, west to NW. California and SE. Washington.

Comments
Lightest in color of all the western chipmunks, it often lives in the driest habitats. An excellent climber, it ascends trees to sun itself and may even nest in them. Its distinctive call is a series of high-pitched chipping notes.

Yellow-pine Chipmunk
Eutamias amoenus
334

7⅛–9⅝" (18.1–24.5 cm) long. Brightly colored, from tawny to pinkish cinnamon, with distinct stripes; light stripes white or grayish, dark stripes usually black. Sides and underside of tail brownish yellow. Top of head brown. Ears blackish in front, whitish behind.

Sign
Remnants of nuts; burrow openings with no loose soil at entrances.

Breeding
Mates in April; 5–7 naked and blind young born May–early June in a nest of leaves, grass, lichen, and feathers.

Habitat
Open coniferous forests, particularly ponderosa (yellow) pine.

Range
S. British Columbia south to N. California, east to W. Montana and NW. Wyoming; in the yellow pine zone.

Comments
In the open forests where the sun casts sharp shadows, the well-defined stripes of the Yellow-pine Chipmunk afford protective coloration. Before winter, it puts on little fat, suggesting that it may not hibernate, or at least does not do so for long; some individuals are active even on snow. This is one of 20 species of western chipmunks, many with relatively limited geographic ranges. When more than one species of chipmunk inhabit the same area, they are usually segregated by habitat or behavior, thereby avoiding competition.

Golden-mantled Ground Squirrel
Spermophilus lateralis
335

9⅛–12⅛" (23–30.8 cm) long. Chipmunklike. Back gray, brownish, or buff; belly whitish. Head and shoulders coppery red, forming "golden mantle." On sides 1 white stripe bordered by black stripes; no facial stripes.

Breeding
1 litter per year of 4–6 young born in early summer.

Habitat
Moist coniferous or mixed forest; in mountains to above timberline.

Range
SE. British Columbia and SW. Alberta south through much of western United States, east to SE. Wyoming, W. Colorado, N. and W. New Mexico.

Comments
Usually silent, the Golden-mantled Ground Squirrel can chirp and squeal with fright and growls when fighting. Its varied diet includes green vegetation and insects, although seeds, nuts, and fruits are the mainstay. It nests in shallow burrows up to 100′ long that often open under or near a log, tree roots, or boulder. It hibernates from about October to May, depending on latitude.

Northern Flying Squirrel
Glaucomys sabrinus
336

10⅜–14½″ (26.3–36.8 cm) long. Small. Very soft fur, rich brown above, white below. A loose fold of skin between fore and hind legs. Large black eyes.

Sign
Nuts stored on stumps or about tree bases.

Breeding
Mates in late winter; gestation of about 40 days; litter of 2–5 young born in spring, often in hollow stump or limb, sometimes in bark nest in conifer crotch. Sometimes a second litter in late summer.

Habitat
Coniferous forests, mixed forests; sometimes in hardwoods where old or dead trees have woodpecker-type nesting holes, especially in stumps 6–20′ high with holes near top.

Range
E. Alaska, S. Yukon, S. Northwest Territories, southern tier of Canadian provinces, Labrador; south in western United States through California, Idaho, Montana, Utah, and N. Wyoming; in eastern United States to Minnesota, Wisconsin, Michigan, New England, and New York, and through Appalachian Mountains.

Comments
This squirrel is quite common, but because it is nocturnal, it is seldom seen. It makes a nest of shredded bark in tree hollows and may cap an abandoned bird's nest to provide a temporary shelter. It spreads its legs and stretches its flight skin in gliding from tree to tree, pulling upright at the last instant to land gently.

Bushy-tailed Woodrat
Neotoma cinerea
337

11½–18½″ (29.2–47.2 cm) long. Varies from pale grayish to blackish above, but often brownish peppered with black hairs; whitish below. Tail squirrel-like, bushy, and flattened.

Sign
Stick houses, usually concealed in rock crevices or beneath boulders or fallen logs.

Habitat
Rocky situations; coniferous forests.

Range
Northwestern United States from N. California and NW. New Mexico north to SW. North Dakota and Washington, then north through extreme SW. Saskatchewan, SW. Alberta, British Columbia, extreme SW. Mackenzie, and SE. Yukon.

Comments
This is the original "pack rat," the species in which the trading habit is most pronounced. It has a strong preference for shiny objects and will drop whatever else it may have in favor of carrying off a coin or a spoon. In coniferous forests this woodrat may build its house as high as 50′ up a tree.

Hoary Bat
Lasiurus cinereus
338

4–6" (10.2–5.2 cm) long. Light brown above with tips of fur heavily frosted white; throat buff. Ears short and rounded, with black, naked rims. Interfemoral membranes well furred above.

Habitat
Hangs from evergreen branches.

Range
Throughout continental United States except for peninsular Florida; also found in southern Canada.

Comments
Although it is the most widely distributed U.S. bat, the Hoary occurs only in small numbers and is rarely seen. It emerges late in the evening and eats mostly moths.

Western Gray Squirrel
Sciurus griseus
339

17½–23¼" (44.5–59.3 cm) long. Gray with numerous white-tipped hairs above; belly white. Backs of ears reddish brown. Long bushy tail with bands of gray, white, and black, especially below.

Sign
Large leaf nests, obvious in winter, often high in trees. Remains of pinecones and acorns.

Breeding
1 litter of 3–5 young born between March and June.

Habitat
Woodlands, low-elevation pine or mixed forests.

Range
Pacific states, from Washington to California.

Comments
This squirrel is active all year but during bad storms may remain in its nest. In summer it uses a nest of shredded bark and sticks, usually at least 20' above the ground; in winter it probably lives in a tree hollow. Pinecones, acorns and other nuts, some fungi, berries, and insects are chief foods. Its hoarse barking call is heard mostly in late summer.

Douglas' Squirrel
Tamiasciurus douglasii
340

10⅝–14" (27–35.5 cm) long. Upper parts reddish gray or brownish gray grading into chestnut-brown on middle of back; underparts orangish to grayish. Grayer in winter. Tail above like back, except last third blackish; tail below rusty in center, bordered by a broad black band with whitish edge. Blackish line on sides in summer, indistinct or absent in winter. Small ear tufts in winter.

Sign
Summer nests resembling large balls in trees; middens (piles of cone remnants). Tracks similar to those of the Red Squirrel.

Breeding
Mates in early spring; litters usually of 4–6 young in May or

June; sometimes a second litter. Young venture out in August; families remain together for much of first year.

Habitat
Primarily coniferous forests.

Range
SW. British Columbia, W. Washington, W. Oregon, N. California.

Comments
Very active throughout the year, it runs about through trees and on the ground, though during bad storms it will remain in its nest. It builds a summer nest mainly of mosses and lichens, twigs, and shredded bark, but sometimes caps deserted bird's nest; in winter it nests in tree holes. Noisier than most squirrels, it has a large repertoire of calls, including a trill.

Red Squirrel
Tamiasciurus hudsonicus
341

10⅝–15¼″ (27–38.5 cm) long. Smallest tree squirrel in its range. Rust-red to grayish red above, brightest on sides; white or grayish white below. Tail similar to back color but outlined with broad black band edged with white. In summer, coat is duller and a black line separates reddish back from whitish belly. In winter, large ear tufts.

Sign
Piles of cone remnants; small holes in earth; tree nests, especially in conifer stands, often built of grass and bark. Tracks: In mud, hindprint about 1½″ long, with 5 toes printing; foreprints half as long, with 4 toes printing. In rapid bounds, front tracks appear between hind; in slow bounds, front tracks slightly behind hind. Straddle 4″.

Breeding
Mates in late winter after animated nuptial chases. 3–5 young born in March or April; sometimes a second litter in August or September.

Habitat
Often abundant in coniferous forests, mixed forests, or hardwoods.

Range
Throughout much of Canada and Alaska; in the United States through Rocky Mountain states, in the Northeast south to Iowa, N. Illinois, N. Indiana, N. Ohio, N. Virginia, and south through the Alleghenies.

Comments
In conifer forests it feeds heavily on pine seeds and leaves piles of cone remnants everywhere. Other foods include acorns and other seeds; bird's eggs and young birds; fungi—even amanita mushrooms, which are deadly to man, are often cached in trees. It makes a nest in a hollow tree, fallen tree, hole in the ground, hummock, or tree crotch (like the leaf nests of gray squirrels).

Abert's Squirrel
Sciurus aberti
342

18¼–23″ (46.3–58.4 cm) long. Large. Dark grizzled gray above with darker sides, reddish back; belly white. Tail above similar to back but with whitish cast, bordered with white; white below. Tasseled ear reddish on back with tufts or "tassels" extending beyond eartips.

Sign
Nests about 1′ in diameter, high in trees, especially in pine or juniper. Remains of pinecones and gnawed twigs.

Breeding
Mating chases may be seen in February or March. Litter (usually of about 4 young) born in March or April; young are on their own by late June.

Habitat
Ponderosa pine forests or pinyon-juniper woodlands.

Range
Isolated mountainous areas in Arizona, New Mexico, SE. Utah, Colorado; at Grand Canyon in Arizona, only on South Rim.

Comments
On a base of twigs placed in a crotch, Abert's Squirrel builds a tree nest with 2 entrances and lines the inside of the 5″ chamber with shredded bark. It repairs the nest as necessary. Pine seeds and pinyon nuts are chief foods, but it also eats mistletoe, the inner bark of pine, and other vegetable items. Active throughout the winter, in very cold weather it may remain in its nest except for retrieving buried seeds, especially at tree bases where there is no snow.

Marten
Martes americana
343

19¼–26⅞″ (49–68.2 cm) long. Weasel-like. Brownish, varying from dark brown to blond, with paler head and underparts, darker legs, orange or buff throat patch. Long, bushy tail; pointed snout; small ears. Males larger than females.

Sign
Tracks: Like Mink's but slightly larger, 1½–1⅞″ wide; straddle 2½–3″, to 6″ in snow; walking stride 9″ for males, 6″ for females, more than doubles when running.

Breeding
Mates midsummer; delayed implantation; 2–4 young born blind, naked, around April in leaf nest.

Habitat
Forests, particularly coniferous ones.

Range
Most of Canada; in the West, south to N. California through Rocky Mountains; in the East, to northern New England and N. New York.

Comments
Martens are active in early morning, late afternoon, and on

overcast days, traversing a home range of 5–15 square mi.
They spend much of their time in trees. Both sexes establish
scent posts by rubbing their scent glands on branches. Usually
Martens avoid each other; if 2 meet, they bare their teeth and
snarl. They pounce on prey; the Red Squirrel is favored, but
flying squirrels, rabbits, mice, and birds are also taken. The
varied diet also includes carrion, eggs, berries, conifer seeds,
and honey.

Ermine
Mustela erminea
344

7½–13½" (19–34.4 cm) long. Elongated body, dark brown
above, white below. Tail brown with black tip; feet white. In
winter, throughout northern range, white with black tail tip,
nose, and eyes. Males almost twice as large as females.

Sign
Tracks: Hindprints ¾" wide, less than 1" long, usually with
only 4 or 5 toes printing; foreprints slightly wider,
approximately half as long. Hind feet usually placed in or near
foreprints, but prints are sometimes side by side, more often
with one slightly ahead. Straddle 3". Stride varies as ermines
run and bound, often alternating long and short leaps.

Breeding
Mates in July; 4–9 young born blind, with fine hair, in spring
in some protected area, such as under a log, a rockpile, or tree
stump; eyes open at 35 days.

Habitat
Varied: open woodlands, brushy areas, grasslands, wetlands,
farmlands.

Range
Most of Canada south to N. California, W. Colorado, and N.
New Mexico in West, to N. Iowa, Michigan, Pennsylvania,
and Maryland in East.

Comments
Though the Ermine hunts mainly on the ground, often
running on fallen logs, it can climb trees and occasionally even
pursues prey into water. After a rapid dash, it pounces on its
victim with all 4 feet, biting through the neck near the base
of the skull. Mice are its main food, but it also eats shrews,
baby rabbits, and birds. Its den—which may be found
beneath a log, stump, roots, brushpile, or stone wall—usually
has several entrances and contains a nest of vegetation mixed
with hair.

Mink
Mustela vison
345

19¼–28¼" (49.1–72 cm) long. Sleek-bodied with lustrous
fur, uniformly chocolate-brown to black with white spotting
on chin and throat. Tail long, somewhat bushy. Males larger
than females.

Sign
Hole in snow where it plunged after prey; sliding hills marked
by slender troughs in snow.

Den: In streambanks with 4″ openings.
Tracks: Fairly round, 1¼–1¾″ wide, more than 2″ in snow.
In clear print, heel pad and all 5 slightly webbed toes show
separately; semiretractile claws may show. Hind feet 2¼″ long
in mud, 3½″ in snow, and placed nearly in prints of forefeet;
trail of twin prints 12–26″ apart depending on animal's size
and speed.

Breeding
Mates in midwinter, males mating with several females but
eventually living with 1; 3–6 young born blind, naked, in
fur-lined nest in spring; weaned at 5–6 weeks.

Habitat
Along rivers, creeks, lakes, ponds, and marshes.

Range
Most of United States and Canada except Arizona,
S. California, S. Utah, S. New Mexico, and W. Texas.

Comments
Minks of both sexes are hostile to intruders, and males fight
viciously in or out of breeding season. They maintain hunting
territories by marking with a fetid discharge from the anal
glands, which is at least as malodorous as a skunk's, although
it does not carry as far. Minks swim very well, often hunting
in ponds and streams, and can climb trees but do so rarely.
Like weasels, Minks kill by biting their victims in the neck.
Muskrats are preferred prey, but many rabbits, mice,
chipmunks, fish, snakes, frogs, young snapping turtles, and
marsh-dwelling birds are taken, and sometimes poultry.

Mountain Beaver
Aplodontia rufa
346

9⅜–18½″ (23.8–47 cm) long. Woodchucklike but smaller,
with a short, heavy body. Dark brown above; lighter brown
below. Blunt head; short legs; small ears and eyes; tiny tail.
5 toes on all feet, with first toe on front foot a flattened nail,
other front toes with very long strong claws.

Sign
Burrows up to 19″ in diameter, surrounded by fan-shaped
earth mounds and pathways; in very wet areas, a "tent" of
sticks covered with leaves and fern fronds erected over burrow
entrances; in late summer, "hay piles" of ferns and other
vegetation up to 2′ high on logs or ground; cylindrical earth
cores, to 6″ in diameter, made during winter tunneling and
left on surface after snow cover melts.
Tracks: Narrow, under 2″ long; hindprints larger than
foreprints and may overlap them. 5 toes on all feet, but small
first toe on forefeet may not print.

Breeding
Mates late winter; 1 litter of 3–5 young (usually 4 or 5) born
in early spring, weaned by autumn, disperse soon after.

Habitat
Moist forests, especially near streams.

Range
Extreme SW. British Columbia, W. Washington,
W. Oregon, N. California, extreme west-central Nevada.

Comments
The common name "Mountain-beaver" is misleading, as this rodent is neither a beaver nor does it prefer a mountainous habitat. Active throughout the year, this animal is mostly nocturnal. Its home range is small, averaging about one-third of an acre, and it remains within a few yards of cover. Its labyrinthine burrow system is usually shallow, often near cover, and used by many other animals.

Beaver
Castor canadensis
347

35½–46″ (90–117 cm) long. Very large rodent. Dark brown. Large black scaly tail, horizontally flattened, paddle-shaped. Large hind feet, black, webbed, with inner 2 nails cleft. Small eyes and ears.

Sign
Alarm signal: Tail "slaps" on water loud enough to be heard at a considerable distance. Dams and domelike lodges of woven sticks, reeds, branches, and saplings, caulked with mud. Scent mounds: heaps of mud, sticks, and sedges or grass, up to 1′ high, 3′ wide, where Beavers deposit scent from anal glands, apparently to mark family territory. Logs and twigs peeled where bark is eaten; felled trees; gnawed tree trunks.
Tracks: Distinctive when not obliterated by wide drag mark of tail. Usually only 3 or 4 of the 5 toes print, leaving wide, splay-toed track 3″ long. Webbed hind feet leave fan-shaped track often more than 5″ wide at widest part, at least twice as long as forefeet; webbing usually shows in soft mud.

Breeding
Believed to pair for life, it mates late January–late February, and 4 months later a litter of 1–8 kits (usually 4 or 5) are born well furred, with eyes open, and weighing about 1 lb. They may take to the water inside their lodge within a half hour and are skillful swimmers within a week.

Habitat
Rivers, streams, marshes, lakes, and ponds.

Range
Most of Canada and United States, except for much of S. California, Nevada, and most of Florida.

Comments
Active throughout the year, the Beaver is primarily nocturnal. Beavers living along a river generally make burrows with an underwater entrance in the riverbank; those in streams, lakes, and ponds usually build dams that incorporate a lodge, which has one or more underwater entrances and living quarters in a hollow near the top. The chief construction materials in the northern parts of its range—poplar, aspen, willow, birch, and maple—are also the preferred foods. To fell a tree, the Beaver

gnaws around it biting out chips in a deep groove. Small trees 2–6″ in diameter are usually selected, but larger ones may be felled; a willow 5″ thick can be cut down in 3 minutes.

River Otter
Lutra canadensis
348

35–51⅛″ (88.9–131.3 cm) long. Elongated body. Dark brown (looks black when wet) with paler belly; throat often silver-gray; prominent whitish whiskers. Long tail thick at base and gradually tapering to a point; feet webbed. Males larger than females.

Sign
Holes in snow where otter plunged in flight from predator, rough trough where otter plowed through loose snow.
Rolling places: Areas of flattened vegetation up to 6′ wide, with twisted tufts of grass marked with musk and sometimes droppings. Slides on riverbanks 8″ wide, much wider with heavy use. Slides in snow 1′ wide or wider; often on flat ground, as much as 25′ long; sometimes pitted with blurred prints where otter has given itself a push for momentum.
Trail: Meandering, about 8″ wide, between neighboring bodies of water or other favored spots, such as rolling areas or slides. Trail may show sidling walk.
Tracks: 3¼″ wide or more; often show only heel pad and claws; toes fan out widely, but webbing rarely prints, except in mud. Running stride 1–2′.

Breeding
Mates in spring after birth of litter in April or May; delayed implantation; 1–4 young born blind, fully furred in nest of sticks in bank burrow; weaned at 4 months, disperse at 8. Male, evicted while young are small, returns to help care for them when half grown.

Habitat
Primarily along rivers, ponds, and lakes in wooded areas, but will roam far from water.

Range
Alaska and most of Canada south to N. California and N. Utah; in the East, from Newfoundland south to Florida; extirpated from most areas of Midwest.

Comments
The River Otter is normally active by day. Well adapted to its aquatic life, it has a streamlined body, rudderlike tail, and ears and nostrils valved to keep out water. It swims rapidly both underwater and on the surface, moving like a flexible torpedo, either forward or backward, with astonishing grace and power. To observe its surroundings, it raises its head high and treads water. It can remain submerged for several minutes. Also at ease on land, the River Otter runs fairly well, although not as nimbly as the Mink. Its permanent den is often dug into banks, with underwater and exposed entrances, and contains a nest of sticks, grass, reeds, and leaves. It also uses resting places under roots or overhangs, in hollow logs,

burrows of other animals, or Beaver lodges, which if heavily used may also contain a nest. Feeding mainly on fish, often caught in a quick broadside snap, it also eats small mammals, such as mice and terrestrial invertebrates.

Brush Rabbit
Sylvilagus bachmani
349

11⅛–14¾″ (28–37.5 cm) long. Small. Reddish brown mottled with black; lighter in winter but still mottled. Short legs. Small tail. Short dark ears.

Sign
Close-cropped feeding sites; a maze of runways.

Breeding
Breeds February through August; about 5 litters per year of 1–7 offspring (averaging 3). Before leaving nest, mother covers it with blanket of grass. Young mature in 4–5 months.

Habitat
Thick brushy areas, especially where brush has been cut.

Range
West Coast from NW. Oregon to Baja California.

Comments
While the Brush Rabbit is primarily nocturnal, its young are often active by day. It does not dig burrows and rarely retreats into the burrow of another animal, even when pursued, but may climb into low brush to escape.

Snowshoe Hare
Lepus americanus
350

15–20½″ (38.2–52 cm) long. In summer, dark brown, with tail dark above and dusky to white below; in winter, white, sometimes mottled with brown (stays brown all year in W. Washington and Oregon). Moderately long ears black-tipped. Large hind feet with soles well furred, especially in winter.

Sign
In snow, trails packed down as much as 1′.
Tracks: Hindprints wider than other hares in snow, due to snowshoe effect of widely spread toes.

Breeding
2–3 litters per year of 1–6 young (averaging 3).

Habitat
Forests.

Range
Alaska and most of Canada south to N. California, N. New Mexico, N. Minnesota, N. Michigan, N. New Jersey, and south through the Alleghenies.

Comments
The molt by which this hare changes coats is governed by lengthening or shortening periods of daylight. As daylight diminishes in autumn, the hare begins to grow a white-tipped winter coat, at first patchy—excellent camouflage against patchy snow—and by the time large expanses of ground are

blanketed, the hare has turned white to match. When
daylight lengthens in spring, the winter coat is gradually shed
and replaced with brown.

Yellow-bellied Marmot
Marmota flaviventris
351

18½–27⅝″ (47–70 cm) long. Heavy bodied. Yellowish
brown, with yellowish belly. Feet light to dark brown.
Whitish spots between eyes. Buff patches below ear to
shoulders. Tail bushy.

Sign
In open areas burrow entrances 8–9″ wide, with mounds or
fans of packed earth.

Breeding
A litter of about 5 born March–April.

Habitat
Rocky situations; talus slopes; valleys and foothills to 11,000′
elevations.

Range
British Columbia and S. Alberta south through E. California,
west to Colorado and N. New Mexico, north to Montana.

Comments
It lives in a den in a hillside, under a rockpile, in a crevice or
rock shelter; if alarmed, the Yellow-bellied returns to its den
and often chirps or whistles from its position of safety. It feeds
entirely on many kinds of green vegetation.

Hoary Marmot
Marmota caligata
352

17¾–32¼″ (45–82 cm) long. Large. Silver-gray above, with
brownish rump, whitish belly. Distinctive black and whitish
markings on head and shoulders: nose and large patch between
eyes whitish; patches on forehead around eyes and ears black;
and often band behind nose black. Tail large, reddish brown,
bushy. Ears small. Feet black or very dark brown; forefeet may
have white spots.

Sign
Large burrows 9–15″ wide with fans or mounds of dirt.

Breeding
Mating occurs soon after emergence from hibernation; 4–5
young born about a month later.

Habitat
Most often talus slopes in mountains.

Range
Alaska to Yukon south to Washington. N. Idaho,
W. Montana.

Comments
This marmot feeds almost entirely on grasses and many other
kinds of green plants and may chase others from feeding
grounds it considers its own. In late summer, it puts on a
great deal of fat, which sustains it through hibernation. The

silvery fur is good camouflage in its rocky habitat. Its shrill alarm whistle, louder than that of the other marmots and similar to a man's, accounts for the nickname "Whistler."

Raccoon
Procyon lotor
353

23¾–37⅜" (60.3–95 cm) long. Reddish brown above, with much black; grayish below. Distinguished by a bushy tail with 4–6 alternating black and brown or brownish-gray rings and a black mask outlined in white. Ears relatively small.

Sign
Along shores, streams, or ponds, crayfish leavings; in cornfields, broken stalks, shredded husks, scattered kernels, and gnawed cob ends.
Den: Usually in a hollow tree, which may have scat accumulated about its base and trunk scratched or bark torn.
Tracks: Hindprint 3¼–4¼" long, much longer than wide; resembles a miniature human footprint with abnormally long toes. Foreprint much shorter, 3", almost as wide as long; claws show on all 5 toes. Tracks are large for animal's size because Racoon is flat-footed, like bears and men. Stride 6–20", averaging 14". When walking, left hind foot is almost beside right forefoot. When running, makes many short, lumbering bounds, bringing hind feet down ahead of forefeet in a pattern like oversize squirrel tracks.

Breeding
Though Raccoons are sedentary, males travel miles in search of mates. Female accepts only 1 male per season, usually in February in the North, December in the South. He remains in her den a week or more, then seeks another mate. Lethargic during pregnancy, the female prefers to make a leaf nest in large hollow trees but may also use such protected places as culverts, caves, rock clefts, Woodchuck dens, or under wind-thrown trees. Litter of 1–7 young, average 4–5, born April–May, weighing about 2 oz at birth, open eyes at about 3 weeks, clamber about den mouth at 7–8 weeks, are weaned by late summer.

Habitat
Various, but most common along wooded streams.

Range
Southern edge of southern provinces of Canada; most of United States except for portions of the Rocky Mountain states, central Nevada, and Utah.

Comments
Native only to the Americas, the Raccoon is nocturnal and solitary except when breeding or caring for its young. Although territories overlap, when 2 meet, they growl, lower their heads, bare their teeth, and flatten their ears; the fur on the backs of their necks and shoulders stands on end, generally with the result that both back off. During particularly cold spells, the Raccoon may sleep for several days at a time but does not hibernate. Its vocalizations are varied, including

purrs, whimpers, snarls, growls, hisses, screams, and whinnies. Omnivorous, it eats grapes, nuts, insects, voles, other small mammals, birds' eggs, and nestlings.

Ringtail
Bassariscus astutus
354

24½–31⅞″ (61.6–81.1 cm) long. Yellowish gray above; whitish buff below. Body catlike; face somewhat foxlike. Very long, bushy tail with 14–16 bands, alternately black and white, ending with black at tip; black bands do not meet on underside. Relatively large ears and eyes. White or pale eye ring. 5 toes on each foot; claws partially retractile.

Sign
Tree holes, usually small, with a gnawed rim.
Den: In cliffs, between·or under rocks, and in hollow trees, stumps, and logs.
Tracks: Unlike its relatives, the Ringtail leaves no long heel prints. Prints 1–2¾″ long, 2″ wide, catlike, with no noticeable differences between fore- and hindprints. 5 toes on each foot, with no claws showing. Because habitat is usually dry and often rocky, tracks are not easily found.

Breeding
In Texas, mates early April; litter of 2–4 young born late May–early June, sometimes in a nest. After 3–4 weeks, male joins mate in bringing food to den for offspring.

Habitat
Various; most common in rocky situations, such as jumbles of boulders, canyons, talus slopes, rock piles; less common in wooded areas with hollow trees; sometimes about buildings.

Range
SW. Oregon, California, S. Nevada, southern two thirds of Utah, W. Colorado, and S. Kansas south through Arizona, New Mexico, Oklahoma, and Texas.

Comments
In a narrow den often padded with moss, grass, or leaves, the Ringtail sleeps by day. By night the Ringtail ambushes its prey, then pounces, forcing it down with its fore paws and delivering a fatal bite to the neck. It generally begins by devouring the head of its victim.

Porcupine
Erethizon dorsatum
355

25½–36½″ (64.8–93 cm) long. Large chunky body with high-arching back, short legs. Long guard hairs in front half of body; yellowish in the West. Quills on rump and tail. Feet have unique soles with small, pebbly-textured fleshy knobs and long curved claws; 4 toes on forefeet, 5 toes on hind feet.

Sign
Large irregular patches of bark stripped from tree trunks and limbs with neatly gnawed edges, plentiful tooth marks.
Tracks: Distinctive; toe in; pebbled knobs on soles leave stippled impression, long claws mark far ahead of oval main

prints; foreprint, including claw marks, about 2½" long,
hindprint well over 3" long, usually but not always printing
ahead of foreprint. Stride is short and waddling, with prints
5–6" apart; straddle up to 9" wide. In snow, feet may drag
or shuffle, connecting prints. Trail occasionally blurred, as if
swept by a small broom when belly brushes ground and stiff
heavy tail swishes from side to side in waddling walk.

Breeding
Mates mainly in October and November when it is most
vocal, giving a variety of squeaks, groans, and grunts. Mating
occurs in the same fashion as in other mammals, but not until
the female is sufficiently aroused that she relaxes her quills
before raising her tail over her back and presenting herself.
After a gestation period of nearly 7 months—an unusually
long period for a small mammal—the single young is born in
May or June.

Habitat
Conifer forests and associated brush and deciduous woods.

Range
Most of Canada and western United States; in the East, south
to New England, New York, and most of Pennsylvania,
northern half of Michigan, and Wisconsin.

Comments
The solitary Porcupine is active year-round, though in bitter
cold it may den up in a hole in a rocky bluff, sometimes with
other Porcupines in the area. Primarily nocturnal, it may also
rest by day in a hollow tree or log, underground burrow, or
treetop, for it is an excellent if slow and deliberate climber.
On the ground, it has an unhurried, waddling walk, relying
on its quills for protection against predators that can move
more swiftly, though it prefers to retreat or ascend a tree
rather than confront an enemy. On its body there are about
30,000 quills, which are modified hairs solid at tip and base,
hollow for most of the shaft, and loosely attached to a sheet of
voluntary muscles beneath the skin. While a porcupine cannot
throw its quills at an enemy, when forced to fight it erects
them, lowers its head, and lashes out with its tail. If the tail
strikes the enemy, the loosely rooted quills detach easily and
are driven forcefully into the victim, whose body heat causes
the microscopic barblets on the end of the quill to expand and
become ever more firmly embedded.

Striped Skunk
Mephitis mephitis
356

20½–31½" (52.2–80 cm) long. Black with 2 broad white
stripes on back meeting in cap on head and shoulders; thin
white stripe down center of face. Bushy black tail, often with
white tip or fringe. Coloration varies from mostly black to
mostly white. Males larger than females.

Sign
Strong odor if skunk has recently sprayed. Den entrance
sometimes marked with nesting material, snagged hairs. Small

pits in ground or patches of clawed-up earth from foraging
may be skunk signs if confirmed by tracks or hair.
Tracks: Show 5 toes when clear, sometimes claws. Hindprints
1¼–2″ long, less wide, broadest at front, more flat-footed;
foreprints 1–1¾″ long, slightly wider; stride 4–6″ (because
skunk shuffles and waddles, tracks are closer than in other
mustelids, and fore- and hindprints usually do not overlap);
when running stride longer and hind feet print ahead of
forefeet. Trail undulates slightly because of waddling walk.

Breeding
Mates in late winter; in mid-May, 4–7 young born blind,
with very fine hair clearly marked with black-and-white
pattern; weaned at 6–7 weeks.

Habitat
Deserts, woodlands, grassy plains, and suburbs.

Range
Most of United States; southern tier of Canadian provinces.

Comments
Whereas most mammals have evolved coloration that blends
with their environment, the Striped Skunk is boldly colored,
advertising to potential enemies that it is not to be bothered.
Its anal glands hold about a tablespoon of a fetid, oily,
yellowish musk, enough for 5 or 6 jets of spray—though 1 is
usually enough. When threatened, it raises its tail straight up
and sprays scent 10–15′; the mist may reach 3 times as far,
and the smell may carry a mile. Fluid in the eyes causes
intense pain and fleeting loss of vision.

Coati
Nasua nasua
357

33⅜–52¾″ (85–134 cm) long. Grayish brown. Long, thin,
somewhat indistinctly banded tail (6–7 bands). Long, pointed
snout; white toward tip and around eye, sometimes with black
or dark brown patches on upper part. Ears small; dark feet.
Male twice as large as female.

Sign
Tracks: 3″ long, 2″ wide, hind- and foreprints; all with 5 toes;
claws show on foreprints only. Because not quite as fully
plantigrade as the Raccoon, less of hind heel pad registers, and
prints are shorter.

Breeding
Mates January–March; 4–6 young, with coats darker than
adults, born in maternity den in rocky niche or similar shelter
in spring, after gestation of about 77 days.

Habitat
Mountain forests, usually near water; also rocky, wooded
canyons.

Range
Southeastern quarter of Arizona, SW. New Mexico, Big Bend
and Brownsville areas of S. Texas. Abundant in Huachuca,
Patagonia, and Tumacacori mountains of SE. Arizona.

Comments
More active by day and more gregarious than other members
of the raccoon family, Coatis are fairly conspicuous, as they
travel about in troupes of 4–25, usually females and their
young. They hold their long tails high and nearly erect,
except for the curled tip, and their young engage in constant
noisy play, chasing each other up and down trees. As a social
animal, the Coati is much more vocal than the solitary
Raccoon, uttering a variety of snorts, grunts, screams, whines,
and chatters. It spends its days foraging for food.

Wolverine
Gulo gulo
358

31½–44¼" (80–112.5 cm) long. Bulky, somewhat bearlike.
Dark brown, with broad yellowish bands from shoulders back
over hips and meeting at base of tail; light patches in front of
ears. Males larger than females.

Sign
Tracks: If perfect, all 5 toes and semiretractile claws print;
small toe often does not print. Foreprint 4½–7" long, varying
with size of animal or condition of snow, and about as wide;
heel pad often showing 2 lobes, a wide lobe in front of smaller
round lobe, which does not always register; hindprint similar
to foreprint; stride extremely variable; straddle 7–8".

Breeding
Mates April–September; implantation delayed till January;
2–5 young born early spring in some protected area, such as
a thicket or a rock crevice; remain with mother 2 years.

Habitat
Forests; tundras.

Range
Northern Canada south in West to NW. Washington. Spotty
distribution in southeastern United States.

Comments
Perhaps the most powerful mammal for its size, the ferocious
Wolverine is capable of driving even a bear or Cougar from its
kill. It prefers carrion but eats anything it can kill or find,
including Moose or Elk slowed down in heavy snow, Beavers,
deer, Porcupines, birds, squirrels, eggs, roots, and berries. It
trails Caribou herds, eating the remains of wolf kills; follows
trap lines, eating bait, trapped animals, and cached food; and
raids cabins, marking everything it cannot eat with musk and
sometimes urine and droppings. The Wolverine was once
popularly called the "Glutton," but its voracious appetite
may be an adaptation for survival where food is often scarce.

Black Bear
Ursus americanus
359

4½–6¼' (137–188 cm) long. Black to cinnamon with white
blaze on chest. A "blue" phase occurs near Yukatat Bay,
Alaska; and individuals are nearly white on Gribble Island,
Alaska. Snout tan or grizzled; in profile straight or slightly
convex. Males much larger than females.

Sign

Feeding signs are common: logs or stones turned over for insects; decayed stumps or logs torn apart for grubs; ground pawed up for roots; anthills or rodent burrows excavated; berry patches torn up; fruit-tree branches broken; rejected bits of carrion or large prey, such as pieces of skin, often with head or feet attached.

"Bear Trees": Scarred with tooth marks, often as high as a bear can reach when standing on its hind legs; also higher, longer claw slashes, usually diagonal but sometimes vertical or horizontal. In spring, furrowed or shaggy-barked trees used repeatedly and by several bears as shedding posts—to rub away loose hair and relieve itching—show rub marks and snagged hair.

Trails: Those used by generations of bears are well worn, undulating, and marked with depressions.

Tracks: Broad footprints 4″ long, 5″ wide, turning in slightly at the front and showing 5 toes on fore and hind feet. Hindprints 7–9″ long, 5″ wide. Individually, prints (especially hindprints) look as if made by a flat-footed man in moccasins, except that large toe is outermost, smallest toe innermost and occasionally fails to register. In soft earth or mud, claw indentations usually visible just in front of toe marks. Bears have a shuffling walk; hind and front tracks are paired, with hind track several inches before front track on same side. Stride about 1′ long. Sometimes when walking slowly, hind feet either partially or completely overlap foreprints; when running, hind feet brought down well ahead, with gaps of 3′ or more between complete sets of tracks.

Breeding

Mates June–early July; 1 litter of 1–5 (usually twins or triplets) born January–early February, generally every other year.

Habitat

In the West, forests and wooded mountains seldom higher than 7000′ (2100 m).

Range

Most of Canada, Alaska, south on West Coast through N. California, in Rocky Mountain states to Mexico, N. Minnesota, Wisconsin, and Michigan; in New England, New York, and Pennsylvania south through Appalachians; in Southeast, most of Florida, and S. Louisiana.

Comments

This uniquely American bear, although primarily nocturnal, may be seen at any time, day or night, ranging in a home area of 8–10 square miles, sometimes as many as 15. It is solitary except briefly during mating season and when congregating to feed at dumps. Its walk is clumsy, but in its bounding trot it attains surprising speed, with bursts up to 30 mph. A powerful swimmer, it also climbs trees, either for protection or food. Though classed as a carnivore, most of its diet consists of vegetation, including twigs, buds, leaves, nuts, roots, various fruit, corn, berries, and newly sprouted plants. In spring, the bear peels off tree bark to get at the inner, or cambium, layer; it tears apart rotting logs for grubs, beetles, crickets, and ants. Small to medium-size mammals or other vertebrates are also eaten. A good fisherman, the Black Bear often wades in streams or lakes, snagging fish with its jaws or pinning them with a paw. It rips open bee trees to feast on honey, honeycomb, bees, and larvae. In the fall, the bear puts on a good supply of fat, then holes up for the winter in a sheltered place, such as a cave, crevice, hollow tree or log, or the roots of a fallen tree. Bears are often problems around open dumps, becoming dangerous as they lose their fear of man. Occasionally people have been killed by them.

Grizzly Bear, including Brown Bears
Ursus arctos
360

6–7′ (180–213 cm) long. Yellowish brown to black, often with white-tipped hairs, giving grizzled appearance. Hump over shoulders. Facial profile usually somewhat concave.

Sign
Shallowly dug depression and a high, loose mound of branches, earth, or natural debris heaped over it conceal a cache of carrion or a kill. Beware of this sign, for a bear will not be far away. Other signs include overturned rocks, torn-up berry patches, raggedly rooted, round, torn logs, girdled, bark-stripped, clawed, and bitten "bear trees" (marks higher than those made by Black Bears, with largest tooth marks higher than a man's head and claw slashes perhaps twice as high). Hair tufts on trees, which may be polished from rubbing over several seasons. Large, gaping pits indicate that Grizzlies have dug for rodents. A wide, deep snowslide may be made by a Grizzly sliding downhill on its haunches.
Bed: Usually in thickets, oval depression about 1′ deep, 3′ wide, 4′ long, matted with leaves or needles and sometimes small boughs.
Trail: Trampled in tall grass, may undulate, and is marked by deep depressions.
Tracks: Shaped and placed like those of Black Bear but larger and with different claw marks; the long, relatively straight fore claws print farther ahead of toe pads, and hind claws register only occasionally. Hindprint of a large Grizzly may be 10–12″ long and 7–8″ wide in the front; foreprint often as wide, about half as long. In soft mud, tracks may be even larger. Even on hard ground, Alaskan Brown Bears often leave bigger prints, with hind tracks more than 16″ long, 10½″ wide, and sunk 2″ deep in hard sand. Stride averages 2′, may be 8–9′ during a bounding run.

Breeding
Mates late June–early July; 1 litter of 1–4, average 2, born January–March every other year. Young are exceptionally small, the size of rats, and weigh only 1 lb.

Habitat
Semiopen country usually in mountainous areas.

Range
Alaska, Yukon, and Mackenzie District of Northwest Territories south through British Columbia and W. Alberta to Idaho, Montana, and Wyoming.

Comments
Primarily nocturnal, the great, shaggy Grizzly has a low, clumsy walk, swinging its head back and forth, but when necessary it can lope as fast as a horse. Grizzly cubs can climb, though not as nimbly as Black Bear cubs, but lose the ability during their first year. In winter, Grizzlies put on a layer of fat, as much as 400 lbs, and become lethargic. They den up in a protected spot, such as a cave, crevice, hollow tree, or a hollow dug out under a rock, returning year after year to a good den. Not being true hibernators, they can be awakened easily. Omnivorous, they feed on many kinds of plants, including roots or sprouts, fungi, berries, fish, insects, large and small mammals, and carrion. When salmon migrate upstream to spawn, these normally solitary bears congregate along rivers, and vicious fights may erupt among them. More often, they establish dominance through size and threats, spacing themselves out, with the largest, most aggressive individuals taking the choicest stations. The Grizzly is adept at catching fish with a swift snap of its huge jaws. Occasionally it will pin a fish underwater with its fore paws, then thrust its head underwater to clasp the catch in its teeth. It digs insects from rotting logs and small mammals from their burrows, sometimes tearing up much ground in the process. It caches the remains of larger mammals, such as Elk, Moose, Mountain Goats, sheep, or livestock, returning to the cache until all meat is consumed. While it normally avoids man, it is the most unpredictable and dangerous of all bears.

Lynx
Felis lynx
361

29⅛–41⅞″ (74–107 cm) long. Buff or tawny with mixed blackish hairs; underparts cinnamon-brownish. Short tail tipped with black. Long black ear tufts. Large, pale cheek ruffs, whitish with black barring, forming a double-pointed beard at throat. Feet very large and well furred. Males larger than females.

Sign
Scratching posts and kill caches resemble Bobcat's. It creates scent posts by urinating on trees and stumps.
Tracks: Foreprint 3–4¼″ long, almost as wide; hindprint slightly smaller; both with 4 toes, no claws showing. Because of well-furred paws, prints are much larger and rounder than Bobcat's and especially large when toe pads spread and blur in powdery snow. Straddle usually less than 7″, almost as narrow as Bobcat's. Normally short stride 14–16″, but may have long gaps, as Lynx occasionally leaps as if practicing pounce.

Breeding
Mates mid-March–early April; usually 1 litter of 2 young born May–July.

Habitat
Deep forest.

Range
Much of Canada and Alaska south into much of Washington, N. Oregon, N. Idaho, and extreme NW. Montana. Also Rocky Mountain areas of Wyoming and N. Colorado. In the East, northern New England and extreme N. New York; in the Midwest, N. Michigan and N. Wisconsin.

Comments
By day the Lynx rests under a ledge, the roots of a fallen tree, or a low branch. It frequently, and expertly, climbs trees and sometimes rests in them, waiting to leap down on passing prey. The long ear tufts serve as sensitive antennae, enhancing hearing. Large, thickly furred feet permit silent stalking and speed through soft snow, in which some prey may flounder, though not the well-named Snowshoe Hare, the Lynx's chief prey. Big feet also help make the Lynx a powerful swimmer. Its populations are characteristically cyclic, peaking about every 9–10 years, paralleling that of the Snowshoe Hare.

Bobcat
Felis rufus
362

28–49⅜″ (71–125 cm) long. Tawny (grayer in winter), with indistinct black spotting. Short, stubby tail with 2 or 3 black bars and black tip above; pale or white below. Upper legs have dark or black horizontal bars. Face has thin, often broken black lines radiating onto broad cheek ruff. Ears slightly tufted. Males larger than females.

Sign
Scent posts, established by urinating, visible only on snow and identifiable only by tracks; tree trunks used as scratching posts, with low claw marks; a cache covered somewhat haphazardly and scantily with ground litter.

Tracks: Fore- and hindprints about same size, 2″ long, slightly longer than wide, with 4 toes, no claw marks. If clearly outlined, heel pad distinguishes from canine print: dog's or Coyote's is lobed only at rear; Bobcat's is lobed at rear and concave at front, giving print scalloped front and rear edges. Trail very narrow, sometimes as if made by a 2-legged animal, because hind feet are set on, close to, or overlapping foreprints; 9–13″ between prints. This manner of walking may be an adaptation to stalking: hunting as it travels, cat can see where to place its forefeet noiselessly, then brings down hind feet on same spots.

Breeding
Males are sexually active all year, but most females are in heat in February or March. Mates in spring. Litter of 1–7 young, usually 2–3, born late April–early May. Some southern populations produce a second litter.

Habitat
Primarily scrubby country, broken forests, but adapts to swamps, farmlands, and arid lands if rocky or brushy.

Range
Spottily distributed from coast to coast from southern Canada into Mexico. Probably most plentiful in Far West, from Idaho, Utah, and Nevada to Pacific and from Washington to Baja California. Scarce or absent in most of central and lower Midwest.

Comments
Found only in North America, where it is the most common wild cat, the Bobcat gets its common name from its stubby, or "bobbed," tail. It "lies up" by day in a rock cleft, thicket, or other hiding place. The Bobcat is an expert climber. Sometimes it rests on a boulder or a low tree branch, waiting to pounce on small game that passes; its mottled fur provides excellent camouflage. If hard pressed, it will swim. It uses the same hunting pathways repeatedly to prey mostly on the Snowshoe Hare and cottontail rabbit but also eats mice, squirrels, Porcupines, and cave bats.

Mountain Lion
Felis concolor
363

59⅛–108″ (150–274 cm) long. Yellowish to tawny above; white overlaid with buff below. Unspotted. Long tail with black tip. Backs of ears and 2 whisker patches on upper lip dark. Head fairly small; ears small and rounded; feet large. Young buff with black spots.

Sign
Scratches or gashes on trees used as scratching posts. Remains of a kill often loosely covered with branches, leaves, and litter, making a conspicuous cache, to which the cat may return. Tracks: Prints quite round, usually with all 4 lower toes showing but no claw marks, as claws are retracted. Foreprint 3¼–4″ long; hindprint slightly smaller. Lobed heel pad has single scalloped edge at front, double scalloped edge at rear. Tracks usually in a fairly straight line, staggered in pairs, with hind foot track close to or overlapping forefoot track but seldom registering precisely within it. Straddle 8–10″. Longer gaps indicate bounding, when all feet come down close together. In snow, prints slightly larger, sometimes blurred by thicker winter fur, and elongated by foot drag marks; in deep snow, tail may drag and leave trace between prints.

Breeding
No fixed mating season; 1–6 young usually born midsummer in a maternity den lined with moss or vegetation in rock shelters, crevices, rock piles, caves, or other protected place.

Habitat
Originally varied, now generally mountainous areas. Adaptable to hilly northern forests; mountainous, semiarid terrain; subtropical and tropical forests and swamps.

Range
British Columbia and S. Alberta south through W. Wyoming to California and W. Texas. Also S. Texas, Louisiana, S. Alabama, Tennessee, and peninsular Florida.

Comments
The most widely distributed cat in the Americas, the
Mountain Lion is a solitary, strongly territorial hunting
species that requires isolated or undisturbed game-rich
wilderness; it has therefore declined or become extinct in
much of the habitat where it once thrived. Unlike most cats,
it may be active by day in undisturbed areas. A good climber
and excellent jumper (it can leap more than 20'), it swims
only when necessary. It feeds primarily on large mammals,
preferring deer, but also eats Coyotes, Porcupines, Beaver,
mice, marmots, hares, Raccoons, birds, and occasionally
grasshoppers. Sometimes it waits for passing game but more
often travels widely after prey; a male may cover up to 25
miles in a night.

Red Fox
Vulpes vulpes
364, 365, 367

35⅜–40⅜" (90–103 cm) long. Small, doglike. Rusty reddish
above; white underparts, chin, and throat. Long, bushy tail
with white tip. Prominent pointed ears. Back of ear, lower
legs, feet black. Elliptical pupils. Color variations include a
black phase (almost completely black), a silver phase (black
with silver-tipped hairs), a cross phase (reddish brown with a
dark cross across shoulders), and intermediate phases, all with
white-tipped tail.

Sign
Den: Maternity den usually in sparse ground cover; commonly
enlarged den of marmot or Badger on slight rise, providing
view of all approaches, but also in stream bank, slope, or rock
pile; less often in hollow tree or log. Typical earthen mound
has main entrance up to 1' wide, slightly higher, with littered
fan or mound of packed earth and 1–3 less conspicuous
smaller escape holes. Den well marked with excavated earth,
cache mounds where food is buried, holes where food has been
dug up, and scraps of bones and feathers. Dens established
shortly after mating (usually late January or February),
abandoned by late August when families disperse.
Tracks: Similar to those of a small dog. Foreprint about 2¼"
long, hindprint slightly smaller, narrower, more pointed.
Often blurred, especially in winter, with lobes and toes less
distinctly outlined than those of Gray Fox, as Red Fox's feet
are more heavily haired. In heavy snow, tail may brush out
tracks.

Breeding
Mates January–early March. After 51–53 days gestation,
1–10 kits, average 4–8, born March–May in maternity den.
When about 1 month old, they play above ground and feed on
what is brought them by their parents.

Habitat
Varied: mixed cultivated and wooded areas, brushlands.

Range
Most of Canada and United States except for much of West
Coast: Southwest (S. California, N. Nevada, Arizona);

S. Alberta and SW. Saskatchewan to SW. Oklahoma;
NW. Texas and Southeast (coastal North Carolina to
peninsular Florida).

Comments
Even when fairly common, the Red Fox may be difficult to
observe, as it is shy, nervous, and primarily nocturnal.
Omnivorous, it eats whatever is available, feeding heavily on
vegetation in summer and on birds and mammals in winter.
Invertebrates, such as insects, compose about one fourth of its
diet. Food not consumed at once is cached under snow, leaves,
or soft dirt. In winter, adult foxes rarely den up. In the open,
they curl up into a ball, wrapping bushy tail about nose and
foot pads and at times may be completely blanketed with
snow.

Gray Fox
Urocyon cinereoargenteus
366

31½–44¼″ (80–113 cm) long. Grizzled gray above, reddish
below and on back of head; throat white. Tail with black
"mane" on top and black tip; feet rusty-colored. Prominent
ears.

Sign
Tree and scent posts: Marked with urine, noticeable on snow
by spattered urine stains and melting.
Caches: Heaped or loosened dirt, moss, or turf, frequently
paler than surrounding ground; dug-up cache holes are
shallow and wide, since foxes seldom bury very small prey
except near a den in whelping season.
Den: Entrance size varies considerably, as most dens are in
natural cavities, with entrance occasionally marked by snagged
hair or a few telltale bone scraps; several auxiliary or escape
dens nearby. Dens are in rare instances conspicuously marked
with mounds like those of the Red Fox.
Tracks: Similar to those of a small dog. Also similar to Red
Fox's, but often smaller with larger toes and more sharply
defined because of less hair around pads. Foreprint about 1½″
long; hindprint as long, slightly narrower; 4 toes with claws.
On fairly hard ground, hind heel pad leaves only a round dot
if side portions fail to print. A fox digs in when running,
leaving claw marks even in hard ground, where pads do not
print.

Breeding
Mates February–March; 2–7 young, average 3–4, born in
March or April; weaned at 3 months, hunting for themselves
at 4 months, when they weigh about 7 lbs. Male helps tend
young; however, he does not den with them.

Habitat
Varied, but associated much more with wooded and brushy
habitats than are Red Foxes.

Range
E. North and South Dakota, Nebraska, Kansas, Oklahoma,
most of Texas, New Mexico, Arizona, and California, north

through Colorado, S. Utah, S. Nevada, and W. Oregon; eastern United States.

Comments
Although primarily nocturnal, the Gray Fox is sometimes seen foraging by day in brush, thick foliage, or timber. The only American canid with true climbing ability, it occasionally forages in trees and frequently takes refuge in them, especially in leaning or thickly branched ones. Favored den sites include woodlands and among boulders on the slopes of rocky ridges. It digs if necessary but prefers to den in clefts, small caves, rock piles, slash piles, hollow logs, and hollow trees, especially oaks.

Gray Wolf
Canis lupus
368, 369, 372

39½–80⅝″ (100–205 cm) long. Usually grizzled gray but shows great variation in color, ranging from white to black. Long, bushy tail with black tip. Males larger than females.

Sign
Heavily used trails where prey is plentiful.
Scent posts: Scrapes, rocks, or stumps, all marked with urine.
Den: Entrance 20″ x 26″, with burrow 6–30′ deep, often marked by fan or mound of earth and sometimes by bones or scraps of prey brought for pups.
Rest area: Usually a grassy expanse—dry marsh, old burn, or meadow with good mousing and a wide view—where pack gathers when den is vacated; it is marked by scat, tracks, beaten trails, and sometimes diggings where food has been cached and later uncovered.
Tracks: Similar to domestic dog's but larger. Foreprint 4¼–5″ long; hindprint slightly smaller. Walking stride 30″; sometimes hind feet come down in forefeet prints.

Breeding
Mates February–March; 5–14 young, averaging 7, born April–June in den in an enlarged chamber without nesting material; at 1 month pups emerge to play near den entrance guarded by an adult.

Habitat
Open tundra; forests.

Range
Once most of North America, but now only Alaska, Canada, N. Washington, N. Idaho, N. Montana, Isle Royale National Park in Lake Superior, and NE. Minnesota.

Comments
A social animal, the Gray Wolf mates for life and lives in packs of 2–15, usually 4–7, formed primarily of family members and relatives. The strongest male is normally the leader; all members of the pack help to care for the young. The Gray Wolf possesses various whines, yelps, growls, and barks—the usual one short, harsh, and uttered in a brief series; not all wolves are capable of barking. Howls, used to keep the pack together, may be at a constant pitch, rise and

fall, or rise and break off abruptly. A communal howl is heard sometimes in early morning but most often in the evening, when it may stimulate the urge to hunt. Wolves seldom call when actually chasing prey; rather, they stop to vocalize in order to maintain contact and sometimes call to signal arrival at an ambush point toward which other pack members will then attempt to drive prey.

Coyote
Canis latrans
370, 371

41⅜–52" (105–132 cm) long. Grizzled gray or reddish gray with buff underparts; long, rusty or yellowish legs with dark vertical line on lower foreleg; bushy tail with black tip. Ears prominent.

Sign
Dens: Favored sites are riverbanks, well-drained slopes, sides of canyons, or gulches. Den mouths usually 1–2' wide, often marked by mound or fan of earth and radiating tracks.
Tracks: Similar to dog's, but in a nearly straight line; 4 toes, all with claws; foreprint about 2½" long, slightly narrower; hindprint slightly smaller; stride 13" when walking, 24" when trotting, 30" or more when running, often with much wider gaps signifying leaps. Tracks and scat most often seen where runways intersect or on a hillock or open spot, vantage points where Coyotes linger to watch for prey.

Breeding
Mates February–April; may pair for several years or life, especially when populations are low; 1–19 young born April–May; in a crevice or underground burrow.

Habitat
In the West, open plains.

Range
E. Alaska, northern and western Canada, all of western United States, east to at least New England, N. New York, New Jersey, Ohio, Tennessee, and Louisiana. Additional isolated records of Coyotes all over the East.

Comments
The best runner among the canids, the Coyote can leap 14' and cruises normally at 25–30 mph and up to 40 mph for short distances; tagged Coyotes have been known to travel great distances, up to 400 miles. The Coyote runs with its tail down, unlike wolves, which run with tail horizontal. Vocalizations are varied, but the most distinctive are given at dusk, dawn, or during the night and consist of a series of barks and yelps followed by a prolonged howl and ending with short, sharp yaps. Seldom heard in the East but common in the West, this call keeps the band alert to the locations of its members and reunites them when separated. One call usually prompts others to join in, resulting in the familiar chorus heard at night throughout the West.

Mule Deer
Odocoileus hemionus
373

3¾–6½' (116–199 cm) long. Stocky body with sturdy legs. In summer, reddish brown or yellowish brown above; in winter, grayish above. Throat patch, rump patch, inside of ears, inside of legs white; lower parts cream to tan. Large ears, 4¾–6" long (12–15 cm). Bucks' antlers branch equally, each a separate beam forking into 2 tines. Antler spread to 4' (120 cm). 2 major subspecies: Mule Deer with tail white above, tipped with black; Black-tailed Deer, with tail blackish or brown above. Males larger than females.

Sign
Browse marks, buck rubs, scrapes, beds, and droppings similar to those of White-tailed Deer.
Tracks: Fore- and hindprints 3¼" long (males), 2⅜" long (females); walking stride 22–24". Distinctive bounding gait ("stotting"), with all 4 feet coming down together, forefeet printing ahead of hind feet.

Breeding
Bucks are polygamous and have larger home ranges than does, but during the rutting season both bucks and does may leave their home range. Displays and threats often prevent actual conflict between bucks, but vigorous fights do occur when, with antlers enmeshed, each tries to force down the other's head. Even in such battles injuries are rare; usually the loser withdraws. But if antlers become locked, both perish through starvation. After a gestation of 6–7 months, a single fawn is produced by a once-bred doe, while the older does usually have twins. Newborns weigh about 8 lb. For their first month they are kept concealed.

Habitat
Mixed habitats, forest edges, mountains, and foothills.

Range
S. Yukon and Mackenzie south through western United States to Wisconsin and W. Texas.

Comments
These deer have large ears that move independently and almost constantly and account for the common name. Primarily active in mornings, evenings, and on moonlit nights, deer may also be active at midday. Mule Deer are primarily browsers, enjoying fresh grass and herbs when available but depending mainly on a wide variety of shrubs. Mule Deer also relish mushrooms and fruit. Mule Deer have a stiff-legged bounding gait, with back legs then front legs moving together. They are also good swimmers. Deer in mountainous areas migrate up and down seasonally to avoid heavy snows. In summer, they seldom form large herds. The usual groups consist of a doe with her fawn or a doe with twin fawns and a pair of yearlings. When does encounter each other they often fight, so family groups space themselves widely, thereby helping to ensure food and cover for all. Many bucks are solitary, but some band together before and after rutting season. Deer often "yard up," or herd, in winter.

White-tailed Deer
Odocoileus virginianus
374

4½–6¾' (134–206 cm) long. Tan or reddish brown above in summer; grayish brown in winter. Belly, throat, nose band, eye ring, and inside of ears white. Tail brown, edged with white above, often with dark stripe down center, white below. Black spots on sides of chin. Bucks' antlers with main beam forward and several unbranched tines behind; a small brow tine. Antler spread to 3' (90 cm). Does normally lack antlers. Fawns spotted.

Sign
Bed: Shallow, oval, body-size depression in leaves or snow.
"Buck rubs": Polished scars or oblong sections where bark removed from bushes, saplings, or small trees, usually close to ground; made when a buck lowers its head and rubs antlers against a tree to mark territory; trees chosen to fit antlers (for example, a rub on a tree 4–5" in diameter indicates the rub was made by a very large buck).
Raggedly browsed vegetation: Lacking upper incisors, deer rip away vegetation instead of snipping it neatly like rabbits.
Tracks: Like narrow split hearts, pointed end forward, about 2–3" long, dewclaws may print twin dots behind main prints in snow or soft mud. In shallow snow (1" deep), buck may drag its feet, leaving drag marks ahead of prints; in deeper snow, both bucks and does drag feet. Straddle 5–6" wide. Stride, when walking, 1'; when running, 6' or more, and hindprints sometimes register ahead of foreprints; when leaping, 20'.

Habitat
Farmlands, brushy areas, and woods.

Range
Southern half of southern tier of Canadian provinces; most of United States except most of California, Nevada, Utah, N. Arizona, SW. Colorado, and NW. New Mexico.

Comments
If alarmed, the White-tailed Deer raises, or "flags," its tail, exhibiting a large, bright flash of white; this "hightailing" communicates danger to other deer or helps a fawn follow its mother in flight. Although primarily nocturnal, deer may be active at any time, grazing on green plants, including aquatic ones in the summer; eating acorns, beechnuts, and other nuts and corn in the fall; and in winter, browsing on woody vegetation, including the twigs and buds of viburnum, birch, maple, and many conifers. Deer usually bed down near dawn, seeking concealing cover. They are good swimmers and graceful runners, with top speeds to 35 mph, though in flight they do not run great distances but flee to the nearest cover. When nervous, "Whitetails" snort through their noses and stamp their hooves, a telegraphic signal that alerts other deer nearby to danger. Bucks and does herd separately most of the year, but in winter gather together, or "yard up."

Bighorn Sheep
Ovis canadensis
375

Rams: 5¼–6' (160–185 cm) long. Ewes: 4¼–5¼' (128–158 cm) long. Muscular body with thick neck. Color varying from dark brown above in northern mountains to pale tan in deserts; belly, rump patch, back of legs, muzzle, and eye patch white. Short, dark brown tail. Coat shed in patches June–July. Rams have massive brown horns that curve up and back over ears, then down, around, and up past cheeks in a C shape called a "curl." A 7- or 8-year-old may have a full curl, with tips level with horn bases; a few old rams exceed a full curl, but often horns are "broomed"—broken off near tips or deliberately rubbed off on rocks when they begin to block ram's peripheral vision. Ewes' horns are short, slender, never forming more than a half curl. Horn spread to 33" (83 cm). Ewes much smaller than rams.

Sign
Bed: A depression about 4' wide, up to 1' deep, usually smelling of urine, almost always edged with droppings.
Trail: Narrow trails on mountainsides or steep slopes; may be confused with those made by deer or Mountain Goats.
Tracks: Double-lobed prints, 3–3½" long, with hindprints slightly smaller than foreprints; similar to deer's but with straighter edges—less pointed and often more splayed at front, less heart shaped. When walking downhill on soft ground, dewclaws may print 2 dots behind hoof print. Walking gait about 18"; bounding gait on level ground, 15', down steep incline, 30'.

Breeding
As the fall rutting season approaches, rams have butting contests, which increase in frequency as the season progresses. They charge each other at speeds of more than 20 mph, their foreheads crashing with a crack that can be heard for more than a mile, often prompting other rams to similar contests. Butting battles may continue as long as 20 hours. Horn size determines status; fights occur only between rams with horns of similar size. With nose elevated, head cocked to one side, and upper lip curled, rutting males follow any female in heat, stopping occasionally for butting jousts if more than one follows the same ewe. Depending on latitude, the mating season occurs between August and early January. After a gestation of 180 days, usually in spring or early summer, a single well-developed lamb is born with a soft, wooly, light-colored coat and small horn buds. It remains hidden the first week, then follows its mother about, feeding on grasses, and is weaned at 5–6 months.

Habitat
Alpine meadows and foothills near rocky cliffs.

Range
S. British Columbia, SW. Alberta, Idaho, and Montana south to SE. California, Arizona, and New Mexico.

Comments
Bighorns inhabit areas rarely disturbed by man; they are active

by day, feeding in early morning, midday, and evening, lying down and chewing their cud at other times, and retiring to bedding spots for the night. These may be used for years; other hoofed mammals in our range bed down in different spots each night. A good swimmer and an excellent rock climber and jumper, the Bighorn has hooves hard at the outer edge and spongy in the center, providing good traction even on sheer rock. Highly gregarious, it lives in herds usually of about 10 animals, including ewes, lambs, yearlings, and 2-year-olds; in winter, when rams also join the herd, there may be as many as 100 animals, all led by an old ewe. In spring, rams band together and move to separate higher summer ranges, but all Bighorns migrate between high slopes in the summer and valleys in winter. In summer, they feed mainly on grasses and sedges; in winter, on woody plants. Predators include Cougars, Golden Eagles, wolves, Coyotes, bears, Bobcats, and Lynx; but on cliffs, Bighorns easily escape all but the first 2, and the eagles only attack lambs.

Elk
Cervus elaphus
376

6¾–9¾' (203.2–297.2 cm) long. Large deer with slender legs and thick neck. Brown or tan above; darker underparts. Rump patch and tail yellowish brown. Males have dark brown mane on throat and large, many-tined antlers: 6 tines on each side when mature, with main beam up to 5' (150 cm) long. Females lack antlers, are about 25% smaller than males.

Sign
Elk mark the areas they frequent. Seedlings are stripped of bark by cows with their lower incisors or by bulls with the base of their antlers and then rubbed with the sides of chin and muzzle. These posts may serve as territorial markers, warning other Elk to keep out. Duing the rut, thrashed saplings and large shrubs; "rubs" on saplings and small trees made as the animals polish their antlers.
Wallows: Depressions dug in ground by hooves and antlers, where copious urine and feces give a strong, musky odor.
Tracks: Cloven hearts, much larger and rounder than those of White-tailed or Mule deer; somewhat smaller and rounder than those of Moose; 4–4½" long. When walking, hindprints slightly ahead of and partly overlapping foreprints; stride 30–60". When running and bounding, fore- and hindprints are separate and stride up to 14'. In snow or mud, dewclaws often print behind lobed main prints.

Breeding
During the rutting season, late August–November, peaking in October and November, adult bulls join the herd of cows. Bulls clash their racks of antlers in mating jousts, but they are seldom injured, though occasionally there is a major injury or even a death. The most polygamous deer in America and perhaps the world, bull Elk assemble harems of up to 60 cows. After a gestation of about 255–275 days, a cow leaves the herd to give birth usually to 1 calf, sometimes 2, weighing 25–40 lb. After a week the cow rejoins the herd with her

calf, which is entirely dependent on milk for 1 month but may suckle for up to 9 months.

Habitat
Variable: chiefly high, open mountain pastures in summer; lower wooded slopes, often dense woods, in winter.

Range
Vancouver Island, much of central and W. Washington, W. Oregon to NW. California; central Manitoba to south-central Colorado; central Saskatchewan to S. Manitoba. Great numbers in Colorado, Wyoming, Montana, and Washington; isolated populations in California, Nevada, Utah, Arizona, New Mexico, Oklahoma, South Dakota, Minnesota, and Michigan; very small numbers in Pennsylvania and Virginia.

Comments
The Elk is primarily nocturnal but especially active at dusk and dawn. Unlike the much smaller White-tailed Deer, which is often heard crashing through the brush, the Elk moves through the forest rapidly and almost silently. Bulls can run up to 35 mph, and both bulls and cows are strong swimmers. They feed on many kinds of plants but are primarily grazers; east of the continental divide, they feed more heavily on woody vegetation, owing to the scarcity of grasses and forbs. Lichen is also consumed. The availability of food appears to influence the time of mating, the percentage of cows that become pregnant, and the age of puberty. During the nonbreeding season, cows with their young herd separately from bulls; as they approach maturity, juvenile bulls spend less and less time with the cow-dominated herds. The larger herds occur in open areas; smaller groups are found in woods. Wapiti is the original Shawnee name for this species.

Caribou
Rangifer tarandus
377

4½–6¾′ (137–210 cm) long. Coloration variable; generally brown shaggy fur with whitish neck and mane; belly, rump, underside of tail white. Nearly white on Arctic islands; more brownish on tundra, taiga, and forest. Fawns unspotted. Large snout; short, furry ears; short, well-furred tail. Foot pads large and soft in summer, shrunken in winter; rounded hooves. Males and most females with antlers. Bulls' antlers are branched, semipalmated, and have flattened brow tines, 20–62″ (52–158 cm) long. Cows' antlers relatively small and spindly, 9–20″ (23–50 cm) long. Antler spread to 60″ (153 cm).

Sign
Deeply worn trails made during migrations. Rubs on saplings, thrashed bushes, bedding depressions similar to those of other cervids; distinguishable mainly by tracks and locale. Audible clicking sounds when long ankle tendons slide over bones. Tracks: Widely separated crescents, 5″ wide, slightly shorter, almost always followed by dewclaw marks; on thin, crusted snow, only round outlines of hooves may print; hindprints usually overlap foreprints, leaving double impressions 8″ long.

Breeding

In October and November, the polygamous bulls try to establish harems of 12–15 cows and rush about, thrashing bushes with their antlers and battling other bulls. After gestation of 7½–8 months, usually 1 calf, sometimes 2, is born mid-May–early July. It weighs about 11 lbs and is well developed, able to stand in about 30 minutes, run some distance after 90 minutes, and keep up with the herd within 24 hours. It begins to eat solid foods at 2 weeks but may continue to nurse into the winter.

Habitat

Tundra, taiga; farther south where lichens abound in coniferous forests in mountains.

Range

Alaska and much of Canada south through British Columbia to E. Washington and N. Idaho; also N. Alberta and northern two thirds of Saskatchewan and Manitoba; in the East, south to Lake Superior and east to Newfoundland.

Comments

The Caribou of North America, now considered to be the same species as the Reindeer of Europe and Asia, is among the most migratory of all mammals. These gregarious animals usually form homogeneous bands of bulls, cows with calves, or yearlings, but in late winter before the spring migration, after calving, and before the fall migration and rutting, Caribou may gather in groups of 10–100,000 of both sexes and all ages. Especially active in mornings and evenings, in summer Caribou feed on lichens, mushrooms, grasses, sedges, and many other green plants, twigs of birches and willows, and fruit; dropped antlers are avidly eaten by Caribou and rodents. In winter, lichens are the chief food, but horsetails, sedges, and willow and birth twigs are also eaten. Usually quiet, Caribou may give a loud snort and herds of snorting animals may sound like pigs. Caribou swim well, with nearly a third of their body above water; the air-filled hollow hairs of their coat give them great buoyancy. They can run at speeds of nearly 50 mph but cannot maintain such a pace for very long.

Moose
Alces alces
378

6¾–9' (206–279 cm) long. Largest deer in the world. Horse-size. Long, dark brown hair. High, humped shoulders; long, pale legs; stubby tail. Huge pendulous muzzle; large dewlap under chin; large ears. Males much larger than females, with massive palmate antlers, broadly flattened. Antler spread usually 4–5' (120–150 cm); record of 81" (206 cm).

Sign

Browse raggedly torn. Thrashed shrubs and barked trees. Wallows: Cleared depressions in ground, 4' wide, 4' long, 3–4" deep, muddy, smelling of urine, marked with tracks. During the rut bulls urinate and then roll in wallow; cows also roll in it.
Bed: A shallow depression marked by tracks and droppings.

Trail: Wider and deeper than that of smaller deer; more likely to detour around obstructions or entanglements.
Tracks: Cloven prints usually more than 5″ long; 6″ long and 4½″ wide in large bull. Lobes somewhat splayed in snow, mud, or when running. Dewclaws often print behind main prints in snow, mud, or when running, lengthening print to 10″. Stride 3½–5½′ when walking, more than 8′ when trotting or running.

Breeding
During mating season, mid-September–late October, bulls do not gather a harem but stay with one cow for about a week and then with another. Bulls thrash brush with antlers, probably to mark territory. Occasionally they battle, but generally threat displays prompt one to withdraw; if horns interlock, both may perish. After a gestation of 8 months, 1–2 calves are born, light colored but not spotted. Within a couple of weeks they can swim; at about 6 months they are weaned; and just before the birth of new calves they are driven off.

Habitat
Spruce forest, swamps, aspen and willow thickets.

Range
Most of Canada; in the West, Alaska, N. British Columbia and southeast through Rocky Mountains to NE. Utah, and NW. Colorado; in the East south to Maine, Minnesota, and Isle Royale in Lake Superior.

Comments
Moose are solitary in summer, but several may gather near streams and lakes to feed on willows and aquatic vegetation, including the leaves of water lilies. When black flies and mosquitoes torment them, Moose may nearly submerge themselves or roll in a wallow to acquire a protective coating of mud. Good swimmers, they can move at speeds of 6 mph for up to 2 hours at a time. Migrating up and down mountain slopes seasonally, they may herd in winter, packing down snow, which facilitates movement; then they browse on woody plants, including the twigs, buds, and bark of willow, balsam, aspen, dogwood, birch, Cherry Maple, and viburnum. Despite their ungainly appearance, they can run through the forest quietly at speeds up to 35 mph. Vocalizations include a bull's tremendous bellow and the cow's call, which ends in a coughlike moo-agh. A bull's antlers begin growing in April, attain full growth by August, and are shed between December and February. Moose are unpredictable and dangerous. They are normally retiring animals and avoid human contact, but cows with calves are irritable and fiercely protective, and rutting bulls occasionally have charged people, horses, cars, and locomotives.

WILDFLOWERS

From March to October, the western forests put on a brilliant display of color as thousands of wildflowers burst into bloom. Some of these, such as violets, are common and easily recognized; others are unusual, and offer the visitor a special kind of delight. In this section, you will find descriptions of some of the West's most typical and beautiful wildflowers.

Engelmann Aster
Aster engelmannii
379

Stems leafy in the middle, but not below, and branched near top, and at ends of branches, flower heads with a few white or pinkish rays.
Flowers: heads with a yellow disk about 1½–2½" (3.8–6.3 cm) wide; surrounded by about 13 rays; bracts with a strong, raised midvein, pale and stiff at base; June–September.
Leaves: 2–4" (5–10 cm) long, lanceolate, without stalks, not hairy or only lightly hairy, hairs densest on lower side.
Fruit: seedlike, hairy, with a few fine bristles at top.
Height: 1½–5' (45–150 cm).

Habitat
Open places and openings in woods.

Range
Western Canada south to Washington, NE. Nevada, and N. Colorado.

Comments
This is one of a number of tall asters; the stems straight, erect, few in a bunch, branched only near the top.

Stemless Daisy
Townsendia exscapa
380

A dwarf, tufted, nearly stemless plant that has comparatively large flower heads nestled among very narrow leaves, and many white or pinkish rays surrounding a yellow disk.
Flowers: heads 1–2" (2.5–5 cm) wide, with rays ½–¾" (1.3–2 cm) long, bracts ½–⅝" (1.3–1.5 cm) long; March–May.
Leaves: ¾–2" (2–5 cm) long, erect, densely clustered.
Fruit: seedlike, flat, lightly hairy, bearing at top rigid bristles longer than the body.
Height: 1–2" (2.5–5 cm).

Habitat
Dry open plains and barren places in open pinyon and juniper woodland.

Range
Central Canada; south through Montana and North Dakota to W. Texas; west to central and N. Arizona.

Comments
The several species of *Townsendia* are distinguished from the numerous, rather similar ones in the genus *Erigeron* by the fine slender bristles atop the fruit.

Marsh Marigold
Caltha leptosepala
381

There are several leaves at the base of each erect, leafless flowering stem, with usually only 1 white flower at tip.
Flowers: ½–1½" (1.3–3.1 cm) wide; petal-like sepals 5–12; petals absent; stamens many, pistils several; May–August.
Leaves: to 3" (7.5 cm) long, oblong, with minutely scalloped edges, on stalks either shorter than blade or much longer.
Height: 1–8" (2.5–20 cm).

Habitat
Wet places high in the mountains.

Range
Alaska to Oregon, east to Montana and N. New Mexico.

Comments
Marsh Marigolds bloom very close to receding snowbanks.

Western Pasque Flower
Anemone occidentalis
382

A hairy plant with finely divided leaves and several stems that have 1 white or cream flower at tip.
Flowers: 1¼–2″ (3.1–5 cm) wide; sepals 5–8, hairy on back, resembling petals; petals absent; stamens many; May–September.
Leaves: at base and 3 in a whorl on the stems beneath flower, 1½–3″ (3.8–7.5 cm) wide, divided into narrow segments.
Fruit: seedlike base has a hairy style that becomes a silvery plume to 1½″ (3.8 cm) long.
Height: 8–24″ (20–60 cm).

Habitat
Mountain slopes and meadows.

Range
British Columbia to the Sierra Nevada of California; east to NE. Oregon and W. Montana.

Comments
The common name Pasque refers to the Easter or Passover blooming time of other species in this genus.

Bunchberry
Cornus canadensis
383

Stems grow in extensive low patches, with 1 whorl of leaves at top and, just above, a cluster of tiny greenish flowers surrounded by 4 ovate white or pinkish bracts. The flower cluster resembles a single large flower held on a short stalk.
Flowers: bracts to 4″ (10 cm) wide; small flowers in center of head have 4 sepals and 4 petals; June–August.
Leaves: ¾–3″ (2–7.5 cm) long, narrowly ovate.
Fruit: bright red, round, berries in a tight cluster.
Height: 2–8″ (5–20 cm).

Habitat
Moist woods.

Range
Across northern North America; south near the coast and in the mountains to N. California, Idaho, and N. New Mexico.

Comments
Bunchberry makes an excellent ground cover in the moist woodland garden, and is equally attractive in flower or fruit.

Canada Violet
Viola canadensis
384

White, bilaterally symmetrical flowers hang and face outward at tips of short stalks that grow from axils of leaves.
Flowers: nearly 1″ (2.5 cm) wide, the petals almost all white, yellow at the base, 2 bent upward, purplish on backs, 3 lower ones with purple lines near base; of these, the 2 at side hairy

at base and the middle one with a short spur that projects beneath the flower; May–July.
Leaves: blades 1–3″ (2.5–7.5 cm) long, heart-shaped on slender stalks to 1′ (30 cm) long.
Height: 4–16″ (10–40 cm).

Habitat
Moist forest.

Range
From Alaska to Oregon and Arizona, eastward in the Rocky Mountains.

Comments
The yellow petal bases and the flowers growing from axils of upper leaves help distinguish this lovely violet.

Dwarf Bramble
Rubus lasiococcus
385

Trailing, thornless, freely rooting, leafy stems have short, erect flowering stems bearing 1 leaf and 1 or 2 white flowers.
Flowers: about ½″ (1.3 cm) wide; petals 5, broad; stamens many; June–August.
Leaves: 1–2½″ (2.5–6.3 cm) wide, about as long, cleft into 3 lobes, the edges toothed.
Fruit: small red raspberry.
Height: creeper, with stems to 7′ (2.1 m) long, and floral stalks 4″ (10 cm) high.

Habitat
Thickets and woods.

Range
British Columbia to N. California.

Comments
The very similar Strawberry Bramble (*R. pedatus*) has leaves that are either 5-lobed, or 3-lobed with the basal pair deeply divided. It occurs from Alaska to Oregon and Montana.

Richardson's Geranium
Geranium richardsonii
386

This plant's several stems have palmately cleft leaves on long stalks, most near the base, and bear a few white or pale pink flowers in a branched cluster.
Flowers: about 1″ (2.5 cm) wide; petals 5, ½–¾″ (1.3–2 cm) long with purplish veins, the petals hairy on upper side on at least lower half; stamens 10. Branches of flower cluster have purplish-tipped glandular hairs; June–August.
Leaves: 1½–6″ (3.8–15 cm) wide, nearly round blades cleft into 5–7 main segments, each with a few pointed lobes.
Fruit: about 1″ (2.5 cm) long, including slender, pointed center, with 5 lobes at base.
Height: 8–32″ (20–80 cm).

Habitat
Partial shade in woods, from lowlands into the mountains.

Range
SE. British Columbia; south through E. Washington and

Oregon to S. California; east to New Mexico, South Dakota, and Saskatchewan.

Comments
One of the most widespread western geraniums, this species hybridizes with others, often making identification difficult.

Western Trillium
Trillium ovatum
387

A low plant with 1 white flower on a short stalk that grows from the center of a whorl of 3 broad, ovate leaves at top of an otherwise leafless stem.
Flowers: 1½–3" (3.8–7.5 cm) wide; petals 3, ovate, becoming pink or reddish with age; February–June.
Leaves: 2–8" (5–20 cm) long, without stalks at base.
Height: 4–16" (10–40 cm).

Habitat
Along stream banks and on the floor of open or deep woods, from low to rather high elevations.

Range
British Columbia to central California; east to NW. Colorado, Montana, and Alberta.

Comments
Only one other *Trillium* species in the West has a stalk between the flower and the leaves, Klamath Trillium (*T. rivale*), of northwestern California and southwestern Oregon.

Sego Lily
Calochortus nuttallii
388

Erect, unbranched stems with a few leaves are topped by 1–4 showy, white, bell-shaped flowers in an umbel-like cluster.
Flowers: 1–2" (2.5–5 cm) wide; sepals 3, lanceolate, slightly shorter than petals; petals 3, broad, fan-shaped; yellow around the gland at base, marked with reddish brown or purple above the gland; gland circular, surrounded by a fringed membrane; May–July.
Leaves: 2–4" (5–10 cm) long, narrow, the edges rolled up.
Height: 6–18" (15–45 cm).

Habitat
Dry soil on plains, among sagebrush, and in open pine forests.

Range
E. Montana and W. North Dakota; south to E. Idaho and NW. Nebraska; across Utah and W. Colorado to N. Arizona and NW. New Mexico.

Comments
The petals of this species are occasionally magenta or tinged with lilac. This is Utah's state flower.

Washington Lily
Lilium washingtonianum
389

The several large, fragrant, trumpet-shaped flowers, delicate, waxy white or pale pink, often dotted with minute purple spots, bloom at top of a stout leafy stem.

Flowers: 3–4" (7.5–10 cm) wide, with 6 petal-like segments; June–July.
Leaves: 2–4 " (5–10 cm) long, lanceolate, scattered on lower portion of stem, in several whorls on upper part.
Height: 2–7' (60–210 cm).

Habitat
Brush or open forests.

Range
N. Oregon to the mountains of N. California and the southern Sierra Nevada.

Comments
Near Mount Shasta, in northern California, there is a race of this species called the Shasta Lily that has more narrow spaces between the petal-like segments.

Avalanche Lily
Erythronium montanum
390

1–5 showy white flowers nod at end of a stalk that grows from between 2 broadly lanceolate basal leaves.
Flowers: about 2½" (5 cm) wide; 6 petal-like segments that curve back, white except for a yellow band at base, becoming pink with age; stamens 6, protruding from center; June–September.
Leaves: 4–8" (10–20 cm) long, tapered to a distinct stalk.
Height: 6–10" (15–25 cm).

Habitat
Alpine or subalpine meadows and forests.

Range
British Columbia to N. Oregon.

Comments
This mountain species blooms just after the snow melts, often carpeting meadows with its white flowers.

Fringed Grass of Parnassus
Parnassia fimbriata
391

A white or cream, saucer-shaped flower blooms atop each of several stems, with most leaves at base.
Flowers: about 1" (2.5 cm) wide; petals 5, fringed on lower edges; a yellowish, fan-shaped structure with gland-tipped "fingers" between each of the 5 stamens; July–September.
Leaves: to 2" (5 cm) wide, all except the one at midstem with long stalks, broadly heart-shaped or kidney-shaped, with several major veins arching from notched base to tip.
Height: 6–20" (15–50 cm).

Habitat
Wet places in the mountains.

Range
Alaska to central California; east to the Rocky Mountains from New Mexico to Alberta.

Comments
Grass of Parnassus is the translation of the Latin name of a

European species, *Gramen parnassi.* The word *gramen* was used for both herbs and grasses. The 5 fan-shaped, finger-tipped staminodia, or sterile "fingers," of *Parnassia* are distinctive.

Spring Beauty
Claytonia lanceolata
392

A small, slender, delicate plant with 1 pair of succulent leaves at midstem and a loose raceme of white, pink, or rose, bowl-shaped flowers.
Flowers: ¼–¾" (6–20 mm) wide; petals 5, if pale then often with darker veins; sepals 2; stamens 5; April–July.
Leaves: ½–3½" (1.3–8.8 cm) long, narrow, lanceolate, commonly also 1 or 2 narrow leaves near base of stem, but often withered by time of flowering.
Height: 2–10" (5–25 cm).

Habitat
Moist ground, especially near snowbanks, from foothills to high mountains.

Range
British Columbia to S. California; east to the Rocky Mountains from New Mexico to Alberta.

Comments
Spring Beauty hurries to flower, barely waiting for the snow to melt. It grows from a deeply buried spherical corm.

Queen's Cup
Clintonia uniflora
393

1 (rarely 2) white, starlike flower blooms on a short leafless stalk that grows from a basal cluster of 2 or 3 oblong or elliptic, shiny leaves.
Flowers: 1–1½" (2.5–3.8 cm) wide; 6 lanceolate petal-like segments form a broad bell; May–July.
Leaves: 2½–6" (6.3–15 cm) long.
Fruit: lustrous deep blue berry ¼–½" (6–13 mm) long.
Height: 2½–6" (6.3–15 cm).

Habitat
Coniferous forests, often where moist.

Range
Alaska to N. California and inland to the southern Sierra Nevada; east to E. Oregon and W. Montana.

Comments
Generally there are several clusters of leaves in a patch, for the plant produces an extensive system of underground stems.

Northern Fairy Candelabra
Androsace septentrionalis
394

A small plant with a basal rosette of leaves and several erect stalks ending in an open umbel of small white flowers.
Flowers: corolla slightly more than ⅛" (3 mm) wide, with a broad tube and 5 roundish lobes; calyx lobes shorter than tubular part, broadly pointed; May–August.
Leaves: ½–1¼" (1.3–3.1 cm) long, lanceolate, sometimes with low, irregular teeth near tip.
Height: 1–10" (2.5–25 cm).

Habitat
Dry, rocky places.

Range
Throughout the western mountains.

Comments
These plants are often overlooked, for they are small and very slender. Their umbels of flowers resemble little star bursts.

Beautiful Sandwort
Arenaria capillaris
395

A single small, white, starlike flower blooms at the end of each of many slender, forked branches that grow on a main stalk above a leafy, matted base up to 8″ (20 cm) wide.
Flowers: petals 5, ¼–½″ (6–13 mm) wide; sepals 5, bluntly pointed with translucent edges; June–August.
Leaves: ½–2½″ (1.3–6.3 cm) long, very narrow, opposite, most on lower fourth of stem.
Fruit: capsule, with 3 styles and many seeds.
Height: 2–12″ (5–30 cm).

Habitat
From sagebrush plains to rocky mountain slopes.

Range
Alaska to N. Oregon, N. Nevada, and W. Montana.

Comments
The genus name comes from the Latin *arena,* for sand, referring to the preferred soil of many species.

Miner's Lettuce
Montia perfoliata
396

The slender stems of this succulent plant seem to grow through the middle of a single succulent, circular leaf above which is a raceme of tiny, white flowers.
Flowers: ⅛–¼″ (3–6 mm) wide; sepals 2; March–July.
Leaves: circular leaf to 2″ (5 cm) wide; several leaves at base from half to fully the height of the flowering stems, almost uniformly narrow, or with a lanceolate blade and a slender stalk.
Height: 1–14″ (2.5–35 cm).

Habitat
Loose, moist soil in shady places.

Range
British Columbia to Baja California; east to Arizona, Utah, and North and South Dakota.

Comments
The circular stem leaf is actually 2, paired side by side and grown together. Sometimes they are not grown together at all, or grown together only on one side.

Broad-leaved Montia
Montia cordifolia
397

A succulent plant with most leaves at base, but on stem is 1 pair of broadly ovate or heart-shaped leaves, and above these 3–10 white flowers in a very open raceme without bracts.

Flowers: about ½" (1.3 cm) long; petals 5; sepals 2; stamens 5; May–September.
Leaves: ¾–2½" (2–6.3 cm) wide, opposite, those at base on long stalks.
Height: 4–16" (10–40 cm).

Habitat
Wet soil near springs and streams, more common in the mountains.

Range
S. British Columbia to N. California; east to N. Utah and W. Montana.

Comments
All *Montia* species have edible, rather pleasant-tasting leaves.

Wood Nymph
Moneses uniflora
398

A little plant with 1 white or pale pink, saucer-shaped flower nodding from the top.
Flowers: ¾" (2 cm) wide; petals 5, roundish; stamens 10, with swollen bases; greenish ovary with 5 lobes; May–August.
Leaves: ½–1" (1.3–2.5 cm) long, opposite or in whorls of 3 or 4 toward base of stem, nearly round with tiny round teeth above middle.
Height: 2–6" (5–15 cm).

Habitat
Coniferous forests.

Range
Alaska to NW. California; east to the Rocky Mountain region and to the Black Hills; thence south to New Mexico.

Comments
Moneses, from the Greek words *monos* ("single") and *hesis* ("delight"), refers to the single pretty flower.

Elegant Death-camas ⊗
Zigadenus elegans
399

A plant with long, basal, grasslike leaves and cream or greenish-white, bowl-shaped flowers in a raceme or branched flower cluster.
Flowers: about ¾" (2 cm) wide; 6 broad, petal-like segments, each with a greenish, heart-shaped gland at base; flower parts attached around sides of ovary rather than at base; June–August.
Leaves: 6–12" (15–30 cm) long.
Height: 6–28" (15–70 cm).

Habitat
Mountain meadows, rocky slopes, and forests.

Range
Western Canada; south to W. Washington, E. Oregon, Arizona, New Mexico, and Texas.

Comments
Death-camases are among the most infamous western plants,

poisoning many livestock, especially sheep. Indians and early settlers were also poisoned whenever they mistook the bulbs for those of edible species, such as the Camas lily (*Camassia*). The highly poisonous camas *Z. venenosus* grows throughout most of the western United States. It has petal-like segments about ¼″ (6 mm) long, the inner 3 slightly longer and with a short stalk at the base, and stamens about as long as the segments.

Northern Inside-out Flower
Vancouveria hexandra
400

Small, pointed white flowers in open clusters on smooth stalks supported by leafless stems, and leathery, pinnately compound leaves that grow in patches.
Flowers: about ½″ (1.3 cm) long; 6 white sepals (remaining on open flower; more present earlier), sharply bent back at base, but with tips arched outward; 6 white petals shorter than sepals, also bent back. Pistil and 6 stamens form point in center of flower; May–July.
Leaves: 4–16″ (10–40 cm) long, divided 2 or 3 times into 3-lobed leaflets up to 1½″ (3.8 cm) long, nearly as broad.
Height: 6–20″ (15–50 cm).

Habitat
Shady coniferous woods.

Range
W. Washington to NW. California.

Comments
This genus has only 3 species; in mild climates they make excellent ground cover for woodland gardens. Golden Inside-out Flower (*V. chrysantha*) has yellow flowers.

White Globe Lily
Calochortus albus
401

Egg-shaped, white flowers hang in an open, branched cluster.
Flowers: about 1″ (2.5 cm) long; sepals 3, greenish white, often purplish-tinged, lanceolate; petals 3, broad, satiny white; April–June.
Leaves: those on branched stems 2–6″ (5–15 cm) long, the one at base 8–20″ (20–50 cm) long.
Height: 1–2′ (30–60 cm).

Habitat
Shaded, often rocky places, in open woods and brush.

Range
Southern two-thirds of California.

Comments
The several *Calochortus* species with egg-shaped flowers are generally called Globe Lilies, whereas those with more open flowers are known as Mariposa and Star Tulips.

Wartberry Fairybell
Disporum trachycarpum
402

This beautiful woodland plant, with stems branched in a forked manner, has 1 or 2 small, creamy white, narrowly bell-shaped flowers beneath the leaves at the ends of branches.

Flowers: ⅜–⅝" (9–15 mm) long; 6 petal-like segments; style lacks hairs; May–July.
Leaves: 1½–5" (3.8–12.5 cm) long, many, all along stem, ovate, round or indented at base, smooth on upper surface; hairs on edges stick straight out.
Fruit: round berry about ⅜" (9 mm) wide, at first yellow, becoming red.
Height: 1–2' (30–60 cm).

Habitat
Wooded areas, often near streams.

Range
British Columbia to NE. Oregon; east to E. North Dakota; south through the Rocky Mountain region to S. Arizona and W. New Mexico.

Comments
The regularly forked branches of these attractive and orderly plants bear leaves that are mostly oriented horizontally.

Broad-leaved Twayblade
Listera convallarioides
403

A little plant that has at midstem 1 pair of leaves, and above these a slender raceme of about 20 small, green, bilaterally symmetrical flowers.
Flowers: 3 sepals and 2 upper petals much alike, narrowly lanceolate, short, sharply bent backward; lip ⅜–½" (9–13 mm) long, 2 round lobes at end, widest near tip, evenly tapered and then abruptly narrowed to a stalklike base; June–August.
Leaves: ¾–3" (2–7.5 cm) long, elliptic.
Height: 2–14" (5–35 cm).

Habitat
Moist woods.

Range
Sierra Nevada and central Colorado; north to Canada; also S. Arizona.

Comments
The small green flowers attract little insects. The insect trips a "trigger," and pollen with a spot of "glue" is fired onto its body, to be carried to another flower.

Five-point Bishop's Cap
Mitella pentandra
404

A small plant with tiny, greenish flowers in slender racemes and leaves in a basal cluster.
Flowers: about ¼" (6 mm) wide; petals 5, each with a slender central rib from which project at right angles even finer strands, each tiny petal like a fine double comb with sparse, slender teeth; June–August.
Leaves: 1–3" (2.5–7.5 cm) wide, roundish, on long stalks.
Height: 4–16" (10–40 cm).

Habitat
Damp woods, stream banks, and wet meadows.

Range
Alaska to the Sierra Nevada of California; east to Colorado and Alberta.

Comments
There are several species of this dainty little plant, all in damp, shady places in the West.

Round-leaved Rein Orchid
Habenaria orbiculata
405

Between 2 broadly elliptic or round basal leaves, lying on ground, grows a single flower stalk with up to 25 white or greenish-white, bilaterally symmetrical flowers in a raceme. Flowers: upper sepal and 2 upper petals arch forward; 2 sepals at side bent back; lip narrow, ½–¾″ (1.3–2 cm) long, hanging down; slender spur ⅝–1″ (1.5–2.5 cm) long extends back, and often slightly upward, from beneath base of lip; June–August.
Leaves: 2½–6″ (6.3–15 cm) long.
Height: 8–24″ (20–60 cm).

Habitat
Moist floor of forests.

Range
N. Oregon and NW. Montana northward; east across Canada to the eastern United States.

Comments
This species has the largest flowers of all western rein orchids. Several moths feed on nectar in the spur.

Merten's Saxifrage
Saxifraga mertensiana
406

Nearly circular leaf blades with hairy stalks grow in a basal cluster around a branched flower stalk with white flowers. Flowers: nearly ¼″ (6 mm) wide; petals 5, oblong; stamens 10, with clublike stalks and pink anthers; some flowers replaced by pink bulbs; April–August.
Leaves: blades 1–4″ (2.5–10 cm) wide, lobed on the edge, the larger lobes with roundish, shallow teeth; stalks up to 4 times the length of blade; at base of stalk is a membranous sheath around stem.
Height: 4–16″ (10–40 cm).

Habitat
Wet banks or along streams in coniferous woods.

Range
Alaska to central California, central Idaho, and W. Montana.

Comments
The tiny bulbs that replace some flowers in this species can grow into new plants when they drop to the ground.

One-sided Wintergreen
Pyrola secunda
407

This plant forms low patches of shiny, bright green leaves, above which grow racemes of 6–20 whitish-green or white flowers all turned to one side.

Flowers: corolla ¼" (6 mm) long; petals 5, white; stamens 10; June–August.
Leaves: ¼–2½" (1.3–6.3 cm) long, ovate, with minutely scalloped or toothed edges.
Height: 2–8" (5–20 cm).

Habitat
Moist coniferous woods.

Range
Throughout the West.

Comments
Pyrola, from the Latin *pyrus* ("pear tree"), refers to the leaves of some species that resemble those of pears. Leaves remain green throughout the winter, giving the common name.

False Lily of the Valley
Maianthemum dilatatum
408

Grows in low patches and has slender racemes of tiny white flowers held stiffly erect just above heart-shaped leaves.
Flowers: 4 petal-like segments about ⅛" (3 mm) long; stamens 4; May–June.
Leaves: 2–4½" (5–11.3 cm) long, usually 2 on each stem.
Fruit: red berry ¼" (6 mm) wide.
Height: 6–14" 15–35 cm).

Habitat
Moist or shaded places in woods.

Range
Alaska to the North Coast Ranges of California.

Comments
The genus name comes from the Greek *maios* ("May") and *anthemon* ("flower").

False Mitrewort
Tiarella unifoliata
409

Tiny white flowers hang in loose clusters in narrow, branched racemes at tops of leafy stems.
Flowers: about ¼" (6 mm) wide, with a pale green cuplike base about ¹⁄₁₆" (1.5 mm) long, the upper calyx lobe largest; petals 5, white, hairlike, about ⅛" (3 mm) long; stamens 10, white, protruding; May–August.
Leaves: blades to 3½" (8.8 cm) wide, the lower ones, on long stalks, rather triangular, indented and toothed or divided into 3 leaflets which may be deeply cut.
Fruit: capsule that opens by a split between 2 unequal halves.
Height: 8–16" (20–40 cm).

Habitat
Moist woods, along stream banks.

Range
Alaska to central California; east to Idaho and W. Montana.

Comments
The genus name is from the Greek *tiara,* an ancient Persian headdress, which the fruit resembles.

Fringe Cups
Tellima grandiflora
410

Monument Plant
Frasera speciosa
411

False Solomon's Seal
Smilacina racemosa
412

Grows in clumps with most leaves near base, and cream or pale pink, fringed flowers blooming in several long racemes.
Flowers: about ½" (1.3 cm) wide; sepals 5, short; petals 5, white or pink, fringed across end; both are attached to the edge of cuplike base; stamens 10; April–July.
Leaves: 1–4" (2.5–10 cm) wide, roundish, hairy, shallowly lobed and scalloped, those at base on long stalks.
Height: to 32" (80 cm).

Habitat
Moist places in woods.

Range
Alaska to coastal central California; east to N. Idaho.

Comments
This is a beautiful plant of shaded woods, with slender wands of flowers arching upward or standing erect above the rich green foliage. The curious petals are at first white or cream.

A narrowly cone-shaped plant with 1 stout, tall, erect stem, large leaves in evenly spaced whorls, and clusters of 4-lobed, yellowish-green corollas in axils of upper leaves and leaflike bracts.
Flowers: 1–1½" (2.5–3.8 cm) wide; corolla with pointed lobes joined at base, spotted with purple, with 2 oblong glands in the lower central part of each lobe; stamens 4; May–August.
Leaves: at base 10–20" (25–50 cm) long, lanceolate, 3–4 in a whorl; on stem equally spaced, progressively smaller; veins of leaves parallel.
Height: 4–7' (1.2–2.1 m).

Habitat
Rich soil in woodland openings, from moderate to high elevations.

Range
E. Washington to central California; east to W. Texas, E. Wyoming, and Montana; also northern Mexico.

Comments
This tall, rather coarse herb tends to be solitary, growing singly rather than with others of its kind. Found in meadows as well as open woods, Monument Plant is grazed by both Elk and livestock.

Commonly with several leaning, leafy stems, each tipped with a branched, dense, cluster of many tiny, white flowers.
Flowers: 6 ovate petal-like segments about ⅒" (2.5 mm) long; stamens 6, slightly longer; March–July.
Leaves: 2½–8" (6.3–20 cm) long, ovate, clasping stem at base.
Fruit: reddish berries, ¼" (6 mm) long.
Height: 1–3' (30–90 cm).

Habitat
Moist woods from near sea level to moderate mountain elevations.

Range
Throughout the West.

Comments
"True" Solomon's Seal (*Polygonatum* spp.), lilies from the eastern United States, are similar in leaf arrangement, but differ in having flowers in the leaf axils.

California Corn Lily
Veratrum californicum
413

A long, branched, dense cluster of relatively small, whitish or greenish flowers top the stout, leafy stem of this tall plant.
Flowers: 6 petal-like segments ½–¾" (1.3–2 cm) long, each with a V-shaped green gland at base; June–August.
Leaves: 8–12" (20–30 cm) long, numerous, broad, ovate, plaited, without stalks, angled upward.
Height: 4–8' (1.2–2.4 m).

Habitat
Swamps and creek bottoms, wet meadows and moist forests.

Range
W. Washington to S. California; east to New Mexico, Colorado, Wyoming, and Montana.

Comments
California Corn Lily is extremely poisonous. Sheep that eat the plant in the early weeks of gestation produce lambs with deformed heads; the flowers are even poisonous to insects.

Goatsbeard
Aruncus sylvester
414

Large filmy sprays of tiny white flowers nod or arch at the top of stems of this rather tall, leafy plant.
Flowers: less than ⅛" (3 mm) wide; petals 5, white, which drop off; on some plants flowers have only stamens 15–20, on others only pistils 3–5; May–July.
Leaves: large, divided into ovate leaflets to 6" (15 cm) long, the edges with many sharp teeth.
Height: 3–7' (90–210 cm).

Habitat
Moist places in woods.

Range
Alaska to NW. California.

Comments
Both the common name and the genus name (from the Greek *aryngos* for "goat's beard") refer to the long cluster of flowers.

Poker Alumroot
Heuchera cylindrica
415

Leathery leaf blades varying from ovate to broadly heart-shaped on long stalks clustered at base of flower stalks; upper part of plant densely covered with glandular hairs, especially in the narrow, greenish-white flower cluster.

Flowers: a cream or greenish-yellow cup ¼–½" (6–13 mm) deep, with 5 round calyx lobes forming the rim, the lobes on the lower side slightly longer; petals 5 (or fewer, or none), white, shorter than calyx lobes; stamens 5; April–August.
Leaves: 1–3" (2.5–7.5 cm) wide.
Height: 6–36" (15–90 cm).

Habitat
Rocky flats, slopes, and cliffs.

Range
British Columbia to NE. California; east to N. Nevada, Wyoming, and Montana.

Comments
The dense, narrow flower cluster helps distinguish this species from several others. Alumroot species hybridize, making identification of many plants difficult.

Bedstraw
Galium boreale
416

A leafy plant with 4 leaves in each whorl on the 4-sided stems, short branches often in axils, and at ends of branches many round-topped clusters of tiny, white flowers.
Flowers: petals 4, less than ⅛" (3 mm) long, spreading from top of ovary; no sepals; June–August.
Leaves: to 2" (5 cm) long, narrow, with 3 veins.
Height: 8–32" (20–80 cm).

Habitat
Open, moist areas from sea level to high in the mountains.

Range
Alaska to N. California, Arizona, New Mexico, and Texas; also the northern plains and the eastern United States.

Comments
Most *Galium* species have inconspicuous flowers borne singly or in small clusters, but the 4 spreading corolla lobes, the attachment of flower plants above the ovary, and whorled leaves are consistent features. Sweet-scented European species were once used as mattress stuffing, giving the name Bedstraw to all species in the genus.

Baneberry
Actaea rubra
417

Usually branched, with racemes of many small, white flowers in leaf axils or at end of stem.
Flowers: sepals 3–5, quickly drop as flower opens; petals 4 or 5, spatula-shaped, ⅛" (3 mm) long, also drop; stamens many; May–July.
Leaves: few, very large, pinnately and repeatedly divided into sharply toothed leaflets, each ¾–3½" (2–8.8 cm) long.
Fruit: glistening red (or pearly white) berry ¼–½" (6–13 mm) wide.
Height: 1–3' (30–90 cm).

Habitat
Moist woods and along stream banks.

Range
Throughout the West.

Comments
The attractive berries are poisonous, but are not reported to have caused death to humans or livestock in the United States. European species have fatally poisoned children.

Beargrass
Xerophyllum tenax
418

At the top of a stout stalk that grows from a massive bunch of basal leaves bloom many tiny flowers in a dense, broad, raceme.
Flowers: flat petal-like segments about ⅜" (9 mm) long; May–August.
Leaves: basal, approximately 1–2½' (30–75 cm) long, very narrow.
Height: to 5' (1.5 m).

Habitat
Open woods and clearings.

Range
British Columbia to central California; east to Idaho and Montana.

Comments
Indians used the leaves of Beargrass to weave garments and baskets and ate the roasted rootstock.

Vanilla Leaf
Achlys triphylla
419

Pairs of low slender stalks grow in patches, 1 stalk actually a petiole, having at its tip a round leaf blade with 3 broad, fan-shaped leaflets; the other stalk ending in a narrow spike of small white flowers.
Flowers: spike 1–2" (2.5–5 cm) long; the flowers without sepals or petals but with 6–13 white stamens, the outer ones swollen toward tip; April–June.
Leaves: leaflets 2–4" (5–10 cm) long, with blunt teeth on ends, the central leaflet with 3–5 or up to 8 teeth.
Height: 10–20" (25–50 cm).

Habitat
Shady forests, especially where damp.

Range
S. British Columbia to near the coast of N. California.

Comments
When crumpled, the leaves emit a mild vanillalike fragrance. Frontier women used the leaves to freshen washed clothes.

Rattlesnake Plantain
Goodyera oblongifolia
420

A cylindrical cluster of small, pale greenish to white flowers tops a leafless stalk that rises from a rosette of dark leaves, which usually have 1 main white vein.
Flowers: ¼" (6 mm) long; upper sepal and 2 united petals form a hood over cupped lip petal; side sepals ovate, concave; sepals and petals colored alike; May–September.

Leaves: 1–3½" (2.5–8.8 cm) long, ovate to oblong; short, scalelike bracts present on stalk.
Height: to 18" (45 cm).

Habitat
Dry, mossy, or damp forests.

Range
Alaska east to Nova Scotia and south to Mexico.

Comments
The common name of this unusual plant refers to its mottled leaves, which resemble a snake's skin.

Yerba Buena
Satureja douglasii
421

Long, slender, trailing stems with 1 white or pale purplish bilaterally symmetrical flower in each upper leaf axil.
Flowers: corolla about ¼" (6 mm) long, short upper lip projecting forward, with a shallow notch at tip, longer 3-lobed lower lip bent down; stamens 4; April–October.
Leaves: ½–1" (1.3–2.5 cm) long, opposite, roundish.
Height: creeper, the erect stems to 1' (30 cm) high, trailing stems to 2' (60 cm) long.

Habitat
Shaded woods.

Range
S. British Columbia to N. Idaho; south on the western side of the Cascade Range and Sierra Nevada to Baja California.

Comments
The name Yerba Buena, Spanish for "good herb," has been applied to several kinds of mint, especially Spearmint (*Mentha spicata*), but in the West generally refers to *S. douglasii*.

Pearly Everlasting
Anaphalis margaritacea
422

Several evenly leafy woolly stems in a small patch are topped by a crowded, roundish cluster of flower heads with pearly bracts, sometimes with a dark spot at base of each outer bract.
Flowers: heads about ¼" (6 mm) long; flowers minute, on some plants with stamens only, on others only with pistils; June–September.
Leaves: to 5" (12.5 cm) long, narrowly lanceolate, underside densely hairy, top less so or even smooth and dark green.
Height: 8–36" (20–90 cm).

Habitat
Commonly in forest openings but also along roadsides and in fields, from lowlands to high in the mountains.

Range
Most of North America; south to New Mexico, S. California, Arizona, Kansas, and eastern United States.

Comments
The dried stalks with their pearly-white heads are attractive in floral arrangements.

Yarrow
Achillea millefolium
423

An aromatic plant with feathery, fernlike leaves on a tough fibrous stem, and a flattish cluster of small white flower heads at the top.
Flowers: each head with 3–5 roundish white (sometimes pinkish) rays ⅛" (3 mm) long and 10–30 disk flowers; March–October.
Leaves: to 1½" (3.8 cm) wide, blades repeatedly pinnately divided into fine segments.
Height: 12–40" (30–100 cm).

Habitat
Open areas from lowlands to timberline.

Range
Most of temperate North America.

Comments
Among this species' several common names, Milfoil and Plumajillo ("little feather") refer to the divided leaves, while Sneezeweed may derive from the irritating odor.

Nuttall's Pussytoes
Antennaria parvifolia
424

From a small, grayish basal rosette rises an erect, sparsely-leaved flower stalk with clusters of small, rayless, whitish flower heads.
Flowers: heads nearly ½" (1.3 cm) long, the translucent, scalelike bracts barely darkened at the base; July–September.
Leaves: ½–¾" (1.3–2 cm) long, equally hairy on both sides, those in rosettes lanceolate but obviously broader near the top, those on the flower stalk much narrower.
Fruit: seedlike, with 5 white bristles at top.
Height: to 6" (15 cm).

Habitat
Openings in dry forests and on plains.

Range
Western Canada to E. Washington and through the Rocky Mountains and the western plains to Arizona and New Mexico.

Comments
Some plants in this species produce seed in the usual manner, by fertilization of eggs in the ovary; others do not require fertilization.

Yerba de Selva
Whipplea modesta
425

From long, trailing, rooting stems grow many erect shoots, each tipped with a small head of white flowers.
Flowers: 4–6 petals about ⅛" (3 mm) long, spatula-shaped; twice as many stamens; April–June.
Leaves: ½–1" (1.3–2.5 cm) long, opposite, elliptic.
Height: creeper, the erect, leafy, flowering branches 4–8" (10–20 cm) high.

Habitat
In open or light woods, usually in dry and rocky areas.

Range
W. Washington to central California near the Pacific Coast.

Comments
These plants often form dense, low patches on rocky banks or in open, mixed woods of broadleaf trees and conifers.

Fendler's Waterleaf
Hydrophyllum fendleri
426

A fairly coarse plant with 1 stem that has downward-projecting hairs, a few, large, pinnately divided leaves, and white or lavender, bell-shaped flowers in a loose, branched cluster at the top or on stalks growing from leaf axils.
Flowers: ¼–⅜" (6–9 mm) wide; corolla with 5 round lobes at end; stamens 5, projecting; May–August.
Leaves: to 10" (25 cm) long, with 7–15 lanceolate segments bearing 4–8 sharp teeth on each edge; stalks long or short.
Height: 8–32" (20–80 cm).

Habitat
Moist places in brush and open areas from low to high elevations.

Range
S. British Columbia to N. California; east to New Mexico, SE. Utah, S. Wyoming, and central Idaho.

Comments
This is a common, rather plain-looking, woodland plant.

Case's Fitweed
Corydalis caseana
427

A rather soft, almost succulent, tall plant with leafy, hollow stems, large fernlike leaves, and dense racemes of 50–200 bilaterally symmetrical pinkish-white flowers.
Flowers: ¾–1" (2–2.5 cm) long, with 2 tiny sepals that drop off; petals 4, very different, pink or white, purplish at tip: uppermost, as long as the flower, curves upward at front and forms a straight spur behind; lowest forms a scoop in front; inner 2 face one another and enclose 6 stamens and 1 pistil; June–August.
Leaves: 12–20" (30–50 cm) long, triangular in outline, pinnately divided 3 times, with leaflets each ½–2" (1.3–5 cm) long, ovate.
Fruit: pod ½" (1.3 cm) long, plump, hanging.
Height: 2–7' (60–210 cm).

Habitat
Mountains, in shady moist places.

Range
NE. Oregon, Idaho, and Colorado to the central Sierra Nevada of California.

Comments
This species contains alkaloids poisonous to livestock, which particularly affect sheep, since cattle rarely graze where it grows. The pods of this and other species have elastic walls that when touched curl back and explosively eject seeds.

Indian Pipe
Monotropa uniflora
428

Waxy white plant that blackens with age; the several clustered stems are bent like a shepherd's hook at top.
Flowers: about ¾" (2 cm) long; 1 hanging at end of each stem like a narrow bell; petals 5 (4–6), separate; stamens 10; June–August.
Leaves: scales pressed against stem.
Height: 2–10" (5–25 cm).

Habitat
Deep shaded woods.

Range
NW. California to Alaska; east across the northern part of the West.

Comments
These plants were once believed to absorb all nutrients from the duff, but it is now known that they are associated with a fungus, which obtains nutrients directly from the roots of green plants. Indian Pipe, therefore, is a parasite, with the fungus as a "bridge" between it and its host.

Phantom Orchid
Eburophyton austinae
429

A waxy, white, nearly leafless plant with stems in clusters and racemes of 5–20 bilaterally symmetrical white flowers.
Flowers: sepals 3 and upper petals 2, similar, lanceolate, each ½–¾" (1.3–2 cm) long, gently curving inward and surrounding lip; lip divided into 2 parts, constricted in middle, the tip with a yellow fleck; June–August.
Leaves: reduced to sheaths on the lower part of the stem.
Height: 9–20" (22.5–50 cm).

Habitat
Occasional in dense, moist, usually coniferous woods.

Range
N. Washington to the mountains of N. California and the southern Sierra Nevada; east to Idaho.

Comments
This aptly named plant appears ghostly in the dim light of the forest floor. Since it is not green and is therefore incapable of photosynthesis, it absorbs all its nutrients from the forest duff, aided by a fungus in its roots.

Golden Pea
Thermopsis montana
430

A plant with 1 or several hollow stems, slightly or not at all hairy, and yellow flowers in long racemes in upper leaf axils.
Flowers: ¾–1" (2–2.5 cm) long; 1 broad upper petal and 2 lateral petals nearly enclosing 2 bottom petals that are joined and shaped like prow of a boat; 10 stamens, none joined together by their stalks; May–August.
Leaves: compound, with 3 broadly lanceolate leaflets, each 2–4" (5–10 cm) long; a pair of broadly ovate, leaflike stipules occur where leafstalk joins stem.
Fruit: pod 1½–3" (3.8–7.5 cm) long, slender, erect, hairy.
Height: 2–4' (60–120 cm).

Habitat
Meadows or openings in coniferous forests, in dry or moist soil.

Range
British Columbia to N. California; east to Montana and Colorado.

Comments
This genus resembles the lupines, but *Thermopsis* has only 3 leaflets on each leaf; *Lupinus* has more. Golden Peas, while handsome plants, are suspected of being poisonous. There are several western species, some quite hairy.

Bracted Lousewort
Pedicularis bracteosa
431

An erect plant with divided, rather fernlike leaves and bilaterally symmetrical, beaklike flowers in a dense raceme.
Flowers: corolla ½–¾" (1.3–2 cm) long; varies from yellow to purple, maroon, or reddish, its upper lip narrow, arched outward like the prow of an overturned canoe, the lower lip shorter, the 3 lobes projecting forward; June–August.
Leaves: 3–10" (7.5–25 cm) long, fernlike, divided into narrow leaflets with jagged teeth; upper leaves about as large as lower.
Height: to 3' (90 cm).

Habitat
Moist woods and meadows in the mountains.

Range
British Columbia to S. Oregon; east to Colorado, Utah, Montana, and Alberta.

Comments
Western louseworts vary from plants 3' (2.1 m) tall, to miniature ones only 1" (2.5 cm) high. The genus name, from the Latin *pediculus* ("little louse"), alludes to a superstition that livestock that ate these plants would suffer from an infestation of lice.

Yellow Skunk Cabbage
Lysichitum americanum
432

A spike of minute flowers surrounded by a large, conspicuous yellow or cream bract open on one side; grows on a stout stalk in a cluster of giant, erect leaves.
Flowers: bract to 8" (20 cm) long, often appearing before leaves are fully developed; tiny flowers inconspicuous; April–July, often as the snow melts.
Leaves: 1–5' (30–150 cm) long, the stalks usually much shorter than the oval blades.
Height: 12–20" (30–50 cm).

Habitat
Damp places, with or without standing water.

Range
Alaska to near the coast in central California, east to Montana.

Comments
The common name refers to the skunklike odor of the sap and
the fetid odor of the flowers, which draws flies as pollinators.

Meadow Goldenrod
Solidago canadensis
433

Tall, leafy, finely hairy stem has tiny yellow flower heads on
arching branches in a long or flat-topped cluster at top.
Flowers: each head about ⅛″ (3 mm) long, with 3 short rays;
May–September.
Leaves: 2–5″ (5–12.5 cm) long, lanceolate, finely hairy, with
3 prominent veins.
Fruit: seedlike, sparsely hairy, with many pale bristles at top.
Height: 1–5′ (30–150 cm).

Habitat
Meadows and open forest.

Range
Across Canada and throughout the United States.

Comments
This handsome species produces showy displays, usually late in
the summer. Although it and other Goldenrods are commonly
blamed for hay fever, this discomfort is usually caused by
pollen from Ragweed (*Ambrosia* spp.).

Sulfur Paintbrush
Castilleja sulphurea
434

The flower cluster of this leafy plant resembles a ragged, pale
yellow paintbrush, each calyx and the bracts beneath the
flowers brightly colored.
Flowers: tubular calyx with 4 short, pointed lobes; bilaterally
symmetrical corolla ¾–1¼″ (2–3.1 cm) long, relatively
inconspicuous, the lower lip a green bump on the lower side
well above the middle, the upper lip pale, barely extending
beyond the calyx as a short "beak"; June–September.
Leaves: 1–3″ (2.5–7.5 cm) long, lanceolate, usually not cleft
or lobed; bracts of flower cluster similar, but yellowish.
Height: 6–20″ (15–50 cm).

Habitat
Moist meadows and slopes from moderate to high elevations.

Range
S. Alberta and W. Montana to Utah, New Mexico, and
W. South Dakota.

Comments
Most Indian paintbrushes are bright red; this is one of the few
yellow ones.

Silvery Luina
Luina hypoleuca
435

A leafy plant with several stems in a clump, covered with
white wool that is densest on stems and underside of leaves.
Flowers: heads in a branched cluster at tip of each stem, dull
yellowish and rayless, nearly ⅜″ (9 cm) long, with bracts all of
the same length, side by side, barely overlapping; June–
October.

Leaves: 1–2½" (2.5–6.3 cm) long, broadly ovate.
Fruit: seedlike, with soft white bristles at top.
Height: 6–16" (15–40 cm).

Habitat
In rocky places and on cliffs.

Range
Central British Columbia to central California.

Comments
The leaves have a white underside that often contrast with the darker upper surface. This plant must have reminded the botanist who named this genus of another, *Inula,* also white and woolly, for *Luina* is an obvious anagram.

Sulphur Flower
Eriogonum umbellatum
436

Leaves at base, and on long, erect stalks bloom tiny, yellow or cream flowers in balls at ends of branches of an umbel-like cluster.
Flowers: each individual, ball-like cluster 2–4" (5–10 cm) wide, composed of numerous little cups, from which grow several flowers on very slender stalks; flowers about ¼" (6 mm) long, the 6 petal-like lobes hairy on outside; circle of bractlike leaves immediately beneath umbel; June–August.
Leaves: ½–1½" (1.3–3.8 cm) long, clustered at ends of short woody branches, on slender stalks, ovate, 2–3 times as long as wide, very hairy on lower side.
Height: 4–12" (10–30 cm).

Habitat
Dry areas from sagebrush deserts to foothills and alpine ridges.

Range
British Columbia to S. California; east to the eastern flank of the Rocky Mountains from Colorado to Montana.

Comments
Sulphur Flower is highly variable, adding to the difficulties of identification in a complex group of similar western species.

Sierra Sedum
Sedum obtusatum
437

Pale yellow flowers bloom on branched clusters atop reddish stalks that grow from dense basal rosettes of succulent, often reddish-tinged leaves.
Flowers: sepals 5, blunt; petals 5, narrow, pointed, united in their lower fourth, about ⅜" (9 mm) long, yellow at first, but fading to white or pinkish; June–July.
Leaves: ¼–1" (6–25 mm) long, broadest in upper half, rounded or slightly indented at tip; leaves on flower stalk much smaller.
Height: 1–7" (2.5–17.5 cm).

Habitat
Rocky slopes at moderate to high elevations.

Range
S. Oregon to the S. Sierra Nevada.

Comments
Sedum here refers to the tendency of many species to grow low to the ground. One of several rather similar yellow stonecrops found in the mountains of the West.

Deer Weed
Lotus scoparius
438

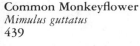

The bunched, erect, tough, green stems have small, pinnately compound leaves and 1–4 yellow flowers in clusters in the upper leaf axils.
Flowers: about ⅜" (9 mm) long; 1 broad upper petal and 2 lateral petals nearly enclosing 2 bottom petals that are joined and shaped like prow of a boat; all 5 often developing a reddish hue as they age; March–August.
Leaves: 3 oblong leaflets, each ¼–½" (6–13 mm) long.
Fruit: pod, slender, curved, with a narrow, knifelike beak and only 2 seeds.
Height: 1–3' (30–90 cm).

Habitat
Dry brushy slopes.

Range
Most of California to N. Baja California.

Comments
This is one of the many species of flowering plants that thrive after fire has ravaged chaparral-covered slopes. It vigorously persists for several years, although it is choked out of most areas by the thick brush that eventually returns. By taking advantage of the open habitat and quickly covering exposed slopes, it helps reduce erosion. Like most other members of the legume family, it has the capacity to enrich the soil with nitrogen.

Common Monkeyflower
Mimulus guttatus
439

An extremely variable, leafy plant ranging from spindly and tiny to large and bushy, with yellow bilaterally symmetrical flowers on slender stalks in upper leaf axils.
Flowers: corolla ½–1½" (1.3–3.8 cm) long, often with reddish spots near opening, 2 lobes of upper lip bent upward, the 3 lobes of lower lip bent downward; at base of lower lip is a hairy hump that almost closes the opening; March–September.
Leaves: ½–4" (1.3–10 cm) long, ovate, opposite, edges with sharp teeth.
Height: to 3' (90 cm).

Habitat
Wet places from sea level to mountains.

Range
Throughout the West.

Comments
In this large genus of several look-alikes with yellow corollas, Common Monkeyflower is distinguished by the longer upper tooth on the angular calyx.

Golden Aster
Chrysopsis villosa
440

A round plant with erect or spreading leafy stems, with yellow flower heads in branched clusters. Stem covered with rough, grayish hairs.
Flowers: heads about 1" (2.5 cm) wide, with yellow rays around yellow disk; May–October.
Leaves: lanceolate, those at midstem ½–1¼" (1.3–3.1 cm) long.
Fruit: seedlike; dingy white bristles in 2 lengths at top, the outer shorter.
Height: 8–20" (20–50 cm).

Habitat
Open plains, rocky slopes, cliffs, from low elevations into coniferous forests; often in dry places.

Range
Canada to S. California; east to Texas, Nebraska, and Wisconsin; south into Mexico.

Comments
This species and its relatives, distinguished by their hairiness, are so common in the West that they are difficult to overlook.

Golden Yarrow
Eriophyllum lanatum
441

A grayish, woolly, leafy plant with several branched stems ending in short leafless stalks and golden-yellow flower heads.
Flowers: heads 1½–2½" (3.8–6.3 cm) wide, with broadly lanceolate bracts prominently ridged on back, and 8–12 broad rays, each ½–¾" (1.3–2 cm) long, around disk; May–July.
Leaves: 1–3" (2.5–7.5 cm) long, irregularly divided into narrow lobes.
Fruit: seedlike, narrow, smooth, with a low crown of scales at top.
Height: 4–24" (10–60 cm).

Habitat
Dry thickets and dry open places.

Range
British Columbia to S. California and W. Nevada; east to NE. Oregon and W. Montana.

Comments
This common and variable species often colors banks along roads with a bright blaze of yellow in drier portions of the West.

Arrowleaf Balsam Root
Balsamorhiza sagittata
442

An almost leafless stalk with 1 large bright yellow flower head at tip grows from a basal cluster of large silvery-gray leaves covered with feltlike hairs.
Flowers: heads 4–5" (10–12.5 cm) wide, with densely woolly bracts, 8–25 rays, each 1–1½" (2.5–3.8 cm) long, and many disk flowers, each enfolded by a parchmentlike scale; May–June.
Leaves: blades to 1' (30 cm) long, on petioles about the same length.

Fruit: seedlike, no hairs or scales at tip.
Height: 8–32″ (20–80 cm).

Habitat
Open hillsides and flats in grasslands, sagebrush, or open pine forest.

Range
British Columbia south through the Sierra Nevada of California; east to W. Montana, W. South Dakota, and Colorado.

Comments
Indians prepared medicine from the roots of this species. The very similar Deltoid Balsam Root (*B. deltoidea*), is found in open places in California, western Oregon, and Washington.

Heartleaf Arnica
Arnica cordifolia
443

Stems with 2–4 pairs of heart-shaped leaves are topped by 1–3 broad yellow heads. Plants in patches.
Flowers: heads 2–3½″ (5–8.8 cm) wide; with 10–15 rays each and many tiny disk flowers; bracts of head have long spreading hairs; April–June, occasionally to September.
Leaves: those on separate, short shoots largest, 1½–5″ (3.8–12.5 cm) long, with long petioles attached at notch; those on flowering stem with short or no petioles.
Fruit: seedlike, with a tuft of white or pale tan hairs at top.
Height: 4–24″ (10–60 cm) tall.

Habitat
In lightly shaded woods.

Range
Alaska to S. California; east to the Rocky Mountains from Canada to New Mexico; also in N. Michigan.

Comments
In alpine areas or in open places along roads, the leaves may be narrower and without the notch at the base of the blade.

Arrowhead Groundsel
Senecio triangularis
444

Broadly or narrowly triangular or arrowhead-shaped leaves, with many sharp teeth on edges, grow on several leafy stems that bear yellow flower heads in a branched cluster at top.
Flowers: heads 1–1½″ (2.5–3.8 cm) wide, with about 8 rays ½″ (1.3 cm) long surrounding the small disk, and bracts mostly all the same length, about ½″ (1.3 cm) long, lined up side by side and not overlapping; June–September.
Leaves: 2–8″ (5–20 cm) long.
Fruit: seedlike, with a tuft of slender white hairs at top.
Height: 1–5′ (30–150 cm).

Habitat
Stream banks and other moist places in the mountains.

Range
Alaska and western Canada; south to S. California, Arizona, and New Mexico.

Comments
As indicated by the common and technical names, the triangular leaves are distinctive.

Golden Columbine
Aquilegia chrysantha
445

Several stems and highly divided leaves form a bushy plant with bright yellow flowers that face upward on long stalks.
Flowers: 1½–3″ (3.8–7.5 cm) wide; sepals 5, long, spreading, lanceolate, petal-like; petals 5, scoop-shaped, with backward-projecting spurs 1½–3″ (3.8–7.5 cm) long; stamens many and styles 5, protruding from center of flower; July–August.
Leaves: large, repeatedly divided, leaflets to 1½″ (3.8 cm) long, about as wide, deeply cleft and lobed on ends.
Height: 1–4′ (30–120 cm).

Habitat
Moist places in sheltered spots.

Range
Arizona to S. Colorado, W. Texas, and northern Mexico.

Comments
Columbine comes from *columbinus,* Latin for "dove," referring to the flower's resemblance to a cluster of 5 doves. The spurs represent the birds' heads and shoulders, the spreading sepals, the wings, the blade of the petal each bird's body.

Glacier Lily
Erythronium grandiflorum
446

1–5 pale to golden yellow flowers hang at end of a stalk that grows from between 2 broadly lanceolate basal leaves.
Flowers: 6 lanceolate petal-like segments 1–2″ (2.5–5 cm) long that curve back behind base of flower; stamens 6, protruding from center; March–August.
Leaves: 4–8″ (10–20 cm) long, gradually tapered to stalk.
Fruit: swollen 3-sided capsule.
Height: 6–12″ (15–30 cm).

Habitat
Sagebrush slopes and mountain forest openings, often near melting snow.

Range
S. British Columbia to N. Oregon; east to W. Colorado, Wyoming, and W. Montana.

Comments
This species often blooms as snow recedes. A form with white or cream petal-like segments with a band of golden yellow at the base grows in southeastern Washington and adjacent Idaho.

Yellow Bell
Fritillaria pudica
447

This dainty little plant has 1 yellow, narrowly bell-shaped flower hanging at the top of the flower stalk.
Flowers: ½–1″ (1.3–2.5 cm) long; 6 petal-like segments; March–June.

Leaves: 2–8" (5–20 cm) long, 2 or more near middle of stem.
Height: 4–12" (10–30 cm).

Habitat
Grasslands, among sagebrush, and in open coniferous woods.

Range
British Columbia; south on the eastern side of the Cascade
Range to N. California; east to Utah, W. North Dakota,
Wyoming, W. Montana, and Alberta.

Comments
A charming, modest lily that can be mistaken for no other;
the yellow bell becomes rusty or purplish as the flower ages.

**Hooker's Evening
Primrose**
Oenothera hookeri
448

A tall, erect, usually unbranched stem with large yellow
flowers in a raceme.
Flowers: 2–3" (5–7.5 cm) wide; sepals 4, reddish; petals 4,
broad; becoming rather orange as they age the following day;
stamens 8; June–September.
Leaves: 6–12" (15–30 cm) long, lanceolate, numerous,
progressively smaller from base to top of stem.
Fruit: slender, rigid pod 1–2" (2.5–5 cm) long.
Height: 2–3' (60–90 cm).

Habitat
Open slopes, road banks, and grassy areas from the plains well
into the mountains.

Range
E. Washington to Baja California; east to W. Texas and
S. Colorado.

Comments
Common Evening Primrose (*O. strigosa*), found throughout
most of the United States, has similar erect stems, but its
petals are less than 1" (2.5 cm) long.

Evergreen Violet
Viola sempervirens
449

Stems creep across ground, producing mats of thick, leathery,
broadly heart-shaped leaves, and bilaterally symmetrical, clear
yellow flowers that face outward, hanging on short stalks
barely as tall as the leaves.
Flowers: about ½" (1.3 cm) wide; petals 5, the 3 lower with
maroon veins near base, the middle one with a short spur
behind it; 2 upper petals bent upward; March–June.
Leaves: ½–1¼" (1.3–3.1 cm) wide, each with finely scalloped
toothed edges, on long stalks.
Height: creeper, flower stalks to 1–5" (2.5–12.5 cm) high,
stems to 1' (30 cm) long.

Habitat
Moist woods.

Range
West of the Cascade Range from British Columbia to S.
Oregon and in the Coast Ranges to central California.

Comments
One of the most common wildflowers within the dim redwood forest, lining many of the trails in the parks of the region. The leaves persist through winter, giving rise to the common name.

Stream Violet
Viola glabella
450

Slender leaning or erect stems with leaves only in upper one third, and bilaterally symmetrical, yellow flowers facing outward, hanging from slender stalks.
Flowers: ½–¾" (1.3–2 cm) wide; petals 5, the 3 lower ones with fine maroon lines at base, of these 3 the lateral ones bearded, the middle one with a short pouch that projects backward under flower; 2 upper petals yellow on backside; March–July.
Leaves: blades 1¼–3½" (3.1–8.8 cm) long, heart-shaped, with finely toothed edges, on long stalks.
Height: 2–12" (5–30 cm).

Habitat
In moist woods or along streams.

Range
Alaska to the southern Sierra Nevada of California, eastward to W. Montana.

Comments
A very common species in moist, shaded places in woods. Most western violets have yellow rather than purple corollas, but all have the perky little flower with a spur or pouch behind the lower petal.

Subalpine Buttercup
Ranunculus eschscholtzii
451

5 shiny, brilliant yellow petals are part of flowers that are sometimes so numerous as nearly to hide the foliage.
Flowers: ¾–1½" (2–3.8 cm) wide; sepals drop as flower opens; June–August.
Leaves: ¼–1¼" (6–31 mm) long, roundish to ovate, varying from having 3 shallow lobes to being highly divided into narrow segments.
Height: 2–10" (5–25 cm).

Habitat
High in mountain meadows and on rocky slopes.

Range
Alaska to S. California; east to Alberta; throughout the Rocky Mountain states to N. New Mexico.

Comments
Subalpine Buttercup has the largest flowers of North American species. There are many buttercups; most have shiny yellow petals, and most are difficult to identify.

California Poppy
Eschscholtzia californica
452

A smooth, bluish-green plant with several stems, fernlike leaves, and usually orange flowers borne singly on a long stalk.
Flowers: 1–2" (2.5–5 cm) wide; petals 4, fan-shaped, deep

orange or yellow-orange, sometimes yellow at tips and orange at base, rarely cream; sepals joined into a cone, which is pushed off as flower opens; stamens many; beneath ovary a flat, conspicuous, pinkish rim; February–September.
Leaves: ¾–2½" (2–6.3 cm) long, divided into narrow segments, on long stalks.
Fruit: capsule 1¼–4" (3.1–10 cm) long, slender, curved.
Height: 8–24" (20–60 cm).

Habitat
Open areas, common on grassy slopes.

Range
S. California to S. Washington; often cultivated.

Comments
On sunny days in spring, California Poppies, the state flower, often turn hillsides orange. Responsive to sunlight, the flowers close at night and on cloudy days. The spicy fragrance attracts mainly beetles, which serve as pollinators. Flowers produced early in the season tend to be larger than those later on.

Fire Poppy
Papaver californicum
453

A single bowl-shaped flower at top of each stem has 4 fan-shaped, reddish-orange petals with a greenish spot at base; before the flowers open, the buds droop.
Flowers: about 1" (2.5 cm) wide; sepals 2, hairy, drop as flower opens; stamens many, yellow; atop nearly cylindric ovary, a cap-shaped stigma with lines radiating from center; April–May.
Leaves: 1¼–3½" (3.1–8.8 cm) long, pinnately divided into few segments with teeth or lobes.
Height: 12–24" (30–60 cm).

Habitat
Open brush and woods, especially after fires.

Range
The Coast Ranges from San Francisco Bay to S. California; not common in the northern half of the range.

Comments
Opium is extracted from the sap of an Old World species of poppy, once commonly (and innocently) grown in gardens and still found scattered in the country.

Scarlet Globemallow
Sphaeralcea coccinea
454

Red-orange or brick-red flowers bloom in narrow clusters and in upper axils on these leafy, branched, velvety-haired plants.
Flowers: 1–1¼" (2.5–3.1 cm) wide; petals 5; stamens many, joined at base, forming a tube around style; April–August.
Leaves: ¾–2" (2–5 cm) wide, nearly round, divided into 3 broad or narrow lobes which may be divided or toothed.
Height: to 20" (50 cm), stems often leaning at base.

Habitat
Open ground in arid grassland and among pinyon and juniper.

Range
Central Canada; south to W. Montana, most of Utah, NE.
Arizona, and most of New Mexico; east to Texas and Iowa.

Comments
Globemallows are common plants on western ranges. The
several species are difficult to distinguish from one another.

Western Wallflower
Erysimum capitatum
455

Erect stems, unbranched or branched in the upper parts, with
narrow leaves, end in a dense raceme of showy orange, burnt
orange, orange-maroon, or yellow flowers.
Flowers: about ¾″ (2 cm) wide, petals 4; March–July.
Leaves: 1–5″ (2.5–12.5 cm) long, in a basal rosette and all
along stem except uppermost parts, narrowly lanceolate, with
small teeth on edges.
Fruit: pod 2–4″ (5–10 cm) long, very slender, with 4 sides,
held erect or nearly so.
Height: 6–36″ (15–90 cm).

Habitat
Dry stony banks, slopes, and open flats.

Range
British Columbia and Idaho; south to S. California and New
Mexico.

Comments
This handsome and variable species intergrades with the more
eastern Plains Wallflower (*E. asperum*).

Orange Agoseris
Agoseris aurantiaca
456

From a basal cluster of leaves grow several leafless stalks with
milky sap, topped by coppery-orange flower heads.
Flowers: head about 1″ (2.5 cm) wide; flowers all of ray type,
those in center of head very short; June–August.
Leaves: 2–14″ (5–35 cm) long, narrow, broadest above
middle, often with a few large teeth.
Fruit: seedlike, with a stalk at tip about as long as the body,
topped by fine silvery bristles.
Height: 4–24″ (10–60 cm).

Habitat
Meadows and grassy openings in coniferous forests in the
mountains.

Range
W. Canada to California and New Mexico.

Comments
This plant is the only orange-flowered *Agoseris*.

Amber Lily
Anthericum torreyi
457

Starlike, yellowish-orange flowers bloom in a narrow open
cluster at top of a leafless stalk that grows from a basal cluster
of several grasslike leaves.
Flowers: about 1″ (2.5 cm) wide; 6 narrow petal-like segments

spread from the base, each with 3–5 greenish or brownish veins down the center; June–November.
Leaves: usually less than ¼" (6 mm) wide, from half to as long as stem.
Height: to 3' (90 cm).

Habitat
Rich soil in canyons, on hills among pinyon and juniper, and in pine forests.

Range
North-central Arizona to central Texas; south into Mexico.

Comments
Of the approximately 300 species of *Anthericum* in the world, only 1 grows in the West.

Tiger Lily
Lilium columbianum
458

A plant with large, showy, mostly orange, nodding flowers at top of a leafy stem.
Flowers: 2–3" (5–7.5 cm) wide; 6 petal-like segments, each long, strongly curved back behind base of flower, yellow-orange to red-orange, spotted with deep red or purple; stamens 6, with anthers less than ¼" (6 mm) long; May–August.
Leaves: 2–4" (5–10 cm) long, narrowly lanceolate, in several whorls, or not in whorls but evenly scattered along stem.
Fruit: plump, 3–sided capsule.
Height: 2–4' (60–120 cm).

Habitat
Prairies, thickets, and open forests.

Range
S. British Columbia to NW. California; east to N. Nevada and N. Idaho.

Comments
This is one of the most popular western wildflowers, often dug for the garden, and in some areas now uncommon.

Rosy Twisted-stalk
Streptopus roseus
459

Small, bell-shaped, pinkish-brown flowers hang on twisted stalks along leafy stems.
Flowers: ¼–½" (6–13 mm) long; 6 petal-like segments, pale greenish brown and spotted or streaked with deep pink; June–July.
Leaves: 1¼–4" (3.1–10 cm) long, broadly lanceolate.
Height: 6–16" (15–40 cm).

Habitat
Moist woods and streambanks.

Range
Alaska to Oregon.

Comments
The arching stems and orderly arrangement of leaves resemble

those of Fairybell (*Disporum*) and False Solomon's Seal (*Smilacina*). *Streptopus* means "twisted foot" in reference to the contorted flower stalk.

Western Meadow Rue
Thalictrum occidentale
460

The branched stems bear highly divided, soft, thin leaves; flowers in open, branched clusters with stamens and pistils on separate plants.
Flowers: about ⅜″ (9 mm) wide; sepals 4–5, greenish brown, eventually dropping off; petals absent; stamens, on plants that have them, hang from purplish, threadlike stalks; May–July.
Leaves: leaflets, each ½–1½″ (1.3–3.8 cm) long, about as wide, usually with 3 lobes, shallowly notched and cleft.
Fruit: pistils develop into small, spreading or reflexed, pointed, narrow fruits.
Height: 1–3′ (30–90 cm).

Habitat
Moist ground, often in shady woods; subalpine meadows.

Range
British Columbia to N. California; east to Colorado, Wyoming, and Montana.

Comments
The very similar Fendler's Meadow Rue (*T. fendleri*) replaces this rue in the Sierra Nevada and southern Rockies.

Pinedrops
Pterospora andromedea
461

The stiffly erect, leafless stems of this reddish-brown plant often grow in clusters, and are covered with glandular hairs. Pale yellowish-brown, egg-shaped flowers in a long raceme.
Flowers: corolla about ¼″ (6 mm) long, with 5 tiny lobes around opening; June–August.
Leaves: represented by scales.
Height: 1–3′ (30–90 cm).

Habitat
Deep humus of coniferous forests, in the West especially common under Ponderosa Pine.

Range
Throughout the West.

Comments
Stems grow for only one year, but remain as dried stalks for several years. The genus name, from Greek words for "winged seeds," refers to the netlike wing at one end of each minute seed that carries it to a new site as it is sprinkled from the capsule.

Mountain Jewel Flower
Streptanthus tortuosus
462

A branched plant with heart-shaped or round leaves and green racemes of flask-shaped, pale yellow or cream to dark brownish-purple flowers.
Flowers: ½″ (1.3 cm) long, petals 4, crinkled, whitish with purple veins; sepals 4; May–August.

Leaves: ¾–3½" (2–8.8 cm) long, clasping, often slightly cupped, concave side downward.
Fruit: slender pod 2½–5" (6.3–12.5 cm) long, arched and spreading.
Height: 8–40" (20–100 cm).

Habitat
Dry rocky slopes.

Range
S. Oregon to S. California, in and west of the Sierra Nevada.

Comments
One of the most widespread and variable species in this western genus. Heartleaf Jewel Flower (*S. cordatus*) is very similar, but grows east of the Sierra Nevada and Cascades.

Long-tailed Wild Ginger
Asarum caudatum
463

A bizarre brown-purplish to yellowish or greenish flower is hidden by heart-shaped leaves growing in pairs from trailing, rooting stems that form dense patches.
Flowers: 1½–5" (3.8–12.5 cm) wide; 1 in each leaf axil, with 3 petal-like lobes ¾–3" (2–7.5 cm) long, tapering out from the bowl-like base to slender tips; stamens 12, tipped with scalelike appendages shorter than pollen sacs; April–July.
Leaves: ¾–4" (2–10 cm) long.
Height: creeper, with leaf stalks 6" (15 cm) high.

Habitat
Moist shaded woods below 5000' (1500 m) elevation.

Range
British Columbia and W. Montana to NE. Oregon; south on the western side of the Cascade Range and the Sierra Nevada to near the coast of central California.

Comments
The aromatic stems and roots were used by early settlers as a substitute for the tropical ginger. There are 2 other western species.

Vase Flower
Clematis hirsutissima
464

A hairy plant generally with several stems in a dense clump, and at the end of each stem a purplish-brown, reddish-lavender, or violet flower hanging like a small, inverted urn.
Flowers: about 1" (2.5 cm) long; sepals 4, leathery, lanceolate, petal-like, hairy on outside, joined at base, their tips flared outward; petals absent; stamens many inside "urn"; April–July.
Leaves: up to 5" (12.5 cm) long, opposite, finely divided, carrotlike.
Fruit: styles form plumes 1–2" (2.5–5 cm) long above the seedlike base, all together forming a shaggy, silvery cluster.
Height: 8–24" (20–60 cm).

Habitat
Grassland, among sagebrush, and in open pine forests.

Range
British Columbia to E. Washington; east to Montana and
Wyoming; south to N. Arizona and New Mexico.

Comments
Unlike most other *Clematis* species, the Vase Flower is not a
vine. Another common name for this species, Lion's Beard,
refers to the shaggy fruit head.

Spotted Coral Root
Corallorhiza maculata
465

1 to many yellowish-, reddish-, or purplish-brown, nearly
leafless stems with several or many bilaterally symmetrical
flowers of the same color in loose racemes.
Flowers: about ¾" (2 cm) wide; 3 sepals and 2 petals
lanceolate, spreading sideways and upward; lip white, usually
purple-spotted, bent downward near base, about ½" (1.3 cm)
long and having 2 small lobes near base; April–September.
Leaves: a few tubular sheaths on stem.
Height: 8–32" (20–80 cm).

Habitat
Shady woods.

Range
Canada south to Guatemala.

Comments
This is the most common coral root in the United States.
Clumps of stems often occur in extensive colonies.

Western Peony
Paeonia brownii
466

A rather fleshy, bluish-green, leafy plant, usually with several
clustered stems, divided leaves, and greenish and reddish-
brown flowers, 1 hanging at end of each stalk.
Flowers: 1–1½" (2.5–3.8 cm) wide; sepals 5 or 6, greenish,
spoon-shaped; petals 5, maroon or bronze in center, green on
margins, about as long as sepals; April–June.
Leaves: blades to 2½" (6.3 cm) long, divided into 3 main
segments on short stalks, segments again divided into 3 parts,
these with lobes at end.
Height: 8–24" (20–60 cm).

Habitat
Chaparral, sagebrush, and pine forests.

Range
E. Washington; south through the northern two thirds of
California; east to Utah, W. Wyoming, and Idaho.

Comments
The genus is named for Paion, Greek god of healing; Indians
made tea from the roots to treat lung ailments.

Mission Bells
Fritillaria lanceolata
467

On an erect stem, leafy in the upper part, leafless below,
bloom several greenish-brown, deeply bowl-shaped flowers.
Flowers: ¾–1½" (2–3.8 cm) long; 6 lanceolate petal-like

segments, brownish, mottled green or yellow; February–June.
Leaves: 1½ to 6″ (3.1–15 cm) long, lanceolate, generally less
than 10 times as long as wide, in several whorls on the stem.
Height: 1–4′ (30–120 cm).

Habitat
Grassy or brushy flats and slopes, or in open woods.

Range
S. British Columbia to S. California; eastward to N. Idaho.

Comments
The genus name comes from Latin *fritillus,* meaning "dice
box," in reference to the short, broad capsule characteristic of
the genus.

Clustered Lady's Slipper
Cypripedium fasciculatum
468

Several short stems in a cluster, each stem with only 2 broad
leaves, and 2–4 drooping, brownish to greenish, bilaterally
symmetrical flowers.
Flowers: about 1½″ (3.8 cm) wide; 3 sepals and 2 petals
similar, the 2 lower sepals joined and appearing as one with 2
tips; lip about ½″ (1.3 cm) long, a greenish pouch streaked or
mottled with purple; April–July.
Leaves: 2–6″ (5–15 cm) long, ovate.
Height: 2–8″ (5–20 cm).

Habitat
Forests at moderately high elevations.

Range
British Columbia southward to central California and N.
Colorado.

Comments
Lady's Slippers attract insects into their pouch, from which
there is only one exit, past the stigma, where pollen from a
previously visited flower is brushed off. Then the insect must
go under one of the anthers, where it will pick up new
pollen.

Roseroot
Sedum rosea
469

A succulent, leafy plant with erect, clustered stems and small
brownish-purple or maroon flowers in bunches at the top.
Flowers: about ⅛″ (3 mm) long; sepals 4, fleshy; petals 4,
fleshy; stamens 8; no ovaries on some plants, 4 ovaries and no
stamens on others. Sometimes there are more parts; June–
August.
Leaves: ¼–1″ (6–25 mm) long, broadly lanceolate, crowded
but equally spaced along stem.
Height: 1¼–12″ (3.1–30 cm).

Habitat
Open areas high in the mountains.

Range
Across northern North America; south in the mountains to S.
California, Nevada, Utah, and N. New Mexico.

Comments
The root has a Rose-like fragrance, giving it its common name.

California Ground Cone
Boschniakia strobilacea
470

An unusual plant resembling a slender, dark reddish-brown pine cone; stands erect on the ground, with cupped, spoonlike bracts, widest near blunt tip.
Flowers: about ⅝″ (1.5 cm) long, bilaterally symmetrical, in axils of bracts; corolla bent at middle of tube, upper lip hoodlike, lower 3-lobed; May–July.
Leaves: bracts among flowers.
Height: 4–10″ (10–25 cm).

Habitat
In forests or brush, associated with the shrub manzanita (*Arctostaphylos*) or the tree madrone (*Arbutus*).

Range
S. California to S. Oregon.

Comments
This species is a perennial parasite that flowers each season and causes large knobs to form on the roots of manzanita and madrone.

Freckled Milkvetch
Astragalus lentigenosus
471

A more or less succulent plant with stems that vary from erect to prostrate and whitish, pinkish, or purplish flowers in racemes.
Flowers: ⅜–¾″ (9–20 mm) long; 1 broad upper petal and 2 lateral petals nearly enclosing 2 bottom petals that are joined and shaped like prow of a boat; spreading or erect; May–July.
Leaves: 11–19 broadly ovate or roundish leaflets ⅜–⅝″ (9–15 mm) long, smooth or lightly hairy on upper surface.
Fruit: pod ½–1½″ (1.3–3.8 cm) long, swollen and leathery-walled or bladdery and thin-walled, 2-chambered, the end flattened sideways into a prominent upcurved beak.
Height: 4–16″ (10–40 cm) long.

Habitat
From deserts and salt flats to open slopes high in the mountains.

Range
Western Canada; south through most of the West to northwestern Mexico.

Comments
One of the most variable of western plants, with numerous types differing in height, flowers, and pods.

Giant Red Paintbrush
Castilleja miniata
472

The flower cluster of this leafy plant resembles a ragged crimson or scarlet paintbrush, calyx and bracts beneath each flower brightly colored.
Flowers: conspicuous, tubular calyx has 4 pointed lobes, cleft

between upper lobes as deep as cleft between lower; bilaterally symmetrical corolla, relatively inconspicuous, ¾–1½" (2–3.8 cm) long, lower lip merely a green bump, upper lip a "beak," at least as long as the pale, tubular lower portion, its edges thin and red; May–September.
Leaves: on stem, to about 4" (10 cm) long, lanceolate, usually without lobes, some of the upper leaves and the colorful bracts with 3 pointed lobes.
Height: 1–3' (30–90 cm).

Habitat
Mountain meadows, thickets, and forest openings.

Range
Throughout the West.

Comments
Most members of this genus are partial parasites on other plants, their roots establishing connections with roots of other species. For this reason, they usually cannot be transplanted.

Red Clintonia
Clintonia andrewsiana
473

An umbel-like cluster of red or reddish lavender, narrowly bell-shaped flowers blooms at the top of a nearly leafless stalk, growing from a basal rosette. Beneath main flower cluster, there may be smaller clusters with only a few flowers.
Flowers: 6 narrow petal-like segments about ½" (1.3 cm) long; May–July.
Leaves: 6–10" (15–25 cm) long, usually 5 or 6, broadly elliptic.
Fruit: deep blue berry to ½" (1.3 cm) long.
Height: 10–20" (25–50 cm).

Habitat
Shaded damp forests near the coast.

Range
Central California to SW. Oregon.

Comments
One of the few wildflowers that grow in the dim light of the Pacific Coast redwood forests. The genus is named for DeWitt Clinton, naturalist and governor of New York in the early 19th century.

Cardinal Flower
Lobelia cardinalis
474

Erect leafy stems, often in clusters, with racemes of flowers resembling flaming red spires.
Flowers: corolla 1–1½" (2.5–3.8 cm) long, bilaterally symmetrical, with 2 small upper lobes and 3 larger lower lobes, the tubular base slit along top and sides; July–October.
Leaves: 2–5" (5–12.5 cm) long, narrowly lanceolate, with fine teeth on edges.
Height: 1–3' (30–90 cm).

Habitat
Moist shady slopes and sunny stream banks.

Range
S. California to S. Utah and W. Texas; north to E. Colorado;
east across most of eastern United States.

Comments
One of the West's most handsome wildflowers, the Cardinal
Flower attracts hummingbirds, which feed on the nectar,
pollinating the flowers.

California Fuchsia
Zauschneria californica
475

A somewhat shrubby green or grayish plant, often with many
branches with brilliant red, trumpet-shaped flowers blooming
in profusion near ends, all oriented in the same direction.
Flowers: 1½–2½" (3.8–6.3 cm) long; 4 red sepals and 4 red
petals growing from a red tubular base; 8 red stamens that
protrude; August–October.
Leaves: ½–1½" (1.3–3.8 cm) long, very narrow and gray
with hair, or broader, lanceolate, and greener.
Height: 1–3' (30–90 cm).

Habitat
Dry slopes and ridges from sea level to high in the mountains;
in the Southwest in damp canyons.

Range
SW. Oregon to Baja California; east to SW. New Mexico.

Comments
This species is related to the popular ornamental fuchsias,
most originally from the American tropics. In California,
species of *Zauschneria* bloom late in the season, after the
summer heat has turned grasses brown and driven most
wildflowers to seed. The flower nectar supplies hummingbirds
with food for the start of their migration.

Scarlet Bugler
Penstemon centranthifolius
476

Few, erect, sparsely leafy stems have bright red, nearly radially
symmetrical, tubular flowers in a long, narrow, but open
cluster near the top.
Flowers: corolla 1–1¼" (2.5–3.1 cm) long, the 5 lobes very
short, barely spreading, round at tips; stamens 5, the fifth
without an anther; April–July.
Leaves: 1¼–3" (3.1–7.5 cm) long, spatula-shaped or
lanceolate, opposite.
Height: 1–4' (30–120 cm).

Habitat
Dry open places in brush, commonly where the soil has been
disturbed.

Range
Coast Ranges from central California to Baja California.

Comments
In certain situations this species will produce extensive, nearly
solid patches of brilliant red. The nearly radially symmetrical
corollas are unusual for this genus.

Skyrocket
Ipomopsis aggregata
477

In upper leaf axils and at tops of sparsely-leaved stems are clusters of showy, bright red or deep pink, trumpet-shaped flowers.
Flowers: corollas ¾–1¼" (2–3.1 cm) long, with 5 pointed lobes; May–September.
Leaves: mostly 1–2" (2.5–5 cm) long, densest near base, pinnately divided into narrow segments.
Height: 6–84" (15–210 cm).

Habitat
Dry slopes from sagebrush to forest.

Range
E. British Columbia to S. California; east to W. Texas; north through the Rocky Mountains and the western edge of the plains to W. North Dakota; also northern Mexico.

Comments
Skyrocket, one of the most common western wildflowers, grows readily from seed; its brilliant red trumpets are handsome in the native garden.

Candystick
Allotropa virgata
478

Lustrous, erect, leafless, scaly stems resembling peppermint sticks have red flowers hanging in a raceme along top.
Flowers: 5 white or reddish petal-like segments about ¼" (6 mm) long form an inverted bowl; May–August.
Leaves: represented by scales.
Height: 4–12" (10–30 cm).

Habitat
Coniferous forests.

Range
British Columbia to the southern Sierra Nevada in California.

Comments
Lacking chlorophyll, these plants absorb nutrients from the rich, thick duff.

Showy Thistle
Cirsium pastoris
479

A white, woolly, prickly plant with crimson flower heads at the ends of the few upper branches terminating the main stem.
Flowers: heads 1½–2½" (3.8–6.3 cm) long, with bracts the same length, tipped with spines; bright red disk flowers extend about 1" (2.5 cm) beyond the bracts; June–September.
Leaves: 4–12" (10–30 cm) long, narrow, pinnately lobed, edges prickly and continuing down the stem as narrow wings.
Fruit: seedlike, with long white hairs at tip, each hair with many smaller hairs along its length.
Height: 2–4' (60–120 cm).

Habitat
Dry open slopes in brushy or grassy areas, or in open woods.

Range
N. California, S. Oregon, and W. Nevada.

Comments
With its red flowers and white foliage, this is perhaps the
handsomest Thistle of a group considered obnoxious weeds.

Snow Plant
Sarcodes sanguinea
480

An unusual plant that is stout, fleshy, entirely bright red,
with bracts overlapping on lower stem and curled among
racemes of flowers above.
Flowers: corolla bell-shaped, ½–¾" (1.3–2 cm) long, with 5
round lobes; April–July.
Leaves: represented by scales.
Height: 8–24" (20–60 cm).

Habitat
Coniferous woods.

Range
S. Oregon to S. California.

Comments
Once seen, never forgotten; the brilliant red is startling in the
filtered sunlight against a dark background of forest duff.

Rocky Mountain Lily
Lilium philadelphicum
481

A plant with 1–3 mostly red, funnel-shaped flowers at top of
an erect, leafy stem.
Flowers: 2–2½" (5–6.3 cm) wide; 6 lanceolate petal-like
segments, red or red-orange near the gently outwardly curved
tips, yellowish and with purple spots at base; June–August.
Leaves: 2–4" (5–10 cm) long, narrowly lanceolate, the lower
ones scattered on stem, upper ones in 1 or 2 whorls.
Height: 12–28" (30–70 cm).

Habitat
Meadows and forests, commonly in aspen groves.

Range
British Columbia to Saskatchewan; south along the eastern
edge of the Rocky Mountains to S. New Mexico; east to
Michigan and Ohio.

Comments
Once much more common than now, the Rocky Mountain
Lily is too often picked by visitors to the mountains.

Scarlet Fritillary
Fritillaria recurva
482

A smooth, gray-green plant with most leaves near the middle
of the stem and, hanging in an open raceme at top, 1–9
scarlet, narrowly bell-shaped flowers.
Flowers: ¾–1¼" (2–3.1 cm) long, tinged on the outside with
purple, inside checkered with yellow; 6 petal-like segments
with tips curved backward; March–July.
Leaves: 1–4" (2.5–10 cm) long, narrow.
Height: 1–3' (30–90 cm).

Habitat
Dry brushy or wooded hillsides.

Range
S. Oregon to central California and W. Nevada.

Comments
One of the few red lilies in the West and the only red Fritillary. *Recurva* refers to the recurved tips of the petal-like segments. However, in the inner parts of the northern Coast Ranges of California there occurs a brilliant red-flowered form whose petal-like segment tips are not recurved.

Red Columbine
Aquilegia formosa
483

Handsome red and yellow flowers hang at ends of branches above this bushy plant with several stems and many leaves.
Flowers: about 2″ (5 cm) wide; sepals 5, petal-like, red, lanceolate, spreading; petals 5, yellow, shaped like sugar scoops, extending into backward-projecting spurs; stamens many, yellow, styles 5, protruding from center; May–August.
Leaves: repeatedly divided into leaflets ¾–1½″ (2–3.8 cm) long, about as wide, each lobed and cleft across ends.
Height: 6–36″ (15–90 cm).

Habitat
Open woods, on banks, near seeps.

Range
S. Alaska to Baja California; east to W. Montana and Utah.

Comments
The species name *formosa,* Latin for "beautiful," aptly describes this large plant, especially when it has hundreds of lovely flowers nodding over it.

Twinflower
Linnaea borealis
484

A matted plant with erect, short, leafless, forked stalks from whose tops hang 2 pink flowers like narrow bells.
Flowers: about ½″ (1.3 cm) long; corolla with 5 round lobes; June–September.
Leaves: ¼–1″ (6–25 mm) long, opposite, broadly elliptic, glossy, sometimes with a few shallow teeth on edges.
Height: creeper, the flower stalks less than 4″ (10 cm) high.

Habitat
Moist forest and brush.

Range
Throughout the western mountains, south to N. California, N. Arizona, and New Mexico; east to W. South Dakota.

Comments
This charming plant makes a good ground cover in the woodland garden.

Few-flowered Shooting Star
Dodecatheon pulchellum
485

A few flowers like deep pink darts point in all directions from an umbel atop a long, erect stalk growing from basal leaves.
Flowers: ¾–1″ (2–2.5 cm) long; corolla with 4 or 5 narrow lobes sharply bent back from a yellowish ring that usually has

dark purplish lines; stamens form yellowish to purplish point of "dart," the tube beneath the anthers not wrinkled, or slightly wrinkled lengthwise; stigma barely broader than stalk; April–August.
Leaves: 2–16" (5–40 cm) long, broadly lanceolate, gradually tapered to long stalks, the margins smooth or with small teeth.
Height: 4–24" (10–60 cm).

Habitat
From coastal prairies to mountain meadows and streamsides.

Range
Throughout the West.

Comments
This is a common species, varying in color of the tube below the anthers, presence or absence of glandular hair on foliage, and shape of the leaves.

Western Bleeding Heart
Dicentra formosa
486

Pink, heart-shaped flowers hang in small, branched clusters above soft, fernlike bluish-green leaves at base.
Flowers: about ¾" (2 cm) long; at base 2 small sepals that drop off; petals 4, pale pink or rose, in 2 pairs: outer 2 with pouch at base, forming outline of heart, with spreading tips, and inner 2 facing one another, with a wavy crest on back, enclosing 6 stamens and 1 pistil; March–July.
Leaves: with long stalks, 9–20" (22.5–50 cm) long, elaborately pinnately compound, leaflets ¾–2" (2–5 cm) long, oblong, cut into divisions about ⅛" (3 mm) wide, soft.
Fruit: pod ½–¾" (1.3–2 cm) long, plump.
Height: 8–18" (20–45 cm).

Habitat
Damp shaded places or, in wetter climates, open woods.

Range
S. British Columbia to central California.

Comments
One of the nursery-trade species. Bleeding Heart (*D. spectabilis*), from Japan, has larger, rosy-red or white flowers, about 1" (2.5 cm) long.

Fairy Slipper
Calypso bulbosa
487

1 mostly pink bilateral flower hangs at tip of an erect, reddish flower stalk that grows above 1 basal leaf.
Flowers: about 1¼" (3.1 cm) long; 3 sepals and 2 upper petals similar, rose-pink, narrowly lanceolate, spreading sideways or upward and also forward. Lip divided into a white, spoonlike tip with reddish-purple spots and a 2-lobed, sacklike base with reddish-purple stripes; March–July.
Leaves: 1¼–2½" (3.1–6.3 cm) long, parallel-veined, tapered to a purplish stalk.
Height: to 8" (20 cm).

Habitat
Thick duff and mossy ground in woods.

Range
N. California, NE. Arizona, and S. New Mexico; north through much of northern North America.

Comments
This species is also called Calypso, for the sea nymph of Homer's *Odyssey*, who detained the willing Odysseus on his return from Troy.

American Vetch
Vicia americana
488

A slender, climbing plant that clings to other vegetation or structures by slender coiling tendrils at the end of each leaf. Loose racemes of 4–10 deep reddish-lavender flowers grow on stalks arising from leaf axils.
Flowers: ½–1¼″ (1.3–3.1 cm) long; 1 broad upper petal and 2 lateral petals nearly enclosing 2 bottom petals that are joined and shaped like the prow of a boat; petals become bluish with age; May–July.
Leaves: pinnately compound, with 8–12 leaflets, each ½–1½″ (1.3–3.8 cm) long.
Height: 2–4′ (60–120 cm).

Habitat
Open places in woods, on road banks, along fences.

Range
Throughout.

Comments
With showy flowers unusually large for the genus, American Vetch resembles many species of *Lathyrus*. In *Vicia*, the hairs surround the tip, resembling a shaving brush; in *Lathyrus*, they are on the upper side, like a little hairbrush.

Purple Loco
Oxytropis lambertii
489

A tufted plant, usually covered with silvery hairs, with dense racemes of bright reddish-lavender flowers held just above the basal leaves by long stalks.
Flowers: ½–1″ (1.3–2.5 cm) long; 1 broad upper petal and 2 lateral petals nearly enclosing 2 bottom petals with a common slender point projecting forward at the tip; June–September.
Leaves: 3–12″ (8–30 cm) long, pinnately compound, with leaflets ¼–1½″ (6–38 mm) long.
Fruit: pod ¾–1¼″ (2–3.1 cm) long, erect, plump, pointed, with a groove on side toward stem.
Height: 4–16″ (10–40 cm).

Habitat
Plains and open areas in pine forests.

Range
On the Great Plains from Canada to Texas; west to the eastern base of the Rocky Mountains in Montana and Wyoming; through the mountains to central Utah and Arizona.

Comments
One of the most dangerously poisonous plants on western ranges, it is lethally toxic to all kinds of livestock.

Great Hedge Nettle
Stachys cooleyae
490

Stout, 4-sided, leafy stems grow in patches and have deep reddish-lavender bilaterally symmetrical flowers in whorls at intervals in a spike at top.
Flowers: corolla ⅝–1″ (1.5–2.5 cm) long, upper lip projecting like a short hood, lower lip 3-lobed, much longer, bent downward; June–August.
Leaves: 2½–6″ (6.3–15 cm) long, opposite, all with stalks, broadly lanceolate, bearing blunt teeth on margins.
Height: 2–5′ (60–150 cm).

Habitat
Swamps and moist low ground from sea level to moderate elevations.

Range
S. British Columbia to S. Oregon, from the eastern slope of the Cascade Range to the Pacific Coast.

Comments
The moist habitat of this species is typical for hedge nettles. Other western species may have smaller, paler flowers and middle and upper leaves without stalks.

Common Owl's Clover
Orthocarpus purpuracens
491

The flower cluster of this erect little plant is rose and yellow, or rose and white, for the floral bracts are velvety and rose-purple on their divided tips.
Flowers: bilaterally symmetrical corollas 1–1¼″ (1.3–3.1 cm) long, each exposing a white or yellow 3-lobed pouch as they "peer" from bracts, strongly angled upward; at end of pouch are 3 tiny teeth; above pouch's upper lip is a short, hooked, velvety, rose-purple beak; March–May.
Leaves: ½–2″ (1.3–5 cm) long, divided into a few very narrow segments.
Fruit: capsule about ½″ (1.3 cm) long.
Height: 4–16″ (10–40 cm).

Habitat
Fields and open wooded areas.

Range
S. California to W. Arizona and northern Mexico.

Comments
Following a wet spring, acre upon acre is carpeted with this beautiful wildflower. The Spanish common name, Escobita, means "little broom," descriptive of the flower cluster.

Elephant Head
Pedicularis groenlandica
492

Dense racemes of flowers that are perfect little pink elephant heads (ears, trunk, and all) bloom on leafy stems.
Flowers: strongly bilaterally symmetrical corolla; exclusive of

the "trunk" about ½" (1.3 cm) long; "trunk" is the upper lip, curving forward well beyond the lower lip, of which 3 lobes form the ears and lower part of the "elephant's head"; June–August.
Leaves: 2–10" (5–25 cm) long, narrow, pinnately divided into sharp-toothed lobes.
Height: to 28" (70 cm).

Habitat
Wet meadows and small cold streams.

Range
Throughout the western mountains.

Comments
The flower's charming structure facilitates pollination while at the same time reducing the chances of hybridization with other species.

Fireweed
Epilobium angustifolium
493

Pink spires of flowers bloom at tops of tall, erect, leafy stems.
Flowers: sepals 4; petals 4, ½–¾" (1.3–2 cm) long, usually deep pink but occasionally white; June–September.
Leaves: 4–6" (10–15 cm) long, with veins joined in loops near edge of leaf.
Fruit: pod 2–3" (5–7.5 cm) long, slender, stands out rigidly from stem.
Height: 2–7' (60–210 cm).

Habitat
Disturbed soil in cool areas, from the lowlands well into the mountains, frequent along highways and in burned areas.

Range
Throughout the West.

Comments
Fireweed often grows in spectacular dense patches, quickly covering unsightly burned or logged areas. Though attractive, it is aggressive in a moist garden, spreading from persistent underground stems.

Scarlet Gaura
Gaura coccinea
494

The leafy stems of this grayish plant are branched, grow in clumps, and bear at the tips reddish-pink, nodding racemes.
Flowers: about ½" (1.3 cm) wide; bilaterally symmetrical; petals 4, narrow, all spreading upward, white in the evening, by midmorning deep pink; stamens 8; May–September.
Leaves: ½–2½" (1.3–6.3 cm) long, crowded, lanceolate.
Fruit: pod less than ½" (1.3 cm) long, hard, shaped somewhat like an old-fashioned toy top.
Height: usually 6–24" (15–60 cm).

Habitat
Sandy soil in grassland and among pinyon and juniper.

Range
Central Canada and W. Montana to Wyoming and Colorado;

southwest to S. California; south to Mexico; east to Minnesota, Missouri, and Texas.

Comments
The whiteness of the newly opened flowers attracts night-flying moths, the primary pollinators of these plants. By early the next day the flowers are pink, the color intensifying throughout the morning. The flower remains open less than a day.

Balloon Flower
Penstemon palmeri
495

A few sparsely leaved, erect, stout stems have swollen white to reddish-pink, bilaterally symmetrical flowers mostly turned to one side in a long, narrow cluster.
Flowers: corolla 1–1½″ (2.5–3.8 cm) long, the short tube at base abruptly expanded into a large swollen chamber with reddish lines on the lower inside, the opening with the 2 upper lobes bent sharply upward, the 3 lower bent downward; 4 stamens with anthers, the fifth without an anther, densely golden-bearded at tip; May–July.
Leaves: largest to 10″ (25 cm) long, lanceolate, opposite, the bases of the paired upper leaves often joined, the stem appearing to go through them.
Height: 2–7′ (60–210 cm).

Habitat
Open rocky areas among sagebrush, pinyon and juniper, or pine woods.

Range
SE. Arizona to central Arizona, S. Utah, and central New Mexico.

Comments
This is one of the most delightful species of *Penstemon,* its cheery puffed-up flowers exquisitely fragrant.

Purple Chinese Houses
Collinsia heterophylla
496

Bilaterally symmetrical flowers in several widely spaced whorls at top of a sparsely leafy stem.
Flowers: about ¾″ (2 cm) long; upper lip of corolla has 2 lavender, pale blue-violet, or white lobes bent upward, with many maroon dots at base; lower lip has 2 violet lobes projecting forward, the third lobe folded between them, hiding the style and 4 stamens; March–June.
Leaves: to 2½″ (6.3 cm) long, few, paired, lanceolate, scalloped on edges.
Height: 1–2′ (30–60 cm).

Habitat
Sandy soil on shaded flats or slopes.

Range
Southern two thirds of California and N. Baja California.

Comments
Few of California's spectacular wildflowers are as charming as

this one. The flowers grow in perfect rings of widely spaced bands around the stem, forming a fairytale pagoda, the "Chinese houses."

Lewis' Monkeyflower
Mimulus lewisii
497

Showy, deep pink to red, bilaterally symmetrical flowers bloom in profusion near the top of this several-stemmed plant.
Flowers: 1¼–2″ (3.1–5 cm) long; corolla with 3 lobes bent down, 2 bent upward, marked with yellow patches of hairs and darker red-violet lines near opening; June–August.
Leaves: 1–4″ (2.5–10 cm) long, with toothed or plain edges, opposite.
Height: 1–3′ (30–90 cm).

Habitat
Wet open places in the mountains.

Range
Western Canada; south to the southern Sierra Nevada in California and to the higher mountains of Utah, Wyoming, and Montana.

Comments
The deep pink to red flowers of this handsome species probably attract hummingbirds during their summer stay in the mountains.

Umbrella Plant
Peltiphyllum peltatum
498

This plant forms large masses of nearly round, jaggedly toothed leaf blades on rough, hairy stalks; small, pink flowers in large, round, branched clusters grow on stalks slightly taller than leaves.
Flowers: petals 5, pink or white, about ¼″ (6 mm) long; stamens 10; pistil with 2 reddish-purple sections; April–June.
Leaves: to 16″ (40 cm) wide.
Height: 2–6′ (60–180 cm).

Habitat
In and along edges of cold streams.

Range
Central Oregon to central California.

Comments
The luxuriant foliage of this plant, which is usually anchored firmly among water-washed rocks, sometimes gives a verdant, almost tropical aspect to mountain streams.

Mountain Globemallow
Iliamna rivularis
499

A stout plant with large, maplelike leaves and showy pink or pinkish-lavender flowers in long, loose racemes at top of stem, and in shorter racemes in upper leaf axils.
Flowers: 1–2″ (2.5–5 cm) wide; petals 5; many stamens joined at base, forming a tube around branched style, each branch ending in a tiny knob; June–August.
Leaves: 2–8″ (5–20 cm) wide, nearly round, 5 or 7 triangular lobes.

Fruit: many segments in a ring, each containing 3 or 4 seeds.
Height: 3–7' (90–210 cm).

Habitat
Springs and along mountain streams.

Range
British Columbia through E. Washington to E. Oregon; east
to Montana; south to Utah and Colorado.

Comments
The several western globemallow species are commonly found
in wet places, recognizable by their maplelike leaves and pink
or rose petals.

Little Pipsissewa
Chimaphila menziesii
500

1–3 shallowly bowl-shaped, pink or pinkish-green flowers
hang at ends of branches above leathery, dark green leaves,
atop this low plant.
Flowers: about ½" (1.3 cm) wide; petals 5, roundish; stamens
10, the bases of the stalks swollen and hairy; June–August.
Leaves: ¾–2½" (2–6.3 cm) long, lanceolate, commonly with
small sharp teeth on edges.
Height: 2–6" (5–15 cm).

Habitat
Coniferous woods.

Range
British Columbia to S. California.

Comments
The genus name refers to the evergreen nature of the plant.
The common name Pipsissewa is believed to be derived from
the Cree Indian word *pipisisikweu,* meaning "it breaks into
small pieces"; the plant was once used in preparations for
breaking up kidney stones or gallstones.

Western Starflower
Trientalis latifolia
501

A delicate stem has a whorl of 3–8 ovate leaves at top, in the
center of which blooms 1 or several pink, star-shaped flowers,
each on its own threadlike stalk.
Flowers: corolla about ½" (1.3 cm) wide, with 5–9 pointed
lobes; April–June.
Leaves: 1¼–4" (3.1–10 cm) long.
Height: 4–10" (10–25 cm).

Habitat
Open woods and prairies.

Range
British Columbia; south through the northern two thirds of
California; east to N. Idaho.

Comments
An alternative name, Indian Potato, refers to the small
underground swelling at the base of the stem; modern
references do not mention edibility, so caution is advised.

Mustang Clover
Linanthus montanus
502

Erect stems have a dense cluster of prickly bracts near top and long, pink, trumpet-shaped flowers projecting from bracts.
Flowers: about ¾″ (2 cm) wide, 1–2″ (2.5–5 cm) long, paler in center, with purple spot at base of each of 5 lobes; outside of tube minutely glandular-hairy; May–August.
Leaves: ¾–1¼″ (2–3.1 cm) long, opposite, palmately divided into 5–11 lobes, each pair like a ring of needles around stem.
Height: 4–24″ (10–60 cm).

Habitat
Dry gravelly places in open woodland.

Range
Western slope of the Sierra Nevada in California.

Comments
The unusually long flowers of this species make it one of the showiest of this California-based genus.

Red Maids
Calandrinia ciliata
503

Small, brilliant, bright reddish-pink, shallowly bowl-shaped flowers bloom on short stalks growing from axils of upper leaves on this succulent plant with spreading or erect stems.
Flowers: about ½″ (1.3 cm) wide; petals 5, sepals 2, with coarse hairs; April–May.
Leaves: ½–3″ (1.3–7.5 cm) long, narrow, upper ones much smaller.
Height: 2–16″ (5–40 cm).

Habitat
Open places where the soil is moist, at least early in the year; often with weeds.

Range
California to Washington; east to SW. New Mexico.

Comments
This species is a member of a large genus of the western Americas and Australia. The genus was named for a Swiss botanist of the 18th century, J. L. Calandrini.

Indian Pink
Silene californica
504

Flowers with fringed, bright red petals resemble brilliant pinwheels at the ends of branches on erect or trailing stems.
Flowers: 1–1½″ (2.5–3.8 cm) wide; a calyx broad, tubular, ⅝–1″ (1.5–2.5 cm) long, with 5 pointed teeth; petals 5, divided by small scales in middle, the broad upper part with deep notches at end, the slender lower part as long as calyx; May–July.
Leaves: 1¼–3″ (3.1–7.5 cm) long, opposite, ovate.
Fruit: capsule, not longer than calyx.
Height: 6–16″ (15–40 cm).

Habitat
Rocky open woods.

Range
Northern two thirds of California into SW. Oregon.

Comments
One of the showiest of western wildflowers, Indian Pink is widespread but usually not numerous.

Showy Daisy
Erigeron speciosus
505

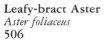

A leafy stem branches near the top into leafless stalks, each with 1 flower head at the end, with many narrow pink, lavender, or white rays surrounding a yellow disk.
Flowers: heads 1½–2" (3.8–5 cm) wide, with bracts all about the same length and lined up side by side, not overlapping like shingles; rays ½–¾" (1.3–2 cm) long; June–September.
Leaves: lower 3 to 6" (7.5–15 cm) long, lanceolate, smooth, commonly with 3 veins, the bases joined to the stem about halfway around and therefore slightly clasping.
Fruit: seedlike, with fragile, fine bristles at top.
Height: 1–3' (30–90 cm).

Habitat
Openings in forests or in lightly wooded areas at low to middle elevations.

Range
S. British Columbia to Oregon; east to New Mexico, South Dakota, and Montana.

Comments
This *Erigeron* has one of the showiest heads, reflected in the species name, *speciosus,* which means "pretty." The similar Hairy Showy Daisy (*E. subtrinervis*) has spreading hairs over most of the stem and leaves.

Leafy-bract Aster
Aster foliaceus
506

Leafy stems with ascending branches, terminated by several flower heads, each with many narrow lavender or purple rays.
Flowers: heads 1–2" (2.5–5 cm) wide; rays surround a yellow disk. Bracts around head overlapping; often additional outer, rather leafy, large bracts; July–September.
Leaves: 5–8" (12.5–20 cm) long, basal ones lanceolate, gradually narrowing to stalklike base, those at midstem with bases partly surrounding and clasping stem.
Fruit: seedlike, smooth or sparsely hairy on surface, topped by a tuft of fine hairs.
Height: 8–20" (20–50 cm).

Habitat
Moist places in woods, on road banks, and in mountain meadows.

Range
Alaska to central California, Arizona, and New Mexico.

Comments
Asters, which take their name from the Greek word for star, have flower heads that resemble those of Fleabanes (*Erigeron*), another large and complex western genus. The bracts of *Aster,* however, usually vary in length, overlapping like shingles on a roof. Many asters are tall and leafy; few *Erigeron* are.

Hooker's Onion
Allium acuminatum
507

An umbel of pink or deep pink flowers grows at the top of a leafless stalk. Plant has a strong onion odor.
Flowers: about ½″ (1.3 cm) long; 6 petal-like segments, each with a long point, inner 3 segments slightly taller than outer 3, edges with very small, almost microscopic teeth; 2 papery, pointed bracts beneath umbel; May–July.
Leaves: 4–6″ (10–15 cm) long, 2 or 3, basal, very narrow.
Height: 4–12″ (10–30 cm).

Habitat
Open, often rocky slopes, among brush and trees.

Range
British Columbia to central California and S. Arizona; east to S. Wyoming and W. Colorado.

Comments
One of the most common of the many western wild onions, all of which have edible bulbs, though some are extremely potent or unpalatable. In the early days of the West, Indians saved at least one exploration party from scurvy by alerting the ill explorers to the curative properties of wild onions.

Redwood Sorrel
Oxalis oregana
508

A low plant in patches, with 3 heart-shaped leaflets on each leaf and 1 funnel-shaped, white or rose-pink flower at end of each stalk; leaf and flower stalks both about the same length and attached to the plant at ground level.
Flowers: ½–¾″ (1.3–2 cm) wide; petals 5, often with purple veins; April–September.
Leaves: leaflets ½–1½″ (1.3–3.8 cm) long, often with pale blotch in center, attached by points to tip of erect stalk.
Height: 2–7″ (5–17.5 cm).

Habitat
Forest shade.

Range
Coastal central California to Washington; east to the eastern side of the Cascade Range.

Comments
This species forms lush, solid, inviting carpets on the cool floor of coastal redwood forests. The sour juice is characteristic of this genus, and gives the generic name, from the Greek *oxys* ("sour").

Spreading Dogbane
Apocynum androsaemifolium
509

A branched, bushy plant with drooping pairs of leaves, and small, pink, bell-shaped flowers in short open clusters at ends of stems or in axils. Milky sap.
Flowers: corolla ¼–⅜″ (6–9 mm) long, with 5 outward-curved tips on rim; June–September.
Leaves: 1–2½″ (2.5–6.3 cm) long, ovate.
Fruit: 2 slender pods, 5–7″ (12.5–17.5 cm) long, each containing many seeds with long silky hairs.
Height: 8–20″ (20–50 cm).

Habitat
Dry soil, mostly in coniferous forests at low or medium elevations.

Range
Throughout the West.

Comments
The popular name Dogbane is derived from the Greek word *apocynum,* meaning "noxious to dogs." Distasteful and poisonous, this species is avoided by animals.

Cliff Penstemon
Penstemon rupicola
510

A few large, brilliant pink or rose, bilaterally symmetrical flowers in many racemes often form a dense display above thick mats of stems and leaves.
Flowers: corolla 1–1½" (2.5–3.8 cm) long, with 5 lobes, 2 bent upward, 3 bent downward; 4 stamens with long wool on anthers, the fifth stamen has no anther, but may have a few hairs at tip; May–August.
Leaves: ½–¾" (1.3–2 cm) long, opposite, ovate, thick, with small, irregular teeth on edges.
Height: creeper, flower stalks to 4" (10 cm) high.

Habitat
Rock slopes, ledges, and cliffs.

Range
Central Washington to California.

Comments
Although there are only a few flowers in any one raceme, there are many racemes, and in full bloom the plant is a swatch of bright, glowing pink.

Farewell to Spring
Clarkia amoena
511

An open plant with showy, pink, cup-shaped flowers in a loose inflorescence.
Flowers: sepals 4, reddish, remain attached by tips, twisted to one side; petals 4, fan-shaped, ¾–1½" (2–3.8 cm) wide, each often with a red-purple blotch in center; stamens 8; June–August.
Leaves: ¾–3" (2–7.5 cm) long, lanceolate.
Height: 6–36" (15–90 cm).

Habitat
Dry grassy slopes and openings in brush and woods.

Range
S. British Columbia to central California.

Comments
As the lush grass watered by spring rains begins to turn gold in the dry heat of summer, Farewell to Spring begins to flower. The flowers close at night, and reopen in the morning. The genus name honors Captain William Clark of the Lewis and Clark expedition to the Northwest in 1806.

Pussy Paws
Calyptridium umbellatum
512

Pink clusters of densely packed flowers at ends of ascending or prostrate stems resemble upturned pads of cat's feet.
Flowers: sepals 2, pale pink, papery and translucent, become larger, to ½" (1.3 cm) long; petals 4, quickly withering, pinkish, ¼" (6 mm) long; stamens 3; May–August.
Leaves: ¾–3" (2–7.5 cm) long, narrow, in a dense rosette.
Height: creeper, with branching stalks 2–10" (5–25 cm) high.

Habitat
Dry, sunny places in coniferous forests.

Range
British Columbia to Baja California; east to Utah, Wyoming, and Montana.

Comments
Stems often lie on the ground with the relatively heavy "pussy paws" forming a perfect ring around the leaf rosette.

Bitterroot
Lewisia rediviva
513

A low, little plant with big, deep pink to white flowers on short stalks, nearly within a rosette of narrow succulent leaves.
Flowers: 1½–2½" (3.8–6.3 cm) wide; petals 12–18; sepals 6–8; stamens 30–50; at middle of each flower stalk is a ring of 5–8 narrow bracts; May–July.
Leaves: ½–2" (1.3–5 cm) long.
Height: ½–2" (1.3–5 cm).

Habitat
Open places among sagebrush or pines.

Range
British Columbia to S. California; east to Colorado and Montana.

Comments
Of the several pretty species of ground-hugging *Lewisias,* this is one of the most showy.

Colorado Four O'Clock
Mirabilis multiflora
514

Vibrant deep pink, broadly tubular flowers bloom in 5-lobed cups growing in leaf axils of this bushy plant.
Flowers: about 1" (2.5 cm) wide; petal-like calyx has 5 lobes; stamens 5; April–September.
Leaves: 1–4" (2.5–10 cm) long, opposite, broadly ovate or heart-shaped, with short stalks.
Fruit: seedlike, ½" (1.3 cm) long, roundish, brown or black.
Height: to 18" (45 cm).

Habitat
Open areas with juniper and pinyon; deserts; grassland.

Range
S. California to S. Colorado; south into northern Mexico.

Comments
Flowers open in the evening. The large root was chewed or powdered by Indians and applied as a poultice.

Tufted Phlox
Phlox caespitosa
515

Low, tufted, slightly woody plant with prickly, needlelike leaves and pale purple, pink, or white flowers.
Flowers: narrowly tubular corolla base ¼–½" (6–13 mm) long, the flared, 5-lobed end ½–¾" (1.3–2 cm) wide; calyx with 5 narrow, pointed lobes joined by a flat translucent membrane; April–June.
Leaves: ¼–½" (6–13 mm) long, not divided, opposite.
Height: 2–6" (5–15 cm).

Habitat
Dry, open pine woods, sometimes among sagebrush.

Range
S. British Columbia to central Washington, NE. Oregon, N. Idaho, and NW. Montana.

Comments
Tufted Phlox resembles small Granite Gilia (*Leptodactylon pungens*), which has leaves divided into needlelike segments.

Baby Blue Eyes
Nemophila menziesii
516

A low plant with pale or clear blue, bowl-shaped flowers that bloom singly on slender stalks growing near the ends of slender, leaning, branched stems.
Flowers: ½–1½" (1.3–3.8 cm) wide; corolla with 5 broad, pale or bright blue petals, often paler near base, generally with small black spots; stamens 5; style with 2 branches at tip; March–June.
Leaves: ¾–2" (2–5 cm) long, opposite, oblong, pinnately divided into segments with teeth along edges.
Height: 4–12" (10–30 cm).

Habitat
Grassy hillsides and among brush.

Range
Central Oregon to S. California.

Comments
One of the most charming and best-known spring wildflowers in California, it is often included in commercial wildflower seed mixtures and has long been cultivated in England. The equally delightful Five Spot (*N. maculata*) of central California has white petals with a large blue-violet spot at the base.

Hound's Tongue
Cynoglossum grande
517

Several smooth stems with large ovate leaves on long stalks mostly near the base, and loose clusters of deep blue flowers on branches at the top.
Flowers: corolla about ½" (1.3 cm) wide, with 5 petals joined into a funnel with 5 white, 2-lobed pads around opening of tube; March–June.
Leaves: blades 3–16" (7.5–40 cm) long, ovate, a few hairs on upper side, many on lower.
Fruit: divided into 4 hard, roundish nutlets ¼" (6 mm) long, with tiny barbed prickles all over surface.
Height: 12–32" (30–80 cm).

Habitat
Dry shaded places in woods.

Range
S. California to W. Washington.

Comments
The common name refers to the shape of the broad leaves.
Indians used preparations from the root to treat burns and
stomach aches. There are several species, all with blue or
maroon flowers and large rough nutlets that stick to clothing.

Blue Violet
Viola adunca
518

A small plant with Pansy-like, bluish-violet flowers that hang
at tips of slender stalks.
Flowers: ½–¾" (1.3–2 cm) wide; petals 5, upper 2 bent
upward, the lower 3 white at base, outer ones with white
hairs. A slender spur extends backward; April–August.
Leaves: blades, ½–1¼" (1.3–3.1 cm) long, on stalks, dark
green, rather thick, ovate or heart-shaped, finely scalloped on
edges; in tufts at base.
Height: up to 4" (10 cm).

Habitat
Meadows, open woods, and open slopes from sea level to
timberline.

Range
Canada; south to S. California, Arizona, New Mexico, the
northern Great Plains.

Comments
Violets are very popular wildflowers and garden plants,
romantically described as "shrinking" because of the way the
petals fold in. Species are often difficult to identify as they
may hybridize, producing intermediate forms.

Blue-eyed Grass
Sisyrinchium angustifolium
519

Several delicate, blue or deep blue-violet flowers in 2 broad
bracts top a flat stem, generally only 1 flower at a time in
bloom; stems taller than the clusters of narrow, sword-shaped
leaves near base.
Flowers: ½–1½" (1–3.8 cm) wide; 6 petal-like segments,
each with a fine point on the otherwise blunt or notched tip;
April–September.
Leaves: 2–10" (5–25 cm) long, ⅛–¼" (3–6 mm) wide.
Height: 4–20" (10–50 cm).

Habitat
Moist places (at least early in the season), generally in the
open, from lowlands well into the mountains.

Range
Throughout the West.

Comments
One of the most perplexing groups of plants, with many,
often intergrading, variants named as species.

Western Blue Flax
Linum perenne
520

An open plant with mostly unbranched leafy stems and delicate blue flowers blooming on slender stalks near the top.
Flowers: ¾–1½" (2–3.8 cm) wide; petals 5, broad; stamens 5; styles 5, longer than stamens; March–September.
Leaves: ½–1¼" (1.3–3.1 cm) long, narrow, with only 1 vein.
Height: 6–32" (15–80 cm).

Habitat
Well-drained soil in prairies, meadows, and open mountain slopes and ledges.

Range
Alaska to S. California; east to W. Texas, central Kansas, and Saskatchewan; also northern Mexico.

Comments
Several Indian tribes used Western Blue Flax for making cordage. Common Flax (*L. usitatissimum*), from which linen is made and linseed oil is obtained, often grows in the wild, "escaping" from cultivation. It has blue petals about ½" (1.3 cm) long and leaves with 3 veins.

Cusick's Speedwell
Veronica cusickii
521

Erect stems grow in little patches and deep blue-violet, flat flowers bloom on hairlike stalks in racemes.
Flowers: corolla about ½" (1.3 cm) wide, 4 lobes, the lowest the narrowest; stamens 2, spread apart; style more than ¼" (6 mm) long; July–August.
Leaves: ½–1" (1.3–2.5 cm) long, opposite, shiny, ovate.
Height: 2–8" (5–20 cm).

Habitat
Open, moist areas in the mountains.

Range
W. Washington to NE. Oregon and the Sierra Nevada of California; east to N. Idaho and W. Montana.

Comments
This perky little wildflower is common along mountain trails. In other species—some weeds in lawns or ditches—the corolla varies from nearly white to clear blue.

Western Polemonium
Polemonium occidentale
522

Many broadly funnel-shaped, sky-blue flowers are crowded in a branched cluster near top of this leafy plant.
Flowers: corolla ½–¾" (1.3–2 cm) wide, with 5 round lobes; June–August.
Leaves: narrow, pinnately compound, bearing 19–27 lanceolate leaflets, each ½–1½" (1.3–3.8 cm) long.
Height: 1–3' (30–90 cm).

Habitat
Wet places at moderate elevations.

Range
British Columbia to S. California; east to Colorado and Alberta.

Comments
The leaves resemble long overlapping ladders, giving a common name for the genus, Jacob's ladder.

Blue Anemone
Anemone oregana
523

Forms open patches and has an erect stem with 1 usually bluish-lavender flower.
Flowers: 1–1½" (2.5–3.8 cm) wide; sepals 5–8, long, generally bluish lavender, but varying to reddish lavender or pale pink (rarely white), resembling petals; no true petals; stamens 35–100; March–June.
Leaves: 1 at base and 3 in a whorl on stem, divided into 3 leaflets to 3" (7.5 cm) long, each often deeply divided and toothed.
Height: 4–12" (10–30 cm).

Habitat
Open woods and brushy hillsides.

Range
N. Washington to central Oregon.

Comments
The Blue Anemone spreads by stout underground stems. It intergrades with the white-flowered Western Wood Anemone (*A. lyallii*).

Common Camas
Camassia quamash
524

Light to deep blue-violet, star-shaped flowers in a raceme; several narrow, grasslike leaves grow mostly near the base.
Flowers: 1½–2½" (3.8–6.3 cm) wide; slightly bilaterally symmetrical; 6 narrow petal-like segments, lower ones tend to curve out from the stem more strongly than do upper ones; April–June.
Leaves: to 2' (60 cm) long.
Height: 12–20" (30–50 cm).

Habitat
Moist meadows.

Range
S. British Columbia to N. California; east to N. Utah, Wyoming, and Montana.

Comments
This species is sometimes so frequent as to color entire meadows blue violet. Indians pit-roasted the bland bulbs with other leaves, and also boiled them, which yielded a good syrup.

Felwort
Swertia perennis
525

Several erect stems, with most leaves at base, and starlike, pale bluish-purple flowers with greenish or white spots in an open, branched, but narrow cluster at the top.
Flowers: about ¾" (2 cm) wide; corolla with 5 pointed lobes joined at base; 2 fringed glands at base of each lobe; very short, thick style; July–September.

Leaves: at base 2–8″ (5–20 cm) long, the lanceolate blades tapered to a slender stalk; 1 or 2 pairs of smaller leaves on stem.
Height: 2–20″ (5–50 cm).

Habitat
Meadows and moist places at high mountain elevations.

Range
Alaska to the southern Sierra Nevada of California; east to New Mexico; north through the Rocky Mountains to Canada.

Comments
The genus is named for E. Sweert, a 16th-century Dutch gardener and author.

Nuttall's Larkspur
Delphinium nuttallianum
526

Generally only 1 stem with a few leaves, mostly at base, and blue bilateral flowers in one or several open racemes.
Flowers: about 1″ (2.5 cm) wide; sepals 5, blue, with ovate blades, the uppermost also bearing a backward-projecting spur ½–1″ (1.3–2.5 cm) long; petals 4, blue or white with blue marks, about ³⁄₁₆″ (5 mm) long, deeply notched on lower edge, upper petals white or bluish, angling upward from center of flower; March–July.
Leaves: to 3″ (7.5 cm) wide, nearly round, palmately divided into narrow, forked lobes.
Height: 4–16″ (10–40 cm).

Habitat
Well-drained soil in sagebrush deserts and open pine forests.

Range
British Columbia to N. California; east to Colorado, Nebraska, Wyoming, and Montana.

Comments
Representative of a host of low larkspur species with blue or blue-violet flowers occurring in many habitats, from dry California grasslands and chaparral to southwestern deserts and high mountaintops. In the West they are second only to locoweeds (*Astragalus* and *Oxytropis*) as a livestock poison, especially among cattle.

Douglas' Iris
Iris douglasiana
527

Large, reddish-purple, pinkish, white or cream flowers (with lilac veins) bloom on stout, branched stalks rising from clumps of sword-shaped leaves.
Flowers: 3–4″ (7.5–10 cm) wide; sepals 3, long, resembling petals, curved downward; petals 3, erect, about same length as sepals and slightly narrower; sepals and petals join to form a tube at base ½–1″ (1.3–2.5 cm) long. Pair of bracts beneath flower grow nearly opposite one another, bases not separated by space on stem; March–May.
Leaves: to 3′ (90 cm) long, usually shorter, ¾″ (2 cm) wide, flexible, tough.
Height: 6–32″ (15–80 cm).

Habitat
Grassy slopes and open brush.

Range
Coast Ranges from S. Oregon to central California.

Comments
A common iris in the redwood region. *Iris,* Greek for "rainbow," refers to the variegated colors of the flowers. A member of Juno's court and goddess of the rainbow, Iris so impressed Juno with her purity that she was commemorated with a flower that blooms with the rainbow colors of her robe.

Tough-leaved Iris
Iris tenax
528

Large, delicate, lavender to deep purple (sometimes white, rarely yellow) flowers, common with dark violet veins, grow at top of short stalks in dense clumps of narrow, tough leaves about the same height.
Flowers: 3–4" (7.5–10 cm) wide; sepals 3, resembling petals, curved downward; petals 3, erect, slightly shorter than sepals; sepals and petals join to form a tube at base ¼–½" (6–13 mm) long; bracts beneath flower joined to stem at distinctly different levels; April–June.
Leaves: to 16" (40 cm) long.
Height: to 16" (40 cm).

Habitat
Pastures, fields, and open areas in forests.

Range
SW. Washington to NW. California, west of the Cascade Range.

Comments
In the Willamette Valley of Oregon these handsome flowers provide brilliant color displays along highways. *Tenax,* Latin for "tenacious," refers to the tough leaves; Indians used fibers from the edges of the leaves of some western species to make strong, pliable rope and cord.

Western Dayflower
Commelina dianthifolia
529

Flowers with 3 broad blue petals protrude from a broad folded leaf at the top of a leaning or erect branched stem with narrow leaves.
Flowers: about ¾" (2 cm) wide; petals 3, on short stalks, lower slightly smaller; stamens 6; July–September.
Leaves: to 6" (15 cm) long, narrow, forming a sheath around stem at base; spathe 1–3" (2.5–7.5 cm) long, including a long, narrow tip.
Height: to 20" (50 cm).

Habitat
Rocky soil among pinyon and juniper or in pine woods.

Range
W. Texas to south-central Colorado and eastern half of Arizona; south throughout most of Mexico.

Comments
This species is called Dayflower because 1 flower appears outside the sheath every 1–4 days, opening near dawn and wilting by midday.

Western Monkshood
Aconitum columbianum
530

A usually tall, leafy plant with bilaterally symmetrical, hoodlike, blue or blue-violet flowers in a showy raceme.
Flowers: sepals 5, resembling petals, the uppermost forming a large arched hood ⅝–1¼" (1.5–3.1 cm) long, the 2 at sides broadly oval, the 2 lowermost narrow; petals 2, concealed under hood, with 3 others that generally do not develop; June–August.
Leaves: 2–8" (5–20 cm) wide, palmately lobed and jaggedly toothed.
Height: 1–7' (30–210 cm).

Habitat
Moist woods and subalpine meadows.

Range
Alaska to the Sierra Nevada of California; east to New Mexico, Colorado, South Dakota, and W. Montana.

Comments
Some species have been a source of drugs, and most are poisonous to humans and livestock. A European species of Monkshood (*A. napellus*) is the celebrated "wolfbane" of werewolf lore.

Maiden Blue-eyed Mary
Collinsia parviflora
531

Tiny, blue and white, bilaterally symmetrical flowers bloom on slender stalks in an open cluster on this small, widely branched plant.
Flowers: about ¼" (6 mm) wide; upper lip of corolla has 2 white lobes, bent upward, often tinged with violet near tips; lower lip has 2 blue-violet lobes projecting forward and a middle lobe folded between them, hiding the style and 4 stamens; April–July.
Leaves: to 2" (5 cm) long but usually much shorter, narrowly lanceolate, opposite near base, in whorls of 4 in the flower cluster.
Height: 2–16" (5–40 cm).

Habitat
Open gravelly flats and banks, often in sparse grass.

Range
British Columbia to S. California; east to Colorado, Michigan and Ontario.

Comments
This *Collinsia* has among the smallest flowers in the genus.

Roundleaf Bluebell
Campanula rotundifolia
532

Blue-violet, bell-shaped flowers hang along the top parts of slender, mostly unbranched stems that grow in small patches.
Flowers: corolla ½–1″ (1.3–2.5 cm) long with 5 pointed lobes that gently curve back; style about as long as corolla; June–September.
Leaves: those along stem ½–3″ (1.3–7.5 cm) long, very narrow; those at base with round blades, but usually withered by flowering time.
Height: 4–40″ (10–100 cm).

Habitat
Meadows and rocky slopes at moderate or high elevations.

Range
In nearly all the high western mountains except the Sierra Nevada.

Comments
The genus name, from the Latin *campana* ("bell"), means "little bell." The alternate common name, Harebell, may allude to an association with witches, who were believed able to transform themselves into hares, portents of bad luck when they crossed a person's path.

Explorer's Gentian
Gentiana calycosa
533

Several leafy stems in a clump bear at the top 1–3 blue, broadly funnel-shaped flowers.
Flowers: 1–1½″ (2.5–3.8 cm) long; corolla varies from blue to yellowish green and also often has greenish streaks; 5 pointed, nearly erect lobes, between which are plaits cut into fine segments at end. Bell-shaped calyx with 5 lobes, with a membranous lining; July–October.
Leaves: ½–1¼″ (1.3–3.1 cm) long, opposite, broadly ovate, bases of lower leaves joined, forming sheath around stem.
Height: 2–12″ (5–30 cm).

Habitat
Mountain meadows and stream banks.

Range
British Columbia south to the Sierra Nevada of California; east to the Rocky Mountains of Montana and Canada.

Comments
Gentians are among the most lovely of mountain wildflowers and are rock-garden favorites. The genus honors King Gentius of Illyria, ruler of an ancient country on the east side of the Adriatic Sea, who is reputed to have discovered medicinal virtues in gentians.

Mountain Bluebell
Mertensia ciliata
534

A plant with clumps of leafy stems and loose clusters of narrowly bell-shaped, blue flowers turning pink with age.
Flowers: corolla 5-lobed, ½–¾″ (1.3–2 cm) long, tubular part same length as the bell-like end; May–August.
Leaves: 1¼–6″ (3.1–15 cm) long, tapered at base, the lower ones on long petioles.

Fruit: divided into 4 small, wrinkled segments.
Height: 6–60" (15–150 cm).

Habitat
Stream banks, seeps, and wet meadows.

Range
Central Idaho to central Oregon and the Sierra Nevada; east to
W. Montana, W. Colorado, and N. New Mexico.

Comments
Mertensias are also called Lungworts, after a European species
with spotted leaves that was believed to be a remedy for lung
disease. Similar species differ in the proportions of the corolla.
Panicled Bluebell (*M. paniculata*) is very similar but all leaves
have petioles.

Coyote Mint
Monardella odoratissima
535

A grayish, aromatic plant with erect, bunched, leafy stems
bearing opposite leaves, and small, whitish or pale purple
flowers in a dense head at the top.
Flowers: corolla ⅝" (1.5 cm) long; bilaterally symmetrical,
with 5 lobes, 2 closer together than the other 3; stamens 4,
protruding. Broadly ovate bracts of head are purplish and
membranelike; June–September.
Leaves: to 1¼" (3.1 cm) long, lanceolate.
Height: 6–14" (15–35 cm).

Habitat
Dry slopes and rocky banks, from low elevations to well into
the mountains.

Range
E. Washington to N. Idaho; south to California, Arizona, and
New Mexico.

Comments
Coyote Mint has many races in the West, varying in density of
foliage hairs, breadth of heads, and length of bracts and calyx.

Rydberg's Penstemon
Penstemon rydbergii
536

Small, dark blue-violet, bilaterally symmetrical flowers form 1
or several whorls at or along the upper part of the erect stems.
Flowers: corolla ½–¾" (1.3–2 cm) long, narrowly funnel-
shaped, the 2 upper lobes projecting forward, the 3 lower
spreading downward, hairy near opening on the lower inside;
stamens 4, with anthers, the fifth without an anther, densely
bearded at tip; June–July.
Leaves: 1½–3" (3.8–7.5 cm) long, lanceolate, opposite, those
at midstem without stalks.
Height: 8–24" (20–60 cm).

Habitat
Open mountain slopes.

Range
E. Washington to E. California; east to N. Arizona, Colorado,
Wyoming, and SW. Montana.

Comments
The dark blue-violet whorls of small flowers help distinguish this common *Penstemon* from most other species.

Snow Queen
Synthyris reniformis
537

Several weak, leafless, flowering stems curve upward from a cluster of leaves on long stalks, and in short racemes bloom deep blue-violet, slightly bilaterally symmetrical flowers.
Flowers: corolla about ¼" (6 mm) long, 1 of the 4 slight spreading lobes broader than the rest; stamens 2; March–May.
Leaves: to 3" (7.5 cm) wide, heart-shaped, but the tip round, the edges irregularly scalloped.
Height: to 6" (15 cm).

Habitat
Coniferous woods.

Range
SW. Washington to central California.

Comments
One of the humbler, early-flowering *Synthyris* species; in the dim light of the early-spring woods its low, dark flowers are easily overlooked.

Blue-pod Lupine
Lupinus polyphyllus
538

1 or several, mostly unbranched, stout, hollow stems have violet or blue-violet flowers in dense, long racemes.
Flowers: about ½" (1.3 cm) long; 1 broad upper petal and 2 lateral petals nearly enclosing 2 bottom petals that are joined and shaped like prow of a boat; June–August.
Leaves: palmately compound, generally with 9–13 leaflets, each 1½–4" (3.8–10 cm) long, smooth on upper surface, arranged like wheel spokes.
Height: 2–5' (60–150 cm).

Habitat
Moist meadows and forests, along streams, from lowlands to mountains.

Range
British Columbia to the Coast Ranges of central California; east to Colorado, Montana, and Alberta.

Comments
This somewhat succulent lupine is one of the tallest and lushest western species. It has been crossed with others for beautiful horticultural hybrids. Along with several other lupine species, it is known to be toxic to livestock.

Cascade Penstemon
Penstemon serrulatus
539

Several erect, leafy stems with 1 or several whorls of deep blue to dark purple, bilaterally symmetrical flowers at the top.
Flowers: corolla ¾–1" (2–2.5 cm) long, without hairs, 2 upper lobes bent slightly upward, 3 lower spreading downward; stamens 4, with anthers, the fifth without an anther, golden-hairy at tip; June–August.

Leaves: 1¼–3″ (3.1–7.5 cm) long, opposite, broadly
lanceolate or ovate, not hairy, sharply toothed on edges,
usually without stalks.
Height: 8–28″ (20–70 cm).

Habitat
Moist places from low to moderate elevations.

Range
British Columbia to S. Oregon.

Comments
One of the few members of *Penstemon* to occur west of the
Cascade Range. The species name *serrulatus* refers to the little
teeth on the leaves.

Silky Phacelia
Phacelia sericea
540

A cluster of several erect stems with most leaves near the base,
covered with dense hairs that have a silvery-gray hue. Purple
or dark blue-violet flowers are in many dense, short coils in a
tight cylindrical cluster, which, because of long, protruding
stamens, appears fringed.
Flowers: corolla about ¼″ (6 mm) long, bell-shaped with 5
round lobes; June–August.
Leaves: 1–4″ (2.5–10 cm) long, broadly lanceolate, pinnately
cleft into many narrow lobes.
Height: to 16″ (40 cm).

Habitat
Open or wooded rocky places in the mountains, often at high
elevations.

Range
S. British Columbia to NE. California; east to Alberta, south
in the mountains to Colorado.

Comments
A common mountain wildflower easily distinguished from
other phacelias by its cylindrical, rather than coiled,
inflorescence.

BUTTERFLIES

Every elevation and every type of forest in the West is home to at least a few species of butterflies. Some rest, camouflaged, on the bark of a tree, while others flit from flower to flower, sipping nectar. Even the snow-covered peaks of the Rockies, a forbidding environment, are inhabited by some of these delicate creatures. Included in this section are descriptions of some common and conspicuous butterfly species of the western forests.

Phoebus Parnassian
Parnassius phoebus
541

2⅛–3" (54–76 mm). Male cream- to snow-white with black and gray markings and red spots on both fore wing and hind wing above and below, varying in size and in hue from pale salmon to brilliant scarlet; black spots on outer edge of fore wing. Female dusky or largely transparent, with more black and gray markings and similar spots; has waxy gray or black pouch at tip of abdomen. Antennae of both sexes banded in black and white.

Life Cycle
Chalk-white, button-shaped eggs hatch in summer. Caterpillar, to 1" (25 mm), is black with yellow spots; overwinters and pupates in smooth tan chrysalis protected by loose cocoon in grass tussock or among debris. Life cycle may require 2 years.

Flight
One brood; June–early September, later at higher altitudes.

Habitat
Subalpine meadows, forest openings, sage flats, and tundra.

Range
Subarctic Alaska south to central Sierra Nevada of California and down Rockies to Utah and New Mexico.

Comments
A number of features probably reflect the Phoebus Parnassian's adaptation to life in the arctic-alpine zone with its short, cool summers. The amount of dark gray scaling seems to increase in higher, colder regions, enabling the butterflies to absorb the sun's warmth. Phoebus flies at colder temperatures than many butterflies, sometimes flying even in snowstorms.

Northern Blue
Lycaeides argyrognomon
542, 545

⅞–1¼" (22–32 mm). Above, male bright silvery purple-blue with narrow dark border; female gray-brown with rows of orange spots around margins above. Dirty white to light fawn below; black line along extreme outer margins thin, becoming inflated at veins forming distinct triangular spots; row of silvery blue-green, orange, and black spots just inside margin somewhat pale and reduced, especially in West.

Life Cycle
Pale gray-green egg laid singly.

Flight
One brood; June–August, later at higher elevations.

Habitat
Cool zones in western mountains.

Range
Alaska and Yukon east to Minnesota and Maritimes; British Columbia south to central California in mountains and coastal bogs; Pacific Northwest to S. Colorado in Rockies.

Comments
There are many species of small blue butterflies in the forests

and woodlands of western North America. Most are very
similar in appearance and very difficult to get a close look at.
The Northern Blue is the butterfly that hikers often stir from
muddy spots along trails in the Cascade Range. Novelist
Vladimir Nabokov, an accomplished and respected
lepidopterist, devoted many years of meticulous study of
Northern Blues and their allies.

Ruddy Copper
Chalceria rubidus
543

1⅛–1¼″ (28–32 mm). Male above bright copper, sometimes
with darker cast; female dull gold with black spots and
brownish shading. Below, both sexes nearly white to pale
yellow; fore wing has black spots, hind wing immaculate or
with black dots.

Life Cycle
Largely unknown.

Flight
One brood; July–August.

Habitat
Moderate to high elevations, up to 11,000′ (3355 m) in open,
dry areas; sagebrush near meadows or streams; watercourses.

Range
Sierra–Cascade axis to eastern Rockies and adjacent prairies;
Alberta south to N. Arizona and New Mexico.

Comments
Brilliantly colored and rapid fliers, Ruddy Coppers can be
observed taking nectar at flowers such as wild buckwheats,
rabbit brush, and bush cinquefoil.

Nelson's Hairstreak
Mitoura nelsoni
544

⅞–1″ (22–25 mm). Above, male dark grayish brown with
rust-brown spots near hind-wing tail or over central parts of
wings to varying degree; has bold patch of scent scales; female
rust-brown over most of wings except for bases and margins.
Both sexes below brown, often with pinkish red or purplish
tint and variable white or brown band behind middle of wing,
jagged to straight, prominent to muted. Near tail, a few dots.

Life Cycle
Egg green. Mature caterpillar bright green with yellow
diagonal markings, covered by many bumps and ridges;
blends with foliage. Chrysalis brownish black; overwinters.

Flight
One brood; May–July.

Habitat
Forests and groves of host conifers from sea level to mid-
elevation mountains.

Range
Pacific Coast from British Columbia to Baja California, east
into N. Idaho, E. Oregon, W. Nevada.

Comments
The butterfly long known as Nelson's Hairstreak probably includes other poorly distinguished species—all with host plants other than incense cedar but still in the cypress family.

Queen Alexandra's Sulphur
Colias alexandra
546, 558

1½–1⅞" (38–48 mm). Male clear, lemon-yellow above. Fore wing pointed and yellow-fringed with small black spot near end of fore-wing cell; brighter yellow spot in hind-wing cell; narrow black fore-wing and hind-wing border. Female yellow or white with fainter cell spots and suggestion of dusky, interrupted border on fore wing above. Below, fore wing yellow; hind wing granular, lime- to olive-green with silvery, unrimmed cell spot. Some northern populations are orange.

Life Cycle
Eggs pale yellowish, pitcher-shaped; laid singly. Caterpillar green with lighter and darker lengthwise stripes; overwinters in third stage after remaining dormant through drier part of summer.

Flight
One brood; June–July.

Habitat
Clearings, meadows, roadsides, and other openings, and edges in mountainous ponderosa pine and true fir forests; also sagelands.

Range
British Columbia and Alberta south to Nevada and New Mexico in mountains and Great Basin (yellow populations); Northwest Territories, Manitoba, and South Dakota (orange populations), with mixtures in between.

Comments
When these butterflies congregate by the score at damp earth following a Colorado mountain shower, the stationary green triangles and frenetic yellow blurs create a striking spectacle.

Northwest Ringlet
Coenonympha ampelos
547

1–1⅞" (25–48 mm). Yellow-buff to deep ocher above, clear and unmarked (Great Basin race may be very pale, with whitish males). Below, fore wing ocher, crossed by partial whitish band, frosty olive-gray at tip; hind wing greenish gray or brownish olive crossed by broad, zigzag, and broken cream-colored streak and often light-scaled veins. Usually without eyespots, although sometimes has 1 fore-wing eyespot below and small eyespots in partial row on hind-wing margin below, especially in eastern part of range.

Life Cycle
Egg yellowish. Caterpillar green. Caterpillars of second brood overwinter.

Flight
Two overlapping broods; April–September.

Habitat
Many grassy places, including marshes, mountain forests and meadows, sagelands, maritime bluffs, disturbed areas, pastures, and vacant lots.

Range
S. British Columbia, Washington, Idaho, Oregon, and N. Nevada.

Comments
The Northwest Ringlet seems to dislike too much moisture; it thrives in the arid Columbia Basin, can tolerate the Puget Sound area, but is absent from the very wet Olympic Peninsula and the coast of Washington.

Common Alpine
Erebia epipsodea
548, 549

1¾–2" (44–51 mm). Wings rounded. Above, dark brown, crossed by reddish-orange patches or bands usually containing eyespots with white pupils. 2 eyespots uppermost on fore wing are larger than others. Below, fore wing similar to upper side but paler, or sometimes reddish orange; hind wing usually frosted with gray over outer third, and sometimes also at base; darker brown median band usually not very outstanding. Hind-wing eyespots often ringed with yellow or pale orange.

Life Cycle
Egg pale yellowish white, nearly spherical; laid singly or in small groups. Caterpillar striped green; overwinters when young and resumes feeding in spring, pupating in loose shelter of silk and grass blades.

Flight
One brood; early June–late August for about three weeks, earlier in lowlands and southern part of range and later at higher elevations and latitudes.

Habitat
Mountain meadows, bogs, clearings, and lower arctic-alpine tundra; sage flats; northern prairie parklands; often in association with aspens.

Range
Central Alaska south in Coast Ranges and Rockies to eastern and central Oregon and New Mexico, and east to central Montana and W. Manitoba.

Comments
Strictly a North American species, the Common Alpine occurs farther south than any other New World alpine. While the other Rocky Mountain alpines are confined to the high country, this species flies down almost to the foothills.

Large Wood Nymph
Cercyonis pegala
550, 551

2–2⅞" (52–73 mm). Large. Highly variable. Above, light cocoa-brown to deep chocolate-brown (very pale in northern Great Basin). Below, paler and heavily striated with darker scales. Normally fore wing above and below has 1 or 2 small

to very large black eyespots, often yellow-rimmed, with small
white or large blue pupil; eyespots may lie in a vague or
discrete broad band of bright or dark yellow. Hind wing above
may have small eyespots; hind wing below may have 1 or 2
small eyespots or a full row of 6 eyespots. Hind wing below
usually divided into darker inner and lighter outer portion by
single zigzagged, dark line. Female normally larger, paler,
with bigger eyespots.

Life Cycle
Egg lemon-yellow, keg-shaped, and ribbed. Caterpillar grass-
green, with 4 lengthwise yellow lines, fine, fuzzy pile, and 2
reddish tails; overwinters shortly after hatching. Chrysalis
green, rather plump.

Flight
One brood; generally June–August or September, varying
with locality.

Habitat
Open oak, pine, and other woodlands; meadows, fields, and
along slow watercourses with long, overhanging grasses;
marshes, prairie groves, thickets, and roadsides.

Range
Central Canada to central California, Texas and central
Florida. Absent from Pacific Northwest Coast and much of
Gulf region.

Comments
The Large Wood Nymph occupies much of North America; it
is the largest wood nymph and the only one east of the
Mississippi. Extremely variable, this butterfly has been given
dozens of names. Today, all are considered a single species. As
they perch on tree trunks or boughs to bask or drink sap,
Large Wood Nymphs blend beautifully with the bark. When
disturbed or seeking mates, they fly erratically through tall
grasses, with little speed but great skill and endurance.
Western wood nymphs visit such flowers as alfalfa and spiraea.

Chryxus Arctic
Oeneis chryxus
552

1¾–2" (44–51 mm). Above, tan or tawny-brown to dark
brown; male has dark, bold patch of scent scales across cell
and surrounding dark region sometimes covering much of fore
wing, leaving tawny marginal band. Below, fore wing tawny;
male's fore wing crossed by dark line shaped like a bird's beak
(female has line but much vaguer), mottled and striated brown
and white; hind wing crossed by broad and prominent brown
median band. Usually 2 or 3 eyespots above and below on fore
wing, 1 on outer angle of hind wing.

Life Cycle
Egg white. Mature caterpillar, to 1¼" (32 mm), striped
lengthwise with straw-color, olive, green, brown, and
brownish yellow; overwinters when young, some taking 2
years to mature. Chrysalis pale yellowish brown with dark
brown head and wing cases.

Flight
1 brood; May–August.

Habitat
Arctic and alpine tundra, evergreen forest clearings, mountain meadows and sage flats, northern prairies and parklands, and shaly steep slopes.

Range
Alaska and Yukon south to central California, E. Nevada, and New Mexico (but absent from Oregon), and east to eastern edge of Rockies and Ontario, N. Wisconsin, N. Michigan, Quebec, and Gaspé Peninsula.

Comments
The Chryxus has the broadest tastes and tolerances of any arctic, dwelling in a wide array of places and habitats. Some cut-off populations, such as the ones in the Olympic Mountains of Washington and the northern Sierra Nevada, have become physically distinctive.

Anicia Checkerspot
Occidryas anicia
553, 564

1⅛–1⅞″ (28–47 mm). Fore wing usually rather long. Above, black with numerous orange or cream-colored spots; orange predominates in most places, black at high altitudes, and from Nebraska to Great Basin cream-color and black. Below, fore wing orange with cream-colored bands especially toward edge; hind wing orange with bands of black-rimmed spots.

Life Cycle
Caterpillar feeds in a group in silken nest; overwinters half grown. Mature caterpillar white with black stripes or black with white dots or stripes; has many black branching spines, the back and side spines orange. Chrysalis white with black spots and orange tubercles.

Flight
One brood; April–August, latest at high altitudes.

Habitat
Alpine tundra and ridges, pine forests, grasslands with aspens, mountain meadows, mountain mahogany brush, sagelands.

Range
Western North America between Cascades, Sierra Nevada, and Great Plains, and from Alaska to Mexico.

Comments
Also called the Paintbrush Checkerspot. Over its vast range, the Anicia Checkerspot is one of the most variable butterflies. At different elevations in the same mountains or even the same locality, these butterflies can be quite dissimilar.

Lorquin's Admiral
Basilarchia lorquini
554

2¼–2¾″ (57–70 mm). Smallest admiral. Above, brownish black with cream-colored, off-white bands across all wings and buff to bright or dark rust-orange fore-wing tips, sometimes extending along much of fore-wing margin. Fore-wing cell has white spot. Below, a complex pattern of alternating brick-red and blue-gray bands beyond white band, reddish and gray spots and black lines inside band. Reddish spot bands just inside margin may also show on hind wing above.

Life Cycle
Egg globelike, pale green; deposited near leaf tip. Young caterpillar dark with white saddle. Mature caterpillar mottled olive and yellow-brown with light side band and white back patch; plumelike bristles behind head are smaller than those on other admiral caterpillars, as are humped segments behind them. Chrysalis irregular, lilac-brown in front and whitish behind; has greenish wing cases and dark, raised disk extending above back.

Flight
Two broods in California; April–September. One brood in Northwest; June–September.

Habitat
River bottomlands, canals, and lakeshores; also parks, forest margins, and elsewhere near host plants.

Range
Central British Columbia and SW. Alberta south to Baja California, NE. Nevada, and SE. Idaho.

Comments
Lorquin's Admiral is an abundant West Coast species, avoiding only the wettest coastlines and higher alpine reaches. When basking, it holds its wings open at a 45° angle, periodically opening and closing them altogether. Without warning it will burst into flight, flapping and gliding in an alternating rhythm, often returning to its original perch. These admirals inspect or attack almost anything that passes by, and have been seen to lunge at gulls 20' (6 m) overhead, harass the birds until they fly away, then resume their station.

California Sister
Adelpha bredowii
555

2⅞–3⅜" (73–86 mm). Large. Above, dark brown, narrowly banded with white, the band broken into spots on fore wing; bright orange patch lies on fore-wing tip, neither reaching nor extending down along brown margin. Underside complexly marked with auburn, pale blue, orange, and white bands and spots. Red-brown bars on fore-wing cell and hind wing inside angle.

Life Cycle
Egg spherical. Caterpillar, to 1¼" (32 mm), dark green on back, olive-brown beneath, with 6 pairs of brushy tubercles front to back. Both caterpillar and chrysalis are slightly humpbacked. Chrysalis light brown, with 2 head horns and metallic marks.

Flight
Two broods; April–October. One brood in desert mountains; May–June.

Habitat
Oak groves in middle- and low-elevation mountains; on coast and on offshore islands.

Range
SW. Washington, rarely south to Baja California, through Nevada and Arizona into Colorado, New Mexico, and Kansas.

Comments
The coloring of this butterfly's wings is like that of a nun's habit, inspiring its common name. California Sisters visit buckeye flowers, but take their moisture more often at damp mud, riverside sand, and fallen fruit.

Western Tiger Swallowtail
Pterourus rutulus
556

2¾–3⅞" (70–98 mm). Above and below, lemon-yellow with black tiger-stripes across wings and black yellow-spotted margins. 1 or 2 orange spots and several blue spots near black tail on hind wing; blue continuous all around outer margin of hind wing below. Yellow spots along outer black margin of fore wing below run together into band; uppermost spot on border of hind wing above and below is yellow.

Life Cycle
Egg deep green, shiny, spherical. Caterpillar, to 2" (51 mm), deep to light green, swollen in front, accentuating large yellow eyespots with black and blue pupils. Dark brown chrysalis overwinters slung from a twig or tree trunk.

Flight
February in S. California, May in Washington, normally June–July in mountain areas. Up to three broods in low altitudes and latitudes, one in cooler places with shorter seasons.

Habitat
Widespread, but normally near moisture—canyons, watersides, trails, roadsides, parks and gardens; sagelands and mesas with creeks.

Range
British Columbia south to Baja California, east through Rockies to Black Hills, and High Plains of Colorado and New Mexico. Rare east of Rockies.

Comments
The Western Tiger Swallowtail may be the most conspicuous butterfly in the West. In Western canyons, males of several species of swallowtails gather in spectacular numbers around mud puddles or beside streams, with the Western Tiger usually predominating.

Pine White
Neophasia menapia
557

1¾–2" (44–51 mm). Male and female above white with heavy black markings around fore-wing tips and along leading edge of fore wing; female also shows network of black veins around hind-wing margin above and below; on male this pattern is only below. Fore wing below black at rear margin with pattern of large white spots; female has bright orange or crimson outlining to hind-wing pattern below.

Life Cycle
Green egg tiny, pear-shaped with bright white beads around neck; deposited in rows, unlike singly laid eggs of most whites and sulphurs. Caterpillar dark green with white back and side stripes. Chrysalis slender, green striped with white.

Flight
July–September, most abundant late summer.

Habitat
Pine and fir forests from sea level to mid-montane.

Range
S. British Columbia and Alberta south through mountains and forests into S. California, N. Arizona, central New Mexico, and Black Hills of South Dakota and Nebraska. Absent from northwest coastal forests.

Comments
This strange white normally flutters weakly, high among conifers. It is difficult to see close up, although males and occasional females can be observed as they take nectar on the forest floor in early morning and late afternoon. Except in southern Arizona or Mexico, it is the only white butterfly that frequents pines.

Faunus Anglewing
Polygonia faunus
559

1⅞–2″ (48–51 mm). Wing margins irregular and ragged. Rich dark russet above. Hind wing above has broad, dark margin, crossed by a number of small yellow-orange spots, and edge may be narrowly purplish gray. Fresh individuals have greenish sheen mostly on margin above. 2-toned and striated brownish gray beneath, with 2 rows of blue-green bars and chevrons along outer part usually more pronounced than in other species. Silver-blue comma-shaped mark on hind wing below.

Life Cycle
Egg pale green. Solitary caterpillar, to 1¼″ (32 mm), tan with whitish patches and spines. Chrysalis tan with dusky green streaks and metallic spots. Adult overwinters, sometimes emerging on warm midwinter days.

Flight
One brood; March–April or May at higher altitudes into fall.

Habitat
Sunny glades, roadsides, and especially coniferous woods.

Range
British Columbia south to central California, east through Northwest Territories and Montana to Hudson Bay, Iowa, and Adirondacks, south in Appalachians to N. Georgia.

Comments
The Faunus Anglewing seeks out sunny forest glades for

basking and feeding. This species varies considerably within its range—smaller and grayer in the Northwest Territories, medium-sized and brighter in the Pacific Northwest.

California Tortoiseshell
Nymphalis californica
560

1⅛–2⅜″ (48–60 mm). Wing margins ragged. Above, rich russet with black blotches on fore wing, small white spots on leading edge of fore wing, black and white pair of spots on leading edge of hind wing, margin dark, often with hint of blue. Below, dull barklike brown, lighter outwardly, contrasting with darker base; margin lined with deep blue marks. Fore-wing trailing edge straight.

Life Cycle
Caterpillar velvety black with yellow and blue-black spines and white specks. Chrysalis gray and tan, may have blue cast; horned head.

Flight
One brood in North, two or three farther south.

Habitat
Mountainous terrain below subalpine zone, especially canyons; also lowland forest edges, glades, and parklands.

Range
British Columbia south to S. California, and east to Saskatchewan, Nebraska, and New Mexico; very rarely wandering or introduced into Midwest and Northeast.

Comments
The California Tortoiseshell may be rare or absent from large parts of its range for several years. These dearths are followed by periods of enormous abundance, involving emigrations over immense areas, which seem to be related to population pressures, host plant availability, and climate conditions.

Milbert's Tortoiseshell
Aglais milberti
561

1¾–2″ (44–51 mm). Above and below 2-toned; inner dark and outer light, separated by a sharp border. Above, inner dark area chocolate-brown with 2 red-orange patches along leading edge of fore wing, outer part has yellow band blending into bright orange band. Below, inner area purplish brown; outer band tan. Dark margin above and below punctuated by faint blue bars, has irregular outline.

Life Cycle
Egg pale green; deposited in clusters, often several hundred together. Caterpillars at first live in colonies in silken nests, later become solitary, folding up a leaf to live in. Mature caterpillar black with narrow yellow band above and green side stripes, white speckled with 7 rows of short spines. Chrysalis grayish or greenish tan, thorny. Adults overwinter.

Flight
Two or three broods where season permits; spring, summer, fall.

Habitat
Dry stream beds and canals, riversides, beaches, meadows, alpine rockslides, roads, and trails.

Range
Far North except Alaska, south to S. California, Oklahoma, and West Virginia.

Comments
This unmistakable butterfly prefers northern latitudes and higher altitudes, although it occupies lowlands if they are cool enough. Extremely versatile, it inhabits every kind of place within its range, from cold desert to rain forest and city lot to alpine summit. Milbert's Tortoiseshell may sometimes be seen even in midwinter on a warmish day in many temperate areas.

Great Spangled Fritillary
Speyeria cybele
562, 563

2⅛–3" (54–76 mm). Above, orange with 5 black dashes near fore-wing base; several black dashes near hind-wing base, irregular black band in middle of wing followed by rows of black dots, plus 2 rows of black crescents, the outer in a line along margin. Below, fore wing yellowish orange with black marks similar to upper side and a few silver spots near tip; hind wing reddish brown with silver spots on base and middle of wing, and broad yellow band and silver triangles next to brown margin. Female darker above, especially at base. Western male brighter orange with more pointed fore wing; female straw-colored outwardly, black at base.

Life Cycle
Tiny caterpillar overwinters after hatching from pale brown egg. Caterpillar black with branching spines that are orange at base. Chrysalis mottled dark brown.

Flight
One brood; June to mid-September.

Habitat
In West, moist pine and oak woods, conifer forest openings, and wet meadows; moist meadows and deciduous woods in East.

Range
S. British Columbia south to central California and New Mexico; S. Quebec and Maritimes south to N. Georgia.

Comments
The Great Spangled Fritillary flies swiftly but pauses to take nectar from thistles and other flowers. Females of this and most other fritillaries mate in June or July, but many of them disappear, perhaps hiding under leaves or bark, to reappear in late August and September, when they lay their eggs near violets. By this time, the shorter-lived males, which have emerged from chrysalises a few days or weeks earlier than females, are scarce. This species is among the more common and widespread of several, very similar Fritillaries.

INSECTS AND SPIDERS

By far the most numerous animals on earth, insects and spiders are also fascinating. Some have carved out a niche for themselves as tiny predators in an immense landscape; others inhabit the inner recesses of fallen logs or dwell on the underside of leaves. Included in this section are descriptions of some of the most conspicuous and abundant insects and spiders in western forests.

Golden Buprestid
Buprestis aurulenta
565

½–¾" (14–19 mm). Elongate oval, flattened. Iridescent bluish green to green with red or copper along outer edges of elytra and where elytra meet. Head rounded in front of eyes; antennae threadlike, extending backward beyond upper part of thorax. Larva is yellowish white and has a small head.

Habitat
Coniferous forests.

Range
Rocky Mountains to the Pacific Coast.

Life Cycle
Cylindrical white eggs are laid on bark of twigs. Larvae pupate in a tunnel. Adults chew through bark in June–July.

Comments
Adults are wary and fly quickly, often to bask in the sun on the bark of trees. Although these beetles are beautiful, adults and larvae are very destructive.

Pine and Spruce Engraver Beetles
Ips spp.
566

⅛–¼" (4–6 mm). Cylindrical. Black, brown, or reddish brown, sometimes with fine yellow hair. Head concealed from above by upper part of thorax, but flattened club of antennae project. Front tibiae widen toward tip. Tip of elytra deeply cut and edged with coarse teeth.

Habitat
Coniferous forests.

Range
Throughout North America; individual species more localized.

Life Cycle
Adults cut cylindrical tunnels through bark to feeding area, then expand brood galleries, where eggs are laid. Larvae excavate galleries further in a pattern resembling an engraving when bark is peeled away.

Comments
The tunnels cut by these insects provide openings for fungus, often hastening the death of a tree already in decline.

Bark Beetles
Scolytus spp.
567

⅛–¼" (3–5 mm). Shiny reddish brown, dark brown, or black. Cylindrical, rounded sharply at front of thorax and behind elytra. Concave below at rear of abdomen. Male's abdomen usually has blunt spines below, pointing to rear. Elytra grooved, pitted. Antennae clubbed.

Habitat
Deciduous and mixed forests.

Range
Throughout North America.

Life Cycle
In early spring female cuts holes for eggs in bark of dying or

dead trees and deposits each egg in separate side tunnel of inner bark, hollowed parallel to grain. Larvae bore deeper, overwinter, and pupate in second summer. Adults emerge late summer or fall.

Comments
These beetles do major damage to trees. The European Elm Bark Beetle (*S. multistriatus*), ⅛″ (3 mm), is shiny reddish brown and the male has 1 blunt spine below its abdomen. It carries the fungus that causes Dutch elm disease, and ranges east of the Mississippi and also from Colorado and Nevada to California, north to Washington. The Fir Engraver (*S. ventralis*), ⅛–¼″ (3–5 mm), is black and has no spines. It feeds on both Douglas-fir and true firs from British Columbia south and in the northern Rocky Mountains.

Common Water Strider
Gerris remigis
568

½–⅝″ (12–16 mm). Flattened, elongate. Dark brown to black. Short fore legs. Long slender middle and hind legs. Mostly wingless.

Habitat
Surfaces of ponds, slow streams, and other quiet waters.

Range
Throughout North America.

Life Cycle
Courtship and mating involve communication by ripples in the water's surface film. Female lays parallel rows of cylindrical eggs on an object at water's edge. Nymphs mature in about 5 weeks.

Comments
These insects are called Skaters in Canada and Jesus Bugs in Texas because they "walk" on the water.

Violet Tail
Argia violacea
569

Male 1⅛–1¼″ (28–32 mm), female 1¼″ (32–33 mm). Male's head black; thorax and abdomen violet. Female is dark brown to black. Wings clear.

Habitat
Along slow streams, coves of fast rivers, or weedy lakes.

Range
Throughout the United States and southern Canada.

Life Cycle
Male clasps female by the neck with a pair of pincerlike appendages and beats wings to perch vertically upward from mate. Female dips abdomen into water to lay eggs on underwater leaf. When eggs are deposited, male takes flight like a helicopter, lifting female from the water.

Comments
Also called Violet Dancer. These striking damselflies are often seen flying in tandem over streams and ponds.

Western Flying Adder
Cordulegaster dorsalis
570

2¾–3⅜" (70–85 mm). Wingspan: to 5⅜" (135 mm). Thorax chocolate-brown with yellow markings. Abdomen blackish with line of yellow patches along middle of back.

Habitat
Near woodland streams.

Range
Nevada and California to Alaska.

Life Cycle
Female uses long, strong egg-laying organ at rear end of abdomen to press eggs singly into wet wood or other plant tissues near water's edge. Nymph burrows into silt or sand at stream bottom, then crawls out on some support and transforms to adult as early as late May in the North.

Comments
Between flights the adder often clings beneath a support, hanging at an oblique angle. Chiefly a forest dragonfly.

Short-tailed Ichneumons
Ophion spp.
571

⅜–¾" (10–19 mm). Abdomen long, compressed on sides. Body pale yellow to reddish brown. Antennae and legs long, pale. Wings clear.

Habitat
Forest canopies and shrubby fields.

Range
Worldwide.

Life Cycle
Female hunts for active caterpillar of appropriate host species and lays 1 egg on its body. Ichneumon larva burrows into host, eventually killing it but usually after caterpillar spins its cocoon. Ichneumon larva then pupates inside host's remains. Adults are active May–August. One generation a year.

Comments
Ichneumons fly to artificial lights at night. They are often seen emerging from hosts' cocoons.

**California Oak Gall
Wasps**
Andricus quercuscalifornicus
572

⅛–¼" (3–5 mm). Brown or reddish brown. Compressed on sides. Short "waist." Antennae threadlike. Legs stout. Wings transparent, yellowish.

Habitat
Hardwood forests and city parks.

Range
S. California to Washington.

Life Cycle
Eggs are inserted into soft young twigs. Larvae tunnel inward, causing tree to form hard galls, or swellings, known as "oak apples." Galls are green at first, then turn red or brown, growing to 4" in width.

Comments
This is the largest and best-known gall wasp in the West.
Sometimes other insects, such as Filbertworm (*Melissopus
latiferreanus*) caterpillars, come to live in the large galls.
Infested twigs swollen with galls break off soon after the galls
turn dark brown.

Giant Carpenter Ant
Camponotus laevigatus
573

⅝" (15 mm); workers mostly smaller, queen large. Shiny
black to reddish brown. Antennae elbowed.

Habitat
Deadwood of tree trunks, felled logs, timber, and poles.

Range
Cascade Range and Sierra Nevada, British Columbia to central
California.

Life Cycle
Nests are built in cavities excavated in dead wood. Brood
chambers accommodate eggs, larvae, and pupae inside silken
pupal cases.

Comments
Unlike termites, carpenter ants do not eat wood but tunnel
inside. They eat other insects, honeydew, and plant matter.
Carpenter ants are among the more conspicuous forest insects
and assist in breaking down woody materials to form the
organic compound humus.

Snow Mosquito
Aedes communis
574

¼" (5–6 mm). Brown with dark brown scales and some
golden-yellow to gray scales. Abdomen has dark and light
bands above. Wings have brown scales.

Habitat
Forested regions with shade.

Range
Northern United States and Canada.

Life Cycle
Eggs are dropped on pools of melting snow, hatching early in
spring. Larvae develop in cold water. One generation a year.

Comments
Unlike most mosquitoes, female Snow Mosquitoes are active
even in very cold weather, when the snow is still on the
ground.

Black Flies
Simulium spp.
575

1/16–⅛" (2–4 mm). Humpbacked, head pointing downward.
Grayish brown to shiny black. Antennae thick, often with
many segments. Wings smoky to clear; veins near front
margin heavy, others delicate.

Habitat
Near running water in forests, mountains, and tundra.

Range
Labrador south to Georgia, west to California and Mexico, north to Alaska.

Life Cycle
Eggs are laid on stones or leaves at the edge of rapidly flowing streams, or on the water surface itself. Larvae tumble into water. Fully grown larvae pupate in cocoons that coat rocks in water, resembling moss. Adults burst out, rise on a bubble of trapped air, and fly away in late spring and early summer.

Comments
Biting adults are the bane of the North Country, particularly early in the season. Some species transmit waterfowl malaria, killing large numbers of ducks, geese, swans, and turkeys.

Deer Flies
Chrysops spp.
576

⅜–⅝" (9–15 mm). Body somewhat flattened, head smaller than that of horse fly. Black with yellow-green markings on thorax and most of abdomen. Antennae cylindrical. Eyes bright green or gold with zigzag or other patterns. Hind tibiae have 2 spurs at tip. Wings have distinctive brownish-black pattern. Larva is yellowish or greenish with brown rings.

Habitat
Forests, meadows, roadsides, and suburbs near water.

Range
Throughout North America.

Life Cycle
Shiny black eggs are laid in clusters on leaves of emergent plants just above water. Fully grown larvae pupate in mud at edge of water. Adults emerge May–August.

Comments
A deer fly circles over its intended victim before settling, then immediately bites. Some transmit bacteria that cause tularemia in rabbits, hares, and occasionally people.

Yellow Jackets
Vespula spp.
577

½–⅝" (12–16 mm). Body stout, slightly wider than head. Abdomen narrow where attached to thorax with short "waist." First antennal segment yellow, others black. Head, thorax, and abdomen black and yellow or white. Wings smoky.

Habitat
Meadows and edges of forested land, usually nesting in ground or at ground level in stumps and fallen logs.

Range
Throughout North America; various species more localized.

Life Cycle
In spring mated female constructs small nest and daily brings food to larvae until first brood matures; females are workers. In late summer males develop from unfertilized eggs and mate. When cold weather begins, all but mated females die.

Comments
Yellow jackets can be pests at picnics, and they will carry off bits of food. Females sting repeatedly at the least provocation.

Golden Northern Bumble Bee
Bombus fervidus
578

Male drone ⅜–⅝″ (10–15 mm); workers ½–¾″ (13–18 mm); spring queen ¾–⅞″ (18–23 mm). Robust, hairy. Face and head mostly blackish. Black band between wings. Female is yellow on most of thorax and abdominal segments 1–4, black on 5–6; male is yellow on segments 1–5, black on 6–7. Female has pollen-collecting basket on hind tibia.

Habitat
Clearings in forests, roadsides, and open areas.

Range
British Columbia south to California, east to the Atlantic.

Life Cycle
Queen overwinters until early spring, enters opening in soil to build honeypots and brood cells. Small workers develop first. With warmer weather, new honeypots and brood cells are constructed, producing larger adults. Only young, mated females (new queens) overwinter; the rest of the colony, including old queen, dies. Adults fly May–September.

Comments
The larger American Bumble Bee (*B. pennsylvanicus*) is black behind the wings with yellow on abdominal segments 1–3. It is found in the United States and southern Canada.

Wood Ticks
Dermacentor spp.
579

¼″ (0.6 cm). Body oval, flat, brown or gray, with shield on back behind head; 8 legs in adult, 6 in young.

Habitat
Woodlands and shrubbery beside trails.

Range
Throughout North America.

Life Cycle
Tick clings to plants while extending forelegs to seize passing host; climbs on, then drops off when engorged. If not yet mature, tick molts and repeats process. Mature female, if mated before last big meal, drops eggs, producing larvae.

Comments
This tick can transfer disease organisms, such as Rocky Mountain Spotted Fever, from one host to the next. After a walk through a field, inspect clothing and hair for ticks.

Forest Wolf Spider
Lycosa gulosa
580

Male ⅜″ (10–11 mm), female ⅜–½″ (10–13 mm). Dark brown with grayish-yellow stripe along middle of cephalothorax and narrow grayish-yellow stripe on each side. Male's abdomen has 2 incomplete black stripes on front third. Pedipalps large, hairy.

Habitat
Woods, among litter.

Range
Rocky Mountains east to the Atlantic Coast.

Life Cycle
Female drags eggs in a spherical sac until they hatch.
Spiderlings ride on female until able to fend for themselves.

Comments
This spider hides among litter by day and hunts at night. It
makes no nest or silken shelter, although it secures a dragline
before leaping upon potential prey.

Orb Weavers
Araneus spp.
581

Male ¼" (6 mm), female ⅜–¾" (10–20 mm). Abdomen
bulbous. Brown to orange, with distinctive pattern for each
species. Legs long, brownish, sometimes ringed with black.

Habitat
Among tall grasses and shrubbery.

Range
Throughout North America.

Web
Spiraling orb with nonsticky radiating support lines and sticky
spiral strands in vertical plane.

Life Cycle
Spider usually hangs head downward near center of web, or
remains at a nearby resting site connected to the web by a
signal line. Egg sac is attached to plant near this retreat or on
foliage nearby. Spiderlings disperse after hatching.

Comments
Each night the old web is replaced with a new one, spun in
complete darkness by touch alone.

**Golden Huntsman
Spider**
Olios fasciculatus
582

Male ½–⅝" (12–17 mm), female ¾–⅞" (19–21 mm).
Cephalothorax reddish yellow to golden with short black hair.
Abdomen, coated with gray hair, bears Y-shaped black marks
toward rear.

Habitat
Shady woodlands and thickets.

Range
New Mexico and Utah, west to California.

Life Cycle
Female carries egg sac in jaws until spiderlings emerge and
disperse.

Comments
This species makes no organized webs but wanders in slow
search for prey.

REPTILES AND AMPHIBIANS

The western forests harbor a wide array of handsome and colorful reptiles and amphibians. From the dreaded venomous rattlesnakes, which prey on small mammals, to the brightly colored newts and salamanders of cooler, moister areas, the western forests provide shelter to a diversity of reptiles and amphibians. This section provides descriptions of many of the most frequently seen of these animals.

Mountain Short-horned Lizard
Phrynosoma douglasi hernandesi
583

2½–5⅞" (6.3–14.9 cm). Flat-bodied; head crowned by stubby spines interrupted at rear by deep notch in skull. 1 row of pointed scales fringes trunk. Spines prominent and horizontal. Belly scales smooth. Gray, yellowish, reddish, or reddish brown; 2 rows of large dark spots down back.

Breeding
Litters of 6–31 are born alive, July–August.

Habitat
Varies, from open rocky or sandy plains to forested areas; from sea level to above 9000′ (2700 m).

Range
S. Utah and W. Colorado south into Mexico.

Comments
Diurnal. This lizard is most active during the midday warmth. At night it burrows into the soil. It feeds primarily on ants, but occasionally eats other insects, snails, sow bugs, even small snakes. Other subspecies of *P. douglasi* occur northwest and northeast of the range indicated.

Western Fence Lizard
Sceloporus occidentalis
584

6–9¼" (15.2–23.5 cm). Spiny; scales on back of thigh abruptly smaller. Scales on back same size as those on sides and belly. Olive, brownish, or black, with pattern of paired blotches or wavy crossbars down back and occasionally some striping. Undersurfaces of legs yellowish orange. Blue patches on sides of belly; adult male has blue patch on throat.

Breeding
Mates early spring. Single clutch of 3–14 eggs, laid May–July, hatches July–September.

Habitat
Rocky and mixed forest areas from sea level to above 9000′ (2700 m). Frequents stone fences, fence posts, old buildings.

Range
Central Idaho south through Nevada, west to Pacific Coast.

Subspecies
Northwestern (*S. o. occidentalis*), 2 blue throat patches often with light blue connecting band, belly light; central Washington to central California.
Coast Range (*S. o. bocourti*), throat patches small in males, absent in females; from San Mateo to Santa Barbara County.
Great Basin (*S. o. longipes*), 1 large blue throat patch in males, belly gray to black with blue patches; central Oregon and extreme SE. Washington to central Idaho south through E. California, Nevada, and W. Utah, also central California south along coast into N. Baja California.
Sierra (*S. o. taylori*), entire belly and throat blue in adult males; in Sierra Nevada of California.

Comments
Diurnal. Easily encountered. Commonly called the blue-belly,

it is often seen displaying to attract females or drive off male intruders; it bobs its head and flattens its sides, showing off the blue patches.

Northern Alligator Lizard
Gerrhonotus coeruleus
585

8¾–13" (22.2–33.0 cm). Eyes dark. Distinct fold along sides. Olive to bluish; indistinct crossbands on back or transverse blotches of darker brown. Dark stripes along edges of belly scales. Young have broad light stripe down the back.

Breeding
Live-bearing. Mates in April at low elevations, in June in highlands. Litters of 2–15 are born in 7–10 weeks.

Habitat
Under rotten logs, rocks, or loose bark in cool, moist woodlands to about 10,500' (3200 m).

Range
Along coast and in Sierra Nevada range, N. California to S. British Columbia, southeast into N. Idaho and W. Montana. Disjunct populations in extreme NE. California (Modoc County) and S. Oregon (Lake County).

Subspecies
San Francisco (*G. c. coeruleus*), dark blotches on back, occasionally fused into lengthwise band, back scales strongly keeled; California coast north and south of San Francisco Bay. Sierra (*G. c. palmeri*), dark markings on back indistinct or absent, back scales strongly keeled; Sierra Nevada of California. Northern (*G. c. principis*), nearly unmarked or black on sides with light mid-back lengthwise band, back scales weakly keeled; Cascade Mountains of Oregon and Washington to Victoria Island, southeast into N. Idaho and W. Montana. Shasta (*G. c. shastensis*), many dark blotches on back (sometimes in irregular crossbands), back scales weakly keeled; S. Oregon into Cascades and Sierra Nevada of N. California.

Comments
Diurnal. This species prefers cooler temperatures than most lizards; hence its occurrence at high elevations. It remains active throughout the day, feeding on insects and snails.

Plateau Striped Whiptail
Cnemidophorus velox
586

8–10¾" (20.3–27.3 cm). Slender; 6 or 7 light stripes separated by dark brown or black bands without spots. Back scales small, granular. Throat white or blue-white; chin blue-green. Belly uniform white or pale blue-green. Lengthwise rows of large, smooth rectangular belly scales. Tail light blue.

Breeding
Unisexual; no mating. Clutch of 3–5 eggs, laid June–July, hatches in August.

Habitat
Pinyon-juniper woodland and ponderosa pine forest, 5500–6000' (1600–1800 m).

Range
W. Colorado south to central New Mexico, west to central Arizona, north through SE. Utah.

Comments
Diurnal. While it is foraging in leaf litter beneath bushes this lizard can be approached quite closely before it takes flight.

Western Skink
Eumeces skiltonianus
587

6½–9⁵⁄₁₆″ (16.5–23.7 cm). 4 light stripes extending well onto tail. Broad brown band on back between light stripes; broad dark band on side between light stripes. Tail usually gray or brown; bright blue in juveniles. Breeding male has orange on sides of head, tip of tail.

Breeding
Mates May–June. Clutch of 2–6 eggs is laid in burrows or under rocks, June–July, hatches July–August.

Habitat
Forest, open woodland, and grassy areas, especially where rocks are abundant. Usually under leaf litter, logs, or rocks.

Range
N. Arizona and S. Nevada to S. British Columbia; south along the coast through California into Baja peninsula.

Subspecies
Western (*E. s. skiltonianus*), light stripe on side has dark border along lower edge; S. British Columbia, W. Montana, N. Idaho, E. Washington, Oregon, and N. California, south along coast to San Diego County; Santa Catalina Island.
Coronado Island (*E. s. interparietalis*), dark bands on side extend at least half length of tail; San Diego County, California, into N. Baja California.
Great Basin (*E. s. utahensis*), light stripe on side lacks dark border; extreme SW. Montana, S. Idaho, Nevada, and north-central Arizona.

Comments
Diurnal. The Western Skink feeds on a variety of insects, their larvae, spiders, and earthworms.

Striped Whipsnake
Masticophis taeniatus
588

40–72″ (101.6–182.9 cm). Long, slender, and fast-moving. Dark brown or blackish, white side stripes divided by thin black line; typically with 2 or more continuous or broken light lengthwise stripes on each side. Large head scales edged in white (except in S. Texas). Scales smooth.

Breeding
Courts in early spring. May nest in abandoned rodent burrows. Lays 3–12 eggs, June–July. Young hatch in August.

Habitat
From grassland and arid brushy flatland to rugged mountainous terrain dominated by pinyon-juniper and open pine-oak woodlands; sea level to 9400′ (2850 m).

Range
South-central Washington southeastward in Great Basin to S.
New Mexico and adjacent extreme W. Texas and Mexico.

Comments
When surprised, this speedster quickly vanishes into brush,
rocks, or mammal burrows. During the day, it hunts with
head held high, watching for scurrying lizards or small
mammals.

Striped Racer
Masticophis lateralis
589

30–60" (76.2–152.4 cm). Long and slender; uniform black or
dark brown, with single yellow or orange stripe on each side
extending from neck to tail. Belly yellowish white, becoming
pink under tail. Scales smooth.

Breeding
Mates in spring. 6–11 eggs are laid late May–July, hatch
August–October.

Habitat
Chaparral brushland, desert foothills, open hardwood-pine
forest in the mountains; especially common around
watercourses and ponds; sea level to 7000' (2150 m).

Range
North-central California south along coast and along western
slopes of Sierra Nevada into Baja California.

Subspecies
Three; 2 in our range.
California (*M. l. lateralis*), stripe yellow; W. California, except
San Francisco Bay region; western slopes of Sierra into Baja.
Alameda (*M. l. euryxanthus*), stripe orange; eastern San
Francisco Bay area.

Comments
Active during the day. Swift, agile, and alert predator.
Like other racers, it locates its prey more by sight than smell.
When hunting, it holds its head high off the ground.

Ringneck Snake
Diadophis punctatus
590

10–30" (25.4–76.2 cm). A small, slender snake with a
yellow, cream, or orange neck ring and bright yellow, orange,
or red belly. Back gray, olive, brownish, or black; belly
frequently marked with black spots. Neck ring may be
interrupted, obscure, or occasionally absent. Scale present
between eye and snout. Scales smooth.

Breeding
Mates in spring or fall. Clutches of 1–10 elongate white or
yellowish eggs, 1", are laid June–July in communal nesting
sites. Young hatch in about 8 weeks, at 4–6" (10–15 cm).

Habitat
Moist situations in varied habitats; forest, grassland, rocky
wooded hillsides, chaparral, into upland desert along streams;
sea level to about 7000' (2150 m).

Range
Nova Scotia to Florida Keys, west to the Pacific Coast, south to central Mexico.

Subspecies
Pacific (*D. p. amabilis*), neck ring narrow, numerous belly spots; San Francisco Bay area, California.
San Bernardino (*D. p. modestus*), neck ring narrow, heavy black spotting on belly; northern San Diego County to Los Angeles County, east to San Bernardino Mountains.
Northwestern (*D. p. occidentalis*), neck ring wide, belly lightly spotted; extreme SW. Washington, south along coast to Sonoma County, California. Isolated populations in Idaho and Washington.
Coralbelly (*D. p. pulchellus*), neck ring wide, belly spots few or absent; western slopes of Sierra Nevada, California.
Regal (*D. p. regalis*), neck ring absent; SW. Idaho south through W. Utah, SE. Nevada, Arizona, W. New Mexico, Trans-Pecos region of Texas, and into Mexico. Isolated populations from SE. Idaho to SE. California.
San Diego (*D. p. similis*), neck ring narrow, belly moderately spotted; southwestern San Bernardino County south into Baja California.
Monterey (*D. p. vandenburghi*), neck ring wide, belly spots few and small; Ventura County to Santa Cruz County, California.

Comments
Secretive. Most often seen under flat rocks, logs, or loose bark of dead trees. When threatened, red-bellied forms tightly coil the tail and elevate it to display brightly colored underside.

California Mountain Kingsnake
Lampropeltis zonata
591

20–40" (50.8–101.6 cm). One of our most attractive snakes, ringed with black, white, and red. Red bands bordered by black. Snout black. Scales smooth.

Breeding
Clutches of 3–8 eggs deposited July; hatch in 9–10 weeks. Young about 8" (20 cm) long.

Habitat
Sierra Nevada yellow pine belt, Coast Ranges chaparral, redwood forests south of San Francisco Bay; sea level to 8000' (2450 m).

Range
Kern County, California, north along western slope of Sierra Nevada into SW. Oregon, southward in eastern portion of Coast Ranges to San Francisco Bay area; and south in mountains in scattered populations to N. Baja California. Isolated population in south-central Washington.

Subspecies
Seven; 5 in our range.
St. Helena (*L. z. zonata*), back edge of first white ring is behind last upper lip scale, snout dark, more than 60 percent of red bands continuous across midline of back; Napa, Lake,

Mendocino, and Sonoma counties, California. Intergrades with
Sierra in N. California and SW. Oregon.
Sierra (*L. z. multicincta*), first white ring and snout resemble
St. Helena, less than 60 percent of red bands continuous across
back; western slopes of Sierra Nevada, Shasta County to Kern
County, California.
Coast (*L. z. multifasciata*), like St. Helena, snout marked with
red; Santa Cruz and Santa Clara counties to Ventura and Santa
Barbara counties, California.
San Bernardino (*L. z. parvirubra*), back edge of first white ring
on or in front of last upper lip scale, snout dark, 37 or more
groups of tricolored rings (triads) around body; San Gabriel,
San Bernardino, and San Jacinto mountains, S. California.
San Diego (*L. z. pulchra*), like San Bernardino except 36 or
fewer tricolored rings; mountains of San Diego County, S.
California.

Comments
Diurnal but becomes active at night during warm weather and
sometimes can be seen crossing a road. Hides under rotting
logs and stones near sunlit stretches of rocky streams.

**Sonoran Mountain
Kingsnake**
Lampropeltis pyromelana
592

20–41″ (50.8–104.1 cm). Tricolored kingsnake with red,
black, and white, cream, or yellow bands. Black bands border
red and light bands and become narrow or disappear on sides.
Top of head black; snout light-colored. Scales smooth.

Breeding
Mates in spring. Clutches of 3–6 elongated eggs are deposited
June–July and hatch in about 2½–3 months.

Habitat
Chaparral woodland and pine forests in mountainous regions;
brushy rocky canyons, talus slopes, and near streams and
springs; 2800–9100′ (850–2800 m).

Range
North-central Arizona south into Mexico; isolated populations
in Utah, Nevada, and Arizona.

Subspecies
Four; 3 in our range.
Arizona (*L. p. pyromelana*), usually more than 43 light rings on
body; central and SE. Arizona and SW. New Mexico into
northwestern Mexico.
Utah (*L. p. infralabialis*), half or more of white body rings
cross belly; E. Nevada, central Nevada to Grand Canyon area
of NW. Arizona.
Huachuca (*L. p. woodini*), usually fewer than 43 light rings on
body; Huachuca Mountains, S. Arizona into Mexico.

Comments
Little is known of this handsome species' natural history. It
feeds on lizards and presumably small rodents. Captive
longevity exceeds 18 years. Protected in Arizona.

California Kingsnake
Lampropeltis getulus californiae
593

36–82" (91.4–208.3 cm). A large, chocolate-brown to black kingsnake with bold, light crossbands or a back stripe. Belly ranges from plain white to heavily blotched with dark pigment to plain black. Scales smooth.

Breeding
Mates mid-March (Florida)–June. Clutches of 3–24 creamy white to yellowish elongated eggs are laid mid-May (Florida)–August. Incubation lasts 8½–11½ weeks.

Habitat
Woodlands, chaparral, lower montane forest, as well as lowland, steppe, and scrublands; sea level to 6900' (2100 m).

Range
SW. Oregon south to extreme S. Baja California, east to S. Utah and W. Arizona.

Comments
Active during the day, especially early in the morning or near dusk, but becomes nocturnal in the warm summer months. It is primarily terrestrial, occasionally climbing into shrubs. This strong constrictor is one of many subspecies of the Common Kingsnake, which ranges widely across the United States.

California Red-sided Garter Snake
Thamnophis sirtalis infernalis
594

18–51⅝" (45.7–131.1 cm). Dark ground color with red blotches on sides, indistinct side stripe, and red on top of head. Red blotches or a double row of alternating black spots often present between stripes. Scales keeled.

Breeding
Live-bearing. Mates mostly late March–early May, occasionally in fall. 7–85 young born late June–August, earlier in Florida, to early October in the North.

Habitat
Near water—wet meadows, marshes, irrigation and drainage ditches, damp woodland, farms, parks.

Range
Coastal California, Humboldt County to San Diego County.

Comments
The California Red-sided Garter Snake is but one of several subspecies of the highly variable and widely distributed Common Garter Snake. Five other distinctive subspecies occur in the West alone.

Wandering Garter Snake
Thamnophis elegans vagrans
595

18–42" (45.7–106.7 cm). Gray or olive ground color with narrow, dull yellow or brown back stripe, which fades on tail; light areas between stripes marked with dark spots, sometimes absent. Scales keeled.

Breeding
Live-bearing. Mates in spring; 4–19 young, 6½–9" (16.5–23 cm) long, are born July–September.

Habitat
Moist situations near water; margins of streams, lakes, damp meadows; grasslands to forest; sea level to 10,500′ (3200 m).

Range
SW. Manitoba, SW. South Dakota, and extreme W. Oklahoma west to coastal British Columbia, W. Washington, central Oregon, and east-central California.

Comments
This snake is a subspecies of the variable and widespread Western Terrestrial Garter Snake, which ranges south into Mexico and east to South Dakota and Oklahoma.

Gopher Snake
Pituophis melanoleucus
596

48–100″ (122–254 cm). Large and powerfully built; small head. Light-colored with black, brown, or reddish-brown blotches on back and sides. Snout somewhat pointed, with enlarged scale extending upward between nostrils.

Breeding
Mates in spring. Clutches of 3–24 cream to white eggs are laid in burrows in sandy soil or below large rocks or logs, June–August; hatch in 64–79 days.

Habitat
Dry, sandy pine-oak woodlands and pine flatwoods, cultivated fields, prairies, open brushland, rocky desert, chaparral; sea level to 9000′ (2750 m).

Range
British Columbia, Alberta, and Saskatchewan south to central Mexico; east to Great Lakes, S. Texas, and Florida.

Subspecies
Sonoran (*P. m. affinis*), blotches brown or reddish brown on forepart of body, distinctly darker on rear; extreme south-central Colorado, W. New Mexico, extreme W. Texas, central and S. Arizona, and SE. California south into Mexico.
San Diego (*P. m. annectans*), black blotches on forepart of body fuse together; coastal S. California into Baja.
Pacific (*P. m. catenifer*), dark brown or black blotches on forepart of body separated; interspaces between side blotches suffused with gray; W. Oregon south through W. and central California to Santa Barbara County.
Great Basin (*P. m. deserticola*), wide blotches on forepart of body usually black, connected with side blotches, and creating isolated light blotches on back; south-central British Columbia south through E. Washington, Nevada, SE. California and eastward through Idaho, Utah, N. Arizona, to Wyoming, W. Colorado, and NW. New Mexico.

Comments
Generally diurnal, but may be active at night during hot weather. When confronted, the Gopher Snake hisses loudly, sometimes flattening its head and vibrating its tail, and then lunges at the intruder.

Northern Pacific Rattlesnake ⊗
Crotalus viridis oreganus
597

16–64" (40.6–162.6 cm). Brownish blotches down midline of back surrounded by light border; begin as oval or hexagonal markings, tending to narrow into conspicuous rings near tail.

Breeding
Mates March–May and in fall; 4–21 young, 6–12" (15–30 cm) long, are born August–October.

Habitat
Woodland, chaparral, conifer forest, grassland scrub, rocky places; sea level to 11,000" (3350 m).

Range
South-central British Columbia, E. Washington, west-central Idaho, Oregon (except SE. corner), west of Sierra Nevada in California south to Kern County.

Comments
The Northern Pacific Rattlesnake is a subspecies of the highly variable and widespread Western Rattlesnake, which ranges east to the Great Plains and south into Mexico. Eight other subspecies occur in the West. Active April–October over much of range, and becomes crepuscular and nocturnal during hot summer months. Adults prey chiefly on small mammals; young like lizards and mice.

Sharp-tailed Snake
Contia tenuis
598

10–19" (25.4–28.3 cm). The short spine-tipped tail and alternating black and whitish crossbars on belly quickly identify it. Upper surfaces brown, yellowish brown, reddish brown, or gray, often with an indistinct and lighter colored line at juncture of back and sides. Scales smooth.

Breeding
About 2–8 eggs laid late June–July; young hatch in autumn.

Habitat
Near streams or moist situations: pastures, open meadows, digger pine–blue oak woodland, oak-dominated foothills, and Douglas-fir–vine maple forest; sea level to 6300' (1900 m).

Range
Central California, along Coast Ranges and east of the San Joaquin Valley in Sierra Nevada, north to Willamette Valley, Oregon. Isolated populations in Pierce and Klickitat counties, Washington, and North Pinder Island, British Columbia.

Comments
Surface activity coincides with the rainy season. This snake is most commonly seen beneath logs or rocks, March–early June, after a warm rain. During dry months it retreats underground. Diet is largely restricted to slugs.

Rubber Boa
Charina bottae
599

14–33" (35.6–83.8 cm). Looks rubbery. Short broad snout and short blunt tail give it a 2-headed appearance. Uniformly olive-green, reddish brown, or tan to chocolate-brown. Large scales on top of head. Eyes small with vertical pupils. Scales smooth. In adult males, well-developed vestigial hind limbs called spurs are present near anus; in females, spurs small.

Breeding
Live-bearing; 2–8 young, 7" (17.8 cm) long, are born late August–September.

Habitat
Damp woodland and coniferous forest, large grassy areas, meadows, and moist sandy areas along rocky streams. Sea level to 9200' (2800 m).

Range
British Columbia to S. California and eastward to Montana, Wyoming, and Utah.

Comments
Crepuscular and nocturnal. An accomplished burrower, the Rubber Boa retreats under rocks or into damp sand, hollow rotting logs, or forest litter.

Western Yellowbelly Racer
Coluber constrictor mormon
600

34–77" (86.4–195.5 cm). Large, slender, agile, and fast-moving. Green, olive-green, yellowish brown, or reddish brown above, belly yellow. Young typically gray and conspicuously marked with dark spots on sides and dark gray, brown, or reddish-brown blotches down midline of back.

Breeding
Mates April–late May in most of range. Female lays 5–28 soft, leathery eggs with a rough granular texture in rotting tree stump, sawdust pile, under rocks, or in small mammal tunnel, mid-June–August. Young hatch in 6–9 weeks, July–September, are 8–13" (20–33 cm) long.

Habitat
Open woodland, mountain meadows, rocky wooded hillsides, grassy-bordered streams, and pine flatwoods; sea level to about 7000' (2150).

Range
S. British Columbia to Baja California east to SW. Montana, W. Wyoming, and W. Colorado.

Comments
Diurnal. Racers may be encountered in most any terrestrial situation except atop high mountains and in the hottest deserts. Despite the scientific name, it is not a constrictor.

Roughskin Newt
Taricha granulosa
601

5–8½" (12.7–21.6 cm). Warty skin, light brown to black above, with sharply contrasting yellow to orange belly. Breeding male temporarily develops smooth skin, swollen vent, compressed tail, and toes tipped with black horny layer. Small eyes with dark lower lids.

Breeding
December–July in quiet waters; October–November at higher

elevations. Eggs laid singly on aquatic plants or submerged twigs, hatching in 5–10 weeks. Larvae transform late summer at about 2" (5.1 cm) or overwinter and transform following June or July at 3" (7.6 cm).

Habitat
Ponds, lakes, and slow-moving streams with submerged vegetation and adjacent humid forests or grasslands.

Range
Pacific Coast, from Santa Cruz County, California, to SE. Alaska. Sea level to 9000' (2743 m).

Subspecies
Northern (*T. g. granulosa*), color typically uniform above, although populations in higher altitudes may have random dark blotches, belly with little or no blotching; same range. Crater Lake (*T. g. mazamae*), belly with heavy dark blotching; Crater Lake National Park, Oregon.

Comments
Most aquatic Pacific newt. On land it may be seen wandering abroad on cool humid days, searching for invertebrates.

California Newt
Taricha torosa
602

5–7¾" (12.7–19.7 cm). Resembles Roughskin Newt but has larger eyes and light-colored lower eyelids. Tan to reddish brown above, yellow to orange below. Back and belly colors blend. Breeding male has smooth skin, swollen vent, compressed tail, and toes tipped with black, horny layer.

Breeding
December–May. Female lays 1–2 dozen eggs in spherical masses, on aquatic plants or submerged forest litter. Larvae hatch at about ½" (11 mm), transform in fall at 2¼" (5.7 cm) or following spring when larger.

Habitat
Quiet streams, ponds, and lakes and surrounding evergreen and oak forests along coast. Fast-moving streams through digger pine and blue oak stands in Sierra Nevada foothills.

Range
Coastal California from San Diego to Mendocino County; also western slope of Sierra Nevada. Separate population at Squaw Creek, Shasta County. Near sea level to 7000' (2134 m).

Subspecies
Coast Range (*T. t. torosa*), brown above, light yellow to orange below; San Diego to Mendocino County, California. Sierra (*T. t. sierrae*), reddish brown to dark brown above, deep orange below; western slope of Sierra Nevada.

Comments
This species strikes a warning posture when threatened, revealing its brightly colored underbelly.

Arboreal Salamander
Aneides lugubris
603

4¼–7¼″ (10.8–18.4 cm). Climbing; grayish to chocolate-brown with oversize head. Cream or yellowish spots usually seen above; belly creamy white. Tail somewhat prehensile; toe tips expanded, squarish. 15–16 grooves on sides.

Breeding
Late spring–early summer. 1–2 dozen eggs laid in tree hollow, rotten log, or earthen cavity. Female broods eggs, which hatch in 3–4 months.

Habitat
Live oak woodlands along coast to yellow pine and black oak forests in foothills.

Range
Coast Ranges of California from Humboldt County to Baja California. Also, central Sierra Nevada foothills; South Farallon, Santa Catalina, and Los Coronados islands.

Comments
Champion climber among salamanders. Rarely seen during summer dry season, it hides in moist tree hollows, rodent burrows, caves, and damp basements. Several dozen may share a retreat. It surfaces during fall rains. At night it forages for insects in trees and on the ground amid leaf litter. It may squeak like a mouse when handled, and bites.

Oregon Ensatina
Ensatina eschscholtzi
oregonensis
604

3–5⅞″ (7.6–14.9 cm). Only salamander with tail constricted at base and 5 toes on hind feet. Plain brown or blackish above, whitish or yellowish below, with fine black dots. Base of limbs lighter in color than tips. Belly whitish or flesh-colored. Male's tail often longer than body; female's shorter.

Breeding
Late spring–early summer. Cluster of 7–25 eggs, laid underground, is brooded by female; young hatch at ¾″ (19 mm) in fall or early winter. No aquatic larval stage.

Habitat
Douglas-fir–vine maple forests in northwestern areas. Redwood forest, chaparral, and coast live oak–black walnut woodlands along coast. Yellow pine–black oak–incense-cedar forests of Sierra Nevada. To 10,000′ (3048 m).

Range
SW. British Columbia south through W. Washington, Oregon, and into NW. California.

Comments
When threatened, the Ensatina assumes a stiff-legged, sway-backed stance, with tail elevated and arched. If the tail is seized, it snaps off, allowing escape. Other subspecies, occurring in California and southern Oregon, display an amazing variety of colors and patterns—uniform brown or reddish brown to dark brown or black above, with cream, yellow, or orange spots, blotches, or mottling.

Olympic Salamander
Rhyacotriton olympicus
605

3–4⅝" (7.6–11.7 cm). Smallest mole salamander. Prominent eyes on small head; slim body, short tail. Plain chocolate-brown or mottled olive above. Belly yellowish green or yellow-orange, with variable black flecking. 14–15 grooves on sides. Males have conspicuous squarish lobes near vent.

Breeding
Spring–summer. Clutch size less than 15 eggs. Larvae transform at about 2½" (6.4 cm).

Habitat
Coastal forest in cold, well-shaded permanent streams and spring seepages.

Range
Olympic Peninsula, Washington, to Mendocino County, California.

Subspecies
Northern (*R. o. olympicus*), brown above with white speckles on sides, belly yellow-orange, sometimes with sparse black flecking; W. Washington to NW. Oregon.
Southern (*R. o. variegatus*), olive with brown mottling above, belly yellowish green with heavy black flecking; NW. California, SW. Oregon.
These subspecies intergrade in a diagonal zone from west-central Oregon to Lewis County, Washington.

Comments
Found at the edge or within the splash zone of fast-moving streams amid moss-covered rock rubble. The Tailed Frog often shares its habitat. It eats small insects and spiders.

Long-toed Salamander
Ambystoma macrodactylum
606

4–6⅝" (10–17 cm). Slender, with long toes. Dark brown to black above, with tan, yellow, or olive back stripe that in some subspecies is broken into blotches. Belly sooty to dark brown. Tubercles on feet. 12–13 grooves on sides.

Breeding
January–June, depending on latitude and elevation; in ponds. Eggs laid singly on spike rushes near surface of water, or in small clusters adhering to vegetation or undersides of logs in deepest part of pond. Hatching larvae transform June–August or following summer at 2–4" (48–98 mm).

Habitat
Arid sagebrush communities to moist evergreen forests and alpine meadows; sea level to 9000' (2743 m).

Range
Tuolumne County, California, to SE. Alaska and northeast to W. Montana. Separate populations in Santa Cruz and Monterey counties, California.

Subspecies
Western (*A. m. macrodactylum*), dull greenish to yellowish back stripe, reduced to scattered flecks on head; west-central

Oregon and W. Washington north to Vancouver Island.
Eastern (*A. m. columbianum*), fused bright yellow to tan
blotches form back stripe, head spotted; W. Idaho, central
and E. Oregon and Washington north to SE. Alaska.
Santa Cruz (*A. m. croceum*), black with series of yellow to
orange markings on back, endangered; Santa Cruz and
Monterey counties, California.
Northern (*A. m. krausei*), unbroken yellow back stripe, yellow
spot on eyelids; E. Idaho and W. Montana north to SE.
British Columbia and SW. Alberta.
Southern (*A. m. sigillatum*), fused yellow blotches form broken
back stripe, small spots on head; N. California and SW.
Oregon. Subspecies intergrade where ranges overlap.

Comments
Usually seen under logs or debris near pools, it sometimes
shares breeding sites with the Northwestern Salamander.
Long-toed's egg masses do not support the growth of algae.

Clouded Salamander
Aneides ferreus
607

3–5¼" (7.6–13.3 cm). Slim, long-legged climbing
salamander, with expanded, squarish-tipped toes. 2 color
phases: uniformly dark brown above; or brown "clouded" with
greenish-gray, ash, or coppery blotches. Belly whitish to
brownish, with white flecking. 16–17 grooves on sides.

Breeding
Late spring–early summer; lays 8–17 eggs singly on roof or
side of cavity in rotting log or under bark. Eggs are suspended
separately on mucus stalks, sometimes get tangled. Female
guards eggs, which hatch fall–early winter.

Habitat
Humid coastal redwood, Douglas-fir, and Port-Orford-cedar
forests; frequents margins of clearings. To 5400' (1646 m) in
western slopes of Cascades.

Range
Coastal California and Oregon, from Mendocino County to
Columbia River; Vancouver Island.

Comments
These agile climbers are seen 20 feet (7 m) and higher in trees.
They spend the dry season deep within logs. May be abundant
in clearings, where they hide under bark of standing or fallen
trees, in talus piles, or in moist rock crevices.

Pacific Giant Salamander
Dicamptodon ensatus
608

7–11¾" (17.8–30 cm). Robust and smooth-skinned. Brown
or purplish, with black mottling. Belly light brown to
yellowish white. No foot tubercles.

Breeding
Terrestrial adults breed in spring, in river headwaters. Eggs
laid singly, on submerged timber. Hatching larvae may
transform during or following second year at 3¼–6" (8.9–
15.2 cm). Sexually active larvae mature at about 8" (20.3 cm).

Habitat
Rivers, their tributaries, and surrounding cool, humid forests.

Range
Extreme SW. British Columbia south along coast to Santa Cruz County, California; Rocky Mountains in Idaho and extreme west-central Montana.

Comments
Most salamanders are voiceless, but the Pacific Giant has been known to emit a low-pitched yelp when captured. Land-dwelling adults live under logs, rocks, and forest litter but are sometimes seen crawling on the surface or even climbing in bushes or trees to 8 feet (2.4 m).

Blotched Tiger Salamander
Ambystoma tigrinum melanostictum
609

6–13⅜" (15.2–40 cm). World's largest land-dwelling salamander. Stoutly built, with broad head and small eyes. Body dark with irregular yellow to olive blotches, which may be so extensive as to reduce the ground color to a fine network. Tubercles on soles of feet.

Breeding
Prompted by rain; eggs laid March–June. Mates in temporary pools, fishless ponds, stream backwaters, and lakes soon after ice is out. Egg masses adhere to submerged debris. Hatching larvae transform June–August at about 4" (90–123 mm).

Habitat
Varied: arid sagebrush plains, pine barrens, mountain forests, and damp meadows where ground is easily burrowed; also in mammal and crayfish burrows; sea level to 11,000' (3353 m).

Range
S. British Columbia, central Alberta, and SW. Saskatchewan south to S. Washington, SE. Idaho, S. Wyoming, and N. Nebraska.

Comments
In the West, Tigers are often neotenic—sexually mature while still in the larval stage. Other subspecies of the Tiger Salamander, varying greatly in coloring and pattern, occur throughout much of the United States and adjacent parts of Canada and Mexico. None, however, occur in the Northwest Coastal Forest or Sierran Montane Forest.

Mountain Yellow-legged Frog
Rana muscosa
610

2–3¼" (5.1–8 cm). Brown with black or dark brown spots or lichenlike markings. Ridges at juncture of back and sides may be indistinct. Eardrum smooth. Belly yellow to pale orange. Toes fully webbed and tips dark. Male has swollen "thumbs."

Voice
No vocal sacs; mating call unknown.

Breeding
March–May in lower regions; June–August at higher elevations. Egg masses are attached to vegetation.

Habitat
Sunny stream banks and undisturbed ponds and lakes.

Range
The Sierra Nevada Mountains of California and extreme W. Nevada. Separate population in the San Gabriel, San Bernardino, San Jacinto, and Palomar mountains of S. California.

Comments
This is the only frog in the High Sierras, from 6000–12,000' (1800–3600 m). In the south it occurs from 1200–7500' (365–2300 m). It has a pungent, musky odor. Primarily diurnal.

Red-legged Frog
Rana aurora
611

2–5⅜" (5.1–13.6 cm). Large; reddish brown to gray, with many poorly defined dark specks and blotches. Folds present at juncture of back and sides. Dark mask bordered by light stripe on jaw. Eardrum smooth. Underside yellow, with wash of red on lower abdomen and hind legs. Toes not fully webbed. Male has enlarged forearms and swollen "thumbs."

Voice
Series of weak throaty notes, harsh, lasting 2–3 seconds.

Breeding
January–March. Egg masses laid in permanent bodies of water.

Habitat
Usually found near ponds or other permanent water with extensive vegetation. Also likes damp woods.

Range
Vancouver Island, British Columbia, south along the Pacific Coast west of the Cascade and Sierra mountains to N. Baja California. From sea level to 8000' (2400 m).

Subspecies
Northern (*R. a. aurora*), dark blotches without light centers; British Columbia to N. California.
California (*R. a. draytoni*), dark blotches with light centers; California to Baja California.

Comments
Primarily diurnal. Breeding takes place over a very few days.

Spotted Frog
Rana pretiosa
612

2–4" (5.1–10.2 cm). Large and brown, with ill-defined dark spots, sometimes with light centers. Ridges present at juncture of back and sides. Dark mask is bordered by light stripe on upper jaw. Underside varies from yellow to orange to red, usually with dark mottling on throat. Toes fully webbed. Eyes turned slightly upward. Male has swollen "thumbs."

Voice
A series of short rapid croaks without much carrying power.

Breeding
March–June. Egg clusters free.

Habitat
Mountainous areas near cold streams and lakes.

Range
Extreme SE. Alaska and north-central British Columbia, south to W. Montana, Wyoming, Idaho, and Oregon. Scattered populations in Utah, Nevada, and W. Oregon and Washington.

Comments
Diurnal. It does not regularly frequent ponds and lakes where water is warm enough to allow for extensive growth of emergent vegetation, such as cattails.

Cascades Frog
Rana cascadae
613

1¾–2⁵⁄₁₆″ (4.4–7.5 cm). Small, olive to brown, with black spots on back and legs. Folds present at juncture of back and sides. Dark mask bordered by light jaw stripe. Eardrum smooth. Underside yellow. Toes not fully webbed.

Voice
A low-pitched, raspy series of 4–6 notes a second.

Breeding
May–August.

Habitat
Mountain meadows, streams, ponds, and lakes above 3000′ (900 m), in the water and vegetation around it.

Range
In the Olympic Mountains of Washington and Cascade Mountains of Washington, Oregon, and N. California. To 9000′ (2700 m) near timberline.

Comments
Diurnal. It is frequently seen preying on insects or basking on a rock in or near the water. When threatened, it swims away.

Foothill Yellow-legged Frog
Rana boylei
614

1⅝–3″ (3.9–7.5 cm). Gray to brown to olive, with light-colored band across top of head. Gray mottling may be present on back. Ridges at juncture of back and sides indistinct. Eardrum granular. Lower abdomen and underside of legs yellow. Toes fully webbed. Male has swollen, dark "thumbs."

Voice
Rasping, unmusical note given 4–5 times in rapid series.

Breeding
March–May, when streams have slowed after winter runoff. Egg clusters attached to downstream side of submerged rocks.

Habitat
Aquatic. Prefers gravelly or sandy streams with sunny banks and open woodlands nearby. Sea level to about 6000′ (1800 m).

Range
From W. Oregon to SW. California; Los Angeles County near coast and Kern County inland; absent from the central valley.

Comments
Primarily diurnal. When threatened, it dives quickly to the bottom and hides among the rocks.

Tailed Frog
Ascaphus truei
615

1–2" (2.5–5.1 cm). Usually olive or gray to almost black; many dark spots on back. Dark stripe often runs from snout through eye; snout bears yellowish triangle. Some small tubercles and warts on skin. Toes long and slender; outer toes of hind feet thicker than others. Eye pupil vertical. Male has pear-shaped "tail," a copulatory organ for internal fertilization.

Voice
No vocal sacs.

Breeding
May–September. Eggs attached to downstream side of rocks.

Habitat
Usually clear, cold, swift-flowing mountain streams; sometimes found near water in damp forests or in more open areas in cold, wet weather.

Range
From S. British Columbia south to NW. California; also W. Oregon and Washington east to NW. Montana and Idaho. Many separate populations.

Comments
Aquatic. Sucking mouthparts equip tadpoles for clinging to rocks in strong currents.

Northern Leopard Frog
Rana pipiens
616

2–5" (5.1–12.8 cm). Slender brown or green frog with large, light-edged dark spots between light-colored ridges at juncture of back and sides; ridges continuous to groin. Light stripe on upper jaw. Eardrum without light center.

Voice
A low guttural snore lasting about 3 seconds, followed by several clucking notes.

Breeding
March–June. Egg masses are attached to submerged vegetation or laid on bottom.

Habitat
Streams, ponds, lakes, damp meadows.

Range
Throughout northern North America, except West Coast.

Comments
Primarily nocturnal. When pursued on land, it flees in zigzag leaps to the security of water.

Western Toad
Bufo boreas
617

2½–5″ (6.4–12.8 cm). Large; has oval parotoid glands. Gray to green, with light-colored stripe down middle of back. Warts tinged with red and surrounded by black blotches. Male has pale throat.

Voice
Like the weak peeping of baby chicks. No vocal sacs.

Breeding
January–September, depending on weather. Egg strings are attached to vegetation in shallow, usually still water.

Habitat
Near springs, streams, meadows, woodlands.

Range
Pacific Coast from S. Alaska to Baja California, east to west-central Alberta, Montana, Wyoming, Utah, Colorado, and Nevada.

Subspecies
Boreal (*B. b. boreas*), dark blotches on belly; SE. Alaska south through the Rocky Mountains to central Colorado, and south into N. California in the West.
California (*B. b. halophilus*), with fewer dark blotches on belly, and wide head; north-central California south into N. Baja California.

Comments
Active at twilight. At higher elevations, where nighttime temperatures are low, it is often active during the day. It lives in burrows of its own construction or those of small rodents.

Pacific Treefrog
Hyla regilla
618

¾–2″ (1.9–5.1 cm). Skin rough; varies greatly from green to light tan to black, often with dark spots. Black stripe through eye and usually a dark triangle between the eyes. Large toe pads. Male has gray throat.

Voice
A high-pitched, 2-part musical note.

Breeding
January–August.

Habitat
On the ground among shrubs and grass, close to water.

Range
From S. British Columbia to Baja California east to Montana, Idaho, and Nevada. Also, Channel Islands off S. California.

Comments
This commonly heard frog of the Pacific Coast, active both day and night, is found from sea level to over 10,000′ (3000 m). When Hollywood moviemakers need an authentic outdoor nighttime sound, they often record its call.

GLOSSARY

Abdomen In insects, the hindmost of the 3 subdivisions of the body; in spiders, the hindmost of the 2 subdivisions of the body.

Achene A small, dry, hard fruit that does not open and contains one seed.

Aestivation Dormancy during a hot, dry season.

Alpine Pertaining to or inhabiting mountains.

Alternate Arising singly along the stem, not in pairs.

Annual Having a life cycle completed in one year or season.

Anther The saclike part of a stamen, containing pollen.

Association A group of organisms typically found together in a particular environment.

Axil The angle formed by the upper side of a leaf and the stem from which it grows.

Bench The former wave-cut shore of a river, sea, etc.

Biomass The total weight of all living organisms in a particular area.

Bipinnate With leaflets arranged on side branches off a main axis; twice-pinnate; bipinnately compound.

Bloom A whitish, powdery coating found on certain fruits and leaves.

Boreal Northern; pertaining to the cool, moist coniferous forest region of North America that stretches from Alaska to Newfoundland.

Bract A modified and often scalelike leaf, usually located at the base of a flower, a fruit, or a cluster of flowers or fruits.

Broadleaf Having wide leaves (as distinct from coniferous); pertaining to deciduous trees.

Brood A generation of butterflies hatched from the eggs laid by females of a single generation.

Calcar In bats, a small bone or cartilage that projects from the inner side of the hindfoot into the interfemoral membrane.

Calyx Collective term for the sepals of a flower, usually green.

Cambium In woody plants, the sheath of embryonic cells, between wood and bark, that divides to form new tissue.

Canopy The uppermost level of a forest community, usually formed by the tallest trees.

Capsule A dry, thin-walled fruit containing 2 or more seeds and splitting along natural grooved lines at maturity.

Carapace Upper part of a turtle's shell.

Caste In social insects, a specialized form of adult with a distinct role in the colony.

Catkin A compact and often drooping cluster of reduced, stalkless, and usually unisexual flowers.

Cell The area of a butterfly's wing that is entirely enclosed by veins; also called discal cell.

Cephalothorax The first subdivision of a spider's body, combining the head and the thorax.

Chaparral Low, thick, scrubby growth consisting of evergreen shrubs or low trees; common in semiarid climates.

Climax The plants and animals in a given community that will persist in that community so long as conditions remain stable.

Cloaca In certain vertebrates, such as reptiles, the chamber into which the digestive, urinary, and reproductive systems empty, opening to the outside through the anus.

Clubbed Enlarged toward the tip, clavate.

Colonnade A row of trees, often with stiltlike roots, remaining after the decay and disappearance of nurse logs.

Community In a particular area, all plant and animal organisms living in close association and interacting.

Compound eye One of the paired visual organs consisting of several or many light-sensitive units, or ommatidia, usually clustered in a radiating array.

Conifer A cone-bearing tree of the pine family.

Corolla Collective term for the petals of a flower.

Coverts In birds, small feathers that overlie or cover the bases of the large flight feathers of the wings and tail, or that cover an area or structure (e.g., ear coverts).

Creeper Technically, a trailing shoot that takes root at the nodes; used here to denote any trailing, prostrate plant.

Crepuscular Active at twilight.

Cutin An impermeable, varnishlike covering on the epidermis of plants.

Deciduous Shedding leaves seasonally, and leafless for part of the year.

Dewclaw A functionless digit or "toe," usually on the upper part of a mammal's foot.

Disk The central portion of a butterfly's wing (*adj.* discal).

Diurnal Active during the daytime hours.

Dominant The plant or animal species most abundant in a community or exercising the greatest influence on the environment.

Drone One of a caste of social bees, consisting only of reproductive males.

Drupe A stone fruit; a fleshy fruit with the single seed enveloped by a hard covering (stone).

Duff Decaying organic matter on the forest floor.

Ecosystem A system of ecologically linked animals and plants that have evolved together in a certain environment. The elements of an ecosystem are mutually dependent.

Ecotone The transition area between 2 communities; ecotones contain species from each area as well as organisms unique to it.

Elytron The thickened forewings of beetles, serving as protective covers for the hind wings.

Entire Smooth-edged, not lobed or toothed.

Epiphyte A plant growing on another plant but deriving little or no nutrition from it; also called an air plant.

Exotic Not native to a given area; also, an introduced plant.

Eyespots Spots resembling eyes on winged insects.

Femur The third segment of an insect's leg.

Flight feathers In birds, the long, well-developed feathers of the wings and tail, used during flight. The flight feathers of the wings are divided into primaries, secondaries, and tertials.

Floodplain An area formed by and subject to a river's process of periodic flooding and deposition.

Follicle A dry, 1-celled fruit, splitting at maturity along a single grooved line.

Fungus A plant that lacks chlorophyll and reproduces by means of spores.

Gravid Bearing eggs or developing young; pregnant.

Habitat The place or community where a plant or animal naturally grows and lives.

Hardwood Of a broad-leaved tree (angiosperm) as opposed to a conifer. The wood may be hard or soft.

Head A crowded cluster of flowers on very short stalks, or without stalks as in the Sunflower Family.

Herb A plant with soft, not woody, stems that dies to the ground in winter.

Host plant The food plant of a caterpillar.

Hybrids The offspring of two different varieties, races, species, or genera.

Inflorescence A flower cluster on a plant; especially the arrangement of flowers on a plant.

Intergrades Animals of related and adjoining subspecies that may resemble either form or exhibit a combination of their characteristics.

Introduced Intentionally or accidentally established in an area by man, and not native; exotic or foreign.

Involucre A whorl or circle of bracts beneath a flower or flower cluster.

Lanceolate Shaped like a lance, several times longer than wide, pointed at the tip and broadest near the base.

Larva(e) A post-hatching immature stage that differs in appearance from the adult and must metamorphose before assuming adult characters (e.g., a tadpole).

Leaflet One of the leaflike parts of a compound leaf.

Lichen Any of a large number of small plants made up of an alga and a fungus growing symbiotically.

Litter Surface layer of forest floor, consisting of slightly decomposed organic matter.

Loam A rich soil of clay, silt, sand, and humus.

Lobed Indented on the margins, with the indentations not reaching to the center or base.

Lore In birds, the space between the eye and the base of the bill, sometimes distinctively colored.

Margin The edge of the wing.

Metamorphosis The transformation of an immature to a mature insect.

Molt The periodic loss and replacement of feathers; most species have regular patterns and schedules of molt.

Moraine A formation of boulders, gravel, sand, clay, etc., deposited directly by a glacier.

Nitrogen fixation Conversion by plants of atmospheric nitrogen into a usable form (nitrates) by certain soil bacteria in their nodules.

Node The place on the stem where leaves or branches are attached.

Nurse log A fallen log or snag on which sprouts or seedlings of a tree begin to grow.

Oblanceolate Reverse lanceolate; shaped like a lance, several times longer than wide, broadest near the tip and pointed at the base.

Obovate Reverse ovate; oval, with the broader end at the tip.

Opposite leaves Occurring in pairs at a node, with one leaf on either side of the stem.

Ovary The swollen base of a pistil, within which seeds develop.

Overwinter To go through a period of dormancy during the cold season.

Palmate Having 3 or more divisions or lobes, looking like the outspread fingers of a hand.

Palp A sensory structure associated with an insect's mouthparts.

Parasite A plant or animal living in or on another plant or animal, and deriving its nutrition from the host organism and to the detriment of the host.

Parotoid gland A large glandular structure on each side of the neck or behind the eyes of toads and some salamanders.

Parthenogenesis Reproduction by the development of an unfertilized egg; some animals produce only one sex and reproduce by means of unfertilized eggs.

Pedicel The stalk of an individual flower.

Pedipalp One of the second pair of appendages of the cephalothorax of a spider, usually leglike in a female but enlarged at the tip in a male as a special organ for transferring sperm; used by both sexes for guiding prey to the mouth.

Peduncle The main flower stalk or stem holding an inflorescence.

Perennial Living more than two years; also, any plant that uses the same root system to produce new growth.

Petal Of a flower, the basic unit of the corolla; flat, usually broad, and brightly colored.

Petiole The stalklike part of a leaf, attaching it to the stem.

Pheromones Sex attractant scent molecules produced by the scent scales, or androconia, of some insects and other animals.

Phloem The vascular tissue in a plant that conducts food material.

Pinnate leaf A compound leaf with leaflets along the sides of a common central stalk, much like a feather.

Pioneer species A plant or animal that begins a new cycle of life in a barren area.

Pistil The female organ of a flower, consisting of an ovary, style, and stigma.

Plastron The lower part of a turtle's shell.

Pod A dry, 1-celled fruit, splitting along natural grooved lines, with thicker walls than a capsule.

Podzol Any of an infertile group of soils typical of conifer and mixed forests in cool moist environments. Often covered by a mat of undecayed litter.

Pollen Spores formed in the anthers of a flower that produce the male cells.

Pome A fruit with fleshy outer tissue and a papery-walled, inner chamber containing the seeds.

Prehensile Adapted for grasping or wrapping around; said of the toes, claws, and tails of certain animals.

Primaries The outermost and longest flight feathers on a bird's wing.

Proboscis A prolonged set of mouthparts adapted for reaching into or piercing a food source.

Pupa The inactive stage of insects during which the larva transforms into the adult form, completing its metamorphosis.

Pupation In insects, the transformation from caterpillar to chrysalis or from larva to adult.

Pupil In an eyespot, a marking near the center.

Race A distinctive geographical population, equivalent to a subspecies or variety.

Raceme A long flower cluster on which individual flowers each bloom on a small stalk all along a common, larger, central stalk.

Ray flower The bilaterally symmetrical flowers around the edge of the head in many members of the sunflower family; each ray flower resembles a single petal.

Regular flower With petals and/or sepals arranged around the center, like the spokes of a wheel; always radially symmetrical.

Reproductive In social insects, a member of the caste capable of reproduction; reproductives usually gain wings for brief mating flights, as occurs in termites and ants.

Rhizome A horizontal underground stem, distinguished from roots by the presence of nodes, often enlarged by food storage.

Rosette A crowded cluster of leaves; usually basal, circular, and appearing to grow directly out of the ground.

Samara A dry, 1-seeded fruit with a wing; a key.

Saprophyte A plant lacking chlorophyll and living on dead organic matter.

Scapulars In birds, a group of feathers on the shoulder, along the side of the back.

Scent scales Specialized scales that produce and disperse sex attractants; also called androconia.

Schist Metamorphic rock, such as mica, with foliate layers that break in parallel planes.

Scrub Stunted vegetation growing in sand or infertile soil.

Secondaries In birds, the large flight feathers located in a series along the rear edge of the wing, immediately inward from the primaries.

Sepal A basic unit of the calyx, usually green, but sometimes colored and resembling a petal.

Seral Part of the series of stages in a community from the initial (pioneer) stage to the climax.

Serotinous Late or delayed in developing, and opened by fire; said of the cones of certain pines.

Serpentine Metamorphic rock, typically dull green mottled with red, but often other colors. Serpentine is inhospitable to the growth of most plants.

Sessile leaf A leaf that lacks a petiole, the blade being attached directly to the stem.

Sheath A more or less tubular structure surrounding a part, as the lower portion of a leaf surrounding the stem.

Shrub A woody plant, smaller than a tree, with several stems or trunks arising from a single base; a bush.

Simple eye A light-sensitive organ consisting of a convex lens bulging from the surface of the head, concentrating and guiding light rays to a cup-shaped cluster of photoreceptor cells. Also called an ocellus.

Simple leaf A leaf with a single blade.

Slough A sluggish creek in a tidal flat, marsh, or bottomland.

Soil A mixture of disintegrated rock and organic materials; characteristically broken down as clay, silt, and sand. The organic component is humus.

Spadix A dense spike of tiny flowers, usually enclosed in a spathe, as in members of the arum family.

Spathe A bract or pair of bracts, often large, enclosing the flowers.

Spike An elongated flower cluster, each flower of which is without a stalk.

Spur A stout, spinelike projection, usually movable, such as is present commonly toward the end of the tibia.

Stamen One of the male structures of a flower, consisting of a threadlike filament and a pollen-bearing anther.

Steppe A dry, short-grass prairie, sometimes also with shrubs such as sagebrush.

Stigma The tip of a pistil that receives the pollen.

Stipules Small appendages, often leaflike, on either side of some petioles at the base.

Stolon A stem growing along or under the ground; a runner.

Style The narrow part of the pistil, connecting ovary and stigma.

Subspecies A more or less distinct geographic population of a species that is able to interbreed with other members of the species.

Succession An orderly sequence of plant and animal communities, one group replacing another, ending in a climax, or final stage. The climax is sometimes never reached, because of repeated disturbances, such as fire.

Symbiosis An intimate biological relationship between two species. Symbiosis may take the form of parasitism, where one organism lives at the expense of the other; commensalism, where the presence of one neither helps nor damages the other; and mutualism, where both gain from the relationship.

Taproot The main root of a tree or plant, growing vertically downward, from which smaller, lateral roots extend.

Tarsus In butterflies, the foot section of the leg; it has hooks at the end for clinging; in birds, the lower, usually featherless, part of the leg.

Thorax The subdivision of the body between head and abdomen, consisting of 3 segments (the prothorax, mesothorax, and metathorax) and bearing whatever legs and wings are present.

Timberline A limit, created by climatological, topographical, or environmental factors, beyond which trees do not grow.

Tragus In bats, the lobe that projects upward from the base of the ear.

Transpiration Loss of water by evaporation from leaves and other parts of plants.

Tubercle A raised, wartlike knob.

Umbel A flower cluster in which the individual flower stalks grow from the same point, like the ribs of an umbrella.

Understory The lower foliage layer in a forest, shaded by the canopy. Also the middle- and lower-level plants beneath the canopy, including shrubs, flowers, and seedlings.

Venation The pattern of veins on a wing.

Vent Anus; opening of the cloaca to the outside of the body.

Virgin forest Woodland that exists in its primeval state.

Viviparous reproduction Giving birth to active young that have developed with no identifiable egg stage within the mother.

Whorled A circle of three or more leaves, branches, or pedicels at a node.

Wing bar A conspicuous, crosswise wing mark.

Wing stripe A conspicuous mark running along the opened wing.

Worker One of a caste of social insects, usually incapable of reproduction, that procures and distributes food or provides defense for the colony.

BIBLIOGRAPHY

Arno, Stephen F. and Ramona Hammerly.
Northwest Trees.
Seattle: The Mountaineers, 1977.
Timberline: Alpine and Arctic Forest Frontiers.
Seattle: The Mountaineers, 1984.

Bakker, Elna.
An Island Called California: An Ecological Introduction to Its Natural Communities.
Berkeley: University of California Press, Berkeley, 1972.

Brown, Vinson.
Reading the Woods.
Harrisburg, Pennsylvania: The Stackpole Co., 1969.

Franklin, Jerry F. and C. T. Dyrness.
Natural Vegetation of Oregon and Washington. Portland, Oregon:
U.S. Forest and Range Experiment Station, USDA, 1973.

Kirk, Ruth.
The Olympic Rain Forest.
Seattle: University of Washington Press, 1966.

Lanner, Ronald M.
The Pinon Pine.
Reno: University of Nevada Press, 1981.

McCormick, Jack.
Life of the Forest.
New York: McGraw-Hill Book Co., 1966.
Living Forest.
New York: Harper & Row, 1958.

Peattie, Donald Culross.
A Natural History of Western Trees.
Boston: Houghton Mifflin Co., 1953.

Schwartz, Susan.
Nature in the Northwest.
New York: Prentice-Hall, 1983.

Shelford, Victor E.
The Ecology of North America.
Urbana, Illinois: University of Illinois Press, 1963.

Spurr, S. H.
Forest Ecology.
New York: The Ronald Press Co., 1964.

Watts, May.
Reading the Landscape.
New York: The Macmillan Co., 1966.

Whitney, Stephen.
Sierra Club Naturalist's Guide: The Sierra Nevada.
San Francisco: Sierra Club Books, 1981.

Zwinger, Ann.
Beyond the Aspen Grove, 1st paperback ed.
New York: Harper & Row, 1981.

CREDITS

Photo Credits
The numbers in parentheses are plate numbers. Some photographers have pictures under agency names as well as their own.

David H. Ahrenholz (542 left and right, 559 left and right)
Ronn Altig (339, 349)

Amwest
Dennis Anderson (462, 470, 486, 493 left, 498)
Joseph J. Branney (363) Charles G. Summers, Jr. (370)

Animals Animals
George K. Bryce (581) Zig Leszczynski (584, 587, 591, 592, 608) B. MacDonald (585) C. Perkins (580) John C. Stevenson (357) Stouffer Productions Ltd. (325) Jack Wilburn (610)

William Aplin (220)
Catherine Ardrey (164, 313, 317)
Ray E. Ashton, Jr. (609)
Ron Austing (274, 284, 392)
Karölis Bagdonas (546, 553 left, 557 right)
Stephen F. Bailey (224)
Gregory Ballmer (544, 560 left)
Roger W. Barbour (326, 328)
Bob Barrett (310)
Tom Bean (16)
David W. Behrens (420, 573)
Michael Beug (319, 321)
Les Blacklock (484, 499, 533)
Donna Lee Botsford (211)
Edmund Brodie (327)
Fred Bruemmer (365)
Sonja Bullaty and Angelo Lomeo (38 left, 45 right, 54 left and right, 59 right, 70 left and right, 90 left and right, 93 right, 396)
James R. Butler (332)
Franz J. Camenzind (2nd frontispiece, 4th frontispiece)
Ken Carmichael (223)
Steward Cassidy (355)
David Cavagnaro (37 left and right, 38 right, 39 left, 40 left and right, 41 left, 42 left, 44 left and right, 45 left, 51 left and right, 52 left, 53 left and right, 55 left, 56 left, 57 left, 59 left, 60 left, 61 left, 63 left, 64 left, 65 left, 67 left, 69 left and right, 71 left and right, 74 left and right, 75 left and right, 76 left, 77 left and right, 78 left and right, 79 left, 81 left and right, 82 left, 84 left and right, 85 left, 86 left, 87 left, 88 left, 89 left and right, 91 left and right, 92 left, 93 left, 94 left, 95 right, 97 left and right, 98 left and right, 99 right, 100 left and right, 101 left and right, 102 left and right, 103 left and right, 104 left and right, 105 left and right, 106 left and right, 107 left, 108 left and right, 116–118, 121, 123, 125–132, 134, 137–147, 157, 166, 179, 180, 184, 186, 191, 202, 217, 222)
Norden H. Cheatham (170, 173)
Scooter Cheatham (39 right)

Herbert Clarke (15, 228, 251, 252, 275, 286, 292, 296, 303, 305, 530)

Bruce Coleman, Inc.
Jen and Des Bartlett (540, 561 right) S. C. Bisserot (439) Bill Brooks (203 right) Bob and Clara Calhoun (269, 471, 596, 617) Jack Couffer (337) J. Ebeling (534) John Hoffman (291) R. Schonberg (467) Joy Spurr (149, 419, 539) R. Tidman (314) Wardene Weisser (589, 599) Larry West (403 right)

Ed Cooper (1, 2, 383, 393, 409, 418, 423, 432, 446, 451, 492, 493 right, 505, 515, 532)
Steve Crouch (135, 159, 177, 178)
Thase Daniel (464)
Kent and Donna Dannen (213, 256, 267, 342, 352, 379, 394)
Harry N. Darrow (550, 563 left and right, 579)
Thomas W. Davies (549, 554 left and right, 570)
Frances V. Davis (320)
Edward R. Degginger (335, 356, 361, 577, 588)
David M. Dennis (613)
Jack Dermid (249)
John DiLiberti (545, 560 right)
Larry R. Ditto (227, 260)
Georges Dremeaux (254)

DRK Photo
Stephen J. Krasemann (354, 445, 491)

Harry Engels, (243, 378, 442)
P. R. Ferguson (199, 401, 461 left, 517)
William E. Ferguson (565, 566, 572, 582)
Kenneth W. Fink (258, 276, 279, 307, 309, 331, 341, 369)
Jeff Foott (1st frontispiece, 233, 259, 271, 299, 344)
Jeff Gnass (19, 23, 27)
James M. Greaves (290)
William Grenfell (153)
Pamela J. Harper (133, 156)
Velma Harris (236)
James Hawkings (311)

Grant Heilman Photography (136, 174)

Douglas Henderson (8, 13, 163, 195, 212, 415, 431, 460, 512, 525)
Walter H. Hodge (115, 119)
Noel Holmgren (495 left and right, 536 left and right)
Michael Hopiak (272)
Warren Jacobi (302)
Charles Johnson (188, 204, 218, 385, 386, 395, 425, 429, 448, 450, 455, 463, 472, 476, 483, 490, 496, 504, 511, 519, 522, 526, 537, 538)
William Jordan (73 left and right)
J. Eric Juterbock (586)
G. C. Kelley (232, 263, 360, 373)
Lewis and Dorothy Klein (417, 503)
E. F. Knights (253, 306)

Peter Kresan (18)
Bonnie Kutschenreuter (506)
Frank A. Lang (482)
Wayne Lankinen (225, 265, 282, 304, 308, 312)
Tom and Pat Leeson (4, 242)
Donald J. Leopold (122)
Jack Levy (543 left and right)
William B. Love (593, 595)
C. D. Luckhart (42 right, 61 right, 88 right, 112)
John R. MacGregor (465, 601)
Thomas W. Martin (266, 300)
Anthony Mercieca (226, 235, 241, 246, 248, 257, 261, 278, 281, 294, 295, 362)
Brian Milne (487)
Robert W. Mitchell (568)
C. Allan Morgan (194, 230, 391)
David Muench (Cover, 7, 9, 12, 14, 25, 26, 28–30, 34, 36, 55 right)
Helen M. Mulligan (158)

National Audubon Society Collection/Photo Researchers, Inc. William Bacon III (358) Tom Branch (402, 424, 488) Ken Brate (315, 398, 459) J. Collins (598, 607, 614, 615) Helen Cruickshank (485 left and right) Stephen Dalton (567) R. Dimond (452) Phil A. Dotson (353, 367) Harry Engels (330) Bob Grant (176) Farrell Grehan (453, 461 right) Harold W. Hoffman (477) Inez and George Hollis (411 right) Russ Kinne (497) Stephen J. Krasemann (336) Calvin Larsen (340) B. Lopez (524) Alexander Lowry (334, 389) Karl Maslowski (345) C. Maxwell (183) Tom McHugh (32, 346, 371, 372) Anthony Mercieca (264) John V.A.F. Neal (414) Charlie Ott (203 left) Richard Parker (426, 440, 480) Constance Porter (215) George Porter (612) Louis Quitt (501) Susan Rayfield (502) Miriam Reinhart (50 left) Leonard Lee Rue III (343, 348) Dan Sudia (268) K. H. Switak (603, 618) V. Weinland (171) Myron Wood (381)

Peter Nice (552)
Theodore F. Niehaus (41 right, 469)
Philip Nordin (556, 557 left)
Boyd Norton (5th frontispiece, 10, 11, 17, 21, 24)
Robert and Margaret Orr (400, 412, 421, 436, 449, 466, 516)
Arthur Panzer (231, 234)
H. A. Pengelly (187)
C. W. Perkins (428)
Robert Perron (3)
Robert Potts (456, 489, 509, 518)
Betty Randall (47 left, 62 left, 473 left, 520, 521, 555 left and right)
Betty Randall and Robert Potts (43 left and right, 46 left and right, 47 right, 48 left and right, 49 left and right, 56 right, 57 right, 58 left and right, 60 right, 62 right, 64 right, 67 right, 68 left and right, 72 left and right, 79 right, 80 left

and right, 82 right, 83 left and right, 86 right, 92 right, 94 right, 95 left, 96 left and right, 99 left, 107 right, 162, 172)
William Ratcliffe (201, 399, 514)
Susan Rayfield (197 left and right, 437)
Tim Reeves (403 left)
Alan Resetar (583)
Edward S. Ross (210, 214, 413, 500, 508, 513, 527, 541 left, 547, 548, 564, 571, 574, 575)
Len Rue, Jr. (376)
Leonard Lee Rue III (5, 333, 374, 377)
Kit Scates (316, 324)
Clark Schaack (66 left, 175)
John Shaw (66 right, 561 left, 569, 576, 578)
Ervio Sian (247, 255, 280)
Robert S. Simmons (594, 597, 604–606)
Perry D. Slocum (238)
Arnold Small (20, 22, 33, 237, 283, 285, 288, 289, 293, 301)
Bruce A. Sorrie (240)
Richard Spellenberg (52 right, 63 right, 65 right, 76 right, 87 right, 120, 124, 167, 207, 208, 219, 406, 410 left and right, 435, 479 left and right, 510)
Keith Spencer (562)
Bob and Ira Spring (430, 433, 434, 447)
Joy Spurr (113, 150–152, 154, 160, 165, 181, 189, 190, 192, 198, 206, 209, 216, 221, 322, 387, 388, 390, 397, 404, 405 left and right, 407 left and right, 408, 411 left, 416 left and right, 422, 441, 444, 468, 478, 494, 507, 523, 528)

Tom Stack and Associates
Ron Hormann (458) Rick McIntyre (368)

Alvin E. Staffan (245, 323, 347, 364, 366, 602)
David M. Stone (185)

M. Stouffer Productions (350)

K. H. Switak (600)
Ian C. Tait (262, 270)
T. K. Todsen (380, 384, 443, 457, 474, 475, 481, 529, 531)
Merlin D. Tuttle (338)
Tom J. Ulrich (359)
University of California/Jepson Herbarium (438)
University of Colorado Museum (427, 454)
William Vandivert (329)
Charles S. Webber (473 right, 535)
Richard E. Webster (229)
Wardene Weisser (193, 239, 298, 351, 382)
C. Wershler (541 right)
Larry West (551, 553 right, 558, 616)
Nicholas Wheeler (50 right, 85 right)
Jack Wilburn (3rd frontispiece, 6, 35, 109–111, 114, 148, 155, 161, 168, 169, 182, 200, 205, 244, 375, 611)
Greg Wright (318)

Dale and Marian Zimmerman (31, 196, 250, 273, 277, 287, 297)

Richard G. Zweifel (590)

Illustrations

The drawings of plants were executed primarily by Margaret Kurzius and Mary Jane Spring. The following artists also contributed drawings of plants and tree silhouettes to this guide: Daniel Allen, Bobbi Angell, Dolores R. Santoliquido, and Stephen Whitney. Dot Barlowe contributed the drawings of mammal tracks.

NATIONAL AUDUBON SOCIETY

The mission of the NATIONAL AUDUBON SOCIETY is to conserve and restore natural ecosystems, focusing on birds and other wildlife for the benefit of humanity and the Earth's biological diversity.

We have nearly 500,000 members and an extensive chapter network, plus a staff of scientists, lobbyists, lawyers, policy analysts, and educators. Through our sanctuaries we manage 150,000 acres of critical habitat.

Our award-winning *Audubon* magazine carries outstanding articles and color photography on wildlife, nature, and the environment. We also publish *American Birds,* an ornithological journal, *Audubon Activist,* a newsjournal, and *Audubon Adventures,* a newsletter reaching 600,000 elementary school students. Our *World of Audubon* television shows air on TBS and public television.

For information about how you can become a member, please write or call the Membership Department at:

NATIONAL AUDUBON SOCIETY
700 Broadway, New York, New York 10008
(212) 979-3000 or 1-800-274-4201

CHANTICLEER STAFF

Prepared and produced by Chanticleer Press, Inc.
Founding Publisher: Paul Steiner
Publisher: Andrew Stewart
Managing Editor: Edie Locke
Production Manager: Deirdre Duggan Ventry
Assistant to the Publisher: Kelly Beekman

Staff for this book:

Editor-in-Chief: Gudrun Buettner
Executive Editor: Susan Costello
Managing Editor: Jane Opper
Series Editor: Mary Beth Brewer
Text Editor: Ann Whitman
Associate Editor: Marian Appellof
Assistant Editors: David Allen, Constance Mersel
Editorial Assistant: Karel Birnbaum
Production: Helga Lose, Amy Roche, Frank Grazioli
Art Director: Carol Nehring
Art Associate: Ayn Svoboda
Picture Library: Edward Douglas, Dana Pomfret
Maps and Symbols: Paul Singer
Natural History Consultant: John Farrand, Jr.

Design: Massimo Vignelli

All editorial inquiries should be addressed to:
Chanticleer Press
568 Broadway, Suite #1005A
New York, NY 10012
(212) 941-1522

To purchase this book, or other National Audubon Society
illustrated nature books, please contact:
Alfred A. Knopf
201 East 50th Street
New York, NY 10022
(800) 733-3000